Aging, Rights, and Quality of Life

Aging, Rights, and Quality of Life
Prospects for Older People with Developmental Disabilities

edited by

Stanley S. Herr, J.D., D.Phil.
University of Maryland School of Law
Baltimore

and

Germain Weber, Ph.D.
Institute of Psychology
University of Vienna
Austria

·P A U L·H·
BROOKES
PUBLISHING Cº

Baltimore • London • Toronto • Sydney

Paul H. Brookes Publishing Co.
Post Office Box 10624
Baltimore, Maryland 21285-0624

www.brookespublishing.com

Typeset by Barton Matheson Willse and Worthington, Baltimore, Maryland.
Manufactured in the United States of America by
The Maple Press Company, York, Pennsylvania.

Some of the case studies herein describe actual living people and actual circumstances. In those cases, people's names have been changed to protect their identities, and their stories have been included with permission. Another case study involves a deceased person whose story and actual name were, with his permission, previously a matter of public record. Still other cases are composites or fictional accounts. In those cases, any similarity to actual individuals is coincidental, and no implications should be inferred.

Permission is gratefully acknowledged to use graphic/image appearing on section opener pages courtesy of ClickArt® Incredible Image Pak™, copyright © 1996 The Learning Company, Inc., and its subsidiaries. All rights reserved. Used by permission. ClickArt, Image Pak, and Brøderbund are trademarks and/or registered trademarks of Learning Company Properties Inc.

Cover design by Brushwood Graphics, Inc.

Cover photographs courtesy of Donna Pandolfino.

Library of Congress Cataloging-in-Publication Data

Aging, rights, and quality of life : prospects for older people with developmental disabilities /
    edited by Stanley S. Herr and Germain Weber.
        p.   cm.
    Includes bibliographical references and index.
    ISBN 1-55766-380-7
    1. Developmentally disabled aged—United States.   2. Developmentally disabled
aged—Government policy—United States.   3. Quality of life—United States.
4. Developmentally disabled aged—Civil rights—United States.   I. Herr, Stanley S.
II. Weber, Germain.
HV3009.5.A35A39   1999
362.1'968—dc21   98-50820
                                                                                                                 CIP

British Library Cataloguing in Publication data are available from the British Library.

Contents

About the Editors

Stanley S. Herr, J.D., D.Phil., Professor of Law, University of Maryland School of Law, 500 West Baltimore Street, Baltimore, Maryland 21201. In addition to his position as professor of law at the University of Maryland School of Law, Dr. Herr directs the university's Clinical Law Office program in disability rights. He is also Senior Research Fellow at the Yale Law School's Schell Center for International Human Rights. From 1993 to 1995, he served as the Kennedy Public Policy Fellow in the White House, reporting directly to the Assistant to the President for Domestic Policy. He is President of the American Association on Mental Retardation (AAMR). He is also Co-founder and Vice President of the Homeless Persons Representation Project, Commissioner of the American Bar Association's (ABA's) Commission on Mental and Physical Disability Law, and Chair of the Editorial Advisory Board to the ABA's *Mental and Physical Disability Law Reporter.* Dr. Herr previously served on numerous boards and commissions, including the National Law Center on Homelessness and Poverty and the Maryland Governor's Commission to Revise the Mental Retardation and Developmental Disabilities Law, the Maryland State Bar Association Committee on Legal Aid to Homeless Individuals and Disabled Individuals, and the Legal Advocacy Committee of The Arc of the United States. Previously, he was a Rockefeller Foundation Fellow for Human Rights at Columbia University and a National Legal Services Corporation Fellow at Harvard University. He has taught at Harvard Law School and Catholic University Law School and was a visiting professor and Fulbright Senior Scholar at Tel Aviv University and the Hebrew University in Jerusalem. Dr. Herr has authored more than 100 publications and has lectured widely on topics of law, public policy, ethics, and aging. He received a bachelor's degree *cum laude* from Yale College, a law degree from Yale Law School, and a doctorate of philosophy from Oxford University. A former recipient of the Burton Blatt Award, the Rosemary F. Dybwad International Fellowship Award, and the Sandra Jensen Award, he is a director of the Rosemary F. Dybwad International Fellowship Trust. In 1996, he received the Humanitarian Award from the AAMR. In 1999, Dr. Herr was named a Mary Switzer Distinguished Research Fellow of the U.S. Department of Education's National Institute on Disability and Rehabilitation Research.

Germain Weber, Ph.D., Professor of Psychology, Department of Applied and Clinical Psychology, Institute of Psychology, University of Vienna, Universitätstrasse 7, A-1010 Vienna, Austria. In addition to his position at the Institute of Psychology, Dr. Weber acts as the Co-director in the postgraduate training program for clinical and health psychology at the University of Vienna. As a faculty member of the Centre Universitaire de Luxembourg, he regularly teaches psychology in Luxembourg. He is acting as Vice-President to the Lebenshilfe Österreich, the major Austrian parents' organization serving and advocating on behalf of people with mental retardation. He is Vice-President of the Österreichische Arbeitsgemeinschaft für Rehabilitation (ÖAR), the Austrian umbrella organization for all major organizations in the field of disabilities. He serves on the advisory council to the Verein für Sachwalter-schaft und Patientenanwaltschaft, the major Austrian association in charge of the implementation of, and assistance under, national laws regulating guardianship. Dr. Weber acts as an advisor for many service providers and research and development programs in the field of developmental disabilities in various European countries. Dr. Weber has authored more than 80 publications and has lectured in many countries on the topics of psychology and mental retardation. He received his primary and secondary education in Luxembourg and his higher education, including his doctoral degree, from the University of Vienna. He was a postdoctoral Fulbright Fellow at the State University of New York at Stony Brook before he was given a position as a research assistant at the Ludwig Boltzmann Institute for Brain-Damaged Children in Vienna, directed by Andreas Rett.

About the Contributors

Sean L. Brohawn, J.D., Attorney, Israelson, Salsbury, Clements & Bekman, L.L.C., 300 West Pratt Street, Suite 450, Baltimore, Maryland 21201. Mr. Brohawn is an attorney with the law firm Israelson, Salsbury, Clements & Bekman in Baltimore. Previously, he was a law clerk to Hon. James R. Eyler of the Maryland Court of Special Appeals. He is an honors graduate of the University of Maryland School of Law.

Chris Conliffe, D.Phil., F.R.S.M., Clinical Psychologist, Institute for Counselling and Personal Development, Interpoint, 20-24 York Street, Belfast, Northern Ireland BT15 1AQ, United Kingdom. Dr. Conliffe is Director of the Institute for Counselling and Personal Development (ICPD) and a clinical psychologist. He specializes in the areas of intellectual disabilities and aging but also works actively as a counselor and psychotherapist. The ICPD is highly involved in peace and reconciliation in Northern Ireland. Dr. Conliffe is also a research fellow of the University of Ulster and has published widely on intellectual disabilities.

David DeVries, Gallup Research Assistant, Gallup Research Center, 200 North 11th Street, Lincoln, Nebraska 68508. Mr. DeVries is a graduate of Hastings College, where he majored in experimental psychology. He is working toward a master's degree in survey research and methodology at the University of Nebraska.

Andrea Fritsch, Mag.phil., Clinical Psychologist, Psychiatric Hospital of the City of Vienna–Baumgartner Höhe, Baumgartner Höhe 1, A-1140 Vienna, Austria. Ms. Fritsch works at the Psychiatric Hospital of the City of Vienna, where she developed programs to enhance the adaptive behavior skills of people with mental retardation with long-term admissions. She is especially involved in serving and advocating for adults and older people with developmental disabilities. In addition, she is a research associate on projects run by the University of Vienna that focus on mental health issues of people with mental retardation. She received her magistra degree in psychology from the University of Vienna. In 1996, she received a Rosemary F. Dybwad International Fellowship.

Barbara Gasteiger-Klicpera, Dr.phil., Lecturer in Clinical Psychology, Department of Applied and Clinical Psychology, Institute of Psychology, University of Vienna, Neutorgasse 13, A-1010 Vienna, Austria. Dr. Gasteiger-Klicpera studied psychology at the University of Vienna, where she is a lecturer in clinical psychology. In addition to research in the field of social services for people with developmental disabilities, Dr. Gasteiger-Klicpera is interested in behavior disorders, victimization in children, and aggression.

John Goldmeier, M.S.W., Ph.D., Professor, School of Social Work, University of Maryland at Baltimore, 525 West Redwood Street, Baltimore, Maryland 21201. In addition to being a professor at the School of Social Work at the University of Maryland at Baltimore, Dr. Goldmeier has chaired the school's specialized concentration in aging. He has published widely in the fields of aging and mental health as well as disabilities. He consults regionally, nationally, and internationally.

Vashti Gosling, Research Associate, Health and Community Care Research Unit, University of Liverpool, Brownlow Hill, Liverpool L69 3GB, United Kingdom. As a research associate at the University of Liverpool, Ms. Gosling is carrying out research on vocational training for people with intellectual disabilities in Merseyside, an urban area in northern England. Her doctoral dissertation, being undertaken at the University of Sheffield, focuses on issues of autonomy and participation among consumers with intellectual disabilities.

Barbara A. Hawkins, Ph.D., Associate Professor, Department of Recreation and Park Administration, Indiana University, HPER Building 133, Bloomington, Indiana 47405. Dr. Hawkins's interests are in the areas of life-span development and leisure behavior. Since 1988, she has been engaged in longitudinal research on aging-related change in adults with mental retardation. In the late 1990s, she broadened her activities to include examining cross-cultural aspects of leisure and successful aging in older adults. At Indiana University, she teaches courses on leisure, aging, and research methods.

Tamar Heller, Ph.D., Associate Professor, Associate Head for Academic Affairs, Director of Graduate Studies, Department of Disability and Human Development, University of Illinois at Chicago, 1640 West Roosevelt Road #404, Chicago, Illinois 60608. In addition to her positions in the Department of Disability and Human Development at the University of Illinois at Chicago, Dr. Heller directs the Institute on Disability and Human Development's Aging Studies Program, including its Rehabilitation Research and Training Center (RRTC) on Aging with Mental Retardation. The RRTC is a national center that brings together researchers and advocacy organizations to study disabilities and aging and to promote progressive public policies. Dr. Heller also directs several large-scale federally funded projects on transition issues and support interventions for individuals with developmental disabilities and their families.

Matthew P. Janicki, Ph.D., Research Professor and Co-director, Center on Intellectual Disabilities, University at Albany, 280 Richardson Hall, Albany, New York 12222. In addition to his position at the University at Albany, Dr. Janicki is Associate Director for Technical Assistance at the Rehabilitation Research and Training Center on Aging with Mental Retardation at the University of Illinois at Chicago. Formerly, he was Director for Aging and Special Populations at the New York State Office of Mental Retardation and Developmental Disabilities. He was a Joseph P. Kennedy, Jr., Foundation Public Policy Leadership Fellow, spending a sabbatical year at the National Institute on Aging and the U.S. Senate. Dr. Janicki is the author of numerous books and articles in the areas of aging, rehabilitation, and intellectual and developmental disabilities and has lectured and provided training in aging and intellectual disabilities around the world.

Marshall B. Kapp, J.D., M.P.H., Frederick A. White Distinguished Professor, Departments of Community Health and Psychiatry; Director, Office of Geriatric Medicine and Gerontology, School of Medicine, Wright State University, Box 927, Dayton, Ohio 45401. Dr. Kapp earned a bachelor's degree at The Johns Hopkins University, a law degree with honors at George Washington University School of Law, and a master's degree in public health at the Harvard University School of Public Health. Since August 1980, he has been a faculty member in the School of Medicine at Wright State University (WSU), where he is the Frederick A. White Distinguished Professor of Professional Service and teaches courses on the legal and ethical aspects of health care. He is also Director of WSU's Office of Geriatric Medicine and Gerontology and holds an adjunct faculty appointment at the University of Dayton School of Law.

Christian Klicpera, Dr.med., Dr.phil., Associate University Professor, Department of Applied and Clinical Psychology, Institute of Psychology, University of Vienna, Neutorgasse 13, A-1010 Vienna, Austria. Dr. Klicpera studied medicine and psychology in Vienna and Salzburg. He worked for several years at the Max Planck Institute for Psychiatry in Munich and as a research fellow at the Children's Hospital Medical Center in Boston. He is an associate professor of clinical and applied psychology at the University of Vienna. His main research areas are specific learning disabilities and social services for people with developmental disabilities.

Jason A. Lebsack, Database Coordinator, Department of Family Medicine, University of Nebraska Medical Center, 983075 Nebraska Medical Center, Omaha, Nebraska 68198. In addition to his position at the University of Nebraska Medical Center, Mr. Lebsack is a doctoral student in industrial and organizational psychology at the University of Nebraska.

Mitchell Levitz, Self-Advocacy Coordinator, Capabilities Unlimited Inc., 2495 Erie Avenue, Cincinnati, Ohio 45208. Mr. Levitz is a co-author of the award-winning book *Count Us In: Growing Up with Down Syndrome* (Harcourt Brace & Co., 1994). He is the Self-Advocacy Coordinator for Capabilities Unlimited Inc. and the Editor-in-Chief of *Community Advocacy Press,* a national publication written by and for individuals with developmental disabilities. He is a national advocate on disability issues and serves on numerous policy boards and committees. In 1999, Mr. Levitz received the Special Award of the American Association on Mental Retardation as part of its international awards program.

Barbara L. Ludlow, Ed.D., Professor, Department of Special Education, West Virginia University, 608 East Allen Hall, Post Office Box 6122, Morgantown, West Virginia 26506. Dr. Ludlow is Professor of Special Education at West Virginia University, where she coordinates the distance education graduate training programs in Severe/Multiple Disabilities and Early Intervention. She received her master's degree in special education from the University of Delaware and her doctoral degree in special education from West Virginia University. Her primary research interests address development and evaluation of innovative models of teacher education and legal, ethical, and social issues in developmental disabilities. She co-edited one professional reference book on transition to adult services and another on distance education applications for preparing special education personnel. She is the author of a number of journal articles on topics ranging from early childhood development to strategies for working with children with severe and multiple disabilities. She is the author of four Phi Delta Kappa fastbacks on topics related to special education and has served as a lecturer for chapter meetings since the 1980s.

Lars Molander, Konsult o.e.p.d., Licensed Psychologist, Österängsvägen 14, SE-182 46 Enebyberg, Sweden. Dr. Molander, currently retired, was a clinical psychologist at the Caroline Hospital, a university hospital in Stockholm, from 1952 until 1965 and Chief Psychologist in services for people with intellectual disabilities in Stockholm County Council from 1965 until 1992. He is a former member of the Swedish Psychologists' Association. Dr. Molander is also author or co-author of six books on intellectual disabilities.

Steve Moss, Ph.D., Senior Lecturer, Department of Psychiatric Nursing, Institute of Psychiatry, De Crespigny Park, Denmark Hill, London SE5 8AF, United Kingdom. Dr. Moss has worked since the late 1970s in disability research, primarily in the field of intellectual disabilities. From 1982 to 1990, he worked on an extensive program of research and service development relating to the needs, characteristics, and provision of services to older individuals. Since 1990, his main area of involvement has been the management of projects concerned with the development of new methods for the detection and diagnosis of psychiatric disorders in people with intellectual disabilities. He is widely known in the United States and Europe for his work in both of these fields.

Manfred Nowak, Dr.juris, LL.M., Dr.habil, Professor of Law; Director, Ludwig Boltzmann Institute of Human Rights, University of Vienna, Hessgasse 1, A-1010 Vienna, Austria. Dr. Nowak is a professor of law at the University of Vienna and the Austrian Federal Academy of Public Administration and Director of the Ludwig Boltzmann Institute of Human Rights at the University of Vienna. He is also vice president and judge at the Human Rights Chamber for Bosnia and Herzegovina in Sarajevo, established under the Dayton Peace Agreement; expert member of the United Nations (UN) Working Group on Enforced or Involuntary Disappearances; and member of the International Commission of Jurists. He is author of more than 250 publications in the fields of constitutional and international law, with a special emphasis on human rights. In 1994, he was awarded the UNESCO (UN Educational, Scientific, and Cultural Organization) Prize for the Teaching of Human Rights.

Robert L. Schalock, Ph.D., Professor and Chair, Department of Psychology, Hastings College, 800 Turner Avenue, Hastings, Nebraska 68901. In addition to his positions at Hastings College, Dr. Schalock is an adjunct professor of pediatrics and psychiatry at the University of Nebraska Medical Center. His major research and writing projects have examined the concept of quality of life and the field of outcomes-based evaluation. He is a past president of the American Association on Mental Retardation.

Alan Walker, D.Litt., Professor of Social Policy, Department of Sociological Studies, University of Sheffield, Elmfield, Northumberland Road, Sheffield S10 2TU, United Kingdom. Dr. Walker has been researching and writing in the fields of disability and aging since the early 1970s. In the 1970s, he was a member of the disability rights movement in the United Kingdom and co-founded the Disability Alliance pressure group and authored the *Disability Rights Handbook*. He specializes in social gerontology and in particular the impact of social and economic policies on older people within the European Union and the relationship between family and formal (i.e., paid) caregivers.

Carol Walker, M.A., Professor of Social Policy, Sheffield Hallam University, Collegiate Crescent Campus, Sheffield S10 2BP, United Kingdom. Ms. Walker is Professor of Social Policy at Sheffield Hallam University. She has researched and published widely in the areas of poverty, social security, and quality-of-life issues and service supports for people with intellectual disabilities.

Patricia Noonan Walsh, Ph.D., Director, Centre for the Study of Developmental Disabilities, University College Dublin, National University of Ireland, Roebuck, Belfield, Dublin 4, Republic of Ireland. Dr. Walsh, a native of New York City, is credentialed in special education at Tufts University in Medford, Massachusetts, and in clinical psychology in Dublin, Ireland. She is Director of the Centre for the Study of Developmental Disabilities and Assistant Director of the clinical psychology doctoral program at the National University of Ireland, Dublin. Dr. Walsh is a council member of the International Association for the Scientific Study of Intellectual Disability (IASSID).

Foreword

A good old age is a universal aspiration. Although its ingredients vary from country to country, at its core is respect for the aging person's human rights, dignity, choices, and desire for a decent quality of life. Older people with developmental disabilities require—and deserve—no less. Yet, in too many places and during too many periods of history, the prospect of experiencing old age at all, let alone a good one, for such people was far from certain.

Today the picture is far brighter. With improvements in health care, human services, and legally based supports and public attitudes, more and more individuals with lifelong disabilities are not just surviving but thriving in their later years. *Aging, Rights, and Quality of Life: Prospects for Older People with Developmental Disabilities* reveals the distinctive challenges of assisting members of this group to achieve this kind of fate. This important and far-reaching book connects three powerful engines for change in our field: the human rights approach, the voice of self-advocacy, and the invigorated quest for quality in the lives of people with developmental disabilities. As a pioneering work, it puts these topics into gerontological, cross-cultural, historical, and legal perspectives. Stanley S. Herr and Germain Weber have skillfully woven these themes together to inform and inspire practitioners, family members, researchers, policy makers, and advocates.

In my own life span of now 9 decades, I have witnessed and experienced a great shift in attitudes toward and expectations for the community's most senior members. Successful aging is not just a slogan but a real possibility for many. As a generation, older adults suffer deep loss of loved ones but find solace and support to carry on. They ache with physical infirmities but change some habits and living arrangements to accommodate to their differently balanced individual abilities and disabilities. They reduce their work or social domains—some people more willingly than others—but search for ways to maintain a sense of satisfaction and usefulness in their worlds. Even if some of their voices grow more halting, they may yet influence others.

My age-peers with developmental disabilities—or by whatever name they choose to call themselves—are not fundamentally different. Åke Johansson, who is in his late 60s in 1999, had been forced to live in a Swedish mental retardation institution for 32 years until he literally liberated himself. His life story has since been related in *Åke's Book* (Lundgren, 1993) and offers a moving testimonial to man's capacity for resilience and compassion. "Human dignity is not a matter of intelligence," he concludes. "The important thing is to give the love and knowledge you have to your fellow human beings. This is human dignity to me" (quoted in Lundgren, 1993, p. 125). Mitchell Levitz, a noted American self-advocate whose writing is included in this book, reveals similar maturity and eloquence when he urges individuals with developmental disabilities to become "partners in decision making throughout our lifetime, including issues that will have an impact on us as we get older" (Chapter 16, p. 287). His call for equality is a vivid reminder of the work that lies ahead for all of us, urging changes in policies and practices to "assure that we are entitled to the same options and benefits available to older citizens without developmental disabilities, including the right to retire" (Levitz, 1997, p. 1).

Human rights concerns with regard to the factor of age started with such concerns regarding children. Eglantyne Jebb, founder of the Save the Children International Union, pioneered an early declaration on the rights of children that proclaimed that the child who is "backward [i.e., mentally handicapped] must be helped" (1923, ¶ 2). Within a year, her declaration had been adopted formally by the League of Nations (1924). After this promising start, however, there was a strange loss of momentum. In the field of human rights, there were long delays in recognizing children's rights and even longer lags in paying attention to the rights of older adults, let alone older adults with disabilities. In particular, older adults in mental retardation institutions were treated as if they were children. The thesis of this book, expressed in many ways, challenges that this infantilization of older adults with developmental disabilities is no longer acceptable and that the legal and human rights gains achieved for children and adolescents with developmental disabilities must be extended to those who are at advanced stages of the life cycle.

Despite some parallels with children's rights, there are also many differences in programming, policies, and rights for older adults. American society has a relatively clear road map of rights and services for children. In contrast, for adults—especially for older adults—with developmental disabilities, the legal rights to services and supports are underdeveloped. One reason is that though children with disabilities have always existed, the existence of a large number of older adults with developmental disabilities represents a newer phenomenon, and their problems are not yet being addressed forcefully by political and professional leaders. In this book, editors Herr and Weber and the contributing authors from several different nations help to reduce this inattention. They highlight trends, problems, and prospects for older people with developmental disabilities that arise from these individuals' lengthening life spans.

More than 3 decades ago, in the mid-1960s, one of these trends received an early start. Societies began to move from a preoccupation with the rights and needs of children to a concern for adults. Thus, the International League of Societies for the Mentally Handicapped (ILSMH), in its Third World Congress, first drew attention to the interests of the adult with mental retardation as "a member of society, endowed with both natural and political rights, which no one may curtail but for good and valid cause, in proceedings which protect his interests, no matter how profoundly handicapped he may be" (ILSMH, 1966, p. 163). In fact, this rather basic position statement opened a new era in which services were viewed "as a matter of right, not a benevolence bestowed by the goodness of the Government" (ILSMH, 1966, p. 163). As the holders of these rights age, there are compelling reasons to define what it truly means to "bring justice and a full life" to our oldest members (ILSMH, 1966). More than 3 decades ago, when I spoke those words as Special Rapporteur for the ILSMH (now called Inclusion International), I did not yet realize the magnitude of that task or its implications for those facing the double jeopardy of old age and disability. It is essential that society's struggles not neglect the aging and that the quality of these individuals' lives and liberties be enriched.

This book offers indispensable guidance in that struggle. It reminds us of a new set of three Rs that must be heeded: risks, rights, and remedies. To date, in most parts of the world, the risks for older people with developmental disabilities have far exceeded the availability of effective rights and remedies. The editors and contributors of this book have done an admirable job of identifying the questions—and the answers—that are critical to shifting that balance and positively altering the status quo.

Older adults face a myriad of risk factors. The lengthening life span that poses questions to each individual brings new puzzles to a group once falsely thought of as "eternal children." In balancing their desires for independence and for support, how should service providers and family members honor their choices and still protect them from unscrupulous third parties or from undue hazards? Can, or should, steps be taken to identify people who are vulnerable and minimize significant risks of someone else's exploiting their vulnerability? Can service delivery systems be reoriented to avoid the trauma of relocating members of this group in unreflective and abrupt ways in their old age?

Many older adults have experienced a lonely existence, and the rights movement to date has not addressed these risks and vulnerabilities in a sustained way. These people encounter abandonment, loneliness, decreasing social contacts, and increased vulnerability to physical and psychological neglect by a society that does not know how to respond to them. Often the service system is based on protections and supports for children within a developmental model that is usually understood as an upward movement of increasing competence. Yet, here we are coping with a developmental process that is often marked by diminishing competence. As the graduates of special education programs survive into adulthood and old age, they outlive child-oriented protections and defenders of their human rights such as their parents and siblings. Especially challenging is the need to protect hard-won self-determination in the face of the combination of cognitive impairment and progressive functional decline.

Remedies, in the sense of both individual and society-wide solutions, require both vision and tenacity. They require vision to formulate the concepts, laws, and policies that will permit a good life for older adults with development disabilities. Even more importantly, however, they require tenacity and a practical type of vision, especially good common sense, to translate societal norms into day to day human realities so that people can live in and feel a part of the community.

Aging, Rights, and Quality of Life: Prospects for Older People with Developmental Disabilities is an excellent resource, benchmark, and blueprint in protecting older people's rights and fulfilling their desires. By putting into practice the service innovations and human rights standards it details, practitioners, planners, activists, and academics can work effectively to improve the prospects of a good old age for older adults with developmental disabilities.

Gunnar Dybwad
Professor Emeritus
The Heller School
Brandeis University
Waltham, Massachusetts

REFERENCES

International League of Societies for the Mentally Handicapped (ILSMH). (1966). *Stress on families of the mentally handicapped.* Brussels: Author.

League of Nations. (1924). *World child welfare charter.* Geneva: Author.

Levitz, M. (1997). *Community Advocacy Press, 2,* 1.

Lundgren, K. (1993). *Åke's book: After 32 years in an asylum for mentally deficient people, the long way to freedom and redress begins.* Stockholm: Swedish National Association for Persons with Mental Handicap.

Save the Children International Union. (1923). *Declaration of the rights of the child [Declaration of Geneva].* Geneva: Author.

About Gunnar Dybwad

Gunnar Dybwad, Dr.juris., Professor Emeritus of Human Development, The Heller School, Brandeis University, Waltham, Massachusetts 02254. Dr. Dybwad served as senior staff member of the Center on Human Policy at Syracuse University and as a visiting scholar at the G. Allan Roeher Institute, Downsview, Ontario, Canada. He received a law degree from the Faculty of Laws, University of Halle, Germany, and is a graduate of the New York School of Social Work. He and his wife, Dr. Rosemary Dybwad, were Co-directors of the Mental Retardation Project of the International Union for Child Welfare in Geneva, working as consultants throughout Europe and the Americas. In the United States, Dr. Dybwad served as a consultant to President John F. Kennedy's Special Assistant on Mental Retardation, to the U.S. Public Health Service, the President's Committee on Mental Retardation, and numerous state government agencies. From 1978 to 1982, he was President of the International League of Societies for the Mentally Handicapped, now known as Inclusion International. He is a Fellow of the American Orthopsychiatric Association, the American Sociological Association, the American Public Health Association, and the American Association on Mental Retardation; a member of the Council for Exceptional Children; and Honorary Associate Fellow of the American Academy of Pediatrics, from which he received the C. Anderson Aldrich Award for his activities in the field of child development. He received the honorary degree of Doctor of Public Service from the University of Maryland and the honorary degree of Doctor of Humane Letters from Temple University. Together with his wife, he has received awards for outstanding service from the American Association on Mental Retardation, the International League of Societies for the Mentally Handicapped, the President's Committee on Mental Retardation, the National Association for Retarded Citizens, the Massachusetts Psychological Association, the Pike Institute of Boston University School of Law, the Foundation for Dignity, the Kennedy Foundation International Awards Program, and the International Association for the Scientific Study of Intellectual Disabilities.

Preface

Older people with developmental disabilities face unique challenges. As their needs increase, the strength and number of their family caregivers wane. As institutional "solutions" are discredited or unavailable, the search for community-based alternatives intensifies. As their life spans lengthen and their total numbers increase, the inadequacy of planning and service provision becomes more apparent. The crisis is here and now, reflected in longer waiting lists for services and case studies that tell of individuals' pain and dislocation and the denial of their basic rights.

We designed this book to make more visible the human rights and the societal problems of older people with mental retardation and other developmental disabilities. We sought to identify measures that would ensure humane supports and a good quality of life for them. This cohort too often occupies a bureaucratic and political no man's land in which neither the developmental disabilities field nor the gerontology field takes sufficient leadership. Through an international and interdisciplinary effort, the contributors to this book raise the profile of all those who face the double jeopardy of developmental disabilities and aging.

Some of these people with disabilities are our clients and friends. Some have been our relatives. For Stanley S. Herr, for example, this project began with Ellis Island and his Aunt Rochelle, who never experienced old age. In 1919, on suspicion of her having mental retardation or some other disability, she was barred from entry to the United States, deported to her native Lithuania, and separated from all of her family but for 1 of her 10 siblings. Ultimately, Aunt Rochelle perished in the Holocaust. To have been labeled as *mentally retarded* at that time—even mistakenly so by an all-powerful immigration inspector—could prove to have heartbreaking, even lethal, consequences.

Across central and eastern Europe, there is even at the turn of the 21st century a missing generation of older people with mental retardation. Some were murdered under Operation T-4, the plan to liquidate people within the domains of the Third Reich who were deemed to have mental disabilities or physical deformities. Others succumbed to the ravages of war, dislocation, harsh discrimination, or their own weakened constitutions. Out of these and other indescribable horrors, the world community has slowly built an edifice of human rights. Out of shocking memories, inspiration has come for progressive changes. Thus, professionals in the field of developmental disabilities from many lands have tried to fashion and fund supports that satisfy the rights and needs of older adults with these disabilities.

For Germain Weber, experiences in his family and with a mentor ultimately led him to the co-editorship of this book. As a young child, he witnessed the cognitive and emotional deterioration of his great-grandmother, "Dit." This strongly influenced his decision during his graduate studies in psychology to specialize in developmental neuropsychology and clinical psychology. Later, as a young researcher, he adopted a life-span approach, focusing first on developmental disabilities and later on neurodegenerative conditions of old age. Returning to Europe from a Fulbright fellowship at the State University of New York at Stony Brook, he contacted Dr. Andreas Rett (best known for discovering Rett syndrome) in Vienna. At their first meeting in 1983, Dr. Rett convincingly argued to Dr. Weber that, in the field of developmental disabilities, the issue of aging urgently needed to be explored in terms of basic and applied research as well as in terms of developing systems of social support. Clearly, this was not only a professional challenge but a unique personal challenge as well. In short order, as Dr. Weber put it, "I felt this field to be my home—serving and advocating for those who risked being abandoned to their fate."

This book has its immediate origins in the Sixth International Roundtable on Aging and Intellectual Disabilities, hosted by the University of Vienna in April 1995. The invited participants were asked to focus on aging and rights and the ways in which older people with mental retardation and other developmental disabilities enjoy a varying quality of life in their respective 16 countries. Coincidentally, it was the 50th anniversary of the end of Austria's involvement in the Third Reich and a moment that called for recognizing hard truths about the past and engaging in deep reflection on the place of human rights imperatives and quality assurances for the future. This volume consists of substantially rewritten versions of papers selected from those submitted to the International Roundtable as well as additional invited contributions from senior scholars in the field.

This book focuses on a group that needs the ardent attention of practitioners, researchers, advocates, and policy makers. It analyzes national and international advances in human rights and quality assurance for older people with developmental disabilities. Too often, the precise needs of this population have been overlooked in the scientific literature; policy-planning documents; and the day-to-day tasks of ensuring their basic rights, dignity, and access to humane and stimulating living environments. Although human rights are universal, older people with developmental disabilities at many times and in many places have not enjoyed those rights and promises fully for a variety of reasons. Although this book identifies those gaps, it also records heartening progress. Parents, professionals, self-advocates, and policy makers in various countries have much to learn from each other's innovations in protecting rights; implementing quality assurance measures; and applying concepts of inclusion, the least restrictive environment, and respect for the decision-making capacities of older people with mental retardation and related disabilities.

If this book helps to share that information and improves the prospects of older people with developmental disabilities in achieving a good old age, then it has met its editors' and contributors' goal.

Stanley S. Herr
Germain Weber

Acknowledgments

We are grateful to many individuals who contributed to the evolution and publication of this book. The chapter authors are owed special debts of gratitude for all of their professionalism and patience during the long gestation of this book. The support and hard work initially of Melissa Behm, Theresa Donnelly, Jennifer Kinard, and Heather Shrestha and then January Layman-Wood and Paul Klemt of Paul H. Brookes Publishing Co. helped us to nurture the project and aim for a broad audience.

Aid came from a variety of sources. The University of Vienna hosted the Sixth International Roundtable on Aging and Intellectual Disabilities, which brought many distinguished colleagues together. This academic conference was sponsored by both the University of Vienna and the Lebenshilfe Austria, the national parents' association for people with mental retardation. The Geriatrics and Gerontology Education and Research program (GGEAR) at the University of Maryland at Baltimore and its delightful coordinator, Reba Cornman, provided support and warm encouragement for this book. Senior colleagues John Goldmeier and Gunnar Dybwad offered generous advice and the benefit of their long experience. The research assistance of Linda Coco, Colleen Hogan, and Josh Udler (students at the University of Maryland School of Law) was invaluable. Dean Donald Gifford of the University of Maryland School of Law provided support through the summer research grant program. Finally, DeAnn Gradington-Wallace helped to prepare the manuscript with meticulous care and attention.

We also record here and on the dedication page a debt of love for the inspiration, time, and tolerance that we received from our families as we labored for more than 3 years on this project. They understand a simple truth—happy are they who study how to act justly for those in need. In addition, in the process of writing this book, two families have grown close to each other. Older people with developmental disabilities with whom we are in contact have also inspired us. Through the kind permission of her guardian, one of those individuals—a long-time client of Stanley S. Herr and the student attorneys of the University of Maryland School of Law's Clinical Law Office—appears on the cover of this book. In her face and in her story are tales of the enduring human spirit that scholarly books cannot capture fully. To all of our clients who taught us lessons in resilience and in hope, we add a heartfelt thanks.

To our loved ones,

Raquel Schuster-Herr
David Louis Herr
Deborah Ann Herr
Ilana Ruth Herr

Christiane Weber-Friedmann
Philipp Weber
Martin Weber
David Weber

that they might live in a world
in which each person—old or young—
is treated with dignity and kindness

1

Aging and Developmental Disabilities
Concepts and Global Perspectives

Stanley S. Herr and Germain Weber

Older people with developmental disabilities were born into a world that had far different expectations for them than those of Western societies at the turn of the 21st century. For most of the 20th century, they were not expected to have access to education and habilitation programs that were individualized and guaranteed by law, nor were they expected to be able to make choices or to enjoy the benefits of self-determination. Few were expected to enter the labor market at all, let alone compete with people without disabilities for mainstream jobs. Until the 1970s, few residential options existed for people with developmental disabilities. Many societies did not even expect these individuals to survive past childhood, let alone until old age. Before the advent of self-advocacy and the disability rights movement in the early 1970s, people with developmental disabilities were viewed as people who needed to be sheltered and sequestered from society. Through myths and stereotypes, they were often regarded as "eternal children" who needed to be dealt with in a paternalistic way and to have all decisions made for them by others.

New philosophies and newfound facts that emerged at the end of the 20th century eroded the limiting expectations of the past. As one family member of an individual with developmental disabilities expressed it, "They told us my brother, who has Down syndrome, would not live past 4. Now he's 43 and going strong. They told us he would always need to live in an institution. Now he's in a group home" (M. May, personal communication, September 1998). In contrast with the era before disability rights, when adults with disabilities were expected to go directly from the schools or makeshift substitutes to the welfare rolls, many more individuals with mental retardation are prepared for the labor market and do in fact enter it. In Sweden, for example, the number of such individuals receiving benefits (called *pensions*

1

in Sweden) dropped by 70% over a 22-year period, with the decline being attributed to an increase in job placements (Grunewald, 1997). Thus, this expression of normalization can be justified on economic as well as humanitarian grounds.

A GLOBAL PERSPECTIVE

In some parts of the world, the old paradigms of dependence and despair persist. In developing nations and the emerging states of Eastern Europe, people with developmental disabilities are often viewed, if they are lucky, as objects of charity. They often struggle for a measure of subsistence. Their concerns and aspirations are scarcely visible to the general citizenry. Some are hidden in family members' homes; others are forced to become beggars in the streets.

With the United Nations' (UN's) designation of 1999 as the International Year of Older Persons, disability rights movement activists have an opportunity to focus the international community's attention on the plight of older people with developmental disabilities. Indeed, the Larnaca Resolution (1998) and efforts by the American Association on Mental Retardation (AAMR) and other national and international nongovernmental organizations (NGOs) seek to do just that. They call on the UN and national committees to direct global attention specifically to the rights and needs of older adults with developmental disabilities in countries at all stages of socioeconomic development (Herr, 1998). Although developed countries can focus on raising the quality of life and the level of compliance with sometimes subtle and sophisticated rights of older adults with disabilities, elsewhere the problems that these individuals face are stark. Sheer survival and access to the most basic supports still loom large for many people with disabilities because of their devalued status in their countries and their dire poverty.

Older people with developmental disabilities constitute one of the most vulnerable segments of one of the world's largest minorities: the 500 million adults and children with disabilities. In developed and developing countries alike, older people with developmental disabilities as part of this minority face what UN Secretary-General Kofi Annan termed a "silent crisis" of discrimination compounded by their disproportionate placement "among the poorest strata of society" (1997, unpaginated). The publication of this book during the UN's 1999 International Year of Older Persons offers a resource for mapping the dimensions of this particular crisis and articulating positive alternative futures for older adults with disabilities.

PROSPECTS FOR A GOOD OLD AGE

This book primarily focuses on the prospects for the population with developmental disabilities to reach and enjoy a good old age in relatively affluent countries. It explores some of the major advances in improving the quality of life of older adults with developmental disabilities while ensuring respect for their human and legal rights. It analyzes the relationship between these two areas of concern and shows that they are inextricably connected. Indeed, many measures of quality of life have explicit rights dimensions (see Chapter 6), and many rights require conditions and supports that meet at least a minimum quality standard (see Chapters 2 and 5). The achievement of those rights and quality-of-life benchmarks poses major challenges both to the developmental disabilities field and to society as a whole. The international scope of this enterprise—and of this book—underlines the need to communicate and exchange innovations across national boundaries. Just as normalization and integration concepts once emerged in northern Europe and then influenced practices in many parts of the rest of the world (Hanamura, 1998), so further innovations in theory and practice can spring up anywhere in the world and be disseminated rapidly.

These challenges are exacerbated by well-established, even explosive, demographic trends. Through advances in health care and improvements in living environments, more people with developmental disabilities are living longer and more vigorous lives. More than 2,000 years ago, Cicero commended old age as "the crown of life, our play's last act" (Falconer, 1958, p. 23). For many people with developmental disabilities, the concepts of inclusion, self-determination (Sands & Wehmeyer, 1996), and person-centered planning (Wehmeyer & Sands, 1998) contain the promise of a better last act than the conditions that they experienced in their youth and their younger years. Toward this end, our book presents some examples of good practice in the field of aging and developmental disabilities. As the case studies in this book demonstrate, however, good practice often comes as the product of hard-won lessons after human tragedies and policy confusion have already occurred. In too many cases, the crown of life rests uneasily until vigilant advocacy takes place and succeeds.

DEMOGRAPHICS

Life-expectancy figures for the population with developmental disabilities show that most of that population will experience a life span that is close to that of the population without disabilities. The shift toward a "graying world" is one of the most prominent demographic features that the 21st century will inherit from the 20th. In 1950, barely 8% of the total U.S. population were ages 65 and older. This group's proportionate representation in the U.S. population had reached more than 12% in 1990 and is expected to grow to more than 14% by 2000 (U.S. Senate Special Committee on Aging, 1991). Moreover, the population older than age 65 has become the most rapidly growing age group in wealthy nations. By 2050, the proportionate representation of the younger population (i.e., people up to age 18 years) and the population older than age 65 will be similar: 23% for the younger group and 24% for the older group. These demographic figures represent a huge shift from those of 1900, when the proportionate representation of these groups in the population were 44% for the younger group and 4% for the older group (U.S. Senate Special Committee on Aging, 1991).

During the 20th century, people with developmental disabilities in Western nations experienced dramatic gains in longevity. This fact is revealed by various investigations that were based on samples rather than on total population studies. In 1929, the mean life expectancy for people with Down syndrome was 9 years (Penrose, 1949); in 1930, the mean life expectancy for people with mental retardation in general was approximately 20 years (Carter & Jancar, 1983). By 1986, the life expectancy of people with Down syndrome had increased to 47 years (Dupont, Vaeth, & Videbich, 1986), and by 1980, the life expectancy of people with developmental disabilities in general had increased to 58 years (Carter & Jancar, 1983). By 1996, the life expectancy of people with mental retardation requiring intermittent to limited supports—a group that comprises about 95% of the total number of people who meet the criteria for having mental retardation (Luckasson et al., 1992)—had increased even further: A life-table analysis conducted in California revealed that people with Down syndrome had a life expectancy of 60–64 years and that people with other developmental disabilities had a life expectancy of 70–74 years (Strauss & Eyman, 1996).

It is generally estimated that this population constitutes 4 in 1,000 older adults in the U.S. population. The absolute number of U.S. citizens ages 60 and older with mental retardation may range from 200,000 to 500,000 (Janicki, 1996). Warren (1998) reported that the number of people with mental retardation ages 60 and older is expected to increase from 526,000 to 1,065,000 by 2030. The increasing number of such older people alone is a strong reason for systematically studying the aging process and its impact on people with developmental disabilities.

CORE CONCEPTS AND THEIR INTERRELATIONSHIPS

An overview of the main concepts of aging, rights, and the quality of life of people with developmental disabilities, and the interrelationships among these concepts, is a necessary starting point of this book. Because this is an interdisciplinary and internationally focused book, it is especially important to define terms, adopt a common terminology, and identify areas of agreement and difference. Dybwad, in the Foreword, aptly captures the spirit of the editors' and contributing authors' common enterprise when he observes that older people with developmental disabilities can no longer be treated like children. Beyond this guiding principle, however, there is a compelling need to devise roadmaps and legal frameworks so that the gains of people with disabilities in childhood, young adulthood, and middle age do not wither away in the last phases of the life cycle.

The Sixth International Roundtable on Aging and Intellectual Disabilities convened in Vienna in 1995 to tackle that challenge, focusing on aging and rights. More than 60 researchers, policy makers, and service providers gathered to search for common ground. The papers delivered and discussions that ensued clearly demonstrated the diverse and urgent issues in the fields of aging and developmental disabilities as analyzed by respected leaders from disciplines such as law, psychology, sociology, medicine, public policy, and education.

The Roundtable revealed two striking points of convergence. First was the overall vulnerability of older citizens with developmental disabilities. Second was their need for approaches to provision of supports based on rights and quality-of-life concepts. Prior to the meeting, experts from 16 countries received profiles, called "case studies," of three older people with developmental disabilities, each of whom had a distinct life story and distinct capacities that were described in the profile. These experts were asked to complete a short, standardized questionnaire on where these three individuals would probably live in their home countries (e.g., own apartment, group home, institution). Furthermore, they briefly assessed the quality of life that the three older adults might experience in their home countries. The experts' replies to the questionnaire showed only a few variations among countries, mainly in the degree of institutionalization and the quality of residential facilities. (Eastern European countries were the exception; their supports were significantly poorer than those in the West.) Other variations in the quality of life for older adults with developmental disabilities resulted from the different paradigms on which such facilities (i.e., own apartment, group home, institution) could be expected to operate. A striking observation, however, was that many experts predicted wide disparities in the worst and best environmental conditions to which the individuals would be subjected in their home countries. Some experts assumed that the variation in rights and quality of life within a particular country or region might be far more prominent than even the variation between the countries.

This extreme variability clearly points to the issue of equal opportunities in old age for people with developmental disabilities. It suggests the need for further research to understand the reasons why older adults with developmental disabilities experience a poorer or a richer quality of life in relation to their needs, particularly factors such as choice of residence, day activities, and self-determination that influence the prospects for a poor or a rich life as an older adult with developmental disabilities. Obviously, such an individual may receive more or less adequate environmental support and thus may be exposed to different risks of abuse and neglect.

These observations suggest the need for a closer look at the human rights and legal situations of older adults with developmental disabilities. One needs to ask not only what legal frameworks and legal instruments exist on the international and national levels for older people with developmental disabilities but also how these instruments (e.g., laws, declarations, treaties) are in fact being used to protect them. The responses to the Roundtable's questionnaire indicated that the preconditions and opportunities for full participation in society in various countries are not widely available to older adults with developmental disabilities (see Chapter 14). The basic empirical results also underscored the need to analyze ways to promote a high quality of life in terms of the special needs of this population within the life-span approach described in the following subsection of this chapter.

Aging and Gerontology

From the demographic trends mentioned, it is clear that gerontology is of growing importance in the field of developmental disabilities. Gerontology—the systematic study of the aging process—was first acknowledged in this field only in the mid-1980s and 1990s (Hogg, Moss, & Cooke, 1988; Janicki & Wisniewski, 1985; Seltzer, Krauss, & Janicki, 1994). Gerontology as an interdisciplinary field of study with regard to the general population, however, has a long tradition, and it received heightened interest as life expectancy grew steadily in wealthy nations during the 20th century (Binstock, George, Marshall, & Schulz, 1995; Birren, 1959; Tibbitts, 1960).

Studies and research approach aging as a lifelong process rather than merely as an aspect of older adulthood. This developmental life-span approach is well established in the study of gerontology and offers novel and valuable perspectives for professionals studying the aging process in people with developmental disabilities. Accordingly, a concern with aging should not focus only on senior citizens with developmental disabilities and their so-called golden age. To better understand the vast diversity of the aging process among older adults with developmental disabilities, researchers include children and adults and consider environmental characteristics in their studies. Without knowledge of the entire life span of these individuals, it is hard for researchers to understand the events of any other phase of their lives, especially the phase of old age. One must understand these individuals' earlier stages of life to assist them in coping with the challenges of aging. Those issues include maintaining or developing their personal independence with advancing age, supporting their role transitions, and helping them adapt to changes in family structures or other natural networks.

Aging is characterized by both personal and social processes. Just as biology and psychology largely determine the personal or individual aging process, the impact of social, cultural, and economic factors on the aging process are the domain of social gerontology. With respect to the personal process of aging, older people's beliefs and attitudes may evolve according to their changing needs. This evolution is reflected in the cognitive theory of aging (Thomae, 1970), which states that objective behavioral changes such as emerging health problems are strongly related to subjective changes (i.e., the individual's beliefs).

Obviously, an individual's aging process occurs in a social and ecological context. This context, however, largely determines one's individual and social experiences of aging. Apart from being an academic discipline, gerontology is also a field of practice. Its practice is influenced deeply by public policy with regard to both resource allocation and regulation. Because of the increasing number of older people in general, including those with and without disabilities, the major challenges in the 21st century will be to ensure that public policy adds sufficient resources for older people with developmental disabilities and their families and truly provides for their basic rights. The practice of gerontology is affected by the outcomes of larger political struggles to define the degree of social and economic responsibility for vulnerable, marginalized groups in society. The attitudes of the general public and professionals in the field of gerontology may be referred to as *social solidarity*, the belief that social cohesion is furthered by remembering that the inclusion of people with developmental disabilities is an outcome of persistent advocacy focusing on their rights.

Rights

The basic rights of older adults with developmental disabilities do not essentially differ from the basic rights of individuals in general. Despite this principle of equality, the basic rights of older adults in general are at higher risk of erosion, especially those of older adults with developmental disabilities. These individuals often experience many forms of social discrimination, neglect, and community indifference. Rights are not self-enforcing. It takes knowledge, energy, initiative, and even courage to claim liberty, services, or property as a right rather than as a favor or a concession from powerful people or institutions. Chapter 2, for example, discusses the circumstances of Charles Turner, who fought for compensation for decades of institutional peonage while he was still living in a large state-run residential facility. Before he was willing to make his claim for compensation, Turner sought reassurance over and over again that it was the right thing to do and that it would not lead to his discharge or to any other form of retaliation.

People who have spent a lifetime acquiescing to authority figures do not suddenly feel comfortable in roles that require self-assertion in their later years. Assertion of one's rights is even more demanding than other forms of self-assertion. The Academy Award–winning movie documentary *Best Boy* (Wohl, 1980) and its sequel *Best Man* (Wohl, 1997) suggested, however, that despite parental overprotection in their pasts, older people with developmental disabilities can learn to become more autonomous. Philly Wohl, the subject of these documentary memoirs, moved at age 52 from his mother's home to a group home. At age 70, he claimed the right to recognition of his manhood and membership in his religious community when he underwent a bar mitzvah, the Jewish rite of passage that generally occurs at the age of 13. (At that age, Philly had been placed in an institution briefly.)

As the example of Philly Wohl illustrates, not all rights are legally based or precisely defined. Some statements of rights are framed in language that seems more aspirational than precatory. Thus, Cotten and Spirrison proposed the following bill of rights for older people with developmental disabilities:

- The right to an adequate standard of living, economic security, and protective work.
- The right to humane services designed to help them reach their fullest potential.
- The right to live as independently as they are able and wish in the community of their choice, in as normal a manner as is possible.
- The right to an array of services that is generally available to other elderly groups.
- The right to choose to retire. In addition, the opportunity to retire "to something" rather than just "from something."
- The right to participate as a member of the community, having reciprocal interdependency [of relationships].
- The right to be considered a person and not merely "elderly" or "retarded."
- The right to protected well-being, and to a qualified guardian, when required.
- The right to be involved in setting one's goals and making one's own decisions. The right to fail if necessary.
- The right to a positive future, having enough involvement with life to prevent a preoccupation with death.
- The right to be romantic [rather than] asexual.
- The right to sufficient activity and attention to permit continued integrity of self, individual identity, and purpose.
- The right to an interesting environment and life style, with [the] availability of sufficient mobility to provide a variety of surroundings.
- The right to live and die with dignity. (1986, pp. 164–165)

The preceding bill of rights is still a valid one. The creative and thorough legal advocate can probably find "hard law" consisting of statutes, regulations, and case precedents to back up and make more specific most of these rights. Unfortunately, the average citizen, and even those closest to people with developmental disabilities, may be ignorant of the legal foundations of these rights and the steps necessary to ensure their protection. As a U.S. President's Committee on Mental Retardation report candidly explained, "in many cases the very people in the best position to facilitate the expression of rights for people with mental retardation (paid support staff, families, guardians, etc.) are also very likely to be obstructing the expression of those rights" (Hewitt & O'Nell, 1998, p. 8).

This entourage of staff and family supporters does not need a legal treatise but rather a guide to core issues of rights that can lead to improved quality of life for older people with developmental disabilities. Those issues include but are not limited to rights to habilitation; medical services; protection from abuse and neglect; housing; fair employment; financial entitlement; wholesome living conditions in facilities; nondiscrimination; least restrictive protective services; and a panoply of other rights under state, federal, and international law and standards. For a variety of reasons, children and youth with disabilities often have better access to free legal services programs than do their aging counterparts. Children and youth with disabilities may have clearer statutory entitlement or more vigorous surrogates to demand their rights. Not surprisingly, the largest category of cases handled by the federally mandated Protection and Advocacy Systems (i.e., offices for legal and other advocacy services in the United States) are education cases, which constituted 36% of the total caseload in 1996 and 1997 (Hewitt & O'Nell, 1998). It will take a for-

termining quality of life for older people with developmental disabilities. Feeling safe and secure in one's residence might improve the quality of life of these individuals. Day services and activities should be evaluated with respect to not only their functional characteristics but also whether the activities are meaningful for older adults and whether they relate to individuals' competencies. In addition, the age and health status of caregivers must be considered. This factor is strongly supported by U.S. estimates that more than 80% of people with developmental disabilities who are older than age 60 years live at home with family caregivers (Warren, 1998). Indeed, Braddock (1998) found that 479,862 people, constituting some 25% of the total number of such individuals living with family caregivers, reside with caregivers older than age 60. By analyzing these data, one can assume that the caregivers themselves have reached an advanced age. Many of these older family caregivers might experience major age-related physical health problems that affect not only their own quality of life but also the quality of life of those for whom they care.

In summary, poor health and poor support services are major challenges for older people with developmental disabilities. Research on quality of life does not focus on the fantasy of the long-lasting "golden years" but aims to promote the well-being of older people with developmental disabilities and prevent them from experiencing premature dependency and infirmity. Promoting quality of life thus contributes to reducing costly health services while supporting successful aging and a sense of well-being.

THE ORGANIZATION OF THIS BOOK

The contributing authors of this book are leading researchers in the developmental disabilities field. In the chapters that follow, they address the central issues affecting the rights and quality of life of older adults with developmental disabilities. Supports for such people must be based on effective social policies, modern legal regulations, and the application (i.e., active use) of international human rights declarations. Moreover, quality of life as perceived by the individual is determined by personal needs and regulated by psychological functions. Furthermore, the individual's entourage (i.e., staff, family members, friends) plays a key role in providing and monitoring quality of life for the individual and invoking his or her rights.

This book consists of four parts. Part I addresses human rights and legal considerations, identifying key issues of advocacy and rights enforcement in the context of aging and developmental disabilities. It documents the general recognition of the basic principles of human rights for people with developmental disabilities, describes successful efforts to promote and defend the rights of older people with developmental disabilities, and explores why many experience an untenable diminution in the exercise of their rights as they age.

In Chapter 2, Herr introduces and examines human rights challenges for older people. Through historical and legal perspectives, he presents milestones in international and national advocacy as well as case studies that reveal the many forms of legal protection required by older people who have been classified as having developmental disabilities. In Chapter 3, Nowak focuses on international human rights such as the right to equality, the right to nondiscrimination, and the ever-growing role of general and special human rights in modern disability policy. He traces developments of the 1990s in defining the human rights of older adults and of people with disabilities—including the UN Standard Rules on the Equalization of Opportunities for Persons with Disabilities—and analyzes their implications for older adults with mental retardation.

In Chapter 4, Kapp examines the issue of decision making when caring for older people with developmental disabilities. The issues related to informed consent and surrogate decision making are analyzed according to ethical as well as legal considerations. He reflects on the limitations of future financing of health care services and their implications for this population.

In Chapter 5, Herr analyzes the state of U.S. law at the turn of the 21st century as it affects the rights of older people with developmental disabilities. Herr focuses on four critical areas:

1. The right to protection of fundamental rights through access to counsel and to the system of justice
2. The right to live in least restrictive environments, primarily in the community
3. The rights to humane care and freedom from physical or mental abuse
4. The right to nondiscrimination in obtaining services, jobs, and medical care

In Part II, on quality of life and quality standards, the focus is on concepts and practices that have had a major influence on the developmental disabilities field's drive to promote a more meaningful life for people with developmental disabilities. There is a growing belief that quality of life must be evaluated from the subjective standpoint of the individual. Quality standards, however, are often defined in terms of minimum standards in the residential environment, such as requirements for design of the physical environment and staff qualification. Although there is a vast amount of research on issues related to physical environment and staff qualification as they relate to the individual's quality of life in earlier life stages, little attention has been paid to these issues as they relate to people with developmental disabilities in old age. Part II also presents a close analysis of the relationship between quality of life, quality standards, and rights of older people with developmental disabilities.

Schalock, DeVries, and Lebsack, in Chapter 6, analyze quality-enhancement techniques on the basis of the core dimensions of quality of life for older people with mental retardation. The relationship of quality-of-life concerns to rights principles or rights assertion and program change, which is crucial for people of advanced age, are examined in the framework of successful aging.

In Chapter 7, Hawkins explores how the individual rights of older people with developmental disabilities are threatened by ageism and discrimination. She concludes by offering a standard of a good old age founded on a framework of successful aging for older U.S. citizens. She illustrates this standard with various case studies regarding place of residence and retirement options.

In Chapter 8, Walker, Walker, and Gosling study processes and practices that foster dependency and limit the freedom of older people with developmental disabilities in the British context. They closely examine current practice and service provisions that undermine the person's independence in environments for older people with developmental disabilities and suggest ways to improve their human rights.

In Chapter 9, Klicpera and Gasteiger-Klicpera address major concerns about the organization of services for older people with developmental disabilities and methods of quality assurance. Analyzing factors by which quality of care can be enhanced in a variety of environments, they stress means by which to empower older adults and support these individuals' relatives. They also suggest staff incentives to improve quality and reduce staff resistance to program changes.

Part III identifies service models and innovations that can support older people with developmental disabilities on a daily basis and in times of crisis. There is a general agreement among the chapter authors in Part III to opt for a person-centered paradigm when designing services of support and more closely consider the individual needs of older people who receive care.

Heller, in Chapter 10, examines major challenges that professionals face in responding to the changing needs of older people with developmental disabilities and their families, such as demographic trends, emerging service philosophies, new service and caregiving program models, assistance through technological advances, and self-advocacy for older people with developmental disabilities. In Chapter 11, Moss provides a comprehensive account of the mental health needs of older people with developmental disabilities. Advances in defining, recognizing, and diagnosing mental health problems in this population are presented and discussed. He also addresses models for appropriate services to meet individuals' specific mental health needs. In Chapter 12, Ludlow gives a thorough examination of the various issues related to life after the loss of a loved one. She integrates personal stories of loss with the service, legal, ethical, and practical implications.

In Chapter 13, Molander describes the advances in services and accommodation models in Sweden, one of the leading nations in providing services to older people with mental retardation. From an international perspective, in Chapter 14 Conliffe and Walsh compare the availability of equal opportunities for older people with developmental disabilities with the opportunities for older people without disabilities. They then propose an agenda for collaborative research in this field. Weber and Fritsch, in Chapter 15, explore issues related to the satisfaction of older adults with developmental disabilities with their residential arrangements. First, these authors discuss basic psychological functions conducive to well-being and the relationship between these functions and the quality of life as the older person with developmental disabilities perceives it. Next, they outline residential options for older people in Europe, using case reports of questionable clinical approaches as well as examples of good practice for accommodating older people with developmental disabilities.

Part IV suggests future directions for enhancing the services for, and the self-determination of, older people with developmental disabilities. The themes addressed not only analyze various ways to proceed but also point out major changes in social and health policies that might crucially affect older people with developmental disabilities. Levitz, in Chapter 16, addresses the expectations for a good life in one's older years from the perspective of self-advocates. Chapter 16 contains a survey of self-advocates and eloquently reinforces the call of earlier chapters for professionals to listen more carefully to the expectations of older people with developmental disabilities and to offer these individuals opportunities according to their expressed needs and aspirations. In Chapter 17, Janicki examines the fundamentals of public policies for older adults and the principles of aging with dignity. He emphasizes a planning agenda to meet the needs of an aging population according to changes in ideology and social practicalities. Goldmeier and Herr, in Chapter 18, highlight the concepts of empowerment and inclusion in general. Techniques and actions based on these concepts counter paternalistically operated environments and narrow routines of life. In evaluating the various forms of empowerment, they explore valuable additions to the lives of older people with developmental disabilities. In Chapter 19, Herr and Brohawn focus on systems of managed care and the legal regulation of care decisions made by health maintenance organizations and governmental agencies in the Unites States for older people with developmental disabilities. They discuss leading legal precedents and illustrate effective procedures when consumers complain of health care decisions that place them at risk. In Chapter 20, Herr and Weber weigh the prospects for ensuring rights and quality support at the start of a new millennium. They identify risks, suggest remedies, and conclude with recommendations for treating the subjects of this book with the dignity and humanity they deserve.

TERMINOLOGY

The developmental disabilities field is again at an awkward juncture with regard to the language used to identify people with substantial limitations in intellectual functioning. In the United States, the term *mental retardation* is widely used and carefully defined. According to the AAMR (Luckasson et al., 1992), the definitional elements include significantly subaverage intellectual functioning; concurrent limitations in two or more skill areas such as self-care, home living, and communication; and manifestation of these conditions before age 18 years.

In many other parts of the world, the term *intellectual disability* is used as a synonym or replacement for *mental retardation*. This trend has gained support with the naming of the field's international professional NGO the International Association for the Scientific Study of Intellectual Disability; the interest in that term expressed by the AAMR Board of Directors in 1998; and the search, often elusive, for what some self-advocates and others view as more respectful language than the status quo. The editors of this book have charted a middle ground by generally using the term *developmental disability* in lieu of both of the just-mentioned alternatives. Often the text adopts the variant *developmental disabilities* in recognition of the several distinct clinical conditions that may be encompassed within this legislative and professional rubric (see, e.g., the Developmental Disabilities Assistance and Bill of Rights Act of 1975 [PL 94-103] and its amendments, such as the Developmental Disabilities Assistance and Bill of Rights Act Amendments of 1987 [PL 100-146]). In a technical and legal sense, the terms *mental retardation* and *developmental disability* are not interchangeable, because the U.S. law cited previously, for example, includes within its definition of a developmental disability that which may be attributable to a mental or physical impairment, meets a severity threshold (i.e., results in substantial functional limitations in three or more major life activities), and manifests itself at a later age (i.e., before age 22 years). The editors believe, however, that, for the purposes of this book, the term *developmental disabilities* captures the tone, target population, and broad community of interest that is consistent with their inclusive aims. The goal is not to label individuals but to encourage communication among professionals, researchers, and self-advocates that is sensitive and global in reach.

At times, the chapter authors in this book use different terminology in referring to the laws of their home countries or to specific contexts in which other usages are more appropriate. In general, the term *developmental disabilities* is intended to subsume the categories that in various parts of the world are called *mental retardation* or *intellectual disability*. As Shakespeare wrote, "What's in a

name? That which we call a rose by any other name would smell as sweet"
(1594/1987, Act II, Scene II, lines 43–44, p. 75).

REFERENCES

Annan, K. (1997, 3 December). *Secretary-general's message on International Day of Disabled
    Persons cites discrimination against "world's largest minority"* (United Nations press re-
    lease). New York: United Nations.
Arber, S., & Ginn, J. (Eds.). (1995). *Connecting gender and ageing: A sociological approach.*
    Philadelphia: Open University Press.
Bech, P. (1992). Quality of life measurement in the medical setting. *International Journal of
    Methods in Psychiatric Research, 2,* 139–144.
Binstock, R.H., George, L.K., Marshall, V.W., & Schulz, J.H. (Eds.). (1995). *Handbooks of
    aging series: Handbook of aging and the social sciences* (4th ed.). San Diego: Academic
    Press.
Birren, J.E. (1959). *Handbook of aging and the individual: Psychological and biological as-
    pects.* Chicago: University of Chicago Press.
Braddock, D.L. (1998, September 18). *Aging with developmental disabilities: Demographics
    and policy issues affecting American families.* Statement before the U.S. Senate Special
    Committee on Aging, Washington, DC; summarized in *AAMR News and Notes* (1998/
    November/December), *11*(6), 3–4.
Brown, R.I. (Ed.). (1997). *Quality of life for people with disabilities: Models, research, and
    practice* (2nd ed.). Cheltenham, England: Stanley Thornes Publishers.
Carpenter v. Johnson, No. 3:95cv2778 (WIG) (D. Conn., September 18, 1998) (jury verdict)
    (judgment entered on December 1, 1998, for $1.04 million).
Carter, G., & Jancar, J. (1983). Mortality in the mentally handicapped: A fifty year survey at
    State Park Group Hospitals (1930–1980). *Journal of Mental Deficiency Research, 27,*
    143–156.
Cotten, P.D., & Spirrison, C.L. (1986). The elderly mentally retarded (developmentally dis-
    abled) population: A challenge for the service delivery system. In S.J. Brody & G.E. Ruff,
    Aging and rehabilitation: Advances in the state of the art. New York: Springer Publish-
    ing Co.
Developmental Disabilities Assistance and Bill of Rights Act of 1975, PL 94-103, 42 U.S.C.
    §§ 6000 *et seq.*
Developmental Disabilities Assistance and Bill of Rights Act Amendments of 1987, PL 100-
    146, 42 U.S.C. §§ 6000 *et seq.*
Dupont, A., Vaeth, M., & Videbech, P. (1986). Mortality and life expectancy of Down's syn-
    drome in Denmark. *Journal of Mental Deficiency Research, 30,* 111–120.
Edgerton, B. (1994). Quality of life issues: Some people know how to be old. In M.M. Seltzer,
    M.W. Krauss, & M.P. Janicki (Eds.), *Life course perspectives on adulthood and old age*
    (pp. 53–66). Washington, DC: American Association on Mental Retardation.
Falconer, W.A. (Ed. & Trans.). (1958). *Cicero's Cato major de senectute.* Cambridge, MA:
    Harvard University Press. (Original work written circa 55 B.C.E.)
Felce, D. (1997). Defining and applying the concept of quality of life. *Journal of Intellectual
    Disability Research, 41,* 126–135.
Felce, D., & Perry, J. (1995). Quality of life: Its definition and measurement. *Research in De-
    velopmental Disabilities, 16,* 51–74.
Felce, D., & Perry, J. (1997). Quality of life: The scope of the term and its breadth of mea-
    surement. In R.I. Brown (Ed.), *Quality of life for people with disabilities: Models, research,
    and practice* (2nd ed., pp. 56–71). Cheltenham, England: Stanley Thornes Publishers.
Ferring, D., & Filipp, S.H. (1997). Subjektives Wohlbefinden im Alter: Struktur- und Stabili-
    tätsanalysen [Subjective well-being in old age: Analyses of structure and stability]. *Psycho-
    logische Beiträge, 39,* 236–258.
Goode, D.A. (1988). *Discussing quality of life (QOL): Framework and findings of the Work
    Group on QOL for Persons with Disabilities.* Valhalla, NY: Mental Retardation Institute.
Goode, D.A. (Ed.). (1994). *Quality of life for persons with disabilities: International perspec-
    tives and issues.* Cambridge, MA: Brookline Books.

Grunewald, K. (1997). Effect of social and educational policies on the number of persons with mild mental retardation in Sweden. *Mental Retardation, 35*, 218–220.

Hanamura, H. (1998). *Niels Erik Bank-Mikkelsen: Father of the normalization principle.* Bogense, Denmark: Niels Erik Bank-Mikkelsen Memorial Foundation.

Hatton, C. (1998). Whose quality of life is it anyway? Some problems with the emerging quality of life consensus. *Mental Retardation, 36*, 104–115.

Heinlein, K.B. (1994). Quality of care, quality of life: A rural perspective. *Developmental Disabilities, 32*, 374–376.

Herr, S.S. (1998, September). Life, liberty, and happiness: Part III. Pursuing international dimensions. *AAMR News and Notes, 11*(5), 2, 5.

Hewitt, A., & O'Nell, S. (1998). Speaking up—speaking out. In Y. Bestgen, *With a little help from my friends. . . : A series on contemporary supports to people with mental retardation* (pp. 1–34). Washington, DC: U.S. President's Committee on Mental Retardation.

Hogg, J., & Lambe, L. (1997). An ecological perspective on the quality of life of people with intellectual disabilities as they age. In R.I. Brown (Ed.), *Quality of life for people with disabilities: Models, research and practice* (2nd ed., pp. 201–227). Cheltenham, England: Stanley Thornes Publishers.

Hogg, J., Moss, S., & Cooke, D. (1988). *Ageing and mental handicap.* London: Croom Helm.

Janicki, M.P. (1997). Quality of life for older persons with mental retardation. In R.L. Schalock (Ed.), *Quality of life: Volume II. Application to persons with disabilities* (pp. 105–115). Washington, DC: American Association on Mental Retardation.

Janicki, M.P., & Wisniewski, H.M. (Eds.). (1985). *Aging and developmental disabilities: Issues and approaches.* Baltimore: Paul H. Brookes Publishing Co.

Larnaca Resolution. (1998). International Conference on Intellectual and Developmental Disabilities, Larnaca Cyprus; reprinted in *Journal of Intellectual Disabilities Research, 42*, 262.

Luckasson, R., Coulter, D.L., Polloway, E.A., Reiss, S., Schalock, R.L., Snell, M.E., Spitalnik, D.M., & Stark, J.A. (1992). *Mental retardation: Definitions, classification, and systems of supports* (Special 9th ed.). Washington, DC: American Association on Mental Retardation.

Moss, S. (1994). Quality of life and aging. In D.A. Goode (Ed.), *Quality of life for persons with disabilities* (pp. 218–234). Cambridge, MA: Brookline Books.

Penrose, L. (1949). The incidence of Mongolism in the general population. *Journal of the Mental Sciences, 95*, 685.

Phillips, L.R., Morrison, E.F., & Chao, Y.M. (1990). The QUALICARE Scale: Developing an instrument to measure the quality of home care. *International Journal of Nursing Studies, 27*, 61–75.

Posner, R.A. (1996). *Aging and old age.* Chicago: University of Chicago Press.

Sands, D.J., & Wehmeyer, M.L. (Eds.). (1996). *Self-determination across the life span: Independence and choice for people with disabilities.* Baltimore: Paul H. Brookes Publishing Co.

Schalock, R.L. (Ed.). (1990). *Quality of life: Perspectives and issues.* Washington, DC: American Association on Mental Retardation.

Schalock, R.L. (Ed.). (1996). *Quality of life: Vol. I. Conceptualization and measurement.* Washington, DC: American Association on Mental Retardation.

Schalock, R.L. (Ed.). (1997). *Quality of life: Volume II. Application to persons with disabilities.* Washington, DC: American Association on Mental Retardation.

Seltzer, M.M., Krauss, M.W., & Janicki, M.P. (Eds.). (1994). *Life course perspectives on adulthood and old age.* Washington, DC: American Association on Mental Retardation.

Shakespeare, W. (1987). *Romeo and Juliet.* In S. Barnet & J.A. Bryant (Eds.), *Signet classics.* New York: New American Library. (Original work published 1594)

Strauss, D., & Eyman, R.K. (1996). Mortality of people with mental retardation in California with and without Down syndrome, 1986–1991. *American Journal on Mental Retardation, 100*, 643–653.

Thomae, H. (1970). Theory of aging and cognitive theory of personality. *Human Development, 13*, 1–16.

Thunderborg, K., Allerup, P., Bech, P., & Joyce, C.R.B. (1993). Development of the repertory grid for measurement of individual quality of life in clinical trials. *International Journal of Methods in Psychiatric Research, 3*, 45–56.

Tibbitts, C. (1960). *Handbook of social gerontology: Societal aspects of aging.* Chicago: University of Chicago Press.

United Nations (UN). (1993, December 20). UN standard rules on equalization of opportunities for persons with disabilities. General Assembly 48th Session, Resolution 48/96;
reprinted in United Nations (UN). (1994). *Yearbook of the United Nations 1993* (Vol. 47,
pp. 978–988). Dordrecht, the Netherlands: Martinus Nijhoff Publishers.

U.S. Senate Special Committee on Aging. (1991). *Aging America: Trends and projections
133.* Washington, DC: U.S. Government Printing Office.

Warren, D. (1998). The health care needs of the aging person with mental retardation (Abstract). In S.S. Herr (Ed.), *Abstract of proceedings to the 122nd annual meeting.* Washington, DC: American Association on Mental Retardation.

Wehmeyer, M.L., & Sands, D.J. (Eds.). (1998). *Making it happen: Student involvement in education planning, decision making, and instruction.* Baltimore: Paul H. Brookes Publishing Co.

Wohl, I. (Producer & Director). (1980). *Best boy* [Film]. Beverly Hills, CA: Only Child Motion
Pictures. (Available from Only Child Motion Pictures, Inc., Post Office Box 184, Beverly
Hills, California 90213.)

Wohl, I. (Producer & Director). (1997). *Best man* [Film]. Beverly Hills, CA: Only Child Motion Pictures. (Available from Only Child Motion Pictures, Inc., Post Office Box 184, Beverly Hills, California 90213.)

I

Human Rights and
Legal Considerations

2

Aging and Advocacy

Stanley S. Herr

People with mental retardation and other intellectual disabilities need compassion, but, as history teaches, they also need enforceable rights and devoted advocates. These concepts, once controversial, are widely accepted. Indeed, the American Association on Mental Retardation (AAMR) defines as central elements of its mission advocating for progressive polices and promoting the human rights and dignity of people with mental retardation and related developmental disabilities. This human rights thrust was also reflected in the theme of AAMR's 1998 annual meeting: "In pursuit of life, liberty, and happiness." It is also powerfully articulated in its long line of amicus curiae briefs submitted to the U.S. Supreme Court and other tribunals on issues ranging from zoning approval for group homes in the community to civil commitment standards (e.g., *City of Cleburne v. Cleburne Living Center,* 1985; *Heller v. Doe,* 1993). Although advocates for those with disabilities, and societies as a whole, in many parts of the world have made tangible progress in achieving humane goals for older people with developmental disabilities, this chapter recounts a disturbing history and considers the distance still to be traveled in the pursuit of the life, liberty, and happiness of people with disabilities. Aging people with disabilities in particular should command the human services field's attention because they are not only becoming ever more numerous as their life expectancy improves but also a living legacy of society's past dismal treatment of individuals once relegated to places out of sight and out of mind.

This chapter introduces some of the human rights challenges facing the field and the forms of advocacy for people who are aging and vulnerable. It discusses the need for legal protection and the longstanding problems that have generated appeals to legislatures to reduce waiting lists and to courts to eliminate patterns of abuse. It next identifies some milestones in advocacy at the national and international levels and the implications of those milestones for those with developmental disabilities who are aging. The chapter ends with case studies drawn from the author's legal practice that reveal the importance of long-term advocate–client relationships to support these older individuals in lives of dignity and happiness.

THE NEED FOR LEGAL PROTECTION

Vulnerable aging people need legal support in many forms. They need enforcement of criminal and civil laws designed to deter abuse. In the process of deinstitutionalization, they need vigilant advocates and jurists who insist on compliance with court decrees that set minimum standards of habilitation. In situations in which existing legal and social services provisions are inadequate, advocates for people with developmental disabilities must turn to legislators and executive branch officials for solutions. Some contemporary and historical illustrations of these points follow.

Waiting and Aging

Across North America, there are a growing number of people on waiting lists for residential and vocational or other day services. In 1987, there were an estimated 139,673 individuals on such lists; by 1997, that number had increased to 152,896 (The Arc of the United States: A National Organization on Mental Retardation [hereinafter The Arc], 1997). Another 65,290 had sought support services, amounting to a U.S. total of 218,186 people on waiting lists. In New York State alone, The Arc (1997) reported that 50,225 individuals were on such waiting lists, including approximately 5,500 people waiting for residential services, 30,000 waiting for day or vocational services, and more than 14,000 waiting for other support services. New York State was ranked second nationwide in the United States in terms of the proportion of its population with developmental disabilities on waiting lists (276 per 100,000), and its waiting-list population constituted more than one-fifth of the United States' waiting families (see Chapter 20).

One encouraging response to this problem is an initiative adopted in Maryland. Because Maryland was ranked in the bottom quarter of U.S. states with regard to its high waiting-list population, Maryland Governor Parris Glendening and his administration decided to take dramatic steps toward change. On April 6, 1998, the Maryland legislature adopted the Maryland Governor's Waiting List Initiative as part of the fiscal year 1999 state budget (1998 Md. Laws 109). Under this budgetary plan, Maryland projects that by 2003, more than 5,400 additional people will be served through community-based services. This initiative is an attempt to provide systemic solutions for recurrent problems that people with developmental disabilities and their families confront. The initiative expresses three major objectives:

1. To relieve the intolerable stress and worry that older family caregivers confront as they race to find adequate care and services for their children before their own demise
2. To provide support and day programs for younger parents of children with developmental disabilities
3. To avoid institutionalization by providing community-based supports

Advocates marshaled a variety of arguments to win passage of the initiative. At a February 1998 legislative hearing on a proposal for $68.4 million in new state money for the initiative, they cited studies showing that, in Maryland, "40% of family caregivers are over age 60 and 13% are over 80" (The Arc, 1997, p. 10). They urged adoption of the Maryland Governor's Waiting List Initiative to benefit not only the aged but also the aging. They argued that younger parents without supports and day programs would completely falter. Such parents, along with their older counterparts, risked becoming health care casualties themselves if society continued to fail to provide reasonable habilitation services for their children. This hazard increases when young adults with disabilities turn 21 years of age and "age out" of eligibility for public schooling and when their parents begin to turn frail and become disabled. As one witness dramatically stated, "It is not right to make these parents the prisoners of their children" (University of Maryland, Clinical Law Office, 1998, p. 2). In addition, advocates presented testimony that it is bad public policy to jeopardize the health and sanity of these parents and then later incur the added costs of the parents' disabilities along with those of their adult children with disabilities. The argument fell on receptive ears, and the Maryland General Assembly, without a dissenting vote, approved this impressive initiative. If lawmakers in subsequent legislative sessions concur, new total state and federal expenditures of $118 million over 5 years will result in the serving of all 5,435 people on Maryland's waiting list.

As of 1999, Maryland, New Jersey, and New York State have made the greatest strides in addressing waiting lists for services; New Jersey preceded Maryland, and New York followed these two states (see also discussion in the "Risks" section in Chapter 20). By 2004, New York anticipates creating 4,900 new beds. With the filling of beds that become vacant over time, New York expects to serve a total of 8,000 additional people, including 6,700 people who were on waiting lists as of July 1998 as well as others who will be added through 2003. In the first year, state officials have requested a $25 million appropriation for construction and development of new facilities.

Victimizing the Vulnerable

Abuse and exploitation of aging clients is another endemic problem. In one illustrative case, caregivers were accused of misappropriating the funds of the older consumers they were supposed to serve. In front-page news, headlines blared "Caretakers who prey on the retarded" (Francke, 1998a, p. 1A). The article in the *Baltimore Sun* revealed that Vernon Merryman, age 70 and in a wheelchair, was abandoned with two others in a group home when his caregiver stole cash, checks, clothes, and a company car to buy crack cocaine (Francke, 1998a). Another article stated that 13 residents had been victimized at the home, with one former supervisor stealing nearly $20,000 from four of the residents (Francke, 1998b). Compassion—let alone simple decency and fiscal safeguards—was absent when, in a 6-month period, this individual could loot the accounts of a 71-year-old person with mental retardation who was blind and had diabetes and cerebral palsy. Where compassion fails, the law must provide a mode of redress.

Human Rights Abuses

In the human services field, the law has not always been a reliable source of protection. For example, a few remaining older adults with developmental disabilities may have been, in their early years, the subjects of involuntary sterilization. Particularly in the pre–World War II period, some mental retardation professionals were convinced that sterilization was not only proper from a eugenic viewpoint but also compassionate because it was the key to these individuals' gaining release from an institution.

Misguided, class-biased policy and practice once prevailed in many regions of the United States. As the historian James Trent explained,

> At the 1938 annual meeting of the American Association on Mental Deficiency, G.B. Arnold (1938), a physician at the Virginia State Colony for Epileptics and Feeble-Minded, reported on Virginia's sterilization of its first 1,000 feebleminded clientele, 632 of whom had been paroled. Among these first sterilizations were 609 females and 391 males; and among these, 812 "came from families of the definitely low class—but by 'low class' we mean families whose heads are barely eking out an existence." Arnold reported only 139 patients from middle-class families and 8 from "families whose financial circumstances were definitely superior." Although sterilization might have lost its scientific respectability, it continued to serve the function of allowing a public institution like Virginia's to parole some of its lower-class patients, especially lower-class female patients. Arnold put it bluntly: "We do not now sterilize a patient unless we feel that there is a good chance of his leaving the Colony." (1994, p. 217)

Although legalized abuses change and new forms of social control develop, accounts of wrongful institutionalization still receive notoriety. In 1995, Velma Elliot, a woman who was blind and had cerebral palsy, was discovered to have been diagnosed wrongly with mental retardation when she was 10 years old. As a result, Velma, who was 43 years old when she was released, had been committed to a Texas state institution for 33 years. For most of her life, Velma lived a regimented daily life of waking up at 6:00 A.M., going to bed at 9:00 P.M., eating in a dining hall, sleeping in a dormitory, and being weighed periodically to make sure she was not overeating. She was retested, received a correct diagnosis and later was released from the state institution. Since then, freedom, for Velma, has meant waking up and going to bed when she wants to, eating whatever she likes whenever she feels like it, attending classes to earn a general equivalency diploma, and having a room with a view (Bingham, 1998). Her life in a community-based group home allows her to experience all of that and tell her story of newfound liberties. Yet, these freedoms might not have been possible for her but for plans to close the institution, which led to her being retested to determine where she should live.

Advocacy for the Long Term

It takes more than compassion to let hidden people bloom. In 1972, an alliance of civil rights lawyers and the AAMR mounted the first right to habilitation case. The ongoing litigation in the case, originally known as *Wyatt v. Stickney* (1972), is historically significant for several reasons. It was the first case to establish classwide rights to habilitation for people with mental retardation. It also provided people with mental illness a concrete right to treatment standards. The *Wyatt* litigation is unique both in the sweep of legal rights that it embraced and in the application of those rights to facilities throughout the Alabama state mental health and mental retardation systems. In a series of landmark decisions in the 1970s, the U.S. District Court for the Middle District of Alabama, speaking through Judge Frank M. Johnson, Jr., found the living conditions in Alabama's mental health and mental retardation facilities to be in violation of the most basic U.S. constitutional rights.

In 1997, more than a quarter century after the main consent decrees were entered in *Wyatt,* the federal district court again ruled that Alabama's Department of Mental Health and Mental Retardation still was not in full compliance with the original *Wyatt* standards of care and habilitation.

Numerous egregious shortcomings still plague the Alabama mental health and mental retardation systems. In a 225-page decision, the *Wyatt* court cited problems such as the housing of individuals in unsafe buildings, the failure to follow professional standards in the administration of drugs, gross examples of physical abuse and neglect of individuals, excessive use of restraints on elderly patients, failure to provide people with a least restrictive environment, and the continued institutionalization of hundreds of individuals "for no apparent or good reason" (985 F. Supp. at 1416 [1997]).

Defining the care rights of older adults in Alabama and elsewhere requires a delicate judgment. Although the residents in *Wyatt* were improperly and excessively restrained, leading to injuries and "atrophy of the elderly's mobility" (985 F. Supp. at 1399 [1997]), the court found no bright-line solutions. For elderly residents, decision makers must balance individuals' fragility and risk of injury from falling with their need for humane freedom of movement. The court, however, condemned the disregard of existing treatment standards and the acceptance of individuals' consent to standing orders for restraint when consent was dubious. If individuals cannot "meaningfully assert" their rights, safeguards to authentic or substitute consent must be provided (985 F. Supp. at 1400 [1997]).

Overrestrictiveness was at the heart of the violations of the rights of people with mental retardation. These violations, according to the *Wyatt* court, were costly in both human and fiscal terms. According to the evidence,

> Less restrictive settings, such as community residential placements, where appropriate services and supports are provided, tend to enable greater growth in skills and development for mentally-retarded individuals; whereas institutionalized settings can have adverse effects. Community settings provide a multitude of opportunities for modeling behavior and learning skills that are simply not available in institutions. And it costs on average twice as much to serve an individual with mental retardation in a state-operated institution as compared to serving that individual in the community. (985 F. Supp. at 1417 [1997] [footnotes omitted])

The court went on to hold that the decision for deinstitutionalization must be made on a case-by-case basis, with close attention being paid to the consumer's choice. Judge Myron Thompson concluded as follows:

> [T]he court concludes that the defendants' failure to offer those persons, whom they have institutionalized, an informed choice to live in less restrictive community settings where there is a professional determination that such is appropriate violates the 1986 consent decree. An "informed choice" might include the opportunity to visit community sites, talk with providers, talk with the other consumers, visit community workshops and jobs, and have a trial placement in the living arrangement. Habilitation and normalization require that the plaintiffs have this choice. Because of the defendants' failure to comply with the decree, hundreds of residents are unnecessarily institutionalized. (985 F. Supp. at 1417 [1997])

The court cited disturbing examples of physical abuse and neglect that people with mental disabilities confront in Alabama's institutions. It referred to the death of Jeff M. from choking as "one example of the sometimes fatal consequences from inadequate staffing at meal times" (985 F. Supp. at 1419 [1997]). Another resident "bled to death after being beaten by another resident" (985 F. Supp. at 1420 [1997]). The evidence of neglect was so severe in the latter case that the court concluded that the resident "probably would not have died if he had received prompt medical attention, but the staff person responsible for that area was simply not there for most of that evening" (985 F. Supp. at 1420, 1997). In situations like these, it is a strain to remember that the people who died or suffered from "unexcused abuse and neglect" were living in a facility that was intended to be a protected environment (985 F. Supp. at 1420 [1997]).

The *Wyatt* court specifically noted that these are not isolated incidents. An undercover investigation at one facility led to the 1997 indictments of 24 of its staff for abusing residents. In its summary, the district court's 1997 *Wyatt* opinion concluded that violations of standards prohibiting corporal punishment, mistreatment, and inhumane care have occurred, and noted that

> [The residents in the defendants' institutions] are not safe and are frequently abused and neglected. Staff members punch, hit, and kick defenseless mentally-retarded residents. Furthermore, failure to adequately staff residences leads to abuse and unnecessary injuries. Even more egregious is the fact that the defendants know about these problems, and yet fail to correct them. (985 F. Supp. at 1420 [1997])

With the kind of abuse just described occurring after more than 25 years of federal court involvement in the *Wyatt* litigation, one can only imagine what might have occurred if judicial oversight were completely lacking. Although in the 1997 opinion the state of Alabama was found to have been in compliance with many standards and to have come a long way from its past horrors, the court found that the state still had failed to comply with 20 standards in vital areas of habilitation. Fortunately for people with disabilities in Alabama, the federal court will continue to monitor Alabama's compliance with existing consent decrees in the *Wyatt* litigation. When compassion fails, the law must intervene.

Such intervention is common. Advocates for the aging and others have turned to federal class-action lawsuits for declaratory and injunctive relief for the residents or former residents of large institutions (Hayden, 1997). Virginia, for example, once the site for the test case for the propriety of involuntary sterilization, culminating in the infamous U.S. Supreme Court decision in *Buck v. Bell* (1927), has seen several cases arise in its jurisdiction. In *Davis v. Buckley* (1981), the plaintiff class at Southside Virginia Training Center sought release into the community if the authorities would provide them with residential placements as well as social, education, and rehabilitative programs in their home communities. In sustaining the suit, a distinguished jurist, Judge Robert R. Merhige, Jr., made short shrift of a slew of arguments by the defendants, refusing to divert the complaint to the facility's human rights committee or to a far narrower habeas corpus remedy (i.e., a remedy to free the individual from unlawful confinement). In its preliminary rulings, the court acknowledged that the state may not arbitrarily deny treatment, noting that state officials might have responsibility for "community placements where warranted" (526 F. Supp. 985, 991 [1981]).

Another Virginia case attempted to redress other old wrongs. In *Poe v. Lynchburg Training School and Hospital* (1981), the court held that the plaintiffs, who were inadequately or inaccurately informed of the purpose of the involuntary sterilization procedure that they underwent pursuant to state statute, had a legal claim on which relief could be granted. The relief sought was designed to deal with the medical, emotional, and mental problems that the elderly plaintiffs had suffered and continued to suffer as a result of their sterilization procedures. The law was first enacted in 1924 for certain "mental defectives," and the law on involuntary sterilization was not repealed in Virginia until 1974 (518 F. Supp. 789, 791 [1981]). Diligent advocates in other states have also persevered in spotlighting human and legal rights issues relevant to older people with developmental disabilities.

MILESTONES IN DISABILITY RIGHTS

On the international and national levels, advocates have long struggled to gain recognition of the human and legal rights of people with disabilities, including the rights of older people with developmental disabilities. Specific actions, however, are needed to bring declarations and legal norms to life. In this context, it is vital to recall that the horrors and abuses visited on older adults and people with disabilities in Europe in the 1930s and 1940s served as the impetus for pioneering declarations on universal human rights.

International Action

In the post–World War II era—in reaction to the Holocaust and Nazi eugenics practices and medical experiments, and in an attempt to prevent such lurid events from occurring in the future—the international community took steps to strengthen human rights. Out of these concerns came the United Nations' (UN's) Universal Declaration on Human Rights in 1948 and, in ensuing years, a long line of more particularized human rights statements (see Chapter 3). There is a link between these developments and the subject matter of this book.

In parts of Europe, there is a missing generation—the oldest people with disabilities who perished during and prior to World War II. Even before the victims of the Holocaust were targeted for extermination, there was a domestic war waged on German and Austrian nationals with disabilities. In a horrifying campaign referred to as Action T-4 that began in 1931, some 275,000 children and adults with disabilities were killed and 400,000 individuals were forcibly sterilized under the Nazi regime (Herr, 1981; Wolfensberger, 1981). People with mental retardation were dismissed as "useless eaters" and as having "lives not worth living," the old were murdered in their institutions, and the young were taken from their schools and transported on buses that gassed them with carbon monoxide. Had these horrors been averted or the perpetrators been called to justice sooner, the course of history might have changed fundamentally.

The reaction to such monumental hate crimes was a new attention to human rights. For example, the founding of the UN and the assertiveness of an international parents' movement produced several human rights milestones. As Dybwad observed, one of the earliest projects of the UN was "the formulation of a magna charta for a better world" (1997, p. 2). The UN's Universal Declaration of Human Rights, adopted on December 10, 1948, stated an emphatic "recognition of the inherent dignity and of the equal and inalienable rights of all members of the human family" (p. 2).

In the 1960s, the International League of Societies for the Mentally Handicapped (ILSMH), since renamed Inclusion International, began to articulate the specific rights and particular problems that people with mental disabilities confront in claiming dignity and equality. As also noted in this book's foreword, the ILSMH spoke clearly of the human and legal rights of adults in 1966. The ILSMH hailed public officials who "straight-forwardly . . . proclaimed that the services they were providing came to the retarded as a matter of right, not a benevolence bestowed by the goodness of Government" (ILSMH, 1966, p. 163). Within a few years after making that statement, the ILSMH held a symposium on the legislative aspects of mental retardation, produced recommendations that stressed the individual rights of people with mental retardation as human beings, and promulgated the Declaration of the General and Special Rights of the Mentally Retarded (1968). Three years later, the UN General Assembly adopted that text almost verbatim as the Declaration on the Rights of Mentally Retarded Persons (1971). The vote was 110 to 0 with 9 abstentions. At long last, the rights and concerns of such people, both young and old, had reached the world stage, with their rights being proclaimed without a dissenting vote.

In 1999, older people with disabilities gained heightened international attention. The UN declared 1999 the International Year of Older Persons. Activists in the field of developmental disabilities, joined by the AAMR and other endorsing organizations, have adopted the Larnaca (Cyprus) Resolution (1998), calling on the UN secretary-general and other planners of the 1999 activities to give focused attention to the rights and needs of older people with intellectual and other developmental disabilities. It is hoped that this global effort to raise public awareness of the concerns for the quality of life and the public policy agenda for all older people will include the distinctive concerns for those with lifelong cognitive impairments.

National Action

International standards and discussion have also helped to spur progress in the United States. One of the most dramatic illustrations of this progress is the citation of the UN Declaration on the Rights of Mentally Retarded Persons (1971) by the *Wyatt* judge in the landmark 1972 federal district court decision enforcing the constitutional right of institutionalized people to habilitation. As previously discussed, that litigation continues to this day and has spawned class-action and individual lawsuits in virtually every U.S. jurisdiction.

Another effect of cases like *Wyatt* and *New York State Association for Retarded Children v. Rockefeller* (1973) (the latter being popularly known as the Willowbrook case) is legislative reform. Federal legislation such as the Rehabilitation Act of 1973 (PL 93-112), the Developmental Disabilities Assistance and Bill of Rights Act of 1975 (PL 94-103), and the Education for All Handicapped Children Act of 1975 (PL 94-142) (since renamed the Individuals with Disabilities Education Act [IDEA] of 1990 [PL 101-476]) is marked by a civil rights thrust and a legislative history that bears the imprint of this era of judicial dynamism. The Americans with Disabilities Act (ADA) of 1990 (PL 101-336), though enacted in a later decade, completes the civil rights mission of the earlier legislation by prohibiting private sector discrimination. As more fully described in Chapter 5, U.S. federal legislation has created a floor of equality for Americans with disabilities, including those who are aging or aged.

National action also takes the form of professional and consumer association leadership to change how the public views the aspirations and values of these groups' constituencies. In this regard, the sequence of name changes of a leading consumer group is telling: The National Association for Retarded Children became the Association for Retarded Citizens, which in turn adopted as its trademark "The Arc" with the subscript "A National Organization on Mental Retardation." These changes in terminology reflected a concern for people across the life span and the still-elusive effort to find identifying language that is not viewed as an insult by the people so labeled or by their more ardent supporters. In terms of advocacy and the promotion and protection of individuals' human rights, all of the major organizations in the developmental disabilities field recognize the importance of devoting significant energy to those activities. Indeed, national action increasingly must be coordinated with work at the state and local levels as federal programs devolve to more localized units of government. These trends have significant implications for advocacy for and self-assertion by older people with disabilities and their supporters.

CASE STUDIES OF RIGHTS IN ACTION

Advocacy can be understood best at the local level, closer to where individuals with disabilities live. It is on that level that the constraints, conflicts, and competing values come into especially sharp focus when an advocate seeks to help an individual who is one among many to a service provider. The case studies in the following sections are drawn from the work of the Clinical Law Office at the University of Maryland School of Law (hereinafter referred to as the Clinical Law Office). With the exception of the late Charles Turner, who gave permission before his death to have his story told, the names of individuals discussed in the following sections of this chapter are altered to protect these individuals' confidentiality.

Advocating for Institutional Residents

People living in large public institutions have been the focus of much advocacy since the 1970s. Although class-action lawsuits have gained the most publicity, significant and noteworthy efforts have been made to improve legal and other forms of advocacy for individuals with disabilities. Issues of uncompensated labor, civil commitment, institutional conditions, protection of assets, and other basic rights are among the subject matter encountered. Charles Turner's life involved all of these issues and more.

Charles Turner

At the age of 19, Charles Turner was committed to the Asylum and Training School for the Feebleminded (since renamed the Rosewood Center). On the legal motion of his stepmother, two judges of the Orphan's Court certified that, according to the law then in force, Turner would stay in the institution until his "welfare . . . and the public interest shall justify or call for [his] release or discharge." Committed to the institution on August 8, 1924, Turner remained there for his entire life. Although "Charlie" was institutionalized for 63 years, his disabilities were more physical than mental, including a mild case of infantile paralysis at the time of his commitment and a double amputation of his legs because of an automobile accident decades later. By the time Charlie's deinstitutionalization was under consideration, he was too habituated to his routines and too connected to his girlfriend and familiar surroundings to want to leave. He did, however, want his advocates to win him "a little pension for my retirement." For 55 of his 63 years at Rosewood, Charlie had worked for no pay at various jobs essential to the maintenance of the institution. This practice, known as institutional peonage, was common. According to Charlie, for 6 days each week, he and the other "working boys" of Stump Cottage would haul coal or harvest hay. They labored in the fields, laundries, and other work stations under a plan that was designed to minimize state costs while providing the residents with some occupation. In an account published after his death, here is how Charlie described his long decades of labor:

> They drove us to the barn where you got your work detail. They had some boys for the farm and some lawn boys. I worked on the farm from 7:30 in the morning till 6 at night every day but Sunday. I carried plants to the field for planting. We'd bring in hay, bring in vegetables from the fields. (Herr, 1987b, p. 23A)

Ultimately, Charlie gained a settlement from the state for his many years of unpaid work. With these funds, he was able to take some trips, buy a television for his girlfriend, and purchase some clothes for himself. In his new suit, he received the regional AAMR's Bill Brownlowe Memorial Consumer Award for his achievements and perseverance.

In the twilight of his life, Charlie had won property, love, and a measure of honor. He had his space, his circle of caring professionals, and control over his time. His work ethic still strong, he carried out various tasks such as folding laundry well into his 70s. By then, however, he was working for pay and at hours suited to his age and stamina. Before his death, he had the satisfaction of knowing that he had funds to bequeath and that his girlfriend, Suzie, would be able to enjoy some of the extras that make for a good quality of life. In words that would serve as a memorial, he also received this tribute in his final days:

Requiem for a Rosewood Resident

You waited for us a long time
Waited for us to discover your abundant potential
Waited for us to discover your tortured rights
Waited for us to recover your lost home
Waited for us to advocate your deepest dreams
Gentle good man, you knew we would do better one day (Herr, 1987a, p. 2)

Advocating for Nursing Home Residents

One of the sadder events in the annals of deinstitutionalization was the ill-considered movement of thousands of people with developmental disabilities to custodial nursing facilities. Two clients of the Clinical Law Office, Gretta Herman and Marilyn Palmer, presented cases that starkly revealed the harm of this action.

Gretta Herman

Gretta Herman was committed to the Rosewood Center on August 10, 1933, when she was only 15 years old. According to the admission notes—remarkable for their alliteration and dismissive tone—Gretta's problem was "neglect, uneducated, untrained, undisciplined, unsupervised, and an illegitimate, defective child of an incompetent, feebleminded mother; living in remote, rural, poverty-stricken, degraded circumstances." In the early 1970s, partly as a result of efforts to reduce overcrowding at Rosewood, Gretta and some other older residents were transferred to a bleak nursing facility in a

high-crime area of western Baltimore. When the student-attorney from the
Clinical Law Office and his supervising attorney first met Gretta in 1995,
she was strikingly energetic and in rather good health for a 74-year-old person shunted to the sidelines. In many respects, the nursing facility was more
restrictive and offered less habilitation than her former institutional abode.
She rarely ventured outside, and her world was largely bounded by her bedroom and dayroom. Gretta made clear her desire to move out of the nursing
facility, even taking her student-attorney by the arm and attempting to waltz
out the front door with him.

A move out of the nursing facility to authentic community living would
not be accomplished so readily, however. It would require considerable legal
and factual research to prepare a persuasive legal brief detailing the federal
and state constitutional and statutory grounds for her discharge. The key argument was that her inappropriate stay in a nursing facility violated the
Nursing Home Reform Act of 1987 (PL 100-203), which requires an annual
determination of whether the individual needs nursing-level care and
whether the individual needs specialized services for people with mental retardation. The brief even cited international human rights declarations as
supportive of but not as binding authority for this requested action. It would
take persistent advocacy to get state officials to use one of the scarce community slots for a nursing facility resident such as Gretta. Even after the state officials agreed to place Gretta in a community living arrangement, many more
months of searching, planning, and follow-up advocacy were required to
make it happen.

Gretta was not alone in requiring such placement. Marilyn Palmer had a similar history.

Marilyn Palmer

Marilyn Palmer, too, had lived for decades in the Rosewood Center before
being shifted to the same confining nursing facility as Gretta. Although Marilyn was only in her 50s when her advocates first encountered her, she had
been treated in a way that had exacerbated her disabilities. Rather than being
assisted in walking, Marilyn was left in a wheelchair, which caused her mus-
cles to atrophy, and she was not encouraged to take steps. Rather than being
provided with the technology for assistive communication, Marilyn was
given only a rudimentary sign board to identify her basic wants. In many respects, she regressed as a result of an atmosphere of idleness and stifling routines that made each day numbingly like the previous one. As her advocate
sadly commented, "We don't treat our worst criminals this badly."

Today Gretta and Marilyn live in excellent community-based programs that provide a variety of activities and good living conditions. Gretta lives in a well-furnished
home with two other individuals. The house has a large backyard and staff who enjoy her and accommodate her mischievous personality and changing energy levels.
She likes to ride the van to her day activity center, where no visiting advocate goes
away without receiving a hug from her. Marilyn has also flourished in new surroundings. She walks every day, uses a computerized voice synthesizer that increases

her social interactions, and has a paid job doing assembly work. Her paintings in bright acrylics are beautiful enough to be sold and exhibited. One adorns the walls of the supervising attorney and her former student-attorney from the Clinical Law Office, providing them with vivid reminders of a life rescued and society's promises redeemed.

Advocating for People Living in the Community

Keeping individuals in the community under optimum conditions requires sustained attention. Although the Clinical Law Office could have ended its representation of Marilyn and Gretta once they were settled in homes in ordinary neighborhoods, its staff has continued to advocate for them in annual service plan meetings, guardianship matters, and informal settings. The very factors that led to the misplacement of healthy individuals in nursing facilities—lack of family ties, limited communication skills, and vulnerability because of their isolation—weighed in favor of ongoing advocacy. In the community living arrangements of the turn of the 21st century, the relationships between provider and advocate are essentially cooperative and mutually respectful. The issues are quite varied, such as obtaining the latest assistive technology or setting up a burial fund and making funeral arrangements to spare an individual with disabilities from receiving a pauper's cremation. After careful investigation of costly insurance policies and other options, the Clinical Law Office student-attorney, as part of a team planning effort, was able to make some arrangements for Gretta's last rites, when that time comes. The team from the Clinical Law Office secured funds from a state agency and the service provider, negotiated for reduced funeral costs from a local funeral home, and received a donation of several church-owned plots for individuals without financial means. Most of the issues are more immediate and involve adjusting service plans to meet an aging individual's changing health, social, therapy, recreation, and financial needs.

Betty B.

Betty B. is the most dramatic example of long-term advocacy for older adults with developmental disabilities. At the outset, she was misplaced and mistreated in a state mental hospital. As a result of a federal civil rights class-action suit for the right of institutionalized individuals with mental illness to have access to legal counsel (*Coe v. Hughes*, 1985), Betty B. became a named plaintiff and alleged that she had experienced more than 70 incidents of physical and sexual assaults by other institutionalized individuals at the mental hospital during her 22 years of inappropriate confinement as a person with mild mental retardation and epilepsy. Indeed, the hospital's records acknowledged that she had been placed there because Rosewood had no vacancies at the time she was deemed to require institutionalization. Under a settlement with the state, she gained a unique 12-page contract with the Maryland Developmental Disabilities Administration that enabled her to claim a full range of habilitation services suited to her needs and entitled her to services reasonably necessary for her comfort, care, and treatment, including those that permit "maximum restoration of her adaptive capacity." Since 1985, the Clinical Law Office has represented Betty B. continuously to ensure that she receives the full benefit of this agreement and that her interests are expressed clearly and protected. Although Betty B. is fortunate to have a devoted mother, her mother is exceedingly appreciative of having advocacy assistance available for her daughter. Betty B. is 56 years old, and her mother is 78. Over the years, the advocacy assistance that the Clinical Law Office has provided directly to Betty B. or arranged through the Maryland Trust for Retarded Citizens or others has included responses to medical emergencies, extra staff to prevent falls (i.e., a contact guard), various expressive therapies, estate planning, burial fund planning, provision of social work monitoring, regular advocacy at periodic planning meetings, and many other services small and large. To Betty B.'s mother, the advocates are her "band of angels" who work on behalf of those who desperately need legal advice and help. Unlike many families with aging members with developmental disabilities, Betty B.'s mother knows that a supportive structure is in place for the day when she can no longer look out for her dear yet sometimes demanding daughter.

CONCLUSIONS: FROM CUSTODIAL BACK WARDS TO COMMUNITY BACKYARDS

Advocacy is an important ingredient in the progress that has been made in supporting aging people with disabilities. As this chapter reveals, many types of legal issues and forms of advocacy are relevant to the field of developmental disabilities. That changes in the subfield of aging and developmental disabilities have accelerated as advocacy initiatives have multiplied is no coincidence. Those initiatives have included but have not been limited to actions focused on human rights, public policies, large-scale litigation, individualized legal interventions, casework, public awareness, and professional education. Successful transitions from institutions of all kinds—especially the long distance from custodial back wards to a neighborhood backyard of one's own—requires the blending of several of these advocacy modes. Through such coordinated efforts, the Charlies, Grettas, Marilyns, and Bettys of the world can enjoy some measure of freedom and happiness that so often was lacking in their youth.

Another implication of this research is that long-term relationships with aging individuals with disabilities may be an especially important factor in good advocacy outcomes for members of a vulnerable population. Links between the various advocacy actors are also vital in ensuring that the pledge of the Declaration of Independence to safeguard inalienable rights to life, liberty, and the pursuit of happiness (1776, ¶ 2) includes aging people with ongoing disabilities. In the end, that pledge and its practical application depend on the continuity, conscientiousness, and companionship that an advocate provides to another person. At that junction, law and compassion truly can come together. This human rights mission has both American and international dimensions.

REFERENCES

Americans with Disabilities Act (ADA) of 1990, PL 101-336, 42 U.S.C. §§ 12101 *et seq.*

The Arc of the United States: A National Organization on Mental Retardation. (1997, November). *A status report to the nation on people with mental retardation waiting for community services.* Arlington, TX: Author. (Available from the Arc of the United States, 500 East Border Street, Suite 300, Arlington, TX 76010)

Bingham, L. (1998, February 12). Wrongly institutionalized for 33 years, an Arlington woman finds daylight—and the footlights. *Fort-Worth Star-Telegraph,* p. 1 (Life & Arts section).

Buck v. Bell, 274 U.S. 200 (1927).

City of Cleburne v. Cleburne Living Center, 473 U.S. 432 (1985).

Coe v. Hughes, No. K-83-4248 (D. Md. April 4, 1985) (consent decree).

Davis v. Buckley, 526 F. Supp. 985 (E.D. Va. 1981).

Declaration of Independence. (U.S. 1776).

Developmental Disabilities Assistance and Bill of Rights Act of 1975, PL 94-103, 42 U.S.C. §§ 6000–6083.

Dybwad, G. (1997, October). *From Eglantyne Jebb to Barbara Goode: A historical perspective on human rights for persons with mental handicap.* Paper presented at the Human Rights Conference, Prague, Czech Republic.

Education for All Handicapped Children Act of 1975, PL 94-142, 20 U.S.C. §§ 1400–1485.

Francke, C. (1998a, March 2). Caretakers who prey on the retarded: 13 in Howard agency victimized in 4 years. *Baltimore Sun,* p. 1A.

Francke, C. (1998b, March 3). State, Arc to probe Howard program. *Baltimore Sun,* p. 1B.

Hayden, M.S. (1997). Class-action, civil rights litigation for institutionalized persons with mental retardation and other developmental disabilities: A review. *Mental and Physical Disability Law Reporter, 21,* 411–422.

Heller v. Doe, 509 U.S. 312 (1993).

Herr, S.S. (1981). Rights of disabled persons: International principles and American experiences. *Columbia Human Rights Law Review, 12,* 1–55.

Herr, S.S. (1987a). *Requiem for a Rosewood resident* [Poem and eulogy]. Unpublished manuscript.

Herr, S.S. (1987b, November 6). 63 years in "moral quarantine." *Baltimore Sun,* p. 23A.

Individuals with Disabilities Education Act (IDEA) of 1990, PL 101-476, 20 U.S.C. §§ 1400–1485.

International League of Societies for the Mentally Handicapped (ILSMH). (1966). *Stress on families of the mentally handicapped.* Brussels: Author.

International League of Societies for the Mentally Handicapped (ILSMH). (1968). *Declaration of the general and special rights of the mentally retarded.* Brussels: Author.

Larnaca Resolution. (1998). International Conference on Intellectual and Developmental Disabilities, Larnaca, Cyprus; reprinted in *Journal of Intellectual Disabilities Research, 42,* 262.

1998 Md. Laws 109.

New York State Association for Retarded Children v. Rockefeller, 357 F. Supp. 752 (E.D.N.Y. 1975).

Nursing Home Reform Act of 1987, PL 100-203 (Subtitle C of the Omnibus Budget Reconciliation Act of 1987), 42 U.S.C. § 1396(e)(7)(B)(ii).

Poe v. Lynchburg Training School and Hospital, 518 F. Supp. 789 (W.D. Va. 1981).

Rehabilitation Act of 1973, PL 93-112, 29 U.S.C. §§ 701–784.

Trent, J. (1994). *Inventing the feeble mind: A history of mental retardation in the United States.* Berkeley: University of California Press.

United Nations. (1948). *Universal declaration of human rights.* New York: Author.

United Nations. (1971). Declaration on the rights of mentally retarded persons. In *Yearbook of the United Nations 1971, 25,* 368.

University of Maryland, Clinical Law Office. (1998, February 24). *Statement of University of Maryland Clinical Law Office in support of the FY 1999 Developmental Disabilities Budget to the Maryland General Assembly.* Baltimore: Author.

Wolfensberger, W. (1981). The extermination of handicapped people in World War II Germany. *Mental Retardation, 19,* 1–7.

Wyatt v. Rodgers, 985 F. Supp. 1356 (M.D. Ala. 1997).

Wyatt v. Stickney, 344 F. Supp. 387 (M.D. Ala. 1972), aff'd sub nom. Wyatt v. Aderholt, 503 F.2d 1305 (5th Cir. 1974).

3

International Human Rights Standards
Aging and Disabilities

Manfred Nowak

The philosophy of the international disability movement has undergone funda-mental changes since World War II (Degener, 1995; Lindquist, 1995). For a long time, the individualistic medical approach, which perceived disability as a functional lim-itation similar to illness, prevailed. The main objective of disability policy was to care for and to help the individual with disabilities to cope with his or her situation through therapy and technical or personal support. The person with a disability was the object of protection, not the subject of action. Industrialized societies established special institutions where such people were trained, performed work, and more or less spent their whole lives.

Soon after World War II, this philosophy was criticized for isolating and segre-gating large groups of people with physical and mental disabilities from the rest of society. It was gradually replaced by the concept of normalization and integration, which strongly influenced rehabilitation programs in the 1950s and 1960s as well as the delivery of training, technical aid, and support services to people with disabil-ities. Although this policy aimed at integrating people with disabilities into natural social environments—and, above all, with their families—the emphasis remained on the individual. That is, it considered physical and mental disabilities exclusively or primarily a problem of the respective individuals.

HUMAN RIGHTS AND MODERN DISABILITY POLICY

Only during the late 1960s and 1970s did awareness slowly emerge that the prob-lems of people with disabilities are a result of attitudinal, architectural, and struc-

33

tural barriers in their environment and that the resolution of their problems hinged on the willingness of societies to include or exclude the needs of people with disabilities in every process of design. The best individual therapies, training methods, and services are of little use if the environment is hostile and does not remove the numerous physical, psychological, cultural, legal, and political barriers that prevent people with disabilities from participating in everyday life. For example, my ability to move my wheelchair skillfully does not help me when I am confronted by architectural or legal-entry barriers to places that I wish to visit or use. The best psychotherapeutic treatment does not provide access to jobs or to other countries if labor policies or immigration laws establish barriers for people with mental disabilities. The same holds true, *mutatis mutandis,* for older people, regardless of whether they have received a label of mental retardation.

This environment-related concept of disability gained international support during the United Nations (UN) International Decade of Disabled Persons from 1983 to 1992 and is eloquently reflected in the Standard Rules on the Equalization of Opportunities for Persons with Disabilities (StRE) that the UN General Assembly adopted in 1993 (UN, 1993b). By recognizing the needs for support of the individual and change and adaptation of the surrounding environment, questions of disability were transformed into human rights issues. In fact, the distinction between *disability* and *handicap* exposed the underlying human rights problem. *Handicap* refers to the adverse effects of the environment on the individual with a disability, including a loss or limitation of opportunities to take part in community life on an equal basis with others. Viewed through a human rights lens, people with disabilities are perceived not primarily as objects of care and protection but rather as people with human rights on an equal footing with all others. *Empowerment,* a concept developed in the struggle against racial and gender-based discrimination, is also the key word for people with disabilities who wish to participate actively in the economic, political, social, and cultural spheres of everyday life and to fight against the various types of discrimination and environmental barriers with which they are confronted (see Chapter 19). Human rights of the elderly and people with disabilities create corresponding obligations of national governments to remove obstacles for older people with disabilities, in both the public and private sectors, and to ensure the equalization of opportunities.

GENERAL AND SPECIAL HUMAN RIGHTS

Human rights are usually defined as those civil, political, economic, social, and cultural rights recognized by the international community as minimum conditions that enable people to live with dignity (Kneucker, Nowak, & Tretter, 1992). The international community has moved from mere privileges such as class rights (e.g., the medieval British freedom charters), rights of man (i.e., excluding women, in the original sense of the French and American revolutions), or citizens' rights (e.g., in the socialist concept) to human rights in the sense of rights that everyone enjoys by being human, regardless of race, color, sex, language, religion, nationality, age, political or other opinion, national or social origin, property, birth, or other status. In contrast to the term *fundamental rights,* which refers to rights enshrined in domestic constitutions, *human rights* are based on international customary and treaty law at both the universal and regional levels. Ideally, human rights also should be reflected as fundamental rights in domestic constitutions and bills of rights, but that is not always the case. Because human rights represent only minimum international standards, the exercise of fundamental rights may provide better protection for older people with disabilities.

The fact that human rights in principle apply to every human being does not prevent the international community from creating special rights for particular groups. If such rights are explicitly recognized in the framework of international human rights law, scholars usually refer to them as human rights as well (i.e., the human rights of women, children, older people, people with disabilities). In order to avoid creating new privileges, such special rights can be justified only in the context of the right to equality and nondiscrimination as those rights are laid down, for example, in Article 26 of the International Covenant on Civil and Political Rights of 1966 (and entered into force in 1976) (Nowak, 1993). Equality not only entails the traditional liberal concept of equality before the law but also guarantees a right to equal protection of the law and to effective protection against discrimination by society at large. In other words, the right to equality, understood in the sense of treating equals identically and unequals differently, may require measures of positive discrimination and/or affirmative action (Hendriks, 1995; Nowak, 1993). This principle is the legal basis and justification for creating special human rights for groups of people who traditionally have been victims of discrimination or who are particularly vulnerable for other reasons, such as their age or ethnic origin. Often, both reasons apply because vulnerable groups such as people with disabilities or people with acquired immunodeficiency syndrome (AIDS) are also frequently victims of discrimination. Typical examples of groups who traditionally have been discriminated against are women, Blacks, Jews, minorities, and indigenous peoples; other vulnerable groups include children, older people, aliens, refugees, migrant workers, and people with disabilities.

An analysis of international human rights law shows that even general human rights treaties such as the two UN Covenants and the European or American Convention on Human Rights contain a number of special human rights (Ermacora, Nowak, & Tretter, 1993). For example, the Covenant on Civil and Political Rights (CCPR) of 1966/1976 provides special protection to aliens (Article 13), people charged with a criminal offense (Article 14), children (Article 24), and members of minorities (Article 27). The Covenant on Economic, Social, and Cultural Rights (CESCR) of 1966/1976 lists special rights for trade unions (Article 8), mothers and young people (Article 10), and other groups. Typically, provisions of positive discrimination and special rights for particularly vulnerable groups are laid down in special human rights treaties and instruments (UN, 1993a). These documents include the following:

- International Convention on the Elimination of All Forms of Racial Discrimination (CERD) of 1965/1969
- Convention on the Elimination of All Forms of Discrimination Against Women (CEDAW) of 1979/1981
- Declaration on the Elimination of All Forms of Intolerance and of Discrimination Based on Religion or Belief of 1981
- Convention relating to the Status of Stateless Persons of 1954/1960
- Convention relating to the Status of Refugees of 1951/1954
- Organization for African Unity (OAU) Convention Governing the Specific Aspects of Refugee Problems in Africa of 1969/1974

- International Convention on the Protection of the Rights of All Migrant Workers and Members of Their Families of 1990 (not yet in force)
- Convention on the Rights of the Child of 1989/1990
- Declaration on the Rights of Persons Belonging to National or Ethnic, Religious, and Linguistic Minorities of 1992
- European Framework Convention for the Protection of National Minorities of 1995/1998
- International Labor Organization (ILO) Convention No. 169, concerning Indigenous and Tribal Peoples in Independent Countries of 1989/1991

To date, no special human rights treaty has been created for either older people or people with disabilities, although a convention on the rights of people with disabilities was demanded repeatedly during the UN's International Decade of Disabled Persons. More successful, however, were attempts to draft special human rights instruments for these groups in the framework of so-called international soft law. In this respect, the UN appears to be much more advanced than regional organizations, including the Council of Europe, which deemed it sufficient to add a few provisions to their general treaties in the field of economic, social, and cultural rights.

OLDER PEOPLE AND PEOPLE WITH DISABILITIES IN GENERAL HUMAN RIGHTS TREATIES

A few exceptional documents refer to people with disabilities in human rights treaty law. An early example often mentioned is Article 15 of the European Social Charter (ESC) of 1961/1965, establishing a special right of physically or mentally disabled people to vocational training, rehabilitation, and social resettlement. Because this right is still based on the traditional approach of specialized institutions, however, the Council of Europe redrafted Article 15 in the Revised ESC of 1996 (not yet in force) to establish a right of people with disabilities to independence, social integration, and participation in the life of the community (Degener, 1995). In particular, States shall provide such people, irrespective of age and the nature and origin of their disabilities, with guidance and education, and they shall promote their access to employment and their full social integration and participation in the life of the community.

Article 18(4) of the African Charter on Human and People's Rights of 1981/ 1986 is one of the few treaty provisions referring both to older people and people with disabilities: "The aged and the disabled shall also have the right to special measures of protection in keeping with their physical or moral needs." Not surprisingly, that provision has been included in the context of the protection of the African family, which in Article 18(2) is referred to as "the custodian of morals and traditional values recognized by the community." In other words, the African Charter recognizes the protection of older people and people with disabilities primarily as a traditional function of the family, which is underlined by the duty of every individual, as laid down in Article 29(1), to preserve the harmonious development of the family, to "respect his parents at all times," and to "maintain them in case of need."

In the latter part of the 20th century, special provisions regarding older people and/or people with disabilities were included in other regional human rights treaties, particularly in the context of economic, social, and cultural rights. Articles 17 and 18 of the Organization of American States Protocol of San Salvador of 1988 (not yet in force), which added a number of economic, social, and cultural rights to the American Convention on Human Rights of 1969/1978, provide special protection for people who are elderly or disabled. These provisions reflect a fairly modern approach to providing everyone affected by a diminution of physical or mental capacities with the resources and environment needed for developing their personality, including special work programs, special training for families, and consideration in urban development plans.

In 1988, an Additional Protocol to the European Social Charter was adopted (entered into force in 1992) that stipulates, in Article 4, a special right of elderly people to social protection. In particular, older people shall be enabled to remain full members of society for as long as possible, to choose their lifestyle freely, and to lead independent lives in familiar surroundings for as long as they wish. The Revised ESC of 1996 (not yet in force) contains in Article 15 a fairly modern and comprehensive right of people with disabilities to independence, social integration, and participation in the life of the community, and in Article 23 an equally comprehensive right of elderly people to social protection.

In 1989, the UN adopted a special treaty provision on children with mental or physical disabilities in the framework of the Convention on the Rights of the Child of 1989/1990. Article 23 stipulates that such children should enjoy a full and decent life in conditions that ensure their dignity, promote their self-reliance, and facilitate their active participation in the community. Assistance services should be provided to these children in the fields of education, training, health care, rehabilitation, employment, and recreation.

The Second World Conference on Human Rights, held in Vienna in June 1993, paid much attention to vulnerable groups, including people with disabilities. Although not a binding treaty, the Vienna Declaration and Programme of Action, adopted by consensus by the 171 participating states of the World Conference and endorsed by the UN General Assembly in December 1993, is a major legal and political document that sets the agenda of the UN human rights program well into the 21st century (Nowak, 1994, UN, 1993c, 1994a). Paragraphs 63–65 of the Vienna Declaration and Programme of Action are devoted to the rights of people with disabilities and stress that all human rights unreservedly include people with disabilities. In particular, national governments are urged to eliminate all "socially determined barriers, be they physical, financial, social, or psychological, which exclude or restrict full participation in society."

SPECIAL INSTRUMENTS FOR THE RIGHTS OF OLDER PEOPLE

As early as 1948, Argentina submitted a draft declaration of old age to the UN General Assembly, but no action has been taken on it (UN, 1994b). In 1982, the World Assembly on Aging was held in Vienna (World Assembly on Aging, 1984), and the UN General Assembly endorsed the Vienna International Plan of Action on Aging. Because little progress has been achieved on the implementation of the Vienna Plan of Action, the UN secretary-general outlined an action program on aging for 1992 and beyond that included the development of a practical strategy on aging for the decade 1992–2001; promotional activities such as the annual observance of October 1 as International Day for the Elderly; and the drafting of UN Principles for Older Persons, which the UN General Assembly adopted in 1991 (UN, 1991). The 18 UN Principles are divided into five sections that seek to ensure that older people have independence, participation, care, self-fulfillment, and dignity: In particular, they should be able to live in environments that are safe and adaptable to personal preferences and changing capacities (Principle 5), to reside at home for as long as possible (Principle 6), to remain integrated with society (Principle 7), to enjoy all human rights and fundamental freedoms including privacy when residing in any shelter or care or treatment facility (Principle 14), and to live in dignity and security and to be free from exploitation and physical or mental abuse (Principle 17). Older people should be treated fairly regardless of their age, gender, racial or ethnic background, disability, or other status and should be valued independently of their economic contribution to society (Principle 18).

These UN Principles reflect an environment-related concept of empowerment, integration, and participation of older people. Because the 18 principles were adopted only as typical soft law and are not even in the form of a declaration, they are not legally binding, and no system of monitoring States' compliance with these principles has been established.

SPECIAL INSTRUMENTS FOR THE RIGHTS OF PEOPLE WITH DISABILITIES

The UN and its specialized agencies, in particular the International Labor Organization (ILO), the World Health Organization (WHO), and UNESCO (UN Educational, Scientific, and Cultural Organization), have adopted a number of specific instruments concerning the human rights of people with disabilities and undertaken promotional activities (Degener, 1995; UN, 1994b). This chapter focuses on only the most important developments within the UN.

In 1971, the UN General Assembly proclaimed the Declaration on the Rights of Mentally Retarded Persons (UN, 1971), which stipulates, *inter alia*, that people with mental retardation should live with their own families whenever possible and participate in different forms of community life and that they have rights to protection from exploitation, abuse, and degrading treatment and to proper legal safeguards in case their rights need to be restricted.

Similar provisions can be found in the 1975 Declaration on the Rights of Disabled Persons (UN, 1975), which applies to every person with disabilities, defined as "any person unable to ensure by himself or herself, wholly or partly, the necessities of a normal individual and/or social life, as a result of deficiency, either congenital or not, in his or her physical or mental capabilities." The declaration stresses the self-reliance of the person with disabilities and provides that, in case a stay in a specialized establishment becomes indispensable, the environment and living conditions therein shall be as close as possible to those of the life of a person without disabilities of the same age as the person with disabilities.

In 1976, the UN General Assembly proclaimed 1981 the International Year of Disabled Persons (UN, 1979)[1] which was the starting point for many awareness-raising activities and other developments. In 1982, the UN General Assembly, expressing its deep concern that 500 million people worldwide (400 million of whom were estimated to be living in developing countries) were estimated at that time to

---

[1]Originally, the UN General Assembly referred to the International Year *for* Disabled Persons in General Assembly Resolution 31/123 of December 16, 1976. Because this phraseology signaled the traditional paternalistic attitude toward people with disabilities, it was changed by UN General Assembly Resolution 34/154 of December 17, 1979.

have disabilities of one form or another, adopted the World Programme of Action Concerning Disabled Persons (UN, 1982a) and proclaimed the period 1983–1992 the UN Decade of Disabled Persons (UN, 1982a).

In the course of the decade from 1983 to 1992, a number of high-level expert meetings were held, and the international nongovernmental disability community got a major boost and developed new strategies as a human rights movement. The growing awareness among governments resulted in a number of modern international instruments, albeit not in the form of an international convention on the rights of people with disabilities. In addition to the ILO Convention No. 159, Recommendation No. 168 concerning Vocational Rehabilitation and Employment (Disabled Persons) of 1983, and the Tallin Guidelines for Action on Human Resources Development in the Field of Disability of 1990, the following two outstanding and detailed soft-law instruments deserve special attention. The "Principles for the Protection of Persons with Mental Illness and the Improvement of Mental Health Care" were drafted in the UN Commission on Human Rights and its Sub-Commission on the Prevention of Discrimination and Protection of Minorities and were adopted by the UN General Assembly in 1991 (UN, 1992). The 25 principles stress the civil and political rights of people with mental disabilities (including those living within and outside mental health facilities), in particular the right to be treated with humanity and respect for human dignity, the right to live in the community, the principles of personal autonomy and informed consent to treatment, and the prohibition of discrimination on the ground of mental illness. A major part of the principles is devoted to the voluntary and involuntary admission to, as well as the individual's rights and the conditions in, mental health facilities, including procedural safeguards such as the appointment of a patient's personal representative and counsel, the review of involuntary admission by an independent and impartial review body, regular inspection of mental health facilities, and the right of patients to make complaints through domestic legal procedures.

The most important international human rights instrument specifically addressing the situation of people with disabilities is the Standard Rules on the Equalization of Opportunities for Persons with Disabilities (StRE), which the UN General Assembly adopted in 1993 (UN, 1993b). The StRE were drafted by the Commission for Social Development with the active participation and input of international nongovernmental organizations such as Disabled Peoples' International. Hence, they reflect more than any other international document the environment-related and human rights–inspired concept of disability policy as it was expressed, for instance, at the 3rd World Congress of Disabled Peoples' International held in Vancouver in April 1992, marking the end of the UN Decade of Disabled Persons (Disabled Peoples' International, 1992). In its introduction to the StRE, the UN General Assembly stressed that, although not compulsory, the Standard Rules "can become international customary rules when they are applied by a great number of States with the intention of respecting a rule in international law." This language shows that they have been designed as a substitute for a treaty on the rights of people with disabilities. The introduction also provides modern definitions of *disability* and *handicap* and explains the phrase *equalization of opportunities* as "the process through which the various systems of society and the environment, such as services, activities, information and documentation, are made available to all, particularly to persons with disabilities."

The 22 standard rules are divided into three sections. Section I deals with preconditions for equal participation, such as awareness raising, medical care, and rehabilitation and support services, and aims to reduce the individual's functional limitations and increase the independence of the individual. Section II addresses target areas for equal participation and establishes the obligations of national governments to remove all obstacles that prevent people with disabilities from exercising their human rights and from participating fully in the activities of their society. Most important is Rule 5, which urges national governments to make the physical environment accessible for people with disabilities and to provide access to information and communication. Other rules deal with social security, culture, religion, recreation, sports, and education and employment in inclusive environments. Considerable attention was paid to drafting Rule 9, which promotes the full participation of people with disabilities in family life and their right to personal integrity, sexuality, marriage, and parenthood. For example, it states that people with disabilities must not be denied the opportunity to experience their sexuality, have sexual relationships, and experience parenthood (UN, 1993b). Section III is devoted to domestic implementation measures, including appropriate legislative, economic, planning, training, information, and research activities; the establishment of national coordination committees; the involvement of nongovernmental organizations; and continuous monitoring and evaluation measures.

Although the StRE do not constitute a binding treaty, they establish in Section IV an international monitoring mechanism consisting of a Special Rapporteur appointed by the Commission for Social Development and a panel of experts composed primarily of representatives of international organizations of persons with disabilities. In June 1994, Bengt Lindquist, former Swedish Minister of Social Affairs, was appointed Special Rapporteur with the task of establishing a direct dialogue with governments, local nongovernmental organizations, and national coordinating committees and monitoring States' compliance with the StRE. The Special Rapporteur has no power, however, to force governments to implement their obligations, which are only of a moral and a political, not of a legal, nature. In 1997, the Commission for Social Development reviewed this monitoring mechanism and considered whether to eventually replace it with a more effective one.

CONCLUSIONS

The concise and nonexhaustive survey of the present international human rights law presented in this chapter with respect to older people and people with disabilities leads to the following conclusions:

1. Compared with other vulnerable groups and/or groups who are discriminated against, both older people and people with disabilities have received less attention from the international community. Although children are not more vulnerable than older people or people with disabilities, the UN in 1989 adopted the Convention on the Rights of the Child, which became, within a short time, the human rights treaty with the highest number of States Parties (191) and with a fairly efficient international monitoring mechanism. The UN General Assembly either has rejected similar attempts with respect to people with disabilities and the elderly or has not pursued them further.

2. Owing to the proclamation of an International Year of Disabled Persons (UN, 1979) and the UN International Decade of Disabled Persons (1983–1992) (UN, 1982a) as well as the increasing pressure of the nongovernmental disability

movement that at the end of the 20th century considered itself part of the human rights movement, the rights of people with disabilities received more attention than the rights of older people during the 1980s and 1990s. As far as human rights treaty law is concerned, Article 18 of the 1988 Protocol of San Salvador, Article 15 of the Revised European Social Charter, and Article 23 of the 1989 Convention on the Rights of the Child (which, of course, does not apply to older people) seem to be the strongest provisions concerning people with disabilities. Most important, however, are the detailed and well-drafted StRE (UN, 1993b). The StRE contain specific domestic and international monitoring mechanisms and should therefore be taken into consideration by older people with mental retardation and their representatives as well as nongovernmental organizations that are active in this field. In Paragraph 15 of the introduction to the StRE, the UN General Assembly (1993b) stated that special educational efforts might need to be made with regard to groups such as women, children, the elderly, and particularly vulnerable groups of persons with dual or multiple disabilities. Although the definition of *disability* in paragraph 17 of the introduction explicitly includes mental illness, there are no specific provisions for people with developmental disabilities, and a number of rules seem to apply primarily to people with only physical disabilities.

3. The most important specific instruments for people with mental disabilities are the 1991 Principles for the Protection of Persons with Mental Illness and the Improvement of Mental Health Care. Most of these principles are of direct concern to older people with mental retardation, in particular with regard to the rights to personal integrity, autonomy, and human dignity and including procedural safeguards against inhuman and degrading treatment (Nowak & Suntinger, 1995), abuse, and involuntary admission to mental health facilities.

4. The specific human rights of older people are still less developed than those of people with disabilities. Article 17 of the Protocol of San Salvador and Article 4 of the Additional Protocol to the European Social Charter, both adopted in 1988 with the aim of strengthening economic, social, and cultural rights, are the most far-reaching treaty provisions regarding older adults. The precise formulation of these provisions and the monitoring mechanisms of both treaties are fairly weak, however. More important, therefore, are the rather detailed UN Principles for Older Persons of 1991.

5. There are no specific human rights provisions for older people with mental retardation. The only provisions relating to both older people and people with disabilities are Article 18(4) of the African Charter on Human and People's Rights, which is typical for the traditional maintenance role of the African family; Paragraph 15 of the introduction to the StRE, calling for special attention to older disabled persons; and Principle 18 of the UN Principles for Older Persons, calling for fair treatment of older persons regardless of their disabilities. Because older people with mental retardation fall into the categories of older people and people with disabilities, all of the human rights provisions just mentioned are applicable to them.

6. It should be stressed that older people with mental retardation are human beings with the right to enjoy all general human rights without any discrimination on the ground of their age or their disabilities. They have the same rights to life, physical and mental integrity, privacy, home and family life, freedom of expression and religion, social security, housing or adequate health care as young peo-

ple without disabilities do. Every restriction of the human rights of older people with mental retardation, such as their right to personal freedom in the case of involuntary admission to a residential facility, must be justified by the respective limitation clause in the relevant treaty provision that is equally applicable to other human beings. All of the specific human rights provisions aimed at providing special protection to older people and people with disabilities shall be taken into consideration when such limitation clauses are applied by competent national government authorities or international monitoring bodies.

Universal rights are the keystone to progress. The Vienna Declaration and Programme of Action considers this point by recalling in Article 63 the rights of the disabled person in the context of the principle of universality (UN, 1993c). This chapter, therefore, concludes by citing this provision but at the same time slightly modifying its terminology by substituting the term *older people with disabilities* for *disabled person*:

> The World Conference on Human Rights reaffirms that all human rights and fundamental freedoms are universal and thus unreservedly include [older people with disabilities]. Every person is born equal and has the same right to life and welfare, education and work, living independently and active participation in all aspects of society. Any direct discrimination or other negative discriminatory treatment of an [older adult with disabilities] is therefore a violation of his or her rights.

Compliance with these principles can truly improve the quality of life for older people with disabilities.

REFERENCES

Degener, T. (1995). Disabled persons and human rights: The legal framework. In T. Degener & Y. Koster-Dreese (Eds.), *Human rights and disabled persons: Essays and relevant human rights instruments* (pp. 9–39). Boston: Martinus Nijhoff.

Disabled Peoples' International. (1992, April 21–26). Equalization of opportunities. In *Proceedings of the 3rd World Congress of Disabled Peoples' International.* Vancouver, British Columbia, Canada: Author.

Ermacora, F., Nowak, M., & Tretter, H. (Eds.). (1993). *International human rights: Documents and introductory notes.* Vienna: Law Books in Europe.

Hendriks, A. (1995). The significance of equality and non-discrimination for the protection of the rights and dignity of disabled persons. In T. Degener & Y. Koster-Dreese (Eds.), *Human rights and disabled persons: Essays and relevant human rights instruments* (pp. 40–62). Boston: Martinus Nijhoff.

Kneucker, R., Nowak, M., & Tretter, H. (1992). *Menschenrechte–Grundrechte: Materialien und Texte zur politischen Bildung [Human rights–fundamental rights: Materials and texts for human rights education in schools].* Vienna: Österreichischer Bundesverlag Wien.

Lindquist, B. (1995). Standard rules in the disability field: A new United Nations instrument. In T. Degener & Y. Koster-Dreese (Eds.), *Human rights and disabled persons: Essays and relevant human rights instruments* (pp. 63–68). Boston: Martinus Nijhoff.

Nowak, M. (1993). *U.N. Covenant on Civil and Political Rights: CCPR Commentary.* Arlington, VA: N.P. Engel.

Nowak, M. (Ed.). (1994). *World conference on human rights: The contributions of NGOs, reports, and documents.* Vienna: Manz.

Nowak, M., & Suntinger, W. (1995). The right of disabled persons not to be subjected to torture, inhuman and degrading treatment or punishment. In T. Degener & Y. Koster-Dreese (Eds.), *Human rights and disabled persons: Essays and relevant human rights instruments* (pp. 117–130). Boston: Martinus Nijhoff.

United Nations (UN). (1971). Declaration on the Rights of Mentally Retarded Persons: Resolution adopted by General Assembly, U.N. GAOR, 26th Sess., Agenda Item 12, at 2, U.N. Doc. A/Res/2856 (XXVI).

United Nations (UN). (1975). Declaration on the Rights of Disabled Persons: Resolution adopted by General Assembly, U.N. GAOR, 30th Sess., Agenda Item 12, at 3, U.N. Doc. A/Res/3447 (XXX).

United Nations (UN). (1979). International Year of the Disabled Person: Resolution adopted by General Assembly, U.N. GAOR, 34th Sess., Agenda Item 79, at 4, U.N. Doc. A/Res/34/154.

United Nations (UN). (1982a). Implementation of the World Programme of Action Concerning Disabled Persons: Resolution Adopted by General Assembly, U.N. GAOR, 37th Sess., Agenda Item 89, at 4, U.N. Doc. A/Res/37/53.

United Nations (UN). (1982b). World Programme of Action Concerning Disabled Persons: Resolution Adopted by General Assembly, U.N. GAOR, 37th Sess., Agenda Item 89, at 3, U.N. Doc. A/Res/ 37/52.

United Nations (UN). (1991). Implementation of the International Plan of Action on Aging and Related Activities: Resolution Adopted by General Assembly, U.N. GAOR, 46th Sess., Agenda Item 94 (a), at 5, U.N. Doc. A/Res/26/91.

United Nations (UN). (1992). The Protection of Persons with Mental Illness and the Improvement of Mental Health Care: Resolution Adopted by General Assembly, U.N. GAOR, 46th Sess., Agenda Item 98, at 15, U.N. Doc. A/Res/46/119.

United Nations (UN). (1993a). *Human rights: A compilation of international instruments* (Vol. 1). New York: Author.

United Nations (UN). (1993b). Standard Rules on the Equalization of Opportunities for Persons with Disabilities: Resolution Adopted by General Assembly, U.N. GAOR, 48th Sess., Agenda Item 109, at 28, U.N. Doc. A/Res/48/96.

United Nations (UN). (1993c). Vienna Declaration and Programme of Action: Resolution Adopted by the General Assembly, U.N. Doc. A/CONF. 157/23.

United Nations (UN). (1994a). World Conference on Human Rights: Resolution Adopted by General Assembly, U.N. GAOR, 48th Sess., Agenda Item 114 (b), at 3, U.N. Doc. A/Res/ 48/121.

United Nations (UN) Center for Human Rights. (1994b). *United Nations action in the field of human rights.* New York: Author.

World Assembly on Aging. (1984). *Report of the World Assembly on Aging.* Paris: International Center of Social Gerontology.

4

Health Care Decision Making
Legal and Financial Considerations

Marshall B. Kapp

In the United States, the first serious attention paid to the legal status of people with mental retardation arose in the 1960s and 1970s with regard to issues concerning the right of individuals residing (ordinarily involuntarily) in state institutions to receive various forms of treatment. The right to treatment announced by the courts (*Wyatt v. Stickney*, 1972) and discussed in the legal literature (Herr, 1983) of that period included, but was by no means limited to, various forms of medical treatment. Subsequently, a movement developed in the mental health and mental retardation spheres to push courts and legislatures to recognize a corresponding right of patients[1] to refuse treatment, primarily those involving antipsychotic medications (Appelbaum, 1994).

A number of developments have required modifications in how legal issues that influence the lives of people with mental retardation are identified and analyzed. Most prominent, the dramatic deinstitutionalization movement of the early 1970s through the 1990s (Grob, 1991; Rubenstein, 1994) resulted—despite the strong opposition of many neighborhoods (Winerip, 1994)—in the majority of individuals with mental retardation residing in more community-based living environments (Hill & Lakin, 1986). These environments present a different array of decisions and conflicts regarding medical treatment and corresponding legal and ethical challenges (Kendrick, 1994) from those encountered within the confines of the pre-1970s massive public total institutions.

Demographically, the population with mental retardation is aging rapidly (Janicki & Wisniewski, 1985). Average life expectancies continue to rise for people with

---

[1]Because this chapter discusses issues affecting older adults with mental retardation in their roles as consumers of medical services, the term *patients* is used to describe them.

mental retardation as well as for every other group. The "graying" of U.S. citizens with mental retardation, and thus a clear and inexorable increase in the number of older adults with mental retardation, has important legal implications. As people with mental retardation age, they are more likely to encounter a series of health-related problems that require decisions about the initiation, continuation, withholding, or withdrawal of various forms of medical intervention. The decision-making process entailed in coping with these medical problems often raises vexing questions about informed consent and these individuals' decisional capacity.

In addition, as individuals with mental retardation age, it is decreasingly probable for them to have living, cognitively intact parents. A process of surrogate medical decision making may be necessitated by the inability of the patient with mental retardation to personally make and express medical choices with a sufficient degree of rational understanding and capacity to manipulate relevant information. The unavailability of these individuals' parents may seriously complicate that process. Finally, the financial connotations of providing medical care to older adults with mental retardation who are living in community-based environments take a different form from those that needed to be addressed when there were few residential and intervention choices beyond the use of large state institutions.

This chapter briefly outlines several of the most salient legal and ethical issues arising in the context of medical care for older adults with mental retardation in the United States. The discussion is organized initially around the concept of informed consent, which leads logically to a consideration of surrogate decision-making alternatives that might be appropriate for this population. The chapter concludes with speculation about the special ramifications for older adults with mental retardation and their caregivers of the rapidly changing health care–financing climate that engulfs the United States. Such issues of access to health services are of overarching importance to these older adults (see also Chapter 19).

Because the focus here is on decisions concerning diagnostic and therapeutic interventions for individual patients, questions pertaining to the enrollment of older adults with mental retardation in research projects are beyond the scope of this discussion. The research context entails unique considerations (American College of Physicians, 1989; Levine, 1986) that distinguish it from the personal health care activities that are the topic of this chapter.

INFORMED CONSENT

The doctrine of informed consent is the legal heart and soul of individual health care decision making in the United States. The requirements imposed on health care providers under this doctrine are predicated on a firm ethical foundation.

Rationale and Requirements

Individuals with mental retardation and older adults traditionally have been at significant risk for undertreatment (i.e., medical neglect) (Loewy, 1987) and paradoxically also for overly aggressive treatment, particularly in critical care situations (Schwartz, 1994). The legal doctrine of informed consent, which is predicated on the ethical principle of personal *autonomy* (from the Greek words for *self-rule* or *self-determination*), is intended to correct this sort of situation (Faden, Beauchamp, & King, 1986); it was only in the 1980s and 1990s, however, that the informed consent doctrine began to be applied in a meaningful way to care decisions for older adults with mental retardation.

In late 1992, The Arc of the United States: An Organization on Mental Retardation (hereinafter "The Arc"), adopted a position statement on medical and dental treatment. This statement, slightly revised in 1998, characterized the concept of informed consent succinctly and accurately:

> The decision to accept or refuse treatment requires informed consent. The basic elements of informed consent are competency, knowledge, and voluntariness. The individual or surrogate decision maker should have the legal capacity to give consent. In addition, the decision maker should be provided sufficient information to evaluate and understand the benefits and risks of the proposed treatment. The decision maker should be offered the opportunity to ask questions and receive answers in understandable terms in order to exercise free power of choice. (1992, p. 1)

Informed consent must be free of any element of fraud, deceit, duress, or coercion (The Arc, 1992, 1998). These three essential elements appear in Table 1.

The next section of the chapter delves in some depth into the topic of mental competence or capacity with regard to intervention decision making. Voluntariness in the context of informed consent means simply that the patient must be free to reject participation in the proposed intervention. Health care providers must do all that is possible to minimize any potential intimidation inherent in the provider–patient relationship and in institution–patient relationships when care is provided on an inpatient basis. In addition, they must ensure that advice and recommendations are transmitted in as unpressured and empathetic a manner as possible.

The informed consent doctrine obviously takes its name from the fundamental requirement that the patient's consent be informed. To be legally valid, informed consent demands that the health care provider, before commencing an intervention, must disclose certain information (Rozovsky, 1990). As of 1999, the disclosure standard enforced in a bare majority of U.S. jurisdictions is the "professional," "reasonable physician," or "community" standard. Under this test, the adequacy of disclosure is judged against the amount and type of information that a reasonable, prudent physician would have disclosed under similar circumstances. A large minority of jurisdictions have accepted a more expansive version of information disclosure: the "reasonable patient" or "material risk" standard. This standard dictates that the health services provider communicate the information that an average or "reasonable" patient in the same situation would need and want to make a voluntary and knowledgeable decision. Under this test, the patient must be told about all material risks—that is, those factors that might make a difference to an average, reasonable patient in similar circumstances.

The age of a patient may affect which information is material to that person's decision-making process. For instance, a likely side effect that will not manifest for another 20 years may not be nearly as important to an older patient with mental retardation as it would be to one who is younger. The probability that a particular intervention will be accompanied by a great deal of physical pain or discomfort may make quite a difference to the older patient, however, especially to one who is frail. Health care professionals always ought to consider the physical and mental effects of aging among various other factors when deciding whether information regarding an intervention might be material to a particular person. Within both of the disclo-

Table 1.   Elements of informed consent

1. Competent/capable decision maker
2. Adequate information
3. Voluntariness

sure standards just explained, particular information is identified. These categories of information are

1. Diagnosis
2. Nature and purpose of the proposed intervention
3. Risks, consequences, or perils of the intervention
4. Probability of success (i.e., prognosis with the intervention)
5. Reasonable alternatives
6. Result anticipated if nothing is done
7. Limitations on the providers (e.g., a nursing facility that lacks the in-house ability to perform advanced cardiac life support)
8. Professional advice or recommendations

Decision-Making Competence or Capacity

A strong legal presumption exists in favor of respecting the adult individual's right to make autonomous decisions concerning his or her own life, including choices about medical interventions. (Decision making by and for minors involves a different set of issues that are not covered here.) For people with mental retardation, however, the capacity to make choices may be compromised by impairments in basic knowledge, limited communications skills, self-denial of disability that impedes their willingness to seek assistance from others that might aid in their comprehension of information, and socially induced learned inability to make decisions (Ellis, 1992). As these individuals age, their abilities in this realm may be compromised further by biological factors (e.g., dementia, stroke, depression) (Larson, Lo, & Williams, 1986) and, for those who are institutionalized, by the environments in which they find themselves. Particularly when an illness scenario develops in a hospital or in a long-term care facility, the individual's capacity to make and communicate autonomous choices on important matters may be impaired substantially.

Ensuring that medical decisions are made only by competent decision makers is compelled by society's commitment to an ethical principle that often exists in a state of tension with the previously mentioned principle of autonomy (Howell, 1988). This precept is that of beneficence, or doing good to others. Beneficence teaches people not to nihilistically neglect or abandon people with disabilities to theoretical but unreal autonomy. Rather, in Western jurisprudence, the principle of beneficence is incorporated into the state's legal *parens patriae* power. This inherent government authority empowers society to act affirmatively to protect the well-being of people who cannot protect themselves from potential harm. The *parens patriae* authority is the foundation for a variety of governmental interventions on behalf of people who are declared legally incompetent, including the imposition of involuntary guardianship (Kapp, 1994).

At the same time, the state's authority to intervene is limited sharply. There is a reluctance to cast the state's benevolent helping net too widely in an overprotective way that prematurely or unnecessarily interferes with a person's decision-making prerogatives when he or she still may be able to exercise a high degree of autonomy if permitted to do so. Hence, the state may act under a *parens patriae* justification to intervene in the life of a nonconsenting adult only in the least-restrictive or least-intrusive manner possible and consistent with the legitimate purpose of the intervention (Annas & Densberger, 1984).

Legal competence refers to a relative instead of an absolute degree of ability. To say that a person is *legally incompetent* implies that the individual falls below some minimum level of cognitive potential, not simply that the person has less potential than certain other people. The majority of situations in which the decision-making capacity of an older patient with mental retardation (as well as that of other older patients without disabilities) is called into question are handled on a *de facto* rather than a *de jure* basis. Put differently, in most such cases, the health care team and the health care facility quite properly—and without adverse legal consequences—manage such situations on the basis of working, clinical judgments about an individual's intellectual capacity, usually in conjunction with the family, without formal court involvement in determining and acting on the patient's decision-making impairment. In most circumstances, mental capacity should be addressed as an ethical matter by those who are closest to the patient; resorting to the courts is neither necessary nor desirable, because it frequently is expensive, time consuming, and emotionally draining (Herr & Hopkins, 1994). Judicial involvement in determinations of legal competence should be the exception rather than the rule. The advisability of court involvement depends on a variety of factors in any case. These factors are

1. The severity and prognosis of the individual's mental impairment
2. The complexity and likely consequences of the medical decision to be made
3. The availability or absence of a suitable surrogate
4. The agreement or disagreement among the individual, members of the individual's family, health care providers, and other relevant actors

In some situations, such as that of a patient in a long-term coma or persistent vegetative state, the determination of incompetence is fairly straightforward. In most circumstances, though, clinical presentations of possible incompetence are more cloudy. These circumstances include, in addition to mental retardation, transient disorientation due to acute illness or medication side effects; psychosis or emotional problems; and a physical disability that impairs the individual's communication ability. Much more is entailed in determining an individual's legal status than attaching a diagnostic label to a clinical condition, although the importance of an accurate diagnosis for purposes of prescribing an intervention plan for the underlying medical problem cannot be overestimated (Aylward, Burt, Thorpe, Lai, & Dalton, 1995; Janicki, Heller, Seltzer, & Hogg, 1995).

No single, uniform standard of decisional capacity exists (Roth, Meisel, & Lidz, 1977). The concept has been defined vaguely and variously in statutes and court decisions, although U.S. state legislatures (see, e.g., Cal. Prob. Code, 1998) attempted to instill more precision in the mid- to late 1990s (Sabatino, 1996). In daily practice, the attending physician, exercising a largely unchecked range of discretion, frequently is the one who decides when a person is not capable of making choices and when another individual should become involved, without necessarily using any specific standards for making that determination. Observations of nursing (Weiler, 1991) and social service staff may play an important role in influencing the physician's determination. Psychiatric or psychological consultations (Grisso, 1986) frequently are requested when the patient refuses to comply with the attending physician's recommendation, when the attending physician truly is uncertain about the patient's capacity (Perl & Shelp, 1982) and values the expertise that a consultant would bring, or when the attending physician anticipates that a determination of incapacity may become contentious at some later point.

In determining capacity, the most thoughtful analyses suggest that emphasis be placed on the actual abilities of the patient and the subjective thought process followed in arriving at a "good" or a "bad" decision (Appelbaum & Grisso, 1988). This focus on functional capacity is better than the more common approach (Abernethy, 1984) used previously of predicating competency judgments on the purportedly objective nature of the individual's clinical diagnosis or on agreement or disagreement with the patient's specific choice (Kaplan, Strang, & Ahmed, 1988). Although the patient's decision itself may constitute a red flag signaling the appropriateness of further investigation, and although the medical condition connected with a patient's diagnosis certainly may exert an impact on functional ability, one should not move too readily from outcome or category to conclusions about competence.

In an individualized functional inquiry, a number of fundamental questions need to be posed:

1. Can the person make and communicate, by spoken words or otherwise, choices concerning his or her own medical intervention?
2. Can the person offer any reasons for the choices made?
3. Are the reasons underlying the choice rational? Does the individual start with a plausible premise about the facts surrounding the specific medical situation and reason logically from that premise to a conclusion?
4. Is the individual able to understand the implications (i.e., the likely risks and benefits) of the alternatives presented and the choices that are made as well as the fact that those implications apply to the individual him- or herself?
5. Does the person actually understand the implications of those choices?
6. Are the person's choices authentic? Do they appear to be consistent with that person's previously known values and preferences rather than an aberration resulting directly from illness?

Under the functional approach, the patient need not understand the scientific theory underlying the health care team's recommendations in order to be deemed capable of understanding the information presented to him or her, as long as the patient comprehends the general nature and likely consequences of the choices presented. Also, under this approach, the individual's intellectual capacity must be determined on a decision-specific rather than a global, all-or-nothing basis; that is, a patient may be capable of rationally making certain sorts of decisions but not others. The minimally necessary degree of intellectual and emotional capacity may be visualized as falling somewhere on a sliding scale that depends on the nature of the decisions that the individual faces. Thus, the individual's intellectual capacity should not be treated as an all-or-nothing affair. The patient may be capable enough, despite his or her mental retardation and advancing years, to make the specific decision in question, especially if provided with adequate support and counseling.

Furthermore, it is essential to conceptualize competence in a contextual sense instead of as a static, isolated entity. Competence may improve or deteriorate for a particular patient, including an older adult with mental retardation, according to environmental factors such as the time of day or the day of the week, the perceived coerciveness of the physical location where the decision must be made (Perlin, 1989), temporary acute medical ailments, the presence of other people supporting or pressuring the individual's decision, and reactions to medications. Health care providers are under an obligation to manipulate environmental barriers to capacity whenever possible to maximize the patient's decision-making capacity. Hence, if a decision can be delayed safely until a patient is in a more lucid mental state or if the medication schedule can be altered to facilitate the patient's ability to contemplate choices, then reliance on surrogate decision making (see subsequent discussion) may be avoidable. Moreover, many acute physical or mental problems experienced by older patients with mental retardation that impair their decision-making capacity can successfully be treated medically, and that course should be pursued vigorously before the individual is deemed incompetent (Heikoff, 1986).

As noted previously, many older patients with mental retardation are capable of assisted consent with a little extra time and effort from health care professionals (Caplan, 1985). For instance, a patient who is unable to process complex information as swiftly and efficiently as most other people nevertheless may be able to cope with the complexities of a proposed intervention satisfactorily if given enough time to process the information more fully. The rapidity with which a patient processes information should not be equated automatically with the level of that individual's decision-making capacity.

Advance Health Care Planning: Instruction Directives

A person with mental retardation who has sufficient capacity to make some or all medical decisions may, because of physical or mental illness or involvement in an accident, become decisionally incapacitated at a later point. Statutes in almost every state across the United States permit currently competent individuals to engage in advance health care planning to address that contingency through the timely execution of an instruction directive. (Proxy directives are discussed in the following section.) Instruction directives are variously referred to as *living wills* or *declarations* or by other designations, depending on one's jurisdiction.

Instruction directives provide a mechanism through which currently competent individuals may plan proactively and document their future medical intervention wishes in different circumstances. State statutes that establish this mechanism are implementing the constitutional right, derived from the Fourteenth Amendment due process clause's guarantee of liberty to all people, that the U.S. Supreme Court at least implicitly reaffirmed in the 1990 case of *Cruzan v. Director, Missouri Department of Health*.

Impetus for encouraging qualified patients to engage in this form of advance planning also emanates from the federal Patient Self-Determination Act (PSDA), which Congress passed in 1990 as part of the Omnibus Budget Reconciliation Act (PL 101-508). Among other things, this law requires hospitals, nursing facilities, home health care agencies, hospices, health maintenance organizations (HMOs), and preferred provider organizations (PPOs) that participate in the Medicare or Medicaid programs to ask each patient at the time of admission or enrollment whether that individual has executed an advance directive. If the individual answers no and the patient is deemed currently decisionally capable, then the service provider is obligated by the PSDA to offer the patient an opportunity to execute an advance directive at that time. Service providers are explicitly prohibited from requiring an advance directive as a *quid pro quo* for the patient's receipt of care, however.

Attempts to execute, interpret, and implement instruction directives by or on behalf of older patients with mental retardation are likely to require additional inquiries about the decisional capacity of those patients. Focused on specific points in time, these inquiries may examine the individual's functional abilities in the present or in retrospect. In conducting these inquiries, capacity evaluators must use the same substantive criteria and evaluation techniques as would be employed in the assessment of any other group of patients; in other words, presumptions should not be made simply on the basis of a patient's age or mental retardation diagnosis.

SURROGATE DECISION MAKING

When an older patient with mental retardation lacks the capacity to act autonomously as the ultimate decision maker with regard to specific medical decisions, the legal and ethical requirements for informed consent are by no means negated. Voluntary and informed intervention decisions in such cases, however, must be made by a surrogate or a proxy acting on behalf of the patient. This section outlines various applicable types of surrogate decision making. It is vital to note at the outset that a determination of decisional incapacity and the consequent need for identification and empowerment of a surrogate is by no means a license for ignoring the patient's own beliefs and concerns about intervention thereafter. Ethical principles of respect for people, beneficence, and fidelity or loyalty compel continued communication with any patient who indicates a desire for such interaction, even when the patient's functional impairment is severe enough to prevent him or her from acting as the final legal decision maker.

There are several alternative ways to legally delegate what ordinarily would be the patient's authority to make decisions in order for the surrogate to exercise that power on behalf of the patient who has been deemed incompetent. These delegation mechanisms may be categorized as follows:

1. Delegation of authority beforehand by the patient, through an advance proxy directive
2. Delegation of authority to a surrogate by a court order in the specific case
3. Delegation of authority to a surrogate by operation of a statute
4. Informal delegation of authority to a surrogate as a matter of medical custom

Advance Planning: Proxy Directives

This chapter alludes to the legal device for advance medical planning called the *instruction directive* (i.e., a living will or a declaration). The other main advance planning device available to currently competent individuals who wish to maintain as much control as possible over future medical decisions, even if they subsequently become decisionally incapacitated, is the proxy directive. These directives are authorized for health care purposes by statute in all but a few states. Specifically, the directives take the form of durable power of attorney instruments through which a competent individual (i.e., the principal or maker) authorizes a named agent (i.e., the proxy or attorney in fact) to make decisions on behalf of the principal. The instrument is durable in the sense that (unlike the ordinary power of attorney) its continuing validity is unaffected by the principal's becoming incapacitated after execution of the document. Most durable powers of attorney for health care are springing in nature in that they do not become effective (i.e., they do not "spring" into action) until some specified trigger occurs. Usually, the principal selects a trigger such as "when my physician determines that I am no longer capable of making my own decisions."

Many older adults with mental retardation are capable and, with adequate and timely counseling, desirous of executing a proxy directive when a close family member or a friend is available to serve in the surrogate role. In most situations, less cognitive capacity is required to comprehend that one is appointing a family member or a friend to make medical decisions as one's advocate or helper than is required to understand the complexities of particular medical decisions themselves. A person who may not know which specific medical interventions he or she wants still may be clear about who he or she desires to make those decisions.

Surrogate Decision Making by Court Order: Guardianship

Several of the arguments against excessive resort to the courts for formal adjudications of patient incompetence and judicial appointment of guardians (variously referred to as *conservators* or *committees* in some jurisdictions) are mentioned previously in this chapter. In some cases, however, other forms of surrogate decision making may not work well enough. Family members may disagree among themselves. They may make decisions that seem to be at odds with the earlier expressed or implied preferences of the patient or that clearly appear not to be in the patient's best interests. The family may request a course of conduct that seriously contradicts the sense of ethical integrity guiding the health care professionals or the facility. Many older adults with mental retardation face the mirror image of this situation: the absence of any willing and available family members to step into the role of proxy decision maker.

When such situations occur, judicial appointment of a guardian who is empowered to make decisions on behalf of an individual who has been deemed incompetent may be practically and legally advisable. The least restrictive alternative principle doctrine dictates that guardianship be pursued only as a last resort when less formal mechanisms of substitute decision making have failed or are not feasible under the circumstances, because guardianship 1) often entails an extensive deprivation of an individual's basic rights; 2) may be imposed in the absence of meaningful procedural safeguards; and 3) involves substantial financial, time, and emotional costs.

In addition, remember that courts possess the authority, under either specific state statutes or their inherent equity powers, to create limited or partial guardianships rather than transferring decision-making rights from ward to guardian in a total or plenary fashion. This legal development reflects the idea that decisional capacity should be determined for many people on a functional, decision-specific basis. In order to verify the existence and extent of the guardian's authority, health care providers who are faced with substitute decision makers who purport to be a patient's legal guardian should request to see a copy of the official court order creating the guardianship (Appelbaum, 1982).

Delegation of Authority by Statute Family consent statutes have been enacted in about half of the states across the United States. These statutes empower specifically designated relatives to make particular kinds of medical decisions on behalf of incapacitated people who have not executed an advance directive or who never had the decisional capacity to do so (Menikoff, Sachs, & Siegler, 1992). Even absent such legislation, on the rare occasions when courts have been presented with the issue, they have routinely recognized the authority of the family to exercise the incapacitated person's decision-making rights on his or her behalf; just as important, most of these judicial decisions explicitly establish legal precedents for families to act in future cases without the need for prior court authorization.

Legislation in New York State has permitted experimentation with an interesting program for making medical decisions (other than those involving life-sustaining medical interventions) on behalf of individuals with mental disabilities who reside within state-operated or state-licensed facilities and for whom no other surrogate can be identified (Herr & Hopkins, 1994; Sundram, 1988). The program operates through volunteer panels as a less intrusive alternative to judicial involvement. The primary beneficiaries of New York's Surrogate Decision-Making Committee (SDMC) program have been older adults with mental retardation. If caseloads can be kept at a manageable level, then this model can be transposed to other environments (e.g., nursing facilities) and used in other states.

Delegation of Decision-Making Authority by Custom   As a general matter, in the absence of a specific statute, court order, or advance directive delegating authority to a substitute decision maker, neither the family as a whole nor any of its individual members (nor any nonrelatives, for that matter) has any explicit legal authority to make decisions on behalf of a patient who cannot speak for him- or herself. Nevertheless, it has long been a widely known and implicitly accepted medical custom or convention to rely on families as decision makers for individuals who are deemed incompetent, even without express legal authorization to do so. Even when there is no explicit judicial or legislative authorization in one's own state, the legal risk to a health care provider for a good faith treatment decision made in conjunction with the family of a patient who has been deemed incompetent is slight. Indeed, with only one exception (*In re Storer*, 1981), every court presented with such a question in the context of a concrete case has ratified the family's role in medical decision making.

Standards for Surrogate Decision Making

Once a surrogate decision maker has been identified, that surrogate must identify a particular criterion to use in making decisions affecting the patient who has been incapacitated. There are essentially two sometimes complementary, sometimes conflicting criteria available for this purpose. The traditional approach has been for a surrogate to make decisions that serve what the surrogate feels to be the patient's best interests. In this way, the surrogate acts as a fiduciary or a trustee toward the patient who needs protection by selecting a course of action intended to maximize benefits while minimizing risks. The second approach, of more recent vintage, is ordinarily termed *substituted judgment.* Under this test, the surrogate is expected to try to make the same decisions that the patient would make for him- or herself if he or she were currently able to make and express autonomous choices. Here the surrogate acts primarily as an advocate in assisting the patient to maintain as much personal authenticity (i.e., compatibility with the patient's own wishes) and self-determination as possible. Most state legislation and judicial attitudes emphasize autonomy and therefore favor use of the substituted judgment test when possible.

The substituted judgment approach works well, however, only when the surrogate is able to honestly and accurately deduce what the patient would choose under the current circumstances; this deduction may be based either on direct statements made earlier by the patient or, more typically, on reasonable interpolations from knowing the patient and his or her overall values and beliefs over the course of a lifetime (*Lane v. Candura*, 1978). In many situations, this sort of exercise involves gross speculation at best; there simply is not a specific enough indication of what the patient actually would want under the circumstances that the surrogate confronts. This is especially true when the patient has been diagnosed as having mental retardation requiring extensive or pervasive support and has never possessed the capacity to make and express competent, autonomous choices about medical interventions or a range of other matters. Although the courts in several cases attempted to perform an extremely tortured application of the substituted judgment test on decisions about patients who had never been autonomous (*Superintendent of Belchertown State School v. Saikewicz*, 1977), the more realistic, reasonable approach is for the surrogate to fall back on a best-interests analysis in those situations.

IMPLICATIONS OF A CHANGING HEALTH CARE–FINANCING CLIMATE

This chapter discusses medical decision-making rights and mechanisms for older individuals with mental retardation. A right to make medical decisions, personally or through a surrogate, necessarily implies that there exist meaningful choices from which to select. If one does not enjoy reasonable access to appropriate services in the first place, then any notion of informed consent is purely theoretical. As fundamental aspects of health care financing in the United States continue to undergo a major evolutionary (some would argue revolutionary) change process during the first few years of the 21st century, the entire social, legal, and ethical environment in which health care decision making occurs will force service providers, health care professionals, and others to confront a panoply of difficult dilemmas at both the bedside and public policy levels. Among those dilemmas are questions pertaining to health care access and quality for older adults with mental retardation.

First, these individuals rely heavily on government financing programs, with the most important being Medicare, Medicaid, and Supplemental Security Income, to pay the costs of the medical care and residential and social services that they require to maintain health and function. At the least, the structural and operational aspects (i.e., setting eligibility criteria, determining who meets those criteria) of these programs are highly likely to undergo massive modifications in the near future. Much more basic programmatic overhauls by Congress and the president certainly are possible, with serious implications for the choices available to many older adults with mental retardation.

Second, acute medical care delivery and financing (and perhaps long-term care will be included a bit later) is moving steadily into various forms of managed care, primarily HMOs and PPOs. In essence, managed care entities combine the insurer and provider functions within a single, often for-profit, entity that usually is paid an amount that is set prospectively on a per-patient (per capita) basis. Managed care plans carry significant potential both for improving and for jeopardizing the treatment of older adults with mental retardation who enroll voluntarily (because of economic incentives) or involuntarily (as a result of legislation) in this emerging part of the U.S. health care system (Freeborn & Pope, 1994).

On the positive side, under managed care, the enrolled patient should have access to comprehensive medical services, excluding long-term care but notably including preventive and (depending on the specific plan) mental health care coverage, coordinated by a primary care physician assigned to that patient, without the paperwork and discontinuity that plague many parts of the traditional fee-for-service, retrospective payment system. In addition, financial incentives built into the managed care plan ought to discourage both the patient or the patient's surrogate and health care providers from engaging in unnecessary and inappropriate interventions that consume scarce resources without an adequate demonstration of benefit to the patient.

The chief problem is that the financial incentives for prudence in spending at the heart of managed care may be excessive in some plans (Woolhandler & Himmelstein, 1995). Many fear that these incentives may influence health care providers to shortchange patients in terms of not ordering appropriate diagnostic tests, failing to refer to specialists even when such referral is clinically indicated, and refraining from recommending expensive but potentially therapeutic interventions as a matter of cost containment and profit enhancement. Older adults with mental retardation often need a large amount of remedial medical attention for various ongoing and acute ailments but are not skillful or articulate in negotiating on behalf of their own interests. They also lack a solid and dependable cadre of informed, effective advocates to exercise their rights (see Chapter 19). Hence, this population is likely to be in particular jeopardy with regard to *de facto* discrimination and neglect in the allocation of medical resources under a managed care regime.

CONCLUSIONS

As new models of health care financing and delivery continue to emerge after the turn of the 21st century amid vigorous concern and discussion among members of the public, designers and implementers of these systemic innovations must strive to maximize elements of consumers' choice and control on both the micro and macro levels. To the greatest extent possible, the values and preferences of older adults with mental retardation should be reflected at the bedside and in coverage, eligibility, and quality-of-care policies that emerge from legislatures, regulatory bodies, and corporate boardrooms.

REFERENCES

Abernethy, V. (1984). Compassion, control, and decisions about competency. *American Journal of Psychiatry, 141,* 53–60.

American College of Physicians. (1989). Cognitively impaired subjects. *Annals of Internal Medicine, 111,* 843–848.

Annas, G.J., & Densberger, J. (1984). Competence to refuse medical treatment: Autonomy versus paternalism. *University of Toledo Law Review, 15,* 561–596.

Appelbaum, P.S. (1982). Limitations on guardianship of the mentally disabled. *Hospital and Community Psychiatry, 33,* 183–184.

Appelbaum, P.S. (1994). *Almost a revolution: Mental health law and the limits of change.* New York: Oxford University Press.

Appelbaum, P.S., & Grisso, T. (1988). Assessing patients' capacity to consent to treatment. *New England Journal of Medicine, 319,* 1635–1638.

The Arc of the United States: A National Organization on Mental Retardation. (1992). *Medical and dental treatment: Position statement no. XVIII.* Arlington, TX: Author.

The Arc of the United States: A National Organization on Mental Retardation. (1998). *Medical and dental treatment: Position statement no. XVIII* (Rev. ed.). Arlington, TX: Author.

Aylward, E.H., Burt, D.B., Thorpe, L.U., Lai, F., & Dalton, A.J. (1995). *Diagnosis of dementia in individuals with intellectual disability.* Washington, DC: American Association on Mental Retardation.

Cal. Prob. Code § 811 (1998), 1995 Cal. Stat. ch. 842.

Caplan, A. (1985). Let wisdom find a way. *Generations, 10,* 10–14.

Cruzan v. Missouri Department of Health, 497 U.S. 261, 110 S. Ct. 2841 (1990).

Ellis, J.W. (1992). Decisions by and for people with mental retardation: Balancing considerations of autonomy and protection. *Villanova Law Review, 37,* 1779, 1784–1809.

Faden, R.R., Beauchamp, T.L., & King, N.M.P. (1986). *A history and theory of informed consent.* New York: Oxford University Press.

Freeborn, D.K., & Pope, C.R. (1994). *Promise and performance in managed care: The prepaid group practice model.* Baltimore: The Johns Hopkins University Press.

Grisso, T. (1986). *Perspectives in law and psychology: Vol. 7. Evaluating competencies: forensic assessments and instruments.* New York: Plenum Press.

Grob, G.N. (1991). *From asylum to community: Mental health policy in modern America.* Princeton, NJ: Princeton University Press.

Heikoff, L.E. (1986). Practical management of the demented elderly. *Western Journal of Medicine, 145,* 397–399.

Herr, S.S. (1983). *Rights and advocacy for retarded people.* Lexington, MA: Lexington Books.

Herr, S.S., & Hopkins, B.L. (1994). Health care decision making for persons with disabilities: an alternative to guardianship. *JAMA: Journal of the American Medical Association, 271,* 1017–1018.

Hill, B.K., & Lakin, K.C. (1986). Classification of residential facilities for individuals with mental retardation. *Mental Retardation 24,* 107–115.

Howell, M.C. (1988). Ethical dilemmas encountered in the care of those who are disabled and also old. *Educational Gerontology, 14,* 439–449.

In re Storer, 52 N.Y.2d 363, 420 N.E.2d 64 (N.Y. 1981).

Janicki, M.P., Heller, T., Seltzer, G., & Hogg, J. (1995). *Practice guidelines for the clinical assessment and care management of Alzheimer and other dementias among adults with mental retardation.* Washington, DC: American Association on Mental Retardation.

Janicki, M.P., & Wisniewski, H.M. (Eds.). (1985). *Aging and developmental disabilities: Issues and approaches.* Baltimore: Paul H. Brookes Publishing Co.

Kaplan, K.H., Strang, J.P., & Ahmed, I. (1988). Dementia, mental retardation, and competency to make decisions. *General Hospital Psychiatry, 10,* 385–388.

Kapp, M.B. (1994). Ethical aspects of guardianship. *Clinics in Geriatric Medicine, 10,* 501–512.

Kendrick, M. (1994). Some significant ethical issues in residential services. In C.J. Sundram (Ed.), *Choice and responsibility: Legal and ethical dilemmas in services for persons with mental disabilities* (pp. 101–115). Albany: New York State Commission on Quality of Care for the Mentally Disabled.

Lane v. Candura, 376 N.E.2d 1232 (Mass. App. Ct. 1978).

Larson, E.B., Lo, B., & Williams, M.E. (1986). Evaluation and care of elderly patients with dementia. *Journal of General Internal Medicine, 1,* 116–126.

Levine, R.J. (1986). *Ethics and regulation of clinical research* (2nd ed.). Baltimore: Urban & Schwarzenberg.

Loewy, E.H. (1987). Treatment decisions in the mentally impaired: Limiting but not abandoning treatment. *New England Journal of Medicine, 317,* 1465–1469.

Menikoff, J.A., Sachs, G.A., & Siegler, M. (1992). Beyond advance directives: Health care surrogate laws. *New England Journal of Medicine, 327,* 1165–1169.

Patient Self-Determination Act (PSDA) of 1990, codified as part of the Omnibus Budget Reconciliation Act (OBRA) of 1990, PL 101-508, §§ 4206, 4751, codified at 42 U.S.C. §§ 1395cc (a)(1), 1396a(a).

Perl, M., & Shelp, E.E. (1982). Psychiatric consultation masking moral dilemmas in medicine. *New England Journal of Medicine, 307,* 618–621.

Perlin, M.L. (1989). *Mental disability law: Civil and criminal* (Vol. 2, pp. 244–251). Charlottesville, VA: Michie Co.

Roth, L., Meisel, A., & Lidz, C. (1977). Tests of competency to consent to treatment. *American Journal of Psychiatry, 134,* 279–284.

Rozovsky, F.A. (1990). *Consent to treatment: A practical guide* (2nd ed.). Boston: Little, Brown & Co.

Rubenstein, L.S. (1994). Reflections on freedom, abandonment, and deinstitutionalization. In C.J. Sundram (Ed.), *Choice and responsibility: Legal and ethical dilemmas in services for persons with mental disabilities* (pp. 53–67). Albany: New York State Commission on Quality of Care for the Mentally Disabled.

Sabatino, C. (1996). Competency: Refining our legal fictions. In M. Smyer, K. Warner Schaie, & M.B. Kapp (Eds.), *Older adults' decision-making and the law* (pp. 1–28). New York: Springer Publishing Co.

Schwartz, C.E. (1994). Medical decision-making for people with chronic mental impairments. In C.J. Sundram (Ed.), *Choice and responsibility: Legal and ethical dilemmas in services for persons with mental disabilities* (pp. 135–156). Albany: New York State Commission on Quality of Care for the Mentally Disabled.

Sundram, C.J. (1988). Informed consent for major medical treatment of mentally disabled people: A new approach. *New England Journal of Medicine, 318,* 1368–1373.

Superintendent of Belchertown State School v. Saikewicz, 370 N.E.2d 417 (Mass. 1977).

Weiler, K. (1991). Functional assessment in the determination of the need for a substitute decision maker. *Journal of Professional Nursing, 7*(6), 328.

Winerip, M. (1994). *9 Highland Road.* New York: Pantheon Books.

Woolhandler, S., & Himmelstein, D.U. (1995). Extreme risk: The new corporate proposition for physicians. *New England Journal of Medicine, 333,* 1706–1708.

Wyatt v. Stickney, 344 F. Supp. 373, 344 F. Supp. 387 (M.D. Ala. 1972), enforcing 325 F. Supp. 781, 334 F. Supp. 1341 (M.D. Ala. 1971), aff'd in part, remanded in part, and rev'd in part sub nom. Wyatt v. Aderholt, 503 F.2d 1305 (5th Cir. 1974).

5

Legal Rights and Vulnerable People

Stanley S. Herr

Out of the horror of institutional scandals came the impetus for a revolution in the legal rights for people with developmental disabilities. In the United States, the recognition and assertion of those rights has proved to be one of the most dynamic forces for change. The rights campaign has provoked new ways of assisting and thinking about people with such disabilities. It has marshaled new resources and focused the attention of public policy makers on a field that had been the object of benign—and sometimes not so benign—neglect.

Older people also have been the beneficiaries of this revolution, especially through judicial class actions and legislative reforms. Although vast improvements have occurred since the early 1970s, progress remains uneven. Rather than attempt to survey the entire relevant legal landscape, this chapter focuses on the following four critical areas in the struggle for enforceable legal rights:

1. The right to protection of fundamental rights through access to legal counsel and to the justice system
2. The right to live in least restrictive arrangements, primarily in the community
3. The right to receive humane care and habilitation, along with the corollary of freedom from physical or mental abuse
4. The right to be free from discrimination in obtaining services, jobs, and medical care

There are, of course, many other vital and specialized legal topics of importance to this age cohort, including future planning (i.e., wills, advance directives), Social Security benefits, access to affordable housing, rights to social and health care services, and pension rights for those who have had a work history. Because one goal for aging people with mental retardation is to afford them the same rights, dignity, and opportunities as other aging people, their advocates need to consult the literature in these generic areas of elder law (see Frolik & Barnes, 1992; Strauss & Lederman, 1996).

Although the subject matter of this chapter is of universal appeal, the law and the illustrative cases are drawn from the jurisprudence of the United States. In many ways, advocates for people with disabilities in the United States have used the legal systems of the 50 states and the federal government more aggressively and more persistently than have people in other countries. From the time of Alexis de Tocqueville (1835/1981), one of the U.S. legal system's hallmarks has been the ability to turn political questions into legal questions. As Tocqueville observed, sooner or later all social problems in the United States become problems of law. Thus, the legal and political cultures of the United States lend themselves to resort to formal channels of justice. Older people with developmental disabilities have turned to courts, commissions, and counsel as other insular minorities before them have done.

This phenomenon is not unique to the United States. For example, advocates in Israel have sought judicial relief from unnecessary institutionalization or questioned organ donation from a family member with mental retardation to another family member (Herr, 1992). In Sweden, the Disability Ombudsman and the courts have provided redress for many disability-related grievances (Herr, 1995). In many regions of the world, however, disability rights receive scant attention. In a global survey, the United Nations' (UN's) Special Rapporteur of the Subcommission on the Prevention of Discrimination and Protection of Minorities reported on the acute problem of the "lack of specific effective resources to put an end to the violations" of human rights to which people with disabilities are victimized (Despouy, 1993, p. 10). Although a few countries use supervisory committees to regulate admissions to some mental disability services, the UN report concluded that legal remedies are inadequate in many countries. Despouy also decried the lack of community-based services, which often leads to the confinement of people with disabilities to institutions, urging instead the right of this population to "normalize their lives through the provision of 'alternative residential options' which do not impose restrictions on their freedom and enable them to integrate" (1993, p. 31). In many countries, work on this legal and human rights agenda has begun. Given the extensive body of U.S. law on this subject and the widespread interest in the use of legal remedies, this review of the U.S. experience may help to reveal the potential of such remedies.

SOURCES OF RIGHTS

The U.S. legal system is complex and multitiered. This complexity affects the creation and enforcement of rights for people with disabilities. This section provides an overview of some of the sources of law that apply. Because of the federal nature of this system, there are actually more than 55 systems, comprising the laws of the federal government, the 50 states, the District of Columbia, and various U.S. territories. In view of this array of fora, the litigious nature of American society and the creativity of lawmakers to devise new solutions to changing problems, the law impinging on older people with developmental disabilities and their caregivers and family members is in considerable flux.

Federal Law

By virtue of the U.S. Constitution's supremacy clause and the obvious importance of establishing national legal standards, federal law in the disabilities field has assumed ever-growing importance. Under the U.S. Constitution, for example, the Supreme Court of the United States has articulated strong rights for institutional residents to receive safe custody and adequate training (*Youngberg v. Romeo*, 1982), and for community residents to be free from exclusionary zoning when seeking to reside in group homes (*City of Cleburne v. Cleburne Living Center*, 1985). The lower federal courts have presided over class actions of historic dimensions that have led to the closure or downsizing of institutions and to the insistence on decent standards of care and habilitation (e.g., *Halderman v. Pennhurst State School and Hospital*, 1977; *New York State Association for Retarded Children v. Rockefeller*, 1973; *Wyatt v. Stickney*, 1972).

The U.S. Congress has enacted a long line of statutes that have subsidized or otherwise shaped the field of developmental disabilities. An early example is the Developmental Disabilities Assistance and Bill of Rights Act of 1975 (PL 94-103), which defined the term *developmental disability* as a condition likely to continue indefinitely and to require lifelong services, emphasized rights to least restrictive supports, and established protection and advocacy systems in each state. (See discussion later in this chapter.) The Americans with Disabilities Act (ADA) of 1990 (PL 101-336) continued and expanded the civil rights thrust of disabilities law, mandating nondiscrimination in workplaces of 15 employees or more, in public accommodations, in public services, and in channels of telecommunication. The Social Security Act of 1935 (PL 74-271), with its many amendments and its Medicaid and disability income benefits provisions, remains a critical element in national disability policy and in the lives of older people with developmental disabilities.

Regulations, guidelines, and opinion letters round out the contours of federal disability law. Even in an age of law on CD-ROMs, electronic databases, and well-indexed hard-bound volumes, finding and keeping up with disability law can be challenging for even the most conscientious scholars and practitioners. To help reduce the search time, publications have been created such as the American Bar Association's *Mental and Physical Disability Law Reporter*, which summarize the most significant new cases and statutory developments on a bimonthly basis.

Added to the complexity is the phenomenon of the discrepancy between the law in the books versus the law in action. As a matter of administrative convenience, local customs, and/or economic resource constraints, laws are implemented in ways that can diverge wildly from their plain meanings or the intent of their framers. This divergence can result in a great hazard to the rights and the dignity of people with developmental disabilities who are vulnerable and aged. The line workers—street-level bureaucrats charged with applying the law in federal Social Security offices and other programs—often rely on bulky and frequently outdated operations manuals to which the public has limited access. When large numbers of claimants are handled in a depersonalized way, some of these workers may treat them with indifference or hostility, sometimes even devising their own rules of thumb for denying benefits and leaving the correction of errors to the appeals process (Bennett, 1995). Such problems are not limited to the administration of federal laws. They occur under certain state laws as well and require nuanced and tenacious advocacy responses.

State Law

State law still covers the bulk of topics relevant to older people with developmental disabilities. That law determines whether an individual can be committed to an institution, accepted into a group home, or placed under guardianship. Wills, estates, and other instruments for future planning are also governed by state laws. If a crime is committed by or against a person with a disability, the law of the state in which the crime is alleged to have been committed comes into play. In abuse cases, especially sexual abuse cases, justice for a crime victim with mental retardation is not always sure and swift. In one highly publicized New Jersey case, high school students from privileged socioeconomic circumstances were convicted of a first-degree sexual assault against a woman with a mental age of 8 years. Although this crime could have drawn a 40-year sentence, the defendants—with special sentencing features and time off for good behavior—could be released from prison in only 22–27 months (Lefkowitz, 1997). Furthermore, the defendants were granted bail pending their appeals, further delaying any retribution for a crime that occurred in 1989 but took years to investigate, prosecute, and exhaust appeals. Although the victim was 17 years of age at the time of the assault, the case does not augur well for the protection of people with mental retardation of any age.

In summary, the United States has two distinct types of legal systems: federal and state. Depending on the issue and the specific jurisdiction, at times state law and state judges may afford a more complete or more appropriate remedy for an individual with a mental disability than their federal counterparts. This proved to be the case for the right to refuse antipsychotic medication. In *Mills v. Rogers* (1982), the U.S. Supreme Court declined to decide the issue as a matter of federal constitutional law, and on remand the Massachusetts courts upheld such a right in nonemergency situations. This important state case has produced a line of precedent in which this right to refuse treatment is exercised through court-approved substituted judgment to advance the choices that the individual would have made if competent (*Rogers v. Commissioner of the Department of Mental Health*, 1983). On other issues, such as deinstitutionalization and conditions of confinement, federal courts have had a leading role.

THE RIGHT TO PROTECTION OF FUNDAMENTAL RIGHTS

Legal rights in the books may be of little real use without an advocate to assert them or an official to interpret and implement them. Preventive law is also vital to gain the voluntary, nonadversarial compliance with the law of those charged with duties under statutes, regulations, or court decrees. Preventive activities of this kind include in-service training on rights, quality assurance monitoring, legal services outreach, negotiation, and other alternative means of dispute resolution. Outreach to especially insular and underrepresented minorities such as older people with mental disabilities who are ethnic minorities may be needed to overcome barriers to advocacy services (Mental Health Law Project, 1990). Some rights are so valued, or the rights holders are so vulnerable, that society has made institutional arrangements to safeguard those rights and groups. Some examples are described in the subsections that follow.

The Right to Counsel

When an individual's physical liberty is at stake, provisions for appointed counsel should be available. This right is embedded more firmly in the criminal justice system. States have also extended this principle to civil commitment hearings and related processes because institutionalization has been held to constitute a massive curtailment of liberty (*Humphrey v. Cady*, 1972). Indigence is generally not a factor in extending appointed counsel in these cases, because even an individual with developmental disabilities from an affluent background does not have access to funds. The reason for mandatory appointed counsel is compelling. The provision of counsel is crucial if the right to exercise the litany of procedural rights in the admission process is to be meaningful. Counsel can also investigate alternatives to institutionalization and negotiate for less-intrusive alternatives.

In guardianship proceedings, counsel plays a similar role. The appointed attorney for the alleged incompetent person can ensure that someone speaks up for the rights and interests of the older person with developmental disabilities (*Superintendent of Belchertown State School v. Saikewicz*, 1977). Although other participants in the process may be attentive to those rights and interests, whether to forgo chemotherapy, as in *Saikewicz*, or to obtain medical treatment or protective services in the more typical case, the advocate for the proposed ward should have no conflicts of interest or other factors to dilute his or her zealous representation. This role conception has been powerfully reinforced by the New Jersey Supreme Court, in *In re M.R.* (1994), which outlined specific guidance to lawyers appointed to represent proposed wards with developmental disabilities.

A few states have created systems of advocacy for the residents of mental disability facilities. In Maryland, for example, such services are provided under contract with independent legal services providers in both the mental retardation and the mental health systems. In the latter, under a consent decree in *Coe v. Hughes* (1985) grounded in a theory of right of access to the courts, extensive legal and grievance system services are provided to all residents of state mental health facilities, including those who are older and have dual diagnoses.

Protection and Advocacy Systems

The federal Developmental Disabilities Assistance and Bill of Rights Act of 1975 requires each state to have a system to protect and advocate for the rights of individuals with developmental disabilities. Referred to as protection and advocacy systems (P&As), their purpose is to protect the legal and human rights of such individuals of all ages through a full array of remedies and approaches (see 42 U.S.C. § 6041). These approaches include legal remedies, administrative remedies, information and referral services, investigation of incidents of abuse and neglect, education of policy makers, and other "appropriate remedies or approaches" for individuals receiving habitation services, eligible for such services, or being considered for such services or for a change in living arrangements (42 U.S.C. § 6042[a][2][A][i]). Although P&As have discretion to accept or decline cases, their activities must be consistent with an annual objectives and priority-setting process (42 U.S.C. § 6042[a][D]). Grievance procedures must also be available to clients or prospective clients who believe that they have been denied "full access" to the system's services unfairly (42 U.S.C. § 6042[a][2][E]).

Although individuals who can clamor for services may be better positioned to obtain P&A assistance, a number of statutory safeguards encourage representation of isolated individuals, such as older consumers without caring relatives or friends. P&A advocates must have access to developmental disability facilities at reasonable times and locations (42 U.S.C. § 6042[a][2][H]). They also have other powers of great importance to older clients who are incompetent. For example, P&A advocates are entitled to gain access to all records of any individual with developmental disabilities who 1) because of mental or physical condition, cannot authorize consent to records access; 2) does not have a legal guardian or has the state as his or her legal representative; and 3) is believed to be the victim of abuse or neglect (42 U.S.C. § 6042[I][ii]). P&A offices also may intervene unilaterally on behalf of individuals for whom there is "probable cause" to believe that their health or safety is in "serious and immediate jeopardy" when their legal representative has been contacted, offered assistance, and still fails or refuses to act to resolve the situation (42 U.S.C. § 6042[a][2][I][iii]).

With the courts frequently upholding these wide powers, P&As are in an excellent position to assert the rights of older people with developmental disabilities and others vulnerable to abuse or endangerment. For example, after the Mississippi P&A investigated the placement of an institutional resident in a solitary confinement cell for 5 days and the death of another resident subject to a disciplinary restraining hold, it found that its access to the facility and its residents were sharply restricted. The U.S. Court of Appeals for the Fifth Circuit rejected those restrictions, such as the requirement of a written retainer agreement, pre-interview screening and post-interview debriefing of the resident by a staff member, noting that these devices created "a chilling effect of gigantic proportions" that would intimidate most of the residents (*Mississippi Protection and Advocacy System v. Cotten*, 1991, p. 1057). Thus, the court upheld the residents' rights to an effective system of legal protection and emphatically rejected access restrictions that would have rendered the P&A "comatose if not moribund" (*Mississippi Protection and Advocacy System v. Cotten*, 1991, p. 1059). In New Mexico, the results were the same when the institution's administration sought to limit P&A access to clients or would-be clients with developmental or other disabilities. Under a detailed order, all residents of long-term and other care facilities were guaranteed "regular, frequent access on their living units to P&A for the purpose of obtaining information on legal rights and self advocacy" (*Robbins v. Budke*, 1990, p. 1489). A federal court in Alabama also upheld the right of the P&A to rely on an anonymous telephone call as the basis for probable cause to investigate allegations of wrongdoing in connection with the deaths of two residents (*Alabama Disabilities Advocacy Program v. Tarwater Developmental Center*, 1995). In *Michigan Protection and Advocacy Service v. Miller* (1994), the federal district court held that the P&A was entitled to have access to individuals with developmental and other mental disabilities in facilities other than mental disability facilities. Mere access to an individual's records was not sufficient. Similarly, a state court endorsed the right of Maryland's P&A to gain access to a private developmental disability facility, interview residents through the "most effective communication possible," and confer with staff (*Maryland Disability Law Center v. Mount Washington Pediatric Hospital*, 1995, p. 60). It also held that the P&A's determination of probable cause to investigate abuse and neglect did not require a trial court's prior approval. Finally, on a preliminary motion, a federal court found that involuntarily committed residents of an intermediate mental retardation care facility (ICF-MR) who claimed to be warehoused in a hazardous and dangerous environment had an enforceable private cause of action under the Developmental Disabilities Act to an individualized habilitation plan and to the benefit of the P&A system (*Nicoletti v. Brown*, 1987).

Rights Protection Under the Older Americans Act of 1965

The Older Americans Act (OAA) of 1965 (PL 89-73), as reauthorized by the Older Americans Act (OAA) Amendments of 1992 (PL 102-375), establishes several programs that can protect the rights of vulnerable older people with developmental disabilities. These programs include the Long-Term Care Ombudsman, the elder rights and legal assistance development program, and the elder abuse prevention program.

Unfortunately, these services and activities of the aging network may be underused by the developmental disabilities community. Two of the reasons for this neglect include lack of familiarity with OAA programs and the greater visibility and developmental disabilities focus of the P&A offices. Yet, the comprehensiveness of the term *elder right*—defined as a right of an older individual—and the holistic mission of the elder rights program—"to provide leadership for improving the quality and quantity of legal and advocacy assistance as a means for ensuring a comprehensive elder rights system"—suggests that these OAA resources should be explored more fully by advocates for older people with developmental disabilities (42 U.S.C. §§ 3058bb[1], 3058j[a][1]). Indeed, both the P&As and the elder rights programs are under reciprocal obligations to coordinate their activities (42 U.S.C. § 3058g[(b][6]).

Long-Term Care Ombudsman

Each state is required to have an Office of the State Long-Term Care Ombudsman to resolve complaints that relate to the health, safety, welfare, or rights of residents of nursing facilities, board and care homes, and similar adult care facilities. In addition to this investigative function, the ombudsman is to engage in a host of advocacy activities. These include providing services to residents to protect their rights and well-being, representing their interests before government bodies, seeking legal and administrative remedies, commenting on proposed changes in laws and regulations, recommending any such changes as well as new policies and actions, and developing citizen organizations and resident councils to protect the residents' rights and well-being (42 U.S.C. § 3058g[3] [1995]). Like the P&As, the ombudsman has broad access to long-term facilities and their residents and records, including instances in which a guardian refuses to permit the ombudsman to have access to records and fails to act in a resident's best interests.

The ombudsman process is a vital tool in ensuring that older people have access to the quality of residential services to which they legally are entitled (Flemming, 1991). If the ombudsman is assertive, then he or she can be a true asset and advocate in the cause of residents' rights. Many older individuals with developmental disabilities still live in nursing facilities and, as illustrated in Chapter 2, their rights and interests in obtaining less restrictive, more satisfying living arrangements are often neglected. The ombudsman can help them, for example, by monitoring for compliance with the Preadmission Screening and Annual Resident Review (PASARR) Program. Under this Health Care Financing Administration regulation (Requirements for states and long-term care facilities, 1998), long-term residents of nursing facilities with mental disabilities who do not require that level of care must have the option of receiving alternative appropriate services, including noninstitutional alternatives covered by Medicaid (42 C.F.R. § 483.118[c]). Even if the nursing facility is appropriate, the resident may need the ombudsman's assistance to secure an array of continuous specialized services appropriate to a resident with mental retardation (42 C.F.R. § 483.136). This is but one illustration of a developmental disabilities issue for which the ombudsman's access to data for the purpose of "identifying and resolving significant problems" can be enormously valuable (42 U.S.C. § 3058g[c][1]).

Legal Assistance for Older Individuals

Individuals who are age 60 years or older and have the greatest economic or social need are eligible for federally funded legal services. This economic need means having an income at or below the poverty line; *greatest social need* means having needs that include mental or physical disability, social isolation, language barriers, and limits on the performance of usual daily tasks or the capacity to live independently (42 U.S.C. §§ 3002[29]–3002[30][c][i]). Typically, legal services are provided through a contract with a legal aid office or other nonprofit legal services provider.

The OAA not only authorizes individual representation services but also mandates state-level advocacy on such policy issues as guardianship, surrogate decision making, protective services, public benefits, insurance, and pension and health benefits (42 U.S.C. § 3058j[b][1]). It also defines a state legal assistance developer as a key player in securing the legal rights of older individuals, coordinating the provision of legal assistance, and training the aging network and guardians on elder rights and alternatives to guardianship. In summary, these legal resources can aid elders with developmental disabilities because many possess characteristics of priority candidates for legal services.

Prevention of Elder Abuse, Neglect, and Exploitation

Federal funds are also authorized for programs that seek to prevent the abuse, neglect, and exploitation of older people. These programs target abuse both in facilities and in domestic or other community-based environments. Funded activities include outreach to identify such abusive treatment, public education, data systems development, training with "particular focus on prevention and enhancement of self-determination and autonomy," and support for enforcement of elder abuse and neglect laws (42 U.S.C. § 3058i[b]).

This program—along with the ombudsman; legal services; and the outreach, counseling, and assistance program on insurance and public benefits—represents valuable generic resources that can benefit people with developmental disabilities and their advocates and caregivers. Access to these OAA programs is especially important because these separate programs are mandated to "integrate their efforts and marshal their combined force on behalf of vulnerable older persons" (Hommel, 1994, p. 6).

THE RIGHT TO LEAST RESTRICTIVE LIVING ARRANGEMENTS

Since the early 1970s, legislatures and courts have struggled to devise effective legal remedies for the right of people with developmental disabilities to live in safe, appropriate, and least restrictive environments. Older people with developmental disabilities have much to gain from this right because many were subject to unnecessary segregation for lengthy periods or are at risk of such segregation if their parents or other natural caregivers die or can no longer provide support at home. As a result of powerful changes in laws and public policies as well as the voluntary actions of public and private service providers, considerable progress has been achieved. For instance, a 50-state U.S. survey (Anderson, Laikin, Polister, & Prouty, 1998) shows that, for the first time, one-third of all residential service recipients in the developmental disabilities system in the United States live in homes with three or fewer residents.

Progress in the aggregate, however, does not excuse specific injustices. Indeed, hotly contested litigation is pending in this field for individual and class action plaintiffs (e.g., *Williams v. Wasserman*, 1998). The ADA in particular is subject to judicial and administrative interpretations that clarify the law on an ongoing basis (Richardson, 1998). The relevant case law is discussed briefly in the subsections that follow.

Constitutional Rights

Youngberg v. Romeo (1982) remains the pivotal U.S. Supreme Court precedent. In *Youngberg*, the Court held that people with mental retardation in state custody are entitled, under the Fourteenth Amendment, to conditions of safety, freedom from undue bodily restraint, and training designed to ensure safety and freedom from such bodily restraint. In interpreting this constitutional standard, courts are to determine whether professional judgment was exercised or whether there has been "a substantial departure from accepted professional judgement, practice, or standards" (*Youngberg v. Romeo*, 1982, p. 323).

Applying the *Youngberg* standard to a class of people with mental retardation confined to psychiatric hospitals, a federal court in *Thomas S. v. Flaherty* (1988) ordered comprehensive remedies. In terms of less-restrictive arrangements, the court required discharge for those class members with no mental illness or behavior disorder and "conditions of life which are normal enough to promote rather than detract from one's chances of living with fewer restrictions on one's movement," including freedom from "prolonged isolation from one's normal community" (*Thomas S.*, 1988, p. 1206).

Older people with mental retardation had been harmed severely by the restrictive environments in which they were confined. For example, "Margaret R." was placed in a rest home for the aged, even though the facility had no services for people with mental retardation. After this unsuitable rest home refused to continue her care and returned her to a psychiatric hospital, Margaret R. testified in the *Thomas S.* case to plead for her right to live in the community. The defendants countered that there was no appropriate program for her. Margaret R.'s plight, unfortunately, is not unique. The court found that such placements in rest homes did not meet "minimally acceptable professional standards," and that the traditional reliance on rest homes with no specialized services perpetuated the "revolving door" readmissions of individuals with mental retardation to state psychiatric hospitals (*Thomas S.*, 1988, p. 1195). Another long-term patient, "Mary W.," had been placed on antipsychotic drugs since the 1950s despite having been recognized in 1953 not as psychotic but as "a mentally *deficient* person for whom the hospital has nothing to offer" (*Thomas S.*, 1988, p. 1188, emphasis in original). Over the course of 4 decades, she deteriorated to the point where she could no longer feed herself; could no longer walk because her legs had atrophied after extensive periods of restraint; and could no longer speak, other than "uttering two to four stereotyped, 'parrotlike' words or phrases over and over again" (*Thomas S.*, 1988, p. 1195).

To cure what the judge described as "the lingering effects of historic mistreatment," the *Thomas S.* court ordered special treatment to promote the class members' independence, dignity, and normalization—that is, treatments "as consistent as possible with societal norms" that were geared to their special needs (*Thomas S.*, 1988, pp. 1205, 1207). The court also sought remedies for inhumane living conditions through orders citing overcrowding, atypical environments, total lack of privacy, and "endless days of boredom without variation" (*Thomas S. v. Flaherty,* 1988, p. 1193). Although court orders in such cases have been issued by the reams, the underlying conditions, as the discussion of *Wyatt* in Chapter 2 documents, have abated only slowly and partially.

Statutory Rights

A wide array of federal and state statutes stress inclusion, least restrictive residential options, and living arrangements in homes and communities. Congressional findings under the Developmental Disabilities Assistance and Bill of Rights Act stressed national goals of enabling individuals with developmental disabilities 1) to "live in homes and communities in which such individuals can exercise their full rights and responsibilities as citizens" and 2) to "achieve full integration and inclusion in society" consistent with the individual's priorities and strengths (42 U.S.C. §§ 6000[10][B]–6000[10][F]). Federal policy states that such individuals should have "access to opportunities and the necessary support to be included in community life . . . [and to] live in homes and communities" (42 U.S.C. § 6000[8]). Although the Act articulated a right to treatment, services and habilitation in "the setting that is least restrictive of the individual's personal liberty" (42 U.S.C. § 6009[2]), the U.S. Supreme Court has interpreted that language as not creating enforceable substantive rights that are binding against the states (*Pennhurst State School and Hospital v. Halderman,* 1981). State laws have also expressed legislative policies supportive of community living arrangements. Maryland's developmental disabilities law (1986), for example, calls for normalization, integration "into the ordinary life of communities," and services in the community rather than in institutions (Md. Ann. Code Health-Gen. § 7-102[4][5][7]).

Consistent with such policies, the lower federal courts have approved a number of settlements requiring community placements in cases relying on due process and statutory claims. For example, in *Homeward Bound, Inc. v. Hissom Memorial Center* (1990), a federal court in Oklahoma approved a community service system as an alternative to institutional care. The court based its decision to approve the consent decree not only on Section 504 but also on Social Security Act regulations governing ICF-MRs. The court in *People First of Tennessee v. Tennessee* (1997) also required the deinstitutionalization of some 1,600 residents from three state institutions (one of which later closed). Of special significance to older residents, this decree prohibited interinstitutional transfers to nursing or other facilities. Even the Pennhurst and Willowbrook institutions were eventually closed as consent decrees sealed their fates. In addition, several states with institutional class actions opted to shift completely to community-based care, including the District of Columbia, New Hampshire, New Mexico, Rhode Island, Vermont, and West Virginia. Alaska and Hawaii also did so without litigation. By 2000, more than 110 state institutions will be either closed or scheduled for closure.

The latest statute-based judicial challenge arises from the Medicaid requirement that medical assistance, including residence in an ICF-MR, "shall be furnished with reasonable promptness" (42 U.S.C. § 1396a[a][8]). The court in *Doe v. Chiles* (1998) held that this statutory requirement creates a federal right enforceable under civil rights law. The court also required state officials to have procedures for providing services that ensure a waiting period of no more than 90 days. The evidence in this case showed that the plaintiffs had waited for as long as 10 years for services and that hundreds of eligible people were not being provided with services with any semblance of reasonable promptness. One 39-year-old plaintiff, identified as "Jane Doe 6," was living at home with her parents, who were in their 70s and had their own substantial health problems. Jane's failure to receive timely services caused her, in the court's words, "to lose several skills and fail to develop others," or, as her qualified mental retardation professional (QMRP) put it, to face "escalated isolation with no opportunities for peer development and contact" (*Doe v. Chiles*, 1998, p. 713). The QMRP's wrenching conclusion was that Jane, though a person of many strengths, would see those strengths dissolve each day as services were denied and her isolation deepened.

The court ruled that the right was enforceable because it met a three-part test. It was for the benefit of the recipients, it was not too vague or too amorphous as to be outside the judiciary's competence to enforce, and it clearly imposed an obligation on the state. In countering the state's argument that this right would impede the trend toward community-based services, the court flatly disagreed, stating that the order "does not prevent the [state officials] from continuing to pursue the home and community-based services waiver program" under the Medicaid law (*Doe v. Chiles*, 1998, p. 721). Indeed, the plaintiffs had expressed their willingness, even delight, to accept home-based services if the state exercised its discretion to offer a package of services that "entice people away" from an institutional bed (*Doe v. Chiles*, 1998, p. 721). For some families, there may even be an element of bluff; they demand an ICF-MR placement because the promptness requirement applies to such facilities and then bargain for therapies and supports in the community. This nationally significant precedent reveals the procedural gymnastics that advocates may engage in to pursue community services in a legal and human service system that still has a bias toward institutionalization.

THE RIGHT TO HUMANE CARE AND FREEDOM FROM ABUSE

A dishearteningly long line of cases has addressed problems of abuse, neglect, deterioration, and other forms of inhumane care. At the outset, *Wyatt v. Stickney* (1972) noted that several deaths of residents were caused by inattention and resident-to-resident aggression. Nonfatal forms of abuse included long-term seclusion, physical punishment, undue chemical and physical restraints, and a host of other afflictions and inhumane living conditions that are too numerous to recite. Dybwad, describing his experience as an expert witness, lamented the enduring problems to which he testified in *Wyatt* and the cases that followed:

> Over the next years I was requested to testify in some fifteen other institutional court cases throughout the United States and it was depressing to hear year after year about the same violations of human rights, the same neglect, the same gross violations of human decency, and, alas, the same tolerance of the institutional neglect and brutality by professional staffs. We cannot, we must not overlook the indisputable fact that in all those abominable institutions, there were physicians, psychologists, psychiatrists, social workers and various therapists as well as educators, most of whom were members of professional associations which were committed to codes of ethics. Yet, until the law suits were initiated by outsiders, there had been no protest brought forward by any of the professional associations. (1996, p. 15)

Institutional litigation has continued to address the rights to freedom from unsafe, inhumane, and undue conditions of bodily restraint. Courts have thus framed remedies to the lack of behavioral programs and appropriate staffing that result in excessive aggression, self-abuse, and other physical injuries of residents. They have scrutinized the misuse of antipsychotic drugs, implementing standards for avoiding, minimizing, and treating adverse effects, as well as curbing excessive dosages, poly-pharmacy, and drugs used as chemical restraints or for staff convenience (*Thomas S. v. Flaherty*, 1988). They have outlawed forcing residents to labor at unpaid tasks of institutional maintenance (*Townsend v. Clover Bottom Hospital and School*, 1978; *Wyatt v. Stickney*, 1972). This practice of institutional peonage often affected older residents. For example, Clint Tucker testified before a federal judge at the age of 71 that for 22 years he had hauled garbage away on a 7-days-a-week, 12-hours-a-day basis, followed by years of work in the institution's hospital, kitchen, poultry farm, and other worksites (*Townsend v. Treadway*, 1973). One court also cited deficiencies in the prevention of abuse to residents (including acts of violence such as sexual assault resulting in death, kicking, and puncture wounds) in framing comprehensive remedies (*Jackson v. Fort Stanton Hospital and Training School*, 1990). Such remedies have included transfers of residents to staff-recommended community placements.

Abuses are not limited to state facilities. Because staff turnover rates in some private community-based programs reach as high as 71% annually (Jaskulski & Ebenstein, 1996) and because providers may not always be able to thoroughly screen new direct support workers, shortcomings in care will occur. As noted in Chapter 2, the risks of injuries and even crimes against residents are not hypothetical. Clearly, more attention must be paid to strategies for recruitment, retention, and training of quality frontline staff. As one such staff member observed, "We would not trust our cars to non-experienced mechanics, so why would we entrust the lives of our children . . . siblings . . . friends . . . neighbors to those without the necessary skills and experience?" (Hewitt & O'Neil, 1998, p. 3). Responding to such concerns, an American Association on Mental Retardation study suggested ways to reduce the rate of turnover and to keep high-quality employees (Larson, Lakin, & Bruininks, 1998).

THE RIGHT TO NONDISCRIMINATION

Since 1973, federal laws have barred discrimination against qualified individuals with disabilities. Section 504 of the Rehabilitation Act of 1973 (PL 93-112) categorically states that no otherwise qualified individual with a disability can be excluded from participation, or denied benefits, in any program receiving federal financial assistance solely by reason of the individual's disability. The ADA extends and refines that nondiscrimination mandate to private employers of more than 15 people, to public accommodations such as restaurants and day care services, and to public services provided by state and local governments. Although these laws have had far-reaching impacts, have required self-evaluation, and have elicited voluntary compliance, they have not generated many court cases directly bearing on the nondiscrimination rights of older people with developmental disabilities. This analysis differentiates the pre- and post-ADA resolution of such issues.

Pre-ADA Decisions

Negotiation and other informal methods of resolution can often correct discriminatory practices. For example, when a Young Men's Christian Association (YMCA) program removed a 60-year-old woman from its Greek language adult education course because her physical appearance and residence at a mental retardation institution disturbed other students, a clinical law program launched a vigorous advocacy effort on her behalf. Ultimately, this woman of Greek descent with physical disabilities who was mentally alert was readmitted, and the instructor agreed to foster a more accepting classroom atmosphere (Herr, 1985). At the turn of the 21st century, such issues of access to education or recreation programs can lead to claims under Title III of the ADA, which deals with access to public accommodations.

The Rehabilitation Act's Section 504 and state guardianship law also have been invoked in the sensitive area of medical decision making for people with disabilities. Most of these cases have arisen on behalf of infants rather than for older adults at the twilight of their lives (see, e.g., *United States v. University Hospital, State University of New York*, 1984). One exception is the landmark case of *Superintendent of Belchertown State School v. Saikewicz* (1977). The case involved 67-year-old Joseph Saikewicz—a resident of a state institution who had profound mental retardation and acute leukemia—and the agonizing decision of whether to initiate a course of chemotherapy. Although the case was not framed in nondiscrimination law terms, the central issue was whether an individual who is incompetent to make decisions to refuse medical treatment in appropriate circumstances has the same right to refuse treatment as any other person. Under a substituted judgment test, the Massachusetts Supreme Judicial Court ruled that a guardian could opt for not administering chemotherapy in situations in which the individual cannot be cured, cannot communicate other than through grunts, and is unable to understand the adverse effects of chemotherapy and the other discomforts and disorientations that accompany this treatment.

Post-ADA Decisions

As noted in the previous discussion of less-restrictive alternatives, the ADA has opened new vistas for legal redress of segregation and entrenched discrimination. It also has heightened the visibility and vulnerability of questionable decision making involving the lives and employment prospects for people with developmental disabilities.

Sandra Jensen's double organ transplant illustrates this point dramatically. Initially, a university medical center refused to consider Ms. Jensen for this operation because she had Down syndrome. In the wake of a well-orchestrated advocacy campaign and the risk of Section 504 or ADA complaints, the physicians reversed course, and Ms. Jensen became the world's first known double-organ transplant recipient with mental retardation.

The ADA, however, is no panacea for every claimed injustice. In the employment arena, the American Bar Association Commission on Mental and Physical Disability Law (1998) found that ADA claimants charging job discrimination prevailed in less than 14% of administrative and judicial cases. One of the first such cases by employees with mental retardation followed this pattern when the judge ruled that a company could fire employees because of the misconduct of their job coaches without violating the ADA's requirement of reasonable accommodations (*Equal Employment Opportunity Commission [EEOC] v. Hertz*, 1998). Here, the court reasoned that the employees were unqualified because they required the assistance of full-time job coaches and that the agency arranging supported employment had failed in "picking up the pieces" by not reopening arrangements with

Hertz and substituting another agency to supply other job coaches (*EEOC v. Hertz,* 1998). On summary judgment, the court rejected the EEOC's argument that, because a full-time job coach for the employees with mental retardation could be obtained at no cost to Hertz, a job coach is a reasonable accommodation that should have been provided. However, a settlement in this case ended the litigation, restored the job of one of the employees, provided some back pay, and acknowledged that a job coach could constitute a reasonable accommodation.

Negative decisions have also arisen under Title II of the ADA. A state restriction on attendant programs limiting attendant care services to "mentally alert" individuals resulted in a ruling against such people with certain mental as well as physical disabilities. The U.S. Court of Appeals for the Third Circuit held that the ADA was not violated when the essential nature of the program was to provide greater personal control, independence, and employment opportunities for people with physical disabilities, and that extending the program to those who were not mentally alert would constitute a fundamental alteration of the program (*Easley v. Snider,* 1994). In reversing the trial court's decision in favor of a 53-year-old woman with schizophrenia and a 29-year-old with brain injuries, the court found that allowing the use of surrogates to hire, fire, and control the attendants would shift the entire focus of the program, imposing an undue burden on the state and possibly jeopardizing the entire program by broadening eligibility to all people with physical disabilities. The court reasoned that ADA regulations permit state governments to provide special benefits to certain individuals or a particular class of individuals with disabilities without being obligated to provide those same benefits to other classes of people with disabilities.

Using the ADA to Remedy Unnecessary Segregation

Under Title II of the ADA, precedent is building to outlaw the unnecessary segregation of people with disabilities in state facilities and programs. Federal appellate courts in the southeastern and mid-Atlantic states have issued widely cited opinions that not only reaffirm that the unnecessary segregation of individuals with disabilities in institutions is a form of discrimination under the ADA but also emphasize that claims of lack of funds to comply with the ADA will be subjected to close and skeptical judicial scrutiny. This trend is also reflected in authoritative guidance from the Health Care Financing Administration to state Medicaid directors (Richardson, 1998), as discussed in the subsection that follows.

From Nursing Facilities to Attendant Care

Helen L. v. DiDario (1995) revealed the power of the ADA to spare residents from undue restriction. The breakthrough case involved nursing facility residents who received Medicaid and sought attendant care in order to live at home. Idell S. was a 43-year-old mother of two who was paralyzed from the waist down as a result of meningitis. With attendant care, she could leave the nursing facility's custodial care and return to live with her mature children. In *Helen L.,* the U.S. Court of Appeals for the Third Circuit ordered that result directly. In carefully reviewing the ADA and the Justice Department's longstanding integration regulations under both the ADA and Section 504, a unanimous court held that intentional or overt discrimination was not required to constitute an ADA violation. Benign neglect, indifference, or apathy would suffice, or even a mere showing of breach of the integration regulation. The regulation states that "a public entity shall administer services, programs, and activities in the most integrated setting appropriate to the needs of qualified individuals with disabilities" (28 C.F.R. § 35.130[d]). In insisting on compliance with this rule that has the force of law, the court found that the provision of attendant care would not fundamentally alter the program or burden the state agency, because Idell was already eligible for attendant care. The court was harshly critical of the state's defense of administrative convenience when the requested accommodation would save $34,500 annually, permit a mother to live at home with her children, and not require substantive change in the state care programs. The state's resistance, Judge McKee wrote, was "totally inconsistent with Congress' pronouncement that '[t]he Nation's proper goals regarding individuals with disabilities are to assure equality of opportunity, full participation, [and] independent living . . .'" (citing 42 U.S.C. § 12101[a][8]). The decision in *Helen L.* is final because the U.S. Supreme Court declined to review it. As of June 1998, the case had been cited in 69 other court decisions and 31 legal articles. Overall, it has won overwhelmingly positive reviews.

From Institutions to Community Environments

The same integration mandate has been applied to individuals seeking freedom from custody in mental institutions. The leading case is *L.C. v. Olmstead*, decided by the U.S. Court of Appeals for the Eleventh Circuit (138 F.3rd 893 [1998]). The plaintiffs were L.C., a 27-year-old woman with mental retardation and a secondary diagnosis of schizophrenia, and E.W., a 43-year-old woman with mental retardation and a variety of mental disorders. They sought community-based treatment programs rather than a state mental hospital as their most integrated appropriate setting (*L.C. v. Olmstead*, 1997). The trial and appellate courts concurred that L.C.'s and E.W.'s confinement in this unnecessarily segregated setting violated their rights under the ADA's integration mandate. The Eleventh Circuit then remanded the case to the trial court for further evidentiary findings with regard to whether the community placements could be made without fundamentally altering the state's program.

At this stage, *L.C. v. Olmstead* has established some key principles. First, the statute and its legislative history clearly uphold the regulation's integration mandate. Second, without speaking in terms of deinstitutionalization or imposing discharge as an across-the-board remedy, *L.C.* and other courts hold that when treating professionals for an individual with a disability find that community placement is appropriate for him or her, the ADA "imposes a duty to provide treatment in a community setting—the most integrated setting appropriate to the person's needs" (*L.C. v. Olmstead*, 1997, p. 902). Third, the state's mere assertion that it lacks the funds to provide nondiscriminatory integrated services does not excuse its refusal to comply with the ADA. Both state budget officials and mental disability service officials must act to comply with federal law, and their actions in denying community treatment to these two adults with mental retardation are judged in the context of the state's overall mental health budget. Fourth, courts may take into account additional available Medicaid waiver slots as well as the ability of the state to reap savings from shifting from institutional to community-based care. It is worth noting that in Georgia, where L.C. and E.W. sought community-based care, the federal government had allocated federal funds for 2,100 slots; but the state had used only 700 slots. In short, the state would appear to be hard pressed to show that these two plaintiffs cannot be accommodated reasonably in the community.

In December 1998, the U.S. Supreme Court granted a writ of certiorari to review the *L.C.* decision. By exercising this discretionary power, at least four of the Court's nine justices suggested that there are substantial questions that deserve further review. Initially, the following were the two questions presented:

1. Does the public services portion of the ADA compel the state to provide treatment and habilitation for people with mental disabilities in community placements when appropriate treatment and habilitation can also be provided to them in a state institution?
2. If that portion of the ADA is so construed, does it exceed the enforcement power granted to Congress in Section of the Fourteenth Amendment to the U.S. Constitution? (*Olmstead v. L.C.*, 1998a)

The Court then decided a few days later, however, to restrict review to Question 1 and to drop Question 2 (*Olmstead v. L.C.*, 1998b). Although a final decision was not expected until the end of the Court's 1998 term (in the spring of 1999), this case already has aroused grave concerns about the continuing vitality of the ADA to curb undue institutionalization. The AAMR and many other organizations entered the case as amici curiae to sustain the Act as a tool for community placement and the *L.C.* Eleventh Circuit decision. Although Maryland and 9 other states initially sought review but then declined to join the brief on the merits, 13 states appeared on the opposite side of the case.

In an earlier case that is now beyond high court review, individuals in a Pennsylvania state psychiatric hospital were held to be entitled to appropriate support services in the community. In *Charles Q. v. Houstoun* (1996), the court reasoned that because the plaintiffs were recommended for discharge and their needs could be met in the environment that gives the most freedom, summary judgment should be granted in their favor on their ADA claims. The plaintiffs had not requested a newly devised program, but only that they should be admitted to existing programs.

Steps to Encourage Voluntary Compliance

In light of this strong trend toward integration, federal health officials urged further self-evaluation by state Medicaid directors and voluntary compliance with the ADA. This effort, timed with and in recognition of the eighth anniversary of the ADA, urged the directors to strive to meet the ADA's objectives by "continuing to develop home and community-based service options for people with disabilities to live in integrated settings" (Richardson, 1998). One of those objectives quoted uses the same language forcefully upheld in the *Helen L.* case. Like Judge McKee, HCFA Director Richardson stressed the national goals in ensuring "equality of opportunity, full participation [and] independent living" for people with disabilities (1998, unpaginated). By summarizing the *Helen L.* and *L.C.* cases and by calling for a reinvigorated self-evaluation process that involves Medicaid directors working "in conjunction with the disability community and its representatives" (Richardson, unpaginated, 1998) to ensure that state care policies, procedures, and practices comply with the ADA, the federal government served notice on the states that proactive steps are needed. In particular, it reinforced this message by invoking the authority of the U.S. Attorney General for the proposition that states are required to meet the ADA's "most integrated setting" standard and that steps must be taken "if the treating professional determines that an individual living in a facility could live in the community" (Richardson, 1998). Thus, states, service providers, and disability activists should plan for greater use of community-based resources as a matter of public policy, law, and prudent action to avoid further litigation or controversy.

CONCLUSIONS

The field of developmental disabilities law fully accepts that older people with mental retardation and related disabilities possess an array of legal and human rights. Like their younger counterparts, they increasingly claim services as a matter of right rather than of charity. Legal rights, as distinguished from human rights, are also ascertained and enforced more readily because they arise within well-established systems of state and national laws. The U.S. legislation and litigation summarized in this chapter certainly point to many pathways for helping older people with developmental disabilities to live with dignity in the most integrated environments appropriate to their needs.

Will there be enough well-trained professionals, direct support workers, advocates, and policy makers to guide them along those paths? Will there be enough resources—financial as well as political—to mitigate the double jeopardy that comes with old age accompanied by a developmental disability? The answers are not absolute, but the trends that have developed since 1972 are promising. Legal rights strategies have helped to boost federal and state budgets for community-based care, to energize the field to seek more self-determining options for clients, and to develop quality assurance approaches that do not simply rely on good intentions. Advocacy offices and a growing body of law to protect fundamental rights exist that could have scarcely been imagined even in the 1960s.

Yet the law in many respects remains fluid. Just as Tocqueville (1835/1981) observed, in the United States, new political issues become legal issues. With regard to older people with disabilities, this truth poses new perils and possibilities. Will Supreme Court precedents on assisted suicide (*Vacco v. Quill*, 1997; *Washington v. Glucksberg*, 1997) and the example of Oregon's first known legal assisted-suicide case (Eagan, 1998) put unacceptable pressure on people with mental retardation to prematurely terminate their lives? Will these justices uphold or put the brakes on expansive least-restrictive alternative rulings? Will the devolution of more powers to the states weaken the edifice of federal disability and other civil rights laws nearly 30 years in the making? Will new bioethical and medical advances be shared with people of limited intellectual abilities? Such questions may present future legal rights challenges for people of all ages with developmental disabilities. In the meantime, advocates continue to be engaged in securing access to justice, least restrictive environments, humane services, and nondiscriminatory treatment for older adult consumers. Although the contours of these legal rights may change, the mission of using the law to make the world a better place for older people with developmental disabilities is enduring.

REFERENCES

Alabama Disabilities Advocacy Program v. Tarwater Developmental Center, 894 F. Supp. 424 (M.D. Ala. 1995).

American Bar Association Commission on Mental and Physical Disability Law. (1998, June). Study finds employers win most ADA Title I judicial and administrative complaints. *Mental and Physical Disability Law Reporter, 22*, 403–407.

Americans with Disabilities Act (ADA) of 1990, PL 101-336, 42 U.S.C. §§ 12101–12213.

Anderson, L., Laikin, C., Polister, B., & Prouty, R. (1998). One third of residential service recipients live in homes with three or fewer residents. *Mental Retardation, 36,* 249.

Bennett, S. (1995). "No relief but upon the terms of coming into the House": Controlled spaces, invisible disentitlements, and homelessness in an urban shelter system. *Yale Law Journal, 104,* 2157–2212.

Charles Q. v. Houstoun, 1996 Westlaw 44 7549 (M.D. Pa. 1996).

City of Cleburne v. Cleburne Living Center, 473 U.S. 432 (1985).

Coe v. Hughes, No. K-83-4248 (D. Md. 1985).

Despouy, L. (1993). *Human rights and disabled persons* (UN Pub. No. E.92.XIV.4). New York: United Nations Center for Human Rights.

Developmental Disabilities Assistance and Bill of Rights Act of 1975, PL 94-103, 42 U.S.C. §§ 6000–6083.

Doe v. Chiles, 136 F.3rd 709 (11th Cir. 1998).

Dybwad, G. (1996). From feeblemindedness to self-advocacy: A half century of growth and self-fulfillment. *European Journal on Mental Disability, 3,* 3–18.

Eagan, T. (1998, March 26). First death under an assisted-suicide law. *New York Times,* p. A14.

Easley v. Snider, 36 F.3d 297 (3rd Cir. 1994).

Equal Employment Opportunity Commission v. Hertz, 1998 Westlaw 5694 (E.D. Mich. 1998).

Flemming, A. (1991, January 31). *Older Americans Act Reauthorization Amendments of 1991 Hearing before the Subcommittee on Labor and Human Resources, U.S. Senate.* Washington, DC: U.S. Government Printing Office.

Frolik, L.A., & Barnes, A.P. (1992). *Elderlaw: Cases and materials.* Charlottesville, VA: Michie Co.

Halderman v. Pennhurst State School & Hospital, 446 F. Supp. 1295 (E.D. Pa. 1977), aff'd in part, rev'd and remanded in part, 612 F.2nd 84 (3rd Cir. 1979) (subsequent history omitted; consent decree approved to close institution).

Helen L. v. DiDario, 46 F.3rd 325 (3rd Cir. 1995).

Herr, S.S. (1985). Legal processes and the least restrictive alternative. In M.P. Janicki & H.M. Wisniewski (Eds.), *Aging and developmental disabilities: Issues and approaches* (pp. 77–92). Baltimore: Paul H. Brookes Publishing Co.

Herr, S.S. (1992). Human rights and mental disability: Perspectives on Israel. *Israel Law Review, 26,* 142–194.

Herr, S.S. (1995). Maximizing autonomy: Reforming personal support laws in Sweden and the United States. *Journal of The Association for Persons with Severe Handicaps, 20,* 213–223.

Hewitt, A., & O'Neil, S. (1998). People need people: The direct service work force. *Impact, 10,* 2–3. (Available from the Institute on Community Integration, Research and Training Human Development, 150 Pillsbury Drive, S.E., Minneapolis, Minnesota 55455)

Hommel, P. (1994). 1992 amendments to the Older Americans Act, Part I: Focus on elder rights advocacy in new title VII. *Best Practice Notes on Delivery of Legal Assistance to Older Persons, 6,* 3–20. (Available from the Center for Social Gerontology, 2302 Shelby Avenue, Ann Arbor, Michigan 48103)

Homeward Bound, Inc. v. Hissom Memorial Center, No. 85-C-437-E (N.D. Okla. January 12, 1990).

Humphrey v. Cady, 405 U.S. 504 (1972).

In re M.R., 135 N.J. 155, 638 A.2nd 1274 (1994).

Jackson v. Fort Stanton Hospital & Training School, 757 F. Supp. 1243 (D.N.M. 1990).

Jaskulski, T., & Ebenstein, W. (Eds.). (1996). *Opportunities for excellence: Supporting the frontline workforce.* Washington, DC: President's Committee on Mental Retardation.

Larson, S.A., Lakin, K.C., & Bruininks, R.H. (1998). *Staff recruitment and retention: Study results and intervention strategies.* Washington, DC: American Association on Mental Retardation.

Lefkowitz, B. (1997). *Our guys: The Glen Ridge rape and the secret life of the perfect suburb.* Berkeley: University of California Press.

L.C. v. Olmstead, 1997 Westlaw 148674 (N.D. Ga.), aff'd in part and remanded in part, 138 F.3rd 893 (11th Cir. 1998), cert. granted, 119 S. Ct. 633 (1998).

Md. Code Ann. Health-Gen. §§ 7-101–7-1201 (1986).

Maryland Disability Law Center v. Mount Washington Pediatric Hospital, 106 Md. App. 55, 664 A.2nd 16 (1995).

Mental Health Law Project. (1990). *Outreach and advocacy for black and Hispanic people with mental disabilities.* (Available from the Bazelon Center for Mental Health Law [formerly the Mental Health Law Project], 1101 15th Street, NW, Washington, D.C. 20005)

Michigan Protection & Advocacy Service v. Miller, 849 F. Supp. 1202 (W.D. Mich. 1994).

Mills v. Rogers, 457 U.S. 291 (1982).

Mississippi Protection & Advocacy System v. Cotten, 929 F.2nd 1054 (5th Cir. 1991).

New York State Association for Retarded Children v. Rockefeller, 357 F. Supp. 752 (E.D.N.Y. 1973).

Nicoletti v. Brown, 740 F. Supp. 1268 (N.D. Ohio 1987).

Older Americans Act (OAA) of 1965, PL 89-73, 42 U.S.C. §§ 3001–3058ee (1994).

Older Americans Act (OAA) Amendments of 1992, PL 102-375, 106 Stat. 1195, 42 U.S.C. §§ 3001 *et seq.*

Olmstead v. L.C., No. 98-536, 67 U.S.L.W. 3392, 525 U.S. — (December 14, 1998a).

Olmstead v. L.C., No. 98-536, 525 U.S. — (December 17, 1998b).

Pennhurst State School & Hospital v. Halderman, 451 U.S. 1 (1981).

People First of Tennessee v. Tennessee, No. 3-95-1227 (M.D. Tenn. July 3, 1997).

Rehabilitation Act of 1973, PL 93-112, 29 U.S.C. § 794 (Supp. Pamphlet 1998).

Requirements for states and long-term care facilities, 42 C.F.R. §§ 483.1–483.480 (1998).

Richardson, S.K. (1998, July 29). *President Clinton announces major HCFA initiative* (Policy letter from Sally K. Richardson, Director of the Health Care Financing Administration, to State Medicaid directors [10 paragraphs]). (Available by e-mail from jfa@telesys.tnet.com)

Rogers v. Commissioner of the Department of Mental Health, 458 N.E.2nd 308 (Mass. 1983).

Robbins v. Budke, 739 F. Supp. 1479 (D.N.M. 1990).

Social Security Act of 1935, PL 74-271, 42 U.S.C. §§ 301 *et seq.*

Strauss, P.J., & Lederman, N.M. (1996). *The elder law handbook: A legal and financial survival guide for caregivers and seniors.* New York: Facts on File.

Superintendent of Belchertown State School v. Saikewicz, 370 N.E.2nd 417 (Mass. 1977).

Thomas S. v. Flaherty, 669 F. Supp. 1178 (W.D.N.C. 1988), aff'd, 902 F.2nd 250 (4th Cir. 1990), cert. denied, 111 S. Ct. 373 (1990).

Tocqueville, A. de. (1981). *Democracy in America.* New York: McGraw-Hill. (Original work published 1835)

Townsend v. Clover Bottom Hospital & School, 560 S.W.2nd 623 (Tenn. Sup. Ct. 1978).

Townsend v. Treadway, No. 6500 (M.D. Tenn. September 21, 1973).

United States v. University Hospital, State University of New York, 575 F. Supp. 607 (E.D.N.Y. 1983), aff'd, 729 F.2d 144 (2nd Cir. 1984).

Vacco v. Quill, 117 S. Ct. 2293 (1997).

Washington v. Glucksberg, 521 U.S. 702, 117 S. Ct. 2302 (1997).

Williams v. Wasserman, 937 F. Supp. 524 (D. Md. 1996), decision on merits pending in U.S. District Court for the District of Maryland.

Wyatt v. Stickney, 344 F. Supp. 387 (M.D. Ala. 1972), aff'd sub nom. Wyatt v. Aderholt, 503 F.2nd 1305 (5th Cir. 1974).

Youngberg v. Romeo, 457 U.S. 307 (1982).

II

Quality of Life and Quality Standards

6

Enhancing Quality of Life

Robert L. Schalock, David DeVries, and Jason Lebsack

This chapter has a single thesis: The quality of life of older people with developmental disabilities can be enhanced by applying a number of quality-enhancement techniques based on an understanding of the core dimensions of a life of good quality. The chapter begins with a discussion of some of the challenges that the developmental disabilities field faces with regard to older people with developmental disabilities, challenges that are not qualitatively different from those that all older people face. Thereafter, the concept of quality of life is discussed in reference to its conceptualization, measurement, and application. The chapter concludes with two challenges that individuals working in the field face and the relationship of quality-of-life concerns to rights assertion and program change.

CHALLENGES THAT THE DEVELOPMENTAL DISABILITIES FIELD FACES

The life span of people with developmental disabilities has increased dramatically, raising significant challenges for policy makers and service providers (Arnold, 1991; Bowling, 1993; Brown, 1993; Clark, 1995; Cole, 1986; Harbert & Ginsberg, 1990; Janicki, 1997; Seltzer, Krauss, & Janicki, 1994). Their increased longevity has occurred within the context of three moral dimensions that constitute powerful frameworks that potentially work against older people with developmental disabilities in the contemporary world:

- A sense of respect for and obligation to others that elevates freedom and self-control, places a premium on avoiding suffering, and sees productive activity and family life as central to people's well-being
- The understanding of what makes for a full life and that which older adults value, such as physical and mental well-being, choices, giving and receiving, involvement, and productivity
- A sense of dignity and the respect of others (Taylor, 1989)

81

Unfortunately for older people and particularly for those with disabilities, the preceding moral dimensions can be problematic because most cultures offer few guidelines for either the development of new frameworks or the modification of existing ones to meet the inevitable changes that accompany old age. As Holstein and Cole stated,

> In a simple example, the West's intensely work-oriented society imposes particular burdens of adaptations for the older person whose impairment (combined with societal limitations) impedes living by those norms. Older people may no longer have a family nearby or, if they do, they may not want to be a "burden." They may experience disrespect as their physical and mental frailties accelerate. In many ways, their dignity is perpetually at risk. Thus, they may suffer. For older people, these difficulties assume a unique poignancy. Old age is not just another life state. (1996, p. 15)

As a result, older adults with developmental disabilities frequently have a low status at best in American society and, more typically, are devalued and depersonalized. To quote Hogg,

> Despite a relative increase in inclusion and integration, this has not prevented the population of older people with intellectual disabilities remaining visible and defined. Implicitly, they are viewed as presenting "a problem" or as "a matter of concern," and certainly a "subject worthy of study." Far from merging with the wider population, particularly with older peers without intellectual disabilities, a substantial proportion of people have remained as distinctive as if they were in institutional settings, circumscribed by involvement in specialist services and sometimes denied opportunities for inclusion in the mainstream of society. (1997, p. 137)

As a result of the potential for devaluation and depersonalization, a second challenge facing the field is to protect the rights of older people with developmental disabilities. The Civil Rights movement of the 1960s raised society's collective consciousness to the need for constant vigilance to ensure that disadvantaged groups receive fair and just treatment. In the 1970s, litigation and legislation addressing the specific rights of people with disabilities focused this consciousness for the field of developmental disabilities (Herr, 1983). Because older adults with disabilities and their families are frequently vulnerable to self-imposed guilt and lack of assertiveness, they are not likely to challenge agencies or individuals who are treating them in an unjust and unfair manner (Braddock, 1992; Harbert & Ginsberg, 1990; Perlin, Gould, & Dorfman, 1995; Stratford, 1991; Wolfensberger, 1994). Thus, the following basic human rights for all older Americans need to be reaffirmed:

- Freedom, independence, and free exercise of individual initiative
- An income in retirement to provide an adequate standard of living
- An opportunity for employment in an environment free from discriminatory practices
- An opportunity to participate in the widest range of meaningful civic, educational, recreation, and cultural activities
- Suitable housing
- The needed level of physical and mental health services
- Ready access to effective social services
- Appropriate institutional care when required
- A life and death with dignity (Harbert & Ginsberg, 1990)

Thus, the challenge is clear: to strive for equity, empowerment, and inclusion of older adults with developmental disabilities. Although meeting that challenge is a difficult task, the next section of the chapter discusses how the concept of quality of life provides a model to focus efforts and channel resources.

QUALITY OF LIFE

The concept of quality of life has emerged in the developmental disabilities field as part of the paradigm shift characterized by a transformed vision of what constitutes the life possibilities of people with disabilities; a support paradigm; and an integration of the concept of quality of life with quality enhancement, quality assurance, quality management, and outcome-based evaluation (Schalock, 1994b). Considerable work has been done since 1993 to identify the core dimensions of a life of quality. Based on that work, which is summarized in Schalock (1996a, 1997a), eight core quality-of-life dimensions emerged. These are listed in Table 1.

The appeal and potential of the quality-of-life concept for older people with developmental disabilities are that it provides a fundamentally positive and growth-oriented principle that can be used to develop policy and services and evaluate the social validity of rehabilitation services and supports to older people with developmental disabilities (Berlowitz, Du, Kazis, & Lewis, 1995; Birren, Lubben, Rowe, & Deutchman, 1991; Browne, O'Boyle, McGee, & Joyce, 1994; Clark, 1995; Dorfman, 1995; Nagatomo, Nomaguchi, & Takigawa, 1995; Ross, 1995; Whitehouse & Rabins, 1992). Although still in its infancy, two aspects of the concept of quality of life as related to older people with developmental disabilities are discussed in this section: its measurement and its application.

Quality-of-Life Measurement

As shown in Table 1, quality of life is a multidimensional construct that involves eight core dimensions that can be assessed from either an objective or a subjective perspective. Objective analysis investigates social aspects such as health, education, and standard of living, whereas a subjective analysis focuses on perceptions of life experiences (Edgerton, 1996; Schalock, 1996b; Schalock & Keith, 1993). Because of the lifestyle changes that accompany aging, the emerging trend in quality-of-life measurement for older adults with developmental disabilities is to use the person's stated level of satisfaction as the primary measure of quality of life. Measures of satisfaction have commonly been used as an aggregate of individual life domains (Flanagan, 1978), have shown traitlike stability of subjective well-being (Edgerton, 1996), and have been used to evaluate the level of satisfaction across populations and service delivery recipients (Lehman, 1995).

Two studies (Lebsack, in press; Schalock & Keith, 1993) reflected how the concept of quality of life might be measured among older adults with developmental disabilities. The first example used the Quality of Life Indicator Assessment (Lebsack, in press) (see Table 2) to evaluate the older adult's perceived satisfaction

Table 1.   Core quality-of-life dimensions

Emotional well-being
Interpersonal relationships
Material well-being
Personal development
Physical well-being
Self-determination
Social inclusion
Rights

Table 2.   Quality of Life Indicator Assessment: Core dimensions and indicators

Core dimensions	Indicators	Definitions
Emotional well-being	1. Freedom from fear	Freedom from fear, harm, injury, neglect, or hurt
	2. Spirituality	Opportunity to worship and believe as I wish and act on or pursue my personal belief system
	3. General mood	Happiness, contentment, sadness, or disappointment
	4. Self-concept	A positive opinion about myself; what I think about myself
	5. Freedom from anxiety	Freedom from worry involving aspects of family, friends, where I live, my financial situation
Interpersonal relationships	6. Family	Involvement and relationships with spouse, siblings, children, grandchildren, nieces and nephews, cousins, and great-grandchildren
	7. Friends	Involvement and relationships with my friends and acquaintances
	8. Neighbors and cohabitants	Involvement and relationships with my current and former neighbors and/or others with whom I currently live
	9. Activity personnel	Involvement and relationships with those providing organized activities such as church, Bible study, activities, recreation, and leisure
	10. Caregivers	Involvement and relationships with the doctors, nurses, and caregiving staff
Material well-being	11. Home/residence	Where I currently reside
	12. Money	Money with which to buy things and do activities
	13. Personal items	Availability and use of furniture, pictures, radio, television, and similar items
	14. Clothing	My personal clothing, including under- and outergarments
	15. Insurance	Includes health insurance, hospital coverage, and medication
Personal development	16. Education	Opportunities for developing new skills such as classes, workshops, or activities (e.g., cards, social interactions, games, Bible study)
	17. Activities	Opportunities to engage in arts, crafts, and other activities that allow me to enhance my skills or increase my welfare
	18. Intellectual	Opportunities to use my mind through stimulating activities such as doing crossword puzzles, working with numbers, and engaging in memory exercises
	19. Reading materials	Access to books, magazines, and newspapers
	20. Helping others	Opportunities to help others with chores, go for walks, maintain personal hygiene, and visit people
Physical well-being	21. Physical health	Includes my ability to eat, dress, bathe, walk, and care for myself
	22. Food	Includes how food tastes and looks, the amount of food that I can have, and how food is served
	23. Health care	The quality and quantity of services that I receive from doctors, nurses, and other caregiving staff
	24. Medication level	Includes the types and dosages of medication that I am currently taking
	25. Energy level	The energy I have to do things during the day

(continued)

Table 2.   *(continued)*

Core dimensions	Indicators	Definitions
Self-determination	26. Decisions about daily activities	Freedom to make choices and decisions about the activities that I do during the day
	27. Decisions about what I eat and drink	Freedom to make choices and control decisions about what I eat and drink
	28. Decisions about time	Freedom to make choices and decisions about what I do to fill my time and where I spend my time
	29. Personal opinions	Opportunities to express my personal opinions and values
	30. Goals	Opportunities to achieve the goals that I set for myself such as accomplishing daily tasks (e.g., a hobby, reading, getting around)
Social inclusion	31. Accepted by cohabitants	Being liked and accepted by those with whom I live; having co-habitants involve me in their activities
	32. Accepted by staff	Being liked and accepted by caregiving staff; having staff involve me in conversations
	33. Receiving help from cohabitants	Receiving help or support from those with whom I live
	34. Receiving help from staff	Receiving help or support from caregivers
	35. Participation	Opportunities to be involved with others in parties, outings, and activities
Rights	36. Privacy	Feeling and evidence that others respect my privacy
	37. Input into decisions	Opportunities to affect how the facility is run (e.g., rules, regulations, schedules) or with activities that affect my daily life
	38. Possessions	Opportunities to own things
	09. Legal	Opportunities to receive legal aid, help, or other advocacy assistance
	40. Safety	Protection from negative or potentially harmful events or situations

across the eight core quality-of-life dimensions. Five indicators of each quality-of-life core dimension were developed on the basis of published literature. Each indicator was defined, and respondents were asked to rate their degree of satisfaction with the indicator based on the following five-point Likert scale: 5 = Very satisfied, 4 = Somewhat satisfied, 3 = Neutral (neither satisfied nor dissatisfied), 2 = Somewhat dissatisfied, and 1 = Very dissatisfied. The instrument has been used to provide feedback to program staff regarding high and low areas of satisfaction among residents (Lebsack, in press).

The second example used the Quality of Life Questionnaire (Schalock & Keith, 1993), which is a 40-item questionnaire containing items related to the person's self-assessed levels of independence, productivity, community integration, and satisfaction. This questionnaire has been used with clientele in the Mid-Nebraska Mental Retardation Services program since 1993 as part of its annual review. An analysis of 21 people older than age 60 indicated a 3% drop in assessed quality of life during the 5-year period of the study, with slight decreases in the levels of assessed independence, productivity, and community integration. During the 5 years of the study, however, there was a small gain (1%) in levels of assessed personal satisfaction (Schalock, 1997b).

The assessment research being done in the area of quality of life for older adults is dynamic and varied (Edgerton, 1996; Langer & Rodin, 1976; Lawton, Moss, & Duhamel, 1995; Raphael, 1996). The growing need for this quality-of-life research is appropriate, considering the aging trend of people with developmental disabilities. In this effort, one needs to emphasize that the older adult population should be studied as a unique group of people. Physical limitations, personal backgrounds, cognitive abilities, and especially general beliefs and values should be taken into consideration when devising both evaluation approaches and formats. Subjective and objective quality-of-life measurement should be looked on as separate yet important pursuits (Edgerton, 1996). Because quality of life is a multidimensional construct, it must be studied from multiple perspectives.

Quality-of-Life Application

The emphasis on successful aging has been useful in focusing attention on environmental factors that can improve people's quality of life as they age. Advocates of the successful aging perspective (e.g., Bury & Holme, 1990; Goff, 1993; Grembowski, Patrick, Diehr, & Durham, 1993; Groves & Slack, 1994; McConatha, McConatha, & Dermigny, 1994; Rowe & Kahn, 1987; Schultz & Heckhausen, 1996) emphasized the importance of environmental factors as moderators of the aging process. The following principles are common throughout the literature on successful aging:

- There is much capacity remaining in older adults.
- Knowledge-based interventions (i.e., stressing learning, memory, thinking activities) can offset age-related declines in cognitive mechanisms.
- Optimal aging occurs under development-enhancing and age-friendly environmental conditions.
- Functioning is enhanced through factors such as an active lifestyle, social supports, improved socioeconomic status, and minimal medications.
- Policy makers and service providers need to focus on outcomes that the culture or the person values (Baltes & Baltes, 1990; Raphael, 1996).

Program changes based on the concepts of successful aging and quality of life do not occur in a vacuum. Rather, one needs to take a socioecological perspective that understands change and opportunities as a function of the person's interactions with culture, service philosophy, legislation, service provision, community factors, family, and support structures (Bronfenbrenner, 1979; Hogg, 1997; Keith, 1996; Lawton, DeVoe, Ruth, & Parmelee, 1995). The focus of this chapter, however, is on a number of techniques for enhancing quality of life that are cross-referenced to the eight core quality-of-life dimensions summarized in Table 1.

Table 3 lists a number of quality-of-life enhancement techniques for promoting either successful aging or a good quality of life (e.g., Agich, 1993; Bury & Holme, 1990; Grembowski et al., 1993; Holt & Delman-Jenkins, 1992; Kearney, Krishnan, & Londhe, 1993; Mor-Barak, Miller, & Syme, 1991; Ory & Cox, 1994; Saul, 1993; Schalock, 1994a, 1994b; Sixsmith, Hawley, Stilwell, & Copeland, 1993; Williams, 1991). The quality-of-life enhancement techniques summarized in Table 3 are only illustrative, since options and strategies vary according to the environmental variables described previously. The important point to keep in mind is that there is an assumed direct relationship between the enhancement technique and its impact on the person's successful aging and enhanced quality of life.

Table 3. Quality-of-life enhancement techniques

Dimensions	Exemplary enhancement techniques	
Emotional well-being	Increase safety	Reduce stress
	Promote spirituality	Foster success
	Provide positive feedback	Promote stable, safe, and pre dictable environments
Interpersonal relationships	Promote intimacy and affection	Encourage interactions
	Support family	Foster friendships
		Provide supports
Material well-being	Encourage ownership	Support employment
	Advocate for financial security	Encourage possessions
	Ensure safe environments	
Personal development	Provide education and (re)habilitation	Foster skill development
		Provide purposeful activities
	Teach functional skills	Use assistive technology
	Provide vocational and nonvocational activities	
Physical well-being	Ensure health care	Encourage proper nutrition
	Maximize mobility	Support activities of daily living
	Support opportunities for meaningful recreation and leisure	Promote wellness through physical fitness, nutrition, healthy lifestyles, and stress management
Self-determination	Maximize choices	Assist in developing personal goals
	Encourage personal control	
Social inclusion	Interact with support networks	Provide opportunities for community integration and participation
	Promote positive role functions and lifestyles	Support volunteerism
	Stress normalized and integrated environments	
Rights	Ensure privacy	Afford due process
	Encourage voting	Encourage ownership
	Reduce barriers	Encourage civic responsibilities

Two examples illustrate the heuristic value that quality enhancement techniques have for people and programs alike. First, choice and control (listed under "Self-determination" in Table 2) are viewed as environmental tools for quality enhancement (Hughes, 1993; Schalock, 1994b; Sutton, Factor, Hawkins, Heller, & Seltzer, 1993); loss of control over the planning and implementation of quality-of-life activities are viewed as a major component of the deterioration of self-identity (Saul, 1993). An early study (Langer & Rodin, 1976) of the perceived quality of life of older adults identified two common and recurring themes: control and personal power. In this study, a group of nursing facility residents for whom power over small daily tasks was reinforced were happier, talked more with others, and spent less time in passive activities such as watching others. The group that was given little or no control over the same tasks showed no physical or emotional improvement, and twice as many of them died within an 18-month period.

A second example involves results from the administration of the Quality of Life Indicator Assessment (see Table 2) to a group of 60 older adults who were living in either a semi-independent or a supervised living arrangement. The quality-of-life core dimension that showed the lowest satisfaction scores was personal development, which is consistent with Raphael's findings (1996). Among the five indicators of personal development (education, activities, intellectual, reading materials, and helping others), the lowest mean scores were for education and activities. This result is consistent with published literature reporting that passive activities such as watching television and listening to the radio represent a large portion of the waking day of older adults (Lawton, Moss, & Duhamel, 1995). Implementing more individually tailored intellectual stimulation and physical activities in long-term care programs seems to be an appropriate response to enhance the quality of life of older adults. Personal development activities that can reasonably be increased include creative writing and expressive activities (Reiter, 1994), leisure and recreation pursuits (Hawkins, 1997; Saul, 1993), promoting a healthy lifestyle (Edgerton, Gaston, Kelly, & Ward, 1994; Raphael, 1996; Roth & Morse, 1994), and frequent medication reviews (Garwood, 1997).

CONCLUSIONS

Programmatic changes are beginning to occur in services for older adults with developmental disabilities. Many of the changes described in this book are based on a fuller recognition of the rights of older adults; others are based on the emergence of successful aging programs. Still others are based on an enhanced quality of life that represents a potential inalienable right of all people (Luckasson, 1997). As these changes continue to occur, the gerontology field will be confronted with at least two challenges. First, which outcomes indicate to service providers that they have made a difference in consumers' lives? Second, on which life dimensions should service providers focus?

Outcome Evaluation

Although there is a strong consensus that outcome evaluation of programs for older adults is necessary, there is little agreement about what to measure (Clark, 1991; Ebrahim, 1994; Hughes, 1993; James & Minichiello, 1994; Rai, Jatten, Collias, & Hoefnagels, 1995; Rai & Kelland, 1995; Rockwood, 1995; Schalock, 1995; Stewart & King, 1991). Schultz and Heckhausen, for example, in discussing the outcomes from successful aging programs, stated that

> Some advocates of successful aging focus on outcomes such as cardiovascular and pulmonary functioning and the absence of disability as measures of success. Others emphasize cognitive and intellectual performance as measures of success, whereas still others focus on achievements in physical or artistic domains. [We] feel it is important to focus on criteria of success that are externally measurable and include domains of functioning that have been and continue to be valued by cultures throughout time. These include physical, cognitive, intellectual, affective, and creative functioning, as well as social relations. (1996, p. 707)

Consistent with the preceding suggestion, the outcomes selected to evaluate the quality of life of older adults with disabilities should be based on the eight core quality-of-life dimensions and quality indicators listed in Table 4.

Multidimensionality

Significant changes occur in the psyche as one ages. Tornstam, for example, described the human aging process as encompassing "a general potential toward gero-

Table 4.   Quality-of-life dimensions and quality indicators

Dimension	Indicators	
Emotional well-being	Freedom from fear	Self-concept
	Spirituality	Freedom from anxiety
	General mood	
Interpersonal relationships	Family	Activity personnel
	Friends	Caregivers
	Neighbors	
Material well-being	Home/residence	Clothing
	Money	Insurance
	Personal possessions	
Personal development	Educational	Reading materials
	Activities	Helping others
	Intellectual	
Physical well-being	Physical health	Medication level
	Food	Energy level
	Health care	
Self-determination	Decisions about daily activities	Personal opinions
	Decisions about what I eat and drink	Personal goals
	Decisions about how I spend time	
Social inclusion	Accepted by cohabitants	Receiving help from staff
	Accepted by staff	Participation
	Receiving help from cohabitants	
Rights	Privacy	Compliance with legal and
	Input into decisions	human rights
	Protection of possessions	Safety

transcendance, which implies . . . change, development, and maturation of the self and the identity" (1996, p. 37). A number of competing cultural images and metaphors are used to describe the aging process: the universality of physical decline versus the possibilities of successful aging, aging as a fearful state versus aging creatively, and aging as a lack of productivity versus the "productive aging society" (Holstein & Cole, 1996, p. 14).

The shift toward viewing aging from a successful aging perspective has both positive and negative aspects. On the positive side, it encompasses findings (e.g., Cole, 1986) suggesting that considerable potential exists among most older adults; knowledge-based interventions can offset age-related declines in cognitive mechanisms; optimal aging occurs under development-enhancing and age-friendly environmental conditions; and older adults' functioning is enhanced by factors such as improved lifestyle, social supports, socioeconomic status, and other environmental factors. On the negative side, overreliance on productivity and autonomy may further marginalize older adults, downgrade their interdependency, and result in their being relegated virtually to an existential abyss (Cole, 1986). Thus, the primary challenge is to focus on the multidimensionality of the individual's life and to advocate strongly for those rights, core quality-of-life dimensions, and program changes that result in successful aging and an enhanced quality of life. There is no more worthy goal or outcome for all people, including those older adults who have developmental disabilities.

REFERENCES

Agich, G.J. (1993). *Autonomy and long-term care.* New York: Oxford University Press.

Arnold, S. (1991). Measurement of quality of life in the frail elderly. In J.E. Birren, J. Lubben, J. Rose, & D. Deutchman (Eds.), *The concept and measurement of quality of life in the frail elderly* (pp. 50–74). San Diego: Academic Press.

Baltes, P.B., & Baltes, M.M. (Eds.). (1990). *Successful aging: Perspectives from the behavioral sciences.* New York: Cambridge University Press.

Berlowitz, D.R., Du, W., Kazis, L., & Lewis, S. (1995). Health-related quality of life of nursing home residents: Differences in patient and provider perceptions. *Journal of the American Geriatrics Society, 43*(7), 799–802.

Birren, J.E., Lubben, J., Rowe, J., & Deutchman, D. (Eds.). (1991). *The concept and measurement of quality of life in the frail elderly.* San Diego: Academic Press.

Bowling, A. (1993). The concepts of successful and positive aging. *Family Practice, 10*(4), 449–453.

Braddock, D. (1992). Community mental health and mental retardation services in the United States: A comparative study of resource allocation. *American Journal of Psychiatry, 149*(2), 175–183.

Brown, R.I. (1993). Quality of life issues in aging and intellectual disability. *Australia and New Zealand Journal of Developmental Disabilities, 18*(4), 219–227.

Browne, J.P., O'Boyle, C.A., McGee, H.M., & Joyce, C.R.B. (1994). Individual quality of life in the healthy elderly. *Quality of Life Research: An International Journal of Quality of Life Aspects of Treatment, Care and Rehabilitation, 3,* 235–244.

Bronfenbrenner, U. (1979). *The ecology of human development: Experiments by nature and design.* Cambridge, MA: Harvard University Press.

Bury, M., & Holme, A. (1990). Quality of life and social support in the very old. *Journal of Aging Studies, 4*(4), 345–357.

Clark, P.G. (1991). Ethical dimensions of quality of life in aging: Autonomy vs. collectivism in the United States and Canada. *Gerontologist, 31*(5), 631–639.

Clark, P.G. (1995). Quality of life, values and teamwork in geriatric care: Do we communicate what we mean? *Gerontologist, 35*(3), 402–411.

Cole, T. (1986). Introduction. In T.R. Cole & S.A. Gadow (Eds.), *What does it mean to grow old? Reflections from the humanities* (pp. 3–8). Durham, NC: Duke University Press.

Dorfman, L.T. (1995). Health conditions and perceived quality of life in retirement. *Health and Social Work, 20*(3), 192–199.

Ebrahim, S. (1994). The goals of rehabilitation for older people. *Reviews in Clinical Gerontology, 4*(2) 93–95.

Edgerton, R.B. (1996). A longitudinal-ethnographic research perspective on quality of life. In R.L. Schalock (Ed.), *Quality of life: Vol. I. Conceptualization and measurement* (pp. 83–88). Washington, DC: American Association on Mental Retardation.

Edgerton, R.B., Gaston, M.A., Kelly, H., & Ward, T.W. (1994). Health care for aging people with mental retardation. *Mental Retardation, 32*(2), 146–150.

Flanagan, J.C. (1978). A research approach to improving quality of life. *American Psychologist, 33,* 138–147.

Garwood, M. (1997, September). *Healthy aging for persons with developmental disabilities.* Paper presented at the American Association on Mental Retardation Wisconsin chapter 1997 annual conference, Madison, Wisconsin.

Goff, K. (1993). Creativity and life satisfaction of older adults. *Educational Gerontology, 19*(3), 241–250.

Grembowski, D., Patrick, D., Diehr, P., & Durham, M. (1993). Self-efficacy and health behavior among older adults. *Journal of Health & Social Behavior, 34*(2), 89–104.

Groves, D.L., & Slack, T. (1994). Computers and their application to senior citizen therapy within a nursing home. *Journal of Instructional Psychology, 21*(3), 221–226.

Harbert, A.S., & Ginsberg, L.H. (1990). *Human services for older adults: Concepts and skills* (2nd ed. rev.). Columbia: University of South Carolina Press.

Hawkins, B.A. (1997). Promoting quality of life through leisure and recreation. In R.L. Schalock (Ed.), *Quality of life: Vol. II. Application to persons with disabilities* (pp. 117–130). Washington, DC: American Association on Mental Retardation.

Herr, S.S. (1983). *Rights and advocacy for retarded people.* Lexington, MA: Lexington Books.

Hogg, J. (1997). Intellectual disability and aging: Ecological perspectives from recent research. *Journal of Intellectual Disability Research, 41*(2), 136–143.

Holstein, M.B. & Cole, T.R. (1996). Reflections on age, meaning, and chronic illness. *Journal of Aging and Identity, 1*(1), 7–22.

Holt, M.K., & Delman-Jenkins, M. (1992). Research and implications for practice: Religion, well-being/morale, and coping behavior in later life. *Journal of Applied Gerontology, 11*(1), 101–110.

Hughes, B. (1993). A model for the comprehensive assessment of older people and their care. *British Journal of Social Work, 23,* 345–364.

James, J.E., & Minichiello, V. (1994). Disability and rehabilitation in older persons. *Disability and Rehabilitation: An International Multidisciplinary Journal, 16*(3), 95–97.

Janicki, M.P. (1997). Quality of life for older persons with mental retardation. In R.L. Schalock (Ed.), *Quality of life: Vol. II. Application to persons with disabilities* (pp. 105–116). Washington, DC: American Association on Mental Retardation.

Kearney, G.M., Krishnan, V.H., & Londhe, R.L. (1993). Characteristics of elderly people with a mental handicap living in a mental handicap hospital: A descriptive study. *British Journal of Developmental Disabilities, 39*(76, pt. 1), 31–50.

Keith, K.D. (1996). Measuring quality of life across cultures: Issues and challenges. In R.L. Schalock (Ed.), *Quality of life: Vol. I. Conceptualization and measurement* (pp. 73–82). Washington, DC: American Association on Mental Retardation.

Langer, E.J., & Rodin, J. (1976). The effects of choice and enhanced personal responsibility for the aged: A field experiment in an institutional setting. *Journal of Personality and Social Psychology, 34*(2), 191–198.

Lawton, M.P., DeVoe, M.R., Ruth, M., & Parmelee, P. (1995). Relationship of events and affect in the daily life of an elderly population. *Psychology and Aging, 10,* 469–477.

Lawton, M.P., Moss, M., & Duhamel, L.M. (1995). The quality of daily life among elderly care receivers. *Journal of Applied Gerontology, 14*(2), 150–171.

Lebsack, J. (in press). Quality of life satisfaction in elderly residents of two types of long-term care. *Psi Chi Journal.*

Lehman, A.L. (1995). Demographic influences on quality of life among persons with chronic mental illness. *Evaluation and Program Planning, 18*(2), 155–164.

Luckasson, R. (1997). Foreword. In R.L. Schalock (Ed.), *Quality of life: Vol. II. Application to persons with disabilities* (pp. vii–x). Washington, DC: American Association on Mental Retardation.

McConatha, D., McConatha, J., & Dermigny, R. (1994). The use of interactive computer services to enhance the quality of life for long-term residents. *Gerontologist, 34*(4), 553–556.

Mor-Barak, M.E., Miller, L.S., & Syme, L.S. (1991). Social networks, life events, and health of the poor, frail elderly: A longitudinal study of the buffering versus the direct effect. *Family and Community Health, 14*(2), 1–13.

Nagatomo, I., Nomaguchi, M., & Takigawa, M. (1995). Anxiety and the quality of life in residents of a special nursing home. *International Journal of Geriatric Psychiatry, 10*(7), 541–545.

Ory, M.G., & Cox, D.M. (1994). Forging ahead: Linking health and behavior to improve quality of life in older people. *Social Indicators Research, 33*(1), 89–120.

Perlin, M.L., Gould, K.K., & Dorfman, D.A. (1995). Therapeutic jurisprudence and the civil rights of institutionalized mentally disabled persons: Hopeless oxymoron or path to redemption? *Psychology, Public Policy, and Law, 1*(1), 80–119.

Rai, G.S., Jatten, E. Collias, D., & Hoefnagels, W. (1995). Study to assess quality of life (morals and happiness) in two continuing care facilities: A comparative study in the UK and the Netherlands. *Archives of Gerontology and Geriatrics, 20*(3), 249–253.

Rai, G.S., & Kelland, P. (1995). Quality of life cards: A novel way to measure quality of life in the elderly. *Archives of Gerontology, 21*(3), 285–289.

Raphael, D. (1996). Quality of life of older adults toward the optimization of the aging process. In R. Renwick, I. Brown, & M. Nagler (Eds.), *Quality of life in health promotion and rehabilitation: Conceptual approaches, issues, and applications* (pp. 290–306). Thousand Oaks, CA: Sage Publications.

Reiter, S. (1994). Enhancing the quality of life for the frail elderly: Rx, the poetic prescription. *Journal of Long-Term Health Care: The PRIDE Institute Journal, 13*(2), 12–19.

Rockwood, K. (1995). Interaction of research methods and outcome measures. *Canadian Journal on Aging, 14*(1, Suppl. 1), 151–164.

Ross, L. (1995). The spiritual dimension: Its importance to patients' health, well-being and quality of life and its implications for nursing practice. *International Journal of Nursing Studies, 32*(5), 457–468.

Roth, S.P., & Morse, J.S. (Eds.). (1994). *A life-span approach to nursing care for individuals with developmental disabilities.* Baltimore: Paul H. Brookes Publishing Co.

Rowe, J.W., & Kahn, R.L. (1987). Human aging: Usual and successful. *Science, 237,* 143–149.

Saul, S. (1993). Meaningful life activities for elderly residents of residential health care facilities. *Loss, Grief, and Care, 6,* 79–86.

Schalock, R.L. (1994a). Promoting quality through quality enhancement techniques and outcome based evaluation. *Journal on Developmental Disabilities, 3,* 1–16.

Schalock, R.L. (1994b). Quality of life, quality enhancement, and quality assurance: Implications for program planning and evaluation in the field of mental retardation and developmental disabilities. *Evaluation and Program Planning, 17,* 121–131.

Schalock, R.L. (1995). *Outcome-based evaluation.* New York: Plenum Press.

Schalock, R.L. (Ed.). (1996a). *Quality of life: Vol. I. Conceptualization and measurement.* Washington, DC: American Association on Mental Retardation.

Schalock, R.L. (1996b). Reconsidering the conceptualization and measurement of quality of life. In R.L. Schalock (Ed.), *Quality of life: Vol. I. Conceptualization and measurement* (pp. 123–139). Washington, DC: American Association on Mental Retardation.

Schalock, R.L. (Ed.). (1997a). *Quality of life: Volume II: Application to persons with disabilities.* Washington, DC: American Association on Mental Retardation.

Schalock, R.L. (1997b). The conceptualization and measurement of quality of life: Current status and future considerations. *Journal on Developmental Disabilities, 5*(2), 1–21.

Schalock, R.L., & Keith, K. (1993). *Quality of life questionnaire.* Worthington, OH: IDS Publishing.

Schultz, R., & Heckhausen, J. (1996). A life span model of successful aging. *American Psychologist, 51*(7), 702–714.

Seltzer, M.M., Krauss, M.W., & Janicki, M.P. (Eds.). (1994). *Life course perspectives on adulthood and old age.* Washington, DC: American Association on Mental Retardation.

Sixsmith, A., Hawley, C., Stilwell, J., & Copeland, J. (1993). Delivering "positive care" in nursing homes. *International Journal of Geriatric Psychiatry, 8*(5), 407–412.

Stewart, A.L., & King, A.C. (1991). Evaluating the efficacy of physical activity for influencing quality-of-life outcomes in older adults. *Annals of Behavioral Medicine, 13*(3), 108–116.

Stratford, B. (1991). Human rights and equal opportunities for people with mental handicap—with particular reference to Down syndrome. *International Journal of Disability, Development, and Education, 38*(1), 3–13.

Sutton, E., Factor, A.R., Hawkins, B.A., Heller, T., & Seltzer, G.B. (Eds.). (1993). *Older adults with developmental disabilities: Optimizing choice and change.* Baltimore: Paul H. Brookes Publishing Co.

Taylor, C. (1989). *Sources of the self: The making of the modern identity.* Cambridge, MA: Harvard University Press.

Tornstam, L. (1996). Gerotranscendence: A theory about maturing into old age. *Journal of Aging and Identity, 1*(1), 37–50.

Whitehouse, P.J. & Rabins, P.V. (1992). Quality of life and dementia. *Alzheimer Disease and Associated Disorders, 6*(3), 135–137.

Williams, D.K. (1991). Developing environmental interventions to enhance quality of life for elders and their providers in adult residential care: An overview. *Adult Residential Care Journal, 5,* 185–198.

Wolfensberger, W. (1994). The growing threat to the lives of handicapped people in the context of modernistic values. *Disability and Society, 9*(3), 395–413.

7

Rights, Place of Residence, and Retirement
Lessons from Case Studies on Aging

Barbara A. Hawkins

The demographic pattern of the world's population is shifting because of a striking increase in the number of older people, especially in industrialized countries. For example, the U.S. population older than age 65 expanded tenfold in the 20th century. In 1900, only 3.1 million Americans were older than 65 years of age. At the turn of the 21st century, more than 33.2 million Americans are older than age 65 (Kart, 1997). The 20th century also brought new problems for older U.S. citizens. Among the most prominent challenges that older people face are prejudice and discrimination because younger members of American society are not informed about the rights and needs of individuals who live to old age.

INTRODUCTION

This chapter explores some of the ways in which the basic rights of older adults with developmental disabilities may be in jeopardy because of prejudice and discrimination. The organizing concept of ageism is presented to illustrate the ways in which ageism shapes how the basic rights of older adults may be compromised. Other factors that may amplify threats on the basic rights of older people with de-

This chapter is based on research supported by the Rehabilitation Research and Training Center on Aging with Mental Retardation, which is funded by the National Institute on Disability and Rehabilitation Research of the U.S. Department of Education under Grant No. H133B30069. The opinions contained in this chapter are those of the grantee and do not necessarily reflect those of the U.S. Department of Education.

velopmental disabilities are considered also (e.g., economic power and poverty, education, access to human services). Completing this foundation is a framework for examining successful aging as a standard for a good old age for all older U.S. citizens.

The remaining sections of the chapter present comparative case studies that illustrate basic rights issues regarding place of residence and retirement options for aging adults with developmental disabilities. Ethical dilemmas and successful aging queries are included with each case study. The case studies may be used to stimulate discussion groups for local action and community planning. The chapter concludes with a summary of proposed ideals for promoting human rights with regard to place of residence and retirement choices afforded older adults with developmental disabilities.

The needs and potential of older people are emerging as a global concern at the turn of the 21st century (Sokolovsky, 1997). The overall goal of this chapter is to underscore the importance of shaping the vision of old age and disability, especially as it influences the residential and retirement options for future cohorts of older adults with developmental disabilities.

BASIC RIGHTS IN JEOPARDY

The rights of older people with disabilities may be in jeopardy for many reasons. Two distinct sources of concern are 1) pervasive negative stereotypes and beliefs and 2) direct violations of basic human rights. Each of these topics is discussed in the subsections that follow.

Pervasive Negative Stereotypes and Beliefs as Threats to Basic Rights

Prominent gerontologist Robert Butler brought to people's attention the impact that false stereotypes and inaccurate beliefs have on older citizens (Butler, 1969, 1989; Ferrini & Ferrini, 1993). He coined the term *ageism* to refer to the discrimination that older people experience as a result of negative stereotypes associated with old age. Ageism is the pervasive tendency of younger people to hold prejudicial ideas about older people that are unfounded and can lead to discrimination. These ideas are based on false notions such as all older people are senile, feeble minded, frail, stubborn, asexual, crotchety, rigid, dependent, ill, and noncontributing members of society. In spite of the efforts of gerontologists and practitioners to dispel these notions, they persist (Butler, 1989; Kart, 1997). The potential for prejudice to linger as younger generations struggle to have their needs met in a scenario of shrinking social services and less public financial support presents a growing threat to some members of the older population, particularly to those who are vulnerable. Americans may find themselves involved in a generational competition for limited human services and social resources. The result could mean that people who are vulnerable because of their age, gender, lack of political power, lack of education, or disability may be seen as less worthy and thus may experience increased difficulty in gaining access to needed supports and services.

When mental retardation or developmental disability is combined with an individual's old age, the result is likely to be devastating. Neglect, avoidance, outright rejection, discrimination in housing, and denial of access to services are the manifestations of ageist attitudes (Butler, 1989). Unfortunately, adults with developmental disabilities confront these kinds of discrimination on a regular basis as they age.

Ageism in itself is a central concern of older citizens, especially those who are in their 70s, 80s, and 90s. The effort to maintain involvement in the community is a source of constant advocacy by senior citizens' organizations and coalitions. Some of the concerns that older citizens express are maintaining their financial independence, achieving social and civic influence, obtaining adequate health care, and gaining access to a wide range of daily lifestyle options (e.g., work, education, housing, leisure). Vexing questions must be raised: Who is advocating for and safeguarding these rights for older citizens with developmental disabilities? Who is protecting them against false prejudices and discriminatory practices?

The issue of ageism is relevant because the negative effects of society's false beliefs and misinformation about older adults are magnified for individuals who lack

- Educational achievement
- Economic power and property
- Adequate social networks (i.e., family, friends, acquaintances) and civic involvement
- Access to the wide array of generic services offered in communities

Older people with developmental disabilities live each day in greater jeopardy of experiencing prejudice, discrimination, and neglect than do most members of the older adult population without developmental disabilities. The majority of older citizens without disabilities are not sick and do not live in nursing facilities or institutions. They are independent, and many remain vital and active. Some older adults, however, are impoverished and at risk of neglect based on their gender, age, race, and/or disability. One of the most vulnerable segments of the older adult population is those people who have struggled for a lifetime to overcome disenfranchisement based on their label of mental retardation or developmental disability. These individuals lack self-determination, the right to exercise free choice, and the willingness of others to let them exercise personal control over major aspects of their lives. Furthermore, they typically are not meaningfully involved in civic affairs or the decision-making processes that shape the provision of the human services that they receive.

If service providers are to take the initiative in supporting the social, residential, and daily environments of older people with developmental disabilities, they must first alter the negative stereotypes, misunderstandings, and distortions in society that affect these members of the older adult population. Older adults with developmental disabilities experience a form of double jeopardy with regard to ageism: the discrimination of younger, uninformed generations and rejection by their peers without disabilities. Butler (1989) aptly pointed out that all efforts to improve quality of life are moot if the negative forces of ageism are not addressed first. Thus, it is important in creating a vision for the future to first focus on removing ageist attitudes and behaviors toward people with developmental disabilities. Entrenched ageism poses a significant threat to any effort to promote empowerment for personal control, freedom of choice, and self-determination regarding residence and retirement options later in life.

Direct Violations of Basic Human Rights

An enduring shared premise of U.S. citizenship is the individual's right to life, liberty, and the pursuit of happiness. This foundation has come to mean many things to many different members of the U.S. population. For older adults, the premise embodies the following essential ideas:

- A sense of personal dignity
- Respect from others
- Expression of freedom of personal choice
- Self-determination in matters concerning life and daily activities
- A sense of personal control over one's own life and destiny
- The pursuit of happiness
- Access to the services and provisions afforded by American society and government

These manifestations of human rights will continue to increase in importance to older people in the 21st century as the trend toward longer life expectancy continues to swell the older adult segment of the population. Society will be confronted increasingly with issues related to recognizing and protecting the human rights of older adults.

Freedom is at the heart of human rights in old age, especially for older people with developmental disabilities. Freedom is a value that is inherently understood in Western culture but not particularly well defined (Patterson, 1991). Patterson distinguished among three types of freedom: personal, sovereign, and civic. These three types of freedom are particularly helpful to bear in mind when examining freedom in the lives of older people with developmental disabilities. Personal freedom is simply the capacity to do as one wishes insofar as one can. Sovereign freedom is the power to act as one pleases in spite of the wishes of others. Finally, civic freedom is "the capacity of adult members of a community to participate in its life and governance" (Patterson, 1991, p. 4). The fact remains, however, that nobody is entirely free; furthermore, constraints (whether natural, physical, legal, moral, or societal) influence the degree of freedom that any individual experiences (Turnbull, Ellis, Boggs, Brooks, & Biklen, 1981). The degree of freedom or constraint that older people experience, especially older adults with developmental disabilities, is a major influence on whether they have a good or a difficult old age.

Older adults with developmental disabilities have little chance to express these three types of freedom in their lives; that is, their lives are characterized more by constraint than by freedom. For example, people with developmental disabilities typically are provided with fewer opportunities to make decisions about which daily activities they pursue with regard to work, leisure, home, and community life (Edgerton, 1994). These citizens are heavily dependent on caregivers' decisions and control. They have little to no self-determination. Exacerbating the situation is that little is known about the constraints that impede the expression of personal, sovereign, and civic freedom by adults with developmental disabilities (Hawkins, 1998).

Hawkins (1998) found that intrapersonal constraints had the least influence on the pursuit of new leisure activities by a sample of older adults with mental retardation as compared with the impact of interpersonal and structural barriers. Intrapersonal constraints to self-determination in leisure were factors such as being too tired, too old, or too sick; concern about feelings of guilt; and fear of being ridiculed or of hurting oneself. Interpersonal constraints were related to who made the decision about which activities individuals engaged in (i.e., others decided), being too busy or not having enough available time, not having money, and not having access to friends with whom to engage in activities. Structural constraints included not having equipment or facilities for engaging in activities, not having anyone to teach the activity or anyone with whom to do the activities, and not knowing how to do the activities. Interpersonal and structural constraints were far more frequently cited as the reason why new leisure activity involvement was prevented, and each of these types of constraint reflected encumbrances on sovereign and civic freedom. In this study, older adults with developmental disabilities were keenly aware of which leisure activities they wanted to engage in as well as those interpersonal and structural factors that prevented them from pursuing their choices. The lack of sovereign freedom was evident among this sample.

Previous research substantiated that people with mental retardation are capable of developing preferences, acting on personal interests, and demonstrating self-determination (Edgerton, 1994; Kishi, Teelucksingh, Zollers, Park-Lee, & Meyer, 1988; Mahon, 1994; Newton, Horner, & Lund, 1991; Wehmeyer & Metzler, 1995). The research of Hawkins (1998), however, provided evidence that aging adults with mental retardation have little opportunity to experience freedom in the form of self-determined leisure activities. Other research (e.g., Dattilo & Schleien, 1994; Sands & Kozleski, 1994; Wehmeyer & Metzler, 1995) suggested that people with mental retardation may need additional supports in order to develop the knowledge and skills necessary to independently and freely engage in some aspects of typical daily life. The salient point is that all older people desire to exercise their personal, sovereign, and civic freedoms (Patterson, 1991); but most older people with developmental disabilities do not tend to experience freedom. These freedoms are manifested in the form of essential rights in old age, which are listed previously in this chapter. Collectively, when these rights are realized fully, the chances of attaining a personally acceptable quality of life or a good old age are greater than they are in their absence or if they are compromised.

There is no doubt that massive, complex, global social change will continually reshape the life circumstances and life outcomes of older people (Riley & Riley, 1989). "To advance the quality of aging, interventions are needed not only in the life course of individuals but, even more critically, in the social matrix in which these lives are embedded" (Riley & Riley, 1989, p. 15). For older adults with developmental disabilities, efforts of caregivers to teach, facilitate, and support self-determination in daily life decisions in order to promote a good old age are more effective when ageist stereotypes are replaced with more appropriate views of these members of society. Instrumental in this process is the recognition of human rights in old age as well as the active promotion of these rights. A social matrix that is grounded in the protection and promotion of human rights is more likely to promote successful aging for all older citizens.

SUCCESSFUL AGING: A GOOD OLD AGE

Butler (1989) stated that a dignified and healthy older adulthood is characterized by a healthy, active lifestyle; family members who provide primary caregiving; and policy makers and government officials at all levels who are active in promoting and protecting a high quality of life for older adults. Older people who remain productive, contributing members of society for as long as possible tend to experience a higher level of perceived satisfaction with life than those who have no sense of having a role in the community. In addition, individuals who enjoy their family as the primary caregiving unit tend to view their senior years as quality years. Butler further emphasized the importance of cultivating communities that are "rich with strong informal networks of friendly visitors and volunteers and businesses" (1989, p. 147). Finally, policy makers and government officials at all levels need to be active in promoting and protecting a high quality of life for older citizens.

Fry and colleagues (1997) affirmed four areas as consistently connected with a good old age in a cross-cultural study involving eight communities in four diverse cultures: Botswana, Hong Kong, Ireland, and the United States. The following are the four major factors that were found to produce either a good old age or a difficult old age:

1. Reliable physical health and functioning
2. Material security
3. Family and kinship networks
4. Sociality

Health and physical functioning included the capacity to engage in activities in which the individual wanted to be involved and the energy, strength, and vitality necessary to continue daily activities. Material security included pensions, retirement benefits, money, and other indications of material wealth and stability. In less-developed cultures, material wealth was expressed in terms of an adequate subsistence with regard to food, shelter, warmth, and protection against environmental threats.

Family and kinship networks underscored the importance of a strong social structure in promoting a good old age or in triggering difficulties when families were absent or did not fulfill their roles. Sociality may be interpreted differently across cultures; but in all of the communities that Fry and colleagues (1997) studied, sociality was instrumental to either a good or a difficult old age. *Sociality* primarily refers to areas of one's life that provide for positive affect or a sense of well-being. Being vital and active in meaningful leisure activities, the freedom of choice to do as one pleases, and being with others are typical characteristics of sociality that are associated with a good old age. Feelings of loneliness, crankiness, and self-pity are characteristic of a difficult old age. In summary, Fry and colleagues portrayed a good old age in the United States as being vital, active, and involved with others and experiencing good health and a comfortable pension: "[H]ealth problems can erode success in one's elder years, bringing social withdrawal and a more self-centered old age" (1997, p. 118).

The gerontology literature has identified seven markers of successful aging:

1. Length of life
2. Positive mental health status
3. Good overall physical health
4. Sustained cognitive effectiveness
5. Personal control over one's life and destiny
6. Sustained social competence and productive involvement
7. High perceived satisfaction with life (Baltes & Baltes, 1990)

Although these seven elements may represent an ideal state of successful aging that is rarely achieved among the population of older adults, they provide direction for instrumental understanding of those factors that undermine quality of life in older adulthood. All people must cope with the influence of environmental, genetic, pathogenic, and historical factors that may undermine an optimal state of successful aging. The status of an older individual can be described along the continuum from pathology to normal aging to optimal aging according to these seven markers. The goal is to promote conditions that support normal to optimal aging for as many aging individuals as is possible within a given community.

Successful aging for older adults with developmental disabilities can be promoted by merging key factors connected with the successful aging concept with ideas associated with quality of life as described in the mental retardation literature (Schalock, 1996, 1997; Taylor & Bogdan, 1996). Central ingredients that support successful aging for adults with developmental disabilities are

- Health status
- Perceived life satisfaction
- The opportunity to be a contributing member of society, or community membership

Providing the foundation for these elements are the essential human rights of self-determination, control, and opportunities for free choice (Edgerton, 1990; Rodin & Langer, 1977). A stable health status is grounded in the World Health Organization's definition of *health* as "a state of complete physical, mental and social well-being, not merely the absence of disease or infirmity" (1947, p. 2). The second component, perceived life satisfaction, focuses on positive affective states that are subjectively determined based on how the individual views his or her own life circumstances and outcomes. The third component of a good old age, community membership, involves both the perception and the reality that one has a socially valued role in the family, the community, and the larger social context as well as the actual means to participate as a contributing member. Aging successfully, or a good old age, is characterized by a continual process of acceptance, adaptation, and supports by the social matrix that surrounds the older person, thus maximizing the potential of the three elements. The importance of adaptation is a persistent theme in both the gerontology and developmental disabilities literature and continues throughout the life course. In old age, adaptation is optimal when human rights are acknowledged, protected, and promoted with the goal of a good old age.

Edgerton (1994) pointed out that those individuals with mental retardation who have lived most of their adult lives independently in community environments display unpredictable patterns of adaptation compared with those individuals who have lived predictable, regimented lives governed by caregiving service systems. He suggested that the latter case shows one important feature: These individuals are given significantly fewer opportunities to exercise self-determination and decision making compared with the former group of independent individuals. The central point in Edgerton's work is that people who have not had their free will constrained and who have been able to shape their own destiny fare much better! At the heart of this illustration is the impact that imposed dependency versus self-determination has on the individual's life quality and outcomes in later maturity. Liberty, or the exercising of free will and self-determination, is a fundamental right of law-abiding U.S. citizens. This right has not been experienced widely by aging adults with developmental disabilities, thus impairing their chances for successful aging.

One of the greatest challenges is determining how to promote the essential components of a good old age or successful aging for older adults with developmental disabilities, especially when public support of social services appears to be undergoing tremendous devolution. When the foundations that support successful aging are undermined or repressed, then a difficult old age is the result. At the crux of supporting successful aging for adults with developmental disabilities are the essential human rights of self-determination, freedom of choice, and personal control of one's life.

CASE STUDIES

The following case studies illustrate some of the life circumstances that may compromise the potential for achieving a good old age for adults with developmental disabilities. Each case is drawn from a 10-year study of aging adults with mental retardation (Hawkins & Eklund, 1994). Each case contains ethical and successful aging questions at the end of the study that are intended to assist the reader in identifying the basic human rights dilemma of the case. There is no one right answer to each of these questions; several alternative solutions may be viable. There are, however, probably few simple solutions when the dilemma involves the interests of more than one person. Readers are encouraged to avoid pat answers by using the cases to stimulate discussion with other professionals, community members, families, and people with disabilities in a search for a deeper understanding of the issues as well as to generate a broader, more creative set of potential solutions.

The cases may be applied easily in discussion groups, community forums, or focus groups as a stimulus for creating the preferred future in services and supports to aging adults with disabilities. In this sense, the solutions should be community-specific. Readers are encouraged to seek answers to the questions that reflect the core shared value that older people with mental retardation are entitled to the protection of their basic human rights. Group discussion can help to uncover ageist attitudes and remove them from the social consciousness of the community in which these individuals live. By working with other professionals and citizens in the community, attitudes can be clarified by facts and a system of community supports that promote a good old age is thus more likely to emerge. By using these case studies within agencies and community planning activities, grass-roots change may help citizens seek and attain a high quality of life for all members of the community. Although these are cases of people from specific places, they can be used at the local level to identify and clarify issues and to create the preferred social matrix for many communities.

When using these cases in discussion groups, the following guidelines may be helpful (see Muskavitch, 1998, for additional guidelines on writing and using case studies). Select the case, identify its issues, and state the main goals that the group hopes to achieve. Identify and involve in the group individuals who will be considered the main stakeholders because they will relate to the case in some relevant way. In other words, identify the key decision maker(s) and the critical participants in the case, and find surrogates who will identify with these roles. Ask the question, Who else would be concerned about this case or have a stake in how it is resolved? Add these individuals to the group. Keep in mind that effective group discussions depend on maintaining a manageable size for the discussion group; for example, 5–12 members is a reasonable group size.

Determine the forum for your discussion group. For example, will the discussion group be a workshop, a public forum, or an agency-based discussion? Will it take place during a single session or span several sessions? Will the discussion result in a specific outcome or product, such as a position paper, an article in the local newspaper, or a policy statement for a local human services organization? Then develop strategies to evaluate and discuss the case within the forum that you have planned. Are fact finders important? If so, designate responsible participants to collect the information needed. Is all of the information known that needs to be known? If not, bring in additional information that pertains to the local context in which the case is discussed. Restate the most important ethical issues of your situation. Modify the case if it seems appropriate and useful to do so in order to meet local needs and goals. Use group process techniques to formulate and agree on which rights and principles will provide the foundation for the final outcome(s). What values and rights need to be protected and promoted? Seek a preferred future, one in which all participants feel that they can live and one that promotes an optimal quality of life for all members of the community. Create alternative scenarios as a means of considering other perspectives. Encourage social responsibility and human values.

Clarence: The Choice of Where I Live

Clarence lived at home all of his life. When his brother and sisters grew up and left home to live on their own, he stayed with his parents because that is what they wanted for him. Clarence liked this arrangement, too. When Clarence was 60 years old, he did not often go to the day center anymore. He stayed at home with his mother most of the time. His father had died 4 years earlier, and his mother needed Clarence to help her maintain the home. So, he was pretty happy staying at home and doing things for his mother because she needed him.

One day, Clarence's mother became ill. He was frightened and called in a neighbor to look at his mother. The neighbor immediately knew that it was a crisis. Clarence's mother had had a massive stroke; she was on the living room floor, and her physical condition was grave. The neighbor called the local emergency medical service and then began to talk with Clarence about what was happening.

Clarence's mother was 89 years old and in frail physical condition; but prior to her stroke, her mind had been sharp. The fact of the matter was that Clarence and his mother had gotten along by being fairly private about their daily activities. Upon a closer look, it was clear that Clarence was carrying a significant responsibility in the care of his mother and their home. Clarence's parents had made no attempt to make arrangements for Clarence to live elsewhere, although it had been decided previously that he would not live with any of his siblings.

Clarence had been diagnosed with mental retardation requiring intermittent to limited support. The etiology of his mental retardation was Down syndrome. His health always had been generally good; but more recently he was not seen as having enough vitality to continue to work, so he discontinued working when he was 52. At age 56, Clarence stopped going to day programs at the local center for people with developmental disabilities.

After Clarence's mother was hospitalized for her stroke, medical personnel and Clarence's siblings determined that it was time to move her into a skilled nursing facility. The local agency that had provided work and day programming for Clarence stepped in to help his siblings decide what to do with him. During this time, Clarence had become morose and withdrawn and sometimes was openly aggressive toward others. Each time one of his sisters would attempt to talk with him, Clarence would just say that he wanted to live with Mother. When his sisters would suggest looking into some of the group homes around town or in the communities in which each of them lived, Clarence became openly aggressive. He was insistent that he should live with his mother.

Ethical dilemma: Where should Clarence live? Who should decide? What supports are in place to assist in resolving this dilemma?

Successful aging: What parts of Clarence's life support successful aging? What events take place in the case study that support successful aging or lead to a difficult old age for Clarence?

Loyola: To Retire or Not to Retire, What Is My Preference?

Loyola is 62 years old, is in moderately good health, and lives in a group home with five other adults who have developmental disabilities. She is an affable woman who enjoys friendships with many people, both at work and at home. She is a single child of parents who married late in life. Both of her parents are no longer alive, and her cousins live in neighboring states. Her two cousins from her mother's sister's family remain in contact with Loyola. Both of Loyola's cousins are older than she is (both are in their 70s), and they make only one trip per year to visit her. Loyola considers the people with whom she lives to be her immediate family.

Loyola was diagnosed as having mental retardation requiring limited support and has had recurrent bouts with arthritis since she was in her mid-50s. More frequently, arthritis in her hands makes the fine-motor work that she did at the local work center nearly impossible for her to do. The staff at the center dropped lots of hints to Loyola about retiring. They pointed out that she would have much more time to do the activities that she enjoyed the most if she retired. Loyola was hesitant about retiring. She enjoyed her work, the camaraderie with her companions at work, and the small income that she received from her job. Her favorite free-time activities involved talking on the telephone with her work friends, occasionally going out to eat or to a movie with either her housemates or friends from work, and going shopping on the weekends.

Loyola always had been assertive about what she liked and disliked as well as what she preferred to do and what she was not pleased at having to do. She was unsure about retiring from work, especially because all of her other housemates were still working. Loyola was the oldest of the residents living in her home. No one has told Loyola that she may need to move when she retires; staff are concerned that she will become depressed if she must move.

For the most part, Loyola does not voluntarily talk about retirement. She sees retirement as the loss of her discretionary income, the loss of contact with her close friends, the loss of daily social interaction, and the gain of more time at home when everyone else is at work. These do not seem like good options for Loyola, although she does think that a shorter work day might give her some time to rest in the afternoon. When her hands really hurt, she is tired and in pain during the afternoons at work, and usually she goes to bed early at night, right after dinner.

Ethical dilemma: Should the work center and/or group home staff force the issue of retirement with Loyola? What strategies can be used to help Loyola reframe what retirement could be for her?

Successful aging: Is Loyola experiencing successful aging? What events take place in the case study that could change her successful aging status?

Janet: What Kind of Lifestyle Do I Desire?

Janet, a 40-year-old woman with Down syndrome, lives with her parents on a 60-acre farm in a rural area. Her parents encouraged Janet to obtain supportive employment at a McDonald's in a small town about 8 miles from their home. Janet likes her job of 5 years and dearly loves her parents. Her brother is a physician in Chicago with a wife and two teenage children. She sees him only when he comes to visit her parents. Janet has a fairly active social life with her parents, who are in their early 70s. They regularly attend church activities and also are active in events sponsored by the local farmer's organization. People who attend these activities know Janet and treat her kindly.

Janet had consistently tested at a level of functional independence that indicated her need for supports and supervision to be minimal. Her work performance is rated highly by the supervisor and her fellow workers. She believes that she could manage to live on her own or with a roommate, provided that her parents gave her some support with managing her bills and shopping. She has helped her mother with cooking and cleaning at the farmhouse all of her life.

Janet's parents tell her that they see no reason for her to move out on her own. They are happy to take her anywhere she wants to go. They feel that her life is good the way it is, so, as the saying goes, "Why upset the apple cart?" They are concerned that she does not possess the decision-making abilities necessary to live on her own or to live with someone else. They believe that she would be vulnerable to being taken advantage of by a roommate. Janet would like to date more and engage in activities with people more her own age. She does not say this to her parents because she thinks that they would not approve or that she would hurt their feelings.

Ethical dilemma: Should Janet be supported to move away from home? What are her options for exploring this possibility?

Successful aging: Given that life is pretty good as it is for Janet, what are her prospects for the future, especially considering the components of successful aging presented earlier in this chapter? Describe what you think will be the remainder of Janet's life story.

Tom: Do You Hear What I Say?

Tom moved out of the state hospital to a group home when he was 58 years old. It was a big change for Tom, one that he will never forget. He still talks about the day that he moved, even though it was 7 years ago. At age 65, Tom is preparing for another important change in his life: retirement.

For the past 7 years, Tom has worked at the local sheltered work center. He has been a good worker, but he has expressed an interest in doing something different for a change. When Tom turned 60, the staff at his group home began to take him with another resident to the local senior center one night per week to play Bingo. Tom was partnered with an older adult volunteer at the senior center who taught him how to play the game. As time went by on Bingo nights, the people at the center got to know Tom and his roommate. Tom opened up and began to show a new side to his personality. Eventually, Tom displayed a wonderful sense of generosity and kindness in helping other seniors who were having difficulty with mobility or in using their hands. Now Tom is a regular at the center, even during events other than Bingo night.

Tom has developed several special friendships with other adults who attend the center. With one older woman, for example, he listens to old-time music. Sometimes he helps in the kitchen by taking out the trash or washing the dishes. He enjoys greeting folks at the door during special events. Tom would like to do some regular volunteer work at the center as well as participate in the exercise class 3 days per week. Consequently, he has been asking his group home staff whether he can go to the center rather than to work.

Tom clearly has demonstrated a place in the social fabric of his community. He consistently indicates that he would like to change his lifestyle in terms of work and daily activity choices. There is even the provision with his service agency for him to stay where he is living, should he choose to retire. The future seems to hold an important change for Tom—retirement and a new direction in activities at the senior center.

Ethical dilemma: Does Tom's case present any ethical dilemmas?
Successful aging: What parts of Tom's life indicate a successful aging status? What events take place in the case study that support successful aging or will lead to a difficult old age for Tom?

INTERPRETATIONS FOR RIGHTS, PLACE OF RESIDENCE, AND RETIREMENT

The case studies in the previous section underscore the role of freedom in fostering self-determination, choice, and personal control over one's life and destiny. In each instance, the individual portrayed has definite preferences about where he or she wishes to live and in which activities he or she wants to engage on a daily basis. The case studies also suggest the tendency of caregivers (family members or professionals) to assume control and make decisions on behalf of the individual, thus constraining the individual from experiencing freedom. In a caregiving role, it is understandable that decisions are made that are thought to be in the best interest of the person receiving care. As is true for older adults without disabilities, however, the sustained practice of making decisions for another person leads to learned helplessness and a dependency relationship, which are manifestations of a lack of freedom. In too many cases of older adults with developmental disabilities, this kind of relationship unnecessarily exists. In order to promulgate the experience of freedom in terms of self-determination, choice, and personal control, change is needed. Then, perhaps, the stage will be set for a good old age that is characterized by successful aging for older adults with developmental disabilities.

CONCLUSIONS: VISIONS FOR THE FUTURE

A vision for the future is built on a set of axioms or principles that all members of a community believe in and work tirelessly to protect. The following are exemplars that may assist readers as they use the ideas presented in this chapter and this book in shaping a preferred future for themselves and the communities in which they live:

1. Adults with developmental disabilities should assume a central role in the process of exploring and deciding where and with whom they wish to live. Aging in place is an important concept in the preservation of physical, mental, and emotional health in advanced old age. This principle should be communicated clearly to older adults with developmental disabilities when they are making personal choices.
2. Adults with developmental disabilities are able to accept and adapt to change when provided with supports. Supports are distinct and different from someone else making the decisions for the person with a disability. A system of supports that is founded on the principles of empowerment for exercising freedom of choice and control over life decisions promotes a good old age for adults with developmental disabilities as they age.
3. Older adults with developmental disabilities need and want opportunities to be part of their communities—social, productive, and civic. The availability of meaningful roles and opportunities should be part of the social fabric of each community in which aging adults with disabilities live.
4. Revised social policies and professional practices that recognize and actively promote the exercise of personal, sovereign, and civic freedoms by adults with developmental disabilities are needed.

Research into freedom as promoted by a system of supports will place the disabilities and aging fields at the threshold of creating a whole new social context from which service providers' understanding of and perspectives on the process of aging can serve to create a good old age for citizens with developmental disabilities. Carefully designed investigations and evaluations of model programs will provide evidence of the values, attitudes, behaviors, and social practices that promote optimal physical and mental health, social well-being, and a sense of successful aging for adults with developmental disabilities. The results from research and model practices will be instrumental in

- Shaping necessary public policies that protect and serve the rights of older adults with developmental disabilities
- Guiding professional practices that effectively serve the growing diversity of older adults
- Adding new understanding to the knowledge base about successful aging for older adults with developmental disabilities

The process of creating local community change that builds a social matrix in which all citizens' human rights are protected and promoted is requisite to safeguarding a good old age for all.

REFERENCES

Baltes, P.B., & Baltes, M.M. (1990). *Successful aging: Perspectives from the behavioral sciences.* New York: Cambridge University Press.
Butler, R.N. (1969). Ageism: Another form of bigotry. *Gerontologist, 9,* 243–246.
Butler, R.N. (1989). Dispelling ageism: The cross-cutting intervention. In M.W. Riley & J.W. Riley, Jr. (Eds.), *The quality of aging: Strategies for interventions: The Annals of the American Academy of Political and Social Science* (Vol. 503, pp. 138–147). Thousand Oaks, CA: Sage Publications.
Dattilo, J., & Schleien, S.J. (1994). Understanding leisure services for individuals with mental retardation. *Mental Retardation, 32*(1), 53–59.
Edgerton, R.B. (1990). Quality of life from a longitudinal perspective. In R.L. Schalock (Ed.), *Quality of life: Perspectives and issues* (pp. 149–160). Washington, DC: American Association on Mental Retardation.
Edgerton, R.B. (1994). Quality of life issues: Some people know how to be old. In M.M. Seltzer, M.W. Krauss, & M.P. Janicki (Eds.), *Life course perspectives on adulthood and old age* (pp. 53–66). Washington, DC: American Association on Mental Retardation.
Ferrini, A.F., & Ferrini, R.L. (1993). *Health in the later years* (2nd ed.). Madison, WI: Brown & Benchmark.
Fry, C.L., Dickerson-Putman, J., Draper, P., Ikels, C., Keith, J., Glascock, A.P., & Harpending, H.C. (1997). Culture and the meaning of a good old age. In J. Sokolovsky (Ed.), *The cultural context of aging: Worldwide perspectives* (2nd ed., pp. 99–123). Westport, CT: Bergin & Garvey.
Hawkins, B.A. (1998). Constraints on leisure: Adults with mental retardation. *Abstracts of Proceedings of the American Association on Mental Retardation* (p. 72). Washington, DC: American Association on Mental Retardation.
Hawkins, B.A., & Eklund, S.J. (1994). Aging-related change in adults with mental retardation. In *The Arc Research Brief.* Arlington, TX: The Arc National Headquarters.
Kart, C.S. (1997). *The realities of aging: An introduction to gerontology* (5th ed.). Needham Heights, MA: Allyn & Bacon.
Kishi, G., Teelucksingh, B., Zollers, N., Park-Lee, S., & Meyer, L. (1988). Daily decision-making in community residences: A social comparison of adults with and without mental retardation. *American Journal on Mental Retardation, 92,* 430–435.
Mahon, M.J. (1994). The use of self-control techniques to facilitate self-determination skills during leisure in adolescents and young adults with mild and moderate mental retardation. *Therapeutic Recreation Journal, 28*(2), 58–72.
Muskavitch, K.M.T. (1998). *Some pointers on writing and using case studies.* Unpublished manuscript, Indiana University, Bloomington.
Newton, S.J., Horner, R.H., & Lund, L. (1991). Honoring activity preferences in individualized plan development: A descriptive analysis. *Journal of The Association for Persons with Severe Handicaps, 16,* 207–212.
Patterson, O. (1991). *Freedom: Vol. I. Freedom in the making of Western culture.* New York: Basic Books.
Riley, M.W., & Riley, J.W., Jr. (Eds.). (1989). *The quality of aging: Strategies for interventions: The Annals of the American Academy of Political and Social Science* (Vol. 503). Thousand Oaks, CA: Sage Publications.
Rodin, J., & Langer, E.J. (1977). Long-term effects of a control-relevant intervention with the institutionalized aged. *Journal of Personality and Social Psychology, 35,* 897–902.
Sands, D.J., & Kozleski, E.B. (1994). Quality of life differences between adults with and without disabilities. *Education and Training in Mental Retardation and Developmental Disabilities, 29*(2), 90–101.
Schalock, R.L. (Ed.). (1996). *Quality of life: Vol. I. Conceptualization and measurement.* Washington, DC: American Association on Mental Retardation.

Schalock, R.L. (Ed.). (1997). *Quality of life: Vol. II. Application to persons with disabilities.* Washington, DC: American Association on Mental Retardation.

Sokolovsky, J. (Ed.). (1997). *The cultural context of aging: Worldwide perspectives* (2nd ed.). Westport, CT: Bergin & Garvey.

Taylor, S.J., & Bogdan, R. (1996). Quality of life and the individual's perspective. In R.L. Schalock (Ed.), *Quality of life: Vol. I. Conceptualization and measurement* (pp. 11–22). Washington, DC: American Association on Mental Retardation.

Turnbull, H.R., Ellis, J.W., Boggs, E.M., Brooks, P.O., & Biklen, D.P. (1981). *The least restrictive alternative: Principles and practices.* Washington, DC: American Association on Mental Deficiency.

Wehmeyer, M.L., & Metzler, C.A. (1995). How self-determined are people with mental retardation? The National Consumer Survey. *Mental Retardation, 33*(2), 111–119.

World Health Organization (WHO). (1947). Constitution of the World Health Organization: Following the amelioration of false attitudes. *Chronicles of WHO, 1*, 2.

8

Quality of Life as a Matter of Human Rights

Alan Walker, Carol Walker, and Vashti Gosling

Human rights can be gauged by the lives that vulnerable people lead. This chapter reports some findings from field research that the chapter authors conducted in Britain on the quality of life of older people with intellectual disabilities.[1] A key aim of this research was to examine the circumstances of different groups of people with intellectual disabilities who were living in the community and, in particular, the role of health and social services provision in determining their quality of life. This investigation raises critical questions about the approaches adopted by service providers toward this new consumer group that can have the effect of restricting their basic human rights. At the extreme, older people with intellectual disabilities experience a form of double jeopardy because they find themselves being rejected by providers of services for those with intellectual disabilities on the one hand and services for older people on the other.

Until the 1990s, the issue of aging among people with intellectual disabilities received relatively little attention in Britain from the academic community (with the notable exception of Hogg, Moss, and Cooke [1988]) or from policy makers. Social scientists (Martin, Meltzer, & Eliot, 1988; Townsend, 1981a) have recognized the high incidence of disability in old age and looked at the experience of those with physical disabilities as they get older (Zarb, 1991; Zarb & Oliver, 1993); but research on people with intellectual disabilities, particularly the series of studies of hospital closure and relocation following the British government's care in the community program (see, e.g., Booth, Simons, & Booth, 1990; Korman & Glennerster, 1990), did not discuss the aging dimension.

---

[1]The term *learning difficulty* is preferred in Britain, but *intellectual disability* is used throughout this chapter to be consistent with other chapters in this book.

In Walker, Walker, and Ryan (1996), two of the authors of this chapter examined some of the policy implications of growing numbers of people with intellectual disabilities living into older age. This chapter focuses on the processes and principles within the health and social services domain that operate to enhance the dependency and limit the freedom of older people with intellectual disabilities and that do so, paradoxically, because these individuals are older adults rather than because they are people with intellectual disabilities. First, this chapter examines the human rights context in Britain. Then it considers the complex issue of the quality of life of this group of people. Following that discussion, the principles and practice of service provision for older adults are contrasted with those for people with intellectual disabilities. It is argued that these represent divergent social constructions—of youth and old age—and that, as soon as an individual is transferred from one service provider category to another as a result of chronological aging, the orientation of services provided for them shifts from supporting independence to reproducing dependence. This circumstance leads us to consider how far the principle of normalization, which has underpinned many of the most important developments in service provision for people with intellectual disabilities, remains appropriate for this group as they get older. This discussion entails a sociological critique of normalization but also a recognition of the fact that an application of the concept of normalization to service provision for older people implies a more positive construction of old age and a substantial improvement in the human rights of older people. Finally, the chapter considers whether the alternative concept of social integration is a more appropriate basis on which to organize health and social services for older people with intellectual disabilities.

The empirical basis for this chapter lies in two field projects that two of the chapter's authors conducted in the northwestern region of England. The first looked at the quality of life of people who had been moved out of long-stay hospitals for people with mental disabilities and into the community (Walker, Ryan, & Walker, 1993). The second examined disparities in service provision between different groups of people with intellectual disabilities living in the community, one aspect of which examined the circumstances of older consumers of services (Walker et al., 1996). In the first study, 6 months after the relocation of the person with intellectual disabilities, the views of the individual, a close relative of the individual (if there was one), and the formal caregivers were sought. In the second study, two-thirds of the service users were contacted again 3 years after the individual's relocation; the chapter authors also spoke with 30 people who had been resettled within the community from hostels (i.e., supervised living arrangements) or the family home and 30 people who were living with their families. Half of the people were ages 50 years and older. The age of 50 was chosen to denote the start of older age because that is the point at which the "third age" begins. The northwestern region of England had pursued a policy toward people with intellectual disabilities that had been regarded widely as excellent, mainly because of the opportunities it offered people with intellectual disabilities to develop skills and to live independently, and therefore it was an appropriate location in which to investigate the link between service provision and quality of life.

The main aim of the second research project was to compare the quality of life of different groups of people with intellectual disabilities who were living in the community. Two main sets of comparisons were made. First, a comparison was made of the quality of life and service provision of people living in different care environments in the community: those resettled, with funding, from a hospital; those resettled, usually without funding, from hostels or their family home; and those still living in their family home. The second basis for comparison was age.

HUMAN RIGHTS

There is no written constitution in Britain that embodies the fundamental rights and freedoms of its citizens, although the government endorsed international declarations pertaining to these rights. One such declaration sets forth the rights of people with disabilities (United Nations [UN] Declaration on the Rights of Disabled Persons, 1975), and another sets forth the rights of people with intellectual disabilities (UN Declaration on the Rights of Mentally Retarded Persons, 1971). It is difficult, however, to determine who is responsible for ensuring these rights, and many people with intellectual disabilities are likely to need support to enable them to exercise these rights and to seek redress against the infringement of these rights. As more fully discussed in Chapter 3, international declarations illustrate that there is some consensus about the rights and responsibilities that should belong to members of a nation-state. Marshall (1950) argued that the status of citizenship endowed its holders with basic civil and legal rights, political rights, and social rights. These rights, outlined by Marshall in his model of citizenship, have never been enjoyed fully by people with intellectual disabilities in Britain, and consequently they have not been accorded their rightful status as full citizens.

During various periods of history, people with intellectual disabilities have been defined in negative terms and often have been regarded as less than fully human. Hudson (1988) argued that the reason why this group of people was not afforded the human rights protection that others were is related to the fact that they were not deemed to have a "moral personality"; that is, those with authority to write and pass legislation thought that these individuals were incapable of moral or intellectual development. None of the roles ascribed to people with intellectual disabilities implied that these individuals were accorded the same human rights as people without disabilities (Wolfensberger & Nirje, 1972). Their confinement in large residential institutions, until the 1990s, meant that they lacked even the most basic civil right of liberty. Consequently, many people living in or attending segregated formal care environments have experienced a denial or compromise of allied rights such as the freedom to associate and assemble, either directly or indirectly, as a result of organizational practices that are incompatible with such rights.

Post–World War II health and support services were built on a belief in the incompetence of people with intellectual disabilities to make decisions about their own needs, so service providers were concerned primarily with protecting these individuals from risk. The implication of this provision was to deny people any responsibility in the organization of their own lives. Consequently, people with intellectual disabilities historically have been denied the civil, political, and social rights that Marshall considered fundamental to citizenship, both because these rights are not enshrined in legislation and because of practical difficulties that may prevent this population from exercising them. The right to vote, for example, is an element of citizenship that covers the majority of the adult population and one that many people with intellectual disabilities have in the past effectively been denied because of the lack of support or awareness of staff or caregivers, and obstacles in the registration process and the structural environment (Ward, 1987). Many people with in-

tellectual disabilities have also been denied the rights to economic welfare and security; to have a job, education, or meaningful and stimulating daily activities; to
participate in the culture of society; and to form intimate relationships and have
families. The denial of these fundamental rights has been justified by viewing these
individuals as nonadults who are incapable of greater independence and personal autonomy. Scandals in the late 1960s brought to light human rights abuses in large residential facilities, together with the failure to provide for basic needs such as food,
clothing, and personal and emotional needs (Ryan & Thomas, 1987). The British
government's white paper *Better Services for the Mentally Handicapped* (Department of Health and Social Security [DHSS], 1971) responded to these exposures and
initiated plans for the reduction of the hospital population, stating that people with
intellectual disabilities should not be "unnecessarily segregated." This signified the
beginning of a change in attitude of the British government toward this group.

New philosophies of care, primarily normalization, sought to address some of
the discrimination that this group of consumers faced. Normalization was influential in the founding of campaigning groups such as the Campaign for the Mentally
Handicapped (since renamed Values in Action), in the work of The King's Fund Center, and in the expression of the principles of the model of care proposed in the Jay
Committee report (1979a, 1979b), which was an official inquiry into mental handicap nursing and care. Both this report and *An Ordinary Life* (King's Fund Center,
1980) represented a shift in attitudes toward people with intellectual disabilities in
Britain and a challenge to existing medically dominated services, and both express
this change by referring to the rights of this group of consumers. Essentially, the
concept of ordinary life recognizes that people with intellectual disabilities have the
same value as other human beings and the same rights as other citizens; that living
with others in the community is both a need and a right; and, finally, that services
must recognize individuality and provide for individual needs (Towell, 1988). Similarly, the Jay Committee Report stated that "mentally handicapped people have a
right to enjoy normal patterns of life within the community" and "a right to be
treated as individuals" (1979b, p. 35). The Jay Report acknowledged, however, the
need for increased public spending in the short term for any meaningful changes to
occur and a commitment to make these issues priorities at the national level. In
1979, the incoming Thatcher government was hostile to any increase in public expenditure, so progress was slow. The greatest evidence of these principles in practice
has been in residential environments, particularly independent living schemes and
small, staffed group homes. Deinstitutionalization and the incorporation of normalization into the service language, however, do not necessarily equal "an ordinary
life," and other aspects of people's lives after resettlement often are still far from
"ordinary" (Race, 1995).

Few people with intellectual disabilities ever choose where they live or with
whom, and they continue to be placed in existing programs of residential and day
services despite the rhetorical focus on the individual's choices and needs. Group
homes are not necessarily small and may themselves become micro-institutions
(Sinson, 1993), with the staff–user relationship remaining essentially unchanged.
People with intellectual disabilities also continue to be discriminated against in the
labor market and to attend some form of day service or college throughout their
adult lives. The implementation of the National Health Service and Community
Care Act of 1990 (ch. 19) did not necessarily increase real choice for consumers in
the form of individual care packages, as the rhetoric at the time of its passage sug-

gested, and the market that it established in health and social care may mean that services become less responsive to individual consumers (Ward, 1987). The professionalization of these services has continued as professionals have redefined their roles in the lives of consumers. Many people with intellectual disabilities still have little control over other aspects of their daily lives, such as handling their own money (Davis, Eley, Flynn, Flynn, & Roberts, 1995) or having opportunities to participate in social or leisure activities in their local communities (Brown & Smith, 1992). Some of these restrictions may result from family members' or staff members' attempts to protect them or from fixed ideas about what the person is capable of as well as from structural barriers and resource shortages.

There is also evidence that people with intellectual disabilities continue to be denied fundamental moral rights such as the rights to life, to procreate, and to parent (Hudson, 1988). They are discriminated against by medical and social work professionals who make judgments about the value of their lives, which has resulted in cases of compulsory sterilization (*Re B.O. SC Fol. 13 [a Minor]* [House of Lords, May 1, 1987], cited in Hudson, 1988, p. 233); removal of a child from the care of his or her parents with intellectual disabilities because of a social service department decision that such a married couple were incapable of parenting (upheld by a Birmingham High Court Ruling, cited in Hudson, 1988, p. 234); and denial of people with Down syndrome the opportunity to be assessed for receiving organ transplants. Some sections of the disability community have criticized routine antenatal screening for Down syndrome and other disabilities for the purpose of assessing whether to abort such pregnancies when they occur, and particularly how the media debates about such issues neglect to consider their feelings.

These examples indicate that the lives of people with intellectual disabilities are not valued as highly as those of people without disabilities and that the denial of their human rights is therefore less contentious and, in some cases, is seen as justifiable. The fundamental human rights of people with intellectual disabilities are sometimes reduced in media debates to the status of "claim rights"; for example, a person's right to life is discussed in terms of the financial cost of caring for them over a lifetime (Hudson, 1988). The denial of their human rights has been justified on the grounds that, for a person who is incapable of recognizing or appreciating human rights, the loss of those rights is less significant than it is for others. This point has been raised in cases of compulsory sterilization, together with the assertion that the consequences of nonintervention would result in increased supervision and therefore a violation of a different kind (Hudson, 1988). In short, many people with intellectual disabilities continue to lack similar opportunities, lifestyles, expectations, and rights as their contemporaries without disabilities.

British governments have addressed discrimination against sections of the population (women and ethnic minorities) by specific Acts of Parliament, but until the 1980s chose not to do so with regard to people with disabilities. Legal sanctions have been rejected, and the voluntary approach has been the strategy that the governments have pursued with regard to discrimination against people with disabilities in most policy areas. For example, public transport providers have been targeted by the government through education and persuasion and a voluntary quota system and Code of Good Practice (1984) established for employers to follow. This has long been considered inadequate by organizations of people with disabilities who have called for comprehensive antidiscrimination legislation to secure the rights of all people with disabilities in all aspects of their lives. They also called for a Freedom of Information Act and greater funding of their organizations (Oliver, 1986). It is questionable how far the Disability Discrimination Act of 1995 (ch. 50) will go in bringing the rights of people with disabilities into line with those of the rest of the British population. The Act covers areas of employment and the provision of goods, facilities, and services to the general public, although full implementation of the legislation has been staggered over several years. It renders unlawful employers' refusal to provide specialized equipment for employees with disabilities or information in appropriate formats for job applicants with disabilities. There are numerous loopholes in the Act for employers, however, such as the provision stating that discrimination by potential or actual employers is unlawful "unless there is a good reason," which is vague and open to abuse. Commentators with disabilities had called for clearer definitions of reasonable accommodation in order to clarify the employers' permitted defenses for engaging in discrimination (i.e., undue hardship to the organization, safety issues) (Bynoe, Oliver, & Barnes, 1991). Furthermore, the legislation applies only to employers with more than 20 employees. The legislation covering the provision of public goods, services, and facilities does not apply if the customer is incapable of understanding the terms of a contract, which excludes many people with intellectual disabilities. Some report that the Act has split the disability community. Some of the larger organizations argued that though the Act is far from ideal, it is a valuable progression, whereas "others see it as a sop and a denial of full civil rights for disabled people" (Brindle, 1996). A spokesperson from the British Council of Organizations of Disabled People (BCODP) has even suggested that the Act amounted to "legalized discrimination" (Brindle, 1996, p. 6). Much of the objection centers on the previous government's refusal to set up a disability rights commission (similar to those on racial equality and equal opportunities) to enforce the Act and the setting up instead of a relatively powerless advisory body, the National Disability Council. The opposition Labor Party at the time did state, however, its commitment to establishing such a commission upon its accession to power (Brindle, 1996).

RIGHT TO QUALITY OF LIFE

Measuring quality of life is fraught with difficulty. It has been said that there are as many definitions of "quality of life" as there are people (Liu, 1976, cited in Felce & Perry, 1995). A review of 80 quality-of-life scales found little agreement between their authors (Felce & Perry, 1995). Although it is proving difficult to agree on an objective definition, however, there is general agreement on five areas that contribute to an individual's quality of life: physical well-being, social well-being, emotional well-being, material well-being, and development and activity (Felce & Perry, 1995). These main categories subsume a total of 32 subsidiary categories. The operationalization of such a model, therefore, would be extremely complex.

    In the research conducted by this chapter's authors, three areas that broadly fall under the headings of material and social well-being and development and activity were the focus. These are consistent with the model of the five accomplishments and ordinary life model on which policy in the northwestern region of England is based (see below). Both center around the human rights goals of enabling individuals with disabilities not only to live in but also to be fully integrated within their local communities and of providing them with opportunities to be involved in decisions that affect their everyday lives. This philosophy can be equated with the notion of autonomy that, along with physical health, Doyal and Gough defined as being the two basic human needs:

> Physical survival and personal autonomy are the preconditions for any individual action in any culture, they constitute the most basic human needs—those which must be satisfied to some degree before actors can effectively participate in their form of life to achieve any other valued goals. (1991, p. 54)

Autonomy is denied to the majority of people with intellectual disabilities. By virtue of their social status and the response of society to their disabilities, these individuals are not rewarded as they get older with greater control over their own actions. Indeed, the aging process may be associated with an increasing denial of their human rights. They are often treated as if they were perpetual children, with others making decisions on their behalf. Although the normalization model has been criticized for making people with intellectual disabilities fit into an unwelcoming and discriminatory society rather than expecting society to adapt to the diverse needs of all of its members, it has been influential in helping to put the consumer at the center of the debate, arguing that consumers, regardless of their level of disability, should be encouraged and enabled to participate as much as possible in the organization of their everyday lives.

Doyal and Gough argued that the basic needs of disempowered groups are no different from those of anyone else; however, disempowered groups need "additional and specific satisfiers" to address the "additional threats to their health and autonomy" that they face (1991, p. 74). This point is particularly relevant for people with intellectual disabilities, as shown by a consideration of the three prerequisites for individual autonomy: understanding, cognitive and emotional capacity, and opportunity. In all three respects, people with intellectual disabilities are disadvantaged or excluded. According to Doyal and Gough, understanding is dependent on effective teaching and learning from others; if not taught or if badly taught, the individual is "objectively disabled" (1991, p. 63). Cognitive and emotional capacity, they argued, is dependent on a number of factors, including the intellectual capability to formulate aims, the confidence to want to act and to participate in everyday life, and an understanding of the constraints on the success of their actions—none of which can be automatically assumed of people with intellectual disabilities.

Opportunity is dependent on meaningful choices and the range of opportunities available for significant action. Again, these are factors that can never be taken for granted with regard to this group of people. In considering the quality of life of people with intellectual disabilities and in particular the degree of autonomy that they possess, an important consideration is whether the failure to enable them to meet their full potential in relation to understanding, cognitive and emotional capacity, and opportunity is a result of their own developmental disabilities, whether it is socially constructed, or a mixture of both.

A further important question to address when discussing quality of life for people with intellectual disabilities is whether objective or subjective measures should be used. Objective measures have their limitations and dangers. In particular, it is important that they are as open and comprehensive as possible. Although acknowledging the special circumstances of people with intellectual disabilities, these objective measures must not reflect any common misconceptions or stereotypes, in particular with regard to gender, race, age, or disability.

As Felce and Perry (1995) pointed out, "Obtaining an answer is a necessary but not sufficient condition of sound interviewing." For the reasons discussed previously, any subjective assessment that a person with intellectual disabilities makes may be problematic because of their limited life experience, their frequent acquiescence in the presence of authority figures, and their limited comprehension or communication skills. Relying on information from a third party is also problematic, however. If the third party knows the person well, then they are not disinterested; if they do not, then they are even less likely to be able to represent the person's views accurately. Felce and Perry (1995) argued that any third party should share key characteristics, such as age, gender, race, and shared experience. In the research reported here, this chapter's authors could obtain information from only those people who were involved—namely, the consumer, where possible, and the person closest to them, which in all cases was a family caregiver or service provider. Any shared characteristics between the two would have been quite coincidental. In order to minimize the potential for bias, the views of both groups of people are presented straightforwardly, with the information obtained being neither minimized nor exaggerated.

SERVICE PROVISION

Since the late 1970s in Britain, there has been considerable rhetoric about community care or "aging in place," (i.e., enabling older people to stay in their homes or to live with their families), and there is limited financial help to assist them to do this (Walker, 1981). Nevertheless, the number of older people in residential care has continued to grow, and the levels of domiciliary support necessary to prevent this trend has failed to keep pace with demand (Schorr, 1992; Walker, 1982a).

The idea of a service continuum based on increased dependency and the inevitability of decline in the abilities of the older person has dominated policy thinking and service provision. This continuum is underpinned by discriminatory assumptions that older people progress through a service career from domiciliary to day care to residential care as their disabilities require that they receive increasing levels of support. Thus, despite the British government's emphasis on community care in the 1980s and 1990s, considerable numbers of older people are still cared for in residential environments. Residential care is often the care of last resort and is often used only because community-based services for older people are inadequate. Yet policy makers and service providers still regard residential care as a legitimate form of care provision for older people, and older adults constitute almost the last group for whom residential care is regarded as an acceptable and appropriate model of care.

By contrast, in the intellectual disabilities field as well as in the fields of child care, mental health, and physical disabilities, an accelerating trend away from large, long-term, institutional care toward small-scale group living in the community has developed. This policy shift has been driven by conflicting motives. On the negative side is the desire to cut the costs of care: Community care has long been viewed by British governments as a cheaper option than institutional care, but it was not until the 1980s that this preference was turned into reality in a concerted attempt to close long-stay institutions as part of a general strategy to constrain National Health Service spending (Walker, 1989, 1993). More positively, however, user groups, their representatives, and some service providers have argued that people with intellectual disabilities should be able to lead ordinary lives in local communities.

The Jay Committee report endorsed that view in the late 1970s: "Mentally handicapped people have a right to enjoy normal patterns of life in the community" (1979b, p. 17). Many subsequent reports endorsed similar views.

Normalization

Special relocation into local communities, though essential, is not sufficient to ensure that members of a hitherto devalued and stigmatized group such as people with intellectual disabilities become participating members of those communities. Moreover, the move from large institutions to smaller accommodations does not automatically ensure that the type of care provided will be any less institutional in nature (Brown & Smith, 1992). In the intellectual disabilities field, normalization has been adopted by some as a philosophy and by others as a tool to underpin the development of services that were intended both to overcome segregated and institutionalized forms of care, whatever the environment, and to nurture the independence of the individual. Thus, normalization may be seen as a vehicle by which to promote both the quality of life of people with intellectual disabilities and the human rights of these individuals to freedom, autonomy, and dignity. In Britain and North America, the principles of normalization have widespread, though not uncritical, acceptance (Brown & Smith, 1992; Chappell, 1994) and have had a considerable influence on the development of services for people with intellectual disabilities. The particular operational model of normalization that has had the greatest influence in Britain is the "five accomplishments" model (O'Brien, 1985), and, as noted previously, this model was incorporated into the strategy of care for people with intellectual disabilities that the northwestern region of Britain, the area in which this chapter's authors conducted their research, drew up. (For a description of the five accomplishments model, see page 129.)

Normalization went through several metamorphoses as it traveled from Scandinavia to North America and back to Europe during the 1970s and 1980s (Brown & Smith, 1992). Such has been the dominance of the idea throughout the intellectual disabilities field in Britain that it has been likened to "an evangelical movement, with associated doctrinal squabbles and schisms" (Brown & Smith, 1992, p. xvii), which made many people committed to the human rights of people with intellectual disabilities reluctant to criticize it or to suggest modifications to it. More critical assessments have begun to emerge, however.

The application of normalization to service provision has been criticized for neglecting individuals' gender, class, and race (Brown & Smith, 1992). The same criticism may be leveled with regard to age, though it has not been done hitherto (Walker et al., 1996). Although normalization theories hinge on the position of the individual, in its operationalization through the medium of health and social services, attention is inevitably concentrated on the needs, interests, and expectations of the group and, if inappropriately applied, can lead to stereotyping. Normalization is concerned with what is socially valued. When the reference or peer group in the wider community (i.e., older people without disabilities in this context) itself is not socially valued, however, and when the main models of care provided for the wider group neither aspire to nor achieve the core values of normalization, then, unless challenged, the goals set for older people with intellectual disabilities will be constrained. What standard of normality should be used when what passes for normal is deficient in crucial respects (e.g., poor quality services or material deprivation)? Is what is regarded as normal or what is widely accepted as such a desirable optimum, the result of historical development, or just a matter of resource constraints? This sort of dilemma is familiar to social gerontologists who have questioned, for example, the denial of poverty (Walker, 1980) or of disability (Townsend, 1981a) in old age on the grounds that these are normal features of aging. The research of this chapter's authors (Walker et al., 1993, 1996a) found that care workers tended to treat older people with intellectual disabilities differently from younger people and to have different expectations of the abilities and appropriate lifestyle of this population. This finding has important implications for the nature of the support or care that is provided and, in particular, whether the care of older people with intellectual disabilities is structured on the expectation of dependence rather than on the goal of increasing independence or, ideally, interdependence.

One of the major criticisms made of normalization, particularly from within the liberation movement of people with disabilities in Britain, is that, rather than demanding that the wider society unconditionally accept and integrate its members who are different in any respect, it requires the individual to adapt to the norms of society and "compete in the world of the able-bodied and the able-minded" (Atkinson & Walmsley, 1995, p. 227). Furthermore, normalization assumes that "the values and norms of behavior and appearance in society are worth striving for" (Hattersley, 1991, p. 3). Lawson, as a user of mental health services, shared the doubts of other critics of normalization (Chappell, 1994) when adherence to the principles of normalization implies "conformity to an unjust world" (1991, p. 78) and questioned its value when the predominant value system itself is unacceptable. As Bayley (1991) argued, normalization exists only against a background of years of "abnormalization." Bayley further criticized normalization because of its stress on

> Individualistic achievement or success-orientated societal values, which emphasise people's independence rather than their interdependence, [which] are profoundly unhelpful to people with a mental handicap [and many other people]. Instead the focus should be on valuing the person; this makes it possible to question not just any undervalued social roles experienced by people with a mental handicap, but also the values that society holds which appear to deny such people the opportunity to develop in the way which is best for them. (1991, p. 88)

OLDER PEOPLE VERSUS PEOPLE WITH INTELLECTUAL DISABILITIES

All of these criticisms have particular resonance if they are applied to the situation of older people with intellectual disabilities. The aging of this population has important implications for the concept of normalization, which is based on the premise that people with intellectual disabilities should share life experiences similar to those of their peers in the wider community. The limitations of the normalization concept, however, are clearly demonstrated with regard to older people with intellectual disabilities because the experiences of their reference group—older adults— are themselves limited and restricted by society's attitudes, in particular age discrimination and the association of old age with dependency. Thus, the goals set for older people with intellectual disabilities and the services offered to them are in turn restricted by the socially constructed stereotype of old age as a period of dependency (Townsend, 1981b; Walker, 1980, 1982b).

Balancing Care and Support

The practical human rights implications of the circumstances described in the previous section can be illustrated by a discussion of the findings of the chapter authors' study of older people with intellectual disabilities living in the community. Those in formal care usually lived in small-scale, shared, supported housing, the most popular model of community care that has been adopted in Britain for this group. The chapter authors' research found that, in many important respects, a division occurred in service providers' treatment of older and younger people with intellectual disabilities, a division similar to that which exists between services for older people and those for people with intellectual disabilities as described in the previous section.

People with intellectual disabilities are not a homogeneous group. They vary widely in their levels of physical and developmental abilities and disabilities. The problems that they face in their everyday lives are compounded by the stigma that society places on people with disabilities and, for large numbers, by their enforced social exclusion from the wider community. The kind of assistance that people with intellectual disabilities require therefore varies widely. Some people with severe disabilities need care such as the need for others to undertake tasks on their behalf, including personal care needs, cooking, and preparation for meals (Qureshi & Walker, 1989). In this sense, care is something that is done to the recipient in terms of both tending to the recipient's physical needs and providing emotional support. Other people with intellectual disabilities may not need assistance with physical tasks; but, either because of their level of competence or because of restricted opportunities in the past, they may require support (i.e., the help of others to assist them to do things for themselves). This assistance may involve helping the individuals to gain confidence and then giving them the opportunity to do things for themselves, ranging from routine self-care or household tasks to making decisions and participating in activities in the community. Support, in this sense, is a process of empowerment.

If individuals are to achieve the highest level of independence and integration possible, maintaining the correct balance between care and support is crucial. Insufficient care can undermine the individual's quality of life and can restrict activities for which he or she needs only support. Care, when given unnecessarily, can create dependency (Walker, 1982b). If insufficient or inappropriate support is available, then the individual will not be able to obtain and/or maintain control over important aspects of daily living. Conversely, too much or the wrong type of support may limit the individual's self-determination by being overprotective and thus fosters dependence rather than independence.

Service providers in the chapter authors' study tended to concentrate on the need to care for older people and, therefore, to overstate these individuals' levels of dependency rather than to support them in independent living as the service providers did with younger people. Caregivers frequently espoused a view of older people that was remarkably similar to Cumming and Henry's (1961) disengagement thesis. For example, many service providers assumed that, because older people in general tend to lead more sedentary lives, to go out less often, and to have fewer friends than younger people, they needed to expend less effort in developing activities and fostering the social integration of older adults with intellectual disabilities. By making this assumption, therefore, service providers were limiting the quality of life of older people with intellectual disabilities and unnecessarily restricting their human rights.

Independence versus Dependence

If people with intellectual disabilities are to be enabled to develop independently, considerable attention must be paid to their continuing training needs to ensure

1) that they maintain skills that they have learned and 2) that they are given the opportunity to develop new skills and competencies. Indeed, these should be recognized as basic human rights. In practice, in the chapter authors' study older people with intellectual disabilities tended to receive much less skills training than their younger counterparts. Only 3 in 10 people ages 60 and older were receiving any training or had received any in the preceding 12 months, as compared with 8 out of 10 of those younger than age 60. This included informal domiciliary training as well as formal training courses. Service providers believed that it was less important to help older people to develop new skills or to try to maintain their existing skills than was the case for younger people. In 30% of cases, support workers working with the 60-plus age group thought that training was not an important part of their job, whereas only 5.3% of those working with the 50–59 age group and none working with the younger-than-50 age group shared that view. Not only did service providers deny the equal rights to training of older and younger people but also they were more cautious about older people's ability to learn. Only 18% of the older group who might have benefited from skills development were deemed capable of learning a new skill, as compared with 33% of the younger age group. Such stereotyping, based on the popular misconception "You cannot teach an old dog new tricks," has been found among employers who believe, incorrectly, that older people are harder to train (Taylor & Walker, 1994). In fact, operational research (Belbin, 1965; Belbin & Belbin, 1972; Warr, 1993) showed that older workers are just as capable of being trained as younger ones but require different training methods. Ironically, at the end of the 20th century, the older age groups, on average, were more capable of being trained than the younger group because previous cohorts of people with severe disabilities died before reaching old age; thus, the surviving members of that cohort have milder disabilities and are more readily trainable.

Sometimes the more passive strategy applied to older people was justified by the fact that, as people get older, they should be allowed to sit back and relax. Of course, this is not to suggest that training should be forced on people—though service providers often deem it proper for younger people to be strongly encouraged, if not forced, out of their apathy or lethargy in order to take part in some activity. It is important, however, in terms of human rights that each individual be given the opportunity to pursue his or her own potential as far as he or she would like. By making ageist assumptions, however, service providers can restrict the range of opportunities available to older people and, in doing so, unwittingly deny their human right to equal treatment with younger people. Prior to the 1990s, few people with intellectual disabilities had the opportunity to fully exploit their own potential, especially with regard to independent living skills, because of the institutional and overprotective models of care that were in operation for most of the 20th century. Older people, who have lost out most, have been proved capable of gaining greater control over their own lives if they are given the opportunities and skills to do so. The perceptions and reactions of some caregivers follow:

"His disabilities might handicap him as he gets older, but James should go from strength to strength."
"He's got more capabilities in him."
"No matter what your age, if you need support, you need it."
"The thing is, we don't look on them as older people or disabled people; they are themselves."

A second explanation for the reluctance of caregivers to invest in skills training for older people might be their assumption that this group will become less independent in the future. Only one-third of those working with the older-than-60 age group thought that they would become more independent in the future, whereas three-quarters of those working with the younger-than-50 age group believed that that would be the case. By contrast, one in five thought that those older than age 60 would become less independent, whereas none of the caregivers of the younger-than-50 group thought that that would happen. As our data on older people living with their families and reports from caregivers show, however, older age does not necessarily bring greater dependency. Given the opportunities, older people with intellectual disabilities can develop new skills and interests and adapt to new circumstances. Following are some typical observations that caregivers make:

"He's got quality of life now. He's his own man and can please himself. Healthwise, I think we do better. I think everything is better. . . ."
"I think they're treated as old people, and in their minds they're not. I had them reading and writing, but it's all gone by the way. The staff are very nice people, but they're not helping to make Kenneth independent. He's safe and secure, and he has somebody to look after him, and he is occupied from Monday to Friday . . . ; but you need more than that in life."

The second remark was made by a social worker who had worked with Kenneth when Kenneth lived in a hostel and had assisted Kenneth when he moved into sheltered living accommodations, where there were other people with intellectual disabilities. She was contrasting the way in which she had supported him in the past with the care that he was receiving currently, as well as contrasting the difference between the two approaches with regard to his independence, and suggesting that there is a direct link between ability and opportunity.

Caregivers reported that younger people were more likely than older people to have become more competent and independent. In looking at other parts of the data, however, which are discussed below, their responses clearly are related only partly to the abilities of the person with an intellectual disability; but, equally important, they are related to the lower expectations that caregivers have of them and the more restricted opportunities open to them. Some of these caregivers' remarks may help illustrate this point:

"I feel that younger people should learn more, whereas older people may not need training."
"There aren't so many options for older people. There are less activities for someone who is old and disabled."

Although caregivers said that double discrimination against older people with intellectual disabilities did not exist, in practice it clearly did. This chapter's authors frequently heard statements made by those working with older people that, although well meaning, contained implicitly age-discriminatory assumptions. Some of these statements follow:

"Anthea's old key worker would say she shouldn't be set goals, because she is too old. I don't agree. I think everybody should have the chance."

"[He's] growing old gracefully. [We] can't be so hard now, [he] can relax."
"Easier with younger [people, they're] not as set in their ways."
"Younger people need new things. They need to get out more. Older people are more content."

The attitudes of caregivers who make such assumptions may result in practices that reinforce dependency rather than create empowerment. Contrary to the limited expectations of older people that service providers frequently expressed, the findings of this chapter's authors support previous research (Maaskant et al., 1994) that shows that there is no inevitable relationship between age and dependency. Comparison of the data collected 6 months after resettlement with that collected as part of this study some 3 years later showed that the relationship between age and dependency is not as clear-cut as many caregivers and policy makers believe. Over this period, people in both the younger and older age groups gained in independence according to a number of measures. Approximately one-fifth of the people older than 50 had improved their skills in communication or personal care, and more than one-fourth were better able to use and understand money and were better able to exercise choice. In the majority of cases, there had been no change in skill level. In a minority of cases, there had been some deterioration; but, in fact, this was more of a factor among the younger group than among the older group.

Caregivers reported that the younger age group's behavior had led to increased independence in a number of areas. The only respect in which older people were reported to have more independence was with regard to their participation in household activities. Younger people did better with regard to behavior changes, social skills, and their ability to self-advocate. The slower progress made by older people might be age related but could also be an inevitable outcome of the limited opportunities that are made available to them and the expectations of caregivers. Younger people tended to be encouraged to speak out more for themselves and to act more independently. The contrasts for older people were striking, as the following remarks of caregivers indicate:

"I'm hoping he will become more independent; but I'm worried that, because of his age, he may not."
"I don't think we've got the staff [to enable her to become more independent], but her age is probably something that will hold her back."

This age-discriminatory assumption of service providers regarding decline and increasing dependency has implications for the continued presence of older people with developmental disabilities in the community. Research (Walker et al., 1996) revealed that residential care is considered an appropriate option for an older person with intellectual disabilities in situations in which it would not be deemed so for younger people. One district social care purchaser in the northwestern region of England reported that, though special permission had to be sought from the Regional Health Authority to resettle people from the hospital (though not from a community environment) to a residential care facility (contrary to regional policy guidelines), it was generally accepted that nursing facility provisions could be used.

IMPORTANCE OF MEANINGFUL ACTIVITY

A common feature of the restricted quality of life of most people with intellectual disabilities, and in particular of those living in formal care environments, is a lack of regular, structured activities outside the home. This is also a problem common to many older people without disabilities after retirement. It is not altogether surprising, then, that older people in the study were twice as likely as younger people to have no regular, structured activity outside the home and overall to have fewer regular, organized activities (see Table 1). Even those among the family group who did have greater access to the main day care provision—namely, day centers—there was a major disparity between age groups. Only 9% of the younger-than-50 group had no day provision, as compared with 25% of the 50–59 group and 50% of the older-than-60 group.

This lack of activities outside the home has implications for the rights of people with intellectual disabilities to integration, social contact, and participation in the community. Exclusion from the labor market means that many rely on day services for social contact and engagement; however, day centers are influenced by different models of provision (Barnes, 1990). Normalization does not seem to have had the same impact here as it has in residential services (Race, 1995), and consequently many large day centers still operate in segregation from the wider community in inappropriate locations and buildings. At best, they may offer a chance to learn practical and social skills; at worst, they may function as a means of containment and control. (For many, it is a question of the center being better than nothing.)

The type of structured activities outside the home undertaken by respondents also varied according to age. Day centers within the study did not operate any formal retirement policies, and yet there was what amounts to a tacit retirement policy in operation. People older than 60 years were much less likely to use day centers for people with intellectual disabilities and caregivers themselves reported examples of age discrimination. As one caregiver put it, "[I] don't think it's right that day centers won't take people over 65. The Age Concern one is a charity and doesn't have the same resources. It's not fair to turn round and say 'Happy 65th—you can't come here anymore.'"

Although many existing consumers, especially those living with their families, were able to continue to attend day centers as they got older, new older users were unlikely to be given a place. In addition, this group had less favorable access to further education colleges—one respondent, for example, was refused a place because he was too old—and virtually no access to employment. A survey of supported em-

Table 1. Number of sessions of structured activities in 1 week by age: All respondents

Number of activities	Age range (in years)		
	Younger than 50	50–59	60+
0	14.5%	18.5%	48.4%
1–4	27.4%	40.7%	29.0%
5–8	24.2%	22.2%	9.7%
9+	33.9%	18.5%	12.9%
Total	62.0%	27.0%	31.0%

ployment in the northwestern region of England found that 95% of those who were working were younger than 50. Of the 40 programs in operation, 13 did not support anyone older than 50. The author of the survey concluded, "This is certainly well below the level expended in the non-disabled working population. It could be that, because of the very limited resources available generally, this group is not seen as a priority" (Ashton, 1995, p. 17).

This underrepresentation of older people with intellectual disabilities in supported employment programs reflects the growing marginalization of people older than 50 from the labor market, a circumstance that results from age-discriminatory employment practices. As a consequence of such discrimination, the older people in the study had even fewer opportunities to take part in regular, organized activity outside the home than younger people did.

General services for older people without disabilities might be expected to provide an extra avenue for outside activity for older people with intellectual disabilities. Few older people had much contact with these services, however. Because these services tend to cater to much-older adults, the 50- to 70-year-olds might have been deemed too young to be accepted. There is also, however, a reluctance by the older person's service sector to admit people with intellectual disabilities. As a result, older people with intellectual disabilities fall between the two service sectors: a clear case of double jeopardy.

"I think they are a bit patronized. . . . They are people with learning disabilities first rather than older people. Therefore, if you try to get them into an old people's service, the learning disability precludes them. Community care and day centers provided for the elderly don't cater for those with learning difficulties—they are expected to [fit] in."

"She's too old to go to a day center; but at the over 60s club, they don't want her because of her disability. . . . Nothing there for them. You get the normal older people centers, but they don't welcome people with learning difficulties . . . , [and] the Gateway Clubs [clubs for people with learning difficulties], for instance, are not appropriate for older people."

Three people in their 60s had experienced problems with other people without intellectual disabilities when using older people's services. One man, who lived in a sheltered housing complex for older people, was asked not to go on outings organized for tenants. Another woman who had a reputation for her behavior was asked to stop attending a lunch club. At other activities for older people organized by the Salvation Army, this woman was finding it difficult to fit in, as she described:

Well, I go for my dinner to Salvation Army, but they want you to go to the service. And I go again on a Monday, but I'm not keen on it there, 'cause they don't want to know ye. Monday afternoons, we have a game of bingo. They don't want to know ye, you know how some people are? They just don't want to know ye. The minister and one or two of them's alright.

Caregivers who work with younger people, who had less actual contact with services for older people with intellectual disabilities, had a generally more positive view of the quantity and quality of service provision. This might well reflect the "must be" syndrome (i.e., there "must be" services because the need is so obvious). This is an overoptimistic view that has been proved inaccurate in many areas of service provision. More than two-thirds of those working with people older than 50 thought that the general level of services for older people with intellectual disabilities was poor or very poor, yet several reported the closure of appropriate facilities.

Only 12 people older than the age of 50 received services meant for older people (three were ages 50–59, seven were ages 60–69, and two were older than 70). Seven people were in warden-controlled flats for older people. Five went to a day center for older adults. Most support workers thought that this provision was appropriate, but four were not happy with it. Another four of those older than age 60 living in formal care had been identified as needing some kind of day service for older adults but as yet had been unsuccessful in finding a placement. One woman who had been resettled from one of the large hospitals was turned down after assessment because she already had day care in the form of her home support workers. The comments of one of that woman's caregivers regarding the lack of appropriate facilities are illustrative: "When we are invited to events they are always geared towards younger people. . . . I wouldn't say [services for older people] were very good. Everything just seems geared for younger people." When one consumer was asked what she would want from older people's services, she stressed the need for external activities that provide some structure and variety in day-to-day living: "Well, same as you say, if I could find them somewhere to go during the day, get out the house more. I mean, really, when you've been out the house, you feel a lot better for it. . . . [Otherwise,] you get grumpy and depressed."

Although younger people had made slightly more use of community facilities in the previous month and were considerably more likely to have taken part in a greater number of activities in the previous week (see Table 2), caregivers were more likely to say that people in the younger age group were restricted in their activities by lack of adequate support. Of the younger group, 65% were said to have been unable to do something that they wanted to do because there was no support available as compared with only 46% of those older than age 60. In contrast, 7.5% of caregivers working with the under-50 group and 32% working with the group older than age 60 said that people with intellectual disabilities could not undertake their favorite activities as often as they would like, most commonly because of staff shortages.

Service providers were more likely to report that older people preferred indoor activities such as watching television, listening to music, and knitting, whereas younger people were said to enjoy going to the pub, restaurants, the cinema, and soccer games. Only one quarter of the younger group were said to enjoy home-based activities most compared with more than half of the older group. A similar proportion

Table 2.   Number of activities in the past week by age for those in formal care

Number of activities	Age range (in years)		
	Younger than 50	50–59	60+
0	10.0%	4.3%	11.1%
1–4	22.5%	52.7%	44.4%
5–8	22.5%	17.4%	18.5%
9+	45.0%	26.1%	25.9%
Total	40.0%	23.0%	27.0%

Does not include people living with their families. This group tended to use community facilities less, but this did not seem to vary with age.

of the group older than 60, however, were reported to be able to go out alone, and interviews with the service consumers themselves seemed to indicate that people of all ages enjoyed a mixture of activities inside and outside the home. The following are some typical comments of older adults with developmental disabilities:

"I like going to cricket if it's a nice day. I went on Sunday. We're going on holiday soon as well [age 65]."

"Well, we were [going out], but not at the moment. We don't go out through the week, only if they've got enough staff to take me. The only day I go out is on a Sunday, when I go out with my friends [age 70]."

"Well, I sometimes go to the pub, sometimes to the pub and for a walk, you know. I sometimes go to the cinema with my girlfriend [age 52]."

GROWING OLDER WITHIN THE FAMILY

The issue of increasing numbers of older adults with intellectual disabilities is only slowly being recognized by service providers in Britain. When it has been seen as a policy issue, this view has been precipitated by and identified in terms of the needs not of older adults with intellectual disabilities themselves but of the implications that the aging of their caregivers has for formal service provision. The second project of this chapter's authors included interviews conducted with eight people older than age 50 who were still living with family members. Four lived with a parent, three lived with a sibling, and one lived with her husband. The parents concerned were ages 80, 82, 84, and 93. In the case involving the 93-year-old parent, the daughter with intellectual disabilities lived with her increasingly frail, largely bedridden mother. They managed with the help of the former's brother and especially a sister who called in every day and generally organized the household.

This type of living arrangement also has implications for the older person with intellectual disabilities. Their right to choose not to be a caregiver for an older adult parent may not have been considered because they just fell gradually into this role, or they may have been denied the right to choose the kind of support they might need in order to provide sufficient and appropriate care. People with intellectual disabilities who live with their families may experience a restriction of their rights, particularly independence and autonomy, and may lack control over other aspects of their lives (e.g., managing their own money). Families may have built up over many years the habit of doing things together that may have inhibited the development of other relationships (Richardson & Ritchie, 1989); consequently, when a caregiver becomes an older adult, the person with intellectual disabilities may have restricted opportunities to get out and thus may become socially isolated. Again, this may enhance the need for day services provision for older people with intellectual disabilities.

Several of the older people with intellectual disabilities had faced increased physical disability; two in particular had problems with their eyesight. One other person, whose intellectual disability had been minor for most of his life, had developed a phobia about cancer and needed much more support. Nonetheless, family caregivers did not display the ageist attitudes that were evident among some formal service providers. On the whole, the families were not concerned that their relatives' capabilities would deteriorate because of aging. One specifically thought that the reverse had happened, and, in some cases, the person was assuming greater responsibility in their older age. This is not to say that family caregivers did not see limitations in what their relatives could do to gain greater independence, but rather that age was not regarded as the cause of those limitations. This, the authors of this chapter think, is an important illustration of the differences in the social construction of old age that may sometimes exist between primary (i.e., informal) relationships and secondary (i.e., formal) ones: The former can operate successfully without a simplistic chronological definition of *old age*, whereas such definitions became more and more important in formal relationships, such as the labor market, during the 20th century (Qureshi & Walker, 1989; Townsend, 1981b; Walker, 1980, 1982b).

Changes in the relationship between a family caregiver and a relative with intellectual disabilities tended to be due more to the age of the former than that of the latter. In two cases, the roles between the two had reversed, and the daughters with intellectual disabilities began to look after their mothers. One did everything in the house, ranging from shopping to cooking hot meals and handling the bills. The other had more limited abilities but learned to use a microwave with help and to telephone other family members if the need arose. In these instances, when the original caregiver needed to be cared for, the person with an intellectual disability had taken over the caring role and, in so doing, had developed increased independent living skills.

This role reversal is one illustration of how the needs of the caregiver and the person for whom the caregiver is caring can overlap and even conflict in the family situation. It is common for family caregivers not to want their relative with intellectual disabilities to leave home. Often this is because they are not confident of the quality of care that will be provided (Walker & Walker, 1998). In many cases, however, the relationships between the family caregiver and the person with intellectual disabilities are completely interdependent—financially, socially, and practically. Given the particularly intense relationships within such families, it would not be surprising if parents were not reluctant to let their adult child leave home. Although in most cases the reluctance comes from love, decisions might be made on the bases of the parents' wishes and at the expense of the wishes of their adult child. For example, one 85-year-old mother in Walker and Walker's (1998) study had resisted attempts to provide her daughter who had intellectual disabilities with more independent accommodation in the past. Another daughter who had become responsible for providing care for both of them believed she had done so

> selfishly, because she would be on her own. . . . She said, "Oh, [Pamela] would never . . . cope with that. She'd be upset." But it wouldn't, it wasn't [Pamela] who would be upset; it was me mum. . . . She doesn't want to be on her own.

The future of both older caregivers and older people with intellectual disabilities is, of course, an increasingly important issue yet one that both find difficult to confront, even with the support and advice of caregivers. This difficulty may stem from a reluctance or unwillingness on the part of the caregiver, not just that of the relative with an intellectual disability, to look ahead (see Richardson & Ritchie, 1990).

People living with a family caregiver must have worked out plans carefully that can be instituted if and when the caring relationship breaks down as a result of death or ill health. Without such plans, older people with intellectual disabilities who are increasingly likely to face continuing their life after the death of their principal caregiver, experience increased trauma because they have to adjust to the death of their closest relative, the loss of their principal caregiver, and a radical but unprepared-for change in their care and living arrangements. In one case, it had taken the social worker 8 years to persuade an 83-year-old woman looking after her 53-year-old daughter to address the issue of the daughter's future care. At the time of the interview, the daughter could not comprehend the possibility of her mother's death. In this case, the mother had always quietly assumed that her daughter would move into a local hostel when she could no longer provide her daughter's care. The closure of the local hostel left the mother feeling devastated, and she had no idea about alternative provisions for her daughter.

Preparation for future care following the death of the caregiver or for circumstances in which the caregiver can no longer cope with the task is a sensitive issue. Both the caregiver and his or her relative with intellectual disabilities need support and information over a prolonged period. The gaps in service provision and the lack of a long-term relationship with a key worker, which is the experience of most family caregivers, means that such preparation rarely occurs. The system of service provision in Britain, which concentrates resources on crisis intervention, means that families, consumers, and service providers cannot establish a long-term relationship based on trust within which they can begin to address such sensitive issues.

ALTERNATIVE MODELS OF SERVICE PROVISION: FROM NORMALIZATION TO SOCIAL INTEGRATION

Britain has made considerable progress since the 1960s in generating ideas and policies regarding the care and support of people with intellectual disabilities. This progress has been influenced positively by the debate on normalization, which has stressed the basic human rights of this population, such as their being able to live ordinary lives within their communities and being involved in the key decisions that affect them. The practical application of this philosophy to service provision for older people with intellectual disabilities reveals some of the limitations of the philosophy itself and the dilemmas that result from the different traditions of services for people with intellectual disabilities and those for older people with and without disabilities.

The problem with the philosophy of normalization itself is that "normal" service provision may be neither adequate in terms of the quality of life it promotes nor appropriate. Policy makers and service providers have been slow to respond to the specific needs of some groups, such as racial minorities. Alternatively, as with older groups, they have helped to create dependency among older people by not providing sufficient or appropriate support to enable them to maintain independent lives in their own homes. This denial of human rights and reinforcement of dependency is particularly significant for people with intellectual disabilities as they age because Britain's provision of services for people with intellectual disabilities toward the end of the 20th century concentrated not on the segregation and care of this group but on supporting them toward gaining a realization of greater choice and independence. The practical application of the normalization principle may be criticized on several grounds, especially the failure of service providers to enable people to develop additional skills for independent living, with the result that the majority of those in group homes tend to remain there. Nonetheless, there is an aspiration to enhance independence and the individual's right to autonomy that is completely absent from services for older people. Thus, the age-discriminatory assumptions and stereotypes that are built into the traditional pattern of care offered to older people mean that people with intellectual disabilities face more restrictive and possibly more segregated lives when they get older.

The research reported in this chapter shows that many age-discriminatory stereotypes are creeping into intellectual disability services. Age itself was often used by service providers as an explanation for older people's not leading more active lives or not being trained to do more for themselves, despite the fact that, as a whole, the older people in the sample had a wider range of competencies than their younger peers. Perhaps most indicative of the insidious effect of age stereotyping was the fact that reinstitutionalization into older people's homes was accepted readily as a viable option because of a lack of alternatives and the availability of social security funding, although similar residential environments definitely would not even be considered for younger people, on the ground that such provision would be an unacceptable restriction on their development, activities, and overall quality of life. Activities outside the home and social networks were deemed to be less important for older people, because caregivers associated a reduction in outside activities and social networks with the natural process of aging. To the extent that older people become inactive and socially isolated, clearly this circumstance usually does not arise by choice but is one of the aspects of their lives that they most wish to change.

The operational model of normalization that has had greatest influence in Britain is the "five accomplishments" model (O'Brien, 1985); this model was incorporated into the much-commended strategy of care for people with intellectual disabilities that the North Western Regional Health Authority drew up. The five accomplishments represent both a set of quality-of-life and human rights goals toward which consumers should be enabled to progress and a series of baselines for the evaluation of service outcomes:

1. *Community presence:* To enable people with intellectual disabilities to have a physical presence in local communities and have access to typical community facilities
2. *Choice:* To offer people real choices in their lives and enable them to influence key decisions.
3. *Respect:* To ensure that the form of dress, activities, and location of housing are consistent with those of the wider community.
4. *Competence:* To enable each individual to develop his or her full potential within the community environment.
5. *Participation:* To enable each individual to become part of a network of personal relationships, including close friends, family, and links with people without disabilities in the community.

The five accomplishments and other goals of normalization appear to produce positive results compared with those of traditional service provision for older adults, which, as outlined in this chapter, has been based on a model of increasing dependence rather than increasing independence. Despite the criticisms made of normalization, its application to services for older people without disabilities could have as dramatic an impact on services for them as it has had on the development of services for people with intellectual disabilities since the 1970s, and, moreover, its implementation could serve to confront the age-discriminatory construction of services and attitudes toward older people. The need for this becomes more urgent as increasing numbers of people with intellectual disabilities reach old age and, therefore, experience the transition from a superior to an inferior service model.

The principle of normalization, or "ordinary life," is based on allowing each individual to reach the potential of his or her peers. If the age-discriminatory stereotypes that are built into much service provision and exercised by many well-meaning caregivers are not challenged, then the opportunities and advantages that should be offered to older people with intellectual disabilities living in the community, perhaps after years of institutionalization, will be limited merely because of their age and not because of their abilities or, indeed, their inclinations. Those age-discriminatory assumptions that prevail in much of the care of older people without disabilities will create even greater dependency among older people with intellectual disabilities; therefore, this group will not be able to benefit from the more creative and practical support that has allowed some younger people to obtain and retain a degree of independence following relocation from an institution.

Such discriminatory attitudes and policies in service provision restrict the extent to which older people with intellectual disabilities are able to benefit from the normalization model that is regarded as entirely appropriate for their younger counterparts and cast doubt on the usefulness of the concept of normalization when the reference group itself of older adults without disabilities suffers from socially constructed dependency and discrimination. The research reported in this chapter shows that a potentially liberating concept, when applied to older people with intellectual disabilities, can actually create barriers to their participation in their local communities because it embodies a flawed concept of what is typical of people in the older age groups. Instead, service provision for older people with and without intellectual disabilities requires an approach that emphasizes their need for, and right to, social integration. This integration "norm" should be regarded as a basic human right and, when operationalized in terms of a model such as the five accomplishments model, provides the basis for a desirable quality of life.

An emphasis on the right of older people with intellectual disabilities to be integrated as full citizens challenges both the legal basis of human rights in Britain and the dominant model of service provision for older people. It requires legislation to enshrine the basic human rights of this group to community presence, choice, respect, competence, and participation and to outlaw discrimination on the grounds of age. At the service provision level, it necessitates the promotion of good practice with regard to *both* older adults and people with intellectual disabilities.

REFERENCES

Ashton, D. (1995). *Survey of supported employment in the North West*. Clitheroe, England: North West Training Development Team (NWTDT).

Atkinson, D., & Walmsley, J. (1995). A woman's place? Issues of gender. In T. Philpot & L. Ward (Eds.), *Values and visions: Changing ideas in services for people with learning difficulties* (pp. 218–231). Oxford, England: Butterworth Heinemann.

Barnes, C.G. (1990). *Cabbage syndrome: The social construction of dependence*. London: Falmer Press.

Bayley, M. (1991). Normalization or "social role valorization": An adequate philosophy? In S. Baldwin & J. Hattersley (Eds.), *Mental handicap: Social science perspectives* (pp. 82–96). London: Tavistock/Routledge.

Belbin, E., & Belbin, R.M. (1972). *Problems in adult retraining*. London: Heinemann.

Belbin, R.M. (1965). *Training methods for older workers*. Paris: Organization for Economic Cooperation and Development.

Booth, T., Simons, K., & Booth, W. (1990). *Outward bound: Relocation and community care for people with learning difficulties.* Milton Keynes, England: Open University Press.

Brindle, D. (1996, November 27). Shaky step forward. *The Guardian,* p. 6.

Brown, H., & Smith, H.. (1992). *Normalisation: A reader for the nineties.* London: Tavistock/ Routledge.

Bynoe, I., Oliver, M., & Barnes, C. (1991). *Equal rights for disabled people: The case for a new law.* London: Institute for Public Policy Research.

Chappell, A.L. (1994). A question of friendship: Community care and the relationships of people with learning difficulties. *Disability, Handicap, and Society, 9*(4), 419–434.

Cumming, E., & Henry, W.E. (1961). *Growing old: The process of disengagement.* New York: Basic Books.

Davis, A., Eley, R., Flynn, M., Flynn, P., & Roberts, G. (1995). To have and to have not: Addressing issues of poverty. In T. Philpot & L. Ward (Eds.), *Values and visions: Changing ideas in services for people with learning difficulties* (pp. 334–345). Oxford, England: Butterworth Heinemann.

Department of Health and Social Security (DHSS). (1971). *Better services for the mentally handicapped* (Command 4683). London: Her Majesty's Stationery Office.

Disability Discrimination Act, 1995, ch. 50 (Eng.).

Doyal, L., & Gough, I. (1991). *A theory of human need.* New York: Guilford Press.

Felce, D., & Perry, J. (1995). Quality of life: Its definition and measurement. *Research in Developmental Disabilities, 16*(1), 51–74.

Hattersley, J. (1991). The future of normalization. In S. Baldwin & J. Hattersley (Eds.), *Mental handicap: Social science perspectives* (pp. 1–11). London: Tavistock/Routledge.

Hogg, J., Moss, S., & Cooke, D. (1988). *Aging and mental handicap.* London: Croom Helm.

Hudson, B. (1988). Do people with a mental handicap have rights? *Disability, Handicap, and Society, 3*(3), 227–237.

Jay Committee. (1979a). *Inquiry into mental handicap nursing and care* (Vol. 1, Command 7468-I). London: Her Majesty's Stationery Office.

Jay Committee. (1979b). *Report of the committee of enquiry into mental handicap nursing and care* (Command 7468). London: Her Majesty's Stationery Office.

King's Fund Center. (1980). *An ordinary life: Comprehensive locally-based residential services for mentally handicapped people.* London: Author.

Korman, N., & Glennerster, H. (1990). *Hospital closure: A political and economic study.* Milton Keynes, England: Open University Press.

Lawson, M. (1991). A recipient's view. In S. Ramon (Ed.), *Beyond community care: Normalisation and integration work* (pp. 73–90). London: Macmillan/MIND Publications.

Liu, B.C. (1976). *Quality of life indicators in U.S. metropolitan areas: A statistical analysis.* Westport, CT: Praeger.

Maaskant, M., Kessels, A., Frederiks, C., Haveman, M., Lantman, H., Urlings, H., & Stermans, F. (1994, April). *Care dependence and policy purposes.* Paper presented at Older People with Development Disabilities Conference, Dublin, Republic of Ireland.

Marshall, T.H. (1950). *Citizenship and social class.* Cambridge, England: Cambridge University Press.

Martin, J., Meltzer, H., & Eliot, D. (1988). *Prevalence of disability among adults.* London: Her Majesty's Stationery Office.

National Health Service and Community Care Act, 1990, ch. 19 (Eng.).

O'Brien, J. (1985). *A guide to personal futures planning.* Atlanta, GA: Responsive Systems Associates.

Oliver, M. (1986). Social policy and disability: Some theoretical issues. *Disability, Handicap, and Society, 1*(1), 5–17.

Qureshi, H., & Walker, A. (1989). *The caring relationship: Elderly people and their families.* Philadelphia: Temple University Press.

Race, D. (1995). Historical development of service provision. In N. Malin (Ed.), *Services for people with learning disabilities* (pp. 46–78). London: Routledge.

Richardson, A., & Ritchie, J. (1989). *Developing friendships: Enabling people with learning difficulties to make and maintain friends.* London: Policy Studies Institute.

Richardson, A., & Ritchie, J. (1990). Developing friendships. In T. Booth (Ed.), *Better lives: Changing services for people with learning difficulties* (pp. 92–104). Sheffield, England: Social Services Monographs: Research in Practice.

Ryan, J., & Thomas, F. (1987). *The politics of mental handicap* (Rev. ed.). London: Free Association Books.

Schorr, A. (1992). *The personal social services: An outside view.* York, England: Joseph Rowntree Foundation.

Sinson, J. (1993). *Group homes and community integration of developmentally disabled people: Microinstitutionalization?* London: Jessica Kingsley Publishers.

Taylor, P., & Walker, A. (1994). The aging workforce: Employers' attitudes towards older workers. *Work, Employment and Society, 8*(4), 569–591.

Towell, D. (Ed.). (1988). *An ordinary life in practice: Developing comprehensive community-based services for people with learning disabilities.* London: King Edward's Hospital Fund for London.

Townsend, P. (1981a). Elderly people with disabilities. In A. Walker & P. Townsend (Eds.), *Disability in Britain: A manifesto of rights* (pp. 91–118). Oxford, England: Martin Robertson.

Townsend, P. (1981b). The structured dependency of the elderly: The creation of social policy in the twentieth century. *Aging and Society, 1*(1), 5–28.

United Nations (UN). (1971). *Declaration on the Rights of Mentally Retarded Persons.* New York: Author.

United Nations (UN). (1975). *Declaration on the Rights of Disabled Persons.* New York: Author.

Walker, A. (1980). The social creation of poverty and dependency in old age. *Journal of Social Policy, 9*(1), 49–75.

Walker, A. (1981). Community care and the elderly in Great Britain: Theory and practice. *International Journal of Health Services, 11*(4), 541–557.

Walker, A. (Ed.). (1982a). *Community care: The family, the state, and social policy.* Oxford, England: Basil Blackwell/Martin Robertson.

Walker, A. (1982b). Dependency and old age. *Social Policy and Administration, 16*(2), 116–137.

Walker, A. (1989). Community care. In M. McCarthy (Ed.), *The new politics of welfare: An agenda for the 1990s?* (pp. 205–225). London: Macmillan.

Walker, A. (1993). Community care policy: From consensus to conflict. In J. Bornat, C Pereira, D. Pilgrim, & F. Williams (Eds.), *Community care: A reader* (pp. 204–226). London: Macmillan.

Walker, A., Walker, C., & Ryan, T. (1996). Older people with learning difficulties leaving institutional care: A case of double jeopardy. *Aging and Society, 16*(2), 1–26.

Walker, C., Ryan, T., & Walker, A. (1993). *Quality of life after resettlement for people with learning difficulties.* Sheffield, England: Sheffield Hallam University, School of Health and Community Studies.

Walker, C., Ryan, T., & Walker, A. (1996). *Fair shares for all: Disparities in service provision for different groups of people with learning difficulties living in the community.* Brighton, England: Pavilion Publishing/Joseph Rowntree Foundation.

Walker, C., & Walker, A. (1998). *Uncertain futures: People with learning difficulties and their ageing family carers.* Brighton, England: Pavilion Publishing/Joseph Rowntree Foundation.

Ward, L. (1987). *The right to vote?* Bristol, England: West Country Campaign for the Mentally Handicapped (CMH).

Warr, P.B. (1993). Age and employment. In H.C. Triandis, M.D. Dunnette, & L.M. Hough (Eds.), *Handbook of industrial and organizational psychology* (2nd ed., Vol. 4, pp. 485–550). Palo Alto, CA: Consulting Psychologists Press.

Wolfensberger, W., & Nirje, B. (1972). *Normalization: The principle of normalization in human services.* Toronto: National Institute on Mental Retardation.

Zarb, G. (1991). Creating a supportive environment: Meeting the needs of people who are aging with a disability. In M. Oliver (Ed.), *Social work: Disabled people and disabling environments* (pp. 177–203). London: Jessica Kingsley Publishers.

Zarb, G., & Oliver, M. (1993). *Aging with a disability: What do they expect after all these years?* York, England: Joseph Rowntree Foundation.

9

Quality Assurance and Quality Management in Services

Christian Klicpera and Barbara Gasteiger-Klicpera

In the 1990s, there was increasing interest among many professionals in the developmental disabilities field in ensuring a reasonable quality of care, help, and support in the services that people with developmental disabilities (e.g., mental retardation) use and in continuing to increase this quality (Bradley & Bersani, 1990, Goode, 1994; Martin, 1993; Pfeffer & Coote, 1991). This interest extended to the area of services for older adults with developmental disabilities (Moss, 1994; Pilling & Watson, 1995). The organization and the structure of services provided for the older population with mental retardation will be a particularly important task in the 21st century. To be able to offer high-quality services to older adults with developmental disabilities, service providers need to develop quality assurance measures and gear their approach to service provision to the wishes and needs of consumers in the development of all measures for this steadily growing group of people.

This chapter provides an overview of the origins of these concerns. Emphasis is placed on the clients' wishes and the need to ensure quality of care in a variety of environments. It examines not only safeguards against abuse and neglect but also the means by which to empower clients, support relatives, and encourage staff to focus on and improve outcomes. Incentives to improve quality as well as the problems and resistance to such change are discussed. The examples referred to in the different parts of the chapter are based mainly on empirical studies conducted in northern Italy and in Austria.

In looking for the reasons for the increased concern about quality in services for people with disabilities, the first point to note is that the developmental disabilities field has been looking to ensure quality for a considerable time. In the 1950s, professional organizations and associations, particularly those in the United States, concerned with the well-being of people with disabilities formulated standards in-

tended to provide guidelines for the management of large institutions for people
with disabilities. This activity was prompted by the then-growing danger of neglect
of consumers and the limitation of the rights of people with disabilities. Efforts to
formulate standards have continued ever since the 1950s in English-speaking countries. In contrast, in German-speaking countries, professionals and policy makers
have taken notice of debate about services and institutions for people with developmental disabilities; but as of 1999, no binding and specific guidelines for the management of these institutions and services have been developed. Other measures
were also introduced in the 1970s in German-speaking countries to safeguard quality in personal welfare services, such as regular supervisory staff sessions with an
outside consultant.

At first glance, it seems strange that not only quality development but also
quality assurance are being regarded as a priority in many European countries in the
late 1990s, even though services for people with developmental disabilities have
been greatly expanding and efforts to support them have been stepped up steadily
since the 1960s.

SOURCES OF THE CONCERN FOR ACHIEVING QUALITY ASSURANCE

What are the reasons for the lively interest, apparent everywhere in Western societies, in measures to achieve quality assurance? The increased interest in this area is
attributable primarily to the widespread and growing doubt about the quality of services and of all personal welfare services in general (Martin, 1993), and services for
people with disabilities have not been immune to these doubts. Such doubts can be
countered only through appropriate efforts to improve the quality of services.

Another closely connected factor is the pressure that limited public budgets
cause. Because of the significant expansion of services for people with disabilities
in general, costs in this area have mushroomed since the 1960s, and the need for accountability and visibility in the deployment of financial resources has become
more acute. Further expansion of these services, or indeed holding them to their
late 1990s levels, will be possible only if public acceptance of these agencies can be
increased through intensive efforts in the area of quality.

Above all, though, the nature of the preoccupations about quality assurance
have changed, as is clear from the change in the objectives of quality assurance. Ad-
mittedly, protecting clients against abuse and neglect is still a concern; but a further aim is to put into practice certain values and principles regarding the way of
life and the rights of people with disabilities. These principles include, in particular, the principle of "normalization" of living conditions, integration into the community, and lifelong help with development and support for the self-determination
of people with disabilities. Implementation of these principles calls for an ongoing
process of debate. The hoped-for positive effects of implementing these principles
will not come of their own accord but only through a constant effort on the part of
all of those involved. Quality assurance might be a means of supporting this implementation process.

Another significant change from the point of view of quality assurance is the
emphasis on the consumer's wishes. Whereas, in the past, quality assurance was essentially based on the views of experts about what constituted good professional
standards, quality assurance efforts in the late 1990s focus on the expectations of
the consumer, just as quality assurance in a commercial company aims to satisfy

the customer's expectations about the company's products and to supply these products at the lowest possible price through efficient use of resources (Zeithaml, Parasuraman, & Berry, 1990). In the services for people with disabilities, the intention here is to meet clients' needs. It is important to remember, however, that services and supports for older adults with mental retardation are intended for those who often show obvious limitations in articulating their concerns and interests. The task of identifying the concerns of these people and of making these the focal point therefore poses a particular challenge. Consumer surveys must be carefully considered and certainly should not be the sole means of gathering information about consumers. This is partly because services for people with disabilities are long term in nature and because there are few alternatives to them. Thus, the consumer's relationship is marked by dependency.

Although it is important to learn from the quality assurance efforts made in commercial service organizations with respect to the formulation of quality assurance measures, it is also important to bear in mind that the consumers paying for the services are different from the consumers who are using the services. The emphasis on a consumer orientation as a maxim of quality assurance in social services for older adults with mental retardation therefore also means that greater attention must be paid to the concerns and interests of the paying consumer (e.g., family members, public agencies).

Because the paying consumer is usually the state, institutions for older adults with disabilities have a duty of care. Their task is not only to find consumers for the offered services but also to ensure that those most in need are reached. This means making efforts not to exclude anyone whose care poses a particular challenge. It is important, however, to avoid a situation in which people who can get by with less support also take advantage of these services. This duty of care also means that services should have an overview of the needs and concerns of people with disabilities and their families within the catchment area; that is, they should also pay attention to people who do not make use of what is on offer. This is especially true in the area of services for older adults with developmental disabilities, in which special services are likely to be unknown, and therefore not used, by many. In addition, older adults with developmental disabilities may drop out of day centers for people with disabilities and therefore are at high risk of losing personal contact with services for people with mental retardation.

ASSURANCE OF APPROPRIATE CARE FOR ALL OF THOSE WHO NEED IT

This chapter first explores the consequences of service providers' duty of care before discussing quality assurance measures in existing services for older adults with developmental disabilities.

Older Adults with Developmental Disabilities Who Do Not Use Services

In general, social services professionals get involved with only those needs that are presented to them directly, either by the interested parties or through an intermediary body. In certain regions, however—particularly in rural areas—most adults with developmental disabilities live at home without ever taking advantage of the services available to people with disabilities (Innerhofer, Klicpera, & Weber, 1989; Klicpera, Gasteiger-Klicpera, & Innerhofer, 1995; Klicpera & Innerhofer, 1992). Some of these older adults with developmental disabilities have never been to school.

Neither they nor their relatives have had any experience of specific supports (apart from financial assistance) or targeted individual help.

Certain older adults with developmental disabilities may have attended a day center for some time but no longer do so because they or their relatives believed the service was no longer appropriate. Based on interviews (Klicpera et al., 1995) with such people and their relatives, it is clear that, in some cases, support would be entirely necessary and appropriate. In specific terms, this would mean initially getting together with the relatives to discuss help in structuring the day-to-day life and providing an occupation for the individual with a disability and also help with preserving and promoting the person's independence and individual interests. Above all, it would be advisable to discuss ahead of time the question of the longer-term planning of care with the relatives and the person with a disability themselves and to support the family in its decision-making process. For example, the question of who will provide care when the person's parents or, later on, his siblings become old and frail is a major concern for all families. In these respects, the caring relatives all too often find themselves isolated and do not of their own accord take the initiative to address the situation in advance and seek an appropriate solution.

To ensure appropriate care for all those needing it, social services must develop an overview of the social concerns of families with older members with developmental disability within their catchment area and take an active role in approaching the people concerned. In addition, forms of support must be developed that are appropriate for the largest number of people possible for whom the existing services are inaccessible, unsuitable, or unacceptable.

People with Mental Retardation in Homes for Older Adults

In certain regions, many older adults with mental retardation live in homes for older adults when they can no longer get the support that they need from their family. Sometimes the move to the home for older adults is made when they are still relatively young, and sometimes it is made only when they have reached an advanced age. The quality of life for people with developmental disabilities in homes for older adults varies greatly and depends largely on the organization of the home (Klicpera et al., 1995). In certain cases, this can be regarded as an appropriate way of helping people to live their lives, and homes for older adults may also offer older adults with developmental disabilities contact with other people and help them find an occupation of interest. Nevertheless, cooperation with service providers for people with mental retardation is desirable, and in some cases even necessary, so that specific support can be offered in case of difficulties.

Not all homes for older adults are willing to accept older adults with mental retardation, however. Some institutions show extreme reluctance in this regard, a reluctance that may be viewed as discriminatory. Social services providers for people with disabilities have a duty to counter such reluctance with factual information.

People with Mental Retardation Who Are
Cared for in Nursing Facilities and Psychiatric Hospitals

People with mental retardation who live in large institutions drop out of sight easily. In the 1990s, in most Western European countries, major efforts were made to transfer certain consumers from these institutions and integrate them into smaller residential facilities close to the community. Even in countries in which legislators decided that longer-term accommodation in psychiatric institutions was not an appropriate form of care and in which many individuals who had been admitted to such institutions were transferred back to their families or into community-based facilities, such as in Italy, large numbers of older adults with mental retardation remained in these institutions.

Furthermore, a wide range of care philosophies can be observed in nursing facilities, in which people with developmental disabilities live alongside people with ongoing illness and people who need pervasive supports and attention, usually older adults. Often there is little prospect of these people leading more independent day-to-day lives, and their care is limited to the most basic needs. These forms of care have little in common with late 1990s ideas about community-based integration and normalization of living conditions (Klicpera et al., 1995).

In some regions of Western Europe (e.g., South Tyrol), people are admitted to nursing facilities because of a lack of space in community-based residential facilities or because the people with developmental disabilities and their relatives lack adequate information. This particularly affects people who do not attend day services centers and thus do not come into contact with major agencies that offer care in residential facilities. These agencies do not believe that they are directly responsible for providing accommodation in a community-based residential facility for the individual whose former residential and care facility is no longer available to him or her. In these cases, special efforts must be made by informed social workers or physicians to obtain admission to an appropriate residential program. The will to do so may not always be there because of lack of information and lack of awareness of the alternatives. To some extent, nursing facilities are also regarded as catchall solutions for people who cannot manage on their own.

In countries in which smaller, community-based residential facilities have been developed and in which the emphasis has switched to supporting people with disabilities in residential facilities, since the early to mid-1980s, there have been fewer admissions of younger people with mental retardation to larger institutions or homes for older adults. Consequently, in certain regions of Western Europe (e.g., South Tyrol), a disproportionately large number of older adults with mental retardation live in such traditional institutions (Klicpera et al., 1995). Quality assurance for older adults with disabilities therefore must take these institutions into account. Ways of changing the care situation in these institutions and of enabling consumers' representatives to exert more influence should be found.

QUALITY ASSURANCE TO PROTECT AGAINST ABUSE AND NEGLECT

In existing social services, the primary concern of quality assurance is to guarantee protection against neglect and abuse and to guard against degrading and restrictive living conditions for those people who are unable to uphold their rights themselves. The danger of abuse and neglect is always present in service situations in which consumers depend on the services in many different ways; and effective protection can be guaranteed only if this danger is recognized and only if special precautions are taken to investigate suspicions of abuse with regard to necessary care. Older adults with mental retardation and especially older women with developmental disabilities are particularly exposed to the danger of abuse or neglect (Lindley et al., 1995). Formal procedures and clear rules for handling complaints may be of help, particularly if they include protection for the complainant and lead to an independent, thorough investigation of the complainant's concerns. Such complaint systems have not been introduced in all areas of social support services, and, even where they have, care is not always taken to ensure that the interested parties and their relatives are aware of such systems.

Protection is also afforded by regulations that determine, through the use of restrictive measures, which events must be reported to the state supervisory authority or to the central educational authority and how such reports must be handled. By no means do all countries include such rules in their regulations on the management of institutions and agencies offering services of support for people with disabilities.

QUALITY ASSURANCE AS A MEANS OF ENSURING STRUCTURAL AND PROCESS QUALITY

Besides its protective function, quality assurance should also play a proactive role, looking at ways of helping clients to enjoy a higher quality of life and to lead a life within the community that is valued and as satisfactory as possible. There are various ways of achieving this objective. The first way, which one might call the professional route, requires the formulation of guidelines or objectives regarding the work to be done by services and the quality of that work. This can be done by formulating standards that lay down guidelines defining good practice. Subsequently, the services should be examined from the point of view of their structure and the parameters within which they operate with regard to how far they are able to achieve high-quality services and how far the implementation of these measures meets the standards of good practice (Kimmich, 1990).

The formulation of standards has come largely from the professionals and is therefore closely connected with the state of development and degree of organization of staff in services for people with disabilities and the state of development of educational and scientific institutions in this area. This may be one reason why such standards have been formulated in only a few countries and why in many countries they hardly exist at all. When formulating standards, it is also possible to take into account the concerns of interested organizations or of people representing the interests of people with disabilities. One could even say that standards work as guidelines only if they have been formulated jointly by the professional community and professionals representing people with disabilities. It is necessary to discuss them thoroughly and to repeatedly revise them to incorporate innovations and keep up with developments. The standards published in the United States by the Accreditation Council on Services for People with Developmental Disabilities (1990, 1993, 1997), now known as the Council on Quality and Leadership in Supports for People with Disabilities, formulated jointly by the professional associations of experts working in the human services (e.g., teachers, occupational therapists, psychologists, social workers), scientific organizations, and representatives of consumers' interests, can be regarded as a successful example.

Standards as Guidelines for Quality Development

Standards laid down as conditions by state or public authorities have not always been successful, although there have been relatively few systematic studies in this area (e.g., Holburn, 1992). A number of criticisms have been leveled against the definition of standards in a unilateral way:

- *Unmanageability:* The formulation of standards involves a listing of many different aspects. This can lead to a list of hundreds of aspects, which is therefore unmanageable.
- *Priority of external (i.e., physical) conditions:* Because these are easier to define, they are overemphasized and therefore assume excessive importance.
- *Bureaucratization:* To guarantee the verifiability of standards, the written documentation must be extended. This carries the risk of making human services overly bureaucratic.
- *Reactive goal setting:* Because standards are intended primarily to prevent undesirable states of affairs and minimize risks, they tend to discourage innovation and prevent creativity.

These criticisms show that close attention must be paid to the way in which standards are introduced, the manner in which they are handled, and the general conditions under which they are formulated. The positive aspects are likely to prevail if standards are used not to control institutions but rather to serve as guidelines for quality development, combining the verification of standards with ideas, recommendations, or other prospective measures aimed at developing institutions. Standards then provide guidelines for the development of institutions. These involve both general objectives and values, along with specific and detailed recommendations on working methods in the various forms of institutions. Care must be taken, however, to ensure that the standards contain sufficient room to maneuver so that innovations and adaptation to local needs can be made.

The obligation to comply with certain standards should be assumed as a voluntary decision on the part of an institution or sponsor, which thereby demonstrates that it applies certain standards to its own work. This can and should be associated with a certain accreditation system under which the institutions demonstrate that they are at pains to adhere to these guidelines. They would also subject themselves to regular inspection, with the development of proposals for change and special measures (e.g., further training for staff) if an institution fails to meet the guidelines. The Council on Quality and Leadership in Supports for People with Disabilities (1997; formerly known as the Accreditation Council on Services for People with Developmental Disabilities) in the United States and the accreditation system of the National Autistic Society in Great Britain provide examples of how this may be done (Morgan & Reynolds, 1996). These examples are sensible and practicable because the standards define specific guidelines based on a wide-ranging debate, with all of those involved having a say, and they are therefore widely accepted from the outset. The standards are formulated by a body that is independent of the management of the institutions, thereby ensuring that the standards can provide new stimuli rather than simply maintaining the status quo. It is very important, when formulating the standards, that the experiences of professionals, the results of scientific analyses, and the concerns of consumers or of consumers' representatives be taken into account, primarily for the following two reasons:

1. *Standards are value-oriented:* Realistically, standards can be agreed on only in an open debate among all of the parties involved—people with disabilities themselves and their representatives, professional staff working in services, and the management of agencies. This initially requires agreement on certain principles from which the standards themselves can then be derived.

2. *Standards make sense only if their implementation is ensured:* Clear and real-
    istic proposals must be formulated with regard to which measures are neces-
    sary in order to achieve the stated goals. To define standards therefore calls for
    a professional debate about the demands and methods of professional activities
    within the social services.

There seems to be little point in each service provider attempting to formulate
its own quality guidelines. Certain investigations have shown that there is a tendency to omit critical areas or to formulate standards in too general a manner. Therefore, the efforts of representatives of consumers' interests and of scientific organizations are particularly important. It is necessary to look at the growing range of
services made available and the different objectives of those services. In addition,
one should also take into account differing needs resulting from the severity of an
individual's disability and also the individual's age. These efforts to formulate appropriate standards should be accompanied by initiatives to verify empirically indicators of the quality of the care and thereby ensure such quality.

Special Standards for Institutions Serving Older Adults with Mental Disabilities

Most standards at the end of the 20th century do not contain any criteria for special
institutions for older adults with developmental disabilities, such as day services
centers, or guidelines for bringing existing institutions into line with the needs of
older adults with mental retardation. One might introduce additional features for
occupational centers, for example, to meet the desire of consumers for occupational
activities to be extended, perhaps with additional rest periods. It would also be desirable to lay down guidelines concerning medical diagnoses and medical care and
to address the problem of sensory deprivation often encountered in older adults
with developmental disabilities. Specific tasks and problems may require special attention in systems of support aimed at older adults with mental retardation:

*   Traditional daily structures should include a range of features enabling a grad-
    ual transition to a new phase of life in which there is less emphasis on work.
*   Special features should be available that prepare for this new phase of life and
    give clients a realistic idea of how they can organize their life without regular
    work. One should stimulate interests that give a positive structure to their new-
    found free time.
*   This need for a positive structure applies not only to those who are employed
    within daily structures (i.e., traditional environments) for people with disabili-
    ties but also to those whose employment outside the traditional daily structure
    will fade as they grow older.
*   There is also the risk that, as consumers drop out of these daily structures, they
    will lose contact with the agency for special services. Provision must be made
    for such people by providing subsequent care in which allowance is made for
    any emerging needs.

Special needs also arise in the area of accommodation. Generally speaking, the
needs of older adults with mental retardation are not fundamentally different from
those of younger people with disabilities, but the context of their needs or their life
circumstances may be different. A critical aspect in residential facilities for people
with mental retardation is support for contact with relatives, particularly in cases

in which the individual's parents are deceased. In such cases, greater account must be taken of the needs of relatives. If the parents are no longer wholly able to provide the requisite support, then more help must be provided to accommodate the individual in a new environment. Older adults must also be helped to fulfill their need to reminisce, to remember phases of their life, and to communicate their experiences. Preparation for this phase of life should begin at an early stage, perhaps by helping consumers put together a file of keepsakes, a photo album, and other mementos that will later help them to remember those times.

QUALITY ASSURANCE THROUGH EMPOWERMENT OF CONSUMERS

The formulation of standards is only one step in the context of quality assurance measures. According to Pfeffer and Coote (1991) and Walker (1992), it is at least as important to enable clients or their relatives and representatives to have a say in their care. Because the aim of the quality assurance effort is to focus more strongly on the needs of the person with a disability as consumers of the services, it is important to empower them formally within the institutions. People with disabilities and their relatives have a dependent relationship with social services, however. Therefore, the right to have a say does not mean a great deal on its own. To be able to have a say and to have a share in decision making, consumers and their relatives must be adequately and comprehensively informed. Important decisions must be made with them well in advance. Also, care must be taken to ensure that people representing consumers' interests are also able to voice their concerns.

IMPORTANCE OF EXTERNAL EVALUATION
IN THE CONTEXT OF QUALITY ASSURANCE

Another priority in the context of quality assurance is to promote processes that prevent blindness to organizational shortcomings. These are an important addition to internal quality assurance measures. The advantage of internal quality assurance is that it involves a continuous process to ensure that predetermined goals are achieved and discussed measures are implemented. This form of quality assurance is vulnerable, however, to the risks that organizational blindness may set in as a consequence of day-to-day routine and that other ways of organizing the work will be disregarded. To avoid this, it should be possible for ideas and innovations to be accepted from outside the organization. Independent outsiders can give a more objective assessment and express their views more openly. To put this concept into practice, outsiders should be invited to visit the institution to speak to consumers and staff in order to fully acquaint themselves with the institution's methods of working. It may be advantageous to involve several observers in this process so that different points of view and experiences can be incorporated. In this context, it is particularly worth mentioning a model adopted in several places (e.g., Connecticut Department of Mental Retardation, Division of Quality Assurance, 1989). Teams are made up of consumers of other institutions, relatives of people with disabilities, and staff who regularly visit institutions for people with disabilities for 1–2 days, and then record, report, and offer feedback on their findings. When necessary, joint recommendations are formulated with regard to how the work can be improved.

For example, an investigation was carried out in northern Italy in the province of South Tyrol/Alto Adige (Klicpera et al., 1995). This investigation aimed at identifying critical points in the quality of care through participatory observation in residential facilities and through discussions with staff and residents. Some of these points, which we have also observed in other institutions and that are also relevant to older adults with mental retardation, can be summarized as follows:

- There is a tendency toward group treatment that is more conspicuous to outsiders than to caregivers. This may lead to a situation in which there is tacit agreement that all residents of a residential facility should spend all of their free time in the group. In this case, it can be observed that consumers, though they have single rooms, hardly ever use them. In most of the cases, the rooms are not a congenial place in which to stay because they lack adequate furniture to sit, though there is sufficient space for furniture.
- There is lack of encouragement of independence. Fixed routines, insufficient confidence in the abilities of the residents, or lack of the prospect of a more independent form of life lead to a situation in which staff members do more to ensure a smooth daily routine than to enable residents to live as independently as possible.
- There is a tendency to organize everything within the facility rather than make use of resources in the general community or of social life in the environment.
- There is a danger that the interests of the institution prevail over the interests of adult people with developmental disabilities (e.g., in the question of where residents should spend weekends and holidays, whether with relatives or in the residential facility).
- There is a danger that care is determined by the interests of staff (e.g., division of care services between professional caregivers and volunteer personnel).

Some of the preceding dangers arise from the structure or organization of the facility, whereas others have more to do with the approach (e.g., training, motivation) of staff.

QUALITY ASSURANCE THROUGH RESULTS

Quality assurance should also come from the results of work for people with disabilities and ensure that the performances of services contributes to an increase in consumers' quality of life and meets with consumers' satisfaction. One of the basic difficulties in quality assurance of services for people with disabilities, however, is that the results of many personal welfare services often are not easily measurable or reducible to simple indicators. One way of arriving at a more general view, which seems appropriate for more comprehensive services such as those offered in residential facilities, is the concept of quality of life, which can be subdivided further into many different aspects and gauged by means of subjective and objective indicators (Borthwick-Duffy, 1992). One should always start with the needs of the people with disabilities (Bensch & Klicpera, 1994; compare Chapter 6). The individual's preferred lifestyle (including his values and his potential for self-determination) must be taken into account when assessing quality-of-life indicators.

To arrive at usable indicators of the quality of social services for older adults with mental retardation, service providers need to know more about how the articulated needs adjust to the prevailing circumstances and how such needs change with time, especially during the individual's old age. Besides determining the effect on quality of life of various services of a facility by means of objective indicators, measurement of consumers' satisfaction represents an additional form of quality assurance through results. The general dimensions of consumers' expectations, according to Zeithaml and colleagues (1990), provide a good starting point but must be adapted to the specific characteristics of the service in question. Reliability is probably the most important criterion in the assessment of services by clients and their relatives. Consumers must be able to rely on the services and should not have to worry about their being available when needed. Another important dimension is the integrity of the services and the assurance that the well-being and rights of consumers will be taken into account, that they will be treated with respect and kindness, and that financial matters will be dealt with properly. The analysis of consumers' satisfaction should also take into account the extent to which individual consumers' concerns and wishes are understood and dealt with, the speed with which consumers' concerns are responded to, and the satisfaction with the physical appearance of residential facilities and their furniture and other furnishings.

Focusing on the expected results of services should provide a clear direction for work in programs supporting older people with mental retardation. For example, the concept of quality of life can serve as a basis for the planning of individual development and support in which consumers and the people close to them are involved and in which greater importance is attached to planning by virtue of the fact that it is geared to objectives that can be verified. Generally, putting this type of analysis into casework practice should constitute a significant part of the quality assurance effort and enhance the value of and focus greater attention on the activities of frontline staff. This could prevent quality assurance measures from resulting primarily in burgeoning documentation, thus exacerbating the bureaucratic character of the human services.

INCENTIVES TO PROMOTE QUALITY

The preceding discussion was concerned largely with measures in which the quality of services can be defined, determined, or measured and, in a further stage, reported back. It is equally important to ask which incentives can be created to encourage and promote high-quality work and support economical solutions. The following incentives seem worthwhile:

- Convincing all participants that quality is a central concern
- Motivating staff to find and implement ways of improving quality
- Understanding that quality of life cannot be created through regulation and eliciting instead commitment and involvement, not just the objective application of measures, conducive to quality, to foster participation and friendship within a natural social network
- Strengthening the influence of consumers and their right to have a say
- Providing feedback about services because it is essential that staff receive specific feedback on the services they provide; feedback should be regarded as an essential part of all formal quality assurance measures to discuss impressions with staff in a constructive manner immediately afterward
- Basing further training activities on the results of quality assurance measures
- Setting clear priorities with regard to quality assurance measures because not all possible things can be done at once (A great deal of attention was paid to this method of working in the 1990s in the context of efforts to achieve ongoing

quality improvement by identifying individual areas and formulating plans for improvement.)
- Creating incentives for wiser, economical deployment of resources (e.g., visibility of costs incurred in the course of the work, possibility of autonomous deployment of resources)

The traditional methods of quality assurance, such as further training and supervision, will undoubtedly continue to play an important role, particularly if they focus more closely on specifically agreed-on objectives for caregiving. In the future, however, greater attention will be paid to giving staff special incentives for their commitment to caregiving. Such encouragement will naturally come primarily from the fact that the commitment of staff receives particular attention. One should also consider giving committed staff opportunities for professional advancement and acquisition of special skills so that they can then become involved in further training or supervision or assume managerial functions.

Among the ideas adopted from industry, the system of benchmarking is one that may contribute to an improvement in the quality of care (e.g., Keehley, Medlin, MacBride, & Longmie, 1997). The principle of benchmarking involves comparison of a subprocess in one facility with the same subprocess in another facility that is known to perform this subprocess in an exemplary fashion. This assumes that descriptions and detailed analyses of such subprocesses are available and also that the underlying conditions are known. For some tasks (e.g., the integration of people with mental retardation into the world of work, the transition from large residential institutions to some programs aimed at integration into the community), such descriptions are available, though not always with the requisite amount of detail. In Europe, however, such descriptions have not yet been developed in a full range of facilities serving older adults with developmental disabilities.

More comprehensive concepts such as total quality management seem attractive from the point of view of their basic conception and include many of the principles that have been discussed previously, such as continuous attention to quality improvement and the involvement of all staff in the effort to improve quality; but experience with the application of this approach to the field of social services is limited (Martin, 1993; Pollitt, 1996).

PROBLEMS AND RESISTANCE TO QUALITY ASSURANCE

Unfortunately, not everyone shares the concern for quality assurance. Even the public authorities in some countries are reluctant to get involved in this area. This may perhaps be because public administrations in many places do not have the structures or the specialized skills needed to define quality standards and introduce quality assurance measures.

Another significant factor may be the fear that the introduction of quality assurance measures will involve considerable additional cost. This fear largely derives from a misconception, however. Quality assurance is first and foremost an attempt to achieve increased efficiency in the use of available resources. Only if the structural conditions (e.g., the outfitting of institutions) are such that they prevent high-quality work will additional resources be needed.

Another problem is the fact that, in Europe, large organizations representing the interests of people with mental retardation are often simultaneously leading organizations in service provisions for the people with disabilities. It is a challenge for these organizations to formulate specific standards to which they must then adhere. Unfortunately, this easily can result in a tendency to vagueness.

There also may be some resistance from staff. Besides the fear that their work will become more bureaucratic, they may also feel that caregiving is not plannable and therefore is not controllable. In addition, some staff may have some difficulty in dealing with documentation tasks (Klicpera & Bensch, 1995).

CONCLUSIONS

The development of quality assurance for services in the field of mental retardation, and particularly for services for older adults with developmental disabilities, is a task that is only beginning to be addressed. This requires close cooperation, not only among the representatives of consumers' interests, the associations of the different staff professions, and those who back the agencies and the public authorities, but also between applied research and practice.

In the past, the social sciences have helped to ensure that standards for human services address important concerns regarding the improvement of process quality. Little has been done to analyze the effectiveness of quality assurance measures in the services for people with developmental disabilities, however. Applied research and evaluation might be a major help in developing quality assurance. This involves both examination of the objectives of the work and model examples and also the development of suitable methods for the implementation of quality assurance measures, particularly in a field such as human services for older adults with mental retardation, in which experience is limited. Scientific monitoring of the efforts to create appropriate care structures are particularly important. Special attention should be paid to the situation of staff in this arena because their motivation and social and technical skills are crucial to the quality of social services.

REFERENCES

Accreditation Council on Services for People with Developmental Disabilities. (1990). *Standards and interpretation guidelines for services for people with developmental disabilities.* Landover, MD: Author.

Accreditation Council on Services for People with Developmental Disabilities. (1993). *Outcome based performance measures.* Landover, MD: Author.

Bensch, C., & Klicpera, C. (1994). Lebensqualität durch Förderung?! Von der vorbereitenden Förderung einzelner Fertigkeiten zur lebensstilbezogenen Entwicklungsplanung für Menschen mit geistiger Behinderung [Quality of life through educational programming? From preparatory training of specific skills to lifestyle-related developmental planning for people with mental retardation]. *Behinderte in Familie, Schule und Gesellschaft [People with Disabilities in Family, School, and Society], 17*, 39–44.

Borthwick-Duffy, S.A. (1992). Quality of life and quality of care in mental retardation. In L. Rowitz (Ed.), *Mental retardation in the year 2000* (pp. 52–66). New York: Springer-Verlag New York.

Bradley, V.J., & Bersani, H.A. (Eds.). (1990). *Quality assurance for individuals with developmental disabilities: It's everybody's business.* Baltimore: Paul H. Brookes Publishing Co.

Connecticut Department of Mental Retardation, Division of Quality Assurance. (1989). *Program quality review of homes and residences.* Hartford: Author.

Council on Quality and Leadership in Supports for People with Disabilities. (1997). *Personal outcome measures.* Towson, MD: Author.

Goode, D.A. (Ed.). (1994). *Quality of life for persons with disabilities: International perspectives and issues.* Cambridge, MA: Brookline Books.

Holburn, C.S. (1992). Rhetoric and realities in today's CF/MR: Control out of control. *Mental Retardation, 30,* 133–141.

Innerhofer, P., Klicpera, C., & Weber, G. (1989). *Erwachsene Behinderte in der Landwirtschaft: Eine empirische Erhebung über die Eingliederung Behinderter am Bauernhof [Adults with developmental disabilities in farming: An empirical investigation about the integration of adults with developmental disabilities on farms].* Vienna: University of Vienna, Institute of Psychology.

Keehley, P., Medlin, S., MacBride, S., & Longmie, L. (1997). *Benchmarking for best practices in the public sector: Achieving performance breakthroughs in federal, state, and local agencies.* San Francisco: Jossey-Bass.

Kimmich, M.H. (1990). The South Carolina model. In V.J. Bradley & H.A. Bersani, Jr. (Eds.), *Quality assurance for individuals with developmental disabilities: It's everybody's business* (pp. 281–300). Baltimore: Paul H. Brookes Publishing Co.

Klicpera, C., & Bensch, C. (1995). Qualitätssicherung durch Planung und Dokumentation: Gefahren und Chancen [Quality assurance through planning and documentation: Risks and chances]. In A. Evers, K. Leichsenring, & C. Strümpel (Eds.), *Klientenrechte: Sozialpolitische Steuerung der Qualität von Hilfe und Pflege im Alter [Clients' rights: Sociopolitical steering of quality in help and caregiving for older adults]* (Schriftenreihe Soziales Europa Bd. 5 [Social Europe Series, Volume 5], pp. 133–139).Vienna: Bundesministerium für Arbeit und Soziales.

Klicpera, C., Gasteiger-Klicpera, B., & Innerhofer, P. (1995). *Lebenswelten von Menschen mit geistiger Behinderung: Eine empirische Bestandsaufnahme in Südtirol [Spheres of life of people with mental retardation: An empirical investigation in Southern Tyrol].* Heidelberg, Germany: Asanger Verlag.

Klicpera, C., & Innerhofer, P. (1992). *Integration behinderter Menschen in die Arbeitswelt. Neue Formen der Arbeitsintegration und traditionelle Beschäftigungseinrichtungen [Work integration of people with disabilities: New forms of integration in the workplace and traditional occupational facilities].* Heidelberg, Germany: Asanger Verlag.

Lindley, P., Band, J., Gorf, B., Guerrero, M., Walker, D., & Sells, K.G. (1995). What do users think about quality? In D. Pilling & G. Watson (Eds.), *Evaluating quality in services for disabled and old people* (pp. 148–157). London: Jessica Kingsley Publishers.

Martin, L.L. (1993). *Total quality management in human service organizations.* Thousand Oaks, CA: Sage Publications.

Morgan, S.H., & Reynolds, B. (1996). Evaluating services for adults with autism: The Autism Quality Audit and Accreditation Programme. In S.H. Morgan (Ed.), *Adults with autism: A guide to theory and practice* (pp. 53–73). Cambridge, England: Cambridge University Press.

Moss, S. (1994). Quality of life and aging. In D.A. Goode (Ed.), *Quality of life for persons with disabilities: International perspectives and issues* (pp. 218–234). Cambridge, MA: Brookline Books.

Pfeffer, N., & Coote, A. (1991). *Is quality good for you? A critical review of quality assurance in welfare services.* London: Institute for Public Policy Research.

Pilling, D., & Watson, G. (Eds.). (1995). *Disability and rehabilitation series: Vol. 7. Evaluating quality in services for disabled and old people.* London: Jessica Kingsley Publishers.

Pollitt, C. (1996, November). *Business and professional approaches to quality improvement: A comparison of their suitability for personal social services.* Paper presented at the STAKES/European Centre for Social Welfare and Research Seminar, Helsinki, Finland.

Walker, A. (1992). Towards greater user involvement in the social services. In T. Arie (Ed.), *Recent advances in psychogeriatrics* (Vol. 2, pp. 5–18). Edinburgh: Churchill Livingstone.

Zeithaml, V.A., Parasuraman, A., & Berry, L.L. (1990). *Delivering quality service: Balancing customer perceptions and expectations.* New York: Free Press.

III

Service Models and Innovations

10

Emerging Models

Tamar Heller

Most developed countries are shifting their conceptualization of services for older adults with mental retardation toward greater inclusion of these individuals in community life, more recognition of person-centered approaches, and more support in the natural context. This chapter highlights these major advances in services and supports for older adults with mental retardation and their families. It focuses more heavily on the U.S. experience but also includes some examples from other countries.

The goals of services and supports for older adults with mental retardation are to enhance and maintain their physical, social, and emotional well-being. As with the general population, many of these adults and their caregivers experience declines in health and losses in their natural supports as they age. For some subgroups of adults with mental retardation (e.g., adults with Down syndrome), age-related declines occur earlier than they do for the population of older adults without disabilities.

The challenges of support services and intervention programs are to respond to the changing needs of people with mental retardation and their families in the context of societal changes. The following are the contextual changes that are shaping services and supports for this population:

1. Demographic trends
2. Emerging service models
3. Service programs
4. Family caregiving support needs and models

This chapter is supported in part by the Rehabilitation Research and Training Center on Aging with Mental Retardation, University of Illinois at Chicago, through the U.S. Department of Education, National Institute on Disability and Rehabilitation Research Grant No. H133B30069.

5. Technological advances
6. The self-advocacy movement

DEMOGRAPHIC TRENDS

Throughout the developed world, the number of older adults is increasing rapidly at the turn of the 21st century. In the United States, estimates indicate that the percentage of people ages 60 years and older will increase from 17% in 1990 to 25% by 2030 (U.S. Bureau of the Census, 1992). Similarly, the number of older adults with mental retardation also is rising. With improved health and social conditions and new technologies, the life expectancy of adults with mental retardation continues to rise. Most adults with mental retardation other than those with Down syndrome are likely to have a life span similar to that of adults without disabilities (Heller, 1997). With the longer life span comes a longer period of family caregiving. Hence, adults with mental retardation are more likely to outlive their parents than they were before the end of the 20th century (Seltzer & Krauss, 1994). Both of these demographic trends contribute to the burgeoning interest among service providers in developing models that can address issues of aging among adults with mental retardation.

EMERGING SERVICE MODELS

Since the early 1970s, philosophies of serving and supporting people with mental retardation have changed dramatically. Bradley and Knoll (1990) articulated three phases of the development of service philosophies: 1) institutionalization and segregation, 2) deinstitutionalization and community development, and 3) community membership. The first phase emphasized the medical model and the segregation of people with disabilities from the rest of the population. The second phase emphasized the developmental model, with services being offered in specialized environments that helped prepare individuals for integration into less restrictive environments in the community. The third phase of community membership, which is the emerging model in the United States, emphasizes individualized support to help people function in the community and to become wholly integrated into the life of the community. Service delivery in the community membership phase incorporates the following elements:

*   Greater commitment to community and family as resources
*   Emphasis on human relationships and friendship
*   Individualized life plans and person-centered programming
*   Choice and control by people with disabilities
*   An emphasis on quality of life

Only in the 1990s did professionals begin to pay specific attention to older adults with mental retardation. Several alternative philosophies about the conceptualization of services for older adults with mental retardation developed. Some of the models parallel the phases described previously. The most segregated model is one in which specific programs are developed for this group, such as housing developed specifically for older adults with mental retardation or a separate day program created specifically for this group. The second model includes efforts to integrate older adults with mental retardation into the aging network system, including centers, housing, and day programs for older adults. A variant of this model is offering services that are part of mental retardation programs for older adults to older adults in the community who do not have mental retardation. The third model, which fits in with the community membership model, emphasizes individualized programs. These programs can include a wide variety of choices, including staying with mental retardation services, using services for older adults, or using general community services. For example, an individual may choose to conduct leisure activities at a local recreation center and to receive supported living services from the mental retardation service network. The family caregivers may receive support from a local provider of services for older adults. In this model, using a person-centered approach, the needs and preferences of the individual with mental retardation and his or her family drive the process of developing a support plan.

In examining aging and developmental disabilities perspectives in nine countries, Moss (1992) found considerable variation in these countries' embrace of the aging network for this population and in their use of institutional models. For example, in The Netherlands and in Germany, institutional care is a viable and important option in the service system. Haveman and Maaskant (1992) noted that providers of services for older adults without disabilities in The Netherlands lack experience in helping people with developmental disabilities, particularly with regard to people with severe disabilities. In North America, Australia, and Great Britain, there is a strong emphasis on deinstitutionalization and community integration. The population in these countries who live in institutions has decreased drastically since the 1970s, and these countries' community programs have increased markedly.

In the United States, there are numerous examples of successful efforts to integrate older adults with developmental disabilities into aging network services (Janicki, 1994). Arguing against these efforts to bridge the developmental disabilities and service networks for older adults, Blaney (1992) asserted that the aging network programs tend to be inferior to the developmental disabilities programs and often result in more rather than less segregation from people without disabilities in the community. Moss (1992) noted that, in Britain, residential facilities for older adults are often inappropriate for people with developmental disabilities. In these homes, in comparison with homes designed specifically for adults with developmental disabilities, adults received poorer service in terms of individualized programs, community involvement, and leisure pursuits.

In the United States, a national survey (Factor & Anderson, 1992) of innovative day and residential services and service coordination for older adults with mental retardation identified techniques and exemplary programs used to foster person-centered planning and community inclusion. These programs trained individuals with mental retardation in choice making, provided them with information about community resources and service options, and provided assistive technology devices. They used volunteers and allowed individuals to have reduced work schedules to foster individualized approaches.

SERVICE PROGRAMS

The subsections that follow discuss the different types of service programs available to older adults with developmental disabilities.

Residential Services

Toward the end of the 20th century, many developed countries reduced the use of large institutions and increased the use of community-based smaller homes and supported living arrangements. Among European countries, the Scandinavian countries and the United Kingdom decreased the number of older adults with mental retardation living in institutions dramatically between 1980 and 1993 (by an average of 4.25% per year) (Hatton, Emerson, & Kieman, 1995). There was little change among other European countries and some increase in institutionalization rates in The Netherlands (from 2.00 to 2.09 per thousand) and in Poland (from .57 per thousand to .61 per thousand). Although there are wide variations among European countries in the use of large institutions, the trend overall is toward community placement.

In the United States, the rate of older adults with mental retardation living in institutions decreased from .78 per thousand to .45 per thousand during the 1980–1993 period. In the 1990s, 20 U.S. states closed 60 large public institutions, and 5 U.S. states closed down all of their institutions (Braddock, Hemp, Bachelder, & Fujiura, 1995). In addition to the shift into community residences, a change in the types of services offered also occurred. Narrow definitions of residential habilitation or personal care services are shifting to cover a range of services, including personal assistance, supported living, environmental modification, assistive technology, and crisis services.

Another development in housing in the United States is state initiatives in consumer-controlled housing (e.g., Michigan, New Hampshire, Ohio, Rhode Island). In those states that have begun such initiatives, funding is available to assist adults with mental retardation to purchase their own homes with mortgages. These initiatives enable individuals to buy homes with minimal down payments. Also, they allow these individuals to take an active role in choosing the type of housing in which they live.

Despite the shift in resources from the institution to the community models, there has been little growth in the availability of out-of-home residential options. Demographic trends, however, suggest an increasing need for residential services. With the increasing life span of people with mental retardation, there is increasing pressure on the residential service system. In the United States in 1991, the vast majority of people with mental retardation and related developmental disabilities—about 60%—lived in a family home (Fujiura, 1998). Use of the residential service system increases with age, but family care is still the predominant model. Unfortunately, when families do want to make an out-of-home placement, there are long waiting lists for service. Prouty and Lakin (1998) reported that more than 80,000 adults with developmental disabilities in the United States were waiting for residential services in 1997. This figure represented only those people who had official contact with the formal mental retardation service system and thus underestimated actual need for such services. Furthermore, many older adults with mental retardation are not known to the service system. Moss (1992) identified the need for the development of out-of-home residential placement as a major unmet need in all nine of the developed countries that he studied.

Vocational Programs, Day Services, and Retirement Programs

Given that many adults with mental retardation lack regular involvement in day activities, are underemployed, or are involved in sheltered workshops in which they receive low or no pay (Ellis & Rusch, 1991), the prospect of retirement may take on a different meaning for these people from the meaning it has for people who have been employed for much of their adult lives. Retirement in this context seldom refers to actually exiting a work role and receiving pension benefits. For example, in an Australian study (Ashman, Suttie, & Bramley, 1995) of adults with mental retardation ages 55 years and older, the majority had never worked: 19% were working, 24% had worked and were currently retired, fewer than 3% were in supported or typical employment, and 74% relied solely on income from government pensions. In Britain, Moss, Hogg, and Horner (1989) reported that fewer than 3% of adults with mental retardation ages 50 years and older were fully employed, and all were in sheltered workshops. A consumer satisfaction study of 110 employees with mental retardation and other disabilities in supported employment programs in Virginia revealed that participants were relatively young. They ranged in age from 19 to 52 years old, with the average age being 32 years (Kregel & Wehman, 1996).

Several studies (Ashman et al., 1995; Factor, 1989; Heller, Sterns, Sutton, & Factor, 1996) investigated the attitude of adults with mental retardation toward work and retirement. Two U.S. studies that included interviews with older adults with mental retardation indicated that the majority of them wanted to continue working rather than retire (Factor, 1989; Heller et al., 1996). The major reasons were the money that they earned and the camaraderie of the workplace (Factor, 1989). In the Australian study (Ashman et al., 1995), 57% of these older adults with mental retardation who were still working had negative or mixed attitudes toward the prospect of leaving work, and 85% had positive attitudes toward continued employment. These studies indicated that adults with mental retardation often are reluctant to retire. It is not clear to what extent these attitudes toward retirement change as these individuals experience age-related declines in health. In some cases, they may continue working with accommodations at the worksite; in other cases, they may prefer to pursue other activities.

In many parts of the United States and in most other countries, there are few policies or supports that permit individuals with developmental disabilities to retire from programs or activities in which they have been involved and to move into other types of programs or activities. Yet, there is some increased interest in developing retirement programs. For example, a survey in Ohio of counties serving a total of nearly 1,500 older adults with mental retardation (ages 55 years and older), indicated that the number of retirement programs increased from 7 in 1984 to 57 in 1992 (Sutton, Sterns, & Park, 1993). At least two thirds of these programs included activities in centers and nutrition sites for older adults.

Existing retirement programs include approaches that vary in the extent to which they link systems for older adults and those for people with mental retardation (Janicki, 1991). The services for older adults used include older adult center and older adult companion programs, adult day services, church-run or other recreation programs in the community, and preretirement education programs.

The senior center–senior companion model facilitates community integration with other older adults by using staff, volunteers, or friends as mentors to involve these adults in centers for older adults and other community activities. Evaluations (Calkins & Kultgen, 1987; Roberts, 1990) of these programs documented some success in increasing participants' quality of life through increased social integration, enhanced self-esteem, and an increased range of activities.

The adult day services model integrates older adults with mental retardation with severe impairments who cannot participate in the network of services for older adults or in centers for older adults. This program provides day socialization and group activities for people with intense medical needs who do not require 24-

hour nursing care. It is based on the medical model aimed at people with dementia and involves the most segregation of the individual from the life of the community.

The third model, recreational leisure programs, is often administered through a mental retardation agency. These programs usually include retirement coaches or other staff or volunteers who accompany the adult to these activities. These programs vary from group programs to more individualized ones that include the person's informal support network. An example is the Community Living Program of Owen Sound District, Ontario, Canada (Groeneweg, 1992), which aimed to increase the community inclusion of individuals who had retired from the workshop or from typical employment or who had reduced their work hours. After ascertaining individuals' interests, staff provided support to realize and maintain those interests through activities such as library use, trips, weekly luncheons, films, retirement club participation, and bowling.

The fourth model, preretirement education, seeks to increase adults' awareness of later life and retirement issues, including knowledge of community resources, choice-making skills, and leisure and recreation activities (Heller, Sterns, et al., 1996; Hogg, Moss, & Cooke, 1988). Often this model is combined with the previous ones in the development of individualized plans for each of the trainees. An example is the Person-Centered Later Life Planning Project (Heller, Sterns, et al., 1996), which included older adults in Florida, Illinois, and Ohio. This training program offers training in choice making and goal planning and increases awareness of options for health and wellness, leisure activities, work and retirement, living arrangements, and friendships. It includes a training component for staff and families on later–life planning issues. In an empirical study of the program's effectiveness, Heller, Sterns, and colleagues (1996) found that it resulted in increased knowledge of later-life options and increased leisure participation for individuals who were living at home.

The success of any retirement program depends on the follow-up support and resources available in the community. For example, Ashman, Hulme, and Suttie (1990) found that, in Australia, because of the availability of services, those who lived in urban areas were more likely to be involved in community activities than were those who lived in rural areas. In the Later Life Planning Project (Heller, Sterns, et al., 1996), a follow-up on the extent to which individuals had met their chosen goals after 2 years revealed that they were most likely to have attained their recreation goals and least likely to have attained their living arrangement goals. Obstacles to attaining goals were lack of funds, transportation, or people to accompany them to activities and the belief of staff and families that a particular goal was not important or reasonable. When staff or families paid for activities and accompanied them, these individuals were more likely to attain their goals.

Health Care

As older adults with mental retardation experience age-related declines in physical health and develop secondary conditions related to their disabilities, they are likely to require more health care. In the United States, major health care service gaps identified for people with mental retardation include dental care (Jaskulski, Metzler, & Zierman, 1990), home-based medical care, and gynecological care (Minihan & Dean, 1990). Edgerton (1994) noted that, for older adults with mental retardation requiring intermittent supports who are living in the community, inadequate health care is a major threat to their ability to maintain independence. Typical problems include recognizing that there is a health problem, locating medical advice, communicating symptoms, and understanding and complying with a medical professional's instructions.

Many adults living in independent environments have poorer health habits and higher rates of obesity compared with those living in more restrictive environments (Rimmer, Braddock, & Fujiura, 1993; Rimmer, Braddock, & Marks, 1995). The highest rate of obesity in the United States is for adults living in the natural home (55%). For females, this rate is even higher (79%). The extent of obesity in adults with mental retardation differs not only by sex and living arrangement but also by country. For example, Frey and Rimmer (1995) found that the rate of obesity was higher among U.S. adults with mental retardation than among their German counterparts.

Health care professionals need more training to better respond to the health care needs of older adults with mental retardation. A needs assessment of families of adults with Down syndrome (McGuire, 1991) indicated that the major health concerns of families with regard to their relative with Down syndrome centered on health care availability, the need for health screening, and finding health care personnel knowledgeable about Down syndrome and willing to serve adults with this disability. The development of training materials for health care professionals and practice guidelines, such as those that Janicki, Heller, Seltzer, and Hogg (1996) developed for clinical assessment and care management of people with Alzheimer's disease and other dementias, is a step in this direction.

FAMILY CAREGIVING SUPPORT NEEDS AND MODELS

Family members are the most consistent source of caregiving for people with mental retardation across the life span and across most cultures and countries. Yet, sufficient supports for families are often lacking. In the United States, nearly 60% of people with developmental disabilities live with their families (Fujiura, 1998). With age, that percentage decreases because their parents are no longer able to provide care. A British study (Moss & Patel, 1992) indicated that about 32% of adults with mental retardation older than age 40 years lived at home with their families. Estimates in Germany indicated that about half of all adults with mental retardation lived with a family member (Huber, 1990).

Wide discrepancies exist among countries regarding the extent to which older family caregivers are known to the service system. Some estimates of people known to the system in the United States are as low as 40% (Krauss, 1986). In Germany, however, there is more confidence that service providers are aware of nearly all of the families of people with mental retardation (Adam, 1992). Although countries vary in the extent to which families of people with mental retardation are known to the service system, across most locales, there is a consistent and strong need for more residential care and more support for families. This is evidenced in the United States, as it is in many other countries (e.g., in Belgium; Van Walleghem, 1993), by long waiting lists for residential services (Prouty & Lakin, 1998).

Older family caregivers of adults with mental retardation often face the dual strain of caring for their relative with a disability and coping with their own aging process. For these families, the major concerns are continuing to maintain the relative in the family home and planning for the time in the future when the parents can no longer provide care. These concerns were well documented in several studies conducted in the United States (e.g., Heller & Factor, 1993), Ireland (Seltzer et al., 1995), and Belgium (Van Walleghem, 1993). In each of these studies, a major finding that stood out was that families often do not plan for the future. For example, in the Heller and Factor study, nearly three quarters of the family caregivers of adults with mental retardation who were older than age 30 years did not make living arrangement plans for their relatives with mental retardation. Also, families frequently refrained from discussing future care plans with other family members, including the person with mental retardation (e.g., Heller & Factor, 1993; Smith & Tobin, 1989). In a study of a family support program for adults with developmental disabilities in the United States, nearly 61% of family caregivers had never discussed the service plan with their relative (Heller, Smith, & Kopnick, 1992).

Future planning also involves providing for the relative financially and providing for guardianship when the relative is deemed incompetent to make decisions. Smith, Fullmer, and Tobin's (1994) study comparing families who were using day programs for their relative with those who were not using such programs reported that 56% of the user group and 32% of the nonuser group had made guardianship plans. There is some debate about the extent to which guardianship is the best option because it can be a means of stripping people with mental retardation of their rights. Other approaches are limited guardianship or less restrictive options such as mentors and trustees, which are used in Sweden (Herr, 1995). In Sweden, the mentor (*godman*) provides advice and guidance rather than holding complete control of the individual's life or property. The trustee (*forvaltare*) option is similar to guardianship, except that the person retains the right to vote. Another aspect of future planning that is rarely studied is advance directives about who can make health care decisions for someone who later becomes incapacitated.

Family attitudes to future family caregiving are likely to be influenced not only by service quality and availability but also by the sociocultural context of families. For example, in studies (e.g., Markwardt, Heller, Rowitz, & Farber, 1993) across cultures in the United States, African American families were more likely to want to maintain care in the family home than were European American families. In most cases, the parents expected that other siblings would take over the responsibility of caring for their relative with mental retardation. They viewed caregiving for siblings as part of their cultural value of extended-family relationships. Hispanic American families, for example, tended to report less caregiving burden, and African American families tended to report that the siblings of their relative with mental retardation experienced less caregiving burden than European American families reported (Heller, 1994).

In a cross-national comparison, Seltzer and colleagues (1995) reported that, in comparison with older caregivers in the United States, older caregivers in the Republic of Ireland and Northern Ireland were less likely to make future plans and had poorer health, a smaller support network, more parenting stress, and less life satisfaction. Nearly 20% of the mothers of children with mental retardation in the Republic of Ireland reported that there was no one in their personal support networks on whom they could rely for emotional or instrumental assistance. In sharp contrast, the same was true for only 2% of the mothers in the United States or in Northern Ireland. Seltzer and colleagues believed that these striking differences across the countries demonstrated the distinct role that culture plays in shaping parenting experiences. National differences with respect to political stability, religious homogeneity, and economic conditions could have accounted for these differences in caregiving patterns and well-being.

In another cross-national comparison, this time between the United States and The Netherlands, Heller, Haveman, and Van Berkum (1996) found that older parents in The Netherlands were more likely to make future plans and had fewer unmet needs for supports than parents in the United States. This circumstance might be explained by differences between the two countries' service systems. In The Netherlands, the greater use of service coordination, the higher stipends given to families of adults with mental retardation, and the greater availability of residential options could explain parents' greater likelihood of making future plans. In both countries, parents who had higher unmet service needs reported more caregiving burdens.

Major unmet service needs of families caring for adults with mental retardation include information about out-of-home residential options, home-based support services, and estate planning. In a study of older family caregivers in Belgium (Van Walleghem, 1993), the majority of parents reported that they were never informed that home-based support services existed, and many reported frustration with long waiting lists for services. The key needs of families reported in the United States (Heller & Factor, 1994) were for information regarding residential programs, financial plans, and guardianship.

Despite the fact that, in the United States, most people with mental retardation live with family members, total federal spending for family support services is low, representing only 2% of 1996 expenditures for mental retardation services (Braddock, Hemp, Parish, & Westrich, 1998). Although family support comprises a small portion of these expenditures, the total money allocated increased from $171 million to $488 million between 1988 and 1996. Family support includes cash subsidies, respite care, and other supports ranging from family counseling to in-home behavioral support. Most of the innovative family support programs include models of consumer control in which families determine how to spend resources. These are based on the premise that families usually know best what it takes to maintain their relative with developmental disabilities in the family home. By allowing families to pay relatives, neighbors, and friends for support services, family support programs acknowledge the importance of using the informal network. To promote such flexibility, families receive 1) cash subsidies to spend as they choose or within certain parameters or 2) vouchers to acquire supports. Despite the growing interest in experimenting with cash subsidies and vouchers, there is a reluctance to expand these programs substantially. Also, many states limit their initiatives to children with mental retardation. In a U.S. survey, 23 states permitted families to be paid for these services through the Home and Community-Based Waiver (a program included in the Economic Recovery Tax Act (ERTA) of 1981 [PL 97-34]) provided that the individual being paid was not a spouse or parent of a minor. More states noted that they intended to adopt this practice in the future (Smith & Gettings, 1994). In Europe, examples of family support services are the social pedagogical services in The Netherlands, which provide information, advice, and long-term supports, and the *Familienentlastende Dienste* (FEDs, or family support services) in Germany, which provide transportation, information and advice, and respite care.

Few studies have evaluated the effectiveness of family support initiatives for adults. In the United States, these studies (e.g., Herman, 1991; Meyers & Marcenko, 1989; Zimmerman, 1984) primarily examined cash subsidy programs that serve children. They found that these programs resulted in less stress and more life satisfaction for caregivers (Herman, 1991; Meyers & Marcenko, 1989; Zimmerman, 1984) and less need for out-of-home placements (Herman, 1991; Meyers & Marcenko, 1989). A study of a family support program for families of adults with mental retardation in Illinois found that subsidies of about $1,300, combined with service coordination and family control of the service plan and spending decisions resulted in many positive benefits to families during a 4-year period. These benefits included more community integration and improved interpersonal relationships of the adult with mental retardation, fewer unmet service needs, more service satisfaction, and less need for out-of-home placement. Families also reported greater caregiving satisfaction and self-efficacy in caring for their relative with mental retardation (Heller, Ruch-Ross, & Kopnick, 1995). The older caregivers did not differ from the younger caregivers in any of these outcomes, indicating that these programs were just as beneficial for them.

With the trend toward community inclusion of adults with mental retardation, families will continue to play a critical role in enabling adults to live in the community. Family support programs are likely to receive greater attention if out-of-home residential placements become more difficult.

TECHNOLOGICAL ADVANCES

Major technological advances in the field of rehabilitation enable individuals to maintain or to improve functional independence. *Assistive technology* (AT) includes use of equipment (e.g., communication devices, wheelchairs), procedures (e.g., new ways to perform tasks or training in using technology), and environmental modifications (e.g., ramps, grasp bars). Age-related physical declines can lead to functional declines in mobility, communication, activities of daily living, and work skills. Technology for individuals with mental retardation can provide potential benefits, including facilitation of therapeutic regimens, maintenance of physical activities, and increased social participation (Parette & VanBiervliet, 1992). It can aid individuals to age in place without having to move out of their current residence, give up their day or vocational activities, or give up their social network (Galvin & LaBuda, 1991).

Despite technological advances, most older adults without disabilities and older adults with mental retardation do not use AT devices. Most older adult consumers are reluctant to buy products that draw attention to their disabilities (LaBuda, 1988). In a study of older adults with visual, physical, or cognitive impairments who were not living in institutions, Mann, Karuza, Hurren, and Tomita (1993) found a high level of unmet need: an average of two needed AT devices per person. The people with cognitive impairments in their study had a similar number of needed AT devices but used the fewest number of devices (an average of 6 devices used compared with 14 devices among the other groups). People with cognitive impairments were the most dissatisfied with their AT devices: They reported dissatisfaction with at least one third of their devices.

In a national survey, Wehmeyer (1995) found that people with mental retardation generally underuse AT devices, partly because fewer devices are available for people with cognitive versus physical impairments. Second, even when AT devices exist, people with cognitive impairments may have greater difficulty in using them and in understanding instructions regarding use of the devices. Third, staff and family members often are insufficiently aware of AT, funding for assessment, and ways to procure AT devices.

A few studies (DeMello & Mann, 1995; Mendelson, Heller, & Factor, 1995; Pedersen, 1995; Willems & Loebl, 1995) documented the specific needs for and benefits of AT for older adults with mental retardation. Mendelson and colleagues examined the role of AT in facilitating transitions out of nursing facilities and in maintaining functioning so that older adults can age in place. As a result of the Omnibus Budget Reconciliation Act (OBRA) of 1987 (PL 100-203), which mandated that nursing facilities in the United States transfer residents with developmental disabilities who were inappropriately placed in nursing facilities into more appropriate residences, more than 10,000 of these residents have moved out of nursing facilities. In a longitudinal study of the functional limitations and AT needs and use of this group, Mendelson and colleagues found that the greater the prevalence of functional limitations, the less likely people were to move out of nursing facilities. They found that residents had not received needed AT devices. Fewer than 15% of residents with mobility impairments, 4% of those with communication limitations, and 6% of those with limitations in daily activities were using AT devices. The types of equipment that residents most needed were wheelchairs and seating systems. Pedersen (1995) documented a program of providing wheelchair seating for individuals living in skilled nursing facilities, and DeMello and Mann (1995) focused on the use of mobility-related devices by those older adults living in community residences. The latter study found the walker to be the most frequently used and most effective device for this population. Willems and Loebl (1995) presented a case study of the use of adapted controls for the television and videocassette recorder for an individual with severe developmental disabilities about to make a transition from an institution to a community residence. They emphasized the important role of staff in assisting the resident with daily routines and with the ongoing use of the AT device.

The challenge for the developmental disabilities field is to continue developing AT interventions for older adults with developmental disabilities that will enable these individuals to participate fully in the life of their community. This challenge entails not only adequate assessment of functional impairments but also assessments of individuals' environmental context and of ways to support the use of AT in the environments in which people live, work, and play.

THE SELF-ADVOCACY MOVEMENT

In the 1990s, there has been a growing recognition that personal choice and self-advocacy are important goals for adults with mental retardation (Abery & Bruininks, 1990; Pederson, Chaikin, Koehler, Campbell, & Arcand, 1993). The number of People First and other self-advocacy chapters for people with mental retardation in the United States increased from 55 in 1985 to more than 1,000 in 1996 (Hayden & Senese, 1996). Although these groups tend to focus on younger-adult issues, there are a substantial number of middle-age and older adults in these groups. Longhurst (1994) reported that, in 1992, 39% of the members of People First and other self-advocacy chapters were ages 36–50 years and 13% were ages 51 years and older. At a national convention of these chapters in Washington, D.C., in 1994, about 700 self-advocates participated in meetings. Of particular importance was that nearly 50 older adults participated in a speak-out on aging issues held at this conference. Their major concerns centered on their ability to maintain their independence as they got older and to prevent placement in nursing facilities. They spoke most poignantly about the need for supports so that they could continue living at home or in their community residences in the face of their declining health. Also, despite their older age, several of the participants spoke about their desire to obtain meaningful employment.

In most environments, individuals with mental retardation have few opportunities to make meaningful choices regarding their daily lives. Two studies (Heller, Sterns, et al., 1996; Lakin, Burwell, Hayden, & Jackson, 1992) documented these limited opportunities. Lakin and colleagues (1992) found that, among adults with mental retardation living in the community in Minnesota, a majority of adults had no personal choices regarding when they went out with friends (54%) or how they could spend their discretionary income (57%). Only 40% chose their social and leisure activities. Heller, Sterns, and colleagues (1996) found that more than 60% of older adults with mental retardation reported no personal choice regarding their vocational work and that at least 25% reported no personal choice regarding what to eat, when to use the telephone, and whether to clean or to decorate their rooms. Other studies (Heller & Factor, 1993; Sutton et al., 1993; Wehmeyer & Metzler, 1995) showed that adults with mental retardation have little direct involvement in decisions made regarding their retirement (Sutton et al., 1993) and future living arrangement plans (Heller & Factor, 1993). As Wehmeyer and Metzler (1995) noted in their study of adults of all ages, adults with mental retardation are likely to participate in choices and decisions about their lives that are of relatively low importance, such as what they wear; but they are not likely be involved in more important decisions, such as the type of work that they do.

Little empirical research exists regarding ways to increase personal empowerment for adults with mental retardation. Often the behaviors of adults with mental retardation do not match their preferences and desires (Shevin & Klein, 1984). This discrepancy could be attributed to acquiescence, expressive language impairments, and lack of experience in articulating preferences. Research (Heller, Sterns, et al., 1996) demonstrated the efficacy of assertiveness training and decision-making training in developing these individuals' choice-making skills. In their study specifically targeting older adults with mental retardation, Heller, Sterns, and colleagues examined the effectiveness of a 15-week training course in choice making and later-life planning. They found that the personal goals of the trainees (versus a comparison group) were more likely to be reflected in the actual goals developed in their planning meetings with staff and families. In addition to direct instruction in choice making, any choice-making intervention needs to systematically integrate these skills into individuals' lives and to provide opportunities and supports that help to nurture and maintain these skills in their natural environments. Support people play a critical role in enabling individuals to attain their personal goals.

Another useful feature is the development of peer trainers as co-trainers of the curriculum. For this purpose, researchers at the University of Illinois developed the curriculum *Making Choices as We Age: A Peer Training Program* (Heller, Preston, Nelis, Pederson, & Brown, 1995). An empirical test of the usefulness of the peer training intervention indicated that 8 months after completing the training program, trainees increased their knowledge of choice making and increased their choice making in their daily lives (Heller & Nelis, 1996).

CONCLUSIONS: CHALLENGES FOR THE FUTURE

In the 1990s, more attention began to be focused on developing program models that advance the quality of life for older adults with mental retardation. There are still many challenges ahead in the 21st century. Moss (1992) noted that, in many countries, there is an increasing awareness of the need to cater to this group; but there often is a lack of a coherent and firm policy because the needs of these individuals are not well articulated.

The following initiatives need to be advocated:

1. An increase in housing services to reduce waiting lists and expansion of options that offer consumers more control and that allow people to remain in their residence as they become frail
2. Expansion of family support services that respond flexibly to the changing needs of families and that allow families to play a larger role in determining their support needs and in hiring their own support people
3. Fostering of more input from self-advocates by involving them on boards and committees and in training and monitoring services
4. Development of retirement programs that include volunteer options, integration with aging services, and inclusion in the general community
5. Fostering of natural supports through involving friends and more family members of people with mental retardation
6. Provision of supports for aging in place through the use of assistive technology (AT), flexible funding, and flexible programming
7. Stimulation of new service models that include the aging network as one of the options through joint programming, outreach to unserved families, and joint case coordination
8. Development of programs that promote health and wellness through a focus on exercise and nutrition
9. More research on program models for adults with mental retardation to improve current models and to develop new approaches

The emerging models that are most promising are the ones that can balance the preferences and desires of older adults with mental retardation and their families with their often-increasing needs for support as they experience age-related changes and losses. One challenge for both developmental disabilities and service systems for older adults is to develop programs that can accommodate successfully the changing needs of older adults within the environments in which these people live, work, and play. This could entail providing greater personal assistance, more AT devices, or environmental accommodations. It could also entail providing more family supports to enable the family to maintain caregiving or providing supported living services for those individuals who need out-of-home placements. In addition to providing financing for consumer-directed supports, an increasing need exists to develop adequate housing, employment, and health care options from which people with mental retardation and their families can choose. The most successful models coordinate services across the developmental disabilities and aging older adult service systems.

REFERENCES

Abery, B.H., & Bruininks, R.H. (1990). *Enhancing the self-determination of youth with disabilities.* Minneapolis: University of Minnesota, Research and Training Center in Community Living, Institute on Community Integration.

Adam, G.A. (1992). German perspective. In S. Moss (Ed.), *Aging and developmental disabilities: Perspectives from nine countries* (pp. 37–44). Durham: World Rehabilitation Fund/ University of New Hampshire.

Ashman, A.F., Hulme, P., & Suttie, J. (1990). The life circumstances of aged people with an intellectual disability. *Australia and New Zealand Journal of Developmental Disabilities, 16*, 335–347.

Ashman, A.F., Suttie, J.N., & Bramley, J. (1995). Employment, retirement and elderly persons with an intellectual disability. *Journal of Intellectual Disability Research, 39*, 107–116.

Blaney, B. (1992). The search for a conceptual framework. In S. Moss (Ed.), *Aging and developmental disabilities: Perspectives from nine countries* (pp. 93–96). Durham: World Rehabilitation Fund/University of New Hampshire.

Braddock, D., Hemp, R., Bachelder, L., & Fujiura, G. (1995). *The state of the states in developmental disabilities* (4th ed.). Washington, DC: American Association on Mental Retardation.

Braddock, D., Hemp, R., Parish, S., & Westrich, J. (1998). *The state of the states in developmental disabilities* (5th ed.). Washington, DC: American Association on Mental Retardation.

Bradley, V., & Knoll, J. (1990). *Shifting paradigms in services to people with developmental disabilities.* Cambridge, MA: Human Services Research Institute.

Calkins, C.F., & Kultgen, P. (1987). Enhancing the life chances and social developmental networks for older persons with developmental disabilities. In S.F. Gilson, T.L. Goldsbury, & E.H. Faulkner (Eds.), *Three populations of primary focus* (pp. 133–136). Omaha: University of Nebraska.

DeMello, M.A.F., & Mann, W.C. (1995). The use of mobility related devices by older individuals with developmental disabilities living in community residences. *Technology and Disability, 4*, 275–286.

Economic Recovery Tax Act (ERTA) of 1981, PL 97-34, 95 Stat. 172.

Edgerton, R. (1994). Quality of life issues: "Some people know how to be old." In M.M. Seltzer, M.W. Krauss, & M.P. Janicki (Eds.), *Life course perspectives on adulthood and old age* (pp. 53–66). Washington, DC: American Association on Mental Retardation Monograph Series.

Ellis, W.K., & Rusch, F.R. (1991). Supported employment: Current practices and future directions. In J.L. Matson & J.A. Mulick (Eds.), *Handbook of mental retardation* (2nd ed., pp. 479–488). New York: Pergamon Press.

Factor, A.R. (1989). *A statewide needs assessment of older persons with developmental disabilities in Illinois.* Chicago: University of Illinois at Chicago, Institute for the Study of Developmental Disabilities.

Factor, A.R., & Anderson, D. (1992). *Person-centered planning innovative approaches in case management and habilitation planning.* Paper presented at the annual meeting of the American Association on Mental Retardation, New Orleans, LA.

Frey, B., & Rimmer, J.H. (1995). Comparison of body composition between German and American adults with mental retardation. *Medicine and Science in Sport and Exercise, 27*, 1439–1443.

Fujiura, G. (1998). Demography of family households. *American Journal on Mental Retardation, 103*, 225–235.

Galvin, J., & LaBuda, D. (1991). United States health policy issues into the next century. *International Journal of Technology and Aging, 4*, 115–127.

Groeneweg, G. (1992). A Canadian perspective. In S. Moss (Ed.), *Aging and developmental disabilities: Perspectives from nine countries* (pp. 29–36). Durham: World Rehabilitation Fund/University of New Hampshire.

Hatton, C., Emerson, E., & Kieman, C. (1995). Trends and milestones. *Mental Retardation, 33*, 132.

Haveman, M.J., & Maaskant, M.A. (1992). A perspective from The Netherlands. In S. Moss (Ed.), *Aging and developmental disabilities: Perspectives from nine countries* (pp. 65–76). Durham: World Rehabilitation Fund/University of New Hampshire.

Hayden, M.F., & Senese, D. (1996). *Self-advocacy groups: 1996 directory for North America.* Minneapolis: University of Minnesota, Research and Training Center in Community Living, Institute on Community Integration.

Heller, T. (1994). *Multicultural issues and family caregiving for adults with mental retardation.* Paper presented at the annual meeting of the American Society on Aging, San Francisco.

Heller, T. (1997). Aging in persons with mental retardation and their families. In N. Bray (Ed.), *International review of research in mental retardation* (Vol. 20, pp. 99–136). San Diego: Academic Press.

Heller, T., & Factor, A.R. (1993). Support systems, well-being, and placement decision-making among older parents and their adult children with developmental disabilities. In E. Sutton, A.R. Factor, B.A. Hawkins, T. Heller, & G.B. Seltzer (Eds.), *Older adults with developmental disabilities: Optimizing choice and change* (pp. 107–122). Baltimore: Paul H. Brookes Publishing Co.

Heller, T., & Factor, A.R. (1994). Aging family caregivers: Changes in burden and placement desire. *American Journal on Mental Retardation, 98,* 417–426.

Heller, T., Haveman, M., & Van Berkum, G.H. (1996, July). *Subjective and objective caregiving intensity and future planning among aging parents of adults with mental retardation: Comparison of United States and Dutch findings.* Annual meeting of the International Association for the Scientific Study of Intellectual Disability, Helsinki, Finland.

Heller, T., & Nelis, T. (1996, May). *Research, training and leadership partnerships: Professionals and self-advocates working together.* Paper presented at the annual meeting of the American Association on Mental Retardation, San Antonio, TX.

Heller, T., Preston, L., Nelis, T., Pederson, E., & Brown, A. (1995). *Making choices as we age: A peer training program.* Chicago: University of Illinois at Chicago; University of Cincinnati.

Heller, T., Ruch-Ross, H., & Kopnick, N. (1995). *The Illinois Home Based Support Services Programs evaluation report* (Public Policy Monograph Series). Chicago: University of Illinois at Chicago.

Heller, T., Smith, B., & Kopnick, N. (1992). *The impact of a statewide family support program on aging parents of adult children with mental retardation or mental illness.* Paper presented at the annual meeting of the Gerontological Society of America, Washington, DC.

Heller, T., Sterns, H., Sutton, E., & Factor, A.R. (1996). Impact of person-centered later life planning training program for older adults with mental retardation. *Journal of Rehabilitation, 62,* 77–83.

Herman, S. (1991). Use and impact of a cash subsidy program. *Mental Retardation, 29,* 253–258.

Herr, S.S. (1995). Maximizing personal autonomy: Reforming personal support laws in Sweden and the United States. *Journal of The Association for Persons with Severe Handicaps, 20,* 213–223.

Hogg, J., Moss, S., & Cooke, D. (1988). *Ageing and mental handicap.* London: Croom Helm.

Huber, N. (1990). Perspektiven geistig Behinderter menschen im alter nach den Erfahrungen in Vollzeiteinrichtungen [Perspectives of people with intellectual disabilities who are older after their experiences in institutions]. *Aritas, 91,* 221–227.

Janicki, M.P. (1991). *Building the future: Planning and community development in aging and developmental disabilities.* Albany: New York State Office of Mental Retardation and Developmental Disabilities, Community Integration Project in Aging and Developmental Disabilities.

Janicki, M.P. (1994). A vision for the future: Aging and developmental disabilities working together. In D. Vassiliou (Ed.), *Conference proceedings of the National Conference on Aging and Disabilities: A vision for the future* (pp. 7–40). Minot: University of North Dakota.

Janicki, M.P., Heller, T., Seltzer, G., & Hogg, J. (1996). Practice guidelines for the clinical assessment and care management of Alzheimer's and other dementias among adults with intellectual disability. *Journal of Intellectual Disability Research, 40,* 374–382.

Jaskulski, T., Metzler, C., & Zierman, S.A. (1990, May). *Forging a new era: The 1990 reports: A compilation of the policy barriers identified and recommendations made by developmental disabilities councils pursuant to the 1987 requirements in the Developmental Disabilities Assistance and Bill of Rights Act.* Washington, DC: National Association of Developmental Disabilities Councils.

Krauss, M.W. (1986). *Long-term care issues in mental retardation.* Paper presented at the National Institute of Child Health and Human Development and Kennedy Conference, Mental Retardation: Accomplishments and New Frontiers, Bethesda, MD.

Kregel, J., & Wehman, P. (1996, Summer). Supported employment research: Impacting the work outcomes of individuals with disabilities. In K.J. Inge (Ed.), *Improving supported employment outcomes for individuals with the most severe disabilities newsletter* (pp. 1–8). Richmond: Virginia Commonwealth University, Rehabilitation Research and Training Center.

LaBuda, D.R. (1988). *Assistive technology for older adults: Funding resources and delivery systems.* Paper presented at the International Conference of the Association for the Advancement of Rehabilitation Technology, Montréal.

Lakin, K.C., Burwell, B., Hayden, M., & Jackson, M. (1992). *An independent assessment of Minnesota's Medicaid Home and Community Based Services Waiver Program* (Report No. 37). Minneapolis: University of Minnesota, Center for Residential Services and Community Living, Institute on Community Integration.

Longhurst, N. (1994). *The self-help/self-advocacy movement: A demographic study and directory.* Washington, DC: American Association on Mental Retardation.

Mann, W.C., Karuza, J., Hurren, M.D., & Tomita, M. (1993). Needs of home-based older persons for assistive devices. *Technology and Disability, 2,* 1–11.

Markwardt, R., Heller, T, Rowitz, L., & Farber, B. (1993). *Adaptation of African-American families to a member with mental retardation.* Paper presented at the annual meeting of the American Association on Mental Retardation, Washington, DC.

McGuire, D. (1991, September). Survey of psychosocial issues and concerns of persons with Down syndrome. *National Association on Down Syndrome Newsletter,* 1–2.

Mendelson, L.S., Heller, T., & Factor, A. (1995). The transition from nursing homes to community living for people with developmental disabilities: An assessment of the assistive technology needs and usage. *Technology and Disability, 4,* 261–268.

Meyers, J.C., & Marcenko, M.O. (1989). Impact of a cash subsidy program for families of children with severe developmental disabilities. *Mental Retardation, 27,* 383–386.

Minihan, P., & Dean, D. (1990). Meeting the health services needs of persons with mental retardation living in the community. *American Journal of Public Health, 80,* 1043–1048.

Moss, S. (1992). *Aging and developmental disabilities: Perspectives from nine countries.* Durham: World Rehabilitation Fund/University of New Hampshire.

Moss, S., Hogg, J., & Horner, M. (1989). *Residential provision and service patterns in a population of people over the age of 50 years and with severe intellectual impairment: A demographic study of elderly people with mental handicap in Oldham Metropolitan Borough (Part 3).* Manchester, England: University of Manchester, Hester Adrian Research Centre.

Moss, S., & Patel, P. (1992). Prevalence of mental illness in people with learning disability over 50 years of age, and the diagnostic importance of information from carers. *Irish Journal of Psychology, 14,* 26–35.

Omnibus Budget Reconciliation Act (OBRA) of 1987, PL 100-203, 42 U.S.C. §§ 1396 *et seq.*

Parette, H.P., & VanBiervliet, A. (1992). Tentative findings of a study of the technology needs and use patterns of persons with mental retardation. *Journal of Intellectual Disability Research, 36,* 7–27.

Pedersen, J. (1995). Wheelchair seating intervention for persons with developmental disabilities living in a skilled nursing facility: The "Bogard" consent decree. *Technology and Disability, 4,* 269–274.

Pederson, E.L., Chaikin, M., Koehler, D., Campbell, A., & Arcand, M. (1993). Strategies that close the gap between research, planning, and self-advocacy. In E. Sutton, A.R. Factor, B.A. Hawkins, T. Heller, & G.B. Seltzer (Eds.), *Older adults with developmental disabilities: Optimizing choice and change* (pp. 277–325). Baltimore: Paul H. Brookes Publishing Co.

Prouty, R., & Lakin, K.C. (Eds.). (1998). *Residential services for persons with developmental disabilities: Status and trends through 1997.* Minneapolis: University of Minnesota, Research and Training/Center on Community Living, Institute on Community Integration.

Rimmer, J.H., Braddock, D., & Fujiura, G. (1993). Prevalence of obesity in adults with mental retardation: Implications for health promotion and disease prevention. *Mental Retardation, 31,* 105–110.

Rimmer, J.H., Braddock, D., & Marks, B. (1995). Health characteristics and behaviors of adults with mental retardation residing in three living arrangements. *Research in Developmental Disabilities, 16,* 489–499.

Roberts, R.S. (1990, April). *Use of quality of life scales to measure outcomes of a project using volunteers with elderly persons with mental retardation.* Paper presented at the Growing Up and Growing Old Symposium, Institute for Research on Mental Retardation and Brain Aging, Troina, Italy.

Seltzer, M.M., & Krauss, M.W. (1994). Aging parents with coresident adult children: The impact of lifelong caregiving. In M.M. Seltzer, M.W. Krauss, & M.P. Janicki (Eds.), *Life course perspectives on adulthood and old age* (pp. 3–18). Washington, DC: American Association on Mental Retardation Monograph Series.

Seltzer, M.M., Krauss, M.W., Walsh, P., Conliffe, C., Larson, B., Birkbeck, G., Hong, J., & Choi, S.C. (1995). Cross-national comparisons of ageing mothers of adults with intellectual disabilities. *Journal of Intellectual Disability Research, 39,* 408–418.

Shevin, M., & Klein, N.K. (1984). The importance of choice-making skills for students with severe disabilities. *Journal of The Association for Persons with Severe Handicaps, 9,* 159–166.

Smith, G.S., Fullmer, E.M., & Tobin, S.S. (1994). Living outside the system: An exploration of older families who do not use day programs. In M.M. Seltzer, M.W. Krauss, & M.P. Janicki (Eds.), *Life-span development and mental retardation: Implications for individuals, their families, and the human service system* (pp. 19–37). Washington, DC: American Association on Mental Retardation Monograph Series.

Smith, G., & Tobin, S. (1989). Permanency planning among older parents of adults with life-long disabilities. *Journal of Gerontological Social Work, 14,* 35–59.

Smith, G.A., & Gettings, R.M. (1994). *The Home and Community Based Waiver and Community Support Living Arrangement programs: An update on Medicaid's role in supporting people with developmental disabilities in the community.* Alexandria, VA: National Association of State Directors of Developmental Disabilities Services.

Sutton, E., Sterns, H.L., & Park, L.S.S. (1993). Realities of retirement and pre-retirement planning. In E. Sutton, A.R. Factor, B.A. Hawkins, T. Heller, & G.B. Seltzer (Eds.), *Older adults with developmental disabilities: Optimizing choice and change* (pp. 95–106). Baltimore: Paul H. Brookes Publishing Co.

U.S. Bureau of the Census. (1992). *How we're changing: Demographic state of the nation 1992* (Current population reports series P-20, No. 468). Washington, DC: U.S. Government Printing Office.

Van Walleghem, M. (1993). Families with an elderly mentally handicapped child: Results of a qualitative study in Flanders (Belgium). In M.J. Haveman & W.H.E. Buntinx (Eds.), *Family needs and family support in mental retardation: An international perspective* (pp. 73–80). Nijmegen, the Netherlands: Kavanah Press.

Wehmeyer, M.L. (1995). The use of assistive technology by people with mental retardation and barriers to this outcome: A pilot study. *Technology and Disability, 4,* 195–204.

Wehmeyer, M.L., & Metzler, C.A. (1995). How self-determined are people with mental retardation? The national consumer survey. *Mental Retardation, 33,* 111–119.

Willems, B.F., & Loebl, D. (1995). Case study: Adapting a TV/VCR control for a person with severe developmental disability. *Technology and Disability, 4,* 287–294.

Zimmerman, S. (1984). The mental retardation family subsidy program: Its effect on families with a mentally handicapped child. *Family Relations, 33,* 105–118.

11

Mental Health
Issues of Access and Quality of Life

Steve Moss

The significance of mental health and mental illness, for ourselves as individuals and for society as a whole, would be difficult to overestimate. As Berger (1977) wrote, "At any one moment there are more people in hospital for mental illness than for all other diseases combined—including heart disease, cancer, tuberculosis or alcoholism." Although the policy of closing long-term hospitals may have somewhat altered this position, Berger's statement serves to illustrate the sheer scale of the problem. Although people are much more accustomed to reading about scandals concerning human rights abuses while individuals are under treatment, there are in fact major issues concerning the access to and the quality of mental health services for people with intellectual disability. There is a growing recognition of the need to respond more adequately to mental health problems in this population, with a number of countries developing specialist training and clinical services as well as devoting significant resources to research in this field.

Older members of this population are a group to whom increasing attention was paid in the 1980s and 1990s. There is, of course, no clear dividing line in terms of needs between older or younger members of this population, or indeed between people with and without intellectual disability. Nevertheless, aging brings about changes, both with respect to the individual and in relation to society's response to the individual and his or her problems. This chapter discusses the issues that the field needs to address if it is to adequately meet the mental health needs of older people with intellectual disability. In broad terms, these issues can be identified as 1) the problems of defining, recognizing, and diagnosing mental illness in people with intellectual disability; 2) understanding the specific mental health needs of the older segment of this population; and 3) developing appropriate service models to respond to those needs.

In some ways, it is surprising that society has taken so long to respond to the needs of this population, given that it has been known for many years that people with intellectual disability are not only susceptible to mental illness but probably much more so than people without intellectual disability. Tredgold (1908/1970), for instance, estimated that the overall prevalence of mental illness was 26 times higher among people with intellectual disability than among those without.

Why did this early knowledge not result in the development of appropriate specialist services? There is undoubtedly some sort of snowball effect that operates in almost any field of human development whereby a critical mass of public and professional opinion is needed before major change occurs. Scandal and public outcry are, of course, ways in which change can occur more rapidly, as happened in institutional care in the 1960s, leading to the deinstitutionalization and normalization movements. Mental health issues in this population, however, have not led to major scandals like those that brought institutional care into disrepute. As a result, change has been slower, and one can only guess at the impact that this tardiness has had on the quality of life of these individuals and their caregivers.

Seen from this perspective, it becomes clear why progress began to occur only in the 1990s: The mental health of people with intellectual disabilities was an issue whose time had come. In the last quarter of the 20th century, huge achievements were made in the life circumstances of people with intellectual disabilities in aspects such as housing, education, work and leisure opportunities, social engagement, interaction with the community at large, and other social domains. Service providers and to some extent the wider populace, recognize the rights of people with disabilities to a fulfilling life in the wider community. In terms of the order in which these developments occurred, one can say that the major improvements in objective circumstances of people's lives occurred between the mid-1970s and the mid-1980s, and a major shift to subjective quality of life focusing on what consumers of services themselves said they wished for and aspired to occurred between the mid-1980s and the mid-1990s. It is in this latter context that mental health issues have come to greater prominence.

This prefatory discussion suggests that the discussion cannot be restricted solely to issues of service delivery. Mental health is inextricably bound up with quality-of-life issues. A good quality of life tends to protect individuals from mental illness and minimizes the severity of illness when it does occur. Indeed, most people have so many supportive elements contributing to the overall quality of their lives that they are probably unaware of their influence, unless circumstances remove these elements from their lives. The strength of these supports is such that the vast majority of mental illness in the community can be coped with by the individuals themselves and their caregivers and in most cases do not come to the attention of mental health service providers. Obviously, the more severe and debilitating the condition, the more likely that medical help will be sought. Many factors apart from severity of the condition, however, determine whether outside help is sought. Broadly speaking, these are the same factors that contribute to quality of life in the absence of mental illness (e.g., the amount and quality of social support available to the person, the amount of stress in the person's life, the presence or absence of additional physical illness, the effectiveness of the person's coping mechanisms).

Mental health is thus a much broader notion than just the absence of mental illness. Any discussion of the rights of people with disabilities in this context must consider these wider issues—the extent to which the members of this population are being afforded the rights to a quality of life that minimizes the risks of mental illness—as well as the issues of mental health service delivery itself.

DEFINING MENTAL ILLNESS AND MENTAL HEALTH

At first sight, the concepts of health and illness seem like opposite sides of the same coin. Those people who are not healthy are ill; those who are not ill are healthy. This probably does apply to physical health—certainly from the perspective of a physician, who is likely to pronounce a person healthy if no physical illness is found. The doctor believes he or she is able to say this because, in most cases, physical illnesses can be diagnosed clearly. Thus, conditions such as tuberculosis, human immunodeficiency virus (HIV), and syphilis are defined by the presence of an organism, injuries by the presence of physical trauma, and heart disease by measures of cardiovascular functioning that prove to be atypical. In simplistic terms, people tend to think of physical illness as something that, in most cases, can be fixed. People go to the doctor, and the doctor diagnoses the condition and gives the appropriate treatment. At the same time, people may not make the same conclusion as the doctor. One may be pronounced free of physical illness but not feel well. The subjective perception of physical health is thus not as straightforward as its objective diagnosis.

The distinction between subjective and objective perceptions of mental illness is much less straightforward than for physical illness, because subjective factors—what the person says he or she feels—play such a major part in the definition and diagnosis of mental illness. Certainly, there are conditions such as dementia that have associated symptoms of mental illness, but these are clearly the result of characteristic brain damage. Similarly, toxic effects due to drugs can produce symptoms of mental disorder, but they often clear up if the toxicity is removed. Usually, however, one speaks of *mental illness* as something far less clear-cut. The most common mental disorder in the community, for instance, is a mixture of anxiety and depression. It is, of course, highly likely that some people are more susceptible to depression or anxiety than others; but such conditions often relate to life events and general life conditions, such as loss of a close relative, divorce, or loss of a job. In later life, the sense of increasing vulnerability and reducing status in society can make people particularly prone to both depression and anxiety.

Even severe mental disorders such as schizophrenia do not have clear-cut biological bases for their origin. True, schizophrenia tends to run in families, so there is some genetic component; but genetic predisposition does not seem to be enough to ensure that a specific individual will contract the illness. Also, schizophrenia can have so many different symptoms that a nonexpert could easily assume that two cases had completely different disorders. The same goes for depression and anxiety. Some people experience panic attacks, others lose their self-confidence, and still others lose their ability to engage in activities that they once enjoyed. Frequently, people experience a wide range of symptoms relating to a variety of these disorders.

Turning to the notion of mental health, it is clear that this concept is not the direct opposite of mental illness. Published definitions demonstrate that, although the absence of mental illness is a necessary condition, it is only a starting point. Concepts of mental well-being are tied up with notions of appropriate behavior within the given social context, predictability of action, and a reasonable level of integration of the various facets of an individual's personality. In 1975, the American Psychiatric Association's glossary defined *mental health* as

A state of well-being . . . in which the person has effected a reasonably satisfactory integration of his instinctual drives. His integration is acceptable to himself and to the social milieu as reflected in the satisfactory nature of his interpersonal relationships, his level of satisfaction in living, his actual achievement, his flexibility, and the level of maturity he has attained.

In 1948, the World Federation for Mental Health stated,

Mental health is a condition which permits the optimal development, physical, intellectual and emotional, of the individual, so far as this is compatible with that of other individuals. A good society is one that allows this development to its members while at the same time ensuring its own development and being tolerant to other societies.

Note that the two definitions did not even mention mental illness. Lebowitz and Niederehe's (1992) definition, however, is more encompassing of the positive and negative aspects:

Mental health is a broader notion than simply the absence of mental disorder. It implies in addition that the individual functions in desirably positive ways, manifesting some aspects of the ideal of health (even though complete attainment of the ideal may be atypical in a statistical sense). A subjective sense of well-being (as defined by such related notions as happiness, good morale, and life satisfaction) is one of the prominent features. Other aspects of positive mental health include positive self-attitudes, growth and self-actualization, integration of the personality, autonomy, reality perception, and environmental mastery.

Viewed in this way, mental health may be seen as a continuum rather than simply the presence or absence of mental illness. To those working in the field of intellectual disability, many of the concepts noted, such as life satisfaction and environmental mastery, are guiding principles in the development of a better quality of life for these individuals.

AGING, COPING, AND MENTAL ILLNESS

Aging is a process involving many facets. Apart from chronological aging, one can usefully distinguish biological aging, referring to an individual's gradual loss of physiological reserves as she or he gets older; psychological aging, relating to changes in people's adaptive capacities as they get older; and social aging, or the extent to which a person fulfills social and cultural expectations. Laslett (1989) suggested that the life course be divided into four stages:

1. *First Age:* An era of dependence, socialization, immaturity, and education
2. *Second Age:* An age of independence, maturity, responsibility, and earning and saving
3. *Third Age:* An era of personal fulfillment
4. *Fourth Age:* An era in which the individual experiences final dependence, decrepitude, and death

Although the aging process is, by definition, one of continuous change, it is important to recognize that individuals age at different rates with respect to these various facets. Such change can be highly positive, with Third Age aspirations being realized as the individual gets older. Set against such positive psychological and social developments can be factors that militate against such progress. These factors may be long term (e.g., declining health) or may involve major transitions (e.g., bereavement).

Adequate coping mechanisms are central to successful adaptation to change. The ability to cope adequately, however, depends on the person's maintaining a balance between those factors that cause stress and the resources that enable the individual to cope with them, buffering or cushioning the impact of stressors. These resources take many forms (e.g., personal, material, cultural, physical, social, interpersonal) (Murrell & Norris, 1983), and it is in this respect that most people with intellectual disability are at a major disadvantage. By definition, they have lower intellectual abilities, so their ability to acquire effective coping mechanisms is likely to be limited. In addition, the majority (apart from those whose disability is mild) have no spouse and no children and may have little or no contact with their relatives. Their financial circumstances are probably poor, and they are certainly unlikely to have a status or position in society from which they can derive self-esteem. As they age, they may suffer from poor physical health and may also lose members of their family. Because many people with intellectual disability already have impoverished social networks, this latter aspect may have an even greater impact on them than on people without intellectual disability. Overall, it is clear that the social risk factors for mental illness place many members of this population in a vulnerable position.

MENTAL HEALTH PROBLEMS

The study of mental health problems in people with intellectual disability is still in its relative infancy, and, for this reason, there are relatively few sources of accurate information on which one can call, particularly in relation to the specific topic of aging. A reasonable assumption, however, may be that the broad trends for age-related mental illness are similar to those for people without disabilities. Studies of older adults without intellectual disabilities who live in the community indicate that a high proportion, perhaps 20%, of this group who are ages 65 years and older experience definite psychiatric symptoms. Physical illnesses often accompany their psychiatric symptoms, and their physical and psychological symptoms often hinder their activities. Regarding the prevalence of conditions that are of sufficient severity to warrant a diagnosis, a minimum level of 2% is suggested by the fact that data on care show that at least 1.5% of people ages 65 years and older were under psychiatric care from either inpatient or outpatient services (reviewed in Hogg, Moss, & Cooke, 1988). Much higher estimates come from community surveys of psychiatric morbidity on general practice lists or random samples of people without disabilities. Thus, Shepherd, Cooper, and Brown (1966) found psychiatric morbidity rates within a general practice to be 11% for men and 15% for women.

Affective Disorders

Depression is by far the most common mental health problem among older adults without disabilities. Data vary from study to study, depending on population and criteria, although it is generally thought that 15%–20% of older adults without disabilities experience depressive symptoms (Shamoian, 1985). Only 15%–20% of this depressed group will receive treatment, however. Older adults experiencing severe depression show an increased use of medical services, take more psychotropic medications, and are given multiple drugs more often. They see their doctor repeatedly, receive more special investigations, and are admitted to the hospital more frequently.

In relation to people with intellectual disability, a number of studies reported important clinical findings relating to the aging process (see Day & Jancar, 1994, for a review). Affective psychoses (mostly bipolar) tend to start after age 40 and are more common in women. Paranoid psychoses are more likely to start after age 50 and are sometimes associated with temporal lobe epilepsy, severe visual and hearing impairments, and interpersonal difficulties. Patel, Goldberg, and Moss (1993) found 12 individuals of a total sample of 105 to have a diagnosable psychiatric condition (apart from dementia), for an overall prevalence rate of 11.4%. Most of the disorders detected in this older adult population were depression and anxiety—a picture similar to that of the older adult population without disabilities.

Day and Jancar (1994) also drew attention to the importance of environmental and social factors in the genesis of mental illness. These include separation from or the death of a parent, loneliness, and sudden relocation. These life events can lead to depression and anxiety, which can sometimes mistakenly be attributed to dementia.

Dementia

The most obviously age-related mental health problem is dementia. In the population without intellectual disability, epidemiological studies have shown that the prevalence of dementia rises markedly with age, from about 2% in people ages 65–70 to approximately 20% among those older than age 80 (Royal College of Physicians, 1981). Most people working in the intellectual disability field have encountered dementia principally in people with Down syndrome, who are considerably more at risk of contracting Alzheimer's-type dementia than their peers without Down syndrome. There is considerable evidence that the brains of all people with Down syndrome ages 35 and older show the characteristic changes associated with Alzheimer's-type dementia. Not all such individuals, however, show the behavioral and clinical symptoms described in the previous section. Research eventually will clarify why this should be so. In the meantime, it is important to emphasize that, despite changes in the brain due to aging in people with Down syndrome, not all of them will develop dementia.

Despite the high risk for Alzheimer's disease in people with Down syndrome, the absolute number of people with dementia without Down syndrome is probably greater. This is because a disproportionately large number of people with Down syndrome die before they reach age 50. In the Oldham study already referred to, only nine people older than 50 years with Down syndrome were found in a population of 105 individuals. Although the risk for the surviving people with Down syndrome is high, the non-Down population older than 50 years of age is about 10 times as large. These individuals have a dementia risk that is about the same as that of the general population. Unlike those with Down syndrome, these people are not likely to get dementia until they are in their 70s.

The combined prevalence for all diagnosable mental disorders in Patel and colleagues' (1993) study was 21%, a sizable proportion of the total over-50 population. In addition, the data (Moss, Goldberg, Patel, & Wilkin, 1993) on the physical health of this population showed that the group with dementia experienced much poorer physical health than the group average. Health index measures indicated poorer scores for both chronic and acute physical disorders, particularly those involving the central nervous system and gastrointestinal functioning. Many of the individuals with a firm diagnosis of dementia showed deterioration in a wide variety of self-care and community skills domains. These factors, coupled with their generally poor health, suggested that the needs of this particular group of people represent a major use of social services resources.

THE RIGHT TO MENTAL HEALTH

To summarize the discussion in this chapter so far, people with intellectual disability, and older adults with intellectual disability in particular, have elevated risk factors for mental illness. Mental health and mental illness are closely bound up with issues of quality of life, which have gained considerable attention in the 1990s in relation to the specific circumstances of people with intellectual disability. Most people are in the fortunate position of being able to take for granted basic life quality, perhaps questioning it only at times when stress or major negative life events affect us. This is not true for all people, however. Many people with intellectual disability, even if they have a good quality of life, continue to experience the negative effects of past events of their lives. Others may continue to live in adverse circumstances, having little integration with society, perhaps having no friends without disabilities and no contact with their family.

Although no segment of society can be said to benefit from perfect mental health or to have an ideal mental health service, it is nonetheless clear that most people have expectations concerning quality of life and beliefs that they have rights to certain things that improve that quality. Because this chapter has established that people with intellectual disability deserve special attention in relation to mental health, it is pertinent to ask, What is reasonable to demand in terms of basic conditions that can minimize the mental health risks? In this way, one can hopefully pinpoint areas in which improvements can be made.

Broadly speaking, these basic necessities fall into two categories. First, service providers need to ensure a level of quality of life that minimizes mental health risks and cushions the impact of negative life events. Second, high-quality mental health services are needed to help individuals if they do fall ill. These services should be available as rapidly as possible because treatment of mental disorders is most effective when applied early in the development of the disorder. Delaying intervention is likely to contribute to higher levels of persisting clinical, social, and caregiver morbidity (Crow, MacMillan, Johnson, & Johnstone, 1986).

More specifically, quality of life should be such that it provides

- A fulfilling life with opportunities for personal growth and development
- Stress levels that are not excessive
- Adequate social support

High-quality mental health service should provide

- Recognition of mental health problems when they occur
- Expert, prompt assessment

- Appropriate treatment and monitoring of outcomes
- Continued support

These two broad areas, quality of life and mental health services, provide the context for the continuing discussion of mental health issues in this chapter. It is quite clear that many people, not just those with disabilities, have life circumstances that are far from ideal. Boredom, monotony, lack of a sense of autonomy, the stress of increasing job insecurity, and family breakdown all are factors contributing to mental health problems in the community. Their crucial difference from the problems that most people with intellectual disabilities face, however, is that the positive aspects of life of most people without disabilities compensate for their problems. Thus, one might have an unfulfilling job but a rewarding and supportive home life. One's job may be stressful but may also afford high status, positive self-esteem, and an income that helps provide material comfort. People are at greatest risk for developing mental illness when compensating factors are not present. Indeed, this is the reason why older adults are particularly vulnerable. They have retired from work and from the sense of purpose and status that work affords; they may have lost most of their peer group network and may experience physical illness or frailty.

Based on the previous discussion, there appear to be many risk factors relating to the quality of life of older people with intellectual disability. The next section considers some of the findings from studies of quality of life and highlights two factors that have a major bearing on mental health.

QUALITY-OF-LIFE ISSUES

Much of the research on aging and intellectual disability prior to 1985 focused on the poor deal that many older individuals were getting relative to that of their younger peers. Studies of residential service provision in the United States showed low levels of engagement among older adults with intellectual disabilities relative to that found in facilities for younger people, often leading to a situation generating an unnecessary degree of dependency (Baker, Seltzer, & Seltzer, 1977; Willer & Intagliata, 1984). Both Baker and colleagues and Willer and Intagliata found this circumstance to be attributable to age-biased management policies rather than to the abilities of the residents themselves. Based on the views that individuals studied expressed, a number of reports drew attention to perceived negative aspects of these individuals' situations.

Thus, Sands, Kozleski, and Goodwin (1991) studied people with intellectual disability in Colorado, asking about their satisfaction with services and to investigate quality-of-life issues. Many of the adults they surveyed were unhappy with information and referral services and dissatisfied with the quality of education and personal dignity afforded by the community day programs in which they participated. The limited opportunities available to them in choosing where and with whom they lived and how they spent their money constrained the level of independence that they had obtained in adulthood. Participation in the community occurred much less frequently than they themselves desired. Elsewhere, Cattermole, Jahoda, and Markova (1990) reported that choice, privacy, social life, and relationships with their parents and staff emerged as important factors in participants' perception of their quality of life. People with disabilities who moved to community residences were found to have aspirations that encompassed far more than a wish to adapt to life in the community and that their relationships with family and staff were central in achieving such aspirations. From the specific perspective of older people with intellectual disability, an Australian study (Suttie, Ashman, & Bramley, 1993) showed that members of this population experience isolation, concern for their future, depression, a range of medical conditions, and diminishing mobility—concerns that are similar to those that one would expect among any group of older people. Indeed, these expressed concerns encapsulate the two quality-of-life factors that probably have the greatest implications for mental health: physical health and social networks. Many quality-of-life studies of older people found these two factors to be the top priorities of older adults with intellectual disability (Moss, 1994).

Quality of Life and Health

Health is a major influence on quality of life for people of all ages, but its perceived significance tends to change as people age. Generally speaking, younger people are more bound up with the notion of aspiration and progress, and older people are concerned with maintaining the status quo and preventing their worst fears from being realized. In terms of health, young and middle-age individuals tend to focus on fitness, development, and achievement; older people tend to be more concerned with maintaining the status quo—that is, with not becoming any less fit than they are at present rather than aspiring to be even fitter. Overall, the notion of peace of mind about health issues (Nystrom & Andersson-Segesten, 1990) is more relevant for older people than health in the sense of physical perfection.

Contrary to the earlier expectations of research (e.g., Sweeney & Wilson, 1979), many people with intellectual disability stay fit and active throughout their lives. This is due partly to the effect of differential survival (i.e., the tendency of weaker members of the population to die earlier) (Moss, 1991). This leads to the apparent paradox of the older population tending to be in better health and to have higher functional ability than its younger cohorts. At the same time, some individuals do experience poor health and yet survive into their later years (e.g., people with Alzheimer's-type dementia, discussed previously). In effect, the support needs of the older population thus become ever wider, ranging from those who are high functioning and in good health to those who have age-related physical and mental health problems.

The best possible attention to physical health is therefore the first basic right that should be identified. With respect to people with intellectual disability, a major obstacle to this right is that the primary health care system relies heavily on the individual's ability to identify a problem and seek help. This clearly has implications for training of health care personnel at all levels of communication skills. In addition, people with intellectual disability have specific health needs (Moss & Turner, 1995; Turner & Moss, 1996), indicating a further training agenda. These issues are discussed more fully in the section on primary health care in this chapter.

The maintenance of health does not rely solely on health services. The individual's appropriate maintenance of good health with the assistance of caregivers is an essential prerequisite if a good quality of life is to be maintained. There is an increasing emphasis on the maintenance of health for people with intellectual disability through the development and maintenance of a healthy lifestyle (Pitetti, Rimmer, & Fernhall, 1993). Although these initiatives are targeted primarily at physical health, there is no doubt that they are also beneficial to overall quality of life and mental well-being.

Quality of Life and Social Networks

Social networks are a central part of human life, the quality of social interactions being positively associated with psychological well-being in all age groups (Baker, Jodrey, & Intagliata, 1992). Regardless of differing opportunities and constraints in interactions with family members and friends, adults benefit from close personal friendships (Ishii-Kuntz, 1990). A strong social network not only can provide support in the face of stressful life events but also is shown to have a positive effect on perceived quality of life independent of major life events (Mor-Barak, Miller, & Syme, 1991). For older adults, both of these aspects of quality of life are even more crucial than they are for people without intellectual disability (Nagpal & Chadha, 1991), social activity being an important factor in the maintenance of adaptive functioning (Haga, Shibata, Ueno, & Nagai, 1991). Older adults' abilities to cope with the pressures of everyday life, with or without major life events, tend to diminish, so they have an increasing need to rely on their social network for practical assistance (Bowling & Browne, 1991). Also, older people's choices of pleasurable activities tend to focus less on high-energy pursuits and increasingly on family, friends, and the fostering of close relationships through shared tasks (Kelly, 1983).

There is no reason to doubt that older people with intellectual disability value their social contacts just as do their peers without disabilities. Social support, both instrumental and emotional, can play a critical role in enabling individuals to cope and maintain a good quality of life. This does not, however, apply only to family contact; wider friendships are also important. Unfortunately, it is clear from a large number of studies (Azmi, Hatton, Emerson, & Caine, 1997; Llwewllyn, McConnell, & Bye, 1998) that the friendship circle of many people with intellectual disability is often limited to peers with disabilities and/or staff members. These friendships should in no way be devalued, but at the same time there are compelling reasons for encouraging a broader range of contacts. Such contacts can provide these individuals with opportunities to participate in new activities and to extend their experiences and social networks.

The provision of an adequate social network is therefore the second requirement of a basic right to a mentally healthy life. Recognition of the importance of this factor is indicated by the emphasis since the late 1970s on community integration of people with intellectual disability. At the same time, it should be noted that the provision of "normalized" community living does not lead automatically to a broadly based social network ensuring participation and integration. The community experiences that most people take for granted are, for many people with intellectual disability, seriously depleted. Indeed, this also applies to many older individuals without disabilities.

Quality of Life and Psychological Development

Although health and social networks are probably the two most important quality-of-life factors in maintaining mental health, there are other domains that also may be significant. The experience of getting older is central to people's lives, whether as children or in adult life. Even fit older people are not the same as younger people. Their needs and expectations are psychologically different, although these differences may be subtle rather than gross (Moss, 1994). The experience of aging is closely bound up with critical life transitions—growing up, leaving school, getting a job, having a family, retiring, and the like. For many people with intellectual disability, these transitions may be quite different from those of their peers without disabilities. Leaving school has become a meaningful transition for many people with intellectual disability since the mid-1970s. Getting one's first job, getting a promotion, progressing in a career, and retiring, however, are not typical experiences for them. Similarly, Seltzer (1985) made the point that few older people with intellectual disability marry and have children to give them support in later life. This is of particular importance in the present context because it leads to an attenuation of the social network that many older people without disabilities take for granted.

Despite their likely differences from their peers without disabilities, people with intellectual disability do experience critical transitions in their lives. An area that has received increasing attention and that marks an event or transition familiar to all is that of bereavement. People with intellectual disability differ markedly in their understanding of and response to personal loss (Lambe & Hogg, 1995). Many have experienced bereavement and can describe its effects on them. They have attended funerals of relatives and friends. Others are less aware of bereavement and may display little emotion in discussing the loss of family members or friends. In some instances, this reflects overprotection of the person who has not had the opportunity to attend the funeral of the person, with the consequence of unresolved grief.

Coupled with the experience of bereavement is the understanding of one's own mortality. Lipe-Goodson & Goebel (1993) noted that professionals are becoming increasingly sensitive to the need to assist people in recognizing the changes that take place in people with age, including the impending deaths of friends, family, and self. These authors draw a parallel between children's perception of death and that of adults with intellectual disability. Similarly, Myreddi and Narayan (1993) found that young adults with intellectual disability coped best with concrete aspects of death rather than with more abstract issues. Harper and Wadsworth (1993) showed, however, that many adults with intellectual disability display typical grief reactions: a mixture of sadness, anger, anxiety, confusion, and pain. Harper and Wadsworth also found depressive reactions (e.g., crying, fatigue, sleep disruption, loss of appetite) in some individuals, including the occurrence of self-injury as part of the grief reaction in 10%–15% of the people they studied.

The psychological experience of aging in people with intellectual disability is a topic that is by no means fully understood. It must be clear, however, that people's successful adjustment to their changing selves across the life span is part of the process of remaining well balanced and able to cope. This does not imply a passive acceptance of old age or that the aspirations of older people can be discounted. Indeed, this is particularly pertinent for people with intellectual disability, for whom policies in the past have sometimes led to a situation in which older individuals have been required to disengage from more active pursuits, regardless of their own wishes or abilities. To counter this, service providers should consciously adopt a Third Age perspective in both service provision and staff training that focuses not on the maintenance of what exists but on the development of new aspirations and aims.

MENTAL HEALTH SERVICE ISSUES

Having previously discussed the quality-of-life aspects relating to mental health, the chapter discussion next considers some of the issues and problems in the provision of services to people with intellectual disability if they do experience mental illness. A basic right listed previously is that mental health problems should be recognized promptly. This is obviously a fundamental requirement. The best-trained clinician cannot help someone if that person does not present him- or herself for treatment. It is clear, however, that this is one of the first priorities to which service providers must attend because research (Patel, Goldberg, & Moss, 1993) has indicated that there are many undetected cases of mental illness among older people with intellectual disability who should be receiving attention. How does this situation come about?

The Problem of Case Recognition

The identification of mental health problems in the community is not an issue only for people with intellectual disability but is inherent in the nature of mental illness. Unlike physical illness, most types of mental disorder are not characterized by clear boundaries between being well and being ill. Most people have had the experience of circumstances "getting on top of them" and sometimes pushing people to the point where they no longer feel able to cope. In most cases, however, people manage to cope with the help of support networks. Falloon and Fadden (1993) estimated, for instance, that such networks are able to manage 90%–95% of all cases of mental disorder in the community. In this respect, the recognition of psychiatric conditions is highly interactive with the context in which a person lives. Certain social situations lend themselves more to a person's being able to contain or cope with the psychiatric symptoms than others, whereas other social situations may actually produce or exacerbate a person's psychiatric symptoms. Goldberg and Huxley (1980) discussed the factors that determine whether someone with a neurotic disorder becomes a "case." They pointed out that the severity of the person's symptoms is not necessarily directly related to the person's degree of incapacity or interference with the person's day-to-day life. Both interpersonal factors and external social factors may determine whether a given set of symptoms results in presentation of the person's case to a doctor.

For most people without disabilities, the first step is the recognition of the person's problem by the person's family, friends, or colleagues. The onset of a mental illness is often heralded by a person's being unable to hold down a job effectively or being unable to fulfill roles that he or she had previously carried out successfully (e.g., parent, spouse, employee). The general practitioner is the one who decides whether the person 1) has significant mental illness and 2) whether the doctor can treat the person's mental illness or whether a referral to a psychiatrist is indicated.

In comparison with this process, many people with intellectual disability experience far fewer formal role expectations. They usually do not have spouses or children, and their work roles are often less demanding. As a result, significant depression or anxiety may have no dramatic, clearly defined outward manifestations, although distress to the individual may be considerable. Without specialized knowledge, it may be assumed that the symptoms are part of the individual's intellectual disability, with the result that referral to the general practitioner for further psychiatric evaluation may not be made.

The pathway to psychiatric care thus involves at least two steps. First, people who know the individual must notice a significant change in behavior. Second, the person must come to the attention of a medical practitioner. Because of the way this pathway works, certain conditions are more likely to be detected than others. Alcohol abuse or schizophrenia are inherently more noticeable than depression or anxiety because they often result in high-profile behaviors that are obvious and often are a nuisance to others. As a result, the small proportion of people who come to the attention of psychiatric services do not represent a true cross-section of mental illness in the community. This difference is even more noticeable in the intellectually disabled population. The most common reason for referral to a psychiatrist in the United Kingdom is for challenging behavior (Day, 1985), yet research (Patel et al., 1993) indicated that there are probably many people with intellectual disability who have mental illness but whose problems remain undetected. As a result, they have little prospect of receiving appropriate treatment for their condition. The situation is particularly disadvantageous for older individuals because the most prevalent psychiatric conditions of old age—depression and anxiety—can have symptoms that are relatively inconspicuous or may present as physical illnesses.

The preceding discussion indicates the importance of focusing not just on the development of psychiatric techniques but also on improving the pathway by which people with intellectual disability gain appropriate treatment. In this respect, the role of caregivers in recognizing potential symptoms is crucial because they are in the best position to identify significant behavior changes and make appropriate re ferrals. A number of initiatives have been directed specifically toward these issues of recognition and referral. The PAS ADD Checklist (Moss, Prosser, Costello, Simpson, & Patel, 1997) and the MINI PAS-ADD (Prosser, Moss, Costello, Simpson, & Patel, 1997) are two schedules designed to help health and social services staff identify mental health problems in the people for whom they care. Training materials developed by Guy's and St. Thomas's Hospital (Bouras, Murray, Joyce, Kon, & Holt, 1995) in London have been designed to raise the awareness and understanding of staff about a wide range of issues relating to the detection, management, and treatment of mental illness in people with intellectual disability.

The Pivotal Role of Primary Care Services

In the list of basic rights to mental health discussed previously in this chapter, the second component of the right to mental health and a good quality of life is expert, prompt assessment. In this respect, general practitioners have a pivotal role. In the United Kingdom, the House of Commons Social Services Committee made it clear that the continuing capacity of general practitioners to provide primary medical care to people with mental disabilities would in large part determine the success of community care policy (Shepherd, 1993). The World Health Organization Working Groups came to a similar conclusion when it stated that "the primary care team is the cornerstone of community psychiatry" (1973). The significance of the primary health care team reflects the points made previously that the majority of mental illnesses do not come to the attention of a psychiatrist and that the majority of individuals who seek treatment are treated by a health professional other than a psychiatrist.

Primary care for people with intellectual disability has come to increasing prominence because the majority of these individuals no longer live in institutions. Evidence that the health care needs of people with intellectual disability are inadequately met comes from a series of studies undertaken in the United Kingdom and elsewhere (Turner & Moss, 1996). Generally, when people with intellectual disability leave the umbrella of the school medical services, their contact with medical services appears to decrease, with the result that the knowledge of their health needs is correspondingly reduced. In the United Kingdom, the adequacy of primary care services in the detection and management of secondary conditions, preventive care, and prescription practices has been criticized (Cole, 1986; Howells, 1986; Langan, Russell, & Whitfield, 1993; Wilson & Haire, 1990). These studies indicated the presence of a large number of common medical problems that were not known to individuals' general practitioners and/or were not being managed. For many people, the effects of unmanaged visual or hearing impairments compounded their intellectual disability, causing communication difficulties and isolation. Contrary to good practice, many of the people taking antidepressant or anti-epilepsy drugs received them by repeat prescription with no review. Significantly, an American study (Minihan & Dean, 1990) of adults with intellectual disability who lived in community environments found that psychiatric and emotional problems were among the most commonly recorded chronic problems.

From the perspective of a person with intellectual disability, one of the fundamental limitations of the primary health care system is that it relies so heavily on a person's ability to recognize and report symptoms of ill health. People with communication problems may not have the skills to do this, and health care professionals may not have the skills needed to overcome this barrier. Beange and Bauman (1990), in a study of 251 people with intellectual disability attending a health promotion clinic in New South Wales, Australia, reported that the individuals whom they studied failed to present symptoms to general practitioners until their disease was advanced, and they concluded that these individuals could not be expected to arrange their own preventive care. Langan and colleagues (1993) also investigated the problems that people with intellectual disability found in obtaining primary health care in the United Kingdom. They concluded that both users and caregivers may lack the ability to recognize and report symptoms. Rodgers (1994) argued that professionals in primary health care in the United Kingdom may lack the communication skills needed to give appropriate care to people with intellectual disability. Langan and colleagues' survey of 70 general practitioners in western England found that general practitioners generally lacked special expertise for dealing with people with intellectual disability, and almost half believed that further training was appropriate. Similar problems were found in the United States (Harper & Wadsworth, 1992). Harper and Wadsworth argued that health care professionals in the United States often lack the opportunity to gain experience in interacting with people whose ability to express and understand health care information is limited.

Moss and Turner (1995) suggested that there is scope for training programs for primary care team members, consumers, and caregivers, both as separate groups and in terms of coordination and communication. There is a growing literature in the United States (e.g., Harper & Wadsworth, 1992; Wadsworth & Harper, 1991) focusing on the training of staff in this respect. For example, Harper and Wadsworth (1992) reported the evaluation of self-study materials (texts and videotapes) aimed at developing methods of communicating with people with intellectual disability in delivering medical and dental care. Knowledge and skills of physicians, nurses, nursing assistants, and medical students were found to have improved after training, and they were more proactive in interviews. To date, the United Kingdom seems to have made comparatively little progress in this respect.

Psychiatric Services

With regard to the provision of psychiatric services for older adults with intellectual disability, the commitment of service providers must be to provide the best possible mental health services to this population. People with intellectual disability are disadvantaged in two respects. First, the problems of diagnosis and treatment are greatly increased by the presence of intellectual disability and by the linguistic barrier that is often present between patient and clinician. Second, and related to the first point, these additional complications have often led to people's being regarded as unsuitable for receiving treatment by general psychiatric services.

People with intellectual disability are not the only group who have had difficulty in gaining access to appropriate help from specialists. Snowden (1982), for instance, stated,

> An unmistakeable and increasingly troubling aspect of mental health services has been that of restricted access to these services based on social standing. . . . Minorities and those who were poor, rural, chronic mental patients, or too young or too old were poorly served. . . . Working with members of our groups was held to provide little challenge, prestige or income.

People with intellectual disability were not even mentioned in Snowden's book as an underserved group, the recognition of their mental health needs being still in its infancy. Although mental health services are still underdeveloped at the turn of the 21st century, there is a much greater professional interest in the psychiatric profession in the needs of this population. A number of countries have set up specialist training in the psychiatry of intellectual disability. At the same time, it is clear that only a small proportion of the total population with intellectual disabilities who have mental illness is being identified and treated. Referral agents tend to use the services less for specialist consultation and more as a means of reducing their own anxieties and frustrations of difficult cases, many of which have needs that are outside the purview of the service (Falloon & Fadden, 1993). As a result, these specialist psychiatric services spend a lot of their time coping with challenging behavior but remain comparatively unaware of more common mental disorders such as depression and anxiety (Patel et al., 1993). This situation can change only if more effective strategies for recognizing and referring these mental health problems as they occur are introduced.

Assuming that the person's mental health problems have been recognized, the diagnostic process is still fraught with difficulties. A number of researchers and clinicians have asserted that people with intellectual disability manifest the full range of mental health conditions that are represented in the population without disabilities. Eaton and Menolascino (1982) and Reiss (1982) reported surveys of people with mental disabilities attending community-based mental health clinics in Nebraska and Chicago and concluded that people with intellectual disability experience a wide range of emotional disturbances and that the symptoms of specific psychiatric disturbances are essentially the same for people with and without intellectual disability. Sovner and Hurley (1983) similarly concluded that mental illness in this population should not be regarded as fundamentally different from that occurring in individuals without disabilities.

In looking more closely at these assertions, however, it is clear that many diagnostic issues have not been evaluated fully enough to make definitive statements about the prevalence, manifestations, or subjective experiences of mental illness in this population. The linguistic barrier between patient and clinician presents a formidable challenge and is compounded by the fact that mental disorders often do not have clear-cut definitions. Their diagnosis depends on the interaction of a variety of factors: what the people say they are experiencing, what others say about them, how they are seen to behave, and the history of their complaint. For many people with intellectual disability, the first of these factors is usually limited because of reduced communication ability and is often totally absent. As a result, the diagnostic process becomes reliant on third-party reports and observations. The consequence of this circumstance is that the validity of diagnosis for people without verbal communication ability is most uncertain (Moss, 1995; Moss, Prosser, Ibbotson, & Goldberg, 1996). Even the use of the American Psychiatric Association's (1975) glossary in diagnosing this population probably poses more questions than it answers (Sturmey, 1993).

It is not appropriate here to enter into a detailed discussion of diagnostic issues. Suffice it to say that the diagnostic problems are fundamental ones, and one cannot talk with any certainty of the prevalence or the nature of mental health problems in any except the more mildly disabled members of the population. If the individuals with more severe disabilities are to have full rights to good mental health, then effort must be directed in the future toward conducting appropriate research to refine approaches to diagnosis of and treatment for this population.

In terms of planning and organizing mental health services, it is clear that the provision of specialists for people with intellectual disability is increasingly being developed. (See Day, 1994, for an excellent discussion and review of these issues.) Day pointed out that special expertise is required for the accurate diagnosis of mental illness that, in people with intellectual disability, often manifests itself in different ways from those of the population without disabilities. Although theoretically it would be possible to train staff working in services for the general population, the relatively small number of cases gives little opportunity for staff in all of the various disciplines to gain the necessary skills. Specialized psychiatric services are increasingly becoming the preferred option in many countries (see, e.g., Molony, 1993). Despite this trend, however, it should be noted that advocates of normalization (see Day, 1994) support the generic approach, arguing that specialized services lead to stigmatization, labeling, and negative professional attitudes.

Regardless of whether specialists or generic service providers provide interventions for people with intellectual disability, it is clear that the mental health needs of this population are highly complex. As such, diagnostic classification is likely to provide only minimal guidance on the morbidity and quality of life of individuals who experience mental disorders (Falloon & Fadden, 1993). Indeed, this is also true among people without disabilities, and it is apparent that mental health service providers are increasingly recognizing this, adopting a problem-based rather than a strictly diagnostic approach to assessment. Thus, one district in the United Kingdom (Falloon & Fadden, 1993) uses a functional assessment incorporating the following points:

1. Screening for problems that may contribute to continuing vulnerability and stress
2. Analyzing key current problems
3. Setting goals for intervention
4. Formulating intervention strategies
5. Devising methods for monitoring the progress of the treatment

An effective service not only copes with disorders as they occur but also minimizes the likelihood of the disorder's recurrence. Recurrent episodes are more likely either when the person's biological vulnerability is increased or when environmental stress overwhelms the individual's coping capacity. An integrated care approach emphasizes accurate diagnosis as a crucial step that provides a clear direction for biomedical interventions. Following this step, however, the problem-based assessment provides the framework within which to think about long-term prevention of occurrence and maximizing quality of life rather than simply reducing symptoms in the short term. The adoption of such care models is even more important for people with intellectual disability because the majority of them need help to develop and maintain strategies for the long-term maintenance of their mental health.

CONCLUSIONS

This chapter begins by suggesting that people are accustomed to reading about the human rights of people who already receive mental health services rather than the issues of access to the services and social structures that can foster and maintain mental health. Although much of what has been discussed relates to the mental health of people with intellectual disability across the adult life span, the focus on older individuals highlights the significance of a risk factor to which all people are susceptible—the process of aging. Most older adults who are depressed (and there are a lot of them) would probably be depressed in the same set of life circumstances even if they were many years younger. Society should not tolerate individuals' social isolation, lack of purpose, lack of social status, and lack of love; yet many older people live their twilight years in this state. Indeed, it may even be that many older people with intellectual disability fare better than their peers without disabilities because they are lifelong members of an actively supported population.

In some respects, the social risk factors for mental illness that apply to older people without disabilities apply to people with intellectual disability throughout their lives; in that respect, the concept of mental health embodies far more than an absence of mental illness. Society has certainly come a long way in terms of providing better conditions for the fostering and maintenance of mental well-being for its members with disabilities. In terms of the definitions of *mental health* discussed previously in this chapter, however, how many people with intellectual disability would say that they were satisfied with their social relationships, living circumstances, and achievements?

In terms of the formal recognition of mental illness in people with intellectual disability, considerably more progress has been made. The first major step was the acknowledgment that people did not belong in long-stay psychiatric hospitals solely because of their intellectual disability. Since the 1950s and 1960s, many countries have thankfully entered more enlightened times, and most of these inappropriately placed people have been relocated. Unfortunately, better forms of assistance were slow to develop. In the 1970s and 1980s, few specialist services coped with the mental health problems of people with intellectual disability, and generic services frequently washed their hands of the problem either because they did not have the requisite expertise or because they believed that these individuals were better handled by service providers in the intellectual disability field.

In the 1990s, however, all of that changed. The turn of the 21st century marks the *dual diagnosis* phase of service development. This term, originally adopted in the United States to refer to people with a substance abuse problem in addition to a psychiatric disorder, has also been adopted, somewhat confusingly, to refer to people who have co-existing mental illness and intellectual disability. This is, in one sense, a step forward—a formal recognition that a person with intellectual disability can also experience mental illness. One also must be careful not to replace one permanent label with another, possibly even more stigmatizing, one. Outside the context of intellectual disability, people who experience depression or anxiety would never use the term *single diagnosis* to describe their condition. Most of these people would wish to view their condition as one that has the prospect of a cure, at which point the diagnosis would no longer apply. Although it is legitimate to regard some disorders such as autism (and intellectual disability itself) as being lifelong conditions, a large proportion of mental health problems are responsive to treatment. There is a definite danger of the term *dual diagnosis* being used as a permanent label to categorize people, even though the evidence for mental illness is often unsubstantiated, particularly in the case of individuals whose level of intellectual disability is profound. Broadly speaking, it seems reasonable to make a firm diagnosis in those cases in which intervention and service coordination follow directly from the diagnosis. The term *dual diagnosis,* however, does not provide any information about the nature of the condition, its severity, or its prognosis. Once the individual is diagnosed, the diagnosis is likely to remain in a medical record as a permanent label. The more labels a person has, the more irredeemably different from the rest of the population he or she will be perceived. If the concept of a diagnosable condition implies no possibility of a cure, then its use is certainly not a liberalizing force. One patient who was under treatment for 18 years put it eloquently: "Illness is a one-way street, particularly when the experts toss the concept of cure out of the window and congratulate themselves on candour. The idea of illness, of illness that can never go away, is not a dynamic, liberating force. Illness creates victims. While we harbour thoughts of emotional distress as some kind of deadly plague, it is not unrealistic to expect that many so-called victims will lead limited, powerless and unfulfilled lives" (Campbell, 1989).

REFERENCES

American Psychiatric Association, Committee on Public Information. (1975). *A psychiatric glossary: The meaning of terms frequently used in psychiatry* (4th ed.). New York: Basic Books.

Azmi, S., Hatton, C., Emerson, E., & Caine, A. (1997). Listening to adolescents and adults with intellectual disabilities from South Asian communities. *Journal of Applied Research in Intellectual Disabilities, 10,* 250–263.

Baker, F., Jodrey, D., & Intagliata, J. (1992). Social support and quality of life of community support clients. *Community Mental Health Journal, 28,* 397–411.

Baker, B.L., Seltzer, G.B., & Seltzer, M.M. (1977). *As close as possible: Community residences for retarded adults.* Boston: Little, Brown.

Beange, H., & Bauman, A. (1990). Health care for the developmentally disabled: Is it necessary? In W.I. Fraser (Ed.), *Key issues in mental retardation research: Proceedings of the 8th World Congress of the International Association for the Scientific Study of Mental Deficiency (IASSMD).* London: Routledge.

Berger, M.M. (1977). *Working with people called patients.* Philadelphia: Brunner/Mazel.

Bouras, N., Murray, B., Joyce, T., Kon, Y., & Holt, G. (1995). *Mental health in learning disabilities: A training pack for staff working with people who have a dual diagnosis of mental health needs and learning disabilities.* Brighton, England: Pavilion.

Bowling, A., & Browne, P.D. (1991). Social networks, health, and emotional well-being among the oldest old in London. *Journal of Gerontology, 46,* S20–S32.

Campbell, P. (1989). Peter Campbell's story. In A. Brackx & C. Grimshaw (Eds.), *Mental health care in crisis.* London: Pluto Press.

Cattermole, M., Jahoda, A., & Markova, I. (1990). Quality of life for people with learning difficulties moving to community homes. *Disability, Handicap, and Society, 5,* 137–152.

Cole, O. (1986). Medical screening of adults at social recreation centres: Whose responsibility? *Mental Handicap, 14,* 54–56.

Crow, T.J., MacMillan, J.F., Johnson, A.L, & Johnstone, E.C. (1986). A randomised controlled trial of prophylactic neuroleptic treatment. *British Journal of Psychiatry, 148,* 120–127.

Day, K. (1985). Psychiatric disorder in the middle-aged and elderly mentally handicapped. *British Journal of Psychiatry, 147,* 660–667.

Day, K. (1994). Psychiatric services in mental retardation: Generic or specialised provision? In N. Bouras (Ed.), *Mental health in mental retardation: Recent advances and practices.* Cambridge, England: Cambridge University Press.

Day, K., & Jancar, J. (1994). Mental and physical health and ageing in mental handicap: A review. *Journal of Intellectual Disability Research, 38,* 241–256.

Eaton, L.F., & Menolascino, F.J. (1982). Psychiatric disorders in the mentally retarded: Types, problems, and challenges. *American Journal of Psychiatry, 139,* 1297–1303.

Falloon, I.R.H., & Fadden, G. (1993). Integrated mental health care: A comprehensive community based approach. Cambridge, England: Cambridge University Press.

Goldberg, D.P., & Huxley, P. (1980). *Mental illness in the community: The pathway to psychiatric care.* London: Tavistock Publications.

Haga, H., Shibata, H., Ueno, M., & Nagai, H. (1991). Factors contributing to longitudinal changes in activities of daily living (ADL): The Koganei study. *Journal of Cross Cultural Gerontology, 6,* 91–99.

Harper, D.C., & Wadsworth, J.S. (1992). Improving health communication for persons with mental retardation. *Public Health Reports, 107,* 297–302.

Harper, D.C., & Wadsworth, J.S. (1993). Grief in adults with mental retardation: Preliminary findings. *Research in Developmental Disabilities, 14,* 313–330.

Hogg, J., Moss, S., & Cooke, D. (1988). *Ageing and mental handicap.* London: Croom Helm.

Howells, G. (1986). Are the health care needs of mentally handicapped adults being met? *Journal of the Royal College of General Practitioners, 36,* 449–453.

Ishii-Kuntz, M. (1990). Social interaction and psychological well-being: Comparison across stages of adulthood. *International Journal of Aging and Human Development, 30,* 15–36.

Kelly, J.R. (1983). *Leisure identities and interactions.* Boston: Allen & Unwin.

Lambe, L., & Hogg, J. (1995). *Their face to the wind: Service developments for older people with learning disabilities in Grampian region.* Glasgow: ENABLE.

Langan, J., Russell, O., & Whitfield, M. (1993). *Community care and the general practitioner: Primary health care for people with learning disabilities.* Bristol, England: University of Bristol, Norah Fry Research Centre.

Laslett, P. (1989). *A fresh map of life.* London: Weidenfeld & Nicholson.

Lebowitz, B.D., & Niederehe, G. (1992). Concepts and issues in mental health and aging. In J.E. Birren, R.B. Sloane, & G.D. Cohen (Eds.), *Handbook of mental health and aging* (2nd ed., pp. 3–26). London: Academic Press.

Lipe-Goodson, P.S., & Goebel, B.L. (1993). Perception of age and death in mentally retarded adults. *Mental Retardation, 21,* 68–75.

Llwewllyn, G., McConnell, D., & Bye, R. (1998). Perception of service needs by parents with intellectual disability, their significant others, and their service workers. *Research in Developmental Disabilities, 19,* 245–260.

Minihan, P.M., & Dean, D.H. (1990). Meeting the needs for health services of persons with mental retardation living in the community. *American Journal of Public Health, 80,* 1043–1048.

Molony, H. (1993). *Mental health services for people with intellectual disability: Current developments* [Special issue: Ninth World Congress on Intellectual Disability]. *Australia and New Zealand Journal of Developmental Disabilities, 18,* 169–176.

Mor-Barak, M.E., Miller, L.S., & Syme, L.S. (1991). Social networks, life events, and health of the poor, frail elderly: A longitudinal study of the buffering versus the direct effect. *Family and Community Health, 14,* 1–13.

Moss, S.C. (1991). Age and functional abilities of people with mental handicap: Evidence from the Wessex Mental Handicap Register. *Journal of Mental Deficiency Research, 35,* 430–445.

Moss, S.C. (1994). Quality of life and aging. In D.A. Goode (Ed.), *Quality of life for persons with disabilities: International perspectives and issues.* Cambridge, MA: Brookline Books.

Moss, S.C. (1995). Methodological issues in the diagnosis of psychiatric disorders in adults with learning disability. *Thornfield Journal (University of Dublin), 18,* 9–18.

Moss, S.C., Goldberg, D., Patel, P., & Wilkin, D. (1993). Physical morbidity in older people with moderate, severe and profound mental handicap, and its relation to psychiatric morbidity. *Social Psychiatry and Psychiatric Epidemiology, 28,* 32–39.

Moss, S.C., Prosser, H., Costello, H., Simpson, N., & Patel, P. (1997). *The PAS-ADD checklist.* Manchester, England: University of Manchester, Hester Adrian Research Centre.

Moss, S.C., Prosser, H., Ibbotson, B., & Goldberg, D.P. (1996). Respondent and informant accounts of psychiatric symptoms in a sample of patients with learning disability. *Journal of Intellectual Disability Research, 40,* 457–465.

Moss, S.C., & Turner, S. (1995). *The health of people with learning disability* (Report to the Department of Heath). Manchester, England: University of Manchester, Hester Adrian Research Centre.

Murrell, S.A., & Norris, F.H. (1983). Quality of life as the criterion for need assessment and community psychology. *Journal of Community Psychology, 11,* 88–97.

Myreddi, V.A., & Narayan, J. (1993). The concept of death among people with mental handicap. *International Journal of Rehabilitation Research, 16,* 328–330.

Nagpal, N., & Chadha, N.K. (1991). Social support and life satisfaction among aged. *Indian Journal of Psychometry and Education, 22,* 91–100.

Nystrom, A., & Andersson-Segesten, K. (1990). Peace of mind as an important aspect of old people's health. *Scandinavian Journal of Caring Sciences, 4,* 55–62.

Patel, P., Goldberg, D.P., & Moss, S.C. (1993). Psychiatric morbidity in older people with moderate and severe learning disability (mental retardation): Part II. The prevalence study. *British Journal of Psychiatry, 163,* 481–491.

Pitetti, K.H., Rimmer, J.H., & Fernhall, B. (1993). Physical fitness and adults with mental retardation. An overview of current research and future directions. *Sports Medicine, 16,* 23–56.

Prosser, H., Moss, S.C., Costello, H., Simpson, N., & Patel, P. (1997). *The MINI PAS-ADD: A preliminary assessment schedule for the detection of mental health needs in adults with learning disability (mental retardation).* Manchester, England: University of Manchester, Hester Adrian Research Centre.

Reiss, S. (1982). Psychopathology and mental retardation: Survey of a developmental disabilities mental health program. *Mental Retardation, 20,* 128–132.

Rodgers, J. (1994). Primary health care provision for people with learning difficulties. *Health and Social Care, 2,* 11–17.

Royal College of Physicians. (1981). Organic mental impairment in the elderly: Implications for research, education and the provision of services. *Journal of the Royal College of Physicians of London, 102,* 141–167.

Sands, D.J., Kozleski, E.B., & Goodwin, L.D. (1991). Whose needs are we meeting? Results of a consumer satisfaction survey of persons with developmental disabilities in Colorado. *Research in Developmental Disabilities, 12*(3), 297–314.

Seltzer, M.M. (1985). Informal support for aging mentally retarded persons. *American Journal of Mental Deficiency, 90,* 259–265.

Shamoian, C.A. (1985). Assessing depression in elderly patients. *Hospital and Community Psychiatry, 36,* 338–339.

Shepherd, M. (1993). Foreword. In I.R.H. Falloon & G. Fadden, *Integrated mental health care: A comprehensive community based approach.* New York: Cambridge University Press.

Shepherd, M., Cooper, B., & Brown, A.C. (1966). *Psychiatric illness in general practice.* London: Oxford University Press.

Snowden, L.R. (1982). Services to the underserved: An overview of contemporary issues. In L.R. Snowden (Ed.), *Reaching the underserved: Mental health needs of neglected populations.* London: Sage Publications.

Sovner, R., & Hurley, D.A. (1983). Do the mentally retarded suffer from affective illness? *Archives of General Psychiatry, 40,* 61–67.

Sturmey, P. (1993). The use of DSM and ICD diagnostic criteria in people with mental retardation. *Journal of Nervous and Mental Disease, 181,* 38–41.

Suttie, J., Ashman, A.F., & Bramley, J. (1993). Problems undertaking surveys of older people with a disability in Australia. [Special issue: Psychological aspects of ageing: Well-being and vulnerability]. *Irish Journal of Psychology, 14,* 5–24.

Sweeney, D.P., & Wilson, T.Y. (Eds.). (1979). *Double jeopardy: The plight of aging and aged developmentally disabled persons in mid-America: A research monograph.* Ann Arbor: University of Michigan, Institute for the Study of Mental Retardation and Related Disabilities.

Tredgold, A.F. (1970). *Tredgold's mental retardation* (11th ed.). Baltimore: Williams & Wilkins. (Original work published as *Mental deficiency (amentia)* in 1908)

Turner, S., & Moss, S.C. (1996). The health needs of adults with learning disabilities and the health of the nation strategy. *Journal of Intellectual Disability Research, 40,* 438–450.

Wadsworth, J.S., & Harper, D.C. (1991). Increasing the reliability of self-report by adults with moderate mental retardation. *Journal of The Association for Persons with Severe Handicaps, 16,* 228–232.

Willer, B., & Intagliata, J. (1984). Residential care settings for the elderly. In B. Willer & J. Intagliata (Eds.), *Promises and realities for mentally retarded citizens: Life in the community* (pp. 111–146). Baltimore: University Park Press.

Wilson, D., & Haire, A. (1990, 15 December). Health care screening for people with mental handicap living in the community. *British Medical Journal,* 1379–1381.

World Federation for Mental Health. (1948). *Report of the first annual meeting.* Geneva: Author.

World Health Organization Working Groups. (1973). *Psychiatry and primary medical care.* Geneva: World Health Organization.

12

Life After Loss
Legal, Ethical, and Practical Issues

Barbara L. Ludlow

Advances in medical interventions for disabling conditions, along with improved health care across the life span, have significantly increased the life expectancy of people with developmental disabilities. Aging parents, once led to believe that they would be the primary caregivers for their dependent sons and daughters throughout their children's lives, face the likelihood that their children will outlive them and require care outside the family home. Older adults with developmental disabilities, even as they realize the advantages of a longer life, must face the losses associated with aging, including the death of loved ones and relocation from a lifelong residence. These losses present numerous stressors for the individual, the family, and the practitioner and raise a host of legal, ethical, and practical issues that need to be addressed. Thoughtful resolution of these issues is critical to safeguarding the welfare of older people with developmental disabilities and ensuring for them a satisfactory quality of life after loss.

Facing and coping with major life changes and their accompanying losses is a common experience in the lives of older adults. Because people with developmental disabilities are reaching older adulthood in greater numbers, they are experiencing the losses associated with aging. The natural processes of aging may be more stressful for these individuals than for people without disabilities, however, because of their greater dependence on others for everyday support, limited ability to understand what is happening to them resulting from communication or cognition impairments, or societal attitudes that deny them the access to information and support needed for successfully coping with and adjusting to life's losses.

PERSONAL STORIES OF LOSS

Every day, individuals with developmental disabilities, their families, and service providers confront the challenges associated with the death or incapacitation of a caregiver or relocation of residence as a result of loss of the family home, changing service needs, or deinstitutionalization. The following stories represent cases from the professional experiences of the author of this chapter, with names and identifying information changed to protect the privacy of all individuals. These cases are used first to illustrate the many complex issues in situations involving aging, developmental disabilities, and loss and then to serve as examples of the potential impact of services on life after loss.

Ethel

Ethel was a 59-year-old woman with mental retardation requiring limited support whose mother had died within the past year. Ethel had lived all of her life in the family home, helping with housekeeping tasks and caring for her mother after her father's death. The mother's will transferred guardianship of Ethel to a cousin who lived in a neighboring state, specifying that her estate be used to support Ethel in a local nursing facility. Overwhelmed by the loss of her mother's companionship and removal from the only home she had ever known, Ethel became disrespectful of staff and refused to take the insulin injections that she needed to control her adult-onset diabetes. The facility's administrator advised Ethel's cousin to transfer her to a state institution. When Ethel began accusing her cousin of putting her away to steal her mother's money, the facility's staff put her on medication to control what they termed "irrational thoughts and delusions." Frightened by conditions in the institution, Ethel exhibited even more erratic behavior until eventually she was put in restraints for much of the day. She broke several bones while struggling in the restraints and lost a great deal of weight because she refused to eat. A developmental disabilities professional, recognizing Ethel's depression, recommended that she be moved immediately to a community residence and provided with grief counseling, but Ethel died before the transfer could be made.

Arthur

Arthur was an older adult with mental retardation requiring extensive support who lived all of his life in the family home in a small town, maintaining a close relationship with his only brother, Jack. When Arthur's parents reached their 80s, their failing health and loss of strength made his daily care too much of a burden for them and intensified their own caregiving needs. Jack felt that the best solution for everyone would be to put his parents in a nursing facility and to place Arthur in a nearby specialized care facility. Arthur, who was not able to understand the move from his home and belongings and the loss of daily contact with his family, soon became withdrawn. To help assist Arthur in making the transition to his new residence, Jack took some time off from work so that he could visit Arthur several times each day. After Jack's vacation was over, Arthur became upset at the change in his daily routine and the loss of contact with Jack, spending a good deal of time engaged in self-stimulatory behaviors. When Arthur refused to eat for staff, Jack began a routine of stopping by the home twice each day to help Jack eat; but Jack's wife and children complained that he was neglecting their needs and "babying" Arthur unnecessarily. The stress and guilt caused Jack to develop health problems himself, as he struggled with his genuine fear that Arthur would die without his care and his growing belief that his marriage was headed for divorce. Torn by grief over his conflicting responsibilities, Jack was unsure whether to honor his promise to his parents to care for Arthur or to acknowledge his duty to himself and his family.

Martin

Sixty-two-year-old Martin had a diagnosis of cerebral palsy and mental retardation requiring limited support. For the past 15 years, he had lived in the same group facility in a small community and spent his days at the local sheltered workshop or in activities such as shopping, going to the movies, and swimming at the local Young Men's Christian Association (YMCA) pool. Martin and his roommate kept a parakeet as a pet, which they cared for, played with, and showed off proudly to visitors. Over the last several years, Martin had begun to develop age-related health problems that interfered with his ability to perform his job and participate in recreation events. Arthritis increasingly limited his ability to move around and dress himself without assistance, and incontinence caused him to have several embarrassing toileting accidents in public. Abruptly moved to a nursing facility, Martin appeared sad and lost in his new surroundings. The staff, accustomed to caring for older people with greater health care needs, restricted Martin's activities more than necessary, and his physical condition deteriorated further because of his resulting inactivity. The staff were unable to respond to Martin's attempts to speak and sign, increasing his frustration and interfering with their own efforts to communicate with him and get him to comply with requests. Because nursing facility policy prohibited pets, he no longer had even his parakeet to keep him company. Despondent and depressed, Martin's days were spent in his room staring at the television, showing little interest in the other residents or in the few activities provided for him.

Wilma

Wilma, at nearly 60 years old, had lived for more than 30 years in the same large public residential facility. As one of the most communicative and helpful residents of the facility, Wilma was well known to all of the institution's staff, and she enjoyed socializing with them. When a court decree ordered the facility closed, staff began to prepare for the transition of residents to a group home. Although Wilma told people that she was looking forward to the move, she began to exhibit a number of behavior problems that delayed her transfer to the group home. On several occasions, she was found "eloping"— that is, sneaking out of her bedroom window at night and bothering staff and residents in other buildings. She also began to steal and hoard objects, taking things out of purses and off desks and hiding them in her drawer. When she was brought to spend a trial night at the group home, staff reported that she "freaked out," spending the whole night crying and huddled in a corner. The staff concluded that Wilma might be experiencing some dementia due to aging and recommended medication to control her behavior problems.

Regrettably, scenarios like these occur every day because little attention is paid to understanding and responding to the phenomenon of loss associated with aging in people with developmental disabilities. In addition, too many families and practitioners have not taken the time to plan and prepare for the transfer of care following the death or the incapacitation of a caregiver or the transition to a new residence resulting from removal from the family home, changing service needs, or deinstitutionalization.

AGING, DEVELOPMENTAL DISABILITY, AND LOSS

Improvements in health care and social services in the 1970s, 1980s, and 1990s enabled people with developmental disabilities to live ever longer lives. Those individuals who survive to their senior years, however, not only will experience the losses typically associated with aging but also may need to address unique challenges related to their specific disabling conditions. Family and professional caregivers often are unaware of the issues of loss that adults with disabilities must face as they age.

Losses Associated with Aging

Aging as a phenomenon as well as a distinctly human experience is associated with many aspects of loss. Loss is not only inevitable in aging but also a defining characteristic of the last stage of life. Havighurst (1972) identified adjusting to the loss of one's own abilities and the loss of loved ones as the most significant developmental tasks of later life. Viorst (1986) defined *successful aging* as the ability to see these age-related losses as new opportunities for personal growth. Aging, then, may be seen as an intrinsic developmental process that requires coping with significant loss-related stresses in order to find new meaning in life.

One important loss that older adults experience is the gradual diminishment of their physical and sometimes even their mental capabilities. Some decrease in abilities is typical of advancing years, although adequate nutrition, regular exercise, and routine health care as well as maintenance of active interests and social contacts can sustain an individual's functioning at high levels (Kausler, 1991). When the body fails to respond in expected ways and appearance no longer conforms to societal norms of attractiveness, a person is confronted with fundamental changes in the bases for identity and self-esteem (Aiken, 1995; Craik & Salthouse, 1992). Events such as adult children's "leaving the nest" and the older adult's retirement from employment may leave the older adult without the daily routines and tasks that have defined his or her existence for decades (Cavanaugh, 1997; Nouwen & Gaffney, 1974). Older adults must not only adjust to the loss of youth, strength, and health along with changes in social status but also must find new goals and activities to reconstruct their self-identity and develop new goals in life.

Another major loss related to aging is the pressure to relocate to a new residence. Because people tend to view their own home as a place of self-expression, personal privacy and safety, and connection with the community, relocation represents another serious threat to self-identity (Viorst, 1986). Older adults commonly resist relocation actively, which may result in a loss of familiar surroundings, treasured possessions, and cherished friends (Moss, 1994). Most older adults are able to remain in their own home with their needs being met by family members' using natural supports (Ansello & Rose, 1989). Others are able to maintain some control over their lives through assisted living services, in which older adults contract only for the services that they need in the context of retirement communities (Roberto, 1993). Physiological and psychological changes during the aging process, however, may limit an older adult's ability to live independently and require relocation to the residence of an adult child or a care facility (Brody, 1990; Malone & Kropf, 1996). Nevertheless, the desire of older adults to age in place often can be accommodated by in-home supports and services that balance the dual needs of older adults for independence and assistance.

Coping with the loss of significant others is another universal experience of older adults because of the natural ecology of aging. Most adults survive their own parents and other older relatives and so experience the grief associated with the death of someone close to them (Hargrave & Hanna, 1997). The longer a person lives and the older he or she grows, the more occasions there will be to observe the death of contemporaries, such as siblings, spouses, or friends (Hansson & Carpenter, 1994). Some older adults avoid discussing death or, in a vain attempt to conceal their fear of death, refuse to acknowledge the need to grieve (Becker, 1973). Mourning the loss of loved ones, resolving feelings of grief, and coming to terms with one's own impending death, however, are hallmarks of successful aging.

Another aspect of the loss associated with the death of a significant other is a feeling of disorientation or displacement. Most adult children experience feelings of abandonment when a parent dies (Corr, Nabe, & Corr, 1997). A spouse who has provided daily care during many years of married life feels a loss of a sense of purpose after the partner dies (Hansson & Carpenter, 1994). Social support from relatives, friends, and community members is critical to successful adjustment to the death of loved ones (Cutrona, Russell, & Rose, 1986; Thoits, 1986). Older adults who lack informal sources of support or refuse to seek formal support services may experience deterioration in physical and mental health as a result of unresolved grief.

Disability and Age-Related Losses

Dybwad (1962) was one of the first leaders in the field of developmental disabilities to call attention to the unique needs of aging people with disabilities. Much has been learned about aging and developmental disabilities since his call to action. The 1980s and 1990s saw a steady increase in professional examination of the aging process in individuals with developmental disabilities (Janicki & Wisniewski, 1985; Seltzer & Krauss, 1987; Seltzer, Krauss, & Janicki, 1994; Sutton, Factor, Hawkins, Heller, & Seltzer, 1993). A variety of services and programs are available through both the aging and disabilities service systems (Janicki, 1997; Seltzer & Krauss, 1987), but relatively little is known about how older adults with developmental disabilities experience age-related losses or which supports are most effective in helping them adjust to life after loss.

Aging is truly a two-edged sword: As people with developmental disabilities live longer, they also experience both the joys and the sorrows of aging. The life expectancy of the majority of people with developmental disabilities has increased over time across all levels of severity of disabilities (Day & Jancar, 1994; Eyman & Borthwick-Duffy, 1994). In fact, most people with disabilities can be expected to live as long as the rest of the population, largely as a result of improved services and better health care.

Age-related physical, mental, and emotional changes may result in the deterioration of a person's hard-won skills. Many disabling conditions grow worse with age, producing discomfort, pain, or further disability as well as impairing basic functioning to some extent (Adlin, 1993). There is some evidence to suggest that people with disabilities are subject to earlier aging than their peers (Eklund & Martz, 1993; Jacobson, Sutton, & Janicki, 1985; Seltzer & Luchterhand, 1994) and that some disabling conditions increase the risk of dementia associated with aging (Prasher & Chung, 1996; Rasmussen & Sobsey, 1994). Age-related changes in health, behavior, and functional skills create new caregiving challenges that may prompt families to seek out-of-home placement (Black, Cohn, Smull, & Crites, 1985; Essex, Seltzer, & Krauss, 1997; Tausig, 1985). In addition, increasing frailty and risk of injury may reduce an individual's ability to engage in activities of daily living and participate in other valued social and recreation activities (Edgerton, 1994). People with developmental disabilities are likely to be just as troubled by the deterioration of physical and mental abilities as older adults without disabilities, and they may experience similar threats to their self-identity and self-esteem.

Despite the availability of residential facilities in institutions and in community environments, most adults with developmental disabilities spend all of their lives in the family home (Fujuira & Braddock, 1992), largely because of the desire of individual parents to avoid institutionalizing or placing them in a distant residential facility, the lack of sufficient community placements available for children and adults, and sometimes even the reluctance of parents to surrender their caregiving role (Seltzer, 1992). If removal from the home becomes necessary, then older adults with developmental disabilities may be faced with a stressful relocation, often under emergency circumstances.

Families who made the decision years ago to care for their children with disabilities at home believed that they would be able to provide care all of their lives and would ultimately outlive their children. Because of medical advances and improved health care, however, the opposite is true: Most people with developmental disabilities are likely to experience the death of their parents and the transfer of their care to someone else (Seltzer & Krauss, 1994). Out-of-home placement most often occurs because of a family's perceived increase in caregiving burden resulting from the deterioration in the individual's functioning or from the parent's diminished capacity (Ansello & Rose, 1989; Noelker & Somple, 1993). Lack of stable sources of social support in the community puts older adults with developmental disabilities at greater risk for placement in restrictive environments such as nursing facilities or public institutions (Edgerton, 1991; M.M. Seltzer, 1985; Todis, 1992).

Parents of individuals with developmental disabilities often expect siblings or other relatives to assume responsibility for the care of their adult child with developmental disabilities when they become incapacitated or die (Cicirelli, 1982; Goetting, 1986). Yet, they often fail to discuss these expectations with the family member involved or to assist the family member in making specific plans to ensure a smooth and successful transition and to protect the interests of both parties (Seltzer, Begun, Seltzer, & Krauss, 1991). Such failure to prepare can lead to situations in which a life can be endangered or an emergency out-of-home placement is needed (Janicki, Otis, Puccio, Rettig, & Jacobson, 1985; Sherman, 1988).

Any individual who has spent 40, 50, or more years living in the same place with the same people is likely to find an abrupt move quite traumatic. Individuals with developmental disabilities experience additional stress, however, because they often have been permitted little control over their own lives and may feel themselves especially helpless with regard to decisions made by others. Heller (1988) described the transfer trauma associated with insufficient planning and transition prior to residential relocations from the institution to a community living environment. Traumatic reactions may increase the possibility that the person will develop challenging behaviors or even mental disorders that will further interfere with their adjustment (Ryan, 1994). The experience of stress as well as the sense of loss may be even greater for older adults with developmental disabilities, who typically have limited intellectual abilities, poor coping skills, or deteriorating health status.

Older adults with developmental disabilities may experience a loss of self-esteem when they experience a loss of valued social status because of their parents' death or residential relocation. Studies have shown that families often develop a state of interdependence with an adult child with a developmental disability, who may provide emotional support (e.g., attention, comfort, affection) or even instrumental support (e.g., companionship, personal assistance, household help) to his or her parents as the parents grow older (Heller & Factor, 1988, 1993; Seltzer & Krauss, 1994). Adults who are forced to relocate after living in an institution or community residence for many years may have developed evolved social roles that provide them with a sense of self-worth as well as recognition from others (Heller, 1985; Thurman, 1986). In both cases, these individuals may form an adult self-concept based on their daily routines and come to see themselves as capable people performing an important service (Turnbull, Summers, & Brotherson, 1986). When age-related losses result in changes in these activities and a need to redefine themselves, older adults with developmental disabilities may feel a sense of disorientation and despair.

Anyone who suffers the death of a loved one experiences intense emotional reactions of grief and loss, including people with developmental disabilities. Unfortunately, some caregivers, service providers, and even professionals may fail to recognize or to acknowledge the appearance of the typical signs of loss, such as feelings of sadness, hopelessness, or atypical rebellious behavior (Harper & Wadsworth, 1993). Transient depressive states are common in grieving adults, but these behaviors in individuals with developmental disabilities are too often overlooked or attributed to other motives, such as noncompliance (Kloeppel & Hollins, 1989). Such misperceptions could lead to not providing the person with support or counseling or even with comfort to help him or her to cope with grief, refusing medication to help with sleeplessness or negative emotions, or applying an inappropriate and perhaps even cruel intervention to prevent or eliminate the behavior in question.

People with developmental disabilities can experience age-related losses as major stressors, producing changes in the way that they think, feel, or act. Depression, a common human response to stress associated with loss, is typically evidenced in feelings of sadness, hopelessness, and withdrawal behaviors, but also may be manifested as acting-out behaviors that express anger and denial, reactions commonly seen in people with developmental disabilities (Reiss, 1994). Stress can even result in mental disorders or behavior problems, which in turn may be manifested as deterioration in functioning or patterns of maladaptive behavior (Moss, 1994; Stroud & Sutton, 1988).

People with developmental disabilities may be at higher risk for mental disorders because of the way that society responds to them. For example, when an older adult who has no disabilities mourns the loss of a significant other or a lifelong home, he or she generally is provided with some expression of sympathy by relatives and friends, allowed to seek counseling or medical attention to cope with intense feelings and negative thoughts, and encouraged to develop new interests and activities to make life meaningful again. Unfortunately, the individual with a developmental disability who experiences the death of a parent or a traumatic move from home is likely to be ignored by or isolated from other mourners and restricted in opportunities to express feelings of sadness and loss, thus increasing his or her risk of mental disorders.

Unfortunately, mental disorders often go unrecognized in people with developmental disabilities at all stages of life. Although interest in the category of dual diagnosis (i.e., intellectual disability combined with a mental disorder) points to the means for diagnosis and intervention, many clinicians still fail to recognize mental disorders in people with developmental disabilities when they occur (Matson & Barrett, 1993). Diagnostic overshadowing, in which clinicians focus on the individual's overt behavior rather than the underlying problem with feeling or thinking, leads them to attribute the problem to lack of skills or limited understanding associated with the intellectual impairment instead of a cognitive distortion or emotional reaction due to mental illness (Nezu, Nezu, & Gill-Weiss, 1992). Most research (Cherry, Matson, & Paclawskyj, 1997; Foelker & Luke, 1989; Menolascino & Potter, 1989; Pary, 1993), however, suggests that mental disorders occur in older people with developmental disabilities in much the same manner and to the same degree as in the rest of the population. As a result, family members and service providers need to be alert for signs of mental disorders that may occur in older adults with developmental disabilities, especially in situations involving stress and loss.

Older adults with developmental disabilities who experience the shock of a parent's sudden death, abrupt removal from the family home, and unplanned placement in an unfamiliar environment also may be subject to posttraumatic stress disorder (PTSD). PTSD is a cluster of physical and psychological symptoms that can occur either immediately or many years after a severely stressful event (American Psychiatric Association, 1994). Extreme grief at the loss of a loved one, especially if repressed or unresolved, has been associated with PTSD (Horowitz, 1997). Older adults who have experienced some form of abuse at the hands of caregivers may exhibit symptoms of the disorder (Ruskin & Talbott, 1996). Some investigators have noted signs of PTSD in individuals with developmental disabilities who were forced to undergo involuntary residential relocations from an institution to a community living environment (Heller, 1985). Other researchers have identified signs of PTSD in individuals with disabilities who have been victims of physical, psychological, or sexual abuse (Sobsey, 1994). The possibility of PTSD should be considered in older adults with developmental disabilities who display severe reactions to age-related stressors and losses.

LEGAL ISSUES IN AGING, DEVELOPMENTAL DISABILITIES, AND LOSS

A number of pressing and interrelated legal issues may arise following the death or incapacitation of a caregiver of a person with a developmental disability or if the need arises for residential relocation because of the loss of the family home, changing service needs, or deinstitutionalization. These issues center around questions of whether people with developmental disabilities are legally capable of determining their own quality of life or whether someone else needs to offer assistance or even to assume responsibility for making important decisions on their behalf.

Informed Consent and Decision Making

As people age, they face a series of complex decisions about their quality of life, such as when to seek or to refuse medical interventions, how and whether to prolong life in the event of a terminal illness, and even how to arrange for their manner of death. Controversial issues such as consent to life-prolonging treatments, advance directives or living wills, and physician-assisted suicide challenge older adults. These issues are no less applicable to older adults with developmental disabilities, but they are compounded by considerations of the question of whether these individuals have the legal capacity to make such critical decisions.

The presence of a developmental disability often raises serious concerns about an individual's capacity to exercise informed consent. Informed consent is a legal concept with three features: capacity, information, and voluntariness (Turnbull et al., 1977). Consent is conceptualized as a set of functional skills related to specific situations (Kendrick, 1994). This implies that an individual with a developmental disability may be able to make some decisions but not others, whether independently or with support (Sabatino, 1996). A determination of someone's ability to consent should be made in the context of a particular decision or class of decisions and must assess not only whether the individual can make a reasonable judgment but also whether the individual appreciates the consequences of the decision (Flower, 1994). Often it is difficult to determine whether an individual with a developmental disability has adequate understanding and decision-making skills to assess a situation, what kind of information is necessary and sufficient, and whether certain circumstances may represent undue influence by people or events (Herr, 1983). Traditional measures such as intelligence test scores (e.g., IQ scores) or ratings of adaptive behavior provide little guidance in determining a person's decision-making abilities (Kendrick, 1994). Families and service providers need to depend on their knowledge of the person and their prior experience in making similar decisions to recognize when a given situation represents a decision that that person can reasonably be expected to make.

Even when they have the capacity to exercise informed consent, many older people with developmental disabilities lack experience in making important decisions for themselves. In general, people with developmental disabilities are provided with fewer opportunities to engage in decision making because families and caregivers assume that they are not capable or find it easier to act on these individuals' behalf (Edgerton, 1994). Yet, even people with severe disabilities can learn to make decisions if they are provided with information that is geared to their own cognitive and communicative abilities (Grundner, 1986) along with training and support (Heller, Factor, Sterns, & Sutton, 1996). Older adults with developmental disabilities should be allowed and encouraged to make decisions about many aspects of their lives to ensure that they develop and practice the skills that they need for making more crucial decisions.

When older adults with developmental disabilities are not able to give informed consent because of the complexity or the consequences of the decision, they may require assistance from a surrogate decision maker. A surrogate decision maker is an individual who is designated to make difficult or complex decisions (usually involving medical intervention) for another person who is not considered to be capable of making the decision on his or her own (Grundner, 1986; Herr & Hopkins, 1994). Although parents traditionally have been assigned to serve as surrogate decision makers because they are considered to represent the best interests of their children, it is not always clear that this is the case (Herr, 1983). Siblings and other relatives also frequently serve in this capacity, but they too may have conflicting interests. The best solution may be a court order appointing a guardian *pro tempore* or *ad litem*, a disinterested party who can represent the individual alone (Ellis, 1992). Selection of a surrogate decision maker is a serious matter that requires careful consideration of how best to represent the interests of the older adult with a developmental disability.

Guardianship and Control of Affairs

Older adults with developmental disabilities who are incapable of giving informed consent and managing their personal and business affairs may need guardians to serve as their legal representatives and assist them in making important decisions. Assignment of guardianship to parents is all too often a rite of passage for people with developmental disabilities as they enter adulthood (Flower, 1994). A guardian may be assigned to protect the person or the estate or both (Rogers, 1984). The same person may serve in both capacities, but there may be valid reasons for separating these functions and assigning them to two different people (Kindred, 1976). The determination of whether an individual needs a guardian at all or for which functions should rest only on the basis of a demonstrated genuine need for such assistance, and the decision should preserve as much personal freedom as possible while providing adequate protection from harm (Ellis, 1992). People with developmental disabilities should be permitted to participate in selecting a guardian as well as to be involved in decisions that are within their ability to understand (Sabatino, 1996). As a practical matter, older adults with developmental disabilities who have been dependent on their families all of their lives will probably not have had much prior experience to acquire skills for making critical decisions without help (Heller, Factor, et al., 1996). In all events, the older person with a disability should be allowed to retain as much control over decision making as possible by cooperating with the guardian in making assisted decisions whenever possible.

ETHICAL ISSUES

The process of aging and its associated losses raise some ethical issues surrounding the extent to which society recognizes the human rights of people with developmental disabilities and their membership in the community. These issues reflect the perceived social status and roles of people with disabilities, provision of opportunities for choice and control, and potential conflicts with regard to competing interests and values.

Perceived Social Status and Roles

Western culture no longer respects the wisdom of age; it assigns older people a devalued status because of their failure to live up to expectations of physical attractiveness and mental acuity. Butler (1975) defined *ageism* as discriminatory attitudes toward and treatment of older adults resulting in denial of their abilities and accomplishments as well as limitation of their opportunities to participate in social functions. Negative stereotypes of aging and older adults influence how people perceive and respond to them (Tibbits, 1979). Families and professionals alike may be unaware of how their own beliefs about aging may affect their interactions with older adults with developmental disabilities.

The presence of disabilities has long been associated with a devalued social status in most societies. Bogdan and Biklen (1977) coined the term *handicapism* to represent a pattern of denigrating and patronizing treatment of people with developmental disabilities. Individuals with disabilities have been subjected to disadvantage and discrimination by means of pejorative labeling, segregation, institutionalization, and even sterilization (Gartner, 1982; Goffman, 1963/1986; Roth, 1983). Blatt argued that the field of disability services would never be successful until professionals learned to focus on "what people have in common rather than what separates them" (1987, p. 9).

Older adults who also have developmental disabilities are almost certain to be the victims of stigma and stereotyping by others. The combined negative attitudes and demeaning treatment associated with aging and disabilities results in a double stigma (Janicki, 1997) as well as double jeopardy for discrimination (Dickerson, Hamilton, Huber, & Segal, 1979). Older adults with developmental disabilities are acknowledged to constitute the most neglected segment of the traditionally underrepresented population of people with disabilities and the group most likely to be deprived of basic rights (Herr, 1985). Wolfensberger (1985) even questioned whether disability services or aging services subjected older adults to more devalued roles and demeaning treatment.

Fortunately, perceptions of and realities for aging and older adults are rapidly changing. A larger pool of older adults has led to recognition of their potential political and economic power, and increased life expectancy and improved health have enabled many to lead more active and productive lives than before. These developments have significantly enhanced the social status of older adults as a group.

People with developmental disabilities also are experiencing an overall improvement in their social status. In the early 1970s, the United Nations (UN) issued formal declarations affirming the basic rights of people with mental retardation and other disabilities, recognizing them as full members of the human community (Williams & Shoultz, 1984). International standards, successful litigation, and landmark legislation have changed the paradigm of disability services from one of social benevolence to one of civil rights (Herr, 1983). People with developmental disabilities have been recognized as one of a number of minority groups with growing power to ensure that their voices are heard and that their rights are respected (Phillips, 1992).

Family members and professionals need to recognize their own fears of aging and misunderstandings about disabilities and how those beliefs might affect their interactions with older adults with developmental disabilities (Bogdan & Taylor, 1994). They must confront and overcome their own discomfort in coping with later-life concerns in order to approach the losses associated with aging and disabilities with honesty and compassion (Hargrave & Hanna, 1997). They must learn to see the humanity of a person with a developmental disability in terms of his or her unique personality traits, prior experiences, and lifestyle choices (Bogdan & Taylor, 1992). They can help older adults with developmental disabilities to maintain valued social roles in helping with household tasks, providing personal care for people with infirmities, or serving as volunteers in community activities (Wolfensberger, 1985). In addition, they can begin to recognize the desire of all older adults, including those with disabilities, to age with dignity and allow them to exercise choice and control over as many aspects of their lives as possible (Thurman, 1986).

Provision of Opportunities for Choice and Control

One of the fundamental concerns of every older adult is the desire to remain independent and in control of one's own life. Yet, the diminishment of abilities associated with aging may necessitate giving up certain freedoms to ensure safety, such as when an older couple enters a retirement community because they can no longer maintain their house and property. Older adults and their families struggle with the essential tension between autonomy and security, attempting to maximize independence yet ensure safety (Lawton, 1996). Families of older adults with developmental disabilities, however, may be too quick to sacrifice autonomy to guarantee security, just as they have made similar compromises throughout these individuals' lifetime.

The concept of normalization, introduced in 1969 by Nirje (1976) and elaborated by Wolfensberger (1972), produced a fundamental change in the delivery of developmental disability services, moving away from a model of segregation and dependency and toward one of community integration and independence. Recommended practice in disability services recognizes the need for people to exercise choice and control in their lives and urges service providers to promote self-determination in habilitation experiences, residential placements, and employment opportunities (Wehmeyer, 1996). The basic principle underlying independence is that people with developmental disabilities should be provided with the same range of opportunities for choice that are available to other citizens, with due consideration of the person's safety and society's welfare (Cooke, 1996).

Too often, older adults with disabilities have little or no opportunity for choice and control in their lives. Their interactions with family members and professionals tend to be characterized by patronizing and overprotective attitudes as well as limitations and restrictions on choice (Howell, 1988; Sison & Cotten, 1989; Tymchuk, 1979; Walz, Harper, & Wilson, 1986). It also is common for caregivers to coax, compel, or even coerce older adults with developmental disabilities into decisions based on the caregiver's misperceptions about aging or disabilities.

Self-determination is recognized as a critical component of the exercise of choice and control by people with developmental disabilities, especially older adults. Self-determination includes expressing preferences and choices, making decisions, forming a self-identity as a competent person, and developing a belief in the ability to control one's own destiny (Wehmeyer, 1996). To live a self-determined life, an individual needs to be taught decision-making skills, provided with opportunities for choice in routine activities, and helped to participate in person-centered planning processes (Abery & Stancliffe, 1996).

Most individuals with developmental disabilities, however, benefit from some degree of assistance and support in making critical decisions (Thurman, 1986). On the one hand, caregivers must recognize the person's right to the dignity of risk (Perske, 1972), allowing him or her to make mistakes and experience the sometimes negative consequences of an unwise decision; on the other hand, they bear the legal and moral responsibility for protecting people from putting their lives in jeopardy or from causing harm to others (Cooke, 1996). Systematic programs that teach decision-making skills have been effective in helping older adults with developmental disabilities to exercise greater choice and control in their lives (Heller, Preston, Nelis, Brown, & Pederson, 1996; Sutton, Heller, Sterns, Factor, & Miklos, 1996). Family members and professionals alike must be committed to protecting the older adults' right to self-determination through providing opportunities for choice, teaching critical problem-solving skills, and offering assistance with difficult decisions.

Potential Conflicts with Regard to Competing Interests and Values

Both family members and service providers may have competing interests and values that can lead to conflicts resulting in the disadvantage of the older adult with a developmental disability. Competing interests and values may present ethical dilemmas to individuals in deciding on the right course of action to resolve problems related to the losses occasioned by the death or the incapacitation of a caregiver as well as relocation due to loss of the family home, changing service needs, or deinstitutionalization.

One area of competing interests and values centers on money and its appropriate uses. When older adults with disabilities have a significant source of income either from a family inheritance or from public assistance such as Supplemental Security Income, these funds sometimes are used to supplement family income or agency funds rather than to enhance the individual's welfare (Janicki, 1996). So, an older adult with a disability may be forced to live in a sibling's house so that the additional revenue can be used to buy clothing for the sibling's children. In other situations, relatives may seek to have a competent adult with a disability declared incompetent so that they can be put in charge of managing an estate, which can be sold to enrich their own assets. Service providers may encourage an adult with independent financial resources to buy a house to share with a roommate to relieve pressure on the system by making two additional community placements available for those on the waiting list for residential services. Conflicts of interest related to money matters are best avoided by assigning an individual with no claims to the person's money to serve as surrogate decision maker or guardian of the estate (Ellis, 1992).

Day-to-day decisions made by or on behalf of older adults with developmental disabilities also tend to elicit competing interests and values. Boggs (1986) recognized these issues as representing ethical dilemmas in the middle of life, identified them as focusing on issues of choice and control, and warned against overlooking their significance to the individual's quality of life. Older adults with developmental disabilities may prefer a relatively modest lifestyle with a few simple pleasures such as watching television, buying a daily food treat, or caring for a small pet. Family members often urge them to join in their own more conventional, active lifestyles, preferring to acquire material possessions, participate in a whirl of social events, and engage in expensive hobbies like skiing. Service providers, in their dedication to active intervention, may mistakenly program activities into the daily schedule that are irritating to older people. Such misguided attempts to force someone to adopt a nonpreferred lifestyle typically create interpersonal conflicts and may even lead to challenging behaviors.

Because older adults with developmental disabilities often need some degree of assistance with decision making in certain aspects of their lives, the issue of competing interests and values may arise with respect to the processes for reaching such decisions, resolving any differences of opinion, and reaching a satisfactory outcome. A host of ethical dilemmas are presented by the need for surrogate decision making and guardianship orders (Freedman & Freedman, 1994; Rogers, 1984). Surrogates and guardians are legally and ethically bound to make decisions that maximize benefits and minimize risks for the individual (Ellis, 1992). This duty implies that no one should serve as a surrogate or a guardian if there is any chance of conflict between his or her interests and those of the person whom he or she has been designated to assist (Turnbull et al., 1977).

Perhaps the most critical issues related to competing interests and values are those that involve life-or-death decisions. The most dramatic instances of ethical dilemmas arise at what has been termed the edges of life—that is, issues surrounding birth and death (Ramsey, 1978). The approach of death and the act of dying give rise to controversial issues such as the right to refuse intervention, to discontinue life support, to control the manner of dying, or to seek death through assisted suicide. When society's negative attitudes toward disability (Bogdan & Taylor, 1994) are confounded with the average person's fearfulness of death (Becker, 1973), the issues become even more complex. Laws may even constrain the options that family members have when the person for whom they are caring lacks the capacity to make his or her own decisions (Fein, 1997). A person with a disability who does not want to undergo painful or expensive medical interventions may be ordered to submit to them. Caregivers, especially siblings who have promised their dying parents to care for their brother or sister with a disability, may agree out of guilt or anger to life-prolonging interventions in a vain effort to delay the individual's approaching death.

When competing interests and values become evident, it may be helpful for families and service providers to consult with other older adults to gain an older person's perspective (Hargrave & Hanna, 1997). Someone who is 70 years old and has been ill for some time may approach death differently from someone who is in his 40s and is in good health. An individual with deeply held religious convictions may view the suffering associated with a prolonged death in a manner different from one who does not acknowledge the existence of life after death. Another older person may be more sensitive to the desire to age (and perhaps die) with dignity and support the older adult with a developmental disability in expressing his or her own values.

PRACTICAL ISSUES

The many practical issues that need to be addressed when older adults with developmental disabilities confront the losses associated with aging are readily recognized by both family members and service providers. Practical issues are primarily focused on two main concerns: planning for the future and preparing for age-related transitions, as well as arranging for appropriate services to be available to ensure a satisfactory quality of life after loss.

Supports and Services for the Aging Family

Two-generation older families, in which the needs of aging parents and an older adult with developmental disabilities must be addressed, present a new challenge for social services agencies. Professionals from the disability services sector may be tempted to address the needs of the adult with disabilities, neglecting those of the parents; professionals in the aging services sector may consider the needs of the parents rather than those of the dependent adult child (Janicki, 1996). Nevertheless, helping the parents may actually be the key to freeing them to make better caregiving decisions on behalf of their dependent adult child, enhancing everyone's quality of life. In order to become better caregivers, families need information, support, and assistance with new tasks such as financial planning and legal arrangements (Heller & Factor, 1994).

Aging families of older adults with developmental disabilities may not recognize their own needs for service and support. Many families could benefit from assistance (especially care) in maintaining their dependent adult child in the family home as long as possible as well as in preparing for the time when relocation becomes necessary (Janicki, Krauss, Cotten, & Seltzer, 1986; Jennings, 1987). Most existing studies, however, reveal that these families often do not seek assistance (Brubaker, Engelhardt, Brubaker, & Lutzer, 1989; Engelhardt, Brubaker, & Lutzer, 1988; Grant, 1986; Smith, Fullmer, & Tobin, 1994). Some families are unaware that assistance is available or do not know how to gain access to services in their community (Heller, 1994). Many older families are reluctant to request professional help, perhaps because they recall earlier disrespectful, intimidating, or demeaning interactions with professionals (Heller & Factor, 1993). Other families may still fear that the adult may be removed from the family home (Seltzer, 1992) or believe that professionals cannot know what is best for their child (Seltzer & Krauss, 1994). Many families feel a sense of pride in their ability to care for their child without professional assistance or public financial support, or they may feel shame if they have to resort to receiving such support (Krauss & Seltzer, 1993; Smith, Fullmer, & Tobin, 1994).

Service providers must learn to be sensitive to the needs and concerns of aging families if they are to provide effective supports and services. Parents who have cared for dependent adult children with developmental disabilities may have acquired a lifelong suspicion of service agencies and providers (Janicki, 1996). Family support policies should address the needs of these aging families so that resistance can be minimized and collaboration can be ensured (Seltzer, 1992; Seltzer, Krauss, Choi, & Hong, 1996). Effective family supports and services are essential to reducing parents' perceptions of caregiver burden, maintaining the dependent adult child in the family homes, and ensuring that both the aging family and the older adult with a developmental disability maintain a satisfactory quality of life.

Supports and Services for the Older Adult

Older adults with developmental disabilities can best maintain a satisfactory quality of life if they stay active within the limits of their physical and mental abilities. Deconditioning is a common syndrome that occurs with aging when a person's increasing inactivity leads to physical deterioration, such as loss of muscle tone, limited joint flexibility, and conditions such as osteoporosis and pressure sores (Robinson, 1994). Health educators have urged all older adults to counteract this trend by exercising and staying active to prevent disease and disability (Aiken, 1995). Deconditioning is especially problematic among older adults with developmental disabilities, many of whom already are at greater risk for degenerative diseases as a result of conditions such as cerebral palsy, congenital organ impairments, or the long-term effects of taking medications (Eklund & Martz, 1993). Lack of activity is all too common among older people with developmental disabilities, however, because uninformed but well-meaning caregivers may make fewer demands on them. Older adults with disabilities must sustain their activity levels to maintain physical health as well as functional skills (Hawkins, 1994). Active treatment, a cornerstone of effective service provision for children and adults with developmental disabilities, therefore remains a critical component of adequate care for these individuals as they age.

Health care is another major issue for all older adults that increases with advancing age. Most older adults face health concerns such as proper and sufficient nutrition; medication side effects and interactions; and interventions for conditions associated with aging, such as varicose veins, cataracts, and arthritis. Older adults with developmental disabilities may be especially in need of health care because of the nature of many disabling conditions and the variety of interventions that are provided for them (Hawkins, 1994). Yet, the health care needs of older adults with developmental disabilities are too often overlooked or neglected. Some people may be denied routine services on the grounds that they will not enhance these individuals' quality of life, such as when an individual is not fitted with corrective lenses to improve vision because he or she cannot read. Others may be provided with inferior care because of mistaken beliefs that they do not experience pain, such as relying on over-the-counter remedies for foot problems rather than seeking medical attention.

The health promotion, prevention, and intervention programs designed for older adults without disabilities can be equally effective for older people with disabilities (Anderson, 1993; Hawkins, 1994). Health promotion efforts, including weight management through diet and exercise, activities to keep bones strong and joints flexible, and hobbies to increase social contacts are appropriate for older adults with disabilities and can be obtained through centers for older adults and other community aging programs. Prevention activities, such as regular checkups to monitor blood pressure and cholesterol levels and routine screening procedures such as mammograms, pap smears, prostate exams, and blood tests are essential to detecting the presence of disease in early, more treatable stages. Interventions such as physical therapy, medication, and surgery can reduce discomfort and promote functioning.

Permanency Planning

Every older adult must face the challenges of planning for his or her own aging and eventual death. Most human beings, however, find it difficult to confront their own mortality and find many ways to hide this reality from their awareness (Becker, 1973). Many adults harbor a superstitious belief that painful issues such as terminal illness and pending death can be avoided by not thinking about them; hence, they may avoid planning for life after retirement, neglect their health care, or even cancel medical examinations and postpone making a will (Corr et al., 1997). Older parents of adult children with developmental disabilities may be reluctant to make plans because to do so forces them to acknowledge their own approaching death (Walz & Blum, 1994). Yet, planning for the future of an older adult with a developmental disability is essential to ensuring a satisfactory quality of life for these individuals.

Permanency planning is a long-term process that involves identifying the needs of an older adult with a developmental disability, considering a range of alternative options for caregiving, and making arrangements for an array of natural supports and professional services to provide caregiving directed at meeting the individual's needs (Freedman & Freedman, 1994; Heller, 1994). A plan can be prepared to enable the person with a developmental disability to make a gradual transition from the family's care to alternative care before the parent is no longer able to provide care or before the individual's needs change sufficiently to require a modification of caregiving arrangements (Smith, Tobin, & Fullmer, 1995). Planning can make change less stressful for the individual, who can become accustomed to different environments, routines, and caregivers, as well as less worrisome for parents, who are available to oversee the process and be reassured that their dependent adult child's safety and well-being are protected.

Families typically avoid or postpone planning, often waiting until a crisis occurs even to consider what might happen in the future (Heller & Factor, 1988; Kaufman, Adams, & Campbell, 1991). They rarely make specific plans for transferring the responsibility for caring for their dependent adult child in the event that they are no longer able to provide that care themselves (Smith & Tobin, 1989). Although most parents claim to have a vague plan for the future involving some extended-family member, generally they have not discussed this plan at all with the person in question (Heller & Factor, 1991). Families that have made such a plan may not have outlined it in sufficient detail to ensure successful implementation, or they may not have made it adaptable to changing circumstances.

Often parents simply assume that a sibling or other relative will provide care after they die, but they have not assessed in a realistic way whether that is possible or even probable (Freedman, Krauss, & Seltzer, 1997). In other cases, families may assume that public care facilities will be available after their death, with little knowledge of the realities of community facility waiting lists (Heller & Factor, 1993). A person with a developmental disability without a permanency plan in place could end up in an inappropriate placement such as a detention center, a full-care nursing facility, or a mental hospital on either a temporary or a permanent basis (Janicki, 1996). Lack of planning or even inadequate planning may lead to emergency provisions for guardianship, restricting the legal rights and freedom of choice of the adult child with a developmental disability (Freedman & Freedman, 1994: Freedman, Krauss, & Seltzer, 1997).

Permanency planning is a process that should be started well before a crisis is likely to arise. Planning requires not only confronting the inevitability of one's own death but also facing the uncertainty of the dependent adult child's future, thus heightening the parents' stress (Seltzer, Krauss, & Heller, 1991). Families require encouragement, assistance, and support from service providers to engage in permanency planning (Smith, Fullmer, & Tobin, 1994). Family members can benefit from anticipatory guidance, in which they are helped to cope with the possibility of death and make plans for the future (Walz & Blum, 1994). Families can even be encouraged to use the waiting list for a community residence as a transitional phase to prepare for eventual relocation (Essex et al., 1997). Family members and professionals should involve the older adult in the permanency planning process to the maximum extent possible (Heller, Factor, et al., 1996). A permanency plan that is tailored to the family's situation as well as to the older adult's needs is the surest guarantee of a smooth transition to a new caregiver and/or residence as well as the best protection for maintaining a satisfactory quality of life after loss.

Transfer of Caregiving Responsibilities

When aging parents can no longer provide adequate care for older adults with developmental disabilities, the issue of a transfer of caregiving responsibilities needs to be addressed. Some older adults with developmental disabilities may be capable of meeting many of their own day-to-day needs with minimal supervision and support. Others need to be provided with alternative caregiving arrangements and/or relocated to another residence to ensure that they receive appropriate care. Older adults with disabilities should be allowed to accept or to reject a proposed change (Thurman, 1986) and encouraged to participate in the decisions about their new caregiver or residence (Janicki, 1990). All caregiving decisions, however, should be based on the individual's actual needs rather than solely on the fact of aging or the disability condition.

Parents commonly expect siblings to provide care for the adult child with a developmental disability after their death, regardless of whether they have discussed this issue with them (Cicirelli, 1982; Goetting, 1986). Siblings generally make some effort to carry out their parents' wishes for their brother or sister (Gordon, Seltzer,

& Krauss, 1997). Families may prefer siblings to alternative caregivers because the relationship endures over the life span and reflects a common set of shared experiences and values (Zetlin, 1986). Siblings and other relatives may be chosen because they are able to provide both instrumental assistance, helping with daily care or even serving as a surrogate parent, and emotional support (Seltzer, Begun, et al., 1991). Caregivers who are selected by the family may or may not be able to provide the day-to-day care needed by the older adult with developmental disabilities for a variety of personal or financial reasons. In these instances, the surrogate or guardian may prefer to contract for caregiving services with a community agency to provide either in-home care or care in a congregate environment while continuing in their emotional support roles.

Aging in place is a concept that has great value for all older adults, including those with disabilities. Home reflects personal values and lifestyle choices (Kron, 1983), and owning one's own home promotes privacy for oneself and connections with the community (Lawrence, 1987). Familiar surroundings and possessions help older people maintain a sense of their core self, and they generally resist moving or being moved from their family home as long as possible (Moss, 1994). A sense of being at home (O'Connor & Racino, 1993) and belonging to a neighborhood is a critical source of personal identity and social support for people with developmental disabilities (Racino & O'Connor, 1994). Older adults with developmental disabilities have the right to age in place and grow older in their home and community whenever possible.

Some older adults with developmental disabilities can remain in their own homes, whether their home is a house or an apartment, if in-home supports and services are provided. Newer models of residential support for people with developmental disabilities have made this option increasingly available, even for individuals with the most severe disabilities and complex needs (O'Brien, 1994). Alternative community housing options, flexible funding mechanisms, and individualized support systems are allowing adults to pay for personal assistance and homemaking services, share a home with a roommate without disabilities, or participate in cooperative living arrangements with paid staff (O'Connor & Racino, 1993). Person-centered supports, including housing stipends and personal assistance, can be used to promote choice and self-determination in the selection of a residence (Racino & Taylor, 1993). Family members and professionals should respect the desire of the older adult with a developmental disability to remain in the family home and offer supports and services that can make that happen whenever possible.

If the older adult with developmental disabilities requires the full-time supervision provided by congregate care, then an appropriately staffed environment should be selected. Options include group homes and intermediate care facilities designed specifically for people with disabilities or retirement centers or nursing facilities (Janicki, 1996). Programs operated by disability service providers may not be able to accommodate the needs of older people, whereas aging services may not be able to accommodate the specialized needs of people with disabilities (Cotten & Spirrison, 1986; Seltzer & Luchterhand, 1994). Interagency planning and programming are essential to ensuring that the needs of older adults with developmental disabilities are addressed (Ansello & Rose, 1989; Gettings, 1988). Effective interagency collaboration requires that aging specialists and disability service providers be provided with cross-training activities (Gibson, 1991), opportunities for team meetings (Janicki, 1993), and policies and procedures to facilitate joint activity (Hawkins & Eklund,

1989). Collaborative planning and service delivery allows an adult with a developmental disability to be placed in the residential environment that best meets his or her unique needs.

RELOCATION TRANSITION PLANNING

Relocation to a new residence necessarily involves changes in physical surroundings, interpersonal relationships, and daily routines and activities for anyone. The demands of any new environment require the exercise of coping skills in adjusting to new people, places, and events. The longer an individual lives in the same environment, the more stressful the transition is likely to be. Relocation may be particularly difficult for older adults, who may rely on familiar surroundings to assist a failing memory or savor the emotional attachments to people and events of the past (Moss, 1994). As the stress associated with relocating increases, so too does the sense of loss, a fact that is no less true for older adults with developmental disabilities than for those without disabilities.

Many people with disabilities have lived all of their lives in a family home or even an institution, so that relocation represents a dramatic change in nearly all aspects of their daily lives (Heller, 1994). Older adults with developmental disabilities are at great risk for abrupt relocations, when their parents' illness or death creates an emergency need for a new placement (Gordon et al., 1997). Some research suggests that sudden relocation associated with deinstitutionalization may result in increases in mortality and morbidity among older adults with developmental disabilities (Heller, 1994). Other studies have found symptoms similar to PTSD in individuals with developmental disabilities who were transferred from an institution to community environments with little advance warning (Ryan, 1994). The stress experienced during relocation may be short term, enduring only until the person has adjusted to life in the new environment, or it may be long term, persisting for many years. Preparing a relocation plan is an important step in facilitating the transition and reducing stress.

Families and service providers need to engage in relocation transition planning to help the older adult with a developmental disability prepare for and adjust to a change in residence. Whenever possible, the person should participate in selecting the new residence (Thurman, 1986) and in making preparations for the move (Heller & Factor, 1994). The person also should have the opportunity to spend gradually increasing amounts of time in the new residence to become accustomed to the environment and all of its features and demands. At the very least, the person should be allowed to select furniture or other decorative items for the new residence to promote a sense of ownership, choice, and control. If the individual is limited in ability to express him- or herself, a caregiver can still make the effort to consider the individual's known preferences, choosing items consistent with his or her favorite environments and activities. Any relocation will be less stressful if the individual is involved in selecting exciting new opportunities for social, recreational, educational, or vocational activities.

One important aspect of loss associated with relocation is leaving behind treasured friendships. Because people with developmental disabilities spend so much time with service providers and so little time with peers without disabilities, they may form close emotional ties with service providers that amount to friendships (Lutfiyya, 1993). Relocations that involve leaving an adult habilitation program or congregate care facility and/or retiring from supported or sheltered employment positions, therefore, also may involve loss of these staff relationships. People in supported employment positions may have a similar response to leaving co-workers and employers if they are not able to remain on the job after the move. People with disabilities may not have access to transportation, may lack communication and social skills, and may have limited control over their daily schedule, all of which interfere with their ability to continue these valued relationships (Heller, 1994). Consequently, they may need help in maintaining friendships through telephone contact, mail exchange or occasional visits, as well as in building new friendships by becoming involved in a wide range of activities. Adults with developmental disabilities also need assistance in making connections with people in new environments. Staff should design habilitation goals and activities to facilitate the development of relationships with peers with and without disabilities (O'Brien & O'Brien, 1992). Older adult companion programs can be a helpful source of people and activities to promote social contacts and friendships in a new neighborhood or community (Janicki, 1993). Such staff and peer relationships are an important source of social support for older adults with developmental disabilities as they face age-related losses.

Societies have developed a variety of rituals to help people cope with the stress of relocation, such as housewarming gifts and going-away parties. In addition, people use transitional objects to remind them of their lost home and establish themselves in a new residence: A child may bring a stuffed toy to boarding school, an immigrant family may bring a treasured possession from the old country, an older adult woman sets up a photograph of her deceased spouse in the family home or in her room at the nursing facility. These transitional objects help people to maintain their core identities as they evolve to accommodate the demands of a new environment. People also personalize the new environment as much as possible to ease relocation stress: College students use bedspreads and throw pillows to brighten up impersonal, institutional dormitory rooms, and families buy new linens for a new home. Many people sustain traditions in a new location, whether it is through a simple routine such as a bedtime snack of cookies and milk or a more elaborate celebration for a special holiday.

Relocation rituals can be useful in helping an older adult with a developmental disability make the transition to a new residence. Individuals who leave their family home for a new residence should be allowed to bring as many possessions as practicable, especially remembrances of family members. People who leave a large institution for a community residence may not be able to bring many things, but they should be encouraged to find and bring small reminders such as personal trinkets or photographs. Prior to arriving at the new residence, the person should participate in selecting new belongings for the residence—if not furniture, at least decorations such as pictures, pillows, or other ornaments. Individuals who cannot shop or select items by themselves can still choose from two or more items selected by someone else who presents items to them for a final decision. These simple strategies can reduce the pain of loss and help the older adult with a disability to feel more hopeful about life in a new residence.

PROTECTION AGAINST ABUSE

Abuse of older adults is recognized as a growing problem in Western societies, which devalue aging and subject their older members to disadvantaged treatment. Abuse of older adults by family members may be due to the stress of caring for a loved one who is infirm, difficult, or demanding (Barusch, 1991). Many caregiving families in the sandwich generation (i.e., the baby boomers at the turn of the 21st century) are juggling responsibilities for rearing their own children and caring for aging parents, even as they strive to meet career demands and personal needs. Adult children may become uncomfortable when forced to assume a parenting role with their own parents or feel resentful at the additional time and effort required in addition to an already hectic schedule (Barnett, Miller-Perrin, & Perrin, 1997). Abuse of older adults by staff in nursing facilities and other care facilities has been well documented by media exposés. Abuse in these facilities may be due to inadequate screening and training of staff, heavy workloads and little supervision, and an abusive culture transmitted by employees and the features of custodial environments (Aitken & Griffin, 1996).

Older adults with developmental disabilities may face a situation of double jeopardy and greater risk for abuse due to the combination of age and disabilities. People with developmental disabilities are at increased risk for abuse by caregivers throughout their lives and across all environments (Coelho & Dillon, 1990; Crossmaker, 1991). Abuse of these vulnerable individuals may be more common because of their devalued social status, dependency on others for care, and placement in institutions (Sobsey & Mansell, 1990). People with developmental disabilities generally are abused by familiar people rather than by strangers and often by caregivers, including both family members and professionals (Sobsey & Doe, 1991). Families and service providers need to take steps to protect older adults with developmental disabilities from the risk of abuse.

With the prevalence of scandal and abuse of older adults, policy makers and service providers have been sensitized to the need to address the problem of support for caregiving families of older adults. Prevention and intervention efforts have become a national priority in the United States (Breckman & Adelman, 1988). In many states, the government has established an adult protective services system to investigate reports of abuse of older adults or those with disabilities (Aitken & Griffin, 1996). Agencies that provide services to the aging population offer support groups, counseling, in-home assistance, and respite care to reduce family perceptions of caregiving burden and decrease the likelihood of abuse (Barnett et al., 1997).

The best protection against abuse is adequate care and supervision. The care of older adults with developmental disabilities should be entrusted only to caregivers who are trained and licensed to provide the type of care needed. The facility's policies and procedures should ensure that consumers and staff receive adequate supervision and monitoring, especially during activities that require intimate contact or intrusive interventions. The guardian or other individual responsible for the older adult's care should make frequent visits to the home or care facility to review the quality of care that is being provided. The service coordinator assigned by the disability services system also may periodically review services and interview caregivers. Whenever there are concerns about the nature of the care provided, they should be reported immediately to the facility's administrator as well as to the designated adult protective services agency. Minimizing the risks of abuse for the older adult with a developmental disability is important in protecting the individual from physical and emotional harm as well as ensuring a satisfactory quality of life.

GRIEF COUNSELING

Grief is a natural reaction to human loss and a common experience in the lives of older adults. People pass through stages of bereavement, whether adjusting to the loss of their loved ones or to the pending threat of their own death (Kübler-Ross, 1969; Raphael, 1994). When the grief associated with dying and death is unexpressed or repressed, it can lead to physical or mental illness (Humphrey & Zimpher, 1996). All cultures have well-developed rituals to assist people as they adjust to the loss of loved ones (Raphael, 1994). Bereavement rituals may involve prescribed activities for mourning (e.g., sitting with the body, gathering with others for a wake), for noting the death (e.g., publishing a death notice, holding a public burial service), and for behavior following a death in the family (e.g., wearing clothing of a certain color, avoiding contact with others for a specified time period). These important rituals are designed to help the person confront the finality of death, express feelings of grief in socially acceptable ways, receive emotional and instrumental support from others, and begin the process of adjusting to life alone (Corr et al., 1997).

Older adults with developmental disabilities grieve the loss of significant others in much the same way as everyone else. Studies have shown that they are aware of death and its meaning and exhibit a typical range of reactions, including sadness, depression, and loss of interest in activities (G.B. Seltzer, 1985). Expressions of grief are influenced by the cognitive ability to understand the meaning of death as well as communication skills to convey feelings of loss (Kloeppel & Hollins, 1989; Lipe-Goodson & Goebel, 1983). If caregivers fail to recognize behaviors as grief reactions, then they may respond to them inappropriately with punishment and other restrictive measures (Emerson, 1977). When people with developmental disabilities are not provided with natural supports for the grieving process, adjustment problems may result (Wadsworth & Harper, 1991). Serious symptoms of depression or other mental disorders may appear if these individuals are not allowed to discuss death or to participate in bereavement rituals (Turner & Graffam, 1987).

Families and service providers have a responsibility to help older adults with developmental disabilities to mourn the death of loved ones. These adults need social and emotional support to cope with and adjust to the death of loved ones (Castles, 1996; Harper & Wadsworth, 1993). Yet, little is known about what kinds of supports and services would best help them through the mourning process (Gordon et al., 1997). Participation in a religious community has been suggested as an important source of support for people with developmental disabilities facing life's losses (Gaventa, 1986). Grief counseling and anticipatory grieving activities also have been recommended to help individuals prepare for and adjust to the finality of death (Humphrey & Zimpher, 1996). Some agencies have even instituted death education programs for people with developmental disabilities (Barbera, Pitch, & Howell, 1989; Yanok & Beifus, 1993).

Older adults with disabilities should be allowed to participate in bereavement rituals so that they may share the benefits of these ceremonies and customs in resolving their feelings in response to the death of a parent or a significant other. Too often, family members and service providers fail to recognize the person's desire to be consoled or the value of these rituals (Luchterhand & Murphy, 1998). They may even think that participating in ceremonies such as wakes or funerals would be upsetting to an individual with a disability by reminding him or her unnecessarily of the loss. Quite to the contrary, involvement in culturally appropriate bereavement rituals is essential to satisfactory adjustment after the death of a loved one and important in preventing physical and mental health problems due to unresolved grief. Families and professionals need to accept people's need to mourn and provide them with the natural supports to assist them through the stages of bereavement.

ENHANCING LIFE AFTER LOSS

Although families and professionals alike are too often tempted to protect older adults with developmental disabilities from the necessity of coping with the losses associated with aging, such interference denies them important opportunities to learn and grow. Facing the inevitability of death is key to constructing the meaning of life and constitutes an inescapable yet quintessentially human experience. Asking older adults with developmental disabilities to confront this ultimate challenge without providing them with appropriate supports and services, however, is both counterproductive and cruel.

Collaboration between the aging and developmental disabilities service systems is the foundation for provision of a network of supports and services for families and individuals to help them in adjusting to loss. A combination of expertise in aging and in developmental disabilities is most effective in addressing the legal, ethical, and practical issues that situations involving loss raise. When community therapists provide counseling to individuals with developmental disabilities, disability professionals can assist them in interpreting the communication styles and behavior patterns of their clients. Disability service providers may take primary responsibility for transition planning, but they need ideas from aging specialists about supports available for older adults, such as Meals on Wheels programs or group activity centers.

Families need advice and assistance with permanency planning and transition planning to ensure that their dependent adult child's needs will be provided for when they can no longer serve as the primary caregivers. They can benefit from informal supports such as other parents to share their hopes and fears as well as more formal supports such as a legal advisor to help in preparing a will. Individuals with developmental disabilities need opportunities for choice and control in participating in bereavement rituals, deciding which residence to call home, and maintaining their quality of life in everyday activities. Both natural supports, such as transitional objects to ease the stress of relocation and bereavement rituals to allow time for mourning, and professional services, such as counseling sessions to resolve feelings of grief at the death of a parent or transition planning to prepare for a move to a new residence, can make difficult situations easier.

THE SADDEST WORDS ARE THESE: IT MIGHT HAVE BEEN

Had supports and services such as these been made available to the families and individuals profiled in the case studies described at the beginning of this chapter, the stories' endings might have been dramatically different. If service providers had worked to help these people with developmental disabilities and their families to cope with and adjust to the inevitable losses associated with aging and assisted them in planning and preparing for the necessary transitions, then these situations could have been converted to positive growth experiences (see pages 190–192). A second look at these individuals reveals more options and happier outcomes.

Ethel

Ethel's service coordinator convinced her mother to consider a range of options for Ethel's care after her death. Together, they involved Ethel in discussing where she would like to live and what she would like to do when her mother was no longer alive. During the permanency planning process, it was determined that Ethel could remain in the family home with supports. The service coordinator drew up plans for locating a suitable roommate to share living expenses and provide companionship, and he promised to make arrangements for periodic supervision by a human services worker to assist the women as needed. Ethel's mother petitioned the court to appoint a guardian of the estate and asked a local banker to manage Ethel's money after her death. Ethel began to participate in a variety of activities outside the home through the local church and the center for older adults so that she could find new interests and friends. When Ethel's mother died, the service coordinator oversaw the plan's implementation, supported Ethel during the transition, and arranged for counseling to help Ethel cope with her grief.

Arthur

Arthur's parents invited Jack and his family to attend a family meeting to discuss plans for their future and his. When Jack expressed a willingness to assume responsibility for Arthur as well as concerns for his ability to be an effective caregiver, the family sought help from a disability advocate. The advocate explained Arthur's rights to intervention as well as the services available to help families provide care at home. Using financial assistance from the state's family support program along with personal funds, Jack added a room onto his house and purchased some special equipment to make it comfortable and accessible for Arthur. Arthur chose to bring a few cherished possessions from his parents' home. The parents were able to remain in the family home with some in-home nutrition and nursing services as well as to make frequent visits to see Arthur at Jack's house. Arthur enjoyed living with Jack and his wife and daughters because he was able to help with household chores; play games with his nieces; and accompany the family on outings to restaurants, shopping malls, and entertainment centers.

Martin

When Martin's arthritis got worse, his multidisciplinary team decided it was time to revise his individualized habilitation plan. First, they had Martin evaluated by a team of medical specialists, who prescribed medication for his arthritis, altered his diet, and specified a set of daily exercises to minimize discomfort and preserve mobility. Surgery and medication significantly reduced his incontinence, and he learned to wear special pads for extra protection. Then the workshop staff modified Martin's job requirements and work schedule, allowing him to sit during production and take more frequent breaks as well as reducing the number of total hours that he worked each day. The group home supervisor used the extra time to introduce Martin to other activities in the community and to help him get to know people in the local older adults' group. These improvements enabled Martin to remain at the group home with his preferred roommate and pet parakeet and to begin to prepare himself for retirement.

Wilma

Wilma was involved in planning for her transition to a community residence early in the deinstitutionalization process. A team composed of institution staff, community service providers, and relatives met with Wilma to help prepare her for the move. She visited several group homes located in the same community as her family and was able to choose the one that she felt was most comfortable. The group home director introduced her to an older adult companion who promised to help her get involved with recreation activities and social events at the older adult center and other community facilities. Staff at the institution helped Wilma to take photographs of familiar faces and places for a memory album and gave her their telephone numbers so that she could keep in touch with them. A counselor began meeting with Wilma twice a week to discuss her concerns and sort out her feelings about the move. Wilma's relatives helped her to purchase some new furnishings and install them in her room at the group home. Although she was sad to leave her old friends, Wilma quickly adjusted to the community environment and made several new acquaintances.

CONCLUSIONS

Families and service providers can use simple strategies like those described in the previous section to assist older individuals with developmental disabilities as they face the prospects of life after loss, whether the loss is due to their parents' death or incapacitation or residential relocation resulting from their removal from the family home, changing service needs, or deinstitutionalization. Collaboration in arranging for supports and services, common sense in recognizing needs and finding solutions, and compassion in understanding individual reactions to aging and loss are critical elements in addressing the legal, ethical, and practical issues associated with aging, developmental disabilities, and loss. Only through the sensitive and individualized application of natural supports and professional services will aging adults with developmental disabilities be able to maintain a satisfactory quality of life and face their own and others' deaths with dignity.

REFERENCES

Abery, B., & Stancliffe, R. (1996). The ecology of self-determination. In D.J. Sands & M.L. Wehmeyer (Eds.), *Self-determination across the life span: Independence and choice for people with disabilities* (pp. 111–145). Baltimore: Paul H. Brookes Publishing Co.

Adlin, M. (1993). Health care issues. In E. Sutton, A.R. Factor, B.A. Hawkins, T. Heller, & G.B. Seltzer (Eds.), *Older adults with developmental disabilities: Optimizing choices and change* (pp. 49–60). Baltimore: Paul H. Brookes Publishing Co.

Aiken, L.R. (1995). *Aging: An introduction to gerontology.* Thousand Oaks, CA: Sage Publications.

Aitken, L., & Griffin, G. (1996). *Gender issues in elder abuse.* Thousand Oaks, CA: Sage Publications.

American Psychiatric Association. (1994). *Diagnostic and statistical manual of mental disorders* (4th ed.). Washington, DC: Author.

Anderson, D.J. (1993). Health issues. In E. Sutton, A.R. Factor, B.A. Hawkins, T. Heller, & G.B. Seltzer (Eds.), *Older adults with developmental disabilities: Optimizing choice and change* (pp. 29–48). Baltimore: Paul H. Brookes Publishing Co.

Ansello, E.F., & Rose, T. (1989). *Aging and lifelong disabilities: Partnership for the twenty-first century.* College Park: University of Maryland, Center on Aging.

Barbera, T.C., Pitch, R.J., & Howell, M.C. (1989). *Death and dying: A guide for staff serving adults with mental retardation.* Boston: Exceptional Parent Press.

Barnett, O.W., Miller-Perrin, C.L., & Perrin, R.D. (1997). *Family violence across the lifespan: An introduction.* Thousand Oaks, CA: Sage Publications.

Barusch, A.S. (1991). *Elder care: Family training and support.* Thousand Oaks, CA: Sage Publications.

Becker, E. (1973). *The denial of death.* New York: Free Press.

Black, M., Cohn, J., Smull, M., & Crites, L. (1985). Individual and family factors associated with risk of institutionalization of mentally retarded adults. *American Journal of Mental Deficiency, 90,* 271–276.

Blatt, B.R. (1987). *The conquest of mental retardation.* Austin, TX: PRO-ED.

Bogdan, R., & Biklen, D. (1977, March/April). Handicappism. *Social Policy,* 14–19.

Bogdan, R., & Taylor, S.J. (1992). The social construction of humanness: Relationships with severely disabled people. In P.M. Ferguson, D.L. Ferguson, & S.J. Taylor (Eds.), *Interpreting disability: A qualitative reader* (pp. 275–292). New York: Teachers College Press.

Bogdan, R., & Taylor, S.J. (1994). *The social meaning of mental retardation: Two life stories.* New York: Teachers College Press.

Boggs, E.M. (1986). Ethics in the middle of life: An introductory overview. In P.R. Dokecki & R.M. Zaner (Eds.), *Ethics of dealing with persons with severe handicaps: Toward a research agenda* (pp. 1–15). Baltimore: Paul H. Brookes Publishing Co.

Breckman, R.S., & Adelman, R.D. (1988). *Strategies for helping victims of elder mistreatment.* Thousand Oaks, CA: Sage Publications.

Brody, E.M. (1990). The family at risk. In E. Light & B.D. Lebowitz (Eds.), *Alzheimer's disease treatment and family stress: Directions for research* (pp. 2–49). New York: Hemisphere Publishing Corp.

Brubaker, T.H., Engelhardt, J.L., Brubaker, E., & Lutzer, V.D. (1989). Gender differences of older caregivers of adults with mental retardation. *Journal of Applied Gerontology, 8,* 183–191.

Butler, R.N. (1975). *Why survive? Being old in America.* New York: HarperCollins.

Castles, E.E. (1996). *"We're people first": The social and emotional lives of individuals with mental retardation.* Westport, CT: Praeger.

Cavanaugh, J.C. (1997). *Adult development and aging* (3rd ed.). Pacific Grove, CA: Brooks/Cole.

Cherry, K.E., Matson, J.L., & Paclawskyj, T.R. (1997). Psychopathology in older adults with severe and profound mental retardation. *American Journal on Mental Retardation, 101,* 445–458.

Cicirelli, V.C. (1982). Sibling influence throughout the lifespan. In M.E. Lamb & B. Sutton-Smith (Eds.), *Sibling relationships: Their nature and significance across the lifespan* (pp. 267–284). Mahwah, NJ: Lawrence Erlbaum Associates.

Coelho, R.J., & Dillon, N.F. (1990). A survey of elderly persons with developmental disabilities. *Journal of Applied Rehabilitation Counseling, 21,* 9–15.

Cooke, R.E. (1996). Ethics, law, and developmental disabilities. In A.J. Capute & P.J. Accardo (Eds.), *Developmental disabilities in infancy and childhood: Vol. I. Neurodevelopmental diagnosis and treatment* (2nd ed., pp. 609–618). Baltimore: Paul H. Brookes Publishing Co.

Corr, C.A., Nabe, C.M., & Corr, D.M. (1997). *Death and dying, life and living* (2nd ed.). Pacific Grove, CA: Brooks/Cole.

Cotten, P.D., & Spirrison, C.I. (1986). The elderly mentally retarded (developmentally disabled) population: A challenge for the service delivery system. In S.J. Brody & G.E. Ruff (Eds.), *Aging and rehabilitation: Advances in the state of the art* (pp. 112–120). New York: Springer Publishing Co.

Craik, F.I.M., & Salthouse, T.A. (Eds.). (1992). *The handbook of aging and cognition.* Mahwah, NJ: Lawrence Erlbaum Associates.

Crossmaker, M. (1991). Behind locked doors: Institutional sexual abuse. *Sexuality and Disability, 9,* 201–219.

Cutrona, C.E., Russell, D.W., & Rose, J. (1986). Social support and adaptation to stress by the elderly. *Psychology and Aging, 1,* 47–54.

Day, K., & Jancar, J. (1994). Mental and physical health and aging in mental handicap: A review. *Journal of Intellectual Disability Research, 38,* 241–256.

Dickerson, M., Hamilton, J., Huber, R., & Segal, R. (1979). The aged mentally retarded: The invisible client: A challenge to the community. In D.P. Sweeney & T.Y. Wilson (Eds.), *Dou-*

ble jeopardy: The plight of the aging and aged developmentally disabled persons in mid-America: A research monograph (pp. 8–35). Ann Arbor: University of Michigan, Institute for the Study of Mental Retardation and Related Disabilities.

Dybwad, G. (1962). Administrative and legislative problems in the care of the adult and aged mental retardate. *American Journal of Mental Deficiency, 66,* 716–722.

Edgerton, R.B. (1991). Conclusion. In R.B. Edgerton & M.A. Gaston (Eds.), *"I've seen it all!" Lives of older persons with mental retardation in the community* (pp. 268–273). Baltimore: Paul H. Brookes Publishing Co.

Edgerton, R.B. (1994). Quality of life issues: Some people know how to be old. In M.M. Seltzer & M.W. Krauss (Eds.), *Life course perspectives on adulthood and old age* (pp. 53–66). Washington, DC: American Association on Mental Retardation.

Eklund, S.J., & Martz, W.L. (1993). Maintaining optimal functioning. In E. Sutton, A.R. Factor, B.A. Hawkins, T. Heller, & G.B. Seltzer (Eds.), *Older adults with developmental disabilities: Optimizing choice and change* (pp. 3–27). Baltimore: Paul H. Brookes Publishing Co.

Ellis, J.W. (1992). Decisions by and for people with mental retardation: Balancing considerations of autonomy and protection. *Villanova Law Review, 37,* 1779, 1784–1786.

Emerson, P. (1977). Covert grief reaction in mentally retarded clients. *Mental Retardation, 15,* 46–47.

Engelhardt, J., Brubaker, T.H., & Lutzer, V. (1988). Older caregivers of adults with mental retardation: Service utilization. *Mental Retardation, 26,* 191–195.

Essex, E.L., Seltzer, M.M., & Krauss, M.W. (1997). Residential transitions of adults with mental retardation: Predictors of waiting list use and placement. *American Journal on Mental Retardation, 10,* 613–629.

Eyman, R.K., & Borthwick-Duffy, S.A. (1994). Trends in mortality rates and predictions of mortality. In M.M. Seltzer & M.W. Krauss (Eds.), *Life course perspectives on adulthood and old age* (pp. 93–108). Washington, DC: American Association on Mental Retardation.

Fein, E.B. (1997, July 26). Not dead enough to die: Laws force life support on a man who never could consent. *New York Times,* B1, B2.

Flower, C.D. (1994). Legal guardianship: The implications of law, procedure, and policy for the lives of persons with developmental disabilities. In M.F. Hayden & B.H. Abery (Eds.), *Challenges for a service system in transition: Ensuring quality community experiences for persons with developmental disabilities* (pp. 427–447). Baltimore: Paul H. Brookes Publishing Co.

Foelker, G.A., & Luke, E.A. (1989). Mental health issues for the aging mentally retarded population. *Journal of Applied Gerontology, 8,* 242–250.

Freedman, R.I., & Freedman, D.N. (1994). Planning for now and the future: Social, legal, and financial concerns. In M.M. Seltzer & M.W. Krauss (Eds.), *Life course perspectives on adulthood and old age* (pp. 167–184). Washington, DC: American Association on Mental Retardation.

Freedman, R.I., Krauss, M.W., & Seltzer, M.M. (1997). Aging parents' residential plans for adult children with mental retardation. *Mental Retardation, 35,* 114–123.

Fujuira, G.T., & Braddock, D. (1992). Fiscal and demographic trends in mental retardation services: The emergence of the family. In L. Rowitz (Ed.), *Mental retardation in the year 2000* (pp. 316–338). New York: Springer-Verlag New York.

Gartner, A. (1982). Images of the disabled: Disabling images. *Social Policy, 13,* 14–15.

Gaventa, W.C., Jr. (1986). Religious ministries and services with adults with developmental disabilities. In J.A. Summers (Ed.), *The right to grow up: An introduction to adults with developmental disabilities* (pp. 191–226). Baltimore: Paul H. Brookes Publishing Co.

Gettings, R. (1988). Barriers to and opportunities for cooperation between the aging and developmental disabilities services. *Educational Gerontology, 14,* 419–429.

Gibson, J.W. (1991). Aging and developmental disabilities: Service provider health-care training needs. *Educational Gerontology, 17,* 607–619.

Goetting, A. (1986). The developmental tasks of siblingship over the life cycle. *Journal of Marriage and the Family, 48,* 703–714.

Goffman, E. (1986). *Stigma: Notes on the management of spoiled identity.* Upper Saddle River, NJ: Prentice-Hall. (Original work published 1963)

Gordon, R.M., Seltzer, M.M., & Krauss, M.W. (1997). The aftermath of parental death: Changes in the context and quality of life. In R.L. Schalock (Ed.), *Quality of life: Vol. II.*

Application to persons with disabilities (pp. 25–42). Washington, DC: American Association on Mental Retardation.

Grant, G. (1986). Older carers, interdependence and care of mentally handicapped adults. *Aging and Society, 6*, 333–351.

Grundner, T.M. (1986). Working with special populations. In T.M. Grundner, *Informed consent: A tutorial* (pp. 163–173). Owings Mills, MD: National Health Publishing.

Hansson, R.O., & Carpenter, B.N. (1994). *Relationships in old age: Coping with the challenge of transition.* New York: Guilford Press.

Hargrave, T.D., & Hanna, S.M. (Eds.). (1997). *The aging family: New visions in theory, practice, and reality.* Philadelphia: Brunner/Mazel.

Harper, D.C., & Wadsworth, J.S. (1993). Grief in adults with mental retardation: Preliminary findings. *Research in Developmental Disabilities, 14*, 313–330.

Havighurst, R.J. (1972). *Developmental tasks and education* (3rd ed.). New York: David McKay Co.

Hawkins, B.A. (1994). Health promotion for older adults with developmental disabilities. In B.A. Hawkins, S.J. Eklund, & R.P. Gaetani (Eds.), *Aging and developmental disabilities: A training inservice package* (Module 2G). Bloomington: University of Indiana, Institute for the Study of Developmental Disabilities.

Hawkins, B.A., & Eklund, S.J. (1989). Aging and developmental disabilities: Interagency planning for an emerging population. *Journal of Applied Gerontology, 8*, 168–174.

Heller, T. (1985). Residential relocation and reactions of elderly mentally retarded persons. In M.P. Janicki & H.M. Wisniewski (Eds.), *Aging and developmental disabilities: Issues and approaches* (pp. 379–389). Baltimore: Paul H. Brookes Publishing Co.

Heller, T. (1988). Transitions: Coming in and going out of community residences. In M.P. Janicki, M.W. Krauss, & M.M. Seltzer (Eds.), *Community residences for persons with developmental disabilities: Here to stay* (pp. 149–158). Baltimore: Paul H. Brookes Publishing Co.

Heller, T. (1994). Transitions and social adjustment. In B.A. Hawkins, S.J. Eklund, & R.P. Gaetani (Eds.), *Aging and developmental disabilities: A training inservice package* (Module 3A). Bloomington: University of Indiana, Institute for the Study of Developmental Disabilities.

Heller, T., & Factor, A.R. (1988). Permanency planning among black and white family caregivers of older adults with mental retardation. *Mental Retardation, 26*, 203–208.

Heller, T., & Factor, A.R. (1991). Permanency planning for adults with mental retardation living with family caregivers. *American Journal on Mental Retardation, 96*, 163–176.

Heller, T., & Factor, A.R. (1993). Support systems, well-being, and placement decision-making among older parents and their adult children with developmental disabilities. In E. Sutton, A.R. Factor, T. Heller, B.A. Hawkins, & G.B. Seltzer (Eds.), *Older adults with developmental disabilities: Optimizing choice and change* (pp. 107–122). Baltimore: Paul H. Brookes Publishing Co.

Heller, T., & Factor, A.R. (1994). Facilitating future planning and transitions out of the home. In M.M. Seltzer & M.W. Krauss (Eds.), *Life course perspectives on adulthood and old age* (pp. 39–50). Washington, DC: American Association on Mental Retardation.

Heller, T., Factor, A.R., Sterns, H., & Sutton, E. (1996). Impact of person-centered later life planning training program for older adults with mental retardation. *Journal of Rehabilitation, 62*, 77–83.

Heller, T., Preston, L., Nelis, T., Brown, A., & Pederson, E. (1996). *Making choices as we age: A peer training program.* Chicago: University of Illinois at Chicago, Institute on Disability and Human Development.

Herr, S.S. (1983). *Rights and advocacy for retarded people.* Lexington, MA: Lexington Books.

Herr, S.S. (1985). Legal processes and the least restrictive alternative. In M.P. Janicki & H.M. Wisniewski (Eds.), *Aging and developmental disabilities: Issues and approaches* (pp. 77–92). Baltimore: Paul H. Brookes Publishing Co.

Herr, S.S., & Hopkins, B.L. (1994). Health care decision making for persons with disabilities: An alternative to guardianship. *JAMA: Journal of the American Medical Association, 271*(13), 1017–1022.

Horowitz, M.J. (1997). *Stress response syndromes: PTSD, grief, and adjustment disorders* (3rd ed.). Northvale, NJ: Jason Aronson.

Howell, M.C. (1988). Ethical dilemmas encountered in the care of those who are disabled and also old. *Educational Gerontology, 14*, 439–449.

Humphrey, G.M., & Zimpher, D.G. (1996). *Counseling for grief and bereavement.* Thousand Oaks, CA: Sage Publications.

Jacobson, J.W., Sutton, M.S., & Janicki, M.P. (1985). Demography and characteristics of aging and aged mentally retarded persons. In M.P. Janicki & H.M. Wisniewski (Eds.), *Aging and developmental disabilities: Issues and approaches* (pp. 115–142). Baltimore: Paul H. Brookes Publishing Co.

Janicki, M.P. (1990). Growing old with dignity. In R.L. Schalock (Ed.), *Quality of life: Vol. I. Perspectives and issues* (pp. 115–123). Washington, DC: American Association on Mental Retardation.

Janicki, M.P. (1993). *Building the future: Planning and community development in aging and developmental disabilities.* Albany: New York State Office on Mental Retardation and Developmental Disabilities, Community Integration Project in Aging and Developmental Disabilities.

Janicki, M.P. (1996). *Help for caring for older people caring for an adult with a developmental disability: A manual for agencies aiding households with persons with a developmental disability.* Albany: New York State Developmental Disabilities Planning Council.

Janicki, M.P. (1997). Quality of life for older persons with mental retardation. In R.L. Schalock (Ed.), *Quality of life: Volume II: Application to persons with disabilities* (pp. 105–115). Washington, DC: American Association on Mental Retardation.

Janicki, M.P., Krauss, M.W., Cotten, P., & Seltzer, M.M. (1986). Respite services and older adults with developmental disabilities. In C.L. Salisbury & J. Intagliata (Eds.), *Respite care: Support for persons with developmental disabilities and their families* (pp. 51–67). Baltimore: Paul H. Brookes Publishing Co.

Janicki, M.P., Otis, J.P., Puccio, P.S., Rettig, J.H., & Jacobson, J.W. (1985). Service needs among older developmentally disabled persons. In M.P. Janicki & H.M. Wisniewski (Eds.), *Aging and developmental disabilities: Issues and approaches* (pp. 289–304). Baltimore: Paul H. Brookes Publishing Co.

Janicki, M.P., & Wisniewski, H.M. (Eds.). (1985). *Aging and developmental disabilities: Issues and approaches.* Baltimore: Paul H. Brookes Publishing Co.

Jennings, J. (1987). Elderly parents as caregivers for their adult dependent children. *Social Work, 32,* 430–433.

Kaufman, A.V., Adams, J.P., & Campbell, V.A. (1991). Permanency planning by older parents who care for adult children with mental retardation. *Mental Retardation, 29,* 293–300.

Kausler, D.H. (1991). *Experimental psychology, cognition, and human aging* (2nd ed.). New York: Springer-Verlag New York.

Kendrick, M. (1994). Some significant ethical issues in residential services. In C.J. Sundram (Ed.), *Choice and responsibility: Legal and ethical dilemmas in services for persons with mental disabilities* (pp. 101–115). Albany: New York State Commission on Quality of Care for the Mentally Disabled.

Kindred, M. (1976). Guardianship and limitations on capacity. In M. Kindred, J. Cohen, B. Penrod, & T. Shaffer (Eds.), *The mentally retarded citizen and the law* (pp. 62–87). New York: Free Press.

Kloeppel, D., & Hollins, S. (1989). Double handicap: Mental retardation and death in the family. *Death Studies, 13,* 31–38.

Krauss, M.W., & Seltzer, M.M. (1993). Coping strategies among older mothers of adults with retardation: A life-span developmental perspective. In A.P. Turnbull, J.M. Patterson, S.K. Behr, D.L. Murphy, J.G. Marquis, & M.J. Blue-Banning (Eds.), *Cognitive coping, families, and disability* (pp. 173–182). Baltimore: Paul H. Brookes Publishing Co.

Kron, J. (1983). *Home-psych: The social psychology of home and decoration.* New York: Clarkson N. Potter.

Kübler-Ross, E. (1969). *On death and dying.* New York: Macmillan.

Lawrence, R.J. (1987). What makes a house a home? *Environment and Behavior, 19,* 154–168.

Lawton, M.P. (1996). The aging family in a multigenerational perspective. In G.H.S. Singer, L.E. Powers, & A.L. Olson (Eds.), *Family, community, and disability series: Redefining family support: Innovations in public–private partnerships* (pp. 135–149). Baltimore: Paul H. Brookes Publishing Co.

Lipe-Goodson, P.M., & Goebel, B. (1983). Perception of age and death in mentally retarded adults. *Mental Retardation, 21,* 68–75.

Luchterhand, C., & Murphy, N.E. (1998). *Helping adults with mental retardation grieve a death loss.* Philadelphia: Brunner/Mazel.

Lutfiyya, Z.M. (1993). When "staff" and "clients" become friends. In A.N. Amado (Ed.), *Friendships and community connections between people with and without developmental disabilities* (pp. 97–108). Baltimore: Paul H. Brookes Publishing Co.

Malone, M., & Kropf, N. (1996). Growing older. In P.J. McLaughlin & P. Wehman (Eds.), *Mental retardation and developmental disabilities* (2nd ed., pp. 85–112). Austin, TX: PRO-ED.

Matson, J.L., & Barrett, R.P. (Eds.). (1993). *Psychopathology in the mentally retarded* (2nd ed.). Needham Heights, MA: Allyn & Bacon.

Menolascino, F.J., & Potter, J.F. (1989). Mental illness in the elderly mentally retarded. *Journal of Applied Gerontology, 8,* 192–202.

Moss, S. (1994). Quality of life and aging. In D.A. Goode (Ed.), *Quality of life for persons with disabilities: International perspectives and issues* (pp. 218–234). Cambridge, MA: Brookline Books.

Nezu, C.M., Nezu, A.M., & Gill-Weiss, M.J. (1992). *Psychopathology in persons with mental retardation: Clinical guidelines for assessment and treatment.* Champaign, IL: Research Press Co.

Nirje, B. (1976). The normalization principle and its human management implications. In R.B. Kugel & A. Shearer (Eds.), *Changing patterns in residential services for the mentally retarded* (Rev. ed., pp. 179–195). Washington, DC: President's Committee on Mental Retardation. (DHEW Pub. No. [OHD] 76-21015)

Noelker, E.A., & Somple, L.C. (1993). Adults with Down syndrome and Alzheimer's disease: Clinical observations of family caregivers. In K.A. Roberto (Ed.), *The elderly caregiver: Caring for adults with developmental disabilities* (pp. 81–94). Thousand Oaks, CA: Sage Publications.

Nouwen, H.J.M., & Gaffney, W.J. (1974). *Aging.* Garden City, NY: Doubleday.

O'Brien, J. (1994). Down stairs that are never your own: Supporting people with developmental disabilities in their own homes. *Mental Retardation, 32,* 1–6.

O'Brien, J., & O'Brien, C.L. (1992). Members of each other: Perspectives on social support for people with severe disabilities. In J.A. Nisbet (Ed.), *Natural supports in school, at work, and in the community for people with severe disabilities* (pp. 17–63). Baltimore: Paul H. Brookes Publishing Co.

O'Connor, S., & Racino, J.A. (1993). "A home of my own": Community housing options and strategies. In J.A. Racino, P. Walker, & S.J. Taylor (Eds.), *The community participation series: Vol. 2. Housing, support, and community: Choices and strategies for adults with disabilities* (pp. 137–160). Baltimore: Paul H. Brookes Publishing Co.

Pary, R.J. (1993). Acute psychiatric hospital admissions of adults and elderly adults with mental retardation. *American Journal on Mental Retardation, 98,* 434–436.

Perske, R. (1972). The dignity of risk and the mentally retarded. *Mental Retardation, 10,* 24–27.

Phillips, M.J. (1992). "Try harder": The experience of disability and the dilemma of normalization. In P.M. Ferguson, D.L. Ferguson, & S.J. Taylor (Eds.), *Interpreting disability: A qualitative reader* (pp. 213–227). New York: Teachers College Press.

Prasher, V.P., & Chung, M.C. (1996). Causes of age-related decline in adaptive behavior of adults with Down syndrome: Differential diagnoses of dementia. *American Journal on Mental Retardation, 101,* 175–183.

Racino, J.A., & O'Connor, S. (1994). "A home of our own": Homes, neighborhoods, and personal connections. In M.F. Hayden & B.H. Abery (Eds.), *Challenges for a service system in transition: Ensuring quality community experiences for persons with developmental disabilities* (pp. 381–403). Baltimore: Paul H. Brookes Publishing Co.

Racino, J.A., & Taylor, S.J. (1993). "People first": Approaches to housing and support. In J.A. Racino, P. Walker, & S.J. Taylor (Eds.), *The community participation series: Vol. 2. Housing, support, and community: Choices and strategies for adults with disabilities* (pp. 33–56). Baltimore: Paul H. Brookes Publishing Co.

Ramsey, P. (1978). *Ethics at the edges of life: Medical and legal intersections* (Bampton lectures in America series). New Haven, CT: Yale University Press.

Raphael, B. (1994). *The anatomy of bereavement.* Northvale, NJ: Jason Aronson.

Rasmussen, D.E., & Sobsey, D. (1994). Age, adaptive behavior, and Alzheimer disease in Down syndrome: Cross-sectional and longitudinal analyses. *American Journal on Mental Retardation, 99,* 151–165.

Reiss, S. (1994). *Handbook of challenging behavior: Mental health aspects of mental retardation.* Worthington, OH: IDS Publication Corp.

Roberto, K.A. (1993). Review of the caregiving literature. In K.A. Roberto (Ed.), *The elderly caregiver: Caring for adults with developmental disabilities* (pp. 3–20). Thousand Oaks, CA: Sage Publications.

Robinson, K.M. (1994). Rehabilitation services. In B.A. Hawkins, S.J. Eklund, & R.P. Gaetani (Eds.), *Aging and developmental disabilities: A training inservice package* (Module 2B). Bloomington: University of Indiana, Institute for the Study of Developmental Disabilities.

Rogers, P.R. (1984). Understanding the legal concept of guardianship. In T. Apolloni & T.P. Cooke (Eds.), *A new look at guardianship: Protective services that support personalized living* (pp. 35–48). Baltimore: Paul H. Brookes Publishing Co.

Roth, W. (1983). Handicap as a social construct. *Society, 20,* 56–61.

Ruskin, P.E., & Talbott, J.A. (Eds.). (1996). *Aging and posttraumatic stress disorder.* Washington, DC: American Psychiatric Press.

Ryan, R. (1994). Posttraumatic stress disorder in persons with developmental disabilities. *Community Mental Health Journal, 30,* 45–54.

Sabatino, C. (1996). Competency: Refining our legal fictions. In M. Smyer, K.W. Schaie, & M.B. Kapp (Eds.), *Older adults' decision-making and the law* (pp. 1–28). New York: Springer Publishing Co.

Seltzer, G.B. (1985). Selected psychological processes and aging among older developmentally disabled persons. In M.P. Janicki & H.M. Wisniewski (Eds.), *Aging and developmental disabilities: Issues and approaches* (pp. 211–227). Baltimore: Paul H. Brookes Publishing Co.

Seltzer, G.B., Begun, A.L., Seltzer, M.M., & Krauss, M.W. (1991). Adults with mental retardation and their aging mothers: Impacts of siblings. *Family Relations, 40,* 310–317.

Seltzer, G.B., & Luchterhand, C. (1994). Health and well-being of older persons with developmental disabilities: A clinical review. In M.M. Seltzer, M.W. Krauss, & M.P. Janicki (Eds.), *Life course perspectives on adulthood and old age* (pp. 109–142.) Washington, DC: American Association on Mental Retardation.

Seltzer, M.M. (1985). Research in social aspects of aging and developmental disabilities. In M.P. Janicki & H.M. Wisniewski (Eds.), *Aging and developmental disabilities: Issues and approaches* (pp. 161–173). Baltimore: Paul H. Brookes Publishing Co.

Seltzer, M.M. (1992). Family caregiving across the full lifespan. In L. Rowitz (Ed.), *Mental retardation in the year 2000* (pp. 85–100). New York: Springer-Verlag New York.

Seltzer, M.M., & Krauss, M.W. (1987). *Aging and mental retardation: Extending the continuum* (Monographs of the American Association on Mental Retardation No. 9). Washington, DC: American Association on Mental Retardation.

Seltzer, M.M., & Krauss, M.W. (1994). Aging parents with coresident adult children: The impact of lifelong caregiving. In M.M. Seltzer & M.W. Krauss (Eds.), *Life course perspectives on adulthood and old age* (pp. 3–18). Washington, DC: American Association on Mental Retardation.

Seltzer, M.M., Krauss, M.W., Choi, S.C., & Hong, J. (1996). Midlife and laterlife parenting of adult children with mental retardation. In C.D. Ryff & M.M. Seltzer (Eds.), *The parental experience in midlife (The John D. and Catherine T. MacArthur Foundation series on mental health and development: Studies on successful midlife development)* (pp. 316–338). Chicago: University of Chicago Press.

Seltzer, M.M., Krauss, M.W., & Heller, T. (1991). Family caregiving over the life course. In M.P. Janicki & M.W. Krauss (Eds.), *Aging and developmental disabilities: Challenges for the 1990s* (pp. 3–24). Washington, DC: American Association on Mental Retardation.

Seltzer, M.M., Krauss, M.W., & Janicki, M.P. (Eds.). (1994). *Life course perspectives on adulthood and old age.* Washington, DC: American Association on Mental Retardation.

Sherman, B. (1988). Predictors of the decision to place developmentally disabled family members in residential care. *American Journal on Mental Retardation, 92,* 344–351.

Sison, G.F.P., & Cotten, P.D. (1989). The elderly mentally retarded person: Current perspectives and future directions. *Journal of Applied Gerontology, 8,* 151–167.

Smith, G.C., Fullmer, E.M., & Tobin, S.S. (1994). Living outside the system: An exploration of older families who do not use day programs. In M.M. Seltzer, M.W. Krauss, & M.P. Janicki (Eds.), *Life course perspectives on adulthood and old age* (pp. 19–37). Washington, DC: American Association on Mental Retardation.

Smith, G.C., & Tobin, S.S. (1989). Permanency planning among older parents of adults with lifelong disabilities. *Journal of Gerontological Social Work, 14,* 35–59.

Smith, G.C., Tobin, S.S., & Fullmer, E.M. (1995). Elderly mothers caring at home for offspring with mental retardation: A model of permanency planning. *American Journal on Mental Retardation, 99,* 487–499.

Sobsey, D. (1994). *Violence and abuse in the lives of people with disabilities: The end of silent acceptance?* Baltimore: Paul H. Brookes Publishing Co.

Sobsey, D., & Doe, T. (1991). Patterns of sexual abuse and assault. *Journal of Sexuality and Disability, 9,* 243–259.

Sobsey, D., & Mansell, S. (1990). The prevention of sexual abuse of people with developmental disabilities. *Developmental Disabilities Bulletin, 18,* 51–66.

Stroud, M., & Sutton, E. (1988). *Expanding options for older adults with developmental disabilities: A practical guide to achieving community access.* Baltimore: Paul H. Brookes Publishing Co.

Sutton, E., Factor, A.R., Hawkins, B.A., Heller, T., & Seltzer, G.B. (Eds.). (1993). *Older adults with developmental disabilities: Optimizing choice and change.* Baltimore: Paul H. Brookes Publishing Co.

Sutton, E., Heller, T., Sterns, H.L., Factor, A.R., & Miklos, S. (1996). *Person-centered planning for later life: A curriculum for adults with mental retardation.* Chicago: University of Illinois at Chicago, Institute on Disability and Human Development.

Tausig, M. (1985). Factors in family decision-making about placement for developmentally disabled individuals. *American Journal of Mental Deficiency, 89,* 352–361.

Thoits, P.A. (1986). Social support as coping assistance. *Journal of Consulting and Clinical Psychology, 54,* 416–423.

Thurman, E. (1986). Maintaining dignity in later years. In J.A. Summers (Ed.), *The right to grow up: An introduction to adults with developmental disabilities* (pp. 91–115). Baltimore: Paul H. Brookes Publishing Co.

Tibbits, C. (1979). Can we invalidate negative stereotypes of aging? *Gerontologist, 19,* 10–20.

Todis, B. (1992). "Nobody helps!": Lack of perceived support in the lives of elderly people with developmental disabilities. In P.M. Ferguson, D.L. Ferguson, & S.J. Taylor (Eds.), *Interpreting disability: A qualitative reader* (pp. 61–77). New York: Teachers College Press.

Turnbull, A.P., Summers, J.A., & Brotherson, M.J. (1986). Family life cycle: Theoretical and empirical implications and future directions for families with mentally retarded members. In J.J. Gallagher & P.M. Vietze (Eds.), *Families of handicapped persons: Research, programs, and policy issues* (pp. 45–65). Baltimore: Paul H. Brookes Publishing Co.

Turnbull, H.R., III (Ed.), & Biklen, D.P., Boggs, E.M., Ellis, J.W., Keeran, Jr., C.V., & Siedor, G.R. (1977). *Consent handbook* (Special Pub. No. 3). Washington, DC: American Association on Mental Deficiency.

Turner, J.L., & Graffam, J.H. (1987). Deceased loved ones in the dreams of mentally retarded adults. *American Journal on Mental Retardation, 92,* 282–289.

Tymchuk, A.J. (1979). The mentally retarded in later life. In O.J. Kaplan (Ed.), *Psychopathology of aging* (pp. 197–200). San Diego: Academic Press.

Viorst, J. (1986). *Necessary losses.* New York: Simon & Schuster.

Wadsworth, J., & Harper, D. (1991). Grief and bereavement in mental retardation: A need for a new understanding. *Death Studies, 15,* 281–292.

Walz, T., & Blum, N.S. (1994). Social work and counseling services. In B.A. Hawkins, S.J. Eklund, & R.P. Gaetani (Eds.), *Aging and developmental disabilities: A training inservice package* (Module 4A). Bloomington: University of Indiana, Institute for the Study of Developmental Disabilities.

Walz, T., Harper, D., & Wilson, J. (1986). The aging developmentally disabled person: A review. *Gerontologist, 26,* 622–629.

Wehmeyer, M.L. (1996). Self-determination as an educational outcome: Why is it important to children, youth, and adults with disabilities? In D.J. Sands & M.L. Wehmeyer (Eds.), *Self-determination across the lifespan: Independence and choice for people with disabilities* (pp. 17–36). Baltimore: Paul H. Brookes Publishing Co.

Williams, P., & Shoultz, B. (1984). *We can speak for ourselves: Self-advocacy by mentally handicapped people.* Bloomington: Indiana University Press.

Wolfensberger, W. (1972). *Normalization: The principle of normalization in human services.* Toronto: National Institute on Mental Retardation.

Wolfensberger, W. (1985). An overview of social role valorization and some reflections on elderly mentally retarded persons. In M.P. Janicki & H.M. Wisniewski (Eds.), *Aging and developmental disabilities: Issues and approaches* (pp. 61–76). Baltimore: Paul H. Brookes Publishing Co.

Yanok, J., & Beifus, J.A. (1993). Communicating about loss and mourning: Death education for individuals with mental retardation. *Mental Retardation, 33,* 144–147.

Zetlin, A. (1986). Mentally retarded adults and their siblings. *American Journal of Mental Deficiency, 91,* 217–225.

13

Supports and Services in Sweden
Principles and Implications for Reform

Lars Molander

Sweden is one of the world's leading nations in its provision of services and support to older adults with intellectual disabilities. Its legislation has been a tool for progress. This chapter describes the challenges that older adults with intellectual disabilities confront and Sweden's legislative attempts to remove the obstacles that they face. The most dramatic change in Sweden's provision of services and supports to this group of older adults is in its shift away from institutions. Sweden encourages older people with intellectual disabilities to move to small group homes or apartments that are fully staffed.

From the late 1960s through 1999, there was a marked shift in Sweden's population. The birth rate declined, and the number of pensioners increased considerably. In the 1960s, there were twice as many children and adolescents as pensioners. At the turn of the 21st century, these two groups are of approximately equal size. As a result, there is a greater need to provide adequate support and services to older adults, including those with intellectual disabilities (Statistiska Centralbyrån [Statistics Sweden] [SCB], 1997).

RETIREMENT

The usual retirement age in Sweden is 65 years. The SCB's figures from 1997 showed that 1,542,374 individuals of the 8,847,625 total population of Sweden, or 17.43%, were ages 65 years or older (SCB, 1997). This statistic is one of the highest percentages of older adults of any nation in the world. Moreover, the number of people ages 80 years and older has increased by almost 50% since the early 1980s. As in many other countries, there are more women than men among Sweden's older adult population. The majority of people in Sweden between the ages of 65 and 79 years are healthy and active. People ages 80 years and older, however, need more medical care and social support. Therefore, caring for the rapidly growing number of these older people will be a social and economic problem in Sweden in the near future.

In the population as a whole, 90% of all older adults live in their own homes, either by themselves or with their spouses. Few live with their adult children. Most of the time, they can manage well on their own. If necessary, older adults may receive practical help from home helpers from the municipality or from their children or other relatives. Five percent live in homes for older adults that their municipality runs, and another five percent live in long-term care institutions.

In Sweden, older adults' financial position is usually satisfactory, unlike in many other countries. The size of their pensions is partly dependent on their salary during their working years and the number of years that they were employed. Many have a pension equivalent to about 70% of their former income. If the pension is not sufficient to live on, these individuals can receive financial assistance such as housing allowances and pension supplements.

PEOPLE WITH INTELLECTUAL DISABILITIES

As a result of improved social and medical conditions, among other things, in Sweden during the 20th century, the percentage of people with intellectual disabilities decreased; but more of these individuals grew old.

Definition and Prevalence

In Sweden, some 33,000 people of all ages with intellectual disabilities receive special support and services. From an international perspective, this figure, which represents 0.37% of the Swedish population, may seem comparatively low. This low percentage, however, is based on the fact that, in Sweden, the definition of a person with intellectual disabilities is not static (i.e., "once disabled, always disabled"), as it is in many other countries; instead, it is dynamic. In Sweden, to receive a label of intellectual disabilities in a legal sense, a person must meet two criteria:

1. The individual must have experienced delayed intellectual development.
2. As a result of delayed intellectual development, the individual must be in need of some special services.

If the person satisfies both of the preceding criteria, he or she is entitled to the services listed in the Act Concerning Support and Service for Persons with Certain Functional Impairments (Law No. 1993:387), enacted in 1993 and entered into force on January 1, 1994. Consider, for example, a person with Down syndrome who grows up in his parents' home. As a boy, he experiences delayed intellectual development; but if his parents find that they do not need any special help, the child is not labeled with an intellectual disability in the legal sense. As a school pupil and a young adult, he may need special services. As long as he receives these services, he is deemed to have an intellectual disability according to the law. Later in life, he may find a job and an apartment of his own. If he can manage on his own without any special services, then he is no longer considered to have an intellectual disability under the law. He will experience a low level of intellectual ability for all of his life, but he is regarded as having an intellectual disability only when he needs special services.

Pensioners with Intellectual Disabilities

The number of people older than 65 years of age with intellectual disabilities has been growing steadily and as of 1995 represented 6.5% of all people with intellectual disabilities in Sweden (National Board of Health and Welfare, 1996). Compared with the proportion of the Swedish population without disabilities who are older than age 65 (17.43%), however, this figure is still low. One reason for this low percentage is that some adults with moderate intellectual disabilities can manage on their own. Therefore, they are not classified as having intellectual disabilities, because they do not need special services. In addition, before 1930 (the time when many of the older adults living at the end of the 20th century were born), neither obstetrics nor pediatrics were as developed and as successful as they are at the turn of the 21st century. As a result, many children with congenital frailties did not survive birth or early childhood diseases. Moreover, in those days, services for people with disabilities were still undeveloped; consequently, many young people probably never were identified as having intellectual disabilities. Many of these people had multiple disabilities and thus were at greater risk of death, with the result that they have since died.

The predominance of women that is found among the population of older adults without disabilities is not found among the older adults with intellectual disabilities. Among all age groups, there are more males than females up to the 75–79 age range. Above that age, the numbers of men and women in this population are essentially the same (see Figure 1).

Less than 2% of older adults with intellectual disabilities stay with close relatives (see Table 1). Even fewer, however, live in foster homes. Moreover, every sixth older adult with an intellectual disability lives in his or her own home. In addition, almost 4 out of 10 live in group homes, and about the same proportion live in resi-

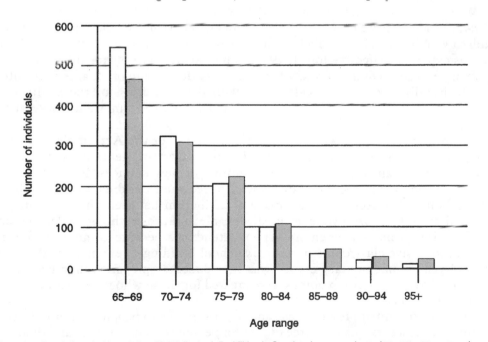

Figure 1.   Population of older adults with intellectual disabilities in Sweden, by age and sex. (□, men; ▨, women.)

Table 1. Where older adults with intellectual disabilities live in Sweden

	Age		All older than
Type of living quarters	65–79	80+	age 65 (in %)
Home of a close relative	36	2	1.6
Foster home	17	5	0.9
Own apartment	354	26	15.7
Group home	822	72	37.0
Institution	729	228	39.7
Other	107	15	5.0
Totals	2,065	348	100.0

Source: Statistics Sweden (1992).

dential homes. Because of the regulations under the Swedish legislation (Law No. 1993:387), many among this population who live in institutions eventually move to group homes. The "Other" category in Table 1 most likely refers to homes for the older adults without disabilities or to community-sponsored long-term care facilities.

LEGISLATION

Since the middle of the 20th century, services to people with intellectual disabilities in Sweden have been mandated by legislation. The purpose of this legislation is to guarantee necessary support and services to everyone who needs them.

Earlier Acts

The first Act in Sweden to benefit people with intellectual disabilities was enacted in 1944 (The Act on Education for the Educable Mentally Retarded, Law No. 1944:477) and effective as of July 1, 1945. It made school attendance compulsory for children who had received a label of educable mentally retarded (EMR). In 1954, the Act was expanded (effective July 1, 1955) to include regulations for the counties to supply care in residential homes, when necessary, for people of all ages with intellectual disabilities and to provide meaningful day activities for the adults who could not find a job (The Act on Education and Care for Certain Mentally Retarded People, Law No. 1954:483).

An important step forward was the third version of the Act, implemented in 1967 (Law No. 1967:940, The Act on Provisions for Certain Mentally Retarded Persons), which contained provisions for a number of new services. It provided personal and economic support to parents who raised their children with disabilities in their home. The Act no longer made a distinction between children with intellectual disabilities who were deemed educable and those who were deemed uneducable: Ten years of elementary school attendance became compulsory for all children. Inclusive classrooms in ordinary school buildings were mandated. A voluntary 4-year supplementary course was introduced to prepare young people for their adult lives. Also, group homes were created for those who no longer needed to live in institutions.

The counties must provide these and other services to people with intellectual disabilities. Most services were free of cost for people with disabilities and their relatives. The counties financed the services by taxing every Swedish taxpayer about

1% of his or her income for these purposes. If a county refused to provide a needed service, a wronged person could contest the denial by appealing to the county administrative court. Maybe a young adult son or daughter wanted to move from the parental home to a group home. If the county agreed that he or she had an intellectual disability and would profit from living in a group home but refused to accommodate him or her because of a lack of places or for economic reasons, the young person (or somebody speaking on his or her behalf) could turn to the court. At the end of the 1980s, there were several hundred such appeals to county administrative courts in Sweden. In four cases out of five, the courts' rulings were in favor of people with disabilities.

The 1986 version of the Act (Law No. 1985:568, The Act on Special Care for Persons with an Intellectual Disability and Others) contained a number of additions. For instance, the Act extended services to people with "childhood psychoses" and to those with brain injuries that, for all intents and purposes, had left them with intellectual disabilities. It was the first Act to regard all people with disabilities to be ordinary citizens with the same rights and obligations as everybody else. On top of that, and because of their disabilities, these individuals were also entitled under the Act to some special supports and services. The Act also prescribed a right for all people with intellectual disabilities to live in ordinary housing areas. If children could not live with their families, they should live in a family home (i.e., a foster home) or a children's home. They must no longer be admitted to an institution. Adults with disabilities could be admitted to an institution only under special circumstances described in the Act. The Act also stated that, as soon as possible, all institutions must be closed down.

The Act of 1993

In the current Act (Law No. 1993:387, Act Concerning Support and Service for Persons with Certain Functional Impairments), the responsibility for supplying services is transferred from the counties to the municipalities. Decisions concerning services can thus be made closer to the people concerned. Also, the number of people who are entitled to support and services has increased and includes many more types of severe and permanent disabilities. Furthermore, the Act entitles a limited number of people with severe disabilities to a personal assistant.

Target Groups   The Act is designed for three groups. The first group (91%) includes people with intellectual disabilities and autism or, in the terminology used in the Act, a condition resembling autism. The second group (2%) incorporates those who have considerable and permanent intellectual or functional impairments due to brain damage that occurred in adulthood and was caused by an external force or a physical illness. The third group (7%) includes those who have some other lasting physical or mental functional impairments that are manifestly not due to typical aging. These are major impairments that cause considerable difficulties in daily life and consequently require extensive supports and services.

Objectives   Law No. 1993:387 seeks to promote equality in living conditions and full participation in community life so that it becomes possible for the individual with an intellectual disability to live as others do. The services are based on the respect for an individual's right to self-determination and privacy. As much as possible, the law intends people with intellectual disabilities to influence the measures provided and to participate in what is decided. If they have special wishes about, for example, how and where to live, how to furnish their room(s), what to do during the day, and how to spend their vacations, these wishes must be taken into consideration as much as possible.

The Act (Law No. 1993:387, § 7) states that such long-term measures must be coordinated and must ensure that the individual shall have good living conditions. Their purpose is to adapt to the individual needs of the recipient of supports and services and to be framed in such a way that they enhance the ability of the individual to live an independent life. All measures are voluntary and shall be provided only if the individual requests them. Thus, against his own will, a person with an intellectual disability cannot be committed compulsorily to an institution. If a person is younger than age 15 years (i.e., not legally competent under Swedish law to make his or her own decisions) or has intellectual disabilities of a severity such that he or she manifestly lacks the ability to form an opinion on the matter, then somebody else must request services on his or her behalf. This request can be made by a person who has custody (e.g., a parent), a contact person, a legal guardian, or a trustee.

Special Supports and Services   The Law No. 1993:387 provisions for special supports and services are varied and wide. These services range from advice to other personal support that requires special knowledge about the problems and conditions governing the life of a person with major and permanent functional impairments. Such advice can be given, for instance, by a psychologist on how the parents best can help their child (e.g., in cases of social and emotional problems). A social worker can inform the person or his or her relatives of their legal rights. People with intellectual disabilities can also receive support from physiotherapists and speech-language pathologists.

The Act also entitles eligible individuals to the support of a personal assistant or financial support for the reasonable costs of hiring such an assistant. Some of the disabilities that this type of aid covers are severe motor disabilities, serious vision or hearing disabilities, severe effects of diabetes or heart or lung diseases, stomach and intestinal diseases, and certain mental illnesses. In addition, if a person needs assistance in an activity such as shopping or going to the movies, then there is an escort service. Someone from the municipality can escort him or her to such activities.

Many people with disabilities are lonely and see only relatives, staff, and other people with disabilities. Therefore, a personal contact who can share their interests may be recommended. Often, people with intellectual disabilities can choose among a number of candidates suggested by the municipality, by friends, or by others. Anybody can become a *contact person*: No special training is required, but a genuine interest in people is important, as is the feeling of the person with a disability that the personal chemistry feels okay. Together, they can do what friends often do—go to the movies or to the theater, attend a rock concert, go for a walk in the park, or have a cup of coffee, for example. At the turn of the 21st century, more than 10,000 people who receive services according to the 1993 Act have contact people. The municipalities pay contact people a small monthly reimbursement for their expenses. In order to provide relief service, someone from the municipality can look after a person with disabilities in his or her home for a few hours. There are also special homes such as the homes of private individuals or short-term facilities run by municipalities in which people with disabilities can stay for a few days.

With regard to children, short periods of supervision may be provided for schoolchildren younger than the age of 12 years. Although this type of supervision is common for children without disabilities up to the age of 12 years, youngsters with disabilities may need further assistance after the age of 12 years. Residential arrangements with special services for children and young adults who need to live away from their parents' home are also available. Another family may take care of a child with a disability and receive a special remuneration for their expenses. If it is not possible to find a "family home" or if the biological parents cannot take care of the child, there are specially staffed homes in apartments or villas for three to five children.

For adults with disabilities, there are residential arrangements with special services. For adults who cannot live by themselves, there are staffed group homes in the form of apartments or small houses (see "Developments and Improvements in Group Homes" and "Group Homes for People with Special Needs" further on in this chapter). Those who are of working age (ages 21–65 years) and have no gainful employment are provided with daily activities. Day activity centers run by the municipality are provided for adults with intellectual disabilities who cannot find a job on the open market or in sheltered employment.

For people with intellectual disabilities, the closing down of the institutions and their transfer to community living arrangements in apartments of their own or in small group homes has been of tremendous importance. For many people with physical disabilities, provision of a personal assistant has opened up a new world to them. Suddenly, they can be like other people, doing things in town, for example, instead of living a confined life in their rooms waiting for the home helper to show up.

Charges   For those who have a national pension in the form of a disability pension, an old-age pension, or some other source of income, reasonable charges for residential arrangements and for recreation or cultural activities may be imposed. These charges must not exceed the actual costs incurred by the municipality, however. In addition, the municipality should ensure that a private individual may retain sufficient funds for his or her personal needs (a "reserved amount").

Responsibilities of the Municipalities   According to Law No. 1993:387, the municipalities are responsible for finding and contacting people who might need special support and services. They are also responsible for informing these individuals of their legal rights and of the services that are available. Most of these services are either free of cost for the person or heavily subsidized because they are financed by tax revenue.

A person with a disability or the person's representative may appeal to a county administrative court if he or she does not receive the support and service that he or she wants and to which he or she is entitled under Law No. 1993:387. The court may then instruct the municipality to supply the necessary supports or services. Appeals to the county administrative courts to receive services under Law No. 1993:387 have been less successful than under the former Act (Law No. 1985:568). During the first 17 months after Law No. 1993:387 was enacted, there were 789 appeals. Only 298 (or 28%) of the judgments were to the advantage of individuals with disabilities; the National Board of Health and Welfare intends to do a follow-up study to find out why (Handikappreformen [Handicap Reform], 1995).

A PLACE TO LIVE

As a consequence of the aims set by Law No. 1967:940, there has been a marked shift in living conditions for people with intellectual disabilities from living in institutions to houses and apartments in the community.

When Institutions Were Popular

Segregating people with intellectual disabilities in institutions, often situated on the outskirts of the community, was an idea that Sweden adopted from 19th century central Europe. In the beginning, these institutions operated on a voluntary basis and were financially supported by national government subsidies or by the counties. With the introduction of the 1954 version of the Act, however, the number of institutions rapidly increased (see Figure 2). Many people accepted these institutions as an effective and rational way to provide the necessary support for people with intellectual disabilities through a skilled staff and essential equipment. Some observers compared them to hospitals, prisons, or military camps in terms of their economies of scale, if not their spartan living conditions.

Alarming Reports

In the 1960s, the National Board of Health and Welfare in Sweden started to receive reports from institution staff and parents about the disadvantages and injurious effects of institutional care on people with disabilities. According to these reports, people with disabilities were often treated as objects and not as people. Moreover, even simple daily routines became bureaucratized *in absurdum*. The direct-care staff often felt helpless, and consequently the residents were the ones who suffered as a result of a bullying or otherwise unhealthy psychological environment. In addition, infections were spread, and thus many people with disabilities in these institutions were always ill. Also, many of the inmates reacted to the big, noisy wards with apathy, aggressive outbursts, or self-destructive behavior.

   Thus, in the 1970s, Sweden made the decision not to increase the number of people with intellectual disabilities in institutions. By the 1980s, encouraged by the positive effects of group homes, the Swedish government decided to close down all of the institutions for people with intellectual disabilities. This directive was included in the Acts of 1986 (Law No. 1985:568) and 1993 (Law No. 1993:387). In January 1996, approximately 1,700 people of all ages still lived in institutions; but only 30 of these individuals were younger than age 20 years (National Board of Health and Welfare, 1996). Only two of the remaining 74 institutions had more than 60 beds, and the majority had less than 30 beds.

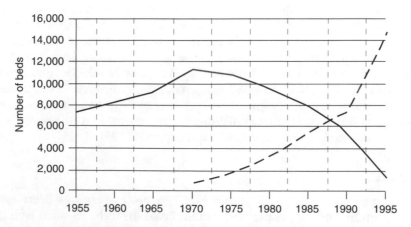

Figure 2.   Number of beds in institutions and group homes in Sweden, 1955–1995. (—, institutions; – – –, group homes.)

Choosing for Others as a Moral Dilemma

According to the 1993 Act, the decision to change the living situation of people with intellectual disabilities should be made only at their own request. "All measures are voluntary and shall be provided only if the individual requests them" (Law No. 1993:387, § 8). Before the decision to close down all institutions was made, however, such questions could not be asked and in fact would have been meaningless. People with intellectual disabilities may not be able to imagine that which they have not experienced. So, the legislators decided for them. Afterward, however, when people with intellectual disabilities had lived in a smaller group arrangement for a year or more, they were able to compare the two forms of living. Hundreds of those residents have been asked if they would like to move back to an institution. So far, no one in this unpublished survey has replied "Yes." Based on these consumers' reactions, the decision to close institutions and replace them with community living arrangements seems to have been a wise one.

All Swedish Institutions Must Be Closed Down

According to Sweden's Acts of 1986 (Law No. 1985:568) and 1993 (Law No. 1993:387), all residential homes and institutions for people with intellectual disabilities must close down as soon as possible. The residents of those institutions are then given an opportunity to move to group homes, where they are to live in common residential areas.

The number of beds in institutions for people with intellectual disabilities reached its maximum around 1970 and then declined steadily through 1995 (see Figure 2). When the process of moving residents out of the institutions began, children and those whose disabilities were considered mild were moved first. At the turn of the 21st century in Sweden, there are virtually no children in such institutions and only a few older teenagers. The next step was to move the young adults and those with moderate disabilities. Most of the people who remain in institutions either have severe intellectual disabilities or are older adults with intellectual disabilities.

The major problem for Sweden at the turn of the 21st century is finding good places for people with intellectual disabilities requiring extensive or pervasive supports and for older adults with intellectual disabilities. In the 1990s, the construction of new houses decreased in Sweden. It was difficult for service providers to find new apartments suitable for people who were moving from institutions and would use those apartments for small-group or clustered living arrangements. If, however, the municipalities themselves want to build houses, then the problem is that, in many districts, the town's planning has reached a stage at which it is difficult to find lots of land in areas that are close to transportation links, shops, and public services. Sometimes the only available lots left are at the edge of the woods and in other remote locations. In spite of such difficulties, knowledgeable experts hope that all Swedish institutions for people with intellectual disabilities will be closed soon after the turn of the 21st century.

Developments and Improvements in Group Homes

When group homes began to open in the 1960s, they tended to be big apartments for about 12–14 men or women. Two people would share rather small rooms (12–15 square meters, or about 130–160 square feet). Often, these apartments were staffed by only two or three people. During the 1970s and throughout the 1980s, group homes developed. They accommodated only four or five people, with men and women living together. Each person had his or her own room. Whenever needed, these homes had more staff members than the group homes of the 1960s.

Then, in around 1985, the National Housing Board prescribed that group homes for people with disabilities and for older adults should be more adequate— preferably a living space of at least 40 square meters (i.e., approximately equal to 430 square feet) for a single person, including a bathroom, a hall, and a closet. Most group homes for people with intellectual disabilities requiring intermittent or limited supports consist of three to five such one-person apartments on the same block. Such apartments are usually combined with a service apartment, in which the staff have their own room and in which there is a big kitchen and dining room and a sitting room with a television. There, tenants can be together, eat their meals whenever they do not want to prepare their own food, play games, and otherwise relax.

In most municipalities in Sweden, there is no waiting list for people who want to move to a group home. There is a definite movement, however, away from the older, obsolete group homes in which many people live together to modern apartments for individuals. Living in group homes has become a popular alternative for many older people with developmental disabilities. At the end of the 1990s, according to interviews with people in charge of closing down institutions, almost all such retirement pensioners lived in group homes.

Group Homes for People with Special Needs

There are some people with intellectual disabilities who have problems of a social and/or emotional nature for whom living in an apartment may not be the best alternative. For them, there are group homes in the form of small houses for three to five people. Each person has a room of his or her own. Such homes are often situated in suburbs and sometimes in rural areas on large lots in order to reduce noise disturbance for neighbors. The staff at these small houses may sometimes exceed 10 people on a rolling schedule.

The need for such group homes is small in Sweden, and there are only a limited number of them. The number of older people with intellectual disabilities who have such emotional and/or social problems seems to be limited, and few of them live in group homes for people with special needs. As discussed subsequently, a related issue is whether specialized group homes for adults with senile dementia should distinguish between those whose disabilities are lifelong and those whose disabilities have arisen in old age.

The Debate About Creating Group Homes Only for Older Adults

In the 1990s, there was some discussion in Sweden about whether group homes for older adults with intellectual disabilities should be provided. There are advantages as well as disadvantages to these types of homes (see Table 2). For instance, older adults often want furniture with higher seats. Many of them also like traditionally styled furniture and would prefer to have their own furniture. In addition, young people may like more subdued lighting indoors, which can be both depressing and harmful for older adults because their eyes do not absorb as much light as they once did. If they are afraid to move about in such a dim light for fear of falling and hurting themselves, they may remain seated all day.

Table 2.   Advantages and disadvantages of group homes for older adults with intellectual disabilities

Advantages	Disadvantages
Staff have special knowledge of older adults.	"Tenants" should live together because they like each other, not because they are of the same age.
Furniture suitable for older adults	
More intense lighting	The older the person with an intellectual disability, the more difficult it is for him or her to cope with change.
Subdued sounds	
Special technical aids	
Near to friends of the same age	

Also, many older adults with intellectual disabilities are isolated. In most cases, their parents have died. Many of these older adults were the only child because their parents feared having more children with intellectual disabilities after they were born. Sometimes these individuals have siblings who have never heard of their sister or brother with disabilities because these individuals were placed in an institution at a young age and then were "forgotten." Moreover, it is unusual for these adults to have a life companion or children. Their network of contacts is sparse. Therefore, proximity to other older adults may make their social contacts easier. It is an advantage if staff are trained both in intellectual disabilities and in geriatrics.

The Debate About Creating Group Homes Only for Older Adults with Senile Dementia

In the 1990s in Sweden, a number of group homes opened for older adults with senile dementia who did not previously have intellectual disabilities. The staff at these homes have special training in how to care for such people. There are special arrangements to prevent "escapes," and there are in these group homes special kinds of large bathrooms in which people with motor disabilities can be cared for. Because of the increasing number of cases of senile dementia, the difference between older adults with and without previous intellectual disabilities becomes smaller. Therefore, it seems unnecessary to open special group homes for older adults with intellectual disabilities as well as special group homes for older people with senile dementia because it is possible to house these two groups together.

DAILY ACTIVITIES

There are three types of daily activities open to people with intellectual disabilities in Sweden: a job in the open market, sheltered employment, or a place in a day activity center. Since people retire on a pension from the first two options at the age of 65 years (if not before), only "daily activities" are open to older adults with intellectual disabilities.

Only 3%–5% of adults of working age (21–65 years of age) with intellectual disabilities have a job in the open market. Others find it is difficult to obtain or to retain jobs in the competitive employment sector, so for them there is sheltered employment. Sheltered employment in Sweden is run by a government foundation. In sheltered employment environments, there are people with many different kinds of disabilities: physical, mental, and/or social. The number of sheltered jobs is limited, however, and only approximately one out of six employees in sheltered employment (17%) has an intellectual disability; the other five have other types of disabilities (e.g., mobility impairments, 32%; mental illness, 17%; somatic diseases other than those falling into the intellectual or developmental disabilities category, 15%; social-medical impairments, 11%; heart and lung diseases, 3%; hearing impairments, 2%; vision impairments, 1%). For those with intellectual disabilities, the goal of these activities is job training. The official goal of these activities for people with other than intellectual disabilities is rehabilitation so that they eventually can obtain an ordinary job in the open market. Those who participate in sheltered employment are paid a monthly salary in accordance with a collective agreement with the Swedish Trade Union Confederation, usually between 11,000 and 12,000 Swedish crowns per month (approximately 1,300–1,500 U.S. dollars or 1,200–1,400 euros per month as of late March 1999).

Many people with intellectual disabilities cannot get a job in a sheltered workshop because they do not have sufficient working capacity and/or it might be difficult for them to find jobs that they can handle. For those who cannot participate in a sheltered workshop, there are special day activity centers. In the 1950s, most day activity centers were large centers for 30–50 people and staff. The "workers" were often trained to be productive, usually working in rather monotonous jobs that required no qualifications, such as assembling thousands and thousands of clothes pegs. Some of these centers still exist, but the activities that take place at them are aimed toward developing the capacities of the person with a disability. The centers also provide adult education, activities that involve artistic creativity, and training in activities of daily living such as dressing and eating.

At the turn of the 21st century in Sweden, many people with intellectual disabilities have jobs in the community in factories, offices, parks, and cafeterias. Unfortunately, they do not have supported employment as in the United States. They are not considered to be "employed" in the same way that people without disabilities are, and they do not receive a salary. They receive only the same "encouragement money" of 35 Swedish crowns (approximately the equivalent of 4.26 U.S. dollars or 3.92 euros as of late March 1999) per day that they would receive for work performed at the day center. This incentive system is designed to encourage work, whether it is performed in the day center or in the general community.

Some 40%–60% (depending on age) of older adults with intellectual disabilities who visited day centers 5 days a week for years went on doing so after they reached age 65—maybe not every day or full days, but regularly (Socialstyrelesens Meddelandeblad [Annual Information Sheets from the National Board of Health and Welfare]). Even though the 1993 Act (Law No. 1993:387) recommends that the centers remain open to older adults with intellectual disabilities for social and activity reasons, they have no legal right to attend them anymore. When one retires in Sweden at age 65, one receives a pension to support oneself financially and is not expected to have a full-time job. If a pensioner wants to supplement his or her pension with extra income, then he or she can do so; but finding a job is not easy for older adults in Sweden at the turn of the 21st century. Because it is typical for older adults to stay at home and have a leisurely life in retirement, older people with intellectual disabilities should be able to have the same type of lifestyle in order to achieve normalization. According to Law No. 1993:387, however, it is *compulsory* for local governments in Sweden to open day centers to all adults (including people under age 65) with intellectual disabilities, but it is *voluntary* for the local governments to let older adults with intellectual disabilities attend the day centers. As a result, some older adults with intellectual disabilities attend the day centers, and some do not. So far, municipalities have reacted differently to the legislation, with some asserting that these older adults should be pensioners and stay at home.

PUBLIC ASSISTANCE

The majority of people with intellectual disabilities do not have an income and cannot support themselves. Instead, they receive a disability pension. When they become 65 years old, their disability pension is converted into a retirement pension. They need the money for their personal expenses, such as clothes, the dentist, personal hygiene articles, magazines, and music recordings. If these individuals live by themselves or in a group home, then they have to pay for food and lodging. If the rent is too expensive, the municipality can grant them an accommodation allowance. According to the Social Services Act (Socialtjänstlagen, Lag SFS 1980:620 [The Social Services Act, Law No. 1980:620]), however, they are guaranteed a minimum amount of money every month for private use. The amount can vary between municipalities but is usually around 25% of the pension of older people with intellectual disabilities.

VOLUNTARY ASSISTANCE

In Sweden, there is little voluntary assistance (i.e., charity). To receive it is to be viewed as a "victim of charity" and to be classified as an "inferior" member of Swedish society. If someone needs services and supports, the general view is that he or she must be entitled to have qualified and trained staff to provide for those services and supports. Too often, only the clever, active, well informed, and affluent can find out how to obtain voluntary help. Most people with disabilities, however, especially the ones who need the most assistance, are not that fortunate. If there is legislation allowing everyone with disabilities to be entitled to certain forms of service, then they or their representatives can demand such assistance. By comparison, students would not accept a system based on their having to seek out voluntary tutors, and people would not tolerate a system wherein people who are ill would be required to seek voluntary medical help for themselves.

CONCLUSIONS: TASKS FOR THE FUTURE

Sweden faces many challenges in its provisions for older adults with intellectual disabilities. First, the number of these individuals is increasing, particularly among those who are older than age 80. The number of older adults with and without disabilities is predicted to increase during the first quarter of the 21st century, especially in the oldest cohort. Sweden needs to plan for different forms of housing for older adults in order to match the needs and choices of these people. Staff must learn about geriatrics as well as intellectual disabilities. They must also understand how to care for dying people and how to talk about sensitive subjects such as death and bereavement.

Services need to be adapted to the distinct needs of older adults. Medical examinations of older adults must be regular, frequent, and performed by doctors who are trained in treating people with disabilities. The environment of older adults with disabilities should be adjusted to their needs and capacities. Older adults should be offered meaningful day activities and a chance to meet new people in order to compensate for their social isolation.

Municipalities in Sweden are responsible for supports and services to people with intellectual disabilities at the very time when they face economic problems. To many politicians and officials, older adults with intellectual disabilities represent a new group of citizens about whom many admit they have limited knowledge. Some people fear that this may mean reduced and/or inadequate services, understaffing, and no access to day activity centers for older adults. If some older adults with intellectual disabilities are admitted to nursing facilities for older adults, then it may appear to be a "normalized" action; but it would certainly mean a regression to forms of living that Sweden has long tried to abandon.

In Sweden as in other industrialized countries, maximizing the autonomy and dignity of adults with intellectual disabilities remains the foremost task. During the first half of the 20th century, adults with intellectual disabilities were treated like children; they were given dolls and teddy bears and had all decisions made for them by others. In the second half of the 20th century, people learned to treat adults with intellectual disabilities as adults and tried to find out what these people want and need. Let us hope that, on the threshold of the 21st century, older adults with intellectual disabilities will begin to be treated with the respect and special care that they deserve.

REFERENCES

Handikappreformen. *Årsrapport 1995 [The Handicap Reform. Annual Report 1995].* Stockholm: National Board of Health and Social Welfare, 1995:5.

Lag SFS 1944:477. Lag om undervisning av bildbara sinneslöa. [Law No. 1944:477 (1944). The Act on Education for the Educable Mentally Retarded.]

Lag SFS 1954:483. Lag om undervisning och vård av vissa psykiskt efterblivna. [Law No. 1954:483. (1954). The Act on Education and Care for Certain Mentally Retarded People.]

Lag SFS 1967:940. Lag angående omsorger om vissa psykiskt utvecklingsstörda. [Law No. 940 (1967). The Act on Provisions for Certain Mentally Retarded Persons.]

Lag SFS 1980:620. Socialtjänstlagen. [Law No. 1980:620. The Social Services Act.]

Lag SFS 1985:568. Lag om särskilda omsorger om psykiskt utvecklingsstörda m fl. [Law No. 568 (1985). The Act on Special Care for Persons with an Intellectual Disability and Others.]

Lag SFS 1993:387. Lag om stöd och service till vissa funktionshindrade. [Law No. 387 (1993). The Act Concerning Support and Service for Persons with Certain Functional Impairments.]

National Board of Health and Social Welfare. (1996). Support and Service for Persons with Certain Functional Impairments on January 1st 1996. Statistiska [Statistics]. Stockholm: Author.

Statistiska Centralbyrån [Statistics Sweden]. (1992). Stockholm: The National Board of Health and Social Welfare.

Statistiska Centralbyrån [Statistics Sweden]. (1996). Stockholm: The National Board of Health and Social Welfare.

Statistiska Centralbyrån [Statistics Sweden]. (1997). Stockholm: The National Board of Health and Social Welfare.

14

An International Perspective on Quality

Chris Conliffe and Patricia Noonan Walsh

Sadie

Sadie lives in the west of Ireland; she is 84 years old. Sadie has been ill for some months, and although she and her husband, Tom, have a large family, she feels that she has no one to talk to about her worries. Two of their children still live at home. Their daughter Anne is 59 years old. Sadie and Tom have never been told exactly what caused Anne's developmental disability, although when she was born, a doctor said that Anne would be a bit "backward" because Sadie, while she was pregnant, had been in contact with someone who had German measles. Anne is at home all day. "She does nothing," Sadie reports. Anne does not attend a day center or workshop of any kind and has always seemed to depend a good deal on Sadie for everything. Sadie and Tom have not made a will, nor is there a financial plan for Anne's support in the future. Another daughter has agreed to look after Anne when Sadie can no longer do so, but Sadie believes it may be better all around, perhaps, if Anne were to live in a residential facility.

A first impression is that Sadie and Anne are two older European women living unremarkable lives at the turn of the 21st century. Yet, their quiet household is distinctive. Anne represents an emergent population of older adults with developmental disabilities who enjoy unprecedented longevity, as do many thousands of citizens of the more industrialized countries. In addition, Sadie is one of the increasing number of older people who have been pressed into unforeseen lifelong service as caregivers for a family member whose years extend far beyond what might have been predicted in the 1930s. By virtue of their gender, age, and economic dependency and the presence of Anne's developmental disability, both women seem to be on the margins of the bright promise of prosperity and social inclusion throughout Europe.

These days, governments in European and other countries not only aspire to their own endurance and the prosperity of their citizens but also endorse more ambitious policies aimed at the social inclusion of all citizens. In the European Union, for example, national governments are urged to foster inclusion by removing economic and social barriers to the full participation of all citizens in everyday life. Equal opportunities for inclusion accordingly should be extended to all individuals, regardless of their age, gender, or perceived dearth of competence (Commission of the European Communities, 1996). It follows that equal opportunities for social inclusion are rightful outcomes for individuals with intellectual and other developmental disabilities. The quality of interventions on their behalf may be determined not by care and comfort but by how well the interventions support individuals to pursue the desired and equal opportunities.

Do Anne's fortunes reflect changed thinking about the status of people with intellectual and other developmental disabilities? The facts that she has survived at all and lives at home mark progress of a kind as the gap narrows between her life expectancy and that of another woman of her age without disabilities. During the 20th century, people with intellectual disabilities acted in a range of social roles: burdens on the public purse, charity cases, recipients of care, objects of scientific scrutiny, immodest users of social services, and exiles in institutions in their own countries. During the 1930s and World War II, many thousands of Europeans with disabilities lost their lives as victims of a lethal form of social exclusion: genocide. In a program known as Action T-4, the Nazis murdered thousands of people with disabilities. Thus, some of these children of the 1930s, because they were killed, never grew old (Friedlander, 1995).

This chapter suggests that human rights may be expressed in the equal opportunities that countries make available to their citizens, not least to aging citizens with developmental disabilities. An international perspective is adopted by examining realities for this group at the turn of the 21st century in a sample of countries represented at the Sixth International Roundtable on Aging and Intellectual Disabilities held in Vienna in 1995. It proposes supports and services for the population of aging individuals with developmental disabilities the quality of which might best be measured by how well those supports and services promote valued personal and social outcomes for this population. A collaborative research agenda is also proposed.

EQUAL OPPORTUNITIES

In the future that Anne and thousands of people like her must share with all Europeans, two relentless forces will curb expressions of social solidarity. First, a widespread surge in life expectancy among people with developmental disabilities is apparent (Health Research Board, 1996; Seltzer, Krauss, & Janicki, 1994). In situations in which families continue to offer primary care to adults with developmental disabilities, demographic trends are coupled with changes in the texture and composition of family life. More women enter the general workforce, often as older men in traditional industrial sectors leave it, sending ripples through the pool of traditional caregivers and altering the next generation of family supports (Phillips, 1996; Shearn & Todd, 1997). Yet, whatever the cause of their disabilities and whether they experience impairments in physical or cognitive functioning, older adults rely primarily on family help and living arrangements to stay in the community rather than be moved into income or public programs (Boaz & Hu, 1997).

In more prosperous, industrialized countries, older adults—including those with developmental disabilities—continue to thrive. As the number of older adults with developmental disabilities grows, concurrent changes in this population are likely (Health Research Board, 1996). According to 1996 statistics, more than 8% of all Irish people with an intellectual disability (i.e., mental retardation) are age 55 years or older, and those between ages 35 and 54 years comprise 28% of all people in Ireland with a level of intellectual disability requiring limited, extensive, or pervasive support (Health Research Board, 1996; Table 1).

In Northern Ireland, more than one in five (22%) people with Down syndrome—a group at increased risk for premature aging—are age 40 years or older (Conliffe, McHugh, Stringer, & Betts, 1998; Janicki, Heller, Seltzer, & Hogg, 1996). Countries that have adopted community-based models of social care gradually fit the needs of an increased number of households with aging members, many of which are led by older adult family members caring for a middle-age man or woman with a developmental disability.

A second constraint on social solidarity is fiscal. Measures to promote social inclusion may prove costly. Demands from special interest groups on systems of social welfare and other nationally funded services compete with one another. Economic success and rising levels of health care sustain the overall increase in numbers of older citizens who clamor for financial supports such as pensions (Lachman, Bennett, Green, Hagemann, & Ramaswamy, 1995). There are other competitors. Prior to the middle of the 20th century, only a small remnant of exceptional individuals—people with severe disabilities and complex health needs—lived past childhood. At the turn of the 21st century, they may thrive and be set to join a cohort of healthy survivors. Survival carries a price, however. Such individuals will persist in their claims for costly health and social services over time. Will these varied groups benefit equally from the trickle-down effects of gradual inclusion? Or will equal opportunities elude marginal citizens such as Anne, Sadie, and their family members?

Until the 1990s, it was assumed that people with developmental disabilities were chiefly dependent by virtue of an intrinsic incapacity to understand and manage their lives in society. Accordingly, they were encouraged to seek lifelong care—so it was thought—to shore them up so that they could live relatively short lives removed from their peers. Life outcomes were impoverished when compared with those valued for all people at the turn of the 21st century, such as the skills needed to support lifelong learning, a network of friends and acquaintances, and the ability

Table 1.   Proportion (%) of Irish adults with intellectual disabilities requiring support, by age group

Age group	1974	1981	1996
20–34 years	26.3	31.6	32.6
35–54 years	19.1	18.4	28.2
55+ years	9.4	8.0	9.7

Source: Health Research Board (1996).

to use community resources (Hardman, McDonnell, & Welch, 1997). By contrast, contemporary approaches to disability reveal the following three core principles:

1. Fundamental human rights apply to all individuals.
2. The interaction between the social and physical environments and an individual with disabilities plays a major part in the individual's life experience and outcomes.
3. Supports provided for people with disabilities should be judged on the outcomes achieved.

These principles are recognized in the United Nations' (UN's) Standard Rules for the Equalization of Opportunities for Persons with Disabilities (StRE), which the UN General Assembly adopted in 1993 (UN, 1994). The 22 rules (see also Chapter 3) underline the dynamic quality of equal opportunities. Equalization is not a fixed reward but rather "the process through which the various systems of society and the environment, such as services, activities, information and documentation are made available to all, particularly persons with disabilities" (UN, 1994, pp. 11–12). These rules, in addition to advocating a rights-based approach to disability favoring equal opportunities, have been endorsed by the European Union: "General health and rehabilitation and preventative strategies should be more closely tied, where appropriate, to the pursuit of equal opportunities" (Commission of the European Communities, 1996, p. 23).

The ideals of the UN and the European Union—social inclusion, for example—often seem too lofty to be grasped in ordinary experience. To bridge the aims that they endorse and the everyday lives of their citizens, national governments shape social policies. The belief that social planning should be driven by the recognition that each person's needs are of equal importance is a core premise underlying the StRE. For many individuals with distinctive needs, such as older adults with developmental disabilities, equal opportunities are made, not born.

Although longitudinal studies in the Netherlands (van Schrojenstein Lantman-de Valk et al., 1997), the United States (Seltzer & Krauss, 1989), and elsewhere continue to yield information about the capabilities and experiences of cohorts of older adults with developmental disabilities over many years, the understanding of the life-course development of this population is still incomplete. Nor is it a straightforward matter to tease out the factors related to the personal capacities and preferences of individuals with complex needs from those reflecting features of the environment and culture in which they live (Hogg, 1997). The following case study illustrates this point.

Jacques

Jacques is 49 years old and frail in appearance. He resists meeting new people. Is this because his speech is indistinct and he is embarrassed? Or is it because his physical stamina inexplicably lets him down when he exerts himself or because he has no income to spend on social outings? Has a life history of being confined to a peaceful, special residence where staff members make all decisions on Jacques's behalf left a lasting mark that is interpreted as indifference? Has Jacques already lived years longer than anyone predicted, with the result that no one really knows what Jacques ought to do now? His apparent resistance to new experiences might well reflect his personal satisfaction with the way he lives now, or it may reflect his lack of skill in communicating his preferences to others or a history of low expectations resulting from a low income and a dearth of learning opportunities. Or, perhaps, is Jacques increasingly withdrawn with the onset of some age-related disorder such as dementia?

The life experiences of older people with developmental disabilities vary not only across individuals but across cultures as well (Seltzer et al., 1995). The authors of the StRE recognized cross-cultural variability in their statement of the need to acknowledge varied cultural contexts within which political decision making takes place as well as the need to acknowledge the diverse life situations of people with disabilities. Regional differences confound matters further (Moss, 1992). In the United States, human rights are assumed to be ultimately individual and irreducible. For European governments, by contrast, attaining human rights is a social goal (Quinn, 1995). The European Union's social policy directly endorses the StRE yet leaves to each country the decision about how to ensure that its own social systems and environments are available to all citizens.

According to the StRE, *equalization of opportunities* means that all systems and services within a society should be made available to all citizens, particularly to those with disabilities. Rules 1 through 4 state the preconditions required for this process. Do they exist only on paper, or have they embedded themselves in the environments in which people with developmental disabilities live and grow old?

PRECONDITIONS FOR EQUAL OPPORTUNITIES

Even within Europe, countries vary markedly in the coverage of social support that they make available to their citizens and in their traditions of family care. In Denmark, a good deal of care for older people is provided by the public sector; but community care policies in the United Kingdom assume steadfast family input into care arrangements (Salvage, 1995). Thus, as O'Shea and Kennelly observed, family care is interwoven with public policy.

> The inadequate nature of community care in many countries means that families must care. There is a moral imperative, which goes beyond altruism and reciprocity, to provide assistance, since, without extensive family support, life would be intolerable for people with disabilities living at home. Residential care would probably be the only option. (1995, p. 9)

Such options have become commonplace in the better-off countries with older adult populations, where, it must be recalled, only a minority of all people with disabilities worldwide live (O'Toole & McConkey, 1995). Yet, the governments of even these apparently prosperous countries must confront their own economic challenges. Governments confront complex social and economic issues involved in the long-term management of intergenerational transfers to fund social and health services (Lachman et al., 1995).

The resource demands made by older adults with disabilities to national governments for health and social services widen in scope and intensify in the range of goals pursued. Individuals expect continuous health and social gain, not merely maintenance of the status quo with regard to their well-being, even while governments charged with providing such services exhort service providers to give value for money. By contrast, countries in eastern and central Europe whose economies are in transition and have younger populations do not entertain such luxurious choices. Their systems of health and social welfare remain in their infancy. In such countries, governments struggle day to day with more-pressing concerns, such as how to build a social safety net of any kind, however thinly woven (Sachs, 1993).

Prosperous or not, national governments are charged with extending equal opportunities to their own citizens. The first four of the StRE rules that the UN (1994) adopted set out the four preconditions that are necessary, if not sufficient, to make participation available to all citizens within states (i.e., countries), including those citizens with disabilities:

- *Rule 1: Awareness raising:* States should take action to raise awareness in society about people with disabilities, their rights, their needs, their potential, and their contributions.
- *Rule 2: Medical care:* States should ensure the provision of effective medical care to people with disabilities.
- *Rule 3: Rehabilitation:* States should ensure the provision of rehabilitation services to people with disabilities in order for them to reach and sustain their optimum level of independence and functioning.
- *Rule 4: Supports:* States should ensure the development and supply of support services, including assistive technology devices for people with disabilities, to help them to increase their level of independence in their daily living and to exercise their rights.

Are these preconditions for equal opportunities—each spelled out in a list of specific guidelines—widespread across social systems? To address this question, professionals from 16 countries were invited to take part in case studies of three aging Europeans with developmental disabilities. Descriptions of Peter, Joseffa, and Ernst outlining the distinctive characteristics and needs of each individual were drawn from documented life histories and sent to participants at the Roundtable on Aging and Developmental Disability sponsored by the Special Interest Research Group on Aging within the International Association for the Scientific Study of Intellectual Disability (IASSID) that took place in Vienna in May 1995. The case study descriptions outline some of the personal characteristics of Peter, Joseffa, and Ernst, but they also illustrate some of the distinctive features that influence the aging process among older people with intellectual disabilities and the ways in which these individuals interact with others and with the environments in which they live.

Peter

For Peter, with his years of relatively independent living and employment, the recent death of a family caregiver sparked an urgent search for a place to live, a search that may be driven by crisis and may not reflect his own preferences. Peter is 51 years old and has Down syndrome. An only child, he lived in his parents' home in a rural area for most of his life. He attended a general education school with students without disabilities. His social behavior is well developed. Peter's verbal language expression is good, and he manages to get around by himself well. As a young adult, Peter was offered a job as a nurse's assistant by the director of a hospital in a nearby city. In common with his former school friends, he commuted to work every day from his village. When Peter was 29 years old, his mother died, and this affected him deeply, leading to a depressive episode that lasted for nearly a year and a half. Peter's father subsequently remarried. Peter remained in the family home but showed regular outbursts of aggression toward his stepmother. When Peter was about 40 years old, his vocational advocate retired, and Peter lost his job.

In 1993, Peter's father (then age 76) became chronically ill, and his stepmother decided that she must give total support to her husband; she told Peter that she could not take care of two people. Because Peter was never trained for independent living, plans for his future residence must be negotiated carefully. Peter had lived a nearly typical existence for all of his life, and he was definitely opposed to entering a home for people with developmental disabilities.

Joseffa

Joseffa has for some years faced the twin challenges of poor communication skills and behavior problems, which from time to time proved difficult to manage. Joseffa was born in 1945 and was placed in a residential home for infants at age 3 months. When she was 3 years old, Joseffa was admitted to a children's home for those with developmental disabilities near a state-run psychiatric facility. There, she was described as "very lively," and some behavior problems were observed, such as biting and not knowing how to play with toys. Joseffa spent her adolescent and adult years in the children's home. A report in 1985 described her as follows: good general condition; rolling gait; no verbal expression and minimal comprehension of language; spends a lot of time on the toilet; nocturnal incontinence; unable to dress herself without help; generally restless, with stereotypical rocking movements; moves mostly with body bent down; occasional outbursts of aggressive behavior; resorts to self-destructive behavior (e.g., self-biting, striking) if she does not get what she wants; and no interest in structured activities.

A few years later, in 1990, Joseffa's social behavior was described as follows: no friendships; no contact with people outside the unit; enjoys being taken for a walk; moves, climbs, holds a pencil, and brushes her teeth correctly; dresses herself and needs only some help with using the toilet; no real interest in work; runs round and does not fit into the structured day program.

Joseffa moved outside the home in 1992 for a few months to a nature camp, where her social behavior improved significantly and her self-destructive behaviors virtually disappeared. In 1993, however, Joseffa's behavior deteriorated, and she sat on the floor a good deal with stereotypical rocking movements, pulling apart any objects placed in her hands. When she was allowed to leave the unit alone—within the confines of the facility—she was calm and happy; if confined, however, Joseffa became aggressive.

Ernst

Ernst presented as someone who periodically experiences serious mental health difficulties and accompanying bouts of hospitalization and medication. Ernst has a moderate level of developmental disabilities and an autistic disorder that was diagnosed at an early age. Although he always has had a problem of sleep disturbance, his physical health is good. Ernst lived in the family home until he was 22 years old; but because of family difficulties, he was admitted to a state developmental center for 5 years. Afterward, he returned home; but when he was 37 years old, upon the death of his mother, Ernst was admitted to a state psychiatric facility as an inpatient. He has a history of receiving interventions with a range of neuroleptic agents. One month prior to his present evaluation, Ernst was discharged to a community living program in which he no longer takes medication.

At age 55 years, Ernst never makes eye contact with other people. He stares into space or engages in stereotypical hand movements. Although he rarely speaks more than one word at a time, his receptive language skills are good. Clinical records compiled at different periods of Ernst's life give some indication of the pattern of his behavior problems. Systematic observations, described in the following list, indicate that Ernst's behavior is characterized by significant, sustained mood swings:

1. His highs—lasting about 2 or 3 months—are characterized by a euphoric mood, intense verbal outbursts, irritability, overactivity, decreased sleep, running away from the residence, and outbursts of physical aggression toward both objects and people.
2. During a low phase, Ernst displays withdrawal, fatigue, depressed mood, and an increased level of self-stimulatory behavior.
3. Regardless of high or low phase, Ernst shows no obvious interest in communicating with other people.

Respondents completed postal questionnaires inviting them to report on the services likely to be available to individuals such as Peter, Joseffa, and Ernst in their own countries. Sixteen countries were represented. There is no reason to infer the generalized validity of the findings of this small survey, and there are many reasons to suggest that the respondents might well have cited the best rather than the commonplace practice in their countries. Nonetheless, an analysis of the content of the responses suggests that the essential preconditions and opportunities for full participation in society are by no means widely available to people like Peter, Joseffa, and Ernst in the 16 countries represented (see Table 2).

The respondents, representing countries as diverse as Austria, the Czech Republic, France, Ireland, The Netherlands, the United Kingdom, and the United States offered details that suggested that some of the terms in the questionnaire held slightly different meanings across cultures. For example, *advocate* might mean either a social worker or a volunteer befriender. Yet, all respondents converged in their views on the outstanding needs of these three individuals. For Peter, a stable home life and occupation are essential. Joseffa requires personal supports, especially in enhancing her communicative competence. Ernst must have more privacy and autonomy even while his complex mental health requirements are evaluated. Personal safety, shelter, and autonomy are basic rights for all individuals. People with disabilities are first and foremost citizens with equal rights and obligations and only secondarily are users of social services.

Commonalties emerge, even across the 16 diverse countries that the respondents in Vienna represented. It is apparent that Peter, Joseffa, and Ernst would bene-

Table 2. Survey of respondents from 16 countries: Sixth International Roundtable on Aging and Intellectual Disabilities, Vienna (1995)

UN rule	Peter	Joseffa	Ernst
Awareness raising	• More likely to take part in own decisions • Advocate likely in 11 countries	• Guardian likely in 11 countries • Advocate assigned in some countries	• Advocate "probable" in 10 countries
Medical care	• Care is worse in four countries than in the scenario	• Care is worse in four countries than in the scenario	• Little provision for mental health problems
Rehabilitation	• Day programs widespread • More access to a trained professional worker	• Personalized procedures less likely	• Less chance of privacy and access to everyday facilities
Support services	• Overall, adequate • Wide range of residential supports likely: group home, independent living (one country only), or possibly a psychiatric hospital	• Overall, just slightly better than those likely for Ernst	• In six countries, supports are not adequate for Ernst

fit from individual attention to their distinctive personal needs, more direct involvement in decisions taken about their own lives, and contact with well-trained professionals from many disciplines. These issues strike at the heart of quality of life, a construct universally identified and increasingly used as a yardstick by which to evaluate outcomes for individuals with developmental disabilities.

It is striking that the items on the questionnaire distributed in Vienna in 1995 corresponded to those included on measures of the quality of life of individuals with developmental disabilities (Felce, 1997). For example, the instrument that Schalock, Keith, Hoffman, and Karan (1989) described asked who chooses the individual's medical care (Item 11), whether the individual believes that he or she earns enough money (Item 18), and whether the individual takes part in an education program (Item 25). Item 22 of the questionnaire that Schalock and colleagues devised asked how much privacy the individual enjoyed. These themes recalled that privacy was one of the least familiar experiences discerned in the older adult lives of Peter, Joseffa, and Ernst.

Challenging behavior, a dual diagnosis of mental health difficulties, permanency planning, and changes in family caregiving are themes that dominated 1990s research in aging and developmental disabilities (Zigman, Seltzer, & Silverman, 1994). Each factor is likely to leave its mark on the daily experiences of older adults, the services provided for their support, and thus their quality of life. Personal experiences and family or social life are in turn filtered through the cultural context in which the person lives and grows older.

John

John was born in 1948, the eldest in a large family. In 1997, he was 49 years of age and had moderate developmental disabilities, including epilepsy and a hearing impairment. When John was born, his mother was told that John would never be able to take his place in "normal" society. John attends a social education center run by Social Services, the local government authority. He is a friendly, outgoing man of whom staff at the center think highly. John excels in horticulture at the center. John and his family live in a troubled area of Northern Ireland. Because of his typical appearance, John has been questioned on the streets by the police; on one occasion, he was taken into police custody. This was a very traumatic experience for John, and a second experience was prevented only by neighbors who intervened with the security forces. John's mother, age 70 years in 1997, receives a good deal of support from Social Services, and she praised John's key workers highly. She worries about the future. One daughter has agreed to take primary responsibility for John in the event of anything happening to their mother.

Ensuring the quality of life of older adults with developmental disabilities and their families in the 1990s assumed a much wider and more systematic application than it had previously. This construct should be central to the evaluation of all programs and supports provided for people with developmental disabilities. The quality of these supports should be judged by how richly they make available life experiences that promote the person's control over his or her physical and social environments, community involvement, and social relationships (Campo, Sharpton, Thompson, & Sexton, 1996).

Notwithstanding their limitations, the case studies suggest four key themes. First, distinctive vulnerabilities abound in the population of older adults with developmental disabilities. These include poor communication skills, the presence of mental health difficulties, or the risk of homelessness. Each factor is likely to exacerbate the interaction of developmental disabilities with demands presented by the developmental tasks of old age. Second, the legal and civic status of older people with developmental disabilities is ambiguous and variable across countries. In some jurisdictions, it seems that individuals in this group may gain grudging welfare but not clear-cut recognition of their human and civil rights.

Third, the social status of Peter, Joseffa, and Ernst (the three individuals considered at the Vienna meeting) is ambiguous. There is a marked disparity between their negligible presence in their communities as compared with that of their peers. None has a spouse or children. None is a tax-paying employee who contributes to the public good.

Fourth, personal agency—that is, the power of individuals to determine their own affairs—is haphazard in its availability. Peter, Joseffa, and Ernst lack opportunities for privacy, autonomy, and access to personalized supports, which are hallmarks of a good quality of life. In particular, little attention was paid to the distinctive needs of older men and women that arise from gender differences in individuals' health and life experiences.

Respondents to the 1995 Vienna survey were challenged to declare their own country's success in building systems to meet the significant needs of the two older men and an older woman with developmental disabilities. Even if some responses overstated the positive, it is apparent that Peter, Joseffa, and Ernst and people like them have survived as best they can with supports devised for others. Yet the UN's StRE declared that each person's needs are unique and that those needs should shape social policy.

OLDER ADULTS WITH DEVELOPMENTAL DISABILITIES
AT THE TURN OF THE 21ST CENTURY

The commonality of the needs of older adults with developmental disabilities transcends national borders. The needs of this population are highlighted throughout the Western world by shared aspirations for inclusive programs of care that take place in the context of the community. To be effective and acceptable, the notion of community must respect national and regional differences. Patterns of care for older adults with developmental disabilities are often enshrined in local tradition and take into account historical variables that planners and practitioners must honor. What is required in both legislation and service provision are balanced programs that clearly identify the shared basic physical, social, and emotional needs that accompany aging and place these needs in the context of national practice.

Increasing life expectancies throughout the Western world should not be a source of surprise, because the population trends shaping this phenomenon have been apparent since the middle of the 20th century. Despite consistent demographic evidence, planners and policy makers have been slow in their response and have not catered adequately to the acceleration of the range of needs that have developed in the older adult population with developmental disabilities (Janicki, 1994).

A succession of well-documented experiments in good-quality living into old age has demonstrated the possibility of caring for older adults with developmental disabilities with dignity. Janicki (1993) set out a comprehensive structure for quality of life among older people with developmental disabilities based on the work of agencies and aging-related university programs in New York and other states throughout the United States. Mittler (1994) emphasized the important function that parents and other family members perform in obtaining and sustaining a good quality of life for older people with developmental disabilities and the need for appropriate support structures to enable their quality of life to continue. She cited international examples of good practice. Even in the richest countries of the West, however, the evidence is that such experiments remain islands of excellence and that uniformity in service provision remains an elusive yet desirable goal.

Documentation available from various countries reveals that, in the general population, the provision of appropriate services for older people with developmental disabilities continues to be insufficient. The traditional service continuum for older people progresses from domiciliary care through day care to residential care. It is ageist in its assumptions and contributes to a political climate in which older adults are perceived solely as a problem and an increasing burden on national budgets (Walker, Walker, & Ryan, 1995).

Vulnerability is a key factor in discussing the lives of older people. Ironically, at the turn of the 21st century, discussion about normalization and community integration for older citizens with developmental disabilities assumes their shared vulnerability with the general population of older people. For some older people with developmental disabilities, the move out of institutional care creates problems for health and social services in providing small-scale living opportunities in the community (Walker et al., 1995). For others living in the family circle, increased longevity brings additional adjustments (McConkey & Murray, 1989). Since the caregiving role may span 5 or even 6 decades, an extra dimension is added to the burden of care because of the shared aging process and its biological, psychological, and social consequences (Smith, Smith, & Toseland, 1991). A convergence of need gradually develops in which both the caregiver and the person receiving care should be able to expect

- Recognition of personal identity
- Space for independent action and free choice
- Social interaction both within and outside the family
- Protection of privacy and the right of choice
- Provision of a level of service that ensures a proper quality of life

The preceding ideals are echoed in government statements around the world, but what about the reality? Research by Hogg, Moss, and Cooke (1988) showed that older people with intellectual disabilities received fewer opportunities in the community than younger people with intellectual disabilities. Walker and colleagues (1995) highlighted the many difficulties that older people with intellectual disabilities face and the double jeopardy that the fragmentation of services for older adults and people with intellectual disabilities causes. Often, people with intellectual disabilities and their families and caregivers are inadequately served by both generic and specialist service providers. The impact varies according to the level and complexity of the individual's disabilities, and it is most keenly felt by the most vulnerable—those with profound and/or multiple disabilities and their caregivers.

As with the general population, there is a danger in putting all older people with developmental disabilities into one category. A more enlightened approach to understanding the developmental potential of all people with developmental disabilities developed in the 1990s. Many among the population of older people with developmental disabilities at the end of the 20th century were regarded as recipients of services, and the structure of the services available to them made these individuals care-dependent (Maaskant, 1993). They are the "walking wounded" who survived a system that is extant in most countries, and they contrast significantly with an emerging group of older adults with developmental disabilities who have greater expectations of life.

The diversity observed among older adults with developmental disabilities indicates a range of needs that must be taken into account when setting criteria for adequate service provision (Hogg et al., 1988). Setting service provision criteria is a fundamental challenge that continues to test the sensitivities of policy planners and service providers. Those charged with implementing policies must cope with the present reality while fashioning structures for the near future that ideally will accommodate choice and independence.

If quality of life is to move out of the realm of rhetoric into reality and if a truly international perspective is to be adopted, then certain conditions must be applied: realistic planning decisions for effective, efficient involvement in services by older adults and their families in the decision-making process; implementation of these decisions in practice; uniformity in the provision of services; and prioritizing need on the basis of evidence. Of course, there are barriers to the implementation of services to promote quality of life among older people with intellectual disabilities. Janicki (1993) attempted to identify these barriers and to set out a comprehensive range of strategies to overcome them. The format of these strategies provides a basis for international implementation that allows for national and regional differences.

IMPLEMENTATION

National policies differ in the strategies that they employ for providing services for older people with developmental disabilities. In Ireland, the government's Review Group on Mental Handicap Services (1990) recognized that these people have needs, as do their peers without disabilities, and recommended that, accordingly, they should have ready access to comprehensively organized services for older adults.

Although family care remains dominant for middle-age and older people with developmental disabilities in most countries, family care is time limited. Families may seek suitable out-of-home placement for many years in advance of the day on which they are no longer able to provide a home for a family member with disabilities. Many searches prove fruitless, leaving older adult parents who are vulnerable themselves to act as primary caregivers into their 80s or 90s (Walsh, Conliffe, & Birkbeck, 1993). It is cautionary for service planners to recall that, at best, special residences for older people with developmental disabilities may not replicate family life easily. At worst, they may find homes only in specialized institutions or in those institutions designed for mixed populations of older adults, homeless people, and people with longstanding psychiatric difficulties. Other rights may thus be transgressed because "institutionalization by its very nature seems to impact quite adversely on a whole range of family rights" (Quinn, 1995, p. 24).

Guidelines for Services

Which guidelines best shape services respecting individual rights among older people with intellectual disabilities? The following paragraphs attempt to answer that question:

- *National systems of support should target social inclusion.* If social inclusion is the desired aim, then welfare systems must be judged afresh. Do they facilitate the participation of individuals with developmental disabilities in national life? Do they enhance equal opportunities for these individuals? Health and social services form a complex system that rests on national policies but that also contributes to the ongoing development of policy. Each country may thus offer choices among generic or specialized services for older people with disabilities in the wider context of answering a basic question: Which form of service is most likely to promote equal opportunities for an individual's full participation in society?
- *Cultural diversity is not age limited.* National and cultural variations abound, as seen in the survey described in this chapter. Within-culture differences also exist, however—for example, in the mix of voluntary or statutory services that have been developed. In addition, global differences exist. A formal, legal approach to equal opportunities that is expressed in antidiscrimination legislation has developed in the United States (Quinn, 1995), where equality is perceived as a heavily person-driven right. By contrast, European approaches to equality construe equality as a social goal to be achieved through substantive interventions. Programs can be devised to build the social structures and supports required to create preconditions for equal opportunities.
- *Equality may be embraced as both a socioeconomic right and a civil right.* Equality is assumed to be universal in its sway, yet adaptable enough in expression to be sensitive to the distinct needs of individuals grouped by virtue of their

gender, culture, or age. The European social ideal of solidarity may be harnessed to the American individual rights–driven model of equality. Marrying these two strategies may be a radical but fruitful alliance that adds value. Such a merger may form the bedrock for stable yet flexible person-centered service planning on behalf of older people with developmental disabilities. Person-centered service provision represents the point at which individual satisfaction, family preferences, and European social policy may yet converge (Commission of the European Communities, 1996).

• *Service quality must be evaluated dynamically to forge continuous improvement.* It may be necessary but is not sufficient to repeat quality exercises year after year without asking whether weighty annual reports on processes do any more than comfort the service providers who pay for the exercise. Rather, services should be evaluated according to their success in achieving social and personal goals for individuals, with outcomes being driven by a passion for social justice, not merely by politically correct platitudes (Kristiansen, 1996). How to identify service goals in consultation with older people and their families, advocates, and caregivers is an ambitious task worthy of the concerted effort that it demands.

CONCLUSIONS

Social inclusion and equal opportunities are aspirations beyond the grasp of citizens in many countries. The emerging voices of older people with developmental disabilities tell societies that they, too, rightfully claim a place in society that brings closer the outcomes that they value. Achieving access to privacy, self-determination, a secure home, a productive role in society, and individualized services requires nothing less than radical change in the way in which aging individuals with developmental disabilities are supported in pursuit of a satisfying quality of life.

Systemwide strategies must be forged at all levels. Alliances must be struck between people who require distinctive supports as they age and those who provide support. The efficacy of engaging citizen advocates, experts in generic aging services, or members of the wider community in pursuing equal opportunities for older people with developmental disabilities is a fruitful area for future research. The success of natural supports in classroom, workplace, and home environments in furthering the inclusion of people with developmental disabilities suggests that this form of personal support may be well adapted to meet the needs of older people with developmental disabilities. Whether older people with developmental disabilities can flourish in their communities with greater reliance on natural supports is another fruitful question for future research.

Other allies must negotiate at the national level. Policy makers prosper only by working in harmony with service providers, given a groundswell of support for accountability in terms of valuable outcomes for older individuals with disabilities. Governments and universities form another beneficial if wary alliance in, for example, continuously building and evaluating systems of evidence-based service provision (Walsh, 1998). Determining how effective collaboration may be in ensuring services of high quality is yet another question for the research agenda.

Finally, new forms of social inclusion must fit the personal and cultural characteristics of Peter, Joseffa, Ernst, John, and thousands more older people like them. As their numbers swell, they will make their homes, earn their living, and craft their places in society in ways that cannot be foreseen. The scope of adult and continuing education has not yet widened to encompass their aspirations. Certainly, universities vary in how avidly they transform themselves into resources for less-traditional groups of students in the wider community, such as older people, professionals, nongraduates, and people with disabilities. Family members, caregivers, and policy makers must ensure that older men and women with developmental disabilities find a role in society that expresses the equal opportunities that are their right.

REFERENCES

Boaz, R.F., & Hu, J. (1997). Determining the amount of help used by disabled elderly persons at home: The role of coping resources. *Journal of Gerontology: Social Sciences, 52B*(6), S317–S324.

Campo, S.F., Sharpton, W.R., Thompson, B., & Sexton, D. (1996). Measurement characteristics of the Quality of Life Index when used with adults who have severe mental retardation. *American Journal on Mental Retardation, 100*(5), 546–550.

Commission of the European Communities. (1996, July 30). *A new European Community disability strategy* (Doc. No. 96/0216). Brussels: Author.

Conliffe, C., McHugh, S., Stringer, K., & Betts, J. (1998). *A survey of the Northern Ireland Down syndrome population.* Belfast, Northern Ireland: Institute for Counselling and Personal Development.

Felce, D. (1997). Defining and applying the concept of quality of life. *Journal of Intellectual Disability Research, 41*(2), 126–135.

Friedlander, H. (1995). *The origins of Nazi genocide: From euthanasia to the final solution.* Chapel Hill: University of North Carolina Press.

Hardman, M.L., McDonnell, J., & Welch, M. (1997). Perspectives on the future of IDEA. *Journal of The Association for Persons with Severe Handicaps, 22*(2), 61–77.

Health Research Board. (1996). *National Intellectual Disability Database annual report.* Dublin, Ireland: Author.

Hogg, J. (1997). Intellectual disability and ageing: Ecological perspectives from recent research. *Journal of Intellectual Disability Research, 41*(2), 136–143.

Hogg, J., Moss, S., & Cooke, D. (1988). *Ageing and mental handicap.* London: Croom Helm.

Janicki, M.P. (1993). *Building the future: Planning and community development in aging and developmental disabilities.* Albany, NY: Community Integration Project in Aging and Developmental Disabilities.

Janicki, M.P. (1994). Policies and supports for older persons with mental retardation. In M.M. Seltzer, M.W. Krauss, & M.P. Janicki (Eds.), *Life course perspectives on adulthood and old age* (pp. 143–165). Washington, DC: American Association on Mental Retardation.

Janicki, M.P., Heller, T., Seltzer, G.B., & Hogg, J. (1996). Practice guidelines for the clinical assessment and care management of Alzheimer's disease and other dementias among adults with intellectual disability. *Journal of Intellectual Disability Research, 40*(4), 374–382.

Kristiansen, K. (1996). Good, better, and decent: Who knows best? In R. McConkey (Ed.), *Innovations in evaluating services for people with intellectual disabilities* (pp. 27–40). Chorley, England: Lisieux-Hall Publications.

Lachman, D., Bennett, A., Green, J.H., Hagemann, R., & Ramaswamy, R. (1995). *Challenges to the Swedish welfare state* (No. 130). Washington, DC: International Monetary Fund.

Maaskant, M.A. (1993). *Mental handicap and ageing.* Dwingeloo, The Netherlands: Kavanah and Maaskant.

McConkey, R., & Murray, E. (1989). Teenagers' reactions to having a brother or sister who is mentally handicapped. In R. McConkey & C. Conliffe (Eds.), *The person with mental handicap* (pp. 61–74). Dublin, Ireland: St. Michael's House/Belfast, Northern Ireland: Institute of Counselling and Personal Development.

Mittler, H. (1994). International initiatives in support of families with a member with learning disabilities. In P. Mittler & H. Mittler (Eds.), *Innovations in family support for people with learning disabilities* (pp. 15–32). Chorley, England: Lisieux-Hall Publications.

Moss, S. (Ed.). (1992). *Aging and developmental disabilities: Perspectives from nine countries.* Durham, NH: International Exchange of Experts and Information in Rehabilitation.

O'Shea, E., & Kennelly, B. (1995). *Caring and theories of welfare economics* (Working paper 7: Economics). Galway, Ireland: University College Galway.

O'Toole, B., & McConkey, R. (Eds.). (1995). *Innovations in developing countries for people with disabilities.* Chorley, England: Lisieux-Hall Publications.

Phillips, J.E. (1996). *Working and caring: Developments at the workplace for family carers of disabled and older people.* Dublin, Ireland: European Foundation for the Improvement of Living and Working Conditions.

Quinn, G. (1995). The International Covenant on Civil and Political Rights and Disability: A conceptual framework. In T. Degener & Y. Koster-Dreese (Eds.), *Human rights and disabled persons: Essays and relevant human rights instruments* (International studies in human rights, Vol. 40, pp. 69–93). Dordrecht, The Netherlands: Martinus Nijhoff.

Review Group on Mental Handicap Services. (1990). *Needs and abilities: A policy for the intellectually disabled.* Dublin, Ireland: Stationery Office.

Sachs, J. (1993). *Poland's jump to the market economy* (Vol. 3 of the Lionel Robbins lectures). Cambridge, MA: MIT Press.

Salvage, A. (1995). *Who will care? Future prospects for family care of older people in the European Union.* Dublin, Ireland: European Foundation for the Improvement of Living and Working Conditions.

Schalock, R.L., Keith, K.D., Hoffman, K., & Karan, O.C. (1989). Quality of life: Its measurement and use. *Mental Retardation, 27,* 25–31.

Seltzer, M.M., & Krauss, M.W. (1989). Aging parents with mentally retarded children: Family risk factors and sources of support. *American Journal on Mental Retardation, 94,* 303–312.

Seltzer, M.M., Krauss, M.W., & Janicki, M.P. (Eds.). (1994). *Life course perspectives on adulthood and old age.* Washington, DC: American Association on Mental Retardation.

Seltzer, M.M., Krauss, M.W., Walsh, P.N., Conliffe, C., Larson, B., Birkbeck, G., Hong, J., & Choi, S.C. (1995). Cross-national comparisons of ageing mothers of adults with intellectual disabilities. *Journal of Intellectual Disability Research, 39*(5), 408–418.

Shearn, J., & Todd, S. (1997). Parental work: An account of the day-to-day activities of parents of adults with learning disabilities. *Journal of Intellectual Disability Research, 41*(4), 285–301.

Smith, G.C., Smith, M.F., & Toseland, R.W. (1991). Problems identified by family caregivers in counseling. *Gerontologist, 31*(1), 15–22.

United Nations (UN). (1994). *The standard rules on the equalization of opportunities for persons with disabilities.* New York: Author.

van Schrojenstein Lantman-de Valk, H.M.J., van den Akker, M., Maaskant, M.A., Haveman, M.H., Urlings, H.F.J., Kessels, A.G.H., & Crebolder, H.F.J.M. (1997). Prevalence and incidence of health problems in people with intellectual disability. *Journal of Intellectual Disability Research, 41*(1) 42–51.

Walker, C., Walker, A., & Ryan, T. (1995). What kind of future? Opportunities for older people with a learning difficulty. In T. Philpot & L. Ward (Eds.), *Values and visions: Changing ideas in services for people with learning difficulties* (pp. 232–243). Oxford, England: Butterworth Heinemann.

Walsh, P.N. (1998, June). *New strategies: Supporting people with intellectual disabilities in Europe.* Keynote presentation at the First National Congress of the Italian Association on Mental Retardation (AIRiM), Brescia, Italy.

Walsh, P.N., Conliffe, C., & Birkbeck, G. (1993). Permanency planning and maternal well-being: A study of caregivers of people with intellectual disability in Ireland and Northern Ireland. *Irish Journal of Psychology, 14*(1), 176–188.

Zigman, W.B., Seltzer, G.B., & Silverman, W.P. (1994). Behavioral and mental health changes associated with aging in adults with mental retardation. In M.M. Seltzer, M.W. Krauss, & M.P. Janicki (Eds.), *Life course perspectives on adulthood and old age* (pp. 67–92). Washington, DC: American Association on Mental Retardation.

15

Challenges for Residential Satisfaction
Options, Choices, and Decision Making

Germain Weber and Andrea Fritsch

Home is central for retired people. In retirement, the focus of a person's life shifts more to the home environment. The home becomes the main place for recreation activities, maintaining friendships, and supporting family ties. For older adults with developmental disabilities, the home environment and its physical attributes have an even more profound impact on their quality of life than they do for older adults without disabilities. The attributes in their living environment—such as physical structure and space, diversity of activities and services, and the ways in which staff relate to and care for them—strongly determine their well-being and satisfaction. Such attributes are central to the realization of such an individual's aspirations and vitally affect that individual's quality of life.

With advancing age, most people with mental retardation experience a series of challenges. There is often disruption in the longstanding structure and daily activities of their lives. There are ruptures in relationships caused not only by retirement but also by the deaths of close relatives and friends. This period is also marked by major decisions such as where and with whom to live. Individuals may not only question their social role as older members of society or as an individual in declining health but also wonder how to fill the many new free hours that come with their new status as older individuals. Their search for meaningful activities and their hopes for successful adjustment to this situation are major ingredients in their pursuit of satisfaction in later life.

The large majority of older adults experience many of these issues. Although old age offers many opportunities for exploring valued experiences for older adults without disabilities, the older population with developmental disabilities is at a higher risk of not experiencing such opportunities. This particular population is more likely to be confined to more routinized and protected environments. Such environments are characterized by a low level of choice-making opportunities in daily routines and individuals' loss of control over their everyday lives.

Clearly, the care and support of older adults with developmental disabilities presents a higher risk for loss of control to that population than they do for older adults without disabilities. Older adults with developmental disabilities often experience the profound loss of control over their lives. Many residential caregiving organizations take away their decision-making authority and their power over the choices in their lives, such as when an older person is forced to move to a more restricted living facility (Blewett, 1980; Edgerton, 1989; O'Brien, 1987). Under these circumstances, the quality of life of these individuals often plummets.

This chapter weaves together detailed observations on the quality of life of older people with developmental disabilities with the emerging scientific literature in two domains: The first focuses on psychological findings that affect quality of life in terms of psychological well-being and centers on decision making and control as perceived by the individual as contributing to his or her well-being, and the second explores major residential options available to older people with developmental disabilities. Based on research data and site visits in 16 countries, this chapter depicts trends in accommodations and analyzes the outcomes of different residential paradigms for the individual's quality of life. The chapter emphasizes how the two domains are tightly interconnected. Neglect of these psychological findings may lead to residential models that fail to respect the individual's expressed needs and capacities for decision making, resulting in needless, unintended deterioration in the older person's quality of life.

DECISION MAKING AND CONTROL:
THE PSYCHOLOGICAL ROOTS OF QUALITY OF LIFE

The overlap between personal well-being or quality of life and decision making or control can be depicted best by introducing Robert's case.

Robert

"Most important to me is to find out what I want and then decide by myself what to do during the day," says Robert, a 63-year-old man with mental retardation requiring limited supports who lives with five other older adults with developmental disabilities. Before moving to his present home in 1989, Robert lived in a large facility in which depersonalized intervention was the standard. In that environment, Robert's individual preferences were ignored. He was unable to learn about and develop his individual identity. Recently, through training in self-determination, Robert acquired skills in decision making. This training assisted him in the transition from the large facility to the group home. During that stressful time, with the help of the skills training, many of Robert's challenging behaviors, aggressive behaviors, and opposing reactions disappeared. The case of Robert reveals important insights and possibilities for the population of older adults with developmental disabilities.

Older people with developmental disabilities are exposed to double discrimination: on the one hand, they are labeled as having developmental disabilities, and, on the other hand, they are referred to as being old (Fitzgerald, 1998). Each stereotype leaves an individual vulnerable to discrimination. For example, the stereotypes related to old age, or *ageism*, reinforce the view that an individual's capacities are decreasing and that the individual is in need of extensive institutional care. Such stereotypes tend to increase these individuals' dependence by raising the risk of lack of funding for this population and accelerating the decline in their opportunities.

Stereotypes affect the expectations of staff members who work with older people with developmental disabilities. The caregivers tend to view these individuals as lacking abilities such as basic decision-making skills. Consequently, staff or close relatives make decisions for these older adults with developmental disabilities. In addition, these decisions usually are not open to review or are not challenged in practice. This kind of stereotyping is the rule in most caregiving environments of older adults with mental retardation, and Robert's experiences, described previously in the case study, are the exception. Most older adults with developmental disabilities lose control over the domain of their personal decision making. This loss of control affects all aspects of their lives and is a central reason for the deterioration in these individuals' quality of life (O'Brien, 1987).

Personal Freedom and Reactance

Choices and decisions are expressions of personal freedom. Research (Harvey, 1976; Hogarth, 1987) in social psychology focuses on the concept of freedom and on free decision making rather than on the individual's being governed by the past. It is important to differentiate between objective and subjective freedoms. Psychological research defines *subjective freedom* as freedom that the individual perceives. Ageism compromises subjective freedom because it erodes the opportunity for older people with developmental disabilities to make decisions about their lives.

The deprivation of an individual's freedom, or even a threat to limit a person's usual behavior options in terms of perceived behavior outcomes, causes most people to respond by what is known as *reactance* (Brehm, 1993; Brehm & Brehm, 1981). Reactance describes a state of irritation and a special motivational state whereby a person aims at restoring the blocked freedom as experienced in concrete situations of daily life. If the person cannot get back to the former level of freedom, then different ways to compensate, depending on the person's coping skills, are observed. Aggressive behavior, outbursts of rage, or, in the younger years, tantrums are observed. Furthermore, reactant behavior appears most prominently when the individual lacks meaningful alternatives (Wicklund, 1974).

Personal Control and Learned Helplessness

Closely related to freedom is the concept of control. According to Rotter's (1954, 1966) theory on locus of control, an individual perceives internal control if he or she believes that an outcome depends largely on his or her own skills or behavior. In contrast, if the person believes that outcomes are independent of his or her behavior, he or she experiences external control—that is, little or no influence on outcomes that affect him- or herself. Based on this theory, Seligman (1992) proposed the concept of learned helplessness. He argued that individuals who are exposed to uncontrollable situations feel and learn a sense of helplessness. This feeling of helplessness may develop into depression.

Major consequences of learned helplessness are related to the individual's emotional regulation and result in sadness and depressive states because the individual perceives the environment in which he or she lives as hard or impossible to influence by him- or herself. Reviews (e.g., Sweeney, Anderson, & Bailey, 1986) of research on attributional style supported the basic hypothesis that people who are depressed show the so-called depressive attributional style. Not all of the research findings related to the concept of learned helplessness are consistent and conclusive. For example, not all people respond with depressive behavior when they are exposed to uncontrollable negative events. Partly in response to these findings (Barnett & Gotlib, 1988; Benassi, Sweeney, & Dufour, 1988), Abramson, Metalsky, and Alloy (1989) proposed a revised theory termed the *hopelessness theory of depression* that is based on the diathesis-stress model and that states that, besides the presence of a stressor, personal vulnerability is involved in depressive states. According to this model, depression may be related to the expectation (i.e., cognitive vulnerability) that a desirable event probably will not occur or that a negative event (i.e., stress) will occur regardless of what the person does. *Hopelessness* refers to the person's expectations about future events as shaped by the person's former experiences and the associated belief that these events are beyond his or her control. The risk for becoming depressed or showing an excess of passive behavior, according to this model, is a function of the explanations and the importance that the person ascribes to these events.

Palmer and Wehmeyer (1998) reported significantly less hopeful expectations for the future in younger adults with mental retardation as compared with their peer group without disabilities. Beliefs about oneself and one's future often shape the individual's learning process and outcome. The use of problem-solving and decision-making skills as well as the opportunity to make choices, are determined by the individual's system of belief. In turn, these individuals' personal belief systems have implications for their development of self-determination (Sands & Wehmeyer, 1996).

Older adults with developmental disabilities experience a higher prevalence of depression than the older adult population without disabilities (see Chapter 11). Although the cognitive explanations for depression (e.g., the causal attributions of the hopelessness model) may play an important role in mood disorders, they represent only one piece of the etiological puzzle in this field. Interpersonal factors and biological factors also must be considered. With respect to the etiology of depressive behavior, dysfunctional interpersonal skills, presumably learned early in life, enhance these individuals' vulnerability to depression later in life.

Quality of Life and Choice Making

Although most of what is known in the field of decision making and control is based on research on people without disabilities, research (White, 1959) documented an adaptive drive for all organisms to develop mastery over the forces around them. The disposition to control outcomes through performance is apparently inherent in human nature. This statement is supported by the observation that usually only minimal interventions are necessary to activate or reestablish the motivation of adults with mental retardation to make their own choices (Switzky & Haywood, 1991). Accordingly, choice making is a crucial consideration with regard to the quality of life of people with developmental disabilities and leads to valuable conclusions and practical applications.

In the 1990s, choice and choice making were central in the development of new approaches to assist people with mental retardation. Empowerment, self-determination, and independence are the main goals in rehabilitation and lifelong education programs. Teaching choice-making skills to individuals with mental retardation is a key technique to assist them in pursuing their personal goals. Bambara and Koger (1996) published a valuable guide offering an excellent introduction to choice making in which they discussed topics such as the identification of an option, selection of a personal choice, modification of a choice, and methods of training the adult population with developmental disabilities in making choices. The training material of Heller, Preston, Nelis, Brown, and Pederson (1996) aims to teach older people with developmental disabilities about choice making, rights and responsibilities, how to make healthy choices, and the use of free time.

Historically, choice for people with mental retardation was rarely recognized or facilitated. The opportunities for decision making and choice making for these individuals were generally absent from their daily routines. Their viewpoints and preferences were generally deemed irrelevant. As a result, these individuals expressed challenging behaviors. This was one of the few ways in which they could express preferences. Difficult or challenging behaviors allow individuals who have little control over their lives to exert some level of control on their environment.

Research published in the 1990s (Belfiore & Toro-Zambrana, 1994; Halle, 1995; Sigafoos, Laurie, & Pennell, 1995) showed that the ability to make choices is not limited to people with mental retardation requiring intermittent or limited supports. In people with mental retardation requiring extensive or pervasive supports, choice making can be observed if adequate choice-making provisions are created (Belfiore & Toro-Zambrana, 1994; Sigafoos, Laurie, & Pennell, 1995). Future research in choice making should focus more closely on the conditions that determine choice selection (Halle, 1995) and on why older adults with developmental disabilities select particular options and not others.

To sum up against the background of this short review on major psychological findings related to choice making, decision making, and control, Robert's statement and his demand for autonomy can be understood better. There might be agreement that *self-determination*—the generic term used here referring to decision making and control—does not mean encouraging a person to act and decide solely according to momentary beliefs, which would indeed come close to encouraging acting-out behaviors. Nor does it mean encouraging individuals to behave solely according to their wishes without considering the effects of their decisions and actions on their immediate environment. Recommended practice in self-determination can best be arrived at by considering key psychological factors such as decision making and control and the satisfying reciprocal relationship between the individual and his or her social environment.

Giving the aging person with a developmental disability the right to make decisions of his or her own and thus fostering the person's opportunities to perceive control over events, is a basic prerequisite for furthering the individual's personal development in old age. Obviously, age does not prevent one from making a wrong decision. Limiting the decision-making process or limiting choice making for older people, however, prevents them from further meaningful developmental experiences that could be a major threat to their perceived quality of life. Furthermore, independence for older people with developmental disabilities may not be about their doing things for themselves but about their choosing how and when tasks are done and by whom (Frost, 1996).

In view of advances in habilitation and community living, an ever-increasing number of the "new" old people with developmental disabilities at the turn of the

21st century show advanced skills in independent daily life according to their experiences in younger adult life. More and more of them, as time goes on, will have strong experiences in self-determination, although their experiences will depend on the economic, social, and philosophical background of the regions in which they live. It might be that these "new" older people with developmental disabilities are at an especially higher risk of losing control in many parts of their final journey because they might be referred to accommodation environments operating in a more restrictive and paternalistic style. Fitzgerald (1998) questioned whether these individuals might be at risk of their needs and aspirations not always being considered best with regard to the decision of where to live their final years and how to spend this new time of freedom.

RESIDENTIAL ACCOMMODATIONS FOR OLD AGE: THE OPTIONS

This section concerns the residential options that older citizens with mental retardation have in most countries as well as the chances that their choices will be considered and the extent to which their quality of life will be challenged by the life-changing decision of where to live.

Peter

"People with disabilities should be free to decide where they want to live," says Peter, who is 61 years old and has lived for the past 12 years in a community-based residential facility with six other people with developmental disabilities, all of whom are over 50 years old. Peter, who has Down syndrome, previously lived with his parents. A worker for 20 years, he has been retired for the past 3 years. Peter had been employed as an assistant in a nursing facility run by the same service provider that operates his present living arrangement.

About 15 years ago, Peter's parents, because of their age and declining health, began to explore options for Peter's transition to an out-of-home placement. Peter, who was accustomed to having an active part in daily decision making while living with his parents, expressed clear signs of uneasiness when visiting small-group homes in which individual decision making was limited. For example, he disapproved of agencies whose policy stated that he could visit his family only once a month and that could not offer him a single room. Also, some of the residential services offered him a place to live only on the condition that he would enter one of the workshops operated by that agency. Although Peter might have been looked at as rather demanding by some of the staff members to whom he was introduced during these visits, his parents supported his assertiveness. They strongly believed that Peter's needs and his individuality should be respected in his future life. The parents were anxious about potential disruptive changes to Peter's lifestyle. They felt that such disruptions might be extremely stressful for him. Because of his parents' advocacy, Peter was spared a most unpleasant life-changing decision. His parents convinced his employer to develop a small, community-based home.

As a result, Peter and his future fellow housemates participated in designing their new residence. For example, they helped to choose the residential area and design the interiors of their rooms. Of the five older people sharing the apartment with Peter, two were friends who had worked with him as assistants in the nursing facility. At age 61, Peter volunteers his services to the nursing facility for about 2 half-days per week. His presence and his services are highly appreciated. Peter enjoys not only getting in touch with his colleagues but also helping others.

The residential staff who care for Peter and his friends pay close attention to maintaining these individuals' independence by encouraging them to assume mutual responsibilities and by offering them time to be in a group for leisure activities or just talking to one another. Peter continues to enjoy deciding what his daily activities will be and having enough time to talk to peers and staff. Although Peter shows consistent preferences, even rituals in some domains (e.g., regularly going through his biographical records), he is afraid that every day might become the same. This risk is best prevented by allowing him to exercise his skills in decision making.

Peter and his friends express a high degree of satisfaction when asked whether they enjoy their lives as older adults. Their satisfaction relates in part to the ways in which they have been prepared for transitions that come with age-related changing needs. Their perception of a good quality of life is determined strongly by the developmental, person-centered approach that fosters self-determination by actively involving them in making informed decisions about their lives (Racino & Taylor, 1993).

General Observations

Unfortunately, the experience of Peter and his friends is still the exception. The norm is not to include older people with mental retardation in deciding where and with whom they shall live. For too many of these individuals, such choices are out of their control. In the face of serious housing shortages for older people and for people with developmental disabilities, they may be forced to endure long waiting lists and "take-it-or-nothing" propositions (see Chapter 2).

The Skewed Distribution of Options   In the 1990s, there were reports of moving older people to less restrictive environments. In the 1970s, advancing age was significantly related to a higher rate of congregate institutional placement in the United States (Scheerenberger, 1982). Although this has begun to change, there are still an insufficient number of freedom-enhancing residential options in the United States and Europe.

In most European countries, no exact figures are known with regard to the percentage of older people with developmental disabilities who use the different residential options. Apart from Sweden, where a general registration for people with mental retardation is carried out, most countries rely on estimates. In Austria, for instance, the number of people with mental retardation is estimated to total 45,000 (Lebenshilfe Österreich, 1994). In 1994, the group of older people (defined as those ages 50 and older) with mental retardation in Austria was estimated to be about 9,500 (Lebenshilfe Österreich, 1994). Also in 1994, only 170 of these older people with developmental disabilities were accommodated in various residential facilities, especially in supervised community-based group homes or in small groups, in different agencies of the largest Austrian association offering all kinds of services in the field of mental retardation. Indeed, these older people represent only a tiny minority of the approximate total of 5,500 cared for in the various agencies of this service provider. From these figures, it can be assumed that the majority of older adults with developmental disabilities in Austria use other accommodation facilities, such as continuing to live with their families or living in institutional environments.

One of the most significant changes within the population with developmental disabilities since the 1970s is the increasing size of the older adult population. As early as 1985, Jacobson, Sutton, and Janicki reported that up to 15.7% of the service population with mental retardation were ages 55 and older in parts of the United States. In European countries (e.g., the United Kingdom), similar rates were reported because people from the United Kingdom were not affected by the Nazis' systematic slaughter of people with mental retardation and other disabilities. As a result of the Nazis' crimes against humanity, a whole generation of people with mental retardation and other disabilities is missing in some regions of Europe. This is one of the reasons why there are regional differences in the types of services available for older people with developmental disabilities in Europe. Another reason for the various levels in the development of services for older people with developmental disabilities in Europe is the differing degrees of social activism and advocacy in different countries.

Although Europe is generally praised for its social system based on solidarity between generations and with regard to minority groups, social policy outcomes may differ substantially between European countries. This difference is especially true in the fields of aging and mental retardation. The different levels of development may be explained not only on the basis of different levels of economic prosperity of a country or a region but also on the cultural characteristics and social attitudes expressed in the local policy decision-making arena.

Unequal Provisions   The lack of suitable housing causes some parents to accept poor living conditions for their older sons and daughters with developmental disabilities. This decision to accept poorer housing ultimately affects their children's quality of life because studies show that an individual's quality of life depends largely on the individual's quality of housing. Gennep (1995) reported that older people living in poorer-quality housing lost adaptive behavior skills and became more dependent. Older people living in better-quality care also became more dependent but did not lose their adaptive behavior skills. *Better-quality housing* refers to the physical condition of the accommodation; designs that positively influence behavioral outcomes (Ferguson, 1997); and safety, comfort, convenience, and accessibility.

In addition, in terms of the impact of a facility's size on individuals' self-determination and deprivation, research (Tossobero, 1995) has shown no correlation with the size of the facility per se but rather with the size of living units. Units with 13 or more residents received high scores in deprivation and limited self-determination. In contrast, units with one to five residents showed the highest-quality scores. These units were predominantly located in urban areas and had staff with the highest levels of training.

Unequal provision of living accommodations persist. While living in community-based residences, younger adults and older people with mental retardation have significantly fewer opportunities than their peers without disabilities to make decisions about matters such as what to eat, what to wear, how to spend free time, and with whom to live (Kishi, Teelucksingh, Zollers, Park-Lee, & Meyer, 1988). Howe, Horner, and Newton (1998) explored the lifestyle quality of adults with mental retardation who were living in supported community-based accommodations versus a matched group of individuals living in traditional residential facilities. The participants of supported living experienced significantly more variety in community activities, participated in more community activities, and preferred community activities more frequently than the individuals living in residential facilities. Furthermore, Howe and colleagues reported that the costs of the two living environments were similar. This clearly shows that prospects for a good quality of life as an older adult with developmental disabilities are determined mainly by residents' daily lives, by events, and by the paradigms through which the services are operated (i.e., by the way in which the funds for running the services are used, not by the level of costs per se).

There is general agreement that the most critical services area for older people with developmental disabilities is their living arrangements. As a 1985 study put it, "[P]eople must have somewhere to live. In many ways, where they live determines the type of services they receive" (Janicki & Wisniewski, 1985, p. 4). The following section outlines the most frequent options in residential accommodations for older people with mental retardation. The section is organized according to community-based small accommodations versus life in facilities with a distinct institutional character. Special attention is paid to how the respective operating principles or theoretical frameworks of the various options affect services and individuals' quality of life. This analysis primarily explores practices and developments in residential accommodations in European countries, along with research reports as well as site visits conducted elsewhere.

Community-Based Accommodations

Two models of community-based accommodations are considered: co-residence with the family and supported, community-based accommodations. These classifications are based on both the size and the location of the accommodation.

Co-residence with the Family   There is little precise research on the number of older people with developmental disabilities who live with their families. Ern (1992) reported from one large region of Germany that, of a total of 2,560 people with developmental disabilities ages 50 years and older in that region, 31.3% lived in professionally supervised facilities, including long term hospitals; 2.9% lived in their own apartments; and the rest (65.8%) lived with their families. Figures from Australia show clear differences with respect to the residential circumstances of older people with developmental disabilities ages 55 years and older. Ashman, Suttie, and Bramley (1995) reported that the majority, 58.8%, resided in large public or private institutions. Only 6.7% continued to live with their parents, and 3.4% lived with unrelated others. The other older people with developmental disabilities used a variety of accommodations characterized as community based. These differences can be explained by the variations in the mean ages of the older cohorts in Australia and Germany. Different family values in general or different familial attitudes determined by the history of genocide toward this population during the Nazi era may perhaps also explain the more frequent residency with the family among older people with mental retardation and other developmental disabilities in Germany.

According to French findings, aging families caring for aging family members with developmental disabilities without any further support are up to 10 times more likely to be found in rural areas than in urban or semiurban areas (Breitenbach, 1997). Although older parents realize that their child's placement outside the family home is inevitable with their advancing age, they often opt to keep their aging child with a developmental disability within the family for as long as possible. This outcome may be explained by families' moral conceptions as well as their view that family life is desired by most older people with developmental disabilities. According to Ern (1992), who interviewed people with mental retardation ages 50–70 years who lived in institutions or large group homes, their predominant thoughts and reflections centered on family life, with the next most frequent concern being health issues.

Many arguments support a life in the family for an older person with mental retardation. They include the benefits of a community-based lifestyle and natural social networks, continuity and constancy in the caregiving the person receives, familiarity of the environment, greater acceptance by the family members, greater respect for the needs of the person, and the contribution of the person with a developmental disability to activities of daily life. In the ideal situation, the older adult with mental retardation continues to experience and perceive the love of his or her relatives, and the person's older family caregivers continue to feel satisfaction in meeting the responsibility for the person's care. Long-term inclusion in the family can also bear risks, however, such as exaggerated (i.e., overprotective) care, a childlike communication style, low competence of relatives in rehabilitation techniques, social isolation, restriction of activities, constant burdens for the parents, and few opportunities for the individual with a disability to interact with peers.

Although programs encourage parents to let adult family members with developmental disabilities leave the parents' home in order to experience adult life, and although there are certain predictors of such out-of-home placement (Heller & Factor, 1994), it is important to acknowledge families as providers of services to older adults with mental retardation and to legitimize and support this role. In the 1990s, programs began to give special attention to helping older people who are caring for an adult with developmental disabilities (Janicki, 1996).

Supported Community-Based Accommodations   Most Western European countries have made the shift from an institutional residential style to small, community-based accommodations run by private agencies. Institutions that are still operated by the national government or by religious orders are more and more the exception. Small, community-based accommodations generally house 4–12 residents.

In Austria, these environments tend to serve between 8 and 12 people. Smaller accommodations are less frequent and only a few older people with mental retardation live on their own. Two types of residential accommodations can be differentiated. One comprises small groups who share an apartment or a family-like home located within an apartment house or in a residential area. The other is a group living as a unit in a larger residential facility for people with developmental disabilities that is located in the community, in theory for the purpose of fostering these individuals' participation in activities and programs open to the general population without disabilities. The latter option is discussed in the section on accommodations of an institutional character because these living environments often permit their residents little participation in the community.

In the greater Vienna area in Austria, older people with mental retardation ages 50–69 years, with a mean age close to 55 years, generally live together with younger adults with mental retardation in age-integrated accommodations (Mühlberger, 1998). Only one service provider offers residential services designed especially for older people with mental retardation. Few of these people enter community-based accommodations of their own volition. Data collected in 1997 showed that, of a total of 128 older adults with mental retardation at a residential facility, only 3.9% entered the facility by their own decision; 18.1% entered primarily because of their parents' motivation; and 30.9% entered because of the death of their parent or other main caregiver. Another 21.7% entered these accommodations as a result of de-institutionalization from psychiatric institutions (Mühlberger, 1998). For the vast majority (59.3%) of these individuals, no special arrangements, such as visiting programs, eased the transition to their new home. Similar results are reported in Australia. Ashman and colleagues (1995) observed that older adults with developmental disabilities play a relatively minor role in determining their future care and residential needs. Less than 10% were actually involved in decision-making processes with regard to their future.

Research (Holland, 1997; Howe, Horner, & Newton, 1998) revealed few if any problems resulting from younger adults and "young-old" people with mental retardation living together. This research, however, has focused on individuals younger than 60 years old. People at midlife have expressed similar needs in terms of daily activities and individual capabilities, but the similarities change with these individuals' advancing age, as do their preferences.

The needs and capabilities of people with mental retardation who are older than age 65 years bear this out. Their needs and preferences are closely linked to age-related changes such as alterations in health, cognitive capacity, and adaptive behavior. Studies show that these needs and preferences are best met in community-based age-similar small groups (Hogg, Moss, & Cooke, 1988). Age-specific needs and preferences are not limited, of course, to older people with developmental disabilities. Older people without disabilities have different needs and wishes than younger people without disabilities, too. They often prefer to live with people of the same age, believing that such an environment offers more respect for their individual needs.

Age is not the only factor distinguishing older adults from others with developmental disabilities. Mühlberger (1998) reported that projects seeking the participation and inclusion of individuals with developmental disabilities older than age 60 years into day center activities of the aging population without disabilities have failed. The older adults without disabilities often opposed sharing their social activities with people with developmental disabilities. Better preparation of older adults without disabilities for interacting with older adults with developmental disabilities might have helped these inclusive activities to succeed. Anderson (1993) reported that both older people with developmental disabilities and their peers without disabilities agreed that social and vocational skills were more important for successful community inclusion than personal, academic, or leisure skills. Another problem concerns deficiencies in caregiving in age-integrated environments. The research (Krauss & Seltzer, 1986) shows a high level of unmet care needs for the older residents, including a lack of general and medical support.

Unfortunately, both age-integrated and age-segregated Viennese agencies seem intent on limiting their admissions of older people with developmental disabilities in the future. They wish to avoid caring for what they perceive as a surplus of older people with developmental disabilities and fail to advocate or to plan for the growing population of older adults with developmental disabilities.

Although these findings should be considered when defining policy and developing programs for older people with mental retardation, they should not be misunderstood as a call for only age-differentiated services (i.e., specialized services) for older adults. Instead, there is a need for a mix of services for older adults that is not different from the services being offered to younger adults, a statement supported by earlier research of Krauss and Seltzer (1986). However, the question is, What are the reasons for the unmet needs and missing supports for older people who live in age-integrated environments? The risks of unmet needs, for example, might be related to the way in which older adults are viewed. Overcoming ageist views and age discrimination still seems to be a major challenge in these environments.

In contrast to Austria and Germany, where professional commitment to community-based services for older people with mental retardation is low (perhaps because of the small proportion of their populations with developmental disabilities), other European countries have developed small, community-based accommodations especially for older people with mental retardation ages 65 and older. These facilities often are equipped with assistive, rehabilitative, and other technological devices. These supports allow an older individual to "age in place" even when the individual requires a great degree of medical and other care. The new accommodations for the older group are located near to where the older people spent most of the earlier part of their lives. This proximity allows them to age in place. The older people can continue to participate according to their needs in a familiar community. Some agencies also respond to the needs of older parents caring for an older person with mental retardation, even offering the option of supported housing facilities for both generations in buildings operated by the same agency.

Finally, the trend of high-functioning younger adults with mental retardation to have their own place to live also merits consideration. With advancing age, many of these people may express fears, such as having problems living alone as an older person (Grant, McGrath, & Ramcharan, 1995). Although living alone might be a successful experience during these individuals' adulthood, this option might no longer meet the needs of an older person with developmental disabilities. As Flynn (1988) reported in an investigation in an urban area, being old and living on their own might even pose additional risk for abuse and exploitation of older adults with developmental disabilities.

Institutional Accommodations

Institutions vary significantly in terms of the type and degree of their institutional characteristics. They range from total institutional environments marked by restrictions and highly protective aims to institutions that are open in some domains to allowing individuals a life of greater independence while retaining institutional features in architecture or in daily congregate activities. The range of such characteristics affect the resident's quality of life (Ferguson, 1997).

Institutional life, by definition, seems discordant with personal independence. Daily activities are regimented from breakfast to bedtime. Goffman's (1961/1990) classic sociological study of asylums concluded that many individual choices are not available to residents of such institutions. The major characteristics he described are still observed in institutional environments: routinization of daily life, separation of staff and inmate worlds, and loss of individuality. Another drawback in institutional environments is the way that they cause loneliness in older people with developmental disabilities and thus promote depressive moods in these individuals. According to Fitzgerald (1998), the largest deficit in protected housing is its impact on residents' personal relationships.

Group and Residential Facilities   In Europe, residential homes differ greatly in scale and style. Some have a capacity for more than 30 people, whereas facilities operated by religious organizations or the national government might have more than 200 places. Occupancy of units within the facility might vary between 8 and 20 people, according to the architectural and structural conditions of the building. The various environments may differ in the choices that residents are permitted to make (e.g., having one's own bedroom with personal items, living in a bedroom completely furnished by the agency, having lunch in the facility's dining room, eating in a monastery-like refectory). As another example of limits in personal decision making, some residential facilities use a catering service that provides the same meals to virtually all of the residents.

In many homes, staff and management form "old people's groups" for people ages 60 years and older in recognition of their need for greater quiet in their living arrangements. Because of lack of funds for special programs of support, however, most of these groups offer their members no special residential activities. Often staff who support these groups lack training in the field of aging. Sometimes these groups suffer from understaffing. As a result, major abuses and human rights violations cannot be ruled out. For example, the older groups, especially those including people with mental retardation requiring extensive or pervasive supports, are referred to the worst-equipped, most decrepit accommodations within the facility. As observed in one of these facilities, the rooms that the group of older adults who were kept inactive most of the time used were equipped with a videotape-monitoring system to allow a small number of personnel to care for them. This response to limited staff resources highlights the risks of discrimination based on age. Through misuse of communication technology, it also represents a gross intrusion on personal intimacy and human dignity.

Accommodations for older people with mental retardation in larger residential facilities still takes place throughout Europe. Not all of the people who officially are discharged from psychiatric hospitals are admitted to community-based small group facilities. Many such people with mental retardation are resettled in residential facilities that are operated under legal regulations for mental retardation services but are physically located on the site of a hospital.

In Australia, where deinstitutionalization occurred earlier than it did in Austria, Ashman and colleagues (1995) reported that only 35% of a cohort analyzed were affected by community-based transfers, whereas the vast majority continued to live in large institutional environments. In addition, older people living in the family and losing their main caregiver are more likely to be admitted to a residential facility than a community-based small-group facility for older people with mental retardation.

In the United States, a disproportionate number of older people with mental retardation are housed in larger facilities (Lakin, Prouty, Braddock, & Anderson, 1997). Although the overall number of people with developmental disabilities living in state institutions decreased by 38.6% from 1977 to 1996, the proportion of people ages 40 years and older increased in the same period from 22.9% to 50.4%. An increasing number of people in this age group have physical impairments and thus present greater care needs such as in eating, dressing, and toileting. Thus, state institutions or other large facilities have become a prominent source of accommodation for a significant part of the older population with developmental disabilities in the United States because community-based residential programs are still insufficient for this age group.

Residential facilities in Europe have their own problems. Even when they are operated in an open manner, older people's opportunities for participation in the larger public environment remain quite restricted. They are often located in rural areas. Often these buildings were used as residential facilities for older adults with disabilities until the older adult population without disabilities was offered new, up-to-date facilities. Not surprisingly, in many of these countries, public funding for residential facilities for older adults with developmental disabilities is limited.

Retirement Facilities and the Use of Other Generic Services   Older adults with developmental disabilities have begun to have access to residential facilities and other services for older adults without disabilities in different regions of Europe. Sadly, abuse of older adults with developmental disabilities by older adults without disabilities has occurred frequently. For example, a 66-year-old woman with Down syndrome exhibited signs of abusive consumption of alcohol a short time after having been admitted to a residential facility (E. Leder, personal communication, June 16, 1998). This problem was not present in her earlier life. It was discovered that the woman had regularly been invited to accompany fellow residents without disabilities in their afternoon activities. Offered a surplus of alcoholic beverages, she was being used merely to amuse her "friends" at the facility. Soon after this discovery, the woman with Down syndrome was transferred to a residential facility for people with developmental disabilities, and her drinking behavior problem then disappeared. In addition to such exploitation, older people with developmental disabilities in residential facilities for older adults are at higher risk for neglect by staff, who are often not trained or lack experience in caring for people with their disabilities.

A few reports detail positive experiences in promoting the inclusion of older people with mental retardation as residents in facilities for older adults. In France, the program referred to as *cohabitation* attempts to integrate relatively independent older adults with mental retardation into facilities for older adults without disabilities (Breitenbach, 1995). One of this program's main goals is to promote relationships among members of both groups. The few relationships that could be observed, however, proved to be predominantly of a functional character. For example, an older person without mental retardation who was mostly confined to his bed enjoyed different services such as the daily delivery of the newspaper by an older person with mental retardation. According to the qualitative report, accompanied by videotape documentation (Fondation de France, 1994), the older person with mobility impairments, while accepting services, had problems engaging in a balanced relationship with the person with a developmental disability. Thus, even well-planned and professionally supported programs aimed at the inclusion of older people with mental retardation in residential facilities for older adults may be of limited impact in terms of their quality of life.

Because of vacancies in ordinary retirement facilities and the shortage of decent accommodations for older people with developmental disabilities, managers of such homes in some regions are offering them places. In most European countries, many retirement facilities are funded directly by the government according to rates of occupancy. As a result, these facilities have a strong interest in having no vacancies because vacancies would affect the funds allocated to them and the number of staff they could employ. The state allowance for a place in a residential facility for older adults is often less than the allowance offered for a person served in an accredited developmental disabilities facility. Given these economic realities, people with developmental disabilities who lack attentive, effective advocates are at risk of receiving low-quality services as they age.

Another risk is posed for older adults with mental retardation in nursing facilities. Some individuals are there despite an absence of need for round-the-clock care. In theory, this kind of accommodation should be reserved for older people with developmental disabilities who have extensive nursing needs (Weber, 1989). Even if they have such needs, staff may lack the training to properly diagnose and cope with their special issues, such as distinguishing Alzheimer's disease from conditions showing similar symptoms. They may not follow required professional standards or may be unfamiliar with research on special features in the course and the symptoms of dementias in people with developmental disabilities (for summaries, see Weber, 1997b; Zigman, Schupf, Haveman, & Silverman, 1995).

In addition, even nursing philosophies that place a high emphasis on the dignity of a person experiencing a dementia, such as the validation model, require adaptations to be used adequately for the care of older adults with developmental disabilities (Urlings et al., 1998). Janicki, Heller, Seltzer, and Hogg (1995) outlined guidelines for assessment practice and service provision with regard to Alzheimer's disease and other dementias in adults with mental retardation. The effectiveness of special nursing facilities for people without mental retardation who have Alzheimer's disease is the subject of an ongoing debate. As a result, general guidance with respect to the accommodation of people with developmental disabilities and dementias cannot be formulated. In contrast, the resettlement of older adults with mental retardation living in nursing facilities and hospitals to other environments is often justified (Walker, Walker, & Ryan, 1996).

In different European countries, misplacement in nursing facilities is reported to occur when the older person with developmental disabilities is admitted to the institution at the same time as the justified referral of his or her older parent. For example, assume that a single, older adult with dementia who is the mother of an individual with mental retardation enters a geriatric facility. Because the admission of a person with mental retardation to that facility cannot be justified on the basis of nursing needs, a misuse of that facility becomes obvious. Although such a referral might be seen as appropriate, considering the fact that these two people lived together all of their lives, the institution fails to consider the special needs of the older adult with mental retardation, whose quality of life inevitably declines.

Psychiatric Institutions Psychiatric hospitals are classic examples of total institutions. The life of an older adult with mental retardation in a large psychiatric facility is best illustrated on an individual basis through a case study.

Hanna

Consider the case of Hanna, a 54-year-old woman with developmental disabilities who entered the psychiatric hospital in the city of Vienna at age 13 years. Hanna had never heard about independence and free choice during her entire life. For 41 years, staff members told her exactly what to wear each morning, regardless of whether she liked the color, and she surely did not buy her own clothes. They told her when and what to eat, regardless of whether she was hungry. They told her on which chair to sit, in which bed to sleep in a dormitory of a dozen people, and when to go to sleep and when to wake up. They decided whether she was allowed to sit in a certain room or whether the daily schedule required her to stay in another place. She never knew about her financial situation; it was never necessary, because staff members knew it for her. She never knew the approximate price of a cup of coffee or of underwear or a pencil, not because her disabilities were so

severe but because staff knew this information for her. Hanna was not allowed to go shopping or to visit a coffee shop by herself anyway, and, of
course, she would not have found her way there—not so much because of
her disability but because others found the way for her. She never learned to
pay with her own money, she never learned to tell time, she never learned to
cross a street correctly and safely, and she never learned how to use public
transportation. Everything was done for Hanna. Because she always had
heard from the people caring for her that she was too old and too sick to do
certain things, this became her main argument against participating in activities. She sat in her chair all day, waiting for time to go by. In the last few
years, staff thought she should have structure in her day and offered her
occupational therapy. After having learned for more than 40 years that she
lacked skills and capabilities, however, Hanna answered only, "No, I'm too
old and too sick."

Hanna does not display major behavioral symptoms on which to frame a reliable
psychiatric diagnosis. In most Western countries, it was traditional until the late
1980s for people with mental retardation who lacked appropriate support from their
families or had nobody around to fight for their cause to be admitted to psychiatric
hospitals merely on the basis of their mental retardation. Psychiatric institutions
generally operated in a way in which consumers' views concerning important life decisions were not considered. Sadly, Hanna's is not a unique case. Almost all of the
longtime residents with developmental disabilities housed in psychiatric hospitals
were never confronted with choices and never developed self-determination skills.
They need balanced assistance that guides them during this learning process but
avoids the next well-meaning imposition by others.

Some older people with developmental disabilities may need temporary treatment in specialized centers for mental health disorders (see Chapter 11). In many
countries, it is accepted, and even defined by law, that a referral of a person with
mental retardation to a psychiatric unit is permitted only on the basis of a valid psychiatric diagnosis. As a matter of recommended practice, often psychiatric units
offer only temporary, limited admissions, with the consumer having the right to return to his former living accommodation, thus preventing long-term hospitalization. Outreach crisis intervention programs have been successfully established as
important tools to respond to psychiatric needs and prevent unjustified referrals
(Shoham-Vardi et al., 1996). These services should be developed especially to meet
the needs of the older population with developmental disabilities and to allow them
to age in place for as long as possible.

Resettlement in Advanced Age

This section analyzes resettlements from psychiatric hospitals as well as the downsizing of such facilities and long-term effects on the lives of older people with developmental disabilities.

Resettlements from Psychiatric Hospitals   Deinstitutionalization can succeed
even in such troubling cases as Hanna's. It is well documented (Collins, 1994; Dagnan, Look, Ruddick, & Jones, 1995; Halpern, Close, & Nelson, 1986) that older people with developmental disabilities who have spent years, even most of their lives,
in large psychiatric facilities, can experience great gains in their quality of life in
properly designed, sensitively applied programs of deinstitutionalization. No evi-

dence exists, however, that all of these individuals will develop self-determination skills as a result of such programs. The development of such skills are more closely related to individuals' level of mental retardation (i.e., the more profound the individual's mental retardation, the less likely that changes in the level of the individual's skills will be achieved) (Eyman & Widaman, 1987).

As compared with the degree of mental retardation, age is not as closely correlated with improvements in adaptive behavior. Therefore, excluding older people with mental retardation from deinstitutionalization programs merely on the basis of their age is a form of ageist discrimination. According to reports (Strauss, Shavelle, Baumeister, & Anderson, 1998), the population transferred to community-based accommodations is at higher risk for neglect cannot be ignored because their mortality may substantially increase after deinstitutionalization. This underscores the need to ensure continuous, consistent, and competent medical care and adequate supports for people with developmental disabilities who undergo transfers from psychiatric institutions.

In Austria, after a major change in the law regulating the admission to psychiatric hospitals was implemented in 1991, the pace of deinstitutionalization programs from long-term state psychiatric hospitals only quickened. Many of the younger adults in such facilities were involved in different projects aimed at their resettlement in community-based small groups. An evaluation (Schober, 1998) report on behavioral outcomes observed differences depending on the philosophy of the resettlement program. Programs focusing predominantly on progress in adaptive behavior and enhanced independence within the first year produced more new behavior problems as compared with the program in which equal attention was paid to individuals' progress in independence and their emotional well-being (Schober, 1998).

Downsizing Deinstitutionalization is often aimed at a major downsizing rather than at closing the institution. Although the benefits for people with developmental disabilities of moving from an institution to a community-based program have often been reported, far less attention has been paid to those who remain in institutions. There may be different reasons why older people should remain in an institution (Larson & Lakin, 1991). For instance, many family members believe that special resources and services are more readily available in institutions or that a move out of an institution may cause stress for an older adult resident. Research (Stancliffe & Abery, 1997) confirms, however, that many of the people who stay in institutions show more challenging behavior at baseline.

Downsizing is often accompanied by some structural and/or programmatic changes within the institution. As an example, in Austria, downsizing was followed by a resettlement in place in many institutions. The physical environment changed from life in residential wards to a life in smaller units (i.e., in residential facilities), with group size varying between 8 and 12 people. The interiors of these units are generally close to the physical characteristics of a family home and hence may show some elements of a normalized environment. Locations within a large psychiatric facility, however, sharply limit residents' experiences and community participation. In addition, the support for these groups remains underdeveloped, with restricted options for meaningful, age-appropriate daily activities or leisure programs. The residents' wishes and aspirations are not respected, and residents do not participate in many areas of daily personal decision making. This kind of resettlement in an institutional environment provides cosmetic improvements but does not eliminate some of the worst features of the institutional environment.

Stancliffe and Hayden (1998) reported on the long-term effects of downsizing on the remaining group in U.S. institutions. Over a 4-year period, they found that therapy services decreased over time while staffing remained the same. In addition, individuals' integration into the community declined significantly, and individuals experienced many moves in residential and day programs within the institution. No significant changes in adaptive behavior were associated with intra-institutional resettlement. Of the medical services used in the community, many were located in state-operated, segregated environments exclusively serving people with developmental disabilities. Finally, per-person expenditures on services increased well in excess of the inflation rate during this period.

Long-Term Effects of Moving   Longitudinal studies (Collins, 1992; Hayden & DePaepe, 1991; Heller, 1985; Walker, Walker, & Ryan, 1993, 1996) reported favorable outcomes with regard to the resettlement of older people with developmental disabilities who left larger institutions for smaller, community-based accommodations. In general, enhancement of adaptive behavior was observed. Other evaluations (Fine, Tangeman, & Woodard, 1990) showed that progress was accompanied by an increase in maladaptive behavior.

In analyzing the long-term effects of deinstitutionalization, especially in the exercise of choice, Stancliffe and Abery (1997) reported that, in the United States, movers exercised significantly more choice, although the movers did not differ at baseline from those who remained in the institution. For both groups, however, the absolute level of choice available was low. Furthermore, the benefits of deinstitutionalization did not differ in accordance with the individual's level of mental retardation. These results are challenged in some areas by U.K. findings. Dagnan and colleagues (1998), in their longitudinal evaluation, found an increase as expressed in different subscales of quality-of-life measurements for the first 41 months, showing a consistent development in quality of life during this period. However, after 53 months, the quality of life leveled off. The areas most affected were leisure and social life. This effect might be due to increased physical constraints lowering levels of activities. In addition, it is important to make continuous efforts to ensure that opportunities are offered and that the level of activity is maintained.

CONCLUSIONS

This chapter first analyzes psychological factors affecting individuals' personal well-being and subjective assessments of their quality of life. Having a say in life decisions as an older adult with developmental disabilities while taking advantage of the ability to select from a decent set of options was shown to be a major agent for increasing a person's psychological well-being. In contrast, an older adult who is deprived of these experiences in everyday life and has little or no perceived control over meaningful and important aspects of his or her life risks losing the joy of living. In such circumstances, activities of everyday life become a matter of complete indifference, and the person may display apathy.

The skewed distribution of accommodation options for older people with developmental disabilities restricts these individuals' prospects for a good old age. In small, community-based accommodations, staff paid greater attention to the needs of older residents. These environments can be labeled as *enabling* environments because they are favorable to individuals' aspirations. In most countries, however, this type of accommodation is limited. Most older people with developmental disabilities still live in pronounced custodial environments. Participation in everyday life (i.e., being effectively involved in decision making, having one's preferences respected) is often unjustifiably restricted. In summary, whether consumers actively take part in the self-defined affairs of everyday life is largely dependent on the type of accommodations in which they live and on the way in which staff serve them.

In addition, findings (Riley & Riley, 1992) on resettlement programs for older people with mental retardation are discussed in this chapter. Riley and Riley analyzed age-differentiated versus age-integrated accommodation models comparing the major consequences affecting an older person's prospects. A typical age-differentiated model (i.e., a model segregating on the basis of age and relegating older adults to "retirement") carries higher risks for older people with developmental disabilities by imposing a role devoid of content. In contrast, age-integrated models are defined by the absence of social barriers linked to age. According to this model, any individual can participate in leisure activities, work, and education programs, notwithstanding the individual's age. The advantage for the individual is that he or she can make a choice from a multitude of different roles. As previously discussed, this is the way in which Peter and his friends enjoy their old age.

Planning and developing services for older people with developmental disabilities is marked by conflicting or ambivalent attitudes of service providers and policy makers (Janicki & Hogg, 1989). These attitudes are often an expression of uncertainty about whether to embrace specialized age-segregated or specialized age-inclusive provisions or whether to further the use of community-based services designed for older adults without disabilities. The proponents of age-specialized services see the advantages in the concentration of professional expertise and the ability to respond to older people's frequently mentioned preferences for enjoying social interaction with their own age group. In contrast, supporters of services developed for older adults without disabilities assume that they can achieve a high degree of social and functional integration by pushing for access to such community-based services. It seems, however, that facilities for older people with mental retardation are often developed pragmatically, particularly in terms of available funding. This approach is justified in retrospect and not on the basis of proactive planning.

The weaknesses of such a pragmatic, emergency-driven approach are obvious. Too many unjustified placements for older people with developmental disabilities in restrictive facilities occur. Too many people languish on long waiting lists for housing. To avoid these problems, forward-thinking planning that applies the concept of the least restrictive alternative is urgently required. Such planning is essential for a population that is so fragile and so prone to being neglected.

In conclusion, aging in place is a right that needs to be promoted effectively. Honoring an individual's right to age in the neighborhood in which the person lived for most of his or her adult years permits the individual to continue to enjoy well-established networks and to avoid problems such as feeling unsafe, out-of-context, dependent, and lonely. This requires a cohesive system of small neighborhood-based living units equipped and operated to provide different levels of support. That type of system offers the best chance of enhancing the individual's independence and nurturing the individual's capacity for self-determination.

REFERENCES

Abramson, L.Y., Metalsky, G.I., & Alloy, L.B. (1989). Hopelessness depression: A theory-based subtype of depression. *Psychological Review, 96,* 358–372.

Anderson, D.J. (1993). Social inclusion of older adults with mental retardation. In E. Sutton, A.R. Factor, B.A. Hawkins, T. Heller, & G.B. Seltzer (Eds.), *Older adults with develop-*

mental disabilities: Optimizing choice and change (pp. 79–93). Baltimore: Paul H. Brookes Publishing Co.

Ashman, A.F., Suttie, J.N., & Bramley, J. (1995). Residential circumstances of older Australians with mental retardation. *American Journal on Mental Retardation, 99,* 356–362.

Bambara, L.M., & Koger, F. (1996). *Opportunities for daily choice making* (Innovation series no. 8). Washington, DC: American Association on Mental Retardation.

Barnett, P., & Gotlib, I.H. (1988). Psychosocial functioning and depression: Distinguishing between antecedents, consequents, and consequences. *Psychological Bulletin, 104,* 97–126.

Belfiore, P.J., & Toro-Zambrana, W. (1994). *Recognizing choices in community settings by people with significant disabilities* (Series: Innovations, no. 1). Washington, DC: American Association on Mental Retardation.

Benassi, V.A., Sweeney, P.D., & Dufour, C.L. (1988). Is there a relation between locus of control orientation and depression? *Journal of Abnormal Psychology, 97,* 357–367.

Blewett, T. (1980, 5 February). The search for identity in a residential home for the elderly. *Social Work Today, 11*(22).

Brehm, J.W. (1993). Control, its loss, and psychological reactance. In G. Weary, F.H. Gleicher, & K.L. Marsh (Eds.), *Control motivation and social cognition* (pp. 3–30). New York: Springer-Verlag New York.

Brehm, S.S., & Brehm, J.W. (1981). *Psychological reactance: A theory of freedom and control.* San Diego: Academic Press.

Breitenbach, N. (1995). *Pouvons-nous vieillir ensemble? Étude sur la cohabitation des personnes handicapées mentales vieillissantes dans les institutions pour personnes âgées [Can we age together? Investigation on the coresidence of older people with mental retardation and older people without mental retardation in homes for older people].* Paris: Fondation de France.

Breitenbach, N. (1997). *Fortes et fragiles. Les familles vieillissantes qui gardent en leur sein un descendant handicapé [Strong and fragile: Older families continuing to live with their adult child with developmental disability].* Paris: Fondation de France.

Collins, J. (1992). *When the eagles fly: A report on the resettlement of people with learning difficulties from long-stay institutions.* London: Values Into Action.

Collins, J. (1994). *Still to be settled: Strategies for the resettlement of people from mental handicap hospitals.* London: Values Into Action.

Dagnan, D., Look, R., Ruddick, L., & Jones, J. (1995). Changes in the quality of life of people with learning disabilities who moved from hospital to live in community based homes. *International Journal of Rehabilitation Research, 18,* 115–122.

Dagnan, D., Ruddick, L., & Jones, J. (1998). A longitudinal study of the quality of life of older people with intellectual disability after leaving hospital. *Journal of Intellectual Disability Research, 42,* 112–121.

Edgerton, R.B. (1989). Ageing in the community: A matter of choice. In A. Brechin & J. Walmsey (Eds.), *Making connections.* London: Hodder and Stoughton/Open University Press.

Ern, M. (1992). *Wege der Annäherung an die Lebenssituation von älterwerdenden und alten Menschen mit geistiger Behinderung [Ways to approach the lives of aging and old people with mental retardation].* Aachen, Germany: Verlag Mainz.

Eyman, R.K., & Widaman, K.F. (1987). Life-span development of institutionalized and community-based mentally retarded persons, revisited. *American Journal of Mental Deficiency, 91,* 559–569.

Ferguson, R.V. (1997). Environmental design and quality of life. In R.I. Brown (Ed.), *Quality of life for people with disabilities: Models, research and practice* (2nd ed., pp. 251–269). Cheltenham, England: Stanley Thornes Publishers.

Fine, M.A., Tangeman, P.J., & Woodard, J. (1990). Changes in adaptive behavior of older adults with mental retardation following deinstitutionalization. *American Journal on Mental Retardation, 94,* 661–668.

Fitzgerald, J. (1998). *Time for freedom? Services for older people with learning difficulties.* London: Centre for Policy on Aging/Values Into Action.

Flynn, M.C. (1988). The social environment of adults living in their own homes. In M.C. Flynn (Ed.), *A place of my own: Independence for adults who are mentally handicapped* (pp. 14–39). London: Cassell.

Fondation de France. (1994). *La cohabitation entre personnes handicapées mentales vieillissantes et personnes âgées en maison de retraite [Co-residence of older persons with men-*

tal retardation and older persons without disabilities in homes for retired persons]. Paris: Author.

Frost, P.A. (1996). Choice and daily activities for people with disabilities. *International Journal of Rehabilitation Research, 19,* 89–91.

Gennep, A. (1995). Ageing and quality of care. *British Journal of Developmental Disabilities, 41,* 73–78.

Goffman, E. (1990). *Asylums: Essays on the social situation of mental patients and other inmates.* New York: Doubleday. (Original work published 1961)

Grant, G., McGrath, M., & Ramcharan, P. (1995). Community inclusion of older people with learning disabilities. *Care in Place, 2*(1), 51–59.

Halle, J. (1995). Innovations in choice-making research: An editorial introduction. *Journal of The Association for Persons with Severe Handicaps, 20,* 173–174.

Halpern, A.S., Close, D.W., & Nelson, D.J. (1986). *On my own: The impact of semi-independent living programs for adults with mental retardation.* Baltimore: Paul H. Brookes Publishing Co.

Harvey, J.H. (1976). Attribution of freedom. In J.H. Harvey, W.J. Ickes, & R.F. Kidd (Eds.), *New directions in attribution research* (Vol. 1, pp. 63–97). Mahwah, NJ: Lawrence Erlbaum Associates.

Hayden, M.F., & DePaepe, P.A. (1991). Medical conditions, level of care needs, and health-related outcomes of persons with mental retardation: A review. *Journal of The Association for Persons with Severe Handicaps, 16,* 188–206.

Heller, T., & Factor, A.R. (1994). Facilitating future planning and transitions out of the home. In M.M. Seltzer, M.W. Krauss, & M.P. Janicki (Eds.), *Life course perspectives on adulthood and old age* (pp. 39–50). Washington, DC: American Association on Mental Retardation.

Heller, T. (1985). Residential relocation and reactions of elderly mentally retarded persons. In M.P. Janicki & H.M. Wisniewski (Eds.), *Aging and developmental disabilities: Issues and approaches* (pp. 379–389). Baltimore: Paul H. Brookes Publishing Co.

Heller, T., Preston, L., Nelis, T., Brown, A., & Pederson, E. (1996). *Making choices as we age: A peer training program.* Chicago: University of Illinois at Chicago, Institute on Disability and Human Development, Clearinghouse on Aging and Developmental Disabilities.

Hogarth, R.M. (1987). *Judgement and choice: The psychology of decision* (2nd ed.). Chichester, England: John Wiley & Sons.

Hogg, J., Moss, S., & Cooke, D. (1988). *Ageing and mental handicap.* London: Chapman and Hall.

Holland, A. (1997). People living in community homes: Their views. *British Journal of Learning Disabilities, 25,* 68–72.

Howe, J., Horner, R.H., & Newton, J.S. (1998). Comparison of supported living and traditional residential services in the State of Oregon. *Mental Retardation, 36,* 1–11.

Jacobson, J.W., Sutton, M.S., & Janicki, M.P. (1985). Demography and characteristics of aging and aged mentally retarded persons. In M.P. Janicki & H.M. Wisniewski (Eds.), *Aging and developmental disabilities: Issues and approaches* (pp. 115–142). Baltimore: Paul H. Brookes Publishing Co.

Janicki, M.P. (Ed.). (1996). *Help for caring for older people caring for adults with a developmental disability.* Albany: New York State Developmental Disability Planning Council.

Janicki, M.P., Heller, T., Seltzer, G.B., & Hogg, J. (1995). *Practice guidelines for the clinical assessment and care management of Alzheimer and other dementias among adults with mental retardation.* Washington, DC: American Association on Mental Retardation.

Janicki, M.P., & Hogg, J. (1989). International research perspectives on aging and mental retardation. *Australia and New Zealand Journal of Developmental Disabilities, 15,* 161–164.

Janicki, M.P., & Wisniewski, H.M. (1985). Some comments on growing older and being developmentally disabled. In M.P. Janicki & H.M. Wisniewski (Eds.), *Aging and developmental disabilities. Issues and approaches* (pp. 1–5). Baltimore: Paul H. Brookes Publishing Co.

Kishi, G., Teelucksingh, B., Zollers, N., Park-Lee, S., & Meyer, L. (1988). Daily decision-making in community residences: A social comparison of adults with and without mental retardation. *American Journal on Mental Retardation, 92,* 430–435.

Krauss, M.W., & Seltzer, M.M. (1986). Comparison of elderly and adult mentally retarded persons in community and institutional settings. *American Journal of Mental Retardation, 91,* 237–243.

Lakin, C., Prouty, B., Braddock, D., & Anderson, L. (1997). State institution populations smaller, older, more impaired. *Mental Retardation, 35,* 231–232.

Larson, S.A., & Lakin, K.C. (1991). Parent attitudes about residential placement before and after deinstitutionalization: A research synthesis. *Journal of The Association of the Severely Handicapped, 16,* 25–38.

Lebenshilfe Österreich [Austrian parents' association for people with mental retardation]. (1994). *Bedürfnisse von alten Menschen mit geistiger Behinderung [The needs of older people with mental retardation].* Vienna: Author.

Mühlberger, P. (1998). *Ältere Menschen mit geistiger Behinderung in den Wohneinrichtungen von Jugend am Werk und Caritas im Raum Wien-Umgebung [Older people with mental retardation living in residential facilities operated by two larger agencies ("Jugend am Werk" and "Caritas") in Vienna and vicinity].* Unpublished thesis, Institute of Psychology, University of Vienna.

O'Brien, J. (1987). A guide to lifestyle planning: Using *The Activities Catalog* to integrate services and natural support systems. In B. Wilcox & G.T. Bellamy (Eds.), *A comprehensive guide to* The Activities Catalog: *An alternative curriculum for youth and adults with severe disabilities* (pp. 175–189). Baltimore: Paul H. Brookes Publishing Co.

Palmer, S.B., & Wehmeyer, M.L. (1998). Students' expectations of the future: Hopelessness as a barrier to self-determination. *Mental Retardation, 36,* 128–136.

Racino, J.A., & Taylor, S.J. (1993). "People first": Approaches to housing and support. In J.A. Racino, P. Walker, S. O'Connor, & S.J. Taylor (Eds.), *Community participation series: Vol. 2. Housing, support, and community: Choices and strategies for adults with disabilities* (pp. 33–56). Baltimore: Paul H. Brookes Publishing Co.

Riley, M., & Riley, J.W. (1992). Individuelles und gesellschaftliches Potential des Alterns [Aging: Individual and societal potentials]. In P.B. Baltes & J. Mitterstraß (Eds.), *Zukunft des Alterns und gesellschaftliche Entwicklung [Future of aging and societal development]* (pp. 437–459). Berlin: Springer-Verlag.

Rotter, J.B. (1954). *Social learning and clinical psychology.* Upper Saddle River, NJ: Prentice-Hall.

Rotter, J.B. (1966). Generalized expectancies for internal versus external control of reinforcement. *Psychological Monographs, 80,* 1.

Sands, D.J., & Wehmeyer, M.L. (Eds.). (1996). *Self-determination across the life span: Independence and choice for people with disabilities.* Baltimore: Paul H. Brookes Publishing Co.

Scheerenberger, R.C. (1982). Public residential services 1981: Status and trends. *Mental Retardation, 20,* 210–215.

Schober, M. (1998). *Ausgliederung von geistig Behinderten aus der Psychiatrie: Eine Evaluation unter Berücksichtigung psychologischer Aspekte [Deinstitutionalization of people with mental retardation from psychiatric institutions: Evaluation of psychological aspects].* Unpublished thesis, Institute of Psychology, University of Vienna, Austria.

Seligman, M.E.P. (1992). *Helplessness: On depression, development, and death.* San Francisco: W.H. Freeman.

Shoham-Vardi, I., Davidson, P.W., Cain, N.N., Sloane-Reeves, J.E., Giesow, V.E., Quijano, L.E., & Houser, K.D. (1996). Factors predicting re-referral following crisis intervention for community-based persons with developmental disabilities and behavioral and psychiatric disorders. *American Journal on Mental Retardation, 101,* 109–117.

Sigafoos, J., Laurie, S., & Pennell, D. (1995). Preliminary assessment of choice making among children with Rett syndrome. *Journal of The Association for Persons with Severe Handicaps, 20,* 175–184.

Stancliffe, R.J., & Abery, B.H. (1997). Longitudinal study of deinstitutionalization and the exercise of choice. *Mental Retardation, 35,* 159–169.

Stancliffe, R.J., & Hayden, M.F. (1998). Longitudinal study of institutional downsizing: Effects on individuals who remain in the institution. *American Journal on Mental Retardation, 102,* 500–510.

Strauss, D., Shavelle, R., Baumeister, A., & Anderson, T.W. (1998). Mortality in persons with developmental disabilities after transfer into community care. *American Journal on Mental Retardation, 102,* 569–581.

Sweeney, P., Anderson, K., & Bailey, S. (1986). Attributional style in depression: A meta-analytic review. *Journal of Personality and Social Psychology, 50,* 974–991.

Switzky, H.N., & Haywood, H.C. (1991). Self-reinforcement schedules in persons with mild mental retardation: Effects of motivational orientation and instructional demands. *Journal of Mental Deficiency Research, 35,* 221–230.

Tossobero, J. (1995). Impact of size revisited: Relation of number of residents to self-determination and deprivatization. *American Journal on Mental Retardation, 100,* 59–67.

Urlings, H., van Schrojenstein Lantman-de Valk, H., Maaskant, M., Breitenbach, N., Vandevelde, J., Weber, G., Moss, S., & Molander, L. (1998). *Volgen: Respectvol omgaan met dementerende mensen met een verstandelijke handicap [Face to face: Respectful coping with dementia in older people with intellectual disability].* Dwingeloo, The Netherlands: Kavanah.

Walker, A., Walker, C., & Ryan, T. (1996). Older people with learning difficulties leaving institutional care: A case of double jeopardy. *Ageing and Society, 16,* 125–150.

Walker, C., Ryan, T., & Walker, A. (1996). *Fair shares for all?* Brighton, England: Pavillon Publishing.

Walker, C., Walker, A., & Ryan, T. (1993). *Quality of life after resettlement for people with learning disabilities* (Report to the North West Regional Health Authority). Manchester, England: North Western Regional Health Authority.

Wcber, G. (1989). Probleme der Vergreisung bei Personen mit geistiger Behinderund [Issues related to extreme old age in people with mental retardation]. *Heilpädagogik [Special Education], 32,* 147–150.

Weber, G. (1997a). *Intellektuelle Behinderung: Grundlagen, klinisch-psychologische Diagnostik und Therapie im Erwachsenenalter [Intellectual disability: Foundations, clinical psychological diagnostics, and therapy in adulthood].* Vienna: WUV-Universitätsverlag.

Weber, G. (1997b). Morbus Alzheimer bei Menschen mit geistiger Behinderung [Alzheimer's disease in people with mental retardation]. In S. Weis & G. Weber (Eds.), *Handbuch Morbus Alzheimer: Neurobiologie, Diagnose und Therapie [Handbook on Alzheimer's disease: Neurobiology, diagnostics, and therapy]* (pp. 1311–1335). Weinheim, Germany: Beltz-PVU.

White, R.W. (1959). Motivation reconsidered: The concept of competence. *Psychological Review, 66,* 297–333.

Wicklund, R.A. (1974). *Freedom and reactance.* Mahwah, NJ: Lawrence Erlbaum Associates.

Zigman, W.B., Schupf, N., Haveman, M., & Silverman, W. (1995). *Epidemiology of Alzheimer disease in mental retardation: Results and recommendations from an international conference.* Washington, DC: American Association on Mental Retardation.

IV

Future Directions

16

Self-Advocacy for a Good Life in Our Older Years

Mitchell Levitz

Just like me, most young people with developmental disabilities are living alone or with family or friends in more diverse communities. We are leading active and productive lives by working or volunteering, participating in community recreation and sports activities, attending religious services, and joining with family and community members for special occasions and events. Many of my friends and I see our lives as being quite typical, even though our social lives may sometimes be more limited. As young adults, we are relatively happy and somewhat active in our own communities and have a variety of opportunities for a good quality of life. In addition, I believe that my generation of young people with developmental disabilities hopes to have the same lifestyle as we get older. Self-advocacy will play a major role in helping to make this happen.

This chapter is about self-advocacy, aging, and claiming our rights to a good life. It focuses on how my generation of people with developmental disabilities can prepare for retirement, face real issues about aging, and create opportunities to help ourselves cope with changes in our lives.

PERSONAL THOUGHTS ABOUT MY LATER YEARS

As I write this chapter at age 26, I believe that I am leading a fulfilling life. In thinking ahead to when I become an older adult, I would like to continue to be active and productive, and I hope that people will respect my wishes then just as they do now. People with developmental disabilities and our supporters have fought long and hard so that we have access to equal rights, are regarded as unique individuals, and are treated with dignity and respect. It concerns me that older adults without disabilities say that aging itself often results in older adults being treated with less dignity and respect. Rather than being looked on as individuals who are experienced in life and living, they are often labeled as senior citizens and viewed as being part of a group of people who no longer are able to contribute, to live independently, or to make individual choices. This attitude sounds too similar to what used to happen to those of us with developmental disabilities. Nonlabeling is one of the principles of the People First self-advocacy movement (see Inclusion International [originally known as the International League of Societies for the Mentally Handicapped (ILSMH)], 1996). This issue is a concern for both individuals with developmental disabilities and older people in general. An important challenge is to eliminate labeling wherever and whenever it occurs. Labeling leads to people thinking that older adults and people with developmental disabilities are limited, and then those people act in ways that do not allow us to maximize our potential.

I am sure that in the future I will to continue to advocate for myself and other people with disabilities to help ensure that aging does not compromise what we have gained through the disability rights movement. One of the areas of self-advocacy that interests me very much is influencing public policy. Like some of my friends and colleagues with developmental disabilities, I have found this area exciting and challenging. I expect that policy work will continue to be both a personal and career goal in my future. I hope to work for many more years with an organization like Capabilities Unlimited, Inc., which provides internships for and hires individuals with developmental disabilities. We train people to gain leadership, career, and self-advocacy skills; serve on policy boards; and participate in legislative advocacy activities. Continuing employment with this kind of organization will also enable me to plan and help fund my retirement years.

When I do finally decide to retire some day, I think that I will enjoy spending time volunteering and being active in my community in any way that I am needed. I have had many role models of well-respected older citizens, such as Gunnar Dybwad (see Foreword) and Justin Dart, who continue to be strong and effective leaders in advocating for the rights of people with disabilities. Walter Rupp, a community organizer for Advocating for Change Together, wrote that "a great deal of legislation is proposed and passed and services are designed without the direct input of the people most affected. Influencing public policy is often time consuming, complicated, and difficult" (1994, p. 4). It is especially exciting for me to realize, however, that the future direction of the disability rights movement will also be shaped by my peers and colleagues from across the United States and around the world. We are learning and developing leadership skills and are beginning to be in the forefront of promoting the rights of individuals of all ages with developmental disabilities. For example, in 1996 and 1997, I was fortunate to attend the Next Generation of Leadership Symposium, sponsored by the U.S. President's Committee on Mental Retardation. This program brings people younger than 35 to Washington, D.C., to work together on developing white papers (i.e., position papers) on disability issues. The symposium is also designed to develop a network of future leaders. The recommendations of such gatherings should influence some policy decisions. In addition, bringing together young potential leaders should have an impact on self-advocacy, human rights, and a better quality of life for my generation of people with developmental disabilities as we strive to influence new directions and promote systems change. Bob Williams, then the Commissioner of the federal Administration on Developmental Disabilities (ADD), described this concept as follows:

People with disabilities and advocates—individually and as a consortium—have advocated, demanded change, educated themselves and others, and have established a firm foundation in the disability policymaking process. . . . The intricate public policy role that people with disabilities have played must now be reinvigorated and must encompass new ideas, new individuals, new thoughts and creativity. . . . There are many exciting milestones yet to be achieved. It is through the knowledge, experience, and solutions offered by people with disabilities and advocates that will continue to help establish disability policy. Every voice counts. (1994, p. 13)

I am sure that politics will continue to be a major interest of mine throughout my lifetime. Perhaps when I have more free time, after I retire from my career, I will be able to volunteer more of my time to support political candidates and work on their campaigns—and, for variation, maybe I will even run for public office myself. After all, Golda Meir became the Prime Minister of Israel when she was 71.

I have also had the opportunity to work as part of a team in helping other people with developmental disabilities to learn and use legislative advocacy skills in order to have an impact on laws, regulations, and policies affecting people with disabilities on the local, state, and national levels. Many examples from U.S. history show that age is no limit in this area. Benjamin Franklin helped frame the U.S. Constitution when he was 81. I watched a television report that highlighted the fact that the American Association of Retired Persons (AARP) is considered the most powerful lobbying organization in the United States. A potential united front could be formed by recruiting older adults and/or retired people with disabilities who are advocates for themselves and others to become active members and leaders in AARP and similar organizations. This kind of integrated community approach could achieve good results based on shared issues related to aging and older adulthood. For example, enforcing the Americans with Disabilities Act (ADA) of 1990 (PL 101-336) and making all public buildings accessible for people who use wheelchairs affects people who face physical challenges, regardless of whether their use of a wheelchair is due to the frailty of aging or a disabling condition such as cerebral palsy or muscular dystrophy.

Like most people with developmental disabilities, it is especially important for me to have good relationships with people in my family and close friends of the family. This should include people who are both older and younger than myself. My family and our close friends have always been supportive, helped me make decisions for myself, and helped me cope with major life changes. Although I am especially close to my grandparents and often turn to them for guidance, they are getting much older. Even though it is hard to think about, I know that my parents and grandparents will not be around forever. I know that I learned a great deal about aging and relationships from my great-grandmother, who passed away a few years ago at the age of 95. I am learning also that it is becoming more important that I develop good relationships with my sisters, cousins, and friends of the family who are close to my age. I hope that if I can find ways to continue to reach out to them, they will be a source of information and support because, as we all grow older together, they will probably experience many of the same problems, concerns, and challenges that I will face. I am also aware that the key people in one's life change over time. We all need to be sure that we continue to maintain and build relationships with the people who care about us and who will provide us with good advice and emotional support, whether they are family, close friends, or advocates.

Of course, we all need to have a little fun in our lives, too. During my free time, these days, like many other people, I enjoy sports. As I get older, I expect to continue to play ping-pong and tennis and go boating, waterskiing, and downhill skiing. Although waterskiing may become more difficult as my body ages, I have heard that there are downhill ski slopes where people ages 70 years and older can ski for free. That is certainly a bonus for getting older and a good motivation to keep myself in good shape! Being a spectator at ballgames is fun, and going to them with family or a group of friends is an enjoyable activity at any age.

PRERETIREMENT YEARS: PLANNING, CHOICES, AND DECISION MAKING

Young people with developmental disabilities are becoming better educated because of increased educational and life opportunities, including school and community inclusion, and greater exposure to modern technology, such as adaptive equipment, computers, and the Internet. Technology is important because it helps us to communicate better and to gain access to information more easily and more independently. This can be particularly useful in knowing our options and choices and making better decisions. Assistive technology is particularly helpful to individuals who, in the past, had more limited access to information and communication because of physical or intellectual challenges. It also has opened the doors to increased participation in all aspects of community life, including greater opportunities for social interactions, recreation, employment, and community volunteer experiences. For example, using a publishing software program has enabled me and my colleagues to publish a national newsletter, *Community Advocacy Press*, written by and for people with developmental disabilities. I have learned new skills such as importing articles by e-mail, editing, layout, scanning photographs, and design. This is an activity that I will be able to use throughout my lifetime for office or home use.

Beginning with early childhood and throughout our school years, having a variety of real-life experiences also helps us to know about and understand the various options available to us. The options include having many opportunities to make decisions and then learning about and coping with the consequences of such decisions. Our right as individuals with developmental disabilities to practice self-determination is more widely accepted. According to Nerney and Shumway, the following principles of self-determination are meant to provide a philosophical foundation for substantive system change that incorporates the values that people with disabilities and their families and friends hold deeply:

1. *Freedom:* The ability for individuals with freely chosen family and/or friends to plan a life with necessary support rather than purchase a program.
2. *Authority:* The ability for a person with a disability (with a social support network or circle if needed) to control a certain sum of dollars in order to purchase these supports.
3. *Support:* The arranging of resources and personnel—both formal and informal— that will assist an individual with a disability to live a life in the community rich in community association and contribution.
4. *Responsibility:* The acceptance of a valued role in a person's community through competitive employment, organizational affiliations, spiritual development and general caring for others in the community, as well as accountability for spending public dollars in ways that are life-enhancing for persons with disabilities. (1996, unpaginated)

I agree with this concept, based on my own experiences growing up in home, school, and community environments that enabled me to practice and acquire skills in self-determination. The support that I had from my family, friends, teachers, co-workers, and the community in having opportunities for self-determination enabled me to develop a sense of self-confidence, self-motivation, and directness. Having opportunities to learn about, understand, and practice self-determination during our younger years helps us to become more skilled in making and carrying out important choices and decisions in our later years.

A starting point for knowing what our choices are and for making decisions is to ask the question, What is self-advocacy? It means speaking out for ourselves and letting people know what we want and need. A second question to ask is, Who is a self-advocate? A self-advocate is a person who speaks about what he or she believes in and someone who is willing to do something about it.

In 1995, the Committee on Self-Advocacy for the ILSMH, since renamed Inclusion International, published a set of beliefs and values of self-advocacy along similar lines. It referred to self-advocacy as beliefs and values of "being a person first, being able to make our own decisions, believing in my value as a person, having other people believe in you as a person" and included the principles of "empowerment, equal opportunity, learning and living together, non-labeling" (Dybwad & Bersani, 1996, p. 14).

Self-advocacy is critical as we age and prepare for changes in our lives. The first step in the planning process is to take responsibility for ourselves to do some research and gather information. We should identify individuals whom we feel comfortable asking for help and those who are knowledgeable and experienced in the areas of aging and planning for the future. For example, if an individual is either employed or looking for employment, he or she can find out about setting up an individual retirement account (IRA) or enrolling in an employer-sponsored retirement plan. The individual needs to figure out and project future income from such a plan. In addition, people with developmental disabilities can explore the options that might be available through work programs and financial support from federal, state, and local governments. We can plan for our retirement by combining government assistance, financial retirement plans, and our earnings. In my opinion, individuals with developmental disabilities should have a goal of being as self-sufficient as possible. Therefore, in planning for the years when we are older, having a job and a career over a period of time may help support us and also enable us to save money to be able to do more during our retirement years. An employment record may also make us eligible for Social Security, medical and health care, and other kinds of benefits and entitlement programs. Being productive and earning money throughout our early years can enable us to have more options and an easier and more enjoyable time in our later years.

If we listen to people with disabilities, three messages become clear (Dybwad & Bersani, 1996). First, we have different concerns than professionals and even our parents have. Second, we value choice, independence, and risk: We know that we are going to make mistakes, and we are willing to accept those mistakes and the penalties and risks of those mistakes. Third, we have dreams for the future. Before we can develop a plan, we must have some clear ideas and know what we want to do when we get older. Consider making a list of these goals and life activities. Next, select and invite people such as family members, a support person, friends, an employment supervisor, a geriatric specialist, a financial expert, and other appropriate people to help us in developing a plan of action. This plan should have actual time frames and designate who will share responsibilities in helping to carry out this plan and help us achieve what we want to do in the future. Various models of person-centered planning demonstrate the idea of gathering information and then setting up a planning process. We should set the agenda, identify our goals, and make choices and decisions for ourselves based on our preferences, interests, and abilities as well as the good information and sound advice we get through this brainstorming activity. One caution, however, is that there may be some strong differences between us as self-advocates and our family members, guardians, surrogates, or professionals. Everyone should try to be calm and patient with one another. The facilitator whom we select for this planning meeting or activity should try to resolve differences of opinion and work out an acceptable compromise on which everyone can agree. Ultimately, however, the final decision should be ours because we are the ones who will be most affected by these decisions.

MAKING HEALTHY CHOICES AS WE GET OLDER

As we get older, our quality of life can get better or worse, depending on the actions that we take throughout our lives, both before and after retirement age. Planning ahead is important. There are many things available to do in the early years, such as regular exercise and staying active, eating healthy foods and watching our weight, getting adequate sleep, and regular medical checkups to help us stay well and treat any health problems before they get worse. If we get ourselves into good shape and follow regular daily routines for healthy living, then we will have an easier time maintaining the lifestyle to which we are accustomed well into our older years. Some people with developmental disabilities have special health care needs and may require extra attention to stay well and prevent potential medical problems. For example, people with Down syndrome such as me often have difficulty in keeping off extra weight and inches during our adult years. Therefore, exercise and eating right are an important part of making healthy choices in our personal lives.

As we get older, we may begin to experience changes such as hearing and vision loss; our bones becoming more brittle and breaking more easily; difficulty in walking up and down stairs; and, sometimes, a harder time in remembering things. It is important to keep our bodies and minds as active as possible. Self-motivation is a key to not getting discouraged as we begin to cope with the changes that come with age. Becoming aware of these new obstacles and other major changes in our lives may make us feel frustrated or sad and even depressed. This experience is not all that different from coping positively with challenges that we have already faced because of our disabilities. It may be a time to use some of the strategies that have helped us overcome some problems in coping with our special needs.

Finding community resources is essential in planning ahead. There are programs available to assist older people who are no longer working and have a fixed and limited income to lead healthy and active lives. Some examples are senior shopping and travel discounts; nutrition, recreation, transportation, and adult day programs; and other services and supports. Older people with developmental disabilities should be entitled to participate in the same community programs that are available to older adults without disabilities. We may not know that these kinds of programs and services are available to us, however. In addition, such programs may not be experienced in including older people with developmental disabilities. We must advocate for ourselves and others to be informed and to ensure that we have the option of full participation in all community activities to which we are entitled. In addition, because the funding for these kinds of programs is constantly in jeopardy, we should be involved in educating local, state, and national governments and organization officials about why these programs and services are critically important to us. This legislative advocacy can be accomplished by writing letters, sending faxes, calling, and visiting our representatives to ask their support to keep these programs in operation or to expand their programs to serve more people. By speaking out, we will help not only older people with developmental disabilities but all older adults.

One of the most important but difficult decisions that people with developmental disabilities may have to make as they get older is where to live in order to get the kinds of supports and assistance that they need. There may come a time when the place where we live, such as at home with our family, in a community residence, or in a supported or independent apartment, may no longer meet our needs. We may gradually have to cope with greater physical, intellectual, or emotional challenges. For our safety and well-being, a professional may suggest that a geriatric living environment may be appropriate. For individuals with intellectual disabilities who have active families, guardians, or surrogates involved and sometimes responsible for making decisions for us, it is important for us to make it clear that we expect to participate to the greatest extent possible. In addition, we should be sure to have a plan in place so that people are aware of our preferences in case of an emergency or an unexpected crisis in which we are not in any position to participate in the decision-making process.

There are different residential options for people as they begin to reach their older years. Some people may decide that they prefer to live in a retirement community or an assisted-living complex or to remain in their own apartment but with extra home care services. Others may require a level of care that is provided only in a skilled nursing facility. In making such critical choices and decisions, we should try to plan ahead by getting information and seeking advice from the people in our lives who care about us and are looking out for our best interests rather than their own.

SELF-ADVOCACY, GROWING OLDER, AND
MAKING MAJOR LIFE CHOICES: NATIONAL SURVEY RESULTS

A national survey developed by Levitz and Nelis (1997) and published on the Age Page of *Community Advocacy Press* solicited information and opinions on aging, rights, self-advocacy, and quality of life for older people with developmental disabilities. Respondents were ages 35 and older. The survey questions are shown in Table 1.

Survey Subjects

Fourteen self-advocates, of whom seven were female and seven were male, responded to the survey. The age range of the respondents was 36–58 years, with the mean age being 46 years. Of the 14 respondents, 13, or 93%, were employed, and one individual was not working. Nine of the respondents were from California, two were from New York State, one was from Pennsylvania, one was from Illinois, and one was from Florida.

Survey Results

Of the 14 respondents, 86% reported that they knew what *self-advocacy* means, and 79% reported that they were members of a self-advocacy group. Here, for exam-

Table 1.   *Community Advocacy Press* national survey questions

---

1. Do you know what *self-advocacy* is?
2. Are you a member of a self-advocacy group?
3. Are you working now, and do you know how much longer you plan to work (until what age)?
4. How are you getting ready for your retirement years, when you may no longer be working or may have health problems?
5. What do you want to do when you retire?
6. Are you retired now?
7. Have people in your life supported your decision to retire? How?
8. What kinds of things or help do you think you will need as you plan to retire?
9. If you plan to do different things when you retire, what kind of support do you think you will need as you plan to retire?
10. Who are you talking to about your retirement?
11. Do you think your self-advocacy skills have helped you or will help you when making your decisions and choices about retirement? How?

Source: Levitz and Nelis (1997).

ple, are some of their answers: "To talk about problems and to solve them," "Sticking up for my own rights," "To stand up for what I believe," and "Speaking up for ourselves."

When individuals were asked "Do you know how much longer you plan to work?" half said yes and half said no. Not only were they equally split in their response to how much longer they planned to work but also the mean ages for both groups were close at 45 and 46, respectively. In response to the question "How are you getting ready for your retirement years?" 50% indicated that they did not know. Those who said that they did know what they planned to do stated that they planned to relax, to travel, to learn independent living skills, and to talk more with their service providers and families about retirement. When asked "What do you want to do when you retire?" 79% stated that they had plans such as to travel, stay at home, and just take it easy. No one in the sample was retired.

The survey found that 25% of the self-advocates had someone supporting their decisions and someone with whom to talk about retirement. Self-advocates reported the people who helped them were friends and staff. Of the self-advocates, 79% had ideas about what they thought was important as they planned for their retirement. Responses included money; health care; and support from family, friends, and staff. Forty-three percent (43%) indicated that they had not yet thought about the types of supports that they might need as they get older. Those who had, said that they would turn to family, friends, and support staff.

Most revealing was that 64% of the respondents reported that they were not talking to anyone about retirement. Two of the self-advocates indicated that they were talking to their self-advocacy groups about how to plan for their future. When self-advocates were asked if their self-advocacy skills helped them as they planned for their retirement, 64% said yes. Some of the ways of planning for the future that were reported were talking with the group, learning how to speak up and talk about their own ideas, making choices, and stating what they think is best for themselves.

We learned from the self-advocates who responded to this survey that more and more self-advocates are beginning to think about their future as they grow older. They are not clear about what will happen to them in old age; but they did indicate that friends, family, and support staff will be important people who can help them.

The role of self-advocacy groups in this process is also important. As people speak up about what is important to them, they also realize that speaking up about their future is helpful. With more than 60% of the self-advocates stating that the self-advocacy skills that they have learned are helping them to make plans for their future, one can only think that as people's self-advocacy skills are increased, preparation for their future retirement will play an important part in determining the outcomes that they experience.

CONCLUSIONS

It is important to us as individuals with developmental disabilities that we be partners in decision making throughout our lifetime, including issues that will have an impact on us as we get older. Access to information that is clear and easy for us to understand is essential for our full participation. In addition, advocacy may be required in order for us to have equal access to community programs for older adults, services, and supports, including high-quality health care. Policies must be supported that protect our health, safety, and well-being; enhance our financial stability; and promote our independence to the greatest extent possible. Policies and regulations should be evaluated to ensure that we are entitled to the same options and benefits available to older adults without developmental disabilities, including the right to retire.

REFERENCES

Americans with Disabilities Act (ADA) of 1990, PL 101-336, 42 U.S.C. §§ 12101 *et seq.*

Dybwad, G., & Bersani, H. (Eds.). (1996). *New voices: Self-advocacy by people with disabilities.* Cambridge, MA: Brookline Books.

Inclusion International. (1996). *The beliefs, values, and principles of self-advocacy.* Cambridge, MA: Brookline Books.

International League of Societies for Persons with Mental Handicaps (ILSMH). (1995). *The beliefs, values, and principles of self-advocacy.* Cambridge, MA: Brookline Books.

Levitz, M., & Nelis, T. (1997). The age page. *Community Advocacy Press, 2*(3), 6.

Nerney, T., & Shumway, D.J. (1996). *Beyond managed care: Self-determination for people with disabilities.* Concord: University of New Hampshire, Institute on Disability/University Affiliated Program.

Rupp, W. (1994). Citizens in action: Self-advocacy and systems change. *Impact, 7,* 4.

Williams, B. (1994). Self-advocates and advocates: Voices for continued change. *Impact, 7*(1), 13.

17

Public Policy and Service Design

Matthew P. Janicki

Aging is one of those inevitable processes of the human condition. As a pundit once noted, the alternative certainly is less attractive. Over the years, humankind has been challenged to make aging a more productive and fulfilling experience. How to do so is a question that has vexed many. Theories have been proposed that help explain what happens during the physical aging process and why some people age early and some age late. Similarly, theories have been advanced to explain how people cope with the psychological and social challenges of aging and why to some it comes with equanimity and to others it comes with trepidation. Of course, these features of aging become more acute as the developed world is faced with the phenomenon of an increasingly "graying" population (United Nations [UN], 1992). A demographic surge in the older adult population will inevitably bring to the forefront many of the social and environmental concerns heretofore not considered major social problems. It is axiomatic that a nation's degree of development is reflected in the manner in which it provides for its older and dependent populations. Such provisions also depend on a nation's cultural beliefs and the extent to which basic human dignity is a valued cultural ingredient.

Of concern here is how public policies that apply to the needs of an older population can be made to apply equally well to older adults with intellectual and developmental disabilities. The aging of any population with lifelong disabilities warrants special consideration, as do the policies that drive the supports that enable them to age with dignity. Thus, this chapter examines the underpinnings of public policies regarding the older adult population and the fundamental constructs that promote aging with dignity. The chapter discusses the following topics:

- Studies indicate that a greater number of adults with developmental disabilities will survive into old age in the future. Such longevity, coupled with demographic bulges such as the baby boom generation, means that there will be increasingly more older people in the years to come. These demographic trends will force governments, advocates, and service providers to plan more purposefully for the needs of an older population.

- Communities need to explore how service capacity can be enhanced to support aging with dignity. Much has yet to be done to overcome cultural and societal biases against older adults and people with disabilities, as exemplified by the often-blatant ageism and discrimination against people with disabilities in many societies. Ironically, models promoting the positive aspects of adaptive aging also promote discrimination against people with disabilities by not recognizing, despite their successful adaptation to a lifelong disability, that older adults with disabilities can age typically and even successfully. Yet, these adults must cope with a lifelong impairment and with being challenged by aging in place, age-related or age-accelerated changes, and the struggle to obtain often-inaccessible age-related services. Aging-related human interest stories, which became more prevalent in the popular press toward the end of the 20th century, give credence to the universality of these difficulties.
- An agenda for planning for the needs of an aging population can be defined. Such an agenda should consider demographics, changing ideologies and social practicalities, and the changing needs of older adults with intellectual disabilities as they age.

This chapter explores the changing nature of the older adult population, identifies the barriers to increased inclusion that these individuals face that are inherent in Western societies and professions, and considers some implications of policy and design issues. To help frame the issues, illustrations derived from the worldwide print media are provided. Underpinning this examination is the belief that, as people with intellectual disabilities age, both societal and personal challenges will determine how productively their aging will take place. Furthermore, the examination is conducted in the context of life course stages, in particular the third and fourth age (Laslett, 1991). The growing similarities of the needs of older people, regardless of whether they have had a lifelong disability, and desires to accommodate older people with intellectual disabilities in a range of community programs and services are considered. Commentary is offered on the application of the theory of successful aging as it applies to people with intellectual disabilities, and it is proposed that the theory needs to consider within its tenets healthy older adults with intellectual disabilities.

For people who enter their third and fourth ages (see definitions of these terms on page 291), clearer public policies and innovative service designs are needed to sustain their skills and functional abilities and to promote their staying healthy and content in a community environment. Public policy makers, researchers, and organizations responsible for intellectual disabilities services must fully address the needs of this group and plan for their future. The culmination of these efforts should lead these individuals to a higher quality of life during older adulthood and a more humane care system that addresses all facets of aging from childhood through senescence. Responding to the individual's needs means going beyond traditional models of care and services and ensuring that older people with disabilities can participate in determining what they need and obtain needed supports and services in a manner that makes them part of the community and promotes the best possible quality of life for as long as possible into old age.

LIFE QUALITY AND GROWING OLD

A greater number of adults with intellectual disabilities than ever before will survive into old age in the 21st century, and, with more awareness of the changing nature of Western societies, more interest is being directed toward the older generations in our populations. This includes interest in an increasingly older population of adults with intellectual and physical disabilities, who present new challenges because of their longevity and increased generational cohort survival. Among these challenges are facing the problems inherent in growing older in a system that has not accommodated older people previously, experiencing the risks of living within a two-generation or multigenerational older family, confronting forces that may impede aging in place, accommodating the transitions associated with new third age activities, and coping with the physical and disease processes associated with the fourth age. These challenges are cross-cutting.

Looking at the evidence of changing demographics and of the projected characteristics of Western nations through 2030, it is clear that significant new demands on health and social planning and services will be made (Peterson, 1999). These services are going to have to bear the brunt of responding to age-associated problems and challenges evident in older people. Thus, how these services respond to the older adult population at the turn of the 21st century will serve as the bellwether for how capably public policies can respond in the long term. Through 2030, the percentage of the developed world's older population is expected to continue to increase substantially. Some predict that the older population, at minimum, will double by 2030, with expected longevity increasing constantly. In some countries, this demographic shift will mean that the older population may make up close to one-third of their overall population. Even in less-developed nations, increases in longevity will mean that the percentage representing the older population will increase notably. Even with this growth, expectations are that future generational cohorts will be different from those who are alive at the turn of the 21st century. The older adults of tomorrow will be healthier, have more financial security, and be much more involved in the life and activities of their communities. The same expectations apply equally to adults with lifelong disabilities. Because of greater longevity due to better health, nutrition, and social conditions, coupled with greater numbers of surviving older adults in each successive generation, more adults with disabilities are expected to live to old age in better health and with greater personal capabilities and assets than their counterparts at the turn of the 21st century.

Given that the life course representing older age has differentiating characteristics, it is useful to explore some of these distinctions. Within this perspective, one can posit ages or stages of life that encompass both social and physical aspects of old age, with each having different personal aspects and public policy implications. Gerontologists have referred to these stages as the *third age* and the *fourth age.* During the life course, the third age is characterized as that period of life involving transition from work to retirement, when most people falling within this stage of life are in general good health, have financial security, and are involved in a greater number of recreational pursuits (Laslett, 1991). In general terms, this age defines the beginning of retirement or a change in lifestyle characterized by greater maturity and leisure. Gerontologists see this life stage among older people who are generally termed the *young-old* and the *middle-old* (generally ages 50–75 years). The

fourth age is characterized as that period of life when adults evidence more pronounced physical decline and experience a greater number of problems with their
health and functioning. This stage begins at around age 75 years or older and includes those older adults considered to be among the *old-old*, although it is highly
variable and its definition may change as successive generations of older adults live
longer and healthier lives. When applying the generalities attributed to these stages,
it is important to remember that aging is highly personal and variable; people do
not age uniformly. Some people may never experience their fourth age, living long,
healthy lives and being what has been termed *successful agers* until they die. Others may die early from disease or other causes and thus never experience a decline.

Within the context of these life-span notions of aging, demographic and longevity changes will place new demands on health and social services systems and will
call into question existing health and social policies and practices (Inclusion International, 1997). These policies need to take into account the expected changes in
demographics as well as the changing character of successive future generations of
adults with disabilities who will be growing old. Yet, for the most part, government
disability-oriented planning structures and service providers have not yet begun to
anticipate and address fully the "graying" of adults with disabilities. In those nations in which there has been planning and support, the planning and support generally have focused on children with disabilities and on helping adults who are of
working age. Even when aging-related services are supported publicly, the inclusion
of older adults with lifelong disabilities has been spotty. In nations without a tradition or a basis of government support for disability services or with undeveloped
health care services, individuals with lifelong disabilities generally may be excluded from the greater community and may not survive into old age. In both types
of environments, the greater society most likely has not yet come to terms with the
survival of older adults with lifelong disabilities; has not made appropriate accommodations in physical access, transportation, and work environments; and has not
promoted actively the inclusion of adults with disabilities in everyday life. Furthermore, even when disability-related services are present, workers who are in
daily contact with adults with disabilities often are unfamiliar with the aging process, and medical practitioners who serve adults are often poorly informed or too
poorly equipped to cope with the presenting medical needs of people with disabilities in old age.

Coping with these types of issues is not easy. In society generally, making the
greater community responsive to aging is a challenge. The UN (1992) undertook a
decade-long effort to make the nations of the world more aware of the impending
demographic changes facing many countries and adopted an activist agenda to make
societies more responsive to the needs of their older citizens. In this context, what
can be done to include older adults with intellectual disabilities within these efforts? First, there needs to be recognition that there exists an ever-growing aging
population with intellectual disabilities and that supports need to be identified,
funded, and individually tailored to enhance the aging with dignity of the individuals who make up this group of older people. Second, once a statement of concern
and acceptance of responsibility is made, then it should be operationalized to ensure
that these activities take place. Such efforts need to be cross-cutting. For example,
such efforts might focus on providing education about the problems associated with
aging as well as special efforts to develop mutual interest among social gerontologists or geriatricians and the disability community with the objective of developing

solutions to issues affecting older adults with disabilities. Third, and equally important, there should be enhanced advocacy to help include people with disabilities and older people who develop disabilities in their old age in the social fabric of their communities. The ideological basis for many of these activities should be framed within the same belief systems that are applied to younger individuals. These systems are based on the notions that, as people age, the most important considerations are helping them to maintain their autonomy; ensuring a safe and healthy living environment; involving them in the greater community; eliminating their isolation; and promoting constant supports from a network of friends, family, and others.

Yet, even within these seemingly universal applications, some disagreement exists within the field with regard to the focus of services. In those nations with dual systems of services—that is, one for older adults and one for people with disabilities—questions have arisen about whether supports should be derived from within the disability community or from services available to all other pensioners or older adults. Some of this debate is influenced by the nature and the quality of naturally occurring supports and services available to any nation's older adults. In some places, they are good; in other places, they are nonexistent or seemingly paltry. When a rich array of community support services are available, there is a natural inclination to seek avenues of inclusion within that network. When services for older adults are sketchy or mostly institutional and of questionable quality, then there may be a justifiable aversion to affiliation with such a support network. Some of this debate is colored by a general aversion to old age, even among well-meaning disability advocates. The basis for this aversion is explored in the next section.

AGEISM AND POSITIVE-VALUED AGE CONCERNS

Many Western societies ascribe a positive value to youth and a negative value to age. Butler (1975), who coined the term *ageism*, noted that ageism is manifested in a wide range of phenomena on both individual and institutional levels in the form of stereotypes and myths, outright disdain and dislike, or simply subtle avoidance of contact; discriminatory practices in housing, employment, and services of all kinds; and epithets, cartoons, and jokes. Ageism thus can represent a pervasive negative societal attitude. It is the blatant prejudice against people who are old and is demonstrated by the emphasis on youth and wellness—the antithesis of the stereotypic perception of older adults.

A parallel negative attitude exists in terms of how some members of American society display attitudes toward people with disabling conditions. The term *handicapism* characterizes this attitude. Handicapism is culture- and generation-bound (i.e., the prevailing beliefs of a cultural group determine the ease of an individual's acceptance of disability). This principle applies to beliefs that generational groups hold. Although many younger people are exposed to people with intellectual or physical disabilities, many older people have not had any interactions with such individuals for the better part of their lives. Their attitudes and values are thus affected by proximity and experience. Handicapism may also stem from personal feelings, such that negative attitudes toward a perceived disability among older adults may stem from a fear that they themselves can or will become infirm and/or develop a disability. Furthermore, different aspects of society may show different levels of acceptance of differentness. People also tend to view disabilities along a basic value continuum with regard to a notion such as typicality (i.e., looking at others in terms of their ability to conform to majority standards, such as in work productivity and conforming value acceptance).

Yet, positive concerns for aging and a greater acceptance of the older population are becoming more prominent as the number of older adults increases. Ageism is still found in many aspects of daily life, but the pernicious negative stereotypes from prior to the 1980s and 1990s are beginning to be replaced by respect for market forces, realization of a need for a coherent public policy to address issues related to aging, and greater sensitivity among younger segments of the population. Market forces, for example, are highly influenced by who buys products, and when older people have discretionary funds and are courted by mercantile interests, this leads to a rise in positive societal perceptions of them. From this circumstance, there is an increasing realization that concern about the state of older people is everybody's responsibility. Witness the following: *The London Daily Telegraph* ("OAPulp," 1997) reported that a well-known rock music star had decided to hold a benefit concert to help raise money for Help the Aged, a London-based charity that helps older people. He is quoted as saying that the effort is "really about the fact that everyone gets old, and that anything that makes young people aware of age issues is good news" ("OAPulp," 1997, p. 3). Such an effort is exceptional and can be used to overcome ageism, a challenge for many nations in which older people, particularly those who are poor and infirm, may hold a devalued status. It can help bring awareness about an age group that often has been marginalized to an age group that needs to know more about aging.

Western cultures value individuals' ability to define their lives and make independent decisions about what they do, where they live, how they spend their time, what they eat, with whom they socialize, and so forth. Of course, realism tempers these freedoms. Income levels define individuals' options for where they live, their experiences and opportunities define what they can do, their social networks define with whom they socialize, and so forth. Older adults with lifelong disabilities may have limited social or financial options that may impinge on how they exercise these decisions. They may also have personal limitations that further constrict the potential exercise of these decisions.

Gerontologists have long debated the qualitative points of old age (Achenbaum, 1986; Neugarten & Neugarten, 1986). There is general recognition, however, that with social and financial supports (e.g., the benefits of the Social Security Act of 1935 [PL 74-271], reasonable pensions, older adult discounts, housing assistance), old age for older adults in the developed world at the turn of the 21st century is easier than it was for older people several generations earlier. With this easier old age comes a more valued societal status. In many instances, this is also the case for older adults with intellectual disabilities. Western societies are changing; they are growing progressively older, and, as such, they should become more accepting of old age. The United States and other Western nations are not yet free from ageism in all of its forms, however. With an increasing number of older citizens, Western societies have made some accommodations for their citizens with disabling conditions, accommodations that can benefit both older adults and people with disabilities; but they have yet to become fully accessible for and fully accepting of people who have disabilities.

What is *successful aging* and how can this concept be applied? From a public policy perspective, planning for the aging of adults with intellectual disabilities takes on many forms. One represents those efforts that are designed to cope with aging as a fact of life—that is, coming to grips with adults who are already in the third or fourth age and whose age-related needs may have been neglected or under-addressed. Another represents those efforts that are designed to help people cope with the inevitability of aging and provide those supports and services that help pre-pare adults for another stage in the life course and the eventualities of aging. Thus, aging-related services can be reactive and apply to people who are already older, or proactive and apply to people who eventually will be older adults. Both of these forms are part of a systematic planning process. The reactive process may already be coping with people who are set in their situations, and the principal focus is to help them stay healthy and age in the most productive manner possible. With the proactive process, however, the principal focus is on enhancing aging because many adults can adapt their lifestyles to promote a healthier and more productive aging process.

The gerontology community looks at aging from the perspective of how it af-fects people or how people manage aging as they grow older (Baltes & Baltes, 1990; Garfein & Herzog, 1995). This perspective also can be used to help understand the impact of aging and how people with lifelong disabilities cope with the changes that aging imposes. Aging is often viewed in terms of whether it is pathological or normal. Pathological aging occurs when adults are affected by diseases or age-related disabilities. A small number of the young-old fall within this categoriza-tion; however, with advancing age, the number increases. Aging that is other than pathological can be seen as normal; this category is further differentiated as either usual or successful. Usual aging is seen as nonpathological (i.e., free of disease), but there is a recognition that there may be a risk or potential of becoming pathologi-cal. Thus, adults who exhibit typical, nonpathological age-associated changes are viewed as usual agers. Most people fall into this categorization of aging. Successful aging, which is presented as the ideal and characterizes a small number of older people, occurs when there is a low risk for pathology and strong evidence of high function. Adults who exhibit little or no loss of function compared with their age peers are seen as successful agers. Because successful aging is seen as the ideal and since the model evolving from this concept has gained broad attention, it is worth exploring, particularly to see whether it has applicability to older adults with intel-lectual disabilities.

The theory of successful aging has been the subject of much discussion (e.g., Baltes & Baltes, 1990; Rowe & Kahn, 1997, 1998; Schulz & Heckhausen, 1996). As presented by Rowe and Kahn (1997, 1998), the model underpinning success-ful aging generally includes three main components: low probability of disease or disease-related disability, high cognitive and physical function capacity, and active engagement with life. The model differentiates how aging affects older adults and whether the adults are functioning adaptively as they age. Crucial to the operation-alization of this concept is to what extent older adults are actively engaged with life.

The model has several components. The first, *low probability of disease,* refers to a dimension that reflects the absence, presence, or severity of risk factors for dis-ease. The second, *high functional level,* draws on a combination of physical and cognitive capacities that are used for examining individuals' potential for personal activity (i.e., what a person can or cannot do). The model draws its basis from what the person actually does that leads him or her to be considered to be aging success-fully. *Active engagement,* the third component, is concerned with interpersonal re-lationships and productive activity. Interpersonal relationships are operationalized by defining contacts and transactions with others, including exchange of information, emotional support, and direct assistance. In this respect, activities are valued regardless of whether they are done for remuneration. The societal value created by the activity is the operational criterion. The model for successful aging thus draws on the confluence of demonstrated good health, capacity for and display of socialization and productivity, and capacity for self-discipline.

In playing out the model, Rowe and Kahn noted that "intrinsic factors alone, while highly significant, do not dominate the determination of risk in advancing age. Extrinsic environmental factors, including elements of lifestyle, play an important role in determining risk for disease" (1997, p. 435). In addition, they noted that genetic contributions to aging play less of a role with advancing age, whereas nongenetic factors increase in influence. The conclusion is that usual aging characteristics are malleable, for Rowe and Kahn stressed the importance of environmental and behavioral factors in determining the risk of disease late in life. Added to this factor is the finding that social relationships in later life have a health-protective aspect, particularly because network membership is a contributing factor. This health-protective aspect comes from two kinds of supportive transactions—socioemotional and instrumental. Socioemotional transactions can include expressions of affection, respect, and other similar social bonding, whereas instrumental transactions can include direct assistance to others, doing chores, and otherwise helping in some manner. Within this framework, a significant health risk factor in older age is isolation, or a lack of social ties; thus, an important contributor to healthier aging in Rowe and Kahn's model is self-efficacy or, simply stated, having control over one's life and activities.

Successful aging thus means having the capacity to maintain one's physical and cognitive health, having control over life choices, and giving of oneself in a manner that is fulfilling and productive. As Strawbridge, Cohen, Shema, and Kaplan (1996) noted, those adults considered to be aging successfully generally have greater involvement in their community, engage in more physical activity, and demonstrate better mental health. In addition, lifelong exercise of control (or autonomy) may be a critical factor in successful aging (Schulz & Heckhausen, 1996), as may the interaction with social structures (Riley, 1998). Given these factors and in terms of this model, what are the implications for growing older with a lifelong disability as evidenced by older adults with intellectual disability? One can argue that such a model may not apply to adults whose well-being is already compromised because of their disability. Rowe and Kahn are silent with regard to how their model applies to people who are aging with a preexisting disability, yet inherent in their conceptualization is the belief that the presence of disability may be incompatible with successful aging. This may not be the case, however, particularly when applied to adults with intellectual disabilities requiring intermittent support whose physical status is not compromised (see Schulz & Heckhausen, 1996). Thus, one can argue that lifelong disability may not be an impediment to healthy or successful aging if there are no significant medical aspects of the disability and if the person has developed productive coping strengths and compensatory mechanisms during adulthood and has maintained lifelong autonomy or control over his or her life activities. Although this proposition has yet to receive attention in the research community, the successful aging model can be applied, if not adapted, to people with intellectual disabilities, particularly if viewed from a life course perspective. Thus, proactive endeavors to help adults gain control of their lives, especially in the area of decision-making and event mastery, may be the key to helping promote successful aging in later life. It would seem that the main areas of particular relevance are the needs to reinforce self-determination and choice as well as to encourage extensive involvement in activities that are both intrinsically rewarding and extrinsically productive for the community.

Successful aging is the combination of avoiding debilitation, disease, and disability (as opposed to impairment); maintaining high physical and cognitive function; and sustaining engagement in social and productive activities. Thus, a range of support strategies must figure in addressing these aspects (Baltes & Lang, 1997). Given this need, supports and services should be designed to help maintain health and physical capacities, provide intellectually and physically stimulating environments, and ensure that social networks and community engagement are utilized to the fullest extent possible. Life after work can involve a great deal of options, and building these into the lifestyles of retirees can, from a planning and financial perspective, be productive and meet the definitional ends of successful aging.

POLICY AND DESIGN ISSUES

A number of initiatives were undertaken in the 1990s that examined the needs of national and local populations of older people with disabilities and explored a range of policy options that warranted action (Older Persons Planning Office, Government of Victoria, 1990; White House Conference on Aging [WHCoA], 1996). These encompassed such disparate concerns as broad system features to social supports and individualized services. For example, one such effort was the 1996 White House Conference on Aging held in the United States (WHCoA, 1996). Although the broader White House Conference addressed generic issues related to America's aging population, a number of preliminary miniconferences were organized that dwelled specifically on issues related to older Americans with intellectual and developmental disabilities (Janicki, 1995). Some of the outcomes of these miniconferences reflected national concerns particular to the United States, but many had universal applications. The following discussion identifies a number of issues with policy and design implications that have roots in the WHCoA.

Implications of Aging

All people age, but each person ages uniquely. Studies show that adults with intellectual disabilities are generally living longer because of better health, nutritional status, and overall living conditions (Janicki, Dalton, Henderson, & Davidson, 1999; van Schronjenstein-Lantman de Valk, 1998; Visser et al., 1997). Some disability-related conditions do not have any significant effect on the aging process. Others cause new problems or "secondary conditions" in later adulthood. Age-related diseases also may affect an older person. Such conditions may compromise how effectively a person lives in his or her community. Perhaps most telling among age-associated problems is the difficulty that older adults with severe physical impairments face. For example, having cerebral palsy over a lifetime can lead to compromised muscle reserve and produce musculoskeletal problems earlier than expected (some say by age 50). These problems may also include ongoing pain, arthritis, problems with walking, and diminished stamina (Turk, Geremski, Rosenbaum, & Weber, 1997). Also, with age, individuals may experience increases in the rate of musculoskeletal and cardiovascular conditions and increases in vision and hearing impairments (Janicki & Dalton, 1998). Such sensory losses can impair communication, self-care, and mobility and have a general impact on adaptive aging in place. Adults with Down syndrome are particularly affected by such age-associated problems earlier in their life span. Many of these individuals experience precocious or premature aging, usually beginning in their late 40s or early 50s, and have a compromised life expectancy. The average age at death for adults with Down syndrome is 55, as compared with an average of about age 65 for adults with other intellectual disabilities (Janicki et al., 1999).

Some age-associated conditions may be particularly pernicious. Studies show that although there is a high risk of dementia, particularly of the Alzheimer's type, among adults with Down syndrome (Dalton, 1995), the overall prevalence of dementia among adults with other forms of intellectual disabilities is probably no greater than it is in the general population (Janicki & Dalton, 1999a). The occurrence of dementia does pose a challenge, however, because it signals a decline in capabilities when most intellectual disability service providers and families still expect continued gains in skill levels. Most intellectual disabilities service providers are not yet prepared to make special accommodations in their care practices for latter-stage dementia care and may be at a loss with regard to where to seek out guidance on which approaches to use. Practice has not resolved the debate between providing specialized community dementia care programs versus providing individual care within existing residential care programs (Janicki & Dalton, 1999b). In addition, the intellectual disabilities field issued special guidelines for assessment and care management in this area (see Janicki, Heller, Seltzer, & Hogg, 1996). Nevertheless, many agency staff are not familiar with recognizing onset features or identifying resources for diagnostic and service coordination advice. Dementia onset and care pose particular problems because most caregivers are unfamiliar with dementia processes and care practices.

These age-associated factors call into question how well adults with intellectual disability age and remain functional. They also may call into question the degree of validity of assumptions about the potential for self-care in old age among adults who have compromised health or who are particularly at risk for age-related problems. Most jurisdictions provide a variety of residential care and housing supports, ranging from group homes and supervised apartment living to supports for people living alone or with family, to which older adults have access. Yet, many community programs are faced with the aging in place of older adults in their care and are seeking specialty assessments for presenting health problems. Some of these problems include changing physical status, cognitive decline or dementia, age-associated mobility or sensory losses, functional decline, and major or terminal diseases or conditions. Geriatric assessments that periodically track physical capability, medications, nutritional status, and cognitive acuteness should be an integral part of any older person's life. Yet, even with expected greater longevity, such medical services are scarce, and people with lifelong disabilities repeatedly experience problems in gaining access to appropriate health care. Witness the following: *The Los Angeles Times* (1997), in a news article entitled "Transplant Patient with Down Syndrome Dies," noted the death of the first adult in the United States with an intellectual disability to receive a major transplant. The woman, a leading self-advocate who lived in California and who had Down syndrome, had been rejected initially for a heart transplant because doctors thought her incapable of handling her own follow-up care. After an advocacy campaign on her behalf, the hospital agreed to the transplant operation. What is disconcerting about this story is that a coalition of advocates had to fight for the transplant. The positive end was that the situation prompted the California General Assembly to pass a bill that would pro- hibit doctors from discriminating against people with disabilities who need trans- plants. The hospital ostensibly had rejected her as a candidate for a heart transplant because it believed that her disability was a barrier to her being to able to care for herself while she recuperated. The unspoken reason was most likely that this was an older woman who happened to have Down syndrome. The issue here was not self-care capability but equal access to life-sustaining health care.

End-of-life care is another issue. With increased longevity and more older adults remaining in community environments, the issue of end-of-life care is beginning to take on more prominence. With end-of-life care comes a range of new legal and pro- grammatic issues, including planning end-of-life care with the use of living wills, advance directives, and the like. The use of such instruments to define how termi- nal illness and treatment are to be handled when one is no longer competent to de- cide on treatment can lead to improved quality of life and dying with dignity (King, 1996). Yet, the potential danger evident when such instruments are not actuated or are not feasible is illustrated in a *New York Times* report entitled "Not Dead Enough to Die: Laws Force Life Support on a Man Who Never Could Consent" (Fein, 1997). This situation involved a 56-year-old man with Down syndrome who lay comatose while his family battled hospital officials over whether he had the right to die with dignity. His brain was barely functioning. According to hospital officials, he could not blink his eyes, swallow food, or make his lungs inflate or deflate on their own. Yet, he had enough brain activity to make scattered waves on a computed tomogra- phy scan. Before the man fell into a coma, he did not make a living will or leave any instructions for his care should he not be able to respond. Given this fact, the hos- pital was keeping his body alive while his mind and soul were no longer of this world. His family was in despair while he continued to lie comatose with no chance of recovery. His sister recounted the family's concern:

> If Jimmy could go back to the life he had, there would be no question here. . . . Jimmy was a happy person. But when these people say the state has to err on the side of life—err on the side of life? This isn't living. Will Jimmy be able to taste his coffee? Will he be able to listen to the country music he loved? No, that was living to Jimmy. (Fein, 1997, p. B2)

This type of dilemma is experienced with ever-greater frequency as families try to cope with health systems unprepared to address end-of-life care and regulatory structures and public policies not yet attuned to these types of issues.

These scenarios were typical of the ones repeatedly raised at the regional mini- conferences making up the WHCoA. In the area of aging and health policy, probably the most outstanding policy and design issue was the general unevenness of the availability of appropriate health care services for older people with disabilities. Without disagreement, the miniconferences fervently endorsed having available and affordable health care, improved access to health care services, and increased train- ing for health care personnel at the graduate-school level as well as in the workplace.

Retirement, Lifestyle Change, and Housing

Another area for consideration is what people do as they age and which general sup- ports may be available. With the pending transition from work to the third age, most disability service providers are challenged to adopt policies enabling older adults with intellectual disabilities to retire or to become more involved in activities and lifestyles suited to pensioners. Helping with retirement and adapting to old age is drawing more attention and requires developing supports that are responsive to the wants and needs of older people. Such supports involve a careful blending of the desires of the individual, available resources, and planning adjustments related to budgetary considerations. Often support needs can be met via existing services or community amenities. These can range from drop-in recreation social centers for people who are retired or who work only part time, to home supports and linking the person to community amenities and other people who share their lifestyle. Such supports also can include helping the person to attend an adult day program based on a community social model.

Thus, providers are recognizing that there is a diversity of need among older adults, even among those individuals with late-life disabilities or impairments associated with old age. From a policy and design framework, the interest that retirement and life course transitions garner depends in great part on the nature of a nation's population demographics and disability services policies. In the United States, this topic is of utmost concern; when the members of the White House miniconferences debated these issues, they raised concerns related to lifestyle and supports for aging in the context of quality of life. Not surprising was that their recommendations covered a great deal of ground under the general rubric of retirement. For example, some were specific and indicated strong support for the elimination of penalties for saving for retirement (with targeted changes to the Social Security Act of 1935 [PL 74-271] specifically eliminating the provisions that severely limit lifetime savings or set asset caps for people with disabilities), for using the Americans with Disabilities Act (ADA) of 1990 (PL 101-336) to expand pension opportunities (and to ensure portability), and for modifying the active treatment requirements of the federal Medicaid program regulations (Medicaid program conditions for intermediate care facilities, 1988) (and thus making them much more flexible in applications to older adults). Other recommendations were applicable more universally, such as expanding volunteering opportunities, providing consumer information on work and retirement options, and ensuring that there is sufficient funding for retirement programs and activities.

Although some are beginning to respond with community support services such as home health and respite, most aging network services have not evolved sufficiently to accommodate people with long-term dependency or physical care needs. Newer practice is to aid older adults with intellectual disabilities in adapting their lifestyles to age-appropriate conditions and situations as they begin to define their preferences. As they age, adults should be given the opportunity to retire from vocational activities or work and become involved in generic community or older adult activities. Such practices are not prevalent around the United States (or in other countries), however, and many older adults may lack any supports as retirees or may be required to be involved in intensive activity programs that are better suited for younger adults. Such programs may be inappropriate for older adults because of older adults' lack of interest in them or because of older adults' changing physical condition. In many instances, program practices may not facilitate having the person involved in older adult–appropriate activities because of conflicting regulations, policies, and funding structures.

Aging in Place

An emerging community living issue that affects families, individuals, and entities providing funding or services is the challenge of providing supports for continued stay in a home or facility while aging in place. This notion refers to the changing needs of people as they age while finding and providing the supports to help people remain where they are. Challenges caused by aging in place are generally due to the increased frailty of older individuals and the demands that increased frailty and diminished ability for self-care make on the family and others who may provide care. Some factors affecting aging in place include increasing physical frailty, diminishing vision and hearing, dementia or other cognitive decline, and restricted mobility. Adults with intellectual disabilities who may be residing at home or on their own may also need special supports as their abilities and needs change with age. Many of these challenges occur when older adults enter the fourth age and experience medical complications or more pronounced physical changes that are not part of normal aging. These changes may be due to the onset of Alzheimer's disease or the progression of certain medical conditions as well as to losses in hearing, vision, or mobility. These changes may make it difficult for adults to remain in their homes without specialized care or assistance. In certain areas, such increased frailty or problems easily may lead to referral to an institutional environment. In most circumstances, such referrals and admissions can be diverted or prevented by providing special assistance to help the adult continue to care for him- or herself at home or, alternatively, by providing the necessary formal or informal assistance that helps keep the adult where he or she is (Lundh & Nolan, 1996).

Where an adult with an intellectual disability lives generally is determined by both social policy and economics. Like older adults in the general population, when adults with intellectual disabilities grow older, they may live in a variety of environments. Increasingly, they seek out housing typically used by older adults and subsidized by local communities. With advanced age, however, the physical barriers present in the home may become more of an issue, and compensation for losses in vision, hearing, and mobility must be considered. Facilities for people who are unable to live independently but who do not need or choose to reside in long-term care environments may include adult care homes, senior assisted housing, group assisted housing, domiciliary care, congregate care, supportive housing, continuing care, life care, residential care, board and care, and personal care facilities (Edelstein, 1995). These types of programs or housing options need to be physically accessible, however, for, as mobility and sensory problems increase with age, the greatest impediment to continued stay is the inability to get around easily and make use of the housing. Private spaces such as bedrooms and bathrooms should be physically accessible and have specialized adaptations for occupants who may have low vision or other eyesight impairments, grasping problems, and movement difficulties. Public spaces such as halls, living rooms, kitchens, and activity rooms also should be accessible to all occupants of the residence.

When faced with problems associated with aging-related frailty or decline, service providers and families may seek admission to a long-term facility for the individual with intellectual disability, particularly if the individual's required degree of care is perceived as exceeding the capacities of these caregivers. Often such referrals are based not on need for nursing care but on the basis of age or a lack of available alternative or accessible housing in the community. Long-term care programs such as nursing facilities may be used when specialized nursing care is indicated for the care of disease or physical condition or terminal illnesses but not for board and care reasons. When faced with severe cognitive decline or compromised mobility and movement, however, caregivers may be challenged to provide continuing care. The need for appropriate alternative care situations requires a great deal of scrutiny if large numbers of older adults with intellectual disabilities are not going to end up living the remainder of their lives in nursing facilities.

In many localities, older adults who are experiencing severe cognitive or physical decline may already be in housing with staff who can provide around-the-clock supervision and care. This situation leads to an interesting question: When such in-home supports are in place, what motivates staff to request transfer or admission of such older adults to nursing facilities—a seemingly prevalent practice? One possible answer may be related to the notion of a threshold or the critical point at which staff feel that care demand conditions are such that they can no longer maintain a sufficient level of care and thus they overwhelmingly request the transfer. This phenomenon also occurs in the general population—families that find that they can no longer cope with providing primary care for a dependent older relative conclude that they can no longer cope with the care demands and request help with getting the relative admitted to a long-term care facility (Mittelman, Ferris, Shulman, Steinberg, & Levin, 1996). Families usually are not paid to provide care, however; so the question is, Why do staff in intellectual disabilities services come to this conclusion? When this type of question is raised, the answer often is that it is not the nature of care but the tolerance and capability of staff that leads them to this conclusion (Janicki & Dalton, 1999a). The nature of care can always be adjusted, just as it is for anyone who lives at home and is sick. Sickness is temporary, though, and the wear and tear on staff who offer personal care in times of illness may not be comparable to that available when the duration is the balance of one's life. With regard to tolerance, it may be that staff perceive having signed on for providing a certain level of care and then find that the demands of the individual exceed that original level. This leads to another question: Why is it that an agency can find ways to provide the most enhanced care for children and adults with multiple intellectual and physical disabilities, but when someone ages and becomes frail or demented, they initiate a referral to a nursing facility? It may be that agencies do not adapt to the changing level of care demands posed by older adults because of inexperience or because of ageism. It may come down to a philosophical or human management model of commitment. This can be ascertained by reviewing to what degree an agency is willing to accept lifetime care management and adapt care practices accordingly when adults age, experience a decline in skills, and develop new care demands.

Individualized supports should become typical for addressing the individual's needs, age, and abilities. Although age-related physical needs are a consideration (e.g., sensory changes, mobility changes, stamina changes), they generally should mirror the overall types of needs that are prevalent among younger people. What may differ is the nature of social needs and networks; these needs and networks are reflected in more age-related individual choices and wants. With maturity, these social needs may be at a different level and may no longer serve as the driving force for actualizing independence. They may be directed more toward a level that helps build on social coreliance with age peers and friends of all ages. Thus, policies and program designs need to reflect some of the more idiosyncratic aspects of age-related needs. These may be found in the degree and nature of supports warranted for older caregivers, newly determined needs for special supports for adults with dementia, and needs related to age-associated cognitive and functional decline as well as to death and dying. Such supports should mirror those found to be appropriate for younger adults. They should include clinical screening and diagnostics for health and physical conditions, adapting or using age-related housing and barrier-free accommodations, and providing services and supports for day activities and use of community amenities that may involve age peers more readily.

In most nations, aging-related service provision is usually dichotomous. Supports or services for older adults are generally structured around a generalist elder care service, whereas long-term care systems and supports or services for adults with disabilities are associated with a specialist disabilities system (Ansello & Rose, 1989; Janicki, 1993; Turner, 1994). In other countries, either neither exists or there is a blending of the two. For example, in the United States, the Older Americans Act of 1965 (PL 89-73) helped to equalize access to age-appropriate services for older adults with disabilities, with many individuals seeking out and using services available within what has become known as the *aging network.* Yet, even with this principle of universal elder care and community supports, implementation is incomplete. In areas where the potential for integrated services exist, the framers of the WHCoA miniconferences urged activities on behalf of adults with disabilities to eliminate barriers to effective integration of older people or to use more fully the resources developed for older people. With this in mind, most of the recommendations stressed better coordination and access. For example, expanding regional or state-level planning and coordination, streamlining national program access and funding, and enabling single points of access for local services were recurring considerations. Others included activities such as simplifying access to information and referral and ensuring that national or state statutes do not discriminate against people who are aging prematurely.

Helping Older Families

Providing supports to those adults who are living at home or with parents, relatives, or friends is one of the more fundamental challenges. A large number of adults with intellectual and developmental disabilities continue to live at home, and, with successive generations, more older people facing this situation will be identified. In this vein, *The Seattle Times* ran an article that asked how long families, as they themselves age, will be able to continue to provide a home for their sons or daughters with intellectual disabilities. The author of the article noted that

> Around the nation [families who are providing care at home] are being referred to as the "hidden families." They are the people who bucked the pressure in the 1930s, 1940s, and 1950s, keeping their developmentally disabled children at home and out of institutions. (Stripling, 1997, p. L3)

The article's author further noted that

> State surveys show that their children are no more or less profoundly retarded than many of the children who moved to institutions. But the parents who incorporated their special-needs children into the family tended to share several traits: good physical health, strong family networks, and strong faith or religious beliefs. Now they share something else. The parents are nearing the end of their lives. Their children, who are enjoying long lives thanks to improved health care, are going to outlive them. Where will these beloved, protected sons and daughters go? (Stripling, 1997, p. L4)

Notwithstanding its emotional tone, the article is indicative of many such stories on this issue that are published with increasing frequency in the world's newspapers. More families like these are caring at home for an adult son or daughter with a disability, and, as they age, they face new and unexpected problems. The family is the most important provider for a son or daughter with a disability, and many adults continue to live with their parents or other relatives as they grow older. The number of families in this situation is relatively large and is expected to increase in the 21st century (Freedman, Krauss, & Seltzer, 1997; Romine, Dale, & Cotten, 1998). Many of these two-generation or multigenerational older adult families (in which the parents are age 60 years or older and a son or daughter with a disability is in his or her 40s or older) may have special needs for assistance because each family member may need help due to their own aging. Many of these families or adult sons or daughters with a disability may not be known to charitable organizations, however, because they have remained at home and may never have been involved with such organizations. It is an all too common situation to be alerted to the existence of these families only after the parents are hospitalized, experience some traumatic event, or die.

Janicki, McCallion, Force, Bishop, and LePore (1998) described four differences between families caring for a parent with an impairment and families caring for a dependent son or daughter. One difference is in the complexity of the problems that such families or households often face. Although some families may present with simple needs (e.g., minimal supports such as respite, transportation, or financial planning information), others have multifarious needs (e.g., multiple caregiving demands such as caring not only for an infirm husband with dementia but also for an adult son with severe intellectual and physical disabilities). Such multigenerational caregiving may be found in other families, but such situations often involve children (who may pose different challenges for their caregivers, but not the challenges associated with personal care for adults).

A second, albeit more idiosyncratic, distinction is what Janicki and colleagues termed the vagaries of financial resources or the unreliability or unpredictability of public funds underpinning any support effort. For example, a government's budget difficulties and a disability agency's resource cutbacks may mean that there are unexpected restrictions on the use of disability-related funds. Reliance on financial resources such as disability-related funds that are not under the direct control of the local agencies designated to help older people can be problematic. Whenever two or more systems attempt to work in concert, there needs to be a realistic appraisal of how each system functions, how it is funded, and which political forces determine its fiscal resources. Joint efforts suffer if one partner withdraws funds that help support the collective activities of the two entities, particularly when families are involved. *The Baltimore Sun* explored such a problem in an article entitled "The Forever Children: Aging Parents Are Haunted by What Lies Ahead" (Suggs, 1997). The article focused on the lives of older parents who are at personal crossroads in struggling with diminishing personal resources to continue to look after their son or daughter (because of their aging and changed life circumstances) and vexing realizations that public services are unable to be responsive to their immediate needs. What makes these parents' dilemmas more acute is the fact that when older families most need supports, the availability of public supports are unpredictable because funds dedicated to helping such families often run out or are unavailable.

A third distinction is household composition and caregiver relationships. Many older households include one or more older adults who are becoming or already have become dysfunctional. In many of these situations, a younger relative who does not live in the same home looks after these older adults. Many people in the baby boom generation (i.e., those adults born between 1946 and 1965) find themselves looking after their older parents who are becoming more reliant on their children as they age. In contrast, in households with an adult with an intellectual disability, caregivers often include not only older parents but also other relatives such as grandparents, cousins, and siblings, as well as nonrelatives and neighbors. In addition, some households may be composed of several generations of the same family, or they may be made up of members who are unrelated. These caregiving relationships are often diverse and complex and reflect household patterns typically found in some immigrant or cultural groups. For example, one can look to the emerging phenomenon of grandparents' assuming greater roles as caregivers for "skipped generation" relatives. Witness the article found in Australia's *Adelaide Advertiser* entitled "Grandparents Under Siege" (1997), which noted that such second-parenting grandparents comprise the majority of surrogate caregivers and in many instances are the heads of households of three-generation families. Yet, as the writer in the *Advertiser* pointed out, such surrogate caregivers often encounter difficulties because of guardianship restrictions, and thus they may not be able to gain access directly to government support funds that are usually made available for the primary caregiver of an adult with an intellectual disability.

The fourth distinction that Janicki, McCallion, and colleagues (1998) noted is the kind of help that these families need to face the inevitable end of their caregiving role. In many typical situations, help with planning may involve seeking a long-term care environment or support solution for one's older adult relative. In contrast, for those people caring for an adult with an intellectual disability, help with planning involves charting a future for that adult. Often there is an almost universal perception among staff coming in contact with such families that most have not planned for the future and, in a sense, that they live from day to day. Yet many older parents express great fear of what may happen to their offspring when they themselves are no longer around (Freedman et al., 1997). Some caregivers assume that their responsibilities will be picked up by other relatives, particularly their child's siblings, upon their incapacity or death. Some may make such formal arrangements, whereas others may defer planning because they feel that they may outlive their offspring. Yet, even among families with younger people, family commitment or planning may not be realized. Witness one situation reported in the Republic of South Africa's *Johannesburg Star* (Khupiso, 1998), in which a father whose wife had died neglected the basic life supports for his son with a profound mental and physical disability. Only when neighbors alarmed by a bad smell coming from the man's dwelling became sufficiently concerned were authorities alerted. When found, the son was in a severe condition of malnutrition, infested with worms, and diseased. Informal family planning and supports obviously were lacking in that situation.

Other authors (Bigby, in press; Seltzer & Krauss, 1994; Smith & Tobin, 1989) discussed the mechanisms and models of family planning. When planning, however rudimentary, is present, the outcomes may be somewhat predictable. Absent planning, however, less predicable outcomes may be evident. An example is the tragedy reported in an article in *The New York Times* entitled "Parents' Deaths Were Fatal to Helpless Son" (1995). Reported was the situation of a 38-year-old man with numerous mental and physical disabilities who lay on his living room couch for a number of days without food or water, unable to help himself as his parents lay dead in the same room. Police reported that the man died some 24–48 hours before the local police climbed through a window of the locked apartment and discovered all three dead. The man's parents, in their 70s, appeared to have died of heart attacks 7–10 days before their bodies were found. The man, who was thought to have had cerebral palsy from birth, had been totally dependent on his parents to feed, dress, and move him. Police said the parents' deaths had left him stranded on the couch, unable to reach a telephone less than 10 feet away. Could such a tragedy have been averted? One can only speculate. If a service system is prepared by knowing "who and what" in terms of providing assistance, however, then this knowledge can be a functional means of helping parents plan for such eventualities.

The issue of aiding families has universal applicability. Thus, it is not surprising that there was a great deal of unanimity at the WHCoA miniconferences with regard to the notion that helping older families is a significant national priority and that providing for these families would help keep intact many families that are at risk of being unable to care for a family member with intellectual disabilities. In urging responsiveness to older families as an overwhelming priority, WHCoA mini-conference participants targeted supports such as making respite care more readily available for caregivers, providing financial supports for aging in place, and offering future planning assistance for families. They also recognized the need to consider abuse prevention activities and the needs of different cultural and ethnic groups and caregivers, to conduct outreach and planning assistance to families, and to provide flexible multigenerational housing options and supports.

CONCLUSIONS

This chapter explores some of the more salient policy and service design issues as well as defines some of the barriers that impede the full inclusion of older people with intellectual and developmental disabilities in the fabric of their communities. It examines the structures that should be in place as core supports for older adults so that they can live in older adulthood with dignity and comfort. It proposes certain criteria for what would be considered minimal expectations, that is, the conditions that other people in the neighborhood or in similar economic situations would have for their living situation and daily lives. These minimal expectations should cover the areas of housing, sustenance (e.g., nutrition), work or activities, physical conditioning, and social connectedness.

To address these needs, the chapter proposes that supports should be directed toward enhancing individuals' capacities to maintain competencies and autonomy in each of these areas. It suggests that, with regard to housing, for example, people need a reasonably clean and safe place to live (e.g., free of neighborhood crime, provisions made for sanitation and heat or relief from heat, easy access for those with walking difficulties, privacy). In terms of sustenance, people need an adequate food supply with sufficient funds to purchase and maintain a suitable diet and provide diversity and variety to enhance their enjoyment of life. In terms of work, they need employment and daily activities that stimulate and challenge them sufficiently and provide for social interactions as well as to provide wages to buy food and pay rent. In terms of physical conditioning, they need sufficient activities and exercise to help keep them physically sound, maintain body mass, and strengthen bone structure. In terms of social connectedness, they need supports to use community amenities, initiate and maintain relationships with peers or neighbors, and provide structures for avoiding social isolation (the bane of older adults).

With regard to the care system, this redefinition may entail a redistribution of day services' funding resources when general intellectual disability day programs are no longer appropriate. It may mean using program models that make better use of what *is* available rather than what *needs to be* available. It may involve working out cooperative agreements with the aging network regarding the use of social programs and in-home older adult care supports. It may involve new outreach efforts to long-term care and health agencies to help provide in-home supports, training for staff, and other supports for community living. Reports of such approaches are beginning to emerge that illustrate how localities are making the effort to prepare for aging in place and ensuring that their service providers are aware of what should be in place when aging is normal and to ameliorate problems when aging is pathological. These efforts include providing funding drawn from intellectual disabilities sources for aging network supports and services (Janicki et al., 1996), using specialty assistance teams drawn from area specialists on dementia care (Antonangeli, 1995), providing for assessment and intervention clinics (Carlsen, Galluzzi, Forman, & Cavalieri, 1994; Chicoine, McGuire, Hebein, & Gilly, 1994; Gambert et al., 1988; Henderson, Davidson, Overeynder, Bishop, & Ladrigan, 1997; McCreary, Fotheringham, Holden, Ouellette-Kuntz, & Robertson, 1993), and financing support services for families (Janicki, McCallion, et al., 1998; Meltzer, 1996).

Increased longevity, coupled with the demographic phenomenon of the pending "senior boom," means that there will be increasingly more older people with lifelong disabilities in the first 30 years of the 21st century. These demographic trends will force governments, advocates, and service providers to plan more constructively for the needs of this older population. Reaching back to the collective experiences of the preconference regional meetings that made up the WHCoA, there was consensus on the dearth of planning and public policy focus on this phenomenon and a lack of awareness among the general population and professionals of the impact of aging on adults with intellectual and developmental disabilities. Furthermore, given that these concerns are being raised around the globe, these perceptions are universal. Most of these fundamental policy issues evidence a greater need to make each nation aging-sensitive. In doing so, each nation can ensure that its citizenry can grow old with the comfort of knowing that they will be supported in their old age and given valued consideration and that they will find that barriers are removed that impede their full access to the communities to which they belong.

Thus, to affect public policies and service design successfully, strategies should be employed that substantially increase public education and thus increase consumer education. National health and social policies related to aging should also place a greater emphasis on the national health services in training health care professionals in aging and developmental disabilities and ensuring that there is aggressive cross-training of workers employed in both aging and disabilities agencies. Only with attention to these policy and design areas will change in the framework of the general milieu in which older people with disabilities find themselves occur and will each community become aging-capable and aging-receptive.

REFERENCES

Achenbaum, W.A. (1986). America as an aging society: Myths and images. *Daedalus, 115*(1), 13–30.

Americans with Disabilities Act (ADA) of 1990, PL 101-336, 42 U.S.C. §§ 12101 *et seq.*

Ansello, E.F., & Rose, T. (1989). *Aging and lifelong disabilities: Partnership for the twenty-first century.* College Park: University of Maryland Center on Aging.

Antonangeli, J.M. (1995). *Of two minds: A guide to the care of people with dual diagnosis of Alzheimer's disease and mental retardation.* Malden, MA: Cooperative for Human Services.

Baltes, P.B., & Baltes, M.M. (Eds.). (1990). *Successful aging: Perspectives from the behavioral sciences.* New York: Cambridge University Press.

Baltes, M.M., & Lang, F.R. (1997). Everyday functioning and successful aging: The impact of resources. *Psychology of Aging, 12,* 433–443.

Bigby, C. (in press). Models of parental planning. In M.P. Janicki & E.F. Ansello (Eds.), *Community supports for older adults with developmental disabilities.* Baltimore: Paul H. Brookes Publishing Co.

Butler, R. (1975). *Why survive? Being old in America.* New York: HarperCollins.

Carlsen, W.R., Galluzzi, K.E., Forman, L.F., & Cavalieri, T.A. (1994). Comprehensive geriatric assessment: Applications for community-residing elderly people with intellectual disability/developmental disabilities. *Mental Retardation, 32,* 334–340.

Chicoine, B., McGuire, D., Hebein, S., & Gilly, D. (1994). Development of a clinic for adults with Down syndrome. *Mental Retardation, 32,* 100–106.

Dalton, A.J. (1995). Alzheimer disease: A health risk of growing older with Down syndrome. In L. Nadel & D. Rosenthal (Eds.), *Down syndrome: Living and learning in the community* (pp. 58–64). New York: Wiley-Liss.

Edelstein, S. (1995). Fair housing laws and group residences for frail older persons. *Conference Papers and Recommendations: Expanding Housing Choices for Older People: An AARP White House Conference on Aging Mini-Conference* (pp. 219–238). Washington, DC: American Association of Retired Persons.

Fein, E.B. (1997, July 25). Not dead enough to die: Laws force life support on a man who never could consent. *New York Times,* pp. B1, B2.

Freedman, R.I., Krauss, M.W., & Seltzer, M.M. (1997). Aging parents' residential plans for adult children with mental retardation. *Mental Retardation, 35,* 114–123.

Gambert, S.R., Crimmins, D., Cameron, D.J., Heghinian, M., Bacon-Prue, A., Gupta, K.L., & Escher, J.E. (1988). Geriatric assessment of the mentally retarded elderly. *New York Medical Quarterly, 8,* 144–147.

Garfein, A.J., & Herzog, A.R. (1995). Robust aging among the young-old, old-old, and oldest-old. *Journal of Gerontology, 50,* S77–S87.

Grandparents under siege: Squaring up for round two of parenting. (1997, August 22). *Adelaide (South Australia) Advertiser,* L6.

Henderson, C.M., Davidson, P.W., Overeynder, J., Bishop, K., & Ladrigan, P. (1997). *Comprehensive geriatric assessment for evaluating functional decline in older adults with intellectual disabilities.* Unpublished manuscript, University of Rochester, Strong Center on Developmental Disabilities, Rochester, NY.

Inclusion International. (1997, April). Needs and appropriate supports for ageing people with mental handicap. *Inclusion: News from Inclusion International, 19,* 23–24.

Janicki, M.P. (1993). *Building the future: Planning and community development in aging and developmental disabilities.* Albany: New York State Office of Mental Retardation and Developmental Disabilities.

Janicki, M.P. (1995). Summary of major White House Conference on Aging recommendations with developmental disabilities as topic. *Challenges Through the Year 2000 and Beyond Post–White House Conference: Proceedings of the Second North Dakota National Conference on Aging and Disabilities* (pp. 24–25). Minot: Minot State University, North Dakota Center for Disabilities.

Janicki, M.P., & Dalton, A.J. (1998). Sensory impairments among older adults with intellectual disability. *Journal of Intellectual and Developmental Disabilities, 23,* 3–11.

Janicki, M.P., & Dalton, A.J. (1999a). Current practice in the assessment and care of persons with intellectual disabilities. In N. Bouras (Ed.), *Psychiatric and behavioral disorders in mental retardation* (pp. 121–153). Cambridge, England: Cambridge University Press.

Janicki, M.P., & Dalton, A.J. (1999b). Dementia and public policy considerations. In M.P. Janicki & A.J. Dalton (Eds.), *Dementia, aging, and intellectual disabilities: A handbook* (pp. 388–414). Philadelphia: Brunner/Mazel.

Janicki, M.P., Dalton, A.J., Henderson, M., & Davidson, P.W. (1999). Mortality and morbidity among older adults with intellectual disabilities: Health services considerations. *Disability and Rehabilitation, 10*(4–5).

Janicki, M.P., Heller, T., Seltzer, G.B., & Hogg, J. (1996). Practice guidelines for the clinical assessment and care management of Alzheimer's disease and other dementias among adults with intellectual disability. *Journal of Intellectual Disability Research, 40,* 374–382.

Janicki, M.P., McCallion, P., Force, L.T., Bishop, K., & LePore P. (1998). Area agency on aging outreach and assistance for households with older carers of an adult with a developmental disability. *Journal of Aging and Social Policy, 10,* 13–36.

Khupiso, V. (1998, January 25). Small boy locked up and left to rot. *Johannesburg Star,* p. 2.

King, N.M.P. (1996). *Making sense of advance directives* (Rev. ed.). Washington, DC: Georgetown University Press.

Laslett, P. (1991). *A fresh map of life: The emergence of the third age.* Cambridge, MA: Harvard University Press.

Lundh, U., & Nolan, M. (1996). Ageing and quality of life: II. Understanding successful ageing. *British Journal of Nursing, 5,* 1291–1295.

McCreary, B.D., Fotheringham, J.B., Holden, J.J.A., Ouellette-Kuntz, H., & Robertson, D.M. (1993). Experiences in an Alzheimer clinic for persons with Down syndrome. In J.M. Berg, H. Karlinsky, & A.J. Holland (Eds.), *Alzheimer disease, Down syndrome, and their relationship* (pp. 115–131). Oxford, England: Oxford University Press.

Medicaid program conditions for intermediate care facilities for the mentally retarded: Final rules, 53 Fed. Reg. 20,448–20,505 (June 3, 1988).

Meltzer, N. (1996). *Washington statewide senior family initiative: A project to assist regions plan for the needs of aging family caregivers of individuals with developmental disabilities.* Seattle, WA: The Arc of King County. (Available from The Arc of King County, 10550 Lake City Way, N.E., Seattle, WA 98125)

Mittelman, M.S., Ferris, S.H., Shulman, E., Steinberg, G., & Levin, B. (1996). A family intervention to delay nursing home placement of patients with Alzheimer disease. A randomized controlled trial. *JAMA: The Journal of the American Medical Association, 276,* 1725–1731.

Neugarten, B.L., & Neugarten, D.A. (1986). Age in the aging society. *Daedalus, 115*(1), 31–49.

OAPulp. (1997, September 16). *London Daily Telegraph,* p. 3.

Older Americans Act of 1965, PL 89-73, 42 U.S.C. §§ 3001 *et seq.*

Older Persons Planning Office, Government of Victoria. (1990). *Looking forward to an older Victoria.* Melbourne, Victoria, Australia: Author.

Parents' deaths were fatal to helpless son. (1995, July 28). *The New York Times,* p. A20.

Peterson, P.G. (1999). Gray dawn: The global aging crisis. *Foreign Affairs, 78*(1), 42–55.

Riley, M.W. (1998). Response to "Successful aging." *Gerontologist, 38,* 151.

Romine, L., Dale, P., & Cotten, P.D. (1998, April). *The elderly Mississippian with a developmental disability: Present and future service needs.* Paper presented at the Fourteenth Annual Conference on the Elderly Handicapped Mississippian, William Carey College, Hattiesburg, Mississippi.

Rowe, J.W., & Kahn, R.L. (1997). Successful aging. *Gerontologist, 37,* 433–440.

Rowe, J.W., & Kahn, R.L. (1998). *Successful aging.* New York: Pantheon Books.

Schulz, R., & Heckhausen, J. (1996). A life span model of successful aging. *American Psychologist, 51,* 702–714.

Seltzer, M.M., & Krauss, M.W. (1994). Aging parents with co-resident adult children: The impact of lifelong caregiving. In M.M. Seltzer, M.W. Krauss, & M.P. Janicki (Eds.), *Life course perspectives on adulthood and old age* (pp. 3–18). Washington, DC: American Association on Mental Retardation.

Smith, G.C., & Tobin, S.S. (1989). Permanency planning among older persons of adults with life-long disabilities. *Journal of Gerontological Social Work, 14,* 35–39.

Social Security Act of 1935, PL 74-271, 42 U.S.C. §§ 301 *et seq.*

Strawbridge, W.J., Cohen, R.D., Shema, S.J., & Kaplan, G.A. (1996). Successful aging: Predictors and associated activities. *American Journal of Epidemiology, 144,* 135–141.

Stripling, S. (1997, June 1). How long are we good for? Parents who have given a lifetime of care to their developmentally disabled children fear for the future. *Seattle Times,* L1, L3–L4.

Suggs, D.K. (1997, March 23). The forever children: Aging parents are haunted by what lies ahead. *Baltimore Sun,* 1A, 14A–15A.

Transplant patient with Down syndrome dies. (1997, May 25). *Los Angeles Times,* p. A12.

Turk, M.A., Geremski, C.A., Rosenbaum, P.F., & Weber, R.J. (1997). The health status of women with cerebral palsy. *Archives of Physical Medicine and Rehabilitation, 78,* S10–S17.

Turner, K.W. (1994). Modeling community inclusion for older adults with developmental disabilities. *Southwest Journal on Aging, 10,* 13–18.

United Nations (UN). (1992). *Proclamation on ageing.* New York: United Nations Department for Policy Coordination and Sustainable Development.

van Schronjenstein Lantman-de Valk, H. (1998). *Health problems in people with intellectual disability.* Maastricht, The Netherlands: University of Maastricht Press.

Visser, F.E., Aldenkamp, A.P., van Huffelen, A.C., Kuilman, M., Overweg, J., & van Wijk, J. (1997). Prospective study of the prevalence of Alzheimer-type dementia in institutionalized individuals with Down syndrome. *American Journal on Mental Retardation, 101,* 400–412.

White House Conference on Aging (WHCoA). (1996). *The road to an aging policy for the 21st century* (Final report). Washington, DC: Author.

18

Empowerment and Inclusion in Planning

John Goldmeier and Stanley S. Herr

Commentators predicted in 1985 that within the following 3 decades, new policy issues would emerge and new frontiers would have to be explored to meet the needs of the growing population of older adults with development disabilities (Lippman & Loberg, 1985). The second of these 3 decades (1995–2005) is upon us. This chapter seeks to point to some possible directions and available options in the quest to develop these new frontiers. The focus of the chapter is on two fundamental ideas that have captured attention: empowerment and inclusion.

INTRODUCTION

Much heterogeneity exists in the population of older people with developmental disabilities. For example, this population includes those with mental retardation, cerebral palsy, epilepsy, or autism. The largest subgroup consists of people with mental retardation, traditionally defined as those individuals whose general intellectual functioning is considered significantly below average (i.e., an IQ score of approximately 70–75 or lower), with the American Association on Mental Retardation's definition (Luckasson et al., 1992) stressing the importance of environmental and other supports to improve the functioning of these individuals. Still, categories related to age, intelligence, and diagnosis in themselves do not describe this population. Rather, it seems more useful to look to the functional characteristics of affected individuals, the degree of autonomy that they can exercise, and the environmental supports that can be made available to them.

In terms of age, *old age* in people with developmental disabilities must also be defined more flexibly. For instance, if age 60 years were used as a criterion, it would tend to exclude people such as those with Down syndrome, who age prematurely, even though the longevity of people with Down syndrome at the turn of the 21st century is increasing (Seltzer & Seltzer, 1992). It would thus be more realistic to follow a more flexible biopsychosocial approach to describing older adults with developmental disabilities such as the one followed in this chapter rather than one that is strictly chronological.

Consideration of philosophical and social policy issues is important also. Relevant here is the concept of structural lag in the rapidly changing contemporary world (Riley & Kahn, 1994). As originally formulated by Merton (1967), the idea of structural lag is that opportunities in the community for individuals to develop their potentialities do not keep pace with their need to do so, suggesting that those opportunities that do exist must be exploited fully. An example might be the situation created by the increasing life expectancy of people with Down syndrome who also have presenile dementia of the Alzheimer's type as contrasted with those who have intellectual impairments but fewer longstanding medical or emotional problems (Bicknell, 1994). Outlets that bring satisfaction and rewards must be created for both of these populations (Scharlach & Kaye, 1997). The challenge then becomes one of how a facility can adapt its services to meet the needs of consumers with multiple and sometimes quite complicated needs.

Fortunately, an expanding knowledge and value base exists that can be explicated in terms of a framework to guide intervention, one that includes concepts such as empowerment and inclusion. To accommodate such a broad perspective, an ecological approach is essential to stress the multiplicity of factors that are generally implicated. An ecological knowledge base allows one to view the person and the person's environment as complex entities consisting of biopsychosocial forces or, put another way, in terms of interactive, cognitive, behavioral, and affective elements (Whittaker & Tracy, 1989). Implicit in an ecological approach is the idea that a goodness of fit between the affected individuals, their families, the larger community, and the programs that are provided must exist and that consumers and need-meeting service providers must not be at cross-purposes with one another.

As for core values, two complementary value orientations traditionally have been paramount (Lowy, 1991). The first holds that the worth and dignity of individuals must be respected and that the uniqueness of each person must be appreciated thoroughly. It follows that the second value, the right to autonomy and self-determination, can be extended more fully when services are offered. In the 1990s, the question of personal autonomy underlying who could give informed consent became a particularly important issue for older adults with developmental disabilities, particularly in health and mental health caregiving environments (American Psychiatric Association, 1985; Dinerstein, Herr, & O'Sullivan, 1999; Rosner & Weinstock, 1990).

More attention is likely to be paid to these value components in the first decade of the 21st century because of questions regarding the maintenance of quality services in a cost-conscious environment. It is already evident that, in the search for optimum standards, such value-laden concepts as quality of life find specific expression in criteria of quality assurance or what the most beneficial alternative may be (Wray, 1990). In the search for the most beneficial alternatives, the developmental disabilities field has moved toward implementing concepts of empowerment and inclusion from institutionalization of individuals far from their homes and kindly intended but often paternalistic and prescriptive suggestions.

EMPOWERMENT

This section discusses the rationale for an empowerment approach, some background regarding how it attained the prominence that it is likely to continue to have, and aspects of how the approach can be implemented on behalf of older people with developmental disabilities. In the first half of the 20th century, there was perhaps acceptance but relatively little recognition that people with developmental disabilities, regardless of age, can be self-determining and productive. In fact, the whole "problem" of disabilities was hidden or denied. The lingering controversy that began in 1997 about whether the Franklin Delano Roosevelt (FDR) memorial should depict the former president in a wheelchair reminded the American public that a conspiracy of silence during his presidency shrouded the fact that he had polio (Gallagher, 1994). FDR and others in his circle of advisors seemed to fear that publicly acknowledging his disability would convey an image of helplessness that would threaten confidence in his leadership. Although this estimate probably sold the public short, in the second half of the 20th century, public attitudes in the United States toward both older adults and people with disabilities as passive individuals who, if they needed services, had to accept those that were dispensed by well-meaning professionals, the experts, were slow to change. The experts made the decisions, informed consumers accordingly, and gave advice on what was to be done. If consumers or their families and caregivers became more active consumers who tried to control the care that was offered, they incurred the risk that help would be withdrawn by those who did not want their authority questioned (Mackelprang & Salsgiver, 1996).

Fortunately, attitudes toward people with mental retardation in the United States began to change in the 1960s and 1970s. In 1962, President Kennedy appointed the Panel on Mental Retardation, which recognized society's responsibility to people with mental retardation by fostering the development of their maximum capacity to bring them as close to the mainstream of independence and "normalcy" as possible (President's Committee on Mental Retardation [PCMR], 1977, p. 105). In individual circumstances in which disabilities could not be overcome, society would have to change through the provision of accommodations or adjustments of social arrangements. By October 1963, two laws—the Maternal and Child Health and Mental Retardation Planning Amendments of 1963 (PL 88-156) and the Mental Retardation Facilities and Community Mental Health Centers Construction Act of 1963 (PL 88-164)—had been signed, signaling an emerging federal role in the financing and improvement of facilities for people with mental retardation in the United States. The real advent of the Civil Rights movement for people with mental retardation in the United States was still almost a decade away, however. In 1972 and 1973, the pioneering lawsuits (e.g., *New York State Association for Retarded Children v. Rockefeller,* 1973; *Townsend v. Treadway,* 1973; *Wyatt v. Stickney,* 1972) upholding these individuals' constitutional rights to education, habilitation, and protection from harm were decided (see Chapter 5). The thrust of this litigation was to individualize plans of habilitation and to outlaw simply containing people in custodial institutions. The doctrine of the least-restrictive alternative meant that the one-size-fits-all philosophy had to be abandoned. Thus, new options began to be explored (Flexer, 1988). Empowering consumers to use those options was the logical next step.

The rationale for an empowerment-based approach is that individuals, their families, or their caregivers should have the opportunity to make their own decisions. Empowering people also presupposes that individuals with developmental disabilities have the right and the capacity, even if individuals' capacity is limited at times, to make choices relevant to their lives. Empowerment-based practice seeks to exploit the areas of strength of individuals, families, or communities in order to use the resourcefulness and resilience that can often be found in people when others seek it (Hartman, 1981). In essence, an empowerment-based approach considers consumers to be experts because, as citizens who interact with the courts, social agencies, hospitals, and other segments of the larger society, they certainly have acquired the necessary experience to make decisions about their lives. This premise applies to older people with developmental disabilities as much as it does to everyone else. Some guidelines derived from the social work literature on empowerment that may be applied to empower older adults with developmental disabilities follow (Simon, 1994).

Expressed Preferences and Demonstrated Needs

The first guideline in empowerment-based practice is that programs should be shaped in response to the expressed preferences and demonstrated needs of consumers and members of their families. The difficulty in how community resources were structured prior to the 1990s was that often the function of an agency providing services was considered primary, and consumers had to adapt to it. The trend at the turn of the 21st century, however, suggests that it is more appropriate to think less about traditional functions and more specifically about how services can be attuned best to consumers' needs. For example, services for older adults with developmental disabilities increasingly must be developed to accommodate their families, which increasingly consist of the "old-old" or the "young-old." It is no longer unusual for a 60-year-old adult with developmental disabilities to live with one or both parents who are in their 80s and still provide their child with important care and support. Nor is it uncommon for "old-old" individuals with intellectual impairments to be cared for by sons or daughters who are in their 60s. A U.S. study conducted in Maryland (Sugg, 1997) suggested that 40% of caregivers of people with developmental disabilities are ages 60 and older. Such situations suggest that there are different clusters of needs, with those who request services usually being the best qualified to say which services might be most helpful. Meeting specific requests for defined needs is empowering for consumers because they are then motivated and enabled to tackle other problems.

The state of Maryland, through a Robert Wood Johnson Foundation demonstration grant, adopted the highly innovative Self-Determination Initiative. The initiative emphasizes four main values: choice and control, individuality, individual rights, and consumer satisfaction. In the words of its developers, this initiative is designed to

- Give people with disabilities substantial control over the services that they receive
- Create partnerships among people with disabilities and their families, service providers, advocates, and Maryland's communities
- Balance the needs and desires of those people who receive services and those who are waiting to receive services
- Reduce the average cost of services and pass on the savings to people who are waiting for services

- Obtain community support for people with developmental disabilities in lives that they have chosen

Similar projects are in operation in 19 states across the United States. So far, results suggest that, "without choice people only appear to be included without really being active partners and empowered and that this type of self-determination initiative is working to enable families and consumers to choose what type of services they want and who will provide them" (J.F. Rosner, personal communication, May 1998).

Accessibility and Availability

Efforts should be made to reach out to find vulnerable populations as part of the process of making programs and services convenient and accessible in the community. Consumers feel a sense of empowerment when programs and services are made convenient and accessible. When access is easier, the likelihood of individuals' continued participation is greater. Accessibility issues became particularly important in the 1990s as new options in the community emerged. Provision of help to families in their homes, respite care, and the development of smaller residential facilities became the preferred service options. Experts express concern, however, that, in the interest of short-run efficiency, some "creaming" is occurring—that is, those with special needs and more complex problems are cast aside in the interest of attaining speedier or easier results (Knoll, 1990). Thus, with older adults with developmental disabilities, planners must devote greater attention to ensuring accessibility for those whose problems require more intensive services and multiple resources. One encouraging sign is that some agencies are willing to support adults with severe disabilities through costly programs in the community. *The New York Times* (Kleinfield, 1997a, 1997b, 1997c), in a Pulitzer Prize–winning front-page series, highlighted such an effort that was made on behalf of James Velez, who, after living for 16 years in an institution, gained a more independent life because of the creativity, perseverance, and commitment of the staff who assisted him.

A broadened definition of *community* that takes an individual's ethnicity into account is also appropriate when questions about the accessibility and availability of programs and services arise. A rising concern worth noting is that as service populations become increasingly diverse, services should be delivered in as culturally competent a manner as possible. The concept of cultural competence suggests that those who provide services should understand and be sympathetic to the cultural values of the consumers whom they serve (Gelfand, 1994). Cultural competence can mean paying attention to consumers' preferences for living in communities or settings in which one ethnic group is more prominent than another. Although, to enhance communication and sociability, effort is often made to match service providers and consumers by race, religion, or language fluency, it must be recognized that this is not always possible, given the diversity of many communities. In this connection, the concept of community also must be rethought to include an enlarged geographic area in which those living in diverse communities in which they are a minority can be included. Consumers' sense of empowerment is also derived from their ethnic identification, and service providers must be aware of this factor.

Mutual Dedication

The empowerment principle suggests that service providers should ask for as much dedication to problem solving from consumers as they do from themselves. The older adult with a developmental disability is empowered when his or her status is elevated from that of a passive recipient of services to that of a contributing partner. In the same way, family members, caregivers, and even collaborating agencies should be recognized as fulfilling a partnership role—in effect, as creating a balanced partnership (Kauppi & Jones, 1985) in which everyone's input is valued.

The professional literature of the 1990s offered some specific guidelines for developing empowering relationships that promote dedication to problem solving. Three guidelines appear to be particularly applicable in empowering older adults with developmental disabilities (Cox, 1994). First, in the decision-making process, professionals should first try to pose options that are possible and then elicit consumers' suggestions or recommendations. Consumers should not be asked to respond positively or negatively without such a backdrop. Second, power struggles should be avoided. The Connecticut Department of Mental Retardation, for example, emphasizes consumers' rights as a way of minimizing problems in helping relationships that stem from questions about power and status (Gant, 1990). Third, when there are impediments in forming professional relationships related to the consumer's ethnicity, these impediments can be addressed by the service provider's encouraging the consumer to draw on the strengths and achievements of the consumer's particular ethnic group. For example, exemplary ways of responding to life's predicaments, which are present in every culture, can be held out as a source of satisfaction and pride. Dedication to problem solving that is shared in equal measure by the consumer and the service provider in the ways described can be empowering simply because of the momentum for change that it creates.

Using Consumers' Wisdom and Experience

The principle of using consumers' wisdom and experience is discussed previously in this chapter; but with respect to older adults with developmental disabilities, it calls for some special considerations. For instance, with this population, outreach should be emphasized, particularly with regard to primary preventive services (Beaver & Miller, 1992). These services include providing information and, if necessary, referral for clients, their families, and caregivers and then following up to be sure that a contact was made. This effort should be collaborative, utilizing consumers' strengths to pursue the means by which to meet more universal or more specific needs. There are many examples of such collaborative efforts. They include the search for solutions to actual or potential health problems, transportation needs, avoidance of becoming a victim of crime, housing needs such as home sharing, or remedies for injustices through legal assistance. These preventive services are offered frequently in the community, traditional centers at which older adults congregate for work or recreation, churches, health centers, or lodges. Older adults with developmental disabilities, their families, or their caregivers will feel encouraged and empowered when they can combine their own knowledge with that of a helper in coping with a variety of situations before a crisis develops.

Creative Intervention

A special sense of creativity and dedication is needed in work with older adults, the more so when they have developmental disabilities. Professionals should not be wedded to one favored intervention method. Instead, they should devise and redevise interventions in response to the unique configuration of requests, issues, and needs that consumers present. A first consideration is the attitude of the caregiver toward consumers. Kastenbaum (1964) first identified the distancing of professionals from the problems of older adults altogether and coined the phrase *the reluctant therapist.*

Fortunately, a considerable change for the better has occurred in that social scientists and professionals have come to realize that older adults have more resilience and competence than they were once thought to have and that older adults also have a right to satisfying and productive lives. In the 1990s in particular, interest in new applications of interventions with older adults increased. Contemporary interventions involve art activities, reminiscence, movement and dance therapy, and activities that involve the senses generally (Holosko & Feit, 1991; Tobin & Gustafson, 1987). Even psychotherapy, which rarely had been attempted with older adults with developmental disabilities prior to the 1990s, began to be advocated (Sadavoy & Leszcz, 1987). The task remains, however, to match such interventions more closely with the needs of older adults with developmental disabilities, whose limitations had been more of a focus than their potentialities prior to the 1990s. Applying a configuration of interventions is empowering because it allows choice and a greater chance of meeting individuals' particular needs. In addition, this framework of interventions also puts the focus on the consumer's whole social network so that one link in the network can reinforce the others.

Leadership

Empowerment-based practice requires not only creativity and initiative but also the demonstration of leadership. Leadership is a dual process. It must be encouraged in the consumer population for purposes of self-advocacy and exercised by service providers.

Encouraging leadership among those in the social network of the older adult with developmental disabilities is necessary so that initiative can be exercised in the type of consumer-responsive partnership described previously (Pederson, Chaikin, Koehler, Campbell, & Arcand, 1993). Another way of encouraging leadership is forming alliances with members of community groups who, as family members or as caregivers, can represent the interests of older adults with developmental disabilities. Finally, some consumers are or want to be more active in their work or recreation environments. Their creative energies can also be mobilized by, for example, organizing them into goal-directed groups to exert influence at legislative hearings (see Chapter 6).

The other aspect of leadership in empowerment-based practice is for practitioners to develop whatever leadership potential exists within themselves. For instance, practitioners can apply qualities that they already possess more deliberately to assume leadership roles to secure services for consumers. In the process, they will use the rich knowledge and experience that they possess in the fields of developmental disabilities and aging as well as their vision of how changes affect the course of peoples' lives. Although questioning how a vision can traverse the distance between that which exists and that which can be attained is appropriate (O'Brien, 1990), the exercise of the type of leadership described here is valid even if not all goals are attained. Partial gains and the process alone can be empowering for both consumers and practitioners.

Patience

Professionals often must be patient in empowerment-based practice with older adults with developmental disabilities. Even under the best of circumstances, a sense of empowerment develops slowly and incrementally from successful experiences in changing previous circumstances. A sense of empowerment also depends greatly on trust in oneself and in others, a quality that may develop slowly in part because previously it may have been weakened by too much dependence on others. Consequently, allowances must be made as consumers and their families test themselves.

To avoid the trap of trying to do too much too soon, proponents of empowerment-based practice (e.g., Cox, 1994) suggested that, in order to increase the consumer's sense of confidence, a little restraint is helpful. For example, Cox (1994) suggested at least four steps to enhance consumers' sense of empowerment. These steps are adapted here for work with older people with developmental disabilities:

1. The capacity and motivation of consumers and those concerned about them are assessed. In this minimally intrusive step, helpers assess the consumer's readiness and ability to solve or ameliorate a problem independently or quasi-independently. For example, if there is a lack of resources, a helping professional might provide the information and point to the resource, leaving it to the consumer, the consumer's family, or the consumer's caregivers to pursue the matter further. The helping professional does not assume that a need for further intervention exists.

2. The professional can encourage ongoing educational efforts in workshops or small-group formats. In this way, the service provider can see whether the knowledge and information transmitted is sufficient for consumers to ameliorate their situations on their own.

3. In situations in which consumers want more active support in pursuing a goal, the helping person may have contact with the consumer more frequently and intensively to provide more follow-up. At the same time, the helping person would have contact with other actual or potential service providers to facilitate important goals.

4. In this step, groups of consumers and their support networks are organized into, for example, advocacy groups to engage in political and community activity designed to achieve more permanent changes in their lives. For example, groups such as the Consortium for Citizens with Developmental Disabilities or The Arc can be supported actively as they pursue disability rights issues and access to health care.

Essentially, by using all of these steps to help consumers take the lead, instilling in consumers the sense of empowerment that derives from having a measure of control in one's life is possible.

INCLUSION

Inclusion is a guiding philosophy for integrating older and younger people with developmental disabilities into the community. Inclusion is an outgrowth of trends for people of all ages who have disabilities. These trends began in the 1980s and 1990s with transfers to less restrictive environments in the community after these people had experienced many years of institutionalization. The idea of inclusion has received much attention (Gibson, Rabkin, & Munson, 1992), even though the concept developed as a logical extension of the principle of normalization, which was first propounded in the United States by Wolfensberger (1972). A related idea, that of educating children with developmental and other disabilities in general classrooms, was mandated by the Education for All Handicapped Children Act of 1975 (PL 94-142) and its successors, the Individuals with Disabilities Education Act (IDEA) of 1990 (PL 101-476), the Individuals with Disabilities Education Act (IDEA) Amendments of 1991 (PL 102-119), and the Individuals with Disabilities Education Act (IDEA) Amendments of 1997 (PL 105-17). This legislation provided some impetus for inclusion at the early stage of the life cycle (Pryor, Kent, McGunn, & LeRoy, 1996). Legislation and case law continue to refine how the principles of inclusion are implemented (see Chapter 5). The passage of the Americans with Disabilities Act (ADA) of 1990 (PL 101-336), for example, was intended to mandate inclusion in work, education, and recreation environments by requiring these environments to be made more accessible for people with disabilities. These ideas— inclusion and normalization—helped produce standards between the 1970s and the end of the 20th century that made it possible for many individuals with developmental disabilities to live in conditions that at least approached those of others in American society (Stroud & Sutton, 1988).

Before some of the philosophical and ethical considerations that affect inclusion are discussed, the types of agencies or service sectors that typically serve older people with developmental disabilities are described next. Three types of such sectors that Seltzer (1988) outlined still seemed prominent at the end of the 1990s. The dominant service sector focuses on people with developmental disabilities. In this sector, services are focused not on age specifically but rather on individuals' functional capacities. Baumeister (1988) reported that this sector provided about two-thirds of the services that older people with developmental disabilities in the United States receive, and there are no data to suggest that this proportion changed substantially in the 1990s. Similarly, the second sector was the age-specialized developmental disabilities sector, which Baumeister found accounted for only 5% of the services provided. The third sector is the aging services sector, in which older adults with developmental disabilities are included along with all other older adults in community-based or institutional facilities. Complementing these three sectors are the other sectors in which older adults with developmental disabilities receive services along with the general population (e.g., the health and mental health sectors). Although the age-integrated developmental disabilities sector seems to be the more firmly established and most inclusive service sector for older adults with developmental disabilities, the development of other sectors, and consumers' use of them, is increasingly important. The following case study illustrates a number of inclusion issues.

Gary, Charles, and James

Gary, age 62 years, was one of three older men with developmental disabilities living together in an apartment. He was referred for counseling services because of impulsive behavior such as taking long walks when upset without telling anyone. He was also known to react with foul language and shoving when he became frustrated with a task at his worksite and when teased, especially by a female co-worker. The referral came from a county agency for citizens of all ages with mental retardation.

This situation arose in the early 1980s, when a state institution for people with mental retardation was about to close. Gary had become quite accustomed to life in the institution. Even after some community living trials, social workers had to use some persuasion to elicit Gary's agreement to leave the institution. With the passage of time, however, there seemed to be little other choice because the institution was closing. The institution's staff matched two other men, James, age 64, and Charles, age 68, with Gary, and all three moved into a supervised two-bedroom apartment made affordable with the Social Security disability payments that the three men received. By the time they were discharged from the institution, the three men had spent an accumulated total of 65 years in that institution alone.

Gary essentially had no family nearby, but once a year he was helped to board a bus to visit a sibling in the Southwest. Indeed, traveling was his strength. When he would leave his apartment after a disagreement with James or Charles, he knew exactly where he was going, usually to a movie at the mall. He also could find his way to the social worker's office, once walking a long stretch when the bus did not come. Gary was quite healthy and well oriented, and his functioning was quite good except for a short-fuse temperament. His impulsiveness had not led to serious injury to himself or to others, but it nevertheless was a problem in his relationships.

Charles, the oldest of the three, was also in good health except for a controllable thyroid condition and poor eyesight, for which he wore eyeglasses. He was an exceptionally good worker and quite strong. He talked proudly of his job as a welder, at which he worked for about 20 hours per week. The job sometimes took him to rural areas like those where he had spent his youth. Charles's job eventually had to be changed because of his weakening eyesight. A brother visited Charles from time to time and brought him clothes and sometimes gifts.

James had cerebral palsy and poor use of one side of his body, so he required some assistance with dressing and moving about. He had his own special armchair by the television set. James was poorly educated but had a relatively high level of intelligence. He was the residential facility's chief organizer: He handled bills that came in the mail, made lists of items for shopping or activities, and helped set agendas for the agency staff worker who visited about two or three times weekly. James came from a large, well-connected local family that usually could be counted on for financial support at budget-setting time. James's family also frequently took James to their home on visits and for holidays. The other two men were sometimes a little jealous of this attention. It seemed, however, that they understood that though James was fortunate to have a concerned family, he was also at a great disadvantage because of his physical limitations. Still, it seemed that Gary's stalking out of the apartment was at times associated with James's put-downs. This problem was given some attention during the contact with the social worker.

Although Gary was the one who had been referred, it quickly became apparent that this was, in a sense, a family situation. An office visit format for Gary lasted only briefly, and "family sessions" soon started—that is, home visits began with Gary's invitation to meet with his roommates. The focus of the social worker's activity over the next 3 years consisted of such visits at intervals of about 3 weeks unless events such as changes in the assigned agency staff member, an illness, or one of Gary's unannounced absences precipitated a crisis. Through counseling and communication, the men learned to handle the common problems of living together, with some of the problems being those that would exist in any family and some being more unique to men, particularly Gary's impulsivity and James's tendency to use put-downs as a way, it seemed, of preserving his own status. With some support, both James and Gary gradually learned to modify their less-positive interactions through more appropriate expression of their feelings and the incidences of Gary's leaving the apartment gradually decreased. Counseling also defused other crises before they escalated. When the situation was reasonably stable, the agency staff member withdrew from the case. Nevertheless, the county agency staff kept informed of the situation because they frequently used it as an example of how older adults with developmental disabilities can live in community-based environments.

Beneficence and Paternalism

The previous case study illustrates the moral dilemmas involved in including older adults with developmental disabilities in a community-based living arrangement in an attempt to establish normalization. Two major philosophical issues are discussed in this section: beneficence (i.e., enhancing the welfare and serving the best interests of others) (Murdach, 1996) and paternalism. Paternalism can include taking action that is contrary to the consumer's wishes that disempowers the consumer by limiting his or her freedom of choice. This dilemma can be reframed by asking, When does paternalism constitute protective intervention that has, to use Beauchamp and Childress' (1994) phrase, a "moral justification"? The question is particularly important in work with people with mental disabilities because, at times, the consumer experiences impairment in the ability to make a reasoned decision. Because such an impairment can put such individuals at risk, not intervening would constitute, in some respects, a moral abdication by the professional that might expose the professional to legal liability.

In the case study of Gary, Charles, and James given previously, pressure to include or to rule out certain options clearly existed at many junctures. The case description began with some persuasion being required to dislodge them from dependence on the institution. Their dependence could not have continued for much longer anyway, because the institution was closing. Then, later, after the three men were offered some choices with regard to living with each other, pressures were entailed in living in a family-like situation. Following these pressures were the expectation that they work or that they participate in socialization experiences, at least to a degree. The three men themselves, the caregiving staff of various agencies, and family members all agreed to these goals for the men's habilitation, and, in fact, as the men's success became more evident, the commitment of all involved to the habilitation approach intensified.

In retrospect, the social worker's persuasion to include the men in the life of the community did seem warranted. Still, the professional must have a moral stance that provides some guidance with regard to how quickly and with what degree of persuasion it is appropriate to intervene without becoming disempowering. One formulation that is implicit in this case study is a model of protective intervention based on an assessment of the risks and benefits (Bradley, 1990). Such a model suggests that only careful, individualized assessment justifies the gradations of assertive intervention shown in the case study presented in this chapter and that, with regard to older adults with developmental disabilities, interventions should be tailored to the degree of the individual's decision-making impairment.

Inclusion versus Isolation

It is useful to contrast the concept of inclusion with its opposite: isolation. In an effort to prevent isolation, it is important to avoid abruptly placing older adults with developmental disabilities in programs that may not have been designed with these individuals in mind and that may not be able to adapt to their needs.

A degree of isolation is not always bad. In a quite original study of older men not restricted to those with disabilities who were living alone, Rubenstein (1986) cited some of the benefits of a singular path. Among the advantages of living and managing alone, the older men in the study reported a sense of independence, a degree of control of the environment, a lack of pressure in the absence of demands to be active at someone else's request, and the sense of continuity with the past by growing old in a familiar environment.

Despite the likelihood that most older adults with developmental disabilities lead more dependent lives than the men described in the Rubenstein study, an analogy can be made with reference to the case study of Gary, Charles, and James in this chapter. The issue is whether support should exist for maintaining the individual in his original home. For example, James's surviving parent, who was quite old, expressed concern about how James's cerebral palsy would be affected by his living with the other two men. She at first wished that James would return home so that she and other family members could care for him. Her wish, however, was not realistic, because others in James's extended family who would be involved in his care had serious doubts that this plan could be implemented. The professionals concerned also had their doubts, and James seemed to be ambivalent at best. One can only speculate about the merits of such a more singular path for James and what it might have added to the meaningfulness of caregiving for his older but failing parent. Weighing questions of self-determination for all those in the consumer's social network seemed to be the key in choosing the most beneficial and least restrictive alternative in this instance.

Normalization and the Life Stages

Normalization, age-appropriateness, and least restrictive alternatives are explicit values in many service programs for older adults with developmental disabilities, especially those programs that seek to include these individuals in the community (Sutton, Sterns, & Park, 1993). These values promote the belief that older adults with developmental disabilities, regardless of their age, should have the opportunity to go through the same growth-producing life stages as everyone else. This belief was an important consideration in the case study described in this chapter. For instance, the original case referral for counseling came about as Gary, after being freed from the constraints that he had experienced during many years of living in an institution, became more interested in establishing heterosexual relationships, an age-appropriate though delayed stage for him. Some of the early activity in this case was therefore focused on helping Gary deal with his feelings about this issue and to express himself in socially appropriate ways, such as by talking rather than by shoving. With Gary and other people with developmental disabilities, such situations may require that more support may be needed to help them master a particular stage of development that has been delayed.

Ultimately, with the greater longevity of this population and the progress of medical science, retirement also becomes an issue. Adults ages 55 and older who no longer desire a program emphasizing work skills should have other alternatives available to them, such as leisure activities, exercise activities, or various community inclusion projects (Hawkins, 1993). Similarly, for Gary, Charles, and James, the agency that provided services to them did not focus on their vocational skills alone; it implemented the increasingly popular philosophy of balancing individuals' vocational and leisure time interests (Stock, 1996).

Requests regarding cohabitation and marriage are a natural result of men's and women's interactions in an inclusive environment. Many people with developmental disabilities age together in family-type living arrangements requiring the types of support that are offered to all other individuals of their age. In Gary's situation, a marriage actually did take place among his circle of acquaintances in the recreation center. Marriage and its impact on people with developmental disabilities, young or old, has been the subject of little discussion or research. Perhaps this is so because to marry or just to live together involves not only private and personal decisions but also decisions that affect the formal and informal support network. Perhaps the issue has not been discussed much because it is a complex and emotional one and because there is fear that public support for programs for both people with disabilities and older adults could be affected adversely if these programs are seen as "too liberal." Evidence exists that these fears may be waning, however, as one large Maryland service provider featured the wedding picture of two of its older adult consumers on its calendar. Future efforts to implement inclusion may stimulate more discussion and the resolution of topics that were once taboo.

The Service Sectors

Of the service sectors discussed previously, the one most concerned with the case of Gary, Charles, and James was the age-inclusive developmental disabilities sector that includes the men in work and recreation groups. Age inclusiveness had been built into that particular program when the men arrived so that, as they aged, adjustments could be made more easily. Thus, for example, the men's programs were modified when the eyesight of one of the men deteriorated, when another required a wheelchair, and when more leisure time activities with less emphasis on work were needed. The age-inclusive environment suited the men because it facilitated the continuation of activities as they became older and enabled them to continue existing friendships and maintain acquaintance groups. An additional advantage was that service coordination and referral were offered so that, as problems arose, the appropriate service referrals were made.

Services in the second sector, the age-specialized developmental disabilities sector, were not used in this case, in part because no such county agency was available. It was fortunate that the men could be included in the age-inclusive developmental disabilities sector just described.

Some efforts were made to include the men in the third sector, the generic aging services sector. In addition to housing, which in the case of Gary, Charles, and James already had been supplied, a center for older adults might have been a focal point. Senior centers are designed to carry out the charge of the Older Americans Act of 1965 (PL 89-73) to provide a broad spectrum of services for all older people. These centers sometimes pose limitations for people with developmental disabilities. Thus, some of their programs cannot be adapted so easily, intellectually or experientially, for older adults such as Gary, Charles, and James, who need a slower pace (Krout, 1989). Nevertheless, the men did participate in senior centers from time to time when the centers offered trips and other activities.

With respect to the other service sectors, such as health and mental health services, Gary, Charles, and James were included as patients in local medical clinics. How these different services affected the lives of the three men is instructive because inclusion, as a philosophy of care, increasingly must be supported by an openness and flexibility on the part of service organizations.

CONCLUSIONS

With the increase in the older adult population, concern about people with developmental disabilities who are aging is increasing. How this concern is to be channeled eventually into programs and services is difficult to predict. Certainly, in the late 1990s, federal funding under the Older Americans Act of 1965 and its subsequent amendments for programs such as housing and senior centers was severely strained. Conservative legislative trends of the 1990s, such as stricter disability benefit reviews that incorporate increasingly narrow federal interpretations affecting children (Janofsky, 1996), were disquieting in that they could lead one to believe that older people with disabilities might be affected next. Whether the political influence of the older population and the constituencies that represent the disability community can be effective in counteracting these trends remains to be seen. State governments are not likely to fill in the gaps. It appears, therefore, that in the 21st century, increasing efforts must be made to empower older people with disabilities, along with their families, caregivers, and service providers, so that together they are better able to advocate for themselves. Success in these efforts should help them to enjoy the options and opportunities available to people without disabilities.

REFERENCES

American Psychiatric Association. (1985). *Principles of medical ethics with annotations especially applicable to psychiatry.* Washington, DC: Author.

Americans with Disabilities Act (ADA) of 1990, PL 101-336, 42 U.S.C. §§ 12101 *et seq.*

Baumeister, A.A. (1988). The new morbidity: implications for prevention. In J.A. Stark, F. Menolascino, H. Albarelli, & V.C. Gray (Eds.), *Mental retardation and mental health: Classification, diagnosis, treatment, services* (pp. 71–80). New York: Springer-Verlag New York.

Beauchamp, T.L., & Childress, J.F. (1994). *Principles of biomedical ethics* (4th ed.). New York: Oxford University Press.

Beaver, M.L., & Miller, D.A. (1992). *Clinical social work practice with the elderly: Primary, secondary, and tertiary intervention* (2nd ed.). Belmont, CA: Wadsworth.

Bicknell, J. (1994). Old age and mental handicap. In J.R.M. Copeland, M.T. Abou-Saleh, & D.G. Blazer (Eds.), *Principles and practice of geriatric psychiatry* (pp. 815–979). New York: John Wiley & Sons.

Bradley, V.J. (1990). Conceptual issues in quality assurance. In V.J. Bradley & H.A. Bersani (Eds.), *Quality assurance for individuals with developmental disabilities: It's everybody's business* (pp. 3–15). Baltimore: Paul H. Brookes Publishing Co.

Cox, E.O. (1994). *Empowerment-oriented social work practice with the elderly.* Pacific Grove, CA: Brooks/Cole.

Dinerstein, R., Herr, S.S., & O'Sullivan, J. (1999). *A guide to consent.* Washington, DC: American Association on Mental Retardation.

Education for All Handicapped Children Act of 1975, PL 94-142, 20 U.S.C. §§ 1400 *et seq.*

Flexer, R. (1988). Rights of persons with developmental disabilities. In M. Stroud & E. Sutton (Eds.), *Expanding options for older adults with developmental disabilities: A practical guide to achieving community access* (pp. 197–207). Baltimore: Paul H. Brookes Publishing Co.

Gallagher, H.G. (1994). *FDR's splendid deception* (Rev. ed.). Arlington, VA: Vandamere Press.

Gant, S.A. (1990). The Connecticut model. In V.J. Bradley & H.A. Bersani (Eds.), *Quality assurance for individuals with developmental disabilities: It's everybody's business* (pp. 302–321). Baltimore: Paul H. Brookes Publishing Co.

Gelfand, D.E. (1994). *Aging and ethnicity: Knowledge and services.* New York: Springer Publishing Co.

Gibson, J.W., Rabkin, J., & Munson, R. (1992). Critical issues in serving the developmentally disabled elderly. *Journal of Gerontological Social Work, 19,* 35–49.

Hartman, A. (1981). The family: A central focus for practice. *Social Work, 26,* 7–15.

Hawkins, B.A. (1993). Leisure participation and life satisfaction of older adults with mental retardation and Down syndrome. In E. Sutton, A.R. Factor, B.A. Hawkins, T. Heller, & G.B. Seltzer (Eds.), *Older adults with developmental disabilities: Optimizing choice and change* (pp. 141–155). Baltimore: Paul H. Brookes Publishing Co.

Holosko, M.J., & Feit, M.D. (Eds.) (1991). *Social work practice with the elderly.* Toronto: Canadian Scholars Press.

Individuals with Disabilities Education Act (IDEA) Amendments of 1991, PL 102-119, 20 U.S.C. §§ 1400 *et seq.*

Individuals with Disabilities Education Act (IDEA) Amendments of 1997, PL 105-17, 20 U.S.C. §§ 1400 *et seq.*

Individuals with Disabilities Education Act (IDEA) of 1990, PL 101-476, 20 U.S.C. §§ 1400 *et seq.*

Janofsky, M. (1996, December 23). Disabled children's families brace for benefit cuts. *New York Times,* p. A12.

Kastenbaum, R. (1964). *New thoughts on old age.* New York: Springer Publishing Co.

Kauppi, D.R., & Jones, K.C. (1985). The role of the community agency in serving older mentally retarded persons. In M.P. Janicki & H.M. Wisniewski (Eds.), *Aging and developmental disabilities: Issues and approaches* (pp. 403–410). Baltimore: Paul H. Brookes Publishing Co.

Kleinfield, N.R. (1997a, June 23). A room of his own: For James Velez, a room of his own at last. *New York Times,* p. A1.

Kleinfield, N.R. (1997b, June 22). A room of his own: Patient's quest for a normal life, at a price. *New York Times,* p. A1.

Kleinfield, N.R. (1997c, June 24). A room of his own: With round-the-clock help, young man joins the world. *New York Times,* p. A1.

Knoll, J.A. (1990). Defining quality in residential services. In V.J. Bradley & H.A. Bersani (Eds.), *Quality assurance for individuals with developmental disabilities: It's everybody's business* (pp. 235–261). Baltimore: Paul H. Brookes Publishing Co.

Krout, J.A. (1989). *Senior centers in America.* Westport, CT: Greenwood Publishing Group.

Lippman, L., & Loberg, D.E. (1985). An overview of developmental disabilities. In M.P. Janicki & H.M. Wisniewski (Eds.), *Aging and developmental disabilities: Issues and approaches* (pp. 41–58). Baltimore: Paul H. Brookes Publishing Co.

Lowy, L. (1991). *Social work with the aging* (2nd ed.). Prospect Heights, IL: Waveland Press.

Luckasson, R., Coulter, D.L., Polloway, E.A., Reiss, S., Schalock, R.L., Snell, M.E., Spitalnik, D.M., & Stark, J.A. (1992). *Mental retardation: Definitions, classification, and systems of supports* (Special 9th ed.). Washington, DC: American Association on Mental Retardation.

Mackelprang, R.W., & Salsgiver, R.O. (1996). People with disabilities and social work: Historical and contemporary issues. *Social Work, 41,* 7–14.

Maternal and Child Health and Mental Retardation Planning Amendments of 1963, PL 88-156, 77 Stat. 273.

Mental Retardation Facilities and Community Mental Health Centers Construction Act of 1963, PL 88-164, 77 Stat. 282.

Merton, R.K. (1967). *Social theory and social structure.* New York: Free Press.

Murdach, A.D. (1996). Beneficence re-examined: Protective intervention in mental health. *Social Work, 41,* 26–32.

New York State Association for Retarded Children v. Rockefeller, 357 F. Supp. 752 (E.D.N.Y. 1973).

O'Brien, J. (1990). Developing high quality services for people with developmental disabilities. In V.J. Bradley & H.A. Bersani (Eds.), *Quality assurance for individuals with developmental disabilities: It's everybody's business* (pp. 17–31). Baltimore: Paul H. Brookes Publishing Co.

Older Americans Act of 1965, PL 89-73, 42 U.S.C. §§ 3001 *et seq.*

Pederson, E.L., Chaikin, M., Koehler, D., Campbell, A., & Arcand, M. (1993). Strategies that close the gap between research, planning, and self-advocacy. In E. Sutton, A.R. Factor, B.A. Hawkins, T. Heller, & G.B. Seltzer (Eds.), *Older adults with developmental disabilities: Optimizing choice and change* (pp. 277–325). Baltimore: Paul H. Brookes Publishing Co.

President's Committee on Mental Retardation (PCMR). (1977). *Mental retardation: Past and present.* Washington, DC: Author.

Pryor, C.B., Kent, C., McGunn, C., & LeRoy, B. (1996). Redesigning social work in inclusive schools. *Social Work, 41,* 668–676.

Riley, M.W., & Kahn, R.L. (1994). Introduction: The mismatch between people and structure. In M.W. Riley, R.L. Kahn, & A. Foner (Eds.), *Age and structural lag: Society's failure to provide meaningful opportunities in work, family, and leisure* (pp. 1–12). New York: John Wiley & Sons.

Rosner, R., & Weinstock, R. (Eds.). (1990). *Ethical practice in psychiatry.* New York: Plenum Press.

Rubenstein, R.L. (1986). *Singular paths: Old men living alone.* New York: Columbia University Press.

Sadavoy, J., & Leszcz, M. (Eds.). (1987). *Treating the elderly with psychotherapy: The scope for change in later life.* Madison, CT: International Universities Press.

Scharlach, A.E., & Kaye, L.W. (1997). *Controversial issues in aging.* Needham Heights, MA: Allyn & Bacon.

Seltzer, M.M. (1988). Standards and patterns of service utilization by elderly persons with mental retardation. *Mental Retardation, 26,* 181–185.

Seltzer, M.M., & Seltzer, G.B. (1992). Aging persons with developmental disabilities. In F.J. Turner (Ed.), *Mental health and the elderly: A social work perspective* (pp. 136–150). New York: Free Press.

Simon, B.L. (1994). *The empowerment tradition in American social work: A history.* New York: Columbia University Press.

Stock, R.W. (1996, December 26). Centers for the elderly enter a new age. *New York Times,* pp. C1, C8.

Stroud, M., & Sutton, E. (1988). *Expanding options for older adults with developmental disabilities: A practical guide to achieving community access.* Baltimore: Paul H. Brookes Publishing Co.

Sugg, D.K. (1997, March 23). The forever children. *Baltimore Sun,* pp. 1A, 14A–15A.

Sutton, E., Sterns, H.L., & Park, L.S.S. (1993). Realities of retirement and pre-retirement planning. In E. Sutton, A.R. Factor, B.A. Hawkins, T. Heller, & G.B. Seltzer (Eds.), *Older adults with developmental disabilities: Optimizing choice and change* (pp. 95–106). Baltimore: Paul H. Brookes Publishing Co.

Tobin, S., & Gustafson, J. (1987). What do we do differently with elderly clients? *Journal of Gerontological Social Work, 10,* 107–120.

Townsend v. Treadway, No. 6500 (M.D. Tenn. September 21, 1973).

Whittaker, J.K., & Tracy, E.M. (1989). *Social treatment: An introduction to interpersonal helping in social work practice* (2nd ed.). Hawthorne, NY: Aldine de Gruyter.

Wolfensberger, W. (1972). *The principle of normalization in the human services.* Toronto: National Institute of Mental Retardation.

Wray, L.D. (1990). The role of quality assurance in public agencies. In V.J. Bradley & H.A. Bersani (Eds.), *Quality assurance for individuals with developmental disabilities: It's everybody's business* (pp. 123–135). Baltimore: Paul H. Brookes Publishing Co.

Wyatt v. Stickney, 344 F. Supp. 387 (M.D. Ala. 1972), aff'd sub nom. Wyatt v. Aderholt, 503 F.2d 1305 (5th Cir. 1974).

19

Managed Care

Stanley S. Herr and Sean L. Brohawn

Managed care in the United States has altered irreversibly the relationship between consumers and their health care providers. Some view it as the answer to the explosive growth of health care costs and as a way to ensure a more efficient use of limited health care resources. Managed care, however, also has demanded increased vigilance and sophistication from consumers, who thus far have consisted primarily of workers receiving managed health care in connection with their employment. The typical managed care enrollee is faced with charting a path through various plans and restrictions, gaining an understanding of rapidly changing health care relationships, and responding to decisions denying requested care or denying payment for care already received.

The rise of publicly funded managed care has only underscored these difficulties. In the 1990s, both the Medicare and Medicaid systems have moved rapidly away from the traditional fee-for-service (FFS) system, toward various forms of managed care. The Medicare and Medicaid systems have introduced growing numbers of people with developmental disabilities to managed care, though many remain unenrolled or partially enrolled. Yet publicly funded managed care has not alleviated the need for savvy decision making and advocacy by or for vulnerable beneficiaries such as older people with developmental disabilities. Given the momentum behind managed care, states must review traditional managed care systems thoroughly to ensure that these systems are appropriate for older individuals with developmental disabilities and fundamentally retool managed health care to account for the health and long-term habilitation needs of this population. And even though Congress had shelved measures for patients' rights as of 1998, proposals for such legislation reappeared at national and state levels. Indeed, the Texas and Missouri state legislatures have given consumers in their states the right to sue HMOs, and Maryland Governor Parris Glendening announced his support for such legislation in his state (Waldron & Zorzi, 1998).

327

Managed care funded through Medicare and Medicaid seeks greater cost efficiency through emphasis on preventive care, coordination of the facets of each individual's care, and cost-conscious management of resources—all facilitated by modern information systems technology. In order for managed care to become a reality
for older people with cognitive or other developmental disabilities, however, it
must use the devices of managed care when appropriate without borrowing too
much from the clinically based models that have defined managed care thus far.
The federal government and state governments must weigh issues such as access to
and quality of care; rights to dispute or appeal adverse care decisions; and methods
of integrating long-term care, personal care services and supports, and the acute
health care needs of older people with developmental disabilities. Maintaining and
improving their outcomes in a system of managed care is a tough challenge not only
for government but also for the health care industry and people with developmental disabilities and their advocates.

This chapter discusses some of the structures and mechanisms that government agencies and managed care entities might employ to ensure both the appropriate delivery of care and the effective review of adverse care decisions. It begins
with a brief introduction to Medicare, Medicaid, and managed care and provides an
overview of the present delivery of acute and long-term care to older adults with
developmental disabilities. Next, it addresses the future of managed care for these
individuals and problems with the wholesale adoption of existing managed care
models. A discussion of the efficacy of grievance procedures and rights to appeal in
reviewing adverse coverage decisions follows. The chapter concludes with an assessment of the utility of managed care devices in serving the health and habilitation needs of older people with developmental disabilities and in supporting their
ability to reside in community environments.

PUBLICLY FUNDED CARE AND
OLDER PEOPLE WITH DEVELOPMENTAL DISABILITIES

There are more than 526,000 adults ages 60 and older with mental retardation or
other developmental disabilities in the United States, and this number may double
by 2030 (American Association on Mental Retardation, 1996). In addition to acute
care services traditionally provided by managed care organizations (MCOs), older
people with developmental disabilities frequently require long-term care for either
chronic health conditions or daily habilitation needs. Much of the long-term habilitative care for older people with developmental disabilities is provided privately by
family, friends, or other informal caregivers (General Accounting Office, 1994). In a
study of the U.S. distribution of all individuals with developmental disabilities by
living arrangement, Braddock (1998) found that 1.89 million live with family caregivers as compared with almost 400,000 in residential facilities. Some forms of long-
term care may be paid for by either Medicare or Medicaid, depending on the type of
service. Medicare generally covers in-home skilled nursing services or therapy following a hospital stay; under Medicaid, states have the option to cover nonmedical
personal care services based in the home or community. In 1995, 31 states chose to
cover personal care services under Medicaid (Kenney, Rajan, & Soscia, 1998).

Although public health care expenditures for people with disabilities rose drastically between the mid-1970s and the end of the 20th century (Health Care Financing Administration [HCFA], 1995), these individuals and in particular individ-

uals with developmental disabilities thus far largely have not been enrolled in comprehensive, mandatory managed care programs. The term *comprehensive* refers to acute health care, long-term care for ongoing health conditions, and habilitative care or personal care services, with the latter being an integral part of the total care needs of many older adults with developmental disabilities and an essential element of any coordinated health care plan. At present, however, there are no operational examples of mandatory, comprehensive managed care for developmental disabilities services for older people (Hemp & Braddock, 1998; Smith & Ashbaugh, 1995). Since 1989, mandatory managed health care combined with long-term care for people with developmental disabilities has been a reality in only one state: Arizona (Hemp & Braddock, 1998). Comparable proposals were considered in Michigan and Rhode Island (Hemp & Braddock, 1998). It is clear that complex decisions lie ahead—not only in how to manage such care but also in how much care to manage.

Medicare

The Medicare program is administered by the U.S. federal government. It covers acute health care for people 65 years of age or older and people younger than age 65 who have a qualifying disability (Social Security Act, 1935/1998). Medicare Part A generally covers hospital care, skilled nursing facility care, and hospice care. Medicare Part B generally covers physicians' charges and laboratory fees, but the average Medicare recipient must pay a premium for Part B coverage.

People age 65 or older qualify for Medicare benefits without an inquiry about disabling conditions. Adults younger than 65 years of age, however, may qualify based on the existence of a disability. Mental retardation as a basis for Medicare eligibility is evaluated on clinical findings alone. Other developmental disabilities are evaluated both on clinical findings and the existence of functional limitations such as difficulties with activities of daily living.

Because people 65 years of age or older automatically qualify for Medicare, HCFA reports data separately for these people and for people younger than age 65 who have a qualifying disability. Undoubtedly, many individuals age 65 or older have disabilities that separately would entitle them to Medicare benefits. As of June 1996, HCFA reported a Medicare enrollment of more than 1.7 million for people ages 55–64 years with a qualifying disability of any kind (HCFA, 1998a). By comparison, more than 33.2 million people were enrolled on the basis of age in June 1996 (HCFA, 1998a).

Medicaid

The Medicaid program is administered primarily by individual states within broad federal guidelines. Accounting for 13% of state spending in 1993, Medicaid is one of the largest single items in many state budgets (White House Conference on Aging, 1995). Each state has discretion to tailor its own Medicaid program, at least 50% of which is funded by the federal government. One obvious consequence of this structure is that, unlike Medicare, each state offers different Medicaid benefits, grievance procedures, and rights of appeal.

Eligibility for Medicaid is means tested. Under the traditional Medicaid program in most states, individuals who receive Supplemental Security Income (SSI) payments because of the existence of a disability generally are eligible for Medicaid. Individuals who are entitled to Medicare Part A who have income at or below the federal poverty level and resources at or below twice the set SSI limit, are termed *categorically needy,* thus qualifying for at least payment of Medicare Part A and Part B premiums and Medicare deductibles and coinsurance (HCFA, 1998b). Medicare recipients who do not meet the criterion for categorical need but are able, because of their medical expenses, to "spend down" to Medicaid financial eligibility are termed *medically needy.* These individuals generally are provided Medicaid payments as a supplement to Medicare coverage, and services are provided by Medicaid providers.

Individuals who are dually eligible for Medicare and Medicaid under either of the previous criteria are termed Qualified Medical Beneficiaries (QMBs) for the categorically needy, and generally non-QMBs for the medically needy (HCFA, 1998b). Because of the high cost of acute and long-term care for older people with developmental disabilities, many people in this population are dually eligible for Medicare and Medicaid assistance, either as QMBs or non-QMBs.

Dually eligible status has important implications for Medicaid coverage. Generally speaking, because states do not contribute to Medicare but contribute as much as 50% toward their own Medicaid programs, they have an interest in providing Medicaid coverage as a supplement to Medicare coverage but no interest in paying for services under Medicaid that could be paid for entirely by the federal government through Medicare (Kenney et al., 1998). States therefore have an incentive to exclude dual eligibles from Medicaid care that can be provided under Medicare. In the 1990s, some states have been able to waive Medicaid restrictions under Medicaid managed care plans in order to coordinate Medicare and Medicaid funding, and the acute and long-term care benefits provided by the two, for the benefit of dually eligible individuals (Smith & Ashbaugh, 1995).

Medicare and Medicaid Managed Care

The term *managed care* refers to "a collection of strategies for containing cost and utilization" of care-related services (Smith & Ashbaugh, 1995, p. 16). Managed care includes "strategies for controlling costs and improving access that focus on primary care and prepaid arrangements as an alternative to traditional, FFS-based, retrospective reimbursement of costs" (Hurley, Freund, & Paul, 1993, p. 6). Managed health care can be as simple as gatekeeping structures that screen access to care or as complex as systems that coordinate all of the various types of acute and long-term care that an individual may need through contracts for the provision of this care at a reduced cost. Managed care may also control direct access to specialists and reduce costly emergency and inpatient care by increasing preventive care (Hurley, Freund, & Paul, 1993). One study of Medicaid MCOs concluded that managed care in Medicaid saves money, and that these savings are greater where states mandate consumers' participation (Hurley, Freund, & Paul, 1993).

In many managed care environments in the public sector, the governmental entity or payor prepays a fixed per-patient or "capitated" sum to MCOs, and in return MCOs assume the risk of covering the ultimate cost of providing the prescribed care to a defined consumer population. This transference of the risk of providing all of the covered care that a certain population needs is a central cost-saving tool of managed care. It allows governments to negotiate a ceiling for health care expenses and thereby predict total costs. MCOs are left with an incentive to provide this risk-based care at the lowest possible cost. Many respond to this challenge in part by focusing on preventive care for acute health problems and coordinating the care of people with complex needs.

Enrollment in a Medicare managed care plan is still optional for beneficiaries. As of December 1995, only approximately 10% of all Medicare beneficiaries were enrolled in a Medicare managed care plan (HCFA, 1998a). There was a rapid shift toward Medicare managed care in the 1990s, however. Although managed care has been an option under Medicare since 1985, the percentage of Medicare beneficiaries enrolled in managed care plans doubled between 1993 and 1996 (Lamphere, Neuman, Langwell, & Sherman, 1997). Of the various types of Medicare managed care, the vast majority of beneficiaries in 1995 were enrolled in a risk-based plan (HCFA, 1998a). Some HMOs have withdrawn from the Medicare program, however, creating disruptions for their beneficiaries (Hilzenrath & Goldstein, 1998).

In contrast to Medicare managed care plans, states can provide Medicaid plans that choose from among many managed care combinations and define the particular services and products to be covered. States may also extend Medicaid coverage to populations previously served by the state's safety net or state-only health insurance programs, thus taking advantage of available federal funding. As with other forms of managed care, states usually restrict the choices of beneficiaries within these programs. To achieve this freedom, states must apply to the U.S. Secretary of the Department of Health and Human Services (HHS) for a waiver of the federal regulations that guarantee freedom of choice in FFS care.

States may alter traditional Medicaid eligibility through two provisions of federal law that permit waivers of existing restrictions. Under both waiver types, states must apply for and periodically renew the exemptions. The first provision, Section 1915(b) of the Social Security Act (PL 74-271), generally permits states to restrict recipients' freedom of choice among providers, and to limit Medicaid-covered services to only designated providers. Under traditional FFS Medicaid, beneficiaries could choose any qualified provider of Medicaid covered services. The 1915(b) waivers are called *freedom of choice waivers* because they restrict this choice.

The Section 1115 research and demonstration waiver permits states to design innovative budget-neutral solutions to various health and welfare problems. Section 1115 programs may replace an entire existing state Medicaid system, thereby mandating participation in the new program for all state Medicaid recipients (Hurley, Freund, & Paul, 1993). It is under Section 1115 Medicaid waivers that states can include previously unserved populations in Medicaid managed care.

As part of the Balanced Budget Act (BBA) of 1997 (PL 105-33), the federal government permits states to place adults with disabilities in mandatory managed care programs without going through the Medicaid waiver process (42 U.S.C. §§ 1395eee, 1396d). The net result of that legislation was a grant of power to states to shift older adults at will into a managed care system with poorer safeguards. The system—payments to, and coverage of benefits under, Programs of All-Inclusive Care for the Elderly (PACE)—applies to adults ages 55 and older and provides for "services to such enrollees through a comprehensive, multidisciplinary health and social services delivery system which integrates acute and long-term care services pursuant to regulations" (42 U.S.C. §§ 1395ee, 1395eee[b][1][C]). It is too early to assess the impact of such mandatory programs on older people with developmental disabilities. At the turn of the 21st century, mandatory enrollment in managed care is initiated on the state level. By either constructing Medicaid waiver plans or implementing a mandatory PACE plan, states are free to require recipients of Medicaid to enroll in MCOs.

PROBLEMS OF MANAGED CARE

Although most older people with developmental disabilities are not enrolled in mandatory managed care programs, the trend is toward their inclusion in such programs. The rising cost of health care is the primary force behind the rise of managed care systems. This trend, coupled with the already expensive care of older people with developmental disabilities, suggests that states and the federal government will be under increasing pressure to bring this group into managed care schemes. The PACE legislation is but one such initiative.

In many ways, however, the managed care environment is not ready to serve all of the acute and long-term health and habilitative needs of people with disabilities. If such a shift were implemented with haste, it would have a profound impact on individuals' rights to services and would likely change significantly how those services are coordinated and provided. In the future, MCOs may emerge that understand the needs of this population better and are better able (and willing) to coordinate complex, heterogeneous services. For this to occur, government payors must make coverage and funding decisions based on care needs rather than on immediate political pressures, and the provision of managed care services to older people with developmental disabilities must be reasonably profitable for participating private sector MCOs.

Financial Climate

Competition is tough in many managed care markets, and it is increasingly difficult for MCOs to survive with the resulting decrease in revenues. Many MCOs will not survive this competition but will merge into ever larger MCOs or cease to exist. Capitation rates for Medicaid populations have been reduced to such an extent that both for-profit and not-for-profit MCOs seeking to serve Medicaid populations frequently must compensate for disappointing earnings with higher rates for private sector patients (New York State Association for Retarded Children [NYSARC], 1998).

One source of such disappointment is the tendency of states to alter the requirements for serving the state's managed care population for unpredictable political and budgetary reasons. One advocacy group claimed that "[d]ecisions on capitated rates . . . are driven by rapidly fluctuating state politics and budget circumstances rather than by actuarial data on the health needs and real costs associated with serving a given population" (NYSARC, 1998, p. 10). In public sector managed care, where capitation rates are relatively low to begin with, the threat of reductions to existing capitation rates that are not tied to the real expenses of providing care may cause MCOs either to cut corners in existing care or to avoid providing care to Medicare and Medicaid populations altogether (Hilzenrath & Goldstein, 1998).

As a group thus far excluded from comprehensive, mandatory managed care, older people with developmental disabilities present problems to governments and MCOs seeking to devise new capitation rates. Bringing them into mainstream managed care means that new provider–consumer relationships and disruptions to existing relationships will occur. Providing interventions for the acute episodes is often complicated by communication difficulties or guardianship issues. Thus, physicians who are accustomed to providing care for the acute conditions of consumers without disabilities may need additional training and time to adjust to serving a broader consumer group.

In addition, MCOs have little experience with capitation rates for the long-term care needs of older people with developmental disabilities and even less experience with rates for habilitative care. The largest MCOs have scant experience in serving people with developmental disabilities in any care environment. These MCOs have decades of experience in predicting the cost of acute care for people who are familiar with managed health care systems. The data that have been collected on the costs of acute care for the typical private sector consumer should not be used to set capitation rates for the acute care of people with disabilities. Instead, the larger MCOs or government payors must conduct new assessments of the costs of the various types of services for people with developmental disabilities. Governments must require such assessments before shifting people with developmental disabilities into prepaid managed care systems. As the 21st century looms, several key questions remain unanswered. How will MCOs define the developmental disabilities population? Which specific formulas will be used to delineate new risk categories? How and to what extent will people with developmental disabilities undergo the transition to managed care?

Some smaller, provider-based MCOs have experienced success with Medicaid managed care for people with developmental disabilities. This suggests that larger MCOs might serve new managed care populations by merging with successful specialty MCOs (NYSARC, 1998). Such provider-based specialty MCOs are more successful because, generally, they are formed from hospitals and providers that have served the developmental disabilities population under the FFS system. They have the experience necessary to understand the needs of people with developmental disabilities and are well versed in coordinating acute, chronic, and habilitative care needs and related services. These providers are also likely to be experienced in dealing with government payors under Medicare and Medicaid. Although such organizations also find it increasingly difficult to survive in a climate of centralization and economies of scale, successful specialty MCOs should find larger MCOs eager to combine, in various ways, with the goal of reaching new markets. In addition, University Affiliated Programs can be a resource to MCOs in diagnosis and assessment, in identifying cost-effective treatments, and in developing practice guidelines and quality assurance indicators (Birenbaum & Cohen, 1998).

This business climate suggests that broader, mandatory inclusion of older people with developmental disabilities in MCOs could take place in the early part of the 21st century as states continue to look for ways to reduce health costs and MCOs become more willing to accept the lower level of payment associated with providing such care. As the overall profitability of managed care declines as a result of competition and market saturation, the marginal profits to be had in publicly funded managed care seem more attractive, especially for larger MCOs that can take advantage of large, centralized administration and information processing (NYSARC, 1998). Although the current climate favors MCOs that can expand their membership, there is still a certain ignorance among larger MCOs of the needs of people with developmental disabilities and a reluctance to contract with government payors for the provision of comprehensive services. Indeed, with the exception of Arizona, no state has both acute and long-term care coverage for this group; however, eight other states do require individuals with disabilities to enroll in Medicaid managed care (Hemp, Braddock, & Westrich, 1998).

Promises of Managed Care

The potential for superior coordination of beneficiaries' health needs makes managed care attractive; it poses a chance to reduce health care costs while improving care outcomes through better management and efficiency. The goal of efficiency is especially attractive in the provision of complex care. In an empirical study of functional outcomes of older people in Medicare risk contracts, six doctors concluded that "administrative efforts in HMOs may smooth the way for elderly enrollees who need more effective management of multiple medical and social problems" (Retchin & Clement, 1992, p. 653). In their view, such management not only can improve overall care but also can alleviate administrative complexities that older individuals receiving multispecialty care often experience. Older people with developmental disabilities and their advocates may also benefit from simplification of care decisions through improved management.

This administrative aspect of managed care has both service-integration and information-tracking implications. Ideally, individuals with complex health needs would receive more appropriate and more efficient services because of cooperation among care providers with diverse expertise. Many individuals with developmental disabilities benefit from service coordination based on the interdisciplinary team model. In the future, however, MCOs may be able to apply computer technology to better assess the use of health services and consumers' outcomes. By contrast, the traditional FFS system tends to place care consistency and assessment in the hands of consumers, notwithstanding their ability to switch providers at any time and leave the results of previous treatments behind.

The prospect of greater coordination, however, raises questions about who will resolve conflicting care recommendations and how much participation of consumers, families, and advocates will be allowed. Should the primary medical care provider or the specialist have the final word on service decisions? Some flexibility is properly left in the hands of the consumer. Although the answers to such questions may not be clear, an approach is suggested by the Medicaid waiver process itself. By implementing localized models of managed care for people with developmental disabilities, states can test various managed care combinations and tailor programs to fit local needs. One such example is Iowa's county-by-county managed care plans, an extremely decentralized approach that is reportedly successful in many of the state's 99 counties. To succeed at this, however, states must assess intrastate differences and the effectiveness of other states' waiver programs as well as their own.

Under managed care, Medicare and Medicaid consumers also can benefit from stricter measures to avoid hospitalization or institutionalization unless absolutely necessary. HMOs typically favor the use of ambulatory care and chronic care services in place of more expensive inpatient care. This emphasis on outpatient care has been linked to reduced hospital use among older adults as well as reduced functional declines for older consumers who are able to avoid long hospital stays (Retchin & Clement, 1992). Professionals recognize that "[o]lder adults with mental retardation have many of the same age related concerns as other older adults" (AAMR, 1996, p. 2). As with the older adult population without disabilities, outpatient care allows people with developmental disabilities to remain in the community, where they can maintain contact with family and friends, and participate in activities such as aging services, recreational programs, and "later-life planning educational programs" (AAMR, 1996, p. 2).

Managed care for older people with developmental disabilities may also expand access to previously uninsured people. The lure of additional federal funding under Medicaid waivers has prompted some states to apply savings from the shift to managed care toward coverage of previously uninsured state residents or coverage of new types of care. Oregon and Kentucky, for example, used waivers to open up Medicaid to all residents living below the federal poverty level. Although states must still pay their share, the Medicaid waivers grant states the discretion to try to reduce uninsured people's reliance on urban safety nets such as emergency rooms. In bringing more of the uninsured population into managed care, states should be able to save money and increase the body of information on poor residents' use of health care services. States cannot determine with certainty the number of uninsured and untreated people with developmental disabilities who might benefit from such an extension of Medicaid eligibility.

Finally, older people with developmental disabilities and their allies potentially could benefit from having an increased voice in decisions that might affect their state's Medicaid enrollees. This greater say can happen through greater representation on MCO boards and payor committees as well as more explicit grievance and appeals processes. When states implement Medicaid waiver plans, they are free to require private companies to include enrollees and advocates on decision-making committees as a condition of participation by such companies and to include these constituencies on state oversight committees. For example, in the development of Maryland's Section 1115 waiver, advocates and consumers were appointed to advisory committees that provided input in the development of Maryland's proposal with assistance from the University of Maryland–Baltimore County Center for Health Program Development. In addition, public hearings were held before and after the proposal was developed. The proposal ultimately included provisions for a consumer hotline and state enforcement of quality standards with the goal of ensuring "routine assessments of patient satisfaction as an integral component" (Wasserman, 1996, p. 27). Frequently, however, such prospective input is advisory only, and there is no guarantee that states will vigorously enforce the standards that are adopted. Although the Maryland plan called for routine assessments of consumer satisfaction in 1996, as of October 1998, no satisfaction assessments had been conducted.

The ultimate option available to dissatisfied consumers is to leave their current plan if a meaningful alternative is offered. Leaving a plan, or exiting, is usually an option for private MCO members who become dissatisfied with their plan (Rodwin, 1996). In the private sector, the exiting reaction has a natural regulating effect: MCOs must improve consumer relations or experience additional market pressure (Hirschman, 1970).

In public sector managed care, however, exit is not always feasible or desirable. In plans offering few provider options, the exit reaction is likely to result only in exchange enrollment, in which individual plans maintain a relatively constant number of enrollees despite movement between the plans. Moreover, as providers themselves withdraw from certain markets, consumer options shrink (Hilzenrath & Goldstein, 1998). Lawmakers must therefore enact meaningful protections tailored to the needs of people with developmental disabilities and require the compliance of MCOs.

Anticipated Problems

At its inception, managed care served the acute health care needs of sophisticated consumers who were willing to surrender some choices in return for cheaper health insurance. In treating people with developmental disabilities, however, it must be stressed that many of the basic assumptions inherent in the design of traditional MCOs either do not fit at all or must be reconsidered. Although the acute care needs of people with developmental disabilities are frequently analogous to the acute care needs of populations traditionally served by managed care, the majority of MCOs have little experience with older people with such disabilities. In any mandatory shift toward managed care for this group, MCOs would have to conduct studies, extrapolate information based on FFS data, and generally overcome the inability or unwillingness to coordinate services for people with developmental disabilities (NYSARC, 1998).

There are many other concerns surrounding the shift to managed care that are specific to vulnerable populations such as older people with developmental disabilities. As previously mentioned, a primary concern is the adjustment of capitation rates to fit the additional expense of complex or comprehensive care. Capitation rates are based on risk adjustment formulas that attempt to categorize services and recipients in order to reliably predict actual expenses. If capitation rates are implemented in ignorance of the actual costs of providing services within the new systems, older people with developmental disabilities may become segregated into a few provider-based MCO plans, eventually causing these plans to incur disproportionate expenses compared with plans able to discourage such enrollment (Holahan, Coughlin, Ku, Lipson, & Rajan, 1995). Appropriate capitation rates thus have important implications for the ultimate quality of services for people with developmental disabilities. Because the body of information on the use and costs of care for people with developmental disabilities is inadequate to the task, fresh risk adjustment formulas must be created.

The issues of adequate dispersal of people with developmental disabilities among existing plans and integration of the care that is provided present several additional concerns. Doctors who are unaccustomed to providing even acute health care to this population may need time to adjust to their new consumers. To address this, capitation rates may take into account, for example, the fact that acute health procedures may require more time for individuals with developmental disabilities.

Other controversies arise if states decide to carve out complex health care or even the population itself from mainstream care. The financial and political climate at the turn of the 21st century suggests that the fuller inclusion of older people with developmental disabilities will continue to occur. So, when consumers and advocates hold on to existing provider relationships by advocating the carving out of entire groups, they risk being pulled into managed care at a later time, when key decisions that they might have influenced have been made already. Carve-outs may nudge people with developmental disabilities from community living environments to more restrictive and more centralized environments. Although managed care is primarily driven by the financial imperative, it can also promote greater inclusion in general health care and superior tracking of service use and care outcomes. Effective service provider–consumer relationships can be maintained through waiver program design, without resorting to mass carve-outs. For this reason, sweeping carve-outs should be used when possible as temporary, transitional structures.

Additional barriers to inclusion of older people with developmental disabilities in managed care stem from the unpredictable consumer behavior of such groups within a managed care system and the inability of MCOs to coordinate complex care effectively for technological and financial reasons. MCOs may also balk at the labor-intensive multidisciplinary assessment and team planning approaches common to the field of developmental disabilities. Anticipated improvements in information systems management technologies are likely to enable MCOs to achieve greater control over service use and better coordinate various levels of care. In addition, the information that is fed into these management systems is likely to improve independently as consolidation, experience, and data collection erode barriers to more inclusive service of people with developmental disabilities. It will eventually be feasible economically, and more possible technologically, to serve older people with developmental disabilities in inclusive, publicly funded managed care environments.

Finally, provisions for the exercise of consumers' voice, grievance procedures, and appeal rights assume the existence of a vigilant consumer—an informed and autonomous individual providing the ultimate quality check. Consumers in MCOs, however, lack purchasing power and may not have the resources, knowledge, or desire to disagree with inappropriate care decisions. This problem may be particularly acute in the population of older adults with developmental disabilities, a group that may also be at unjustified risk of denial of or reduction in medical treatment. For these reasons, advocacy is a crucial issue in the transition to managed care and its ongoing operation.

GRIEVANCE AND APPEALS PROCESSES

One of the most controversial and commonly sought reforms is a stronger grievance and appeals process. Such processes under both Medicare and Medicaid permit frequent review of care and coverage decisions by recipients or their surrogates. The federal government has promulgated regulations that explicitly delineate a formal grievance and appeals process for Medicare. By contrast, Medicaid grievances and appeals are handled at the state level within broad federal guidelines, and therefore they vary among the states. There are many special concerns regarding the navigation of older people with developmental disabilities through the multitiered Medicare appeals process, and additional concerns under Medicaid as notice and fair hearing rights are delegated from states to MCOs.

Medicare regulations require MCOs to maintain internal grievance procedures (42 C.F.R. § 417.436[a][2], 1997). In addition, an adverse decision in response to a coverage or intervention request triggers specific notice provisions. A beneficiary may choose to appeal a coverage decision made by an MCO, invoking in turn a five-level appeal process (42 C.F.R. §§ 417.600–417.638, 1997). Within this appeal process, an aggrieved Medicare recipient has the right to the following:

1. Reconsideration of certain adverse decisions made by the MCO
2. Review of the reconsidered decision by HCFA (conducted by the Network Design Group, an impartial private company contracting with HCFA)
3. Review of HCFA's determination by a federal Administrative Law Judge (ALJ) if "the amount in controversy" (i.e., in dispute) exceeds $100
4. Review of the ALJ's decision by the Departmental Appeals Board
5. Ultimate review in federal district court if the amount in controversy exceeds $1,000

It is important to note that few appeals are actually pursued, and consumers usually lose on appeal. Between 1987 and 1993, approximately six Medicare HMO consumers appealed for judicial review (Stayn, 1994). Of these, two had not exhausted the Medicare grievance and appeal process, and thus the merits of the cases were not reached (*Pasha v. Secure Horizons*, 1991; *Roen v. Sullivan*, 1991).

Under Medicaid, federally mandated grievance and appeals procedures form only a broad framework for individual state action, in contrast to the relatively detailed and specific federal Medicare procedures (42 C.F.R. §§ 431.200–431.250, 434.32, 1997). The discretion granted to states under the Medicaid waivers system seems to have resulted in relatively inaccessible appeals processes (*Perry v. Chen*, 1996). In fact, although federal regulations require MCO grievance procedures (42 C.F.R. § 434.32, 1997) and state-maintained fair hearing procedures (42 C.F.R. §§ 431.200–431.250, 1997), the regulations do not provide explicitly for state or federal judicial review of final state agency determinations. Nevertheless, some Medicaid disputes find their way to federal or state court.

Federal regulations mandate the following guidelines for Medicaid MCO internal grievance procedures:

The contract must provide for an internal grievance procedure that—

(a)   Is approved in writing by the agency;
(b)   Provides for prompt resolution; and
(c)   Assures the participation of individuals with authority to require corrective action. (42 C.F.R. § 434.32, 1997)

In addition, states must maintain hearing systems that provide for either direct hearings before the state agency or local evidentiary hearings with a right of appeal to the state agency. Federal Medicaid regulations also describe requests that trigger the need for a hearing, require states to publish the specific hearing procedures that are adopted, and provide for written notice to recipients "[a]t the time of any action affecting his or her claim" (42 C.F.R. § 431.206(c)(2), 1997). *Action* is defined by the regulations as "a termination, suspension, or reduction of Medicaid eligibility or covered services" (42 C.F.R. § 431.201, 1997).

Medicaid recipients who are not satisfied with state agency determinations may seek judicial review under civil rights law. Section 1983 of the Civil Rights Act of 1871 (42 U.S.C. § 1983, 1994), establishes a private cause of action against any person who, under color of law (i.e., acting with apparent legal authority), abridges rights created by the U.S. Constitution or laws of the United States. In *Wilder v. Virginia Hospital Association* (1990), the U.S. Supreme Court recognized a valid 42 U.S.C. § 1983 cause of action within the context of a Medicaid payment dispute.

Advocates have threshold concerns about the information on and access to state Medicaid grievance and appeals processes, however. The form and content of the notice provided to recipients when care is denied or reduced may effect the number of determinations that are appealed. Enrollees would likely appeal MCO decisions more frequently if they were better informed of their rights. Even after an appeal is pursued, there are sometimes disputes over whether constitutional due process should guide the proceedings.

When official state action is taken resulting in a Medicaid coverage or benefit denial, federal regulations explicitly require states to provide beneficiaries with hearings that meet long-established due process standards. In *Goldberg v. Kelly* (1970), the U.S. Supreme Court required the following standards:

1.   The opportunity to present evidence orally to the hearing official
2.   The opportunity to confront or cross-examine adverse witnesses
3.   The ability to retain an attorney at the claimant's own expense

4. Constraint of the decision-making process by "the legal rules and evidence adduced at the hearing"
5. Adjudication by an impartial decision maker

The preceding Medicaid notice provisions also clearly apply in coverage eligibility determinations.

The U.S. Supreme Court has not yet considered whether official notice and due process are required when individual services are denied or discontinued by a private Medicaid MCO under contract with a state. In *Perry v. Chen* (1996), however, a decision of the U.S. District Court for the District of Arizona, a federal court explicitly extended constitutional due process to such individual service decisions. The court in *Perry* mandated specific written notice under the Medicaid regulations for the denial of doctor-approved individual service requests by an MCO contracting on a capitated basis. The *Perry* court did not consider the issue of consumers' rights when requested services are not approved by the treating physician.

The *Perry* court determined that Arizona had "assigned the entire responsibility for a state-created service" to the MCOs, which were "executing state responsibilities" by providing care to beneficiaries required to receive their Medicaid benefits through state-approved MCOs (1996, p. 1201). The court ultimately enjoined Mabel Chen, as Director of Arizona's Health Care Cost Containment System (AHCCCS), "from failing to provide AHCCCS beneficiaries with written notices and hearing concerning decisions denying medical services" (*Perry v. Chen*, 1996, p. 1205).

Under Medicare, the U.S. Court of Appeals for the Ninth Circuit held that the actions of MCOs contracting with the federal government constituted state action and that inadequate notice to beneficiaries violated due process. The court stated,

> The mere fact that the enrollee may be able to go elsewhere and pay for the services herself is of little comfort to an elderly, poor patient—particularly one who is ill and whose skilled nursing care has been terminated without a specific reason or description of how to appeal. (*Grijalva v. Shalala*, 1998, p. 1121)

Both *Perry* and *Grijalva* involved notice to older adults of the denial of care or denial of payment for care.

These precedents send a clear message to state and federal officials that they are accountable for the administration of their managed care programs, despite the delegation of operations to MCOs. They also underscore the importance of written notice for individual service denials. This notice should contain information regarding recipients' rights of grievance and appeal. Therefore, the Arizona decision may stimulate increased appeals of individual service denials under Medicaid managed care.

The low rate of Medicare and Medicaid MCO appeals can be attributed in part to the difficulty of maintaining such an appeal and the degree of knowledge and initiative required to file, let alone prevail, in the appeals process. Older people with developmental disabilities would have to rely heavily on family, friends, ombudsmen, or counsel as surrogates to review eligibility and treatment decisions and pursue grievances or appeals when necessary. Even savvy surrogates, however, may not understand and invoke these tools. New coordinated advocacy strategies must be explored if this vulnerable population is to make meaningful and systematic use of the right to appeal adverse decisions.

CONCLUSIONS

The developmental disabilities field must closely engage with government payors before they initiate any major changes in health or habilitative services for their older adult consumers who rely on Medicare and Medicaid. Although forms of managed care for the acute health needs of this population are common, long-term care is generally the subject of a carve-out. The managed care climate as the 21st century begins is not conducive to the mandated comprehensive participation of this group. In the future, however, stable, well-funded MCOs that make use of increased knowledge and familiarity with the needs of older people with developmental disabilities, better technology, and close tracking of patient outcomes may serve these people more efficiently and appropriately than the FFS system. People with developmental disabilities and their advocates should welcome these changes to the extent that they result in more effective coordination of services, better data collection and assessment, and improved care outcomes. Indeed, the Arizona experience suggests that a mandated comprehensive system may result in a dramatic expansion of financial resources available for long-term care in a wide range of community-based services (i.e., Arizona's state ranking rose from 49th to 21st in use of community services; see Hemp, Braddock, & Westrich, 1998).

States seeking to administer acute care for people with developmental disabilities in a managed care environment should ensure that it is integrated with other types of care. Following the interdisciplinary team model, providers from all professions involved, along with advocates for the consumer, should meet with the consumer to exchange information on care goals and to plan for consumer-centered outcomes. States should use the broad discretion accorded to them under the Medicaid waiver program to maximize the potential benefits of managed care, such as emphasis on preventive and outpatient care, information collection, and information analysis. The consumer's team of professionals can discuss such information and use it, for example, to assess the effectiveness of prior treatments and work consistently toward service goals.

States should also carefully craft complaint systems that take people with developmental disabilities into account. The timing and form of notice provisions are key elements of informing patients about their rights to have adverse decisions reviewed. By simply permitting MCO plans not to inform patients about these rights when a service denial is made, or by providing insufficient or hypertechnical notice, states discourage formal complaints, especially for people with cognitive disabilities. As the *Perry* court noted, any additional paperwork required in order to provide adequate notice to Medicaid MCO beneficiaries could simply be modeled on the notice provided to Medicaid beneficiaries who have opted into managed care in the past. The additional burden would not be substantial, and the protections afforded would have the greatest impact among the most vulnerable beneficiaries.

In order to allay fears surrounding the shift to managed care for people with disabilities, states planning Medicaid waivers should, among other things, strengthen consumer information management to ensure continuity of care, state accountability, and adequate consumer voice. To achieve the important goal of positive consumer perception of the Medicaid MCO health system, consumers must be consulted and heeded in the program design phase and in periodic system reviews. For their part, advocates for older people with developmental disabilities should help states to develop creative systems that take advantage of managed care's strengths, monitor its weaknesses, and evolve in response to local needs. They and the developmental disabilities community in general must resist following preconceptions that managed care systems are inevitably friends or foes. The field instead must work to ensure that, in concept and detail, new models of care satisfy the unique, local needs of this oldest and least-protected generation.

REFERENCES

American Association on Mental Retardation (AAMR). (1996). *Older adults with mental retardation and their aging family caregivers* [Brochure]. (Available from the AAMR, 44 North Capitol Street, NW, Suite 846, Washington, DC 20001.)

Balanced Budget Act (BBA) of 1997, PL 105-33, 111 Stat. 251.

Birenbaum, A., & Cohen, H. (1998). Managed care and quality health services for people with developmental disabilities: Is there a future for UAPs? *Mental Retardation, 36*, 325–329.

Braddock, D.L. (1998, September 18). *Aging and developmental disabilities: Demographic and policy issues affecting American families* (Statement before the U.S. Senate Committee on Aging). Chicago: University of Illinois at Chicago, Department of Disability and Human Development. (Available from the University of Illinois at Chicago, Department of Disability and Human Development, 1640 West Roosevelt Road, Chicago, IL 60608)

Civil Rights Act of 1871, § 1, 42 U.S.C. § 1983 (1994).

General Accounting Office. (1994). *Long-term care reform: States' views on key elements of well-designed programs for the elderly.* Washington, DC: U.S. Government Printing Office.

Goldberg v. Kelly, 397 U.S. 254 (1970).

Grijalva v. Shalala, 152 F.3rd 1115, 1998 Westlaw 467102 (9th Cir. 1998).

Health Care Financing Administration. (1995). Medicaid payments per user, by eligibility group: Fiscal years 1975–1992 (Statistical Supplement 146). *Health Care Financing Review.*

Health Care Financing Administration. (1998a, May). *HCFA statistics: Populations* [Online]. (Available on the Internet at http://www.hcfa.gov/)

Health Care Financing Administration. (1998b, May). *List and definition of dual eligibles* [On-line]. (Available on the Internet at http://www.hcfa.gov/)

Hemp, R., & Braddock, D.L. (1998). Medicaid managed care and individuals with disabilities: Status report. *Mental Retardation, 36*, 84–85.

Hemp, R., Braddock, D.L., & Westrich, J. (1998). Medicaid, managed care, and developmental disabilities. In D.L. Braddock, R. Hemp, S. Parish, & J. Westrich, *The state of the states in developmental disabilities* (5th ed.). Washington, DC: American Association on Mental Retardation.

Hilzenrath, D., & Goldstein, A. (1998, October 4). Coverage to end for 46,000 as HMOs quit Medicare. *Washington Post*, A1, A12–A13.

Hirschman, A.O. (1970). *Exit, voice, and loyalty.* Cambridge, MA: Harvard University Press.

Holahan, J., Coughlin, T., Ku, L., Lipson, D.J., & Rajan, S. (1995). Insuring the poor through Section 1115 Medicaid waivers. *Health Affairs, 14*, 199–216.

Hurley, R.E., Freund, D.A., & Paul, J.E. (1993). *Managed care in Medicaid.* Ann Arbor, MI: Health Administration Press.

Kenney, G., Rajan, S., & Soscia, S. (1998, January/February). State spending for Medicare and Medicaid home care programs. *Health Affairs*, 201–212.

Lamphere, J., Neuman, P., Langwell, K., & Sherman, D. (1997, May/June). The surge in Medicare managed care: An update. *Health Affairs*, 127–133.

Medical assistance programs, 42 C.F.R. §§ 430–456 (1997).

Medicare program, 42 C.F.R. §§ 405–424 (1997).

New York State Association for Retarded Children (NYSARC). (1998). *Medicaid managed care: Can managed care manage the risk of people with developmental disabilities?* [Monograph]. Albany: Author.

Pasha v. Secure Horizons, No. 90-56256, 1991 Westlaw 138877 (9th Cir. July 26, 1991) (unpublished disposition).

Perry v. Chen, 985 F. Supp. 1197 (D. Ariz. 1996).

Retchin, S.M., & Clement, D.G. (1992). How the elderly fare in HMOs: Outcomes from the Medicare Competition Demonstrations. *Health Services Research, 27*, 651–669.

Rodwin, M.A. (1996). Consumer protection and managed care: Issues, reform proposals, and trade-offs. *Houston Law Review, 32,* 1319–1381.

Roen v. Sullivan, 764 F. Supp. 555 (D. Minn. 1991).

Smith, G., & Ashbaugh, J. (1995). *Managed care and people with developmental disabilities: A guidebook.* Alexandria, VA: National Association of State Directors of Developmental Disabilities Services, Inc. and the Human Services Research Institute.

Social Security Act of 1935, PL 74-271, 42 U.S.C. §§ 1395eee, 1396d (Supp. 1998).

Stayn, S.J. (1994). Securing access to care in health maintenance organizations: Toward a uniform model of grievance and appeal procedures. *Columbia Law Review, 94,* 1674–1720 [Note].

Waldron, T., & Zorzi, W. (1998, October 13). Glendening backs right to sue HMOs. *Baltimore Sun,* 1B, 4B.

Wasserman, M.P. (1996). *Maryland Medicaid reform proposal.* Baltimore: Maryland Department of Health and Mental Hygiene.

White House Conference on Aging. (1995). *Background paper for delegates: Medicaid.* Washington, DC: U.S. Department of Health and Human Services.

Wilder v. Virginia Hospital Association, 496 U.S. 498 (1990).

20

Prospects for Ensuring Rights, Quality Supports, and a Good Old Age

Stanley S. Herr and Germain Weber

Aging people with developmental disabilities have their own visions for their older adult years. For instance Wolfgang S., a middle-age man from Vienna, beautifully described what he expects of a good old age when he no longer routinely works:

> As an older person I wonder about my evening of life. At some point when I will no longer be productive, I don't wish to go to work day-by-day. Therefore it would be fine if there would exist an old people's home for disabled people—a house with elevators large enough for wheelchairs. As there will be more sick persons, more staff are to be employed. For people who cannot leave their home, visiting services should be provided. We should have activities like other pensioners. They go to their club; others go to the park to play chess or have time for gardening. If you are still fit, you can work for extra earnings. Everyday life I figure out as follows: Everyone can sleep as long he likes. If one isn't too old and dependent, he can prepare breakfast on his own. Then one can withdraw to one's room, listening to the radio or watching TV. In a living room one can do handicrafts. After lunch one can have a nap, afterwards receiving a visitor, going for a walk and having a chat. If one isn't tired in the evening, he can undertake something: the state opera, theater, cinema, or one of the wine pubs can be visited. On the whole, during pension there is time for vacation and trips. A pensioner is much more free. (Lebenshilfe Österreich, 1994, p. 15)

Although the elements of a good old age for people with developmental disabilities vary with culture, nationality, and subjective individual preferences, there are some common features. Foremost is the satisfaction of the individual's self-defined needs and preferences. Other elements include emotional and material well-being to provide a stable, supportive, and safe environment; physical well-being achieved through access to good health care and opportunities for exercise; and friendships and personal relationships, including ties to family members and other intimates. Another vital ingredient is the enjoyment of human rights in their broadest dimensions. This enjoyment has both positive aspects, such as rights to health care, and negative aspects, such as freedom from painful intrusions on rights to dignity and privacy. People need the presence of good staff and services to secure the foregoing elements of a good old age. They also need opportunities for personal development to retain, if not expand, cognitive and adaptive skills for the pursuit of a stimulating and varied daily life.

This chapter summarizes some of the challenges for thriving, not just surviving, in old age. It focuses on a distinctive set of challenges to assisting older adults with developmental disabilities and offers recommendations for further action. In elaborating the themes introduced in the foreword, this chapter examines the challenges presented by the three Rs (risks, rights, and remedies) as well as by the goal of achieving outcomes that produce better prospects for quality living for such older people. The first section identifies some risk factors that this population faces, along with critical points of vulnerability. The second section of the chapter focuses on national and international norms along with practical ways to raise human rights awareness and safeguard both human and legal rights. The third section of the chapter discusses remedies in the broad sense of the ways to prevent or to rectify deficiencies in human rights and quality of life. Finally, some observations are offered on prospects for progress through coalition building, visionary leadership, and sheer tenacity.

RISKS

The greatest risk factors arise from the loss of loved ones and, with their deaths, the loss of guidance and practical support. The following is the perspective of a middle-age woman with Down syndrome, expressed through her poetry:

> *I love my father,*
> *But sometimes I wonder about him.*
> *"To get ahead in life,"*
> *Papa would say,*
> *"Don't back down*
> *When your back is against the wall."*
> *Papa has shown me when to be strong*
> *And when to be tender and compassionate.*
> *I wouldn't know what I would do*
> *If something happened to him.*
> *Josephson (1997)*

Parents have their own anxieties, including fears that their older adult child with developmental disabilities will experience disorientation and despair after their deaths. As one parent stated, "I feel like I have 10 good years left, but I guess she'll probably live longer. She took it hard when her daddy died, and I don't know what she'd do if anything happened to me" (Lewin, 1990, p. 32).

As family members age, they may also lose strength and perspective to be effective advocates for their child or other relative with disabilities. Reports of this phenomenon appear in many countries. In Finland, for example, an empirical study of care at home by older adult parents for their sons or daughters with developmental disabilities questioned whether both generations experienced violations of their human rights. Aalto observed that such parents constituted a group that has been "left outside as a result of lack of strength to fight for their rights. This group often faces negligence" (1998, § 2.2). Because of their unfamiliarity with or distrust of contemporary approaches to more independent living by people with disabilities, these older parents often avoid preparations for a son's or daughter's transition to such a life until a crisis strikes. As a result of such late-life transitions, the older person with developmental disabilities often faces institutionalization or experiences deeper adjustment difficulties than might otherwise have occurred. To the extent that older adult parents are satisfied with or resigned to an unsupported status quo, they do not exert pressure for political and service system changes.

Politicians have natural tendencies to respond to more vocal constituencies, so they often neglect the needs of older people with developmental disabilities. Even when parents and legal advocates express outrage at lengthening waiting lists for services and inattention to the population of older adults with developmental disabilities, state governments have been slow to heed their complaints. Commenting at a state budget hearing on a 20-year dip in Virginia's ranking for efforts on behalf of people with mental retardation, one parent testified, "This history suggests that if Virginia were the Titanic, we as a society could be expected to herd all of our mentally retarded citizens into a ballroom to sing 'Nearer My God to Thee' while everyone else raced for the lifeboats" (The Arc, 1998a). New York State presents an example of belated response under fire. Early in 1998, its governor, George Pataki, vetoed a legislative request for more housing for some of the 6,700 people with mental retardation on waiting lists. Perhaps because of election year pressure and the threat of a lawsuit by the New York Lawyers for the Public Interest that would have relied on a federal court precedent from Florida (see Chapter 5 for discussion of *Doe v. Chiles*), New York State adopted a $230 million, 5-year plan to provide housing for about 5,000 people with mental retardation. According to a *New York Times* editorial, members of this group confronted multiple risks:

> Faced with a drastic shortage of this housing [group homes or round-the-clock supervision in other environments], many of these disabled adults are living with aging parents who will soon be unable to support or care for them. Earlier this summer, 26 retarded adults who should have been carefully supervised were found living with improper supervision in a homeless shelter in Westchester County. ("Finally, new housing for the disabled," 1998, p. A26)

Compared with other older adults, people with developmental disabilities are not courted by politicians. Overall, people age 65 or older comprise more than 15% of the voting-age population and have such high rates of voter participation that, in some states, they make up as much as one-third of those who exercise their right to vote. In contrast, their peers with cognitive disabilities traditionally have rarely registered or voted. Thus, retirement villages are must-stop places for politicians to visit, asking residents questions such as, "What are your problems?" and "What do you need?" (Daemmrich, 1998). The population of older adults with mental retardation and related disabilities, however, does not receive similar solicitous attention. For them, political approaches alone are not likely to remedy their major problems.

For similar reasons, the criminal justice system may also fail those older adults who are victims of elder abuse. In the United States, older adults with mental retardation may be neither trained to protect themselves from criminal victimization nor adequately supported as complainants or witnesses in criminal or civil law enforcement processes. Although calls have been made to strengthen their rights to have their cases effectively prosecuted and their testimony appropriately weighed (The Arc, 1998b), many barriers to processing complaints at even earlier stages exist. In many jurisdictions, law enforcement officers may lack the means and training to receive, recognize, and investigate reports of any abuse, let alone elder abuse, of people with mental retardation. Despite the heightened risk of such people being physically or sexually abused, prosecutors may be reluctant to proceed with such cases and have the victim-witness take the stand, even though in theory the presence of mental retardation should not affect a witness' credibility.

Civil legal procedures also may be underused in cases of suspected elder abuse, neglect, or exploitation. First, such problems may not be conceptualized as a legal matter, even though they may consist of serious concerns such as physical assault, threats of assault, abandonment, misappropriation of funds and other property, or severe psychological abuse (Griffiths, Roberts, & Williams, 1993). Second, the victim or members of his or her entourage may not report the matter for fear of retaliation or rupture of important ties. Third, even if recognized and reported by someone as abuse or exploitation, it may be difficult to obtain an advocate for the victim. One reason is that cases of this type for older adults with developmental disabilities may be especially sensitive, complex, and protracted. Furthermore, because such cases seldom promise any financial recovery for the client or the attorney, the potential complainant must find free legal or other advocacy services. Few people with disabilities have the ability to pursue that search; thus, they must rely on the help of friends or Good Samaritans. For example, the University of Maryland School of Law's Clinical Law Office represented an older woman with Down syndrome at the request of a staff member in her group home who had befriended her. The guardian, a family member of the woman with a disability, had refused to release some of her inherited funds for clothing, recreation, and other incidental expenses to improve her quality of life. Only after the expenditure of substantial amounts of *pro bono* time and the filing of court papers for the appointment of a nonrelative co-guardian were the funds released and the additional surrogate appointed. Here, an apparent conflict of interest had existed and gone unresolved for many years. Older people with developmental disabilities face other risks and conflicts in being denied necessary health care treatment. They may confront illegal practices by physicians or dentists who withhold or withdraw treatment based on their disability per se or on stereotypes concerning their disability rather than their physical condition. Their perceived poor quality of life or economic factors may drive these decisions. Managed care organizations may introduce other inequities and greater barriers to getting past the gatekeepers to specialist services. Ashbaugh and Smith (1996) expressed fears that for-profit managed care will allocate fewer resources because of their profit motive and negotiate unreasonable reimbursement rates with providers that will result in care for persons with developmental disabilities that is of marginal quality. Chapter 19 outlines some of the procedural and other reforms that could be instituted to respond to such risks and arbitrary decision making by managed care entities.

Assisted suicide laws add lethal hazards because of the risks of undue influence as well as stereotypes that people with mental retardation and other ongoing disabilities have such poor quality of life that death is preferable for them. In The

Netherlands, an anecdotal report suggested that people with disabilities are disproportionately selected as candidates for euthanasia under such laws, with the argument being made in the report that, in 1996, some 40% of the total number of new-
borns and other people with severe mental retardation who died in The Netherlands
in 1996 did so through the application of active euthanasia (Kummer, 1998). Although these figures seem high, a congressional report on this Dutch experience
captured a similar sense of alarm that assisted suicide can lead to a slippery slope in
which the right to die is transformed into a duty to die (Canady, 1996). In the United
States, The Arc: A National Organization on Mental Retardation (hereinafter "The
Arc"), took a position of strong opposition to physician-assisted suicide for people
with mental retardation. It did so based on its assessments of the risks of coercion
and economic incentives under managed care and other health services systems "for
rationing health care which could lead to the encouragement of physician-assisted
suicide" (The Arc, 1998c, p. 1). Although the issue may not be encountered frequently in practice, it has such emotional, ethical, and legal resonance that it requires vigilant consideration.

In less dramatic ways, older adults may be at risk on a daily basis of harms to
their physical and psychic integrity. They risk regression and idleness by being relegated to nursing facilities, custodial institutions, and other dependency-promoting
environments. In institutional environments, they are more likely to be at risk than
their older adult peers who live in the community (Glendenning, 1993). Even if they
have relatives, the relatives may be reluctant to complain for fear of reprisals such
as threats of discharge. In parts of Europe, for example, the identity of the com-
plainer and the nature of the complaint may be circulated informally to other service providers, which can prejudice the chances of the family member with a disability being accepted into another facility. More generally, through disregard of
their capabilities for self-determination, older adults with developmental disabilities experience harms to their hearts and minds that are not easily undone.

In summary, as long as the old saying, "the squeaky wheel gets the grease,"
holds true, older adults with mental retardation without advocates are in a vulnerable position. That vulnerability runs the gamut from risks of small indignities
to hazards to life itself. Although some losses associated with age are inevitable,
such as the death of loved ones and protectors or declining physical vigor, a humane society can find ways to cushion their impact. The remaining sections of this
chapter discuss the rights and remedies that societies might institute to improve
the prospects for older adults with developmental disabilities and those who care
for them.

RIGHTS

Rights-related activities are one of the great engines for change in the disabilities
field. Such actions include the creation, application, implementation, and revision
of human and legal rights on international and national levels. Some of those rights
are of general application, such as the Universal Declaration of Human Rights or
the domestic law guarantees of equal protection and due process of law enjoyed
under the Fourteenth Amendment to the U.S. Constitution. Other rights have more
circumscribed beneficiaries or are targeted at the prevention of more specialized
wrongs, such as the Americans with Disabilities Act (ADA) of 1990 (PL 101-336),
which takes aim at disability discrimination, or the Developmental Disabilities As-

sistance and Bill of Rights Act of 1975 (PL 94-103), which designates resources for the protection of and advocacy for persons with lifelong disabilities.

International Standards

The international community has established a wide array of binding and nonbinding instruments that can be applied for the protection of the human rights of older adults with developmental disabilities. As Nowak describes in Chapter 3, examples of nonbinding declarations include the United Nations (UN) Declaration on the Rights of Mentally Retarded Persons (1971) and the Standard Rules for the Equalization of Opportunities for Persons with Disabilities (StRE) (1993). Legally binding obligations that the international community promulgates are referred to as *conventions* or *treaties* and become effective when signed and ratified by a designated minimum number of nations. Some of these conventions are international in scope (e.g., the International Covenant on Economic, Social and Cultural Rights [UN, 1966]) whereas others are regional (e.g., the Organization of American States's American Convention on Human Rights, 1969). Although a 1989 convention was age differentiated (UN Convention on the Rights of the Child, 1989), efforts to date to sponsor a convention focused on disability or old age have not succeeded. In 1975, for instance, the UN General Assembly rejected the adoption of a draft convention on the prevention and elimination of all forms of discrimination against persons with disabilities. Instead, as a result of activism stimulated by the UN Decade of Disabled Persons (1983–1992), the StRE were approved with the intention that they would become international customary law when applied by many nations. These standards offered guidance for policy making and reflected moral and political commitments for action at the national government level for the equalization of opportunities for people with disabilities of all ages.

Enforcement Issues

International declarations are not self-enforcing. The StRE created a monitoring mechanism consisting of a special rapporteur to track implementation and a panel of experts to advise him or her. Since 1993, Bengt Lindquist, an ex-Swedish Minister of Social Affairs, has held this post. His observations on the prevalence of noncompliance with international norms bear quoting:

> The ideas and concepts of equality and full participation for persons with disabilities have been developed very far on paper, but not in reality. In all our countries, in all types of living conditions, the consequences of disability interfere in the lives of disabled persons to a degree which is not at all acceptable. . . . When a person is excluded from employment because he is disabled, he is being discriminated against as a human being. (Disabled People's International, Inclusion International, World Blind Union, World Federation of the Deaf, & World Psychiatric Users Federation, 1998, p. 1)

Consciousness Raising

Despite difficulties, activists have taken up the challenge of raising awareness and respect for disability rights. Inclusion International, formerly known as the International League of Societies for Persons with Mental Handicap, has recast itself as an international human rights organization. In broad terms, its statement on "Fundamental Principles of Inclusion" proclaims that "[a]ll people with a mental handicap are citizens of their country, no less entitled than their fellow citizens to consideration, respect and protection under the law" (Lachwitz, 1998, p. 5). More specifically, it calls for integration (they shall "live, learn, work and enjoy life in the community and shall be accepted and valued as any other citizen is accepted or valued") and nondiscrimination (mental handicap shall not, "of itself, justify any form of adverse discrimination") (Lachwitz, 1998, p. 9).

Others who are concerned about older adults with disabilities have tried to apply such human rights precepts to this subfield. Aalto (1998), for example, advocated for the principle that everyone, including the older individual with developmental disabilities, is entitled to an independent life and stated that this principle requires supports for housing transitions; changes in disability policy; and attitudinal, economic, and political changes in order for these individuals to attain equal citizenship. Aalto correctly cautioned that these views "could become empty words if not attached to reality" (1998, § 4).

National Legislative Reforms

Changes in national laws and regulations can lead to new realities. They are also a way to apply international human rights at a national level through the incorporation of international norms in domestic law (Herr, 1977; Lachwitz, 1998). As an example, consider the roots and the ripple effects of the pioneering right to habilitation case of *Wyatt* in the United States (*Wyatt v. Rodgers*, 1997; *Wyatt v. Stickney*, 1972; see Chapter 2). In support of its constitutional analysis for the existence of the right to habilitation, the federal district court in *Wyatt* noted the UN's adoption of the Declaration on the Rights of Mentally Retarded Persons, and its fourth paragraph, which recognized their right to "proper medical care and physical therapy and to such education, training, rehabilitation and guidance" as to develop their "abilities and maximum potential."

With the guidance of the American Association on Mental Retardation (AAMR) and the other amici curiae (friends of the court briefs) in the case, the court went on to order that 49 standards defining habilitation plans, humane environments, and sufficient staffing be fully implemented. The *Wyatt* standards not only influenced the development of case law around the nation but also led to the creation of national and state laws on residents' rights. Its imprint can be found in the Medicaid regulations related to institutions (i.e., the intermediate care facilities for the mentally retarded (ICF-MR), hence the reference to "ICF-MR regs"), the Developmental Disabilities Assistance and Bill of Rights Act of 1975, and the state legislative response to "the moral imperative of cases such as *Wyatt*" (Perlin, 1994, p. 192). This wave of lawmaking certainly reshaped the contours of residential services.

Legal Tools in the United States

Although the United States has enacted landmark legislation for children with disabilities, it has yet to establish legislative frameworks of parallel force and prominence for older adults with disabilities. The Individuals with Disabilities Education Act (IDEA) of 1990 (PL 101-476), originally enacted as the Education for All Handicapped Children Act of 1975 (PL 94-142), is a powerful example of social legislation that literally transformed the way that a primary service for children with disabilities through age 21 is delivered. In contrast, older adults have more diverse service needs, use many types of laws, and do not have an entitlement claim as clear as the right to universal education that children enjoy. Thus, federal laws for older adults tend to be generic in scope and discretionary in the programs funded. For instance, the aging network funded under the Older Americans Act (OAA) of 1965 (PL 89-73) is described as an attempt "to ensure a seamless continuum of quality services" (White House Conference on Aging, 1996, p. 289) that encompass services for nutrition, home and community-based living, advocacy, elder rights protection, health promotion, and transportation. Although the aggregate statistics are impressive (providing, in 1994, more than 1 million legal counseling sessions, 40 million rides, 230 meals, and 12 million responses to requests for information and referral), there is little evidence that people with developmental disabilities are using the OAA programs effectively. Although the United States has 15,000 older adult centers serving 7 million people, it seems doubtful that a proportionate number of people with mental retardation are accommodated within these centers' social and recreation programs. In a few states, discrete community aging initiatives have supported day activities, such as Maryland's use of local older adult centers for 22 older adults with developmental disabilities and the provision of funds to cover extra staff and expenses for serving them (Factor, 1993). Although the mental health needs of older people drew the focused attention of the 1995 White House Conference on Aging (see, e.g., Resolution 16 on "Meeting Mental Health Needs"), the lack of a parallel resolution is another indication of the considerable planning, policy, and legislative work that remains to be done in the aging with developmental disabilities sector.

The U.S. Congress has provided some directions for this work in its consistent expression of basic principles for a national disability policy. This language, reiterated in several major laws, contains the following findings of special resonance for older people with developmental disabilities: "Disability is a natural part of the human experience that does not diminish the right of individuals with developmental disabilities to enjoy the opportunity to live independently, enjoy self-determination, make choices, contribute to society, and experience full integration and inclusion in the . . . mainstream of American society" (42 U.S.C. § 6000[a][2]). The Developmental Disabilities Assistance and Bill of Rights Act Amendments of 1994 (PL 103-230) also added significant national goals in terms of supporting these individuals to pursue meaningful and productive lives. Such goals and the related policy directives for assisted programs include help and encouragement to make informed choices and decisions, to contribute to their family, to have interdependent friendships and relationships with others, to exercise their full rights and responsibilities as citizens living in homes and communities, and to achieve "full integration and inclusion in society, in an individualized manner," consistent with the individual's unique strengths, concerns and capabilities (42 U.S.C. § 6000[a][10]).

This law is important for more than its lofty statements of goals and policies. It backs up these statements with the Protection and Advocacy (P&A) Offices that, as described in Chapter 5, are armed with powers of access to facilities and the authority to pursue legal and other remedies. The law makes specific reference to the broad concept of human rights, requiring states to provide "assurances that the human rights of all individuals with developmental disabilities (especially those individuals without familial protection)" who receive program services have protections consistent with a lengthy bill of rights. Those enumerated rights cover subjects as broad as the right to appropriate treatment, services, and habilitation, their provision in least restrictive environments (LREs), and services meeting standards to ensure "the most favorable possible outcome for those served" (42 U.S.C. § 6009[4]). As a check on the public funding of substandard residential programs, 42 U.S.C. § 6009(3) also calls on state and federal governments to enforce six minimum standards: nourishing diet, medical and dental services, limits on physical restraint, limits on chemical restraints, visits from close relatives without the need for prior notice, and compliance with fire and safety regulations. Although these rights may not provide a private action in court, they can be enforced through federal administrative means (*Pennhurst State School and Hospital v. Halderman*, 1981). In short, the Act does not depend solely on good intentions for the satisfaction of fundamental human rights.

Two major milestones for nondiscrimination on the basis of disability deserve attention. As discussed in Chapter 5, the ADA has the potential to speed integration and end many forms of discrimination to the benefit of both people with disabilities and society at large. The ADA affects wide areas of the economy and generates a burgeoning case law. In one decision (*Immenschuh v. Paragon Group, Inc.*, 1998), for example, a court ruled that a health insurance plan violated the ADA's provisions on public accommodations by refusing to cover a dependent child with Down syndrome. The court awarded $1,500 in damages to the family and issued an injunction that employees and their dependents could not be excluded from the company's health insurance plan solely because of a family member's diagnosis of Down syndrome.

The Fair Housing Amendments Act of 1988 (PL 100-430) is another powerful tool to eradicate discrimination by landlords and municipalities in zoning decisions for group homes. It has been used to prevent county authorities from barring older residents from entering a group home based on generalized allegations of fire safety hazards (*Potomac Group Home Corp. v. Montgomery County*, 1993). Judicial opinions such as the following have made it more difficult for landlords to evict tenants with mental disabilities: a tenant with a panic disorder who relied on a dog as a companion and part of her support system (suit ended with a $100,265 settlement) (Higgins, 1998), a tenant who sought postponement of her eviction hearing until she was released from the hospital (*Anast v. Commonwealth Apartments*, 1997), and five tenants with various mental disabilities who claimed improper terminations by public housing authorities by the denial of legal representation or protective services to protect the tenants' rights (*Blatch v. Franco*, 1998).

Although the *Blatch* case is still in its preliminary stages, it raises a fact pattern directly relevant to the concerns of families caring for aging people with developmental disabilities. The brothers Kevin and Kenneth Blatch had lived in a New York City housing project for nearly their entire lives and had been cared for by their leaseholder mother until her death. Both brothers had schizophrenia, but they alleged that the authorities had tried to downgrade their tenancy status and twice tried to evict them without first contacting any competent relative or the city's protective services agency. Indeed, so incompetent were these plaintiffs that their attorneys had been appointed guardians ad litem (guardians for the purpose of the litigation) at the case's outset even to pursue their FHAA, ADA, and constitutional claims. Together, some half-dozen statutes at the federal level alone contribute to the law against disability discrimination (Colker & Tucker, 1998).

Legal Tools in Europe

European countries have their own legislative accomplishments that deserve study and consideration for adoption elsewhere. Sweden has practically replaced guardianship with mentors (i.e., the *god man*, as this section describes) and trustees. Mentors provide help to people with mental disabilities in managing their legal, financial, or personal affairs without divesting such individuals of their civil rights. Trustees are a protective option of last resort for people who object to the appointment of a *god man* (a Swedish term that translates as "good man" in English) and who have personal or financial interests that would be seriously compromised without the appointment of a surrogate decision maker. With a statutory preference for the voluntary, less-restrictive mode of support, mentors are appointed far more commonly than trustees (28,000 Swedes with mentors versus 4,000 with trustees) (Herr, 1995). Sweden's Act Concerning Support and Service for Persons with Certain Functional Impairments (Law No. 1993:387), enacted in 1993 and effective since January 1, 1994, is another striking legislative innovation. It provides an entitlement to 10 specific support services, including personal assistants, respite services in the home, and housing for adults. Because of a national political consensus favoring greater independence for people with disabilities, such services that were once deemed discretionary are now provided as legal entitlements in Sweden (Herr, 1995). In England, the Disability Discrimination Act of 1995 (ch. 50) covers people with long-term disabilities (duration of 12 months or longer) and affords them rights to nondiscrimination in employment; the selling or renting of a dwelling; and the obtaining of goods, facilities, and services that are made available to members of the public, whether paid for or free. As a template for best practice and strategic planning, the Employers' Forum on Disability (1998) published a 10-point agenda for action and took steps to help implement the Act and improve the job prospects of people with disabilities by making it easier for employers to recruit, retain, and help them to develop as employees. This provides a good example of the civil society where private associations help to fill a gap between the power of the state and the imperatives of the market to improve quality of life and to promote the "rewards of personal and group responsibility" (Wolfe, 1998, p. 23).

REMEDIES

The UN exercised leadership on the issue of aging when its General Assembly called for a practical strategy in the 1990s and focused on implementing selected targets by 2001. By designating October 1 as the International Day for the Elderly and 1999 as the International Year of Older Persons, the UN intended the 1990s to focus on aging just as the 1960s focused on children and youth and the 1980s emphasized people with disabilities.

Making the ingredients for a better old age available in daily life to people with developmental disabilities requires multilevel action. On the micro level, these ingredients include an improved environment in terms of the type of housing, quality of care, quality of staff, and the level of self-determination afforded. On the macro level, dignity in aging demands basic human and legal rights.

Human rights imply human remedies. International disability rights declarations, such as the European Convention for the Protection of Human Rights and Fundamental Freedoms of 1950 (Council of Europe, 1953) and the StRE (1993), constitute moral and sometimes legal commitments to action by the endorsing nations. The values expressed in these documents provide powerful guidelines for governments as they define their own national laws and regulations. For instance, the European Convention states that "[e]veryone's right to life shall be protected by law" (Art. 2) and prohibits "inhumane or degrading treatment or punishment" (Art. 3). Besides offering guidance to governments, such statements need to be considered more carefully by those who are engaged directly in the fields of developmental disabilities and old age, such as service planners, service providers, and other professionals in both the public and private sectors.

To date, too little attention has been directed at disseminating these documents efficiently and using them to train audiences to prevent abuses and change pessimistic attitudes. On a micro level, the human rights documents can promote values that lead to clear goals in planning services and supports. They also can define the principles and mission statements that animate agencies and services for older adults with developmental disabilities. Furthermore, professional associations in the field of mental retardation and related developmental disabilities should focus more systematically on the implications of these values and rights for their members. This review could lead to new publications, training sessions, advocacy actions, and applications of ethics statements in practice.

Goals and Values

There is a long-recognized need for critical thinking on the goals and values of elder care. As the First International Roundtable on Aging and Intellectual Disabilities, held in Boston in 1990, concluded:

> We believe that the integration of older persons with developmental disabilities is a goal to which we should be directing our efforts, but we do not know what service mix is the most effective in reaching this goal. We have not devoted enough critical thinking to answering the question of what we are trying to accomplish through these services. We accept as a fundamental premise the goal of maintaining the functional independence of older persons with developmental disabilities for as long as possible. However, when we enter service environments we find goals that are not as clearly defined. (Seltzer & Janicki, 1991, p. 102)

With gerontology having come to the fore in the field of developmental disabilities only in the 1990s, many issues remain unresolved (see Chapter 1). Uncertainty in the goal-setting process is one of the major issues having profound effects on the outcomes of services. Often, the goals for services for older adults with developmental disabilities are not articulated clearly. The service coordinators and formal caregivers are often themselves uncertain about what *aging* means in general, let alone *aging for persons with developmental disabilities.* As La Rochefoucauld's 17th-century maxim aptly put it, "Few people know how to be old" (1678/1885, maxim 423).

The UN Principles for Older Adults

With respect to clarifying principles and goals, the UN offered a useful starting point. On December 16, 1991, it adopted the UN Principles for Older Persons "in order to add life to the years that have been added to life" (UN, Department of Public Information, 1992). Although primarily designed as guidance for governments in defining their policies for older adults without disabilities, the principles are of equal importance for stimulating progress in the field of aging and developmental disabilities. The resolution lists five principles: independence, participation, care, self-fulfillment, and dignity. In addition to these UN principles, three other principles are of special importance to the older population with developmental disabilities. These are LRE, self-determination, and personal integrity. Together, these eight principles provide a foundation for improving the prospects for older people with developmental disabilities.

Independence   The principle of independence has many dimensions. It calls for opportunities to work and to have a say in determining when and at what pace to withdraw from the labor force. It stipulates access to the necessities of life as well as appropriate educational and training programs to enrich old age. The independence principle calls for living in environments that are safe and suited to personal preferences and changing capacities. It also supports older people's right to reside at home as long as possible.

On the basis of the principle of independence, several actions are recommended. Vocational service providers can establish programs to promote a smoother transition from labor to retirement for older adults with developmental disabilities. To address the changing needs and capacities of aging people with developmental disabilities, specialists can develop appropriate education and training programs to foster and maintain independence. Such programs contribute to aging in place (i.e., remaining in natural environments) as long as possible, a concept strongly supported by the principle of independence.

Participation   The participation principle requires that older adults with developmental disabilities remain integrated in society, participating actively in the formulation and implementation of policies that directly affect their well-being. In addition, they should be able to form movements and associations of older adults.

In the field of developmental disabilities, older people need encouragement to express their opinions on topics affecting their lives as individuals and as members of a group who seek to participate in society. Self-advocacy by older people with developmental disabilities is thus viewed as a major tool for advances in participation (see subsequent discussion in this chapter).

Care   Under the principle of care, the UN urges that older adults should have the benefits of family and community care. They should be ensured protection in accordance with each society's cultural values. Older people should have access to health care to help them maintain or regain their optimum level of physical, mental, and emotional well-being. In addition, they should have access to social and legal services to enhance their autonomy, protection, and care. If necessary, they should be able to use appropriate levels of residential care in a humane and secure environment. Finally, older adults should be able to enjoy human rights and fundamental freedoms when residing in any facility, including full respect for their dignity, beliefs, needs, and privacy as well as their right to make decisions about their care and the quality of their lives.

Realizing this principle requires a greater emphasis on self-determination and a strengthening of the rights of older individuals, including protection from discrimination, neglect, and unduly restrictive institutional care. As further outlined in this chapter, a priority need is the assurance of strong and well-defined advocacy.

Self-Fulfillment   The principle of self-fulfillment promotes the ability of older people to pursue opportunities to develop their personhood fully. This development can occur through access to educational, cultural, spiritual, and recreational resources. People with disabilities may require training to take advantage of a range of leisure opportunities. Self-fulfillment entails not only the continuation of the satisfactions of middle age but aid in developing new interests in one's older years.

Dignity   The principle of dignity states that older people should be able to live with dignity and security, free of exploitation and physical or mental abuse. They should be treated fairly regardless of their age, disability, gender, racial or ethnic background, or other status, and they should be valued independently of their economic contribution to society.

Other Guiding Principles

As previously noted, the support of older people with developmental disabilities also requires consideration of the principles of the LRE, self-determination, and personal integrity.

Least Restrictive Environment   The concept behind the least restrictive alternative (LRA) and its corollary, the LRE, is to reduce unnecessary restrictions in the lives of individuals with disabilities (Turnbull, 1981). The LRA has both legal and professional implications. For example, from the LRA follows the principle of the LRE as a tool for service providers to define and evaluate individually appropriate residential or day services environments for older people with developmental disabilities. This principle is best realized in conjunction with the principle of self-determination.

Self-Determination   Self-determination is a major rallying cry for fostering growth and autonomy for older adults with developmental disabilities. One of the legal roots of this principle is contained in the International Covenant on Civil and Political Rights, which states, "All people have the right of self-determination" (UN, 1966, art. 1).

With respect to people with developmental disabilities, the drive for self-determination has deep resonance. As The Arc defined and espoused it, *self-determination* has several implications:

> People with mental retardation must have opportunities to acquire skills and develop beliefs that enable them to take greater control over their lives. They must have freedom to exercise control and self-determination in their lives with the support they need from friends, family, and individuals they choose. (1998d, unpaginated)

Further-reaching aspects of self-determination are analyzed in the discussion of self-advocacy in a subsequent section of this chapter.

Personal Integrity   *Personal integrity* refers to the needs for personal growth while aging. Developing a successful identity as an older person contributes to personal integrity and self-fulfillment in old age. The converse can produce tragic results. According to Erikson's (1968) developmental life-span model, the failure to develop an identity on the basis of one's life experiences can lead to despair.

Planning for Person-Centered Services

Public Planning   National and regional planning are urgently needed to maximize opportunities that promote healthy and successful aging. This planning must include policies and programs for housing and physical infrastructure, health and hygiene, income security, education and training, social welfare, and family support. Within this context, the plight of older people with developmental disabilities deserves closer attention because of their higher risk for neglect, abuse, and abandonment. Support for informal caregivers, especially family members, is vital because in the United States they care for almost five times as many people as the formal care system but are supported by less than 4% of total developmental disabilities funds (Braddock, 1998). A broader focus on training as well as media awareness programs is needed to educate the public about the complexity and challenges of aging and the inadequate public policy response.

Provider Planning   In planning services, providers frequently must follow government regulations on quality standards. Such regulations may specify the minimum size of living quarters, technical equipment and supports, staffing patterns, and similar details. These characteristics are relatively easy to evaluate and can be viewed as the "hardware" of a service environment. However, the "software" characteristics of a service environment, such as the way in which staff relate to older adults with disabilities and whether consumers have a say in those decisions affecting their lives, often remain undefined. Evaluating the qualitative characteristics of services on a regular basis can be viewed both as a remedy for preventing or detecting neglect and abuse and as a valuable tool for ongoing service development (Benjamin, Capie, & Nossin, 1998).

Certain service providers have a planning advantage. Those providers that offer services for younger adults are in direct touch with their future older customers. This contact allows anticipatory planning in different ways. First, those adults can be asked about their aspirations for the years after retirement. As revealed in this book, adults with intellectual disabilities have a notion of aging, and they often show a high degree of ability to express their views and expectations about the years after retirement (see Chapter 16). Using this easily obtainable data more systematically is surely of major help to establish high-quality services for older adults with disabilities. Second, service providers have at least a broad notion about the size and number of placements needed for older adults with developmental disabilities in the areas in which they are offering services. More rigorous use of these statistics in defining annual or multiyear budgets might increase planning efficiency. In addition, most countries support residential facilities for people with developmental disabilities through public funds. Planning the supply for housing facilities should therefore be conducted with the cooperation of the service providers and the public agencies in charge. Systematic anticipatory planning on this level helps to prevent the extreme shortages of accommodations for older adults with mental retardation, as reported previously in this chapter (see also Chapter 2).

Person-Centered Planning   Adequate planning of services for the older generation of people with developmental disabilities is based on person-centered planning. Person-centered planning values the customer's views and preferences when defining which services to offer, the manner in which they should be offered, and the personnel providing them. According to Sundram (1994), taking advantage of person-centered planning strengthens the general quality of services. Polister, Blake, Prouty, and Lakin (1998), in compiling innovative programs for quality assurance, stressed the consumer-centeredness of human services and earning the trust of the newly empowered consumer. With prophetic force, Dybwad (1985) recognized a fundamental need to define or to articulate the ways in which the service needs of people with developmental disabilities are affected by these individuals' age.

Person-centered planning contrasts starkly with provider-driven planning. Because the views and expectations of people with developmental disabilities are not fully reflected in provider-driven planning, in many cases the services proposed do not fit the needs of those for whom they are designed. Consequently, exclusively provider-defined services might meet the interests of only a small minority of people. This approach may also hinder self-criticism by the agency and its staff, thus perpetuating outmoded practices and perspectives.

One step toward self-determination and empowerment is to place people with developmental disabilities at the center of the process of developing individual goals and plans instead of deciding their future for them during staff meetings behind closed doors (Sutton, Heller, Sterns, Factor, & Miklos, 1997). Hagner, Helm, and Butterworth (1996) described the elements of person-centered planning that should guide the individual to envision and achieve a realistic yet safe self-determined plan. This means tolerating uncertainty, setbacks, false starts, and disagreements, as well as appreciating free choices, increasing self-consciousness, and learning from life experiences. When using person-centered planning, the primary direction comes from the individual. Wherever views can be expressed, he or she should decide where the meetings will be held (e.g., at home, at work, at a community-based center); who should be invited; and what agenda of wishes, plans, preferences, and additional topics should be discussed. Other characteristics of person-centered planning include recognizing one's social relationships as a primary source of support and thus involving family members or friends in planning as opposed to involving only professionals. A trained facilitator (and optimally a co-facilitator) has the role of managing the flow of the discussion; observing the subtle communication of the focal person; ensuring that the participants do not persuade the focal person improperly through strong suggestions; and, if necessary, interpreting nonverbal communication cautiously. Furthermore, the facilitator should focus on the individual's capacities and abilities rather than on limitations and impairments. Whenever feasible, the group should aim for those services and supports that are available to the community at large rather than those designed only for people with developmental disabilities.

Reality often leads to a lack of rich options in the areas of living arrangements, jobs, and leisure activities, to mention only a few domains relevant to people with developmental disabilities. Nevertheless, the aim is to involve the focal persons in every decision-making process concerning their lives. Even in cases of few options, the option selected should be the choice of the individual himself or herself. Even if there is only one alternative to consider, the individual has the right to refuse—the right to say no. Likewise, he or she is no more obligated than other members of society to make irrevocable decisions. Generally, one should be able to change decisions already made without immediately being labeled as unstable and vacillating. Self-determination as well as the other foundations of quality of life are a basic right and not a privilege.

Mobilizing Advocacy Resources

Both individuals with disabilities and their families face many unmet needs for advocacy services. For the former group, many of those needs are real but unrecognized. Earlier sections of this chapter and other parts of this book discuss in detail such needs for lawyers and other advocates who can assist with rights, benefits, future planning, and responses to abuse (see Chapters 1–5 and 19). Family members fill some of those gaps or select professionals who can. As some aging parents experience a weakening of their physical ability to advocate for their adult child, however, they must turn somewhere for assistance. Parents also realize that they will be outlived, often leaving their child without a strong advocate. This knowledge itself is a source of worry and sometimes a stimulant for action.

One solution to these twin needs is the creation of trust arrangements to ensure that a competent advocate and, if necessary, a surrogate decision maker are available to the surviving child with a disability. Individually tailored arrangements can be expensive, however, and can exceed the means of many families that have only modest estates to transfer.

Another, more novel solution is to sponsor collective forms of trust, advocacy, and visiting arrangements. For the sake of convenience, this book refers to those approaches as *legacy projects.* The underlying concept is that families in a state or region would pool their resources to perpetuate visiting, oversight, money management, and advocacy arrangements for older people with developmental disabilities who have lost their primary supporters through death, disability, or serious infirmity. Depending on how well the legacy project is capitalized, it could engage social work, nursing, rehabilitation, legal, and other human services professionals. Even if only some of these services were available on a staff or consultant basis, linkages through pro bono, clinical training, and other altruistic means would be possible. The existence of large volunteer-reliant movements in the broader field, such as Special Olympics, the Arc, the United Cerebral Palsy Associations, and other nonprofits, suggests that recruiting volunteers to assist in visiting and befriending aging people with disabilities is feasible. Volunteers also can be used for highly responsible tasks in making substituted medical and dental care decisions for people with mental impairments. By analogy, New York State law authorizes a surrogate decision-making committee—composed entirely of volunteers—to authorize such treatment when an individual who is incompetent to take that decision lacks another surrogate and the treatment is required in the patient's best interests (Herr & Hopkins, 1995). In summary, through funds generated by the families or through funds raised from donations of cash or in-kind services, legacy projects can be established to meet the lifetime advocacy needs of aging and otherwise unprotected people with developmental disabilities.

The Maryland Trust for Retarded Citizens (MTRC) is one such example. Founded in 1963 and restructured in 1980, it serves 296 members as of the fall of 1998, of whom 30 are receiving active services because of the death of their sponsors. Upon the payment of a $2,000 membership fee, MTRC opens an information file that documents the member's family, medical, and program history and outlines the interests and the goals of the member and the family sponsor. The Trust's Supplemental Services Plans, funded on a fee-for-service basis, provide packages of services with estimated costs ranging from $1,740 for quarterly interventions to $400 for attending an annual team meeting and quarterly telephone calls to service providers. For a fee, during his or her lifetime, the sponsor can also use this service to develop or to monitor care plans.

The MTRC staff is well equipped for these tasks. The staff consists of a director of administration, a clinical supervisor who is a licensed and certified social worker, and three case managers. A highly experienced case worker with a registered nurse degree and licensed social worker associate credentials also performs supplemental services work. For instance, she has advocated for over 10 years for Betty Boe to ensure that this 56-year-old woman's health, therapy, day activity, and residential needs are met in an effective and timely way. (For further details of that case, see Chapter 2.) She also advises the member's mother and attorney, receiving payment for her services from the state under the terms of a settlement agreement. A more typical case involved a 73-year-old member whose father had died and left a bequest directly under a will, thereby jeopardizing the member's Social Security eligibility. MTRC put the member's niece-guardian in contact with an attorney who specialized in estate planning for people with developmental disabilities and who was able to resolve this problem. A Trust case manager also assisted the niece-guardian by attending team meetings, seeking a more suitable residential placement in an assisted living unit for older adults, and keeping the member in the senior center's day activities that she already attended and loved. Other active cases for a man age 75 years and another age 69 years centered on monitoring their living arrangements and medical care needs. With 15 members ages 60 years and older and another 43 members in their 50s, MTRC is likely to be increasingly active in fulfilling its mission of providing active members with lifetime personal advocacy, protecting their legal rights, and helping them through the service delivery maze. Its purpose is also to assist sponsors with transition planning, including the development of the MTRC Sibling Circle, which, as one of its first tasks, is preparing a checklist to assist siblings when they assume a role in their brother's or sister's care. Legacy projects like this are clearly needed in many states and countries.

P&As are another possible base for more legally oriented advocacy approaches. Located in each state and the District of Columbia, these federally mandated advocacy offices exist to provide legal, administrative, and other remedies for people with developmental disabilities of all ages. Under their priority-setting processes, any P&A could decide to give special focus to the rights and public policy needs of such older people. They could also solicit funds from state, foundation, and other sources to develop projects that provide more systematic individual and group representation for this vulnerable and frequently underserved age cohort.

Consortiums or coalitions could also play a role in mobilizing or training advocacy resources to help the people who are the focus of this book. For example, the Maryland Developmental Disabilities Council funded a local chapter of The Arc to organize training sessions for lawyers who are interested in assisting families with estate planning when there is a family member with developmental disabilities. The University of Maryland School of Law has served as a co-sponsor and host for these sessions, and experts have provided their help on a *pro bono* basis. Coalitions on a far broader scale are needed to satisfy national and state advocacy requirements. Consortiums can also play a role in mobilizing or training advocacy groups to help older adults with developmental disabilities.

Encouraging Self-Advocacy

Self-advocacy has become one of the most powerful sources for inducing change in the lives of younger adults with developmental disabilities. In general, self-advocacy encourages people with developmental disabilities to speak out for what they believe in, to express their needs, and to make their own decisions. Self-advocacy enables such people to take control of their lives and to experience adulthood in a more normalized way. Self-advocacy is more than strengthening self-confidence and goes beyond the principle of self-determination as it aims to inform people with developmental disabilities about their rights (see Inclusion International, 1998). Learning about one's rights should also be linked to learning about one's responsibilities. The individual's degree of social participation is dependent largely on his or her abilities to self-advocate and be involved in society at many levels. For example, some self-advocates may desire to register to vote and to cast their ballots in general elections.

Moreover, major advances in self-advocacy require special attention from people in the supporting environment. In encouraging and training people with developmental disabilities to express their thoughts, beliefs, and needs, staff must learn to listen more carefully to what the individual is expressing. Self-advocacy can be promoted best when staff really take the time to listen to the individual and to get to know him or her well. Patience is obviously required because it may take a longer time for people with developmental disabilities to learn and understand matters of importance. The challenge for supporters is to select those communication techniques that enhance self-advocates' understanding so that they can learn to handle new situations successfully and make informed decisions on their own or with requested aid.

Self-advocacy has developed extensively, particularly in the United States (Longhurst, 1994). To date, however, self-advocacy for older adults with developmental disabilities has not yet been generally available. Introducing older adults to existing groups or promoting groups of older self-advocates is of importance to improving the living conditions of this cohort in the future. Maintaining and adapting competencies for self-advocacy in older adults with developmental disabilities should be supported strongly by others in their environment. As depicted in this book, old age presents a multitude of risks that can increase the degree of impairment of older adults with developmental disabilities. Self-advocacy in old age can counter some of those risks by encouraging people to have control over their lives and to question harsh or unjustified treatment. Self-advocacy does not happen spontaneously but requires supporting older adults to develop and maintain skills in advocacy and self-determination.

The quality of life that older adults with disabilities achieve is significantly affected by personal levels of self-determination. Research indicates that age is more positively associated with high scores in quality of life when coupled with more opportunities to make decisions and more integrative activities (Jones, Dagnan, Trower, & Ruddick, 1996). Skills and knowledge in self-determination can be cultivated in multiple ways by service providers, caregivers, relatives, and the individuals themselves (Holub, 1998). In addition, good practice in the field increasingly recognizes and promotes offering choices in community environments even for people with severe disabilities (Belfiore & Toro-Zambrana, 1994).

The call for self-determination is equally relevant in the daily support of older adults as for youth with developmental disabilities. If improperly implemented, however, self-determination can result in additional risks. Allowing an individual's waning self-determination to result in complete withdrawal and disengagement or in staff not responding to obvious and serious medical needs based on the person's reluctance to receive medical assistance are examples of misplaced literalism. There are boundaries between respecting self-determination and neglecting professional duties of care and support (Sundram, 1999). Service providers are urged to develop nuanced understandings of self-determination, together with the older adults whom they serve and these individuals' advocates. Well-defined and clear statements on self-determination, with critical illustrations from daily life, should be part of every facility's operating manuals and training programs. The book and training sessions on the consent doctrine and its applications by the AAMR can also provide a model for meeting this need (Dinerstein, Herr, & O'Sullivan, 1999).

Supporting Older Parents and Other Natural Networks

The need to improve systems of support for older parents and other natural caregivers is imperative. Agencies must respond to the distinctive characteristics of aging families caring for an adult with a developmental disability (Janicki, 1996). Indeed, there are many reasons why older adults with developmental disabilities continue to live with their families. Erös (1991) reported on South Tyrol (a German-speaking province of northern Italy), where 51.1% of the families investigated mentioned that their middle-age or older adult child with mental retardation did not want to live in another place and that the family respected the wish of this family member. Other reasons for their continuing to live in the family home are that close family members indicate that they have a special understanding of the person's needs and a belief that they can respond to these needs best. In addition, the accommodation options for out-of-home placement are limited, resulting in many of these older adults with developmental disabilities being placed on waiting lists and these parents hoping to live to see and support the transition to the new home. Other parents may have made no plans for future residential accommodations because they lack information about the options or they simply repress the issue because it is perceived as an anxiety-provoking burden. Some parents, however, are resigned to the status quo because either the residential options they considered for their older offspring did not meet their expectations or those of their family member or they expect—because of fantasy or problem avoidance—that they can always stay together.

Weber and Rett (1991) reported the views of parents on future accommodations for their middle-age and older adult children with Down syndrome. About one-third of the parents had repressed this issue by the time they were interviewed. They had neither plans nor expectations about future accommodations. Another third expressed the expectation that some other family member would eventually take responsibility for the care of the older family member with developmental disabilities. This expectation seems to be unrealistic in most cases; the literature reports that only 2%–3% of older adults with mental retardation live with a relative other than a parent (Erös, 1991). Similarly, Freedman, Krauss, and Seltzer (1997) reported that more than 50% of older mothers with a mean age close to 70 years had made no plans for future residential accommodation. These data show that support programs for older families caring for older adults with developmental disabilities are indeed an important issue. The issue is further complicated when even parents in their 80s do not make plans for their children's future and instead adopt a wait-and-see approach (Aalto, 1998).

Continuing to live into advancing adulthood in the parents' home is an unquestionable right of the individual with a developmental disability and the parents. Yet, despite many reasons for this long-term co-residency, some result in late transitions or abrupt transitions that often are not successful. These problems range from lack of adequate information on accommodation options to the failure to secure accommodations that fit the individual's specific needs. Providers must also respect and foster the rights of parents and their adult child with a disability to visit each other and otherwise encourage them to reduce late or unprepared transitions.

For those parents who decide to continue to care for their child into advancing age, however, respite and outreach services should be easily available (Colond & Wieseler, 1995). Just as community support services are demonstratively effective in this area with younger families with children with developmental disabilities, special community support services can be developed for older caregiving parents.

Typically, caregiving families come to providers' attention only when a crisis occurs. Magrill, Handley, Gleeson, and Charles instead recommended an "investment in preventive partnership work with families as at the core of meeting the needs of this user group and determining accurate, cost-effective planning for future services" (1997, p. 16). Parents' confidence in their child's future prospects also can be enhanced by this positive early contact with provider staff.

Staffing to Improve Quality of Life

Frontline staff and others are responsible for realizing an agency's philosophy according to its principles and goals. The work responsibilities, however, often outstrip rewards and frequently do not meet the expectations of staff. Improving quality of life for older people with developmental disabilities thus requires the empowerment of the staff.

Prior to empowerment, however, it is essential that staff qualifications match the demands of the job for which individual staff members are hired. Of particular importance is the presence and ongoing development of a shared vision of the knowledge, skills, and attitudes that define the direct support role. Henry, Keys, Balcazar, and Jopp (1996) offered two recommendations: First, recruit only those people whose values are consistent with those of the agency, and second, offer training in the philosophy of the agency.

An agency's philosophy must be believed and implemented by those who are supposed to provide services in its spirit. The philosophy of providing a high quality of life within the community centers on independence, social integration, jobs in the community, self-determination for making life decisions, and making all necessary services easily available. An important variable for the successful implementation of these values is that staff members must identify with and personally commit to these values. Accordingly, when the agency's values change, so too must the attitudes and behavior of staff members.

Consider, for example, staff members who have worked for approximately 20 years in a large residential facility in which the main philosophy has been to keep people with developmental disabilities fed, clean, quiet, and isolated from the rest of society so that they are "not too much bother for anyone." When staff members who are accustomed to this philosophy of containment start working for employers who espouse the mission of empowerment and inclusion, considerable gaps between the ideas of job values and job performance occur. The probable result is a high potential for conflict, low job satisfaction, and a diminishing quality of services and supports. To avoid these difficulties, Henry and colleagues (1996) recommended either training in the philosophy offered by the employer to achieve changes in motivation and attitudes of the employees or recruiting new personnel whose values are consistent with those of the agency. They also discovered that training staff in inclusion philosophy is associated with more positive attitudes of staff members. These results suggest that paying attention to the attitudes of employees might be a key to developing personal beliefs that motivate employees to carry out the desired philosophy in their day-to-day work. Based on their results, Henry and colleagues recommended that agencies carry out job interviews and performance reviews that focus on these values. When searching for staff with already consistent values, Henry and colleagues recommended using their Community Living Attitudes Scale to enable employers to screen out people with negative attitudes toward people with developmental disabilities.

Once qualified staff are hired, training them becomes crucial, given that insufficient training is a frequent reason for staff turnover. Because it is hard to find good, qualified workers, especially in direct service, managers must develop effective training programs. An effective training program increases employees' knowledge and motivation and even addresses ways to handle their personal needs. Effective training must first include a solid background of knowledge in health, psychological, and social issues of aging as well as knowledge and experience in the field of developmental disabilities. For example, an older person needs markedly more time to prepare in the morning. A direct support staff member might feel tempted to help the person wash his or her face because the staff member feels stressed by the activity plan for that day or because friends of the older person are waiting. In that case, the older person who experiences social attention might perceive face washing as caresses. For many people, caressing is an agreeable experience, and the older person might miss this kind of attention. Being washed and experiencing an agreeable state produces, within short time, a strong association. Applying basic knowledge of behavioral gerontology prevents staff from giving support that leads to greater dependency in the older person. For instance, slowing down is a prominent characteristic of the aging process. The major challenge for direct support staff is to restrain themselves from preventing the older person from doing something just for the sake of efficiency.

A second element of effective training is to address staff motivation. One way to strengthen staff motivation is to foster cooperation between staff members and management. Such cooperation can include regular meetings to develop mutual goals and work plans. Defining lifelong education and professional habilitation programs also can increase job satisfaction and lead to better job performance (Massey, Johnson, & Kirk, 1992). The provision of such programs is one way to change staff expectations from viewing their jobs as temporary steppingstones to viewing their work as a source of pride and long-term personal fulfillment. Finally, staff motivation might be influenced by offering clear salary plans based on well-defined goals, competencies, and responsibilities as well as an attractive range of benefits (compare Chapter 9).

Finally, effective training recognizes that good practice entails not only meeting the needs of the clients but also providing active and systematic support for the personal needs of frontline staff, especially those who care for older people with disabilities (Kryspin-Exner, 1997). Indeed, professional qualifications are determined not only by the employees' formal knowledge and practical experience but also by their acquisition of personal competencies, such as effective coping strategies and the ability to manage stress. For instance, training in general stress management techniques is shown to be most effective when it takes into account the emotional needs of the staff and also includes techniques useful to them in handling stress and problems in their private lives.

By providing employees with basic knowledge, motivational assistance, and personal support, employers may reduce turnover and begin to empower the staff to actualize the philosophy of providing a high quality of life to individuals with disabilities. When asking staff to empower the people for whom they are caring, employers should consider that caregivers may expect equivalent treatment from them. Empowerment can take many forms, including management's receptivity to employees' suggestions for improving the work environment and affording them a more professionalized status. This can include the employer's paying for the employees' membership in professional associations such as AAMR, sending employees to off-site training sessions, and supporting the development of a credentialing process for direct support professionals.

Preserving Personal Identity

Quality of life as perceived by older people with developmental disabilities is further influenced by typical age-related personal needs. According to the principle of personal integrity, one of those needs is for personal growth and the development of a successful identity as an older person. A pathway to promote personal integrity is to reflect on one's life—that is, to reconstruct one's life through memories (see Blewett, 1980). The records compiled by most service providers, however, are of little help for those staff members who want to support older adults in reappraising episodes of their own life. Staff may have only limited knowledge about those people and events that were of major importance in an older person's life. In addition, people with developmental disabilities may undergo difficulties in successfully reconstructing those episodes that are of importance to them. In Erikson's terms, they risk "experiencing old age as despair" when their need to reflect on their lives cannot be supported adequately. As a remedy, print-based personal biographies presenting key memories and places might be used. This might help the older person to reorient to the highlights of his or her life as well as to better cope with past critical events. For staff, the personal biography might be of great value because it helps them to know better the person's past and because it allows them to have greater empathy when the person asks for assistance or just seeks somebody with whom to talk. This empowers staff members to better coach the individual in search of personal integrity as he or she tries to sum up his or her past.

Broadening Independence and Honoring Individual Choices

Quality is tightly linked with opportunities and choices. Choices must be realistic and also available, however. This includes being provided with appropriate assistance related to these choices. First, this means helping to convert personal preferences into reality, and second, it means providing assistance in developing indispensable preconditions and skills to be able to make voluntary choices. Examples for such preconditions are easy-to-understand information about the existence of different options, considering the meaning of the different options for one's life, and evaluating how far a certain option best meets the person's needs.

Mature judgment requires information and experience. To achieve this, people with developmental disabilities need careful assistance and empathic guidance in experiencing choice making. The main challenge in assisting and guiding people with developmental disabilities, and especially the older generation, is to consider the ever-present influence of one's own value system. Furthermore, older people can be influenced easily. Especially when that person opts for a choice that implies more staff time and attention, honoring and respecting the person's choices can become a particular challenge.

Independence can be viewed as the amount of permitted input the individual has in decisions with respect to how to live. This includes selection of staff, leisure activities, and activities of daily life. The Colorado investigation by Sands, Kozleski, and Goodwin (1991) reported that individuals with developmental disabilities exclusively experience independence for "lighter" decisions such as weekend or evening activities, clothes, friends, personal decorations, or spending their own money. For the more "weighty" decisions of where to live, choice of jobs, weekday activities, the choice of service agency support staff, or the choice of roommates, family members or staff mostly decide without the person's input. In contrast to their highly ranked aspirations for independence, these aging adults experience only limited levels of independence. This problem might not be due to a developmental disability per se. Precluding older people with or without developmental disabilities from having a respected voice in important decisions about their lives can be viewed as an intentional and structural restriction.

In summary, the main areas in supporting older people with developmental disabilities include preserving personal identity, maintaining independence, having a say in decisions affecting one's life, fostering participation in social life, arranging meaningful daily activities, helping the individual to recall and perceive a full life, and, finally, being assisted in the pursuit of enjoying the benefits of daily life. In this quest, older neighbors with developmental disabilities need powerful and sustained advocacy.

CONCLUSIONS: PROSPECTS FOR PROGRESS

That the road is long does not permit one to hesitate in taking the first steps on the journey. The information is at hand on some of those next steps. As this book demonstrates, the demographic tides continue to crest. Prudent policy makers, service providers, and parents must plan for a future that includes more people with developmental disabilities living longer and vying for scarce resources. Advocates and self-advocates must inform themselves of options and rights that grow seemingly more complex with every passing year. Practitioners, from the most seasoned professionals to the newest direct support workers, must understand those rights and options as well as their own corresponding rights and responsibilities or face legal peril. Politicians face their own peril if they ignore the rights and needs of older people with developmental disabilities, perils such as the risks of being sued, adverse publicity, entanglement with federal regulators, and even rejection at the polls.

Coalitions are essential to bringing about reforms and sustaining a focus on these hidden older people. A Coalition for Older People's Empowerment (COPE) (i.e., a coalition on aging and developmental disabilities or however one would wish to style it), could have many facets and tap many talents. As this book reveals, researchers can offer both qualitative and quantitative analyses of the scope of the problems and possible solutions within the geographic area being considered. Practitioners can shed light on service delivery concerns and best practices for meeting those concerns. Family members are needed to bring out more of the human dimension—including family dynamics and family stresses—and to supply the political power to turn abstract rights into concrete realities. Self-advocates must do the same to put a human face on what otherwise might seem an esoteric, remote, and even dry topic to most outsiders to this field.

Professional advocates have their own expertise to add to any COPE initiatives. In a disciplined fashion, they can present factual, public policy, and legal arguments for why the worthy aims of this group deserve a full response among the many other worthy causes that seek the support of decision makers and the public. Professional associations such as AAMR state chapters can lend their own multidisciplinary support to these persuasive efforts, lobbying legislatures and state officials and joining as amicus curiae (friend of the court) in impact cases. Finally, The Arc, as part of its waiting list campaign or as a distinct initiative, can mobilize a grassroots effort to implement their position that older people with mental retardation should have the same rights, dignity, and opportunities as other older adults (The Arc, 1998a).

Clearly, many reforms are needed to transform the policies and practices for older adults with developmental disabilities from their often substandard state to where they should be. If other experiences with international disability observances are a guide, the 1999 International Year for Older Persons may lead to a UN International Decade for Older Persons, helping to keep the focus on needed reform efforts for years to come. In specifying those reforms, this book highlights some of the good practices and legislative innovations that deserve emulation. For example, the person-centered approach can serve as a most valuable tool to prevent unnecessary relocations to large, so-called highly protected facilities. Legislative milestones such as the U.S. system of P&As and the ADA and Sweden's laws on personal assistance and mentors represent models for international reform. The recognition of gerontology by the AAMR and the new stress on subjective measures of quality of life are other measures of progress.

The time for passive reaction to demographic trends is over. As earlier chapters of this book make clear, with the aging of the baby-boom generation and the expected doubling of the population of older adults with developmental disabilities by 2030, industrialized societies need a substantial increase in the number of less-restrictive accommodations in the early decades of the 21st century. In the face of this urgency, policy confusions in many countries about the strategic objectives of accommodations and services for older adults with developmental disabilities can no longer be tolerated. If, however, policy is to be influenced increasingly by what consumers say, it is necessary to enter into dialogue with them (compare Chapter 16). Research on the quality of provisions is, unfortunately, mostly based on the perspectives of third parties and thus is of limited reliability and use in defining person-centered provisions for older adults with developmental disabilities. The better approach is to include in a direct way their views in the research on quality of life. Some examples of this inclusive methodology are the investigation of Hogg and Lambe (1997), analyzing the views on subjective quality of life of older people with developmental disabilities and the evaluation conducted by James, Hobson, and Bradley (1998) of outcomes in terms of quality of life for accommodation programs from the residents' perspectives. Putting the individual's quality of life at the center of professionals' concerns might finally help policy makers and planners to avoid confusion and drift. These new sources of information will enable them and other leaders to make more valid—and value-based—decisions about the directions that services for older people with developmental disabilities should take. In the end, the challenge is to improve this field so that when the Mitchell Levitzes (see Chapter 16) and other young self-advocates of the world experience old age, they will have the same pluralistic options for a good old age that are prized by all older adults at the turn of the 21st century.

REFERENCES

Aalto, M. (1998). What will happen . . . when his old parents are too tired to go on? A project concerning aged parents with a mentally handicapped person living at home. (Available from Forbundet De Utvecklingsstordas Val (FDUV), Tologatan 27 A 15, 00260 Helsingfors, Finland)

Act Concerning Support and Service for Persons with Certain Functional Impairments [Sweden] (Law No. 1993:387). (1993). [Lag om stöd och service till vissa funktionshindrade (Lag SFS 1993:387).]

Americans with Disabilities Act (ADA) of 1990, PL 101-336, 42 U.S.C. §§ 12101–12213.

Anast v. Commonwealth Apartments, 956 F. Supp. 792 (N.D. Ill. 1997).

The Arc: A National Organization on Mental Retardation. (1998a). Around the nation: A waiting list round-up of activities. *The Arc Today, 47,* 4, 5.

The Arc: A National Organization on Mental Retardation. (1998b). *Justice and fair treatment under the criminal law* (Position paper no. 20, adopted at the 49th annual meeting of The Arc). Arlington, TX: Author.

The Arc: A National Organization on Mental Retardation. (1998c). *Physician-assisted suicide* (Position paper no. 26, adopted at the 49th annual meeting of The Arc). Arlington, TX: Author.

The Arc: A National Organization on Mental Retardation. (1998d). *Self-determination* (Position paper no. 25, adopted at the 49th annual meeting of The Arc, Fort Worth, TX). Arlington, TX: Author.

Ashbaugh, J., & Smith, G. (1996). Beware the managed health-care companies. *Mental Retardation, 34,* 189–193.

Belfiore, P.J., & Toro-Zambrana, W. (1994). *Recognizing choices in community settings by people with significant disabilities* (Innovation series no. 1). Washington, DC: American Association on Mental Retardation.

Benjamin, M., Capie, A., & Nossin, M. (1998). *Measuring the quality of community services. A multi-perspective approach.* Wellington, New Zealand: Standards and Monitoring Services.

Blatch v. Franco, No. 97 Civ. 3918(DC), 1998 Westlaw 265132 (S.D.N.Y., May 26, 1998).

Blewett, T. (1980, February 5). The search for identity in a residential home for the elderly. *Social Work Today, 11*(22).

Braddock, D.L. (1998). *The state of the states in developmental disabilities* (5th ed.). Washington, DC: American Association on Mental Retardation.

Canady, C.T. (1996). Physician-assisted suicide and euthanasia in The Netherlands: A report to the House Judiciary Subcommittee on the Constitution, 104th Cong., 2nd Sess. (Reprinted in Winter 1998 issue of *Issues in Law and Medicine, 14,* 301–324.)

Colker, R., & Tucker, B.P. (1998). *The law of disability discrimination: Cases and materials* (2nd. ed.). Cincinnati, OH: Anderson Publishing Co.

Colond, J.S., & Wieseler, N.A. (1995). Preventing restrictive placements through Community Support Services. *American Journal on Developmental Disabilities, 100,* 201–206.

Council of Europe, European Convention for the Protection of Human Rights and Fundamental Freedoms of 1950, 213 U.N.T.S. 221, E.T.S. 5, entered into force on September 3, 1953.

Daemmrich, J.A. (1998, August 25). When elders speak, the politicians listen. Seniors: Their regular voting habits make them a key constituency, and office-seekers are reacting accordingly. *Baltimore Sun,* pp. 1A, 13A.

Developmental Disabilities Assistance and Bill of Rights Act Amendments of 1994, PL 103-230, 42 U.S.C. §§ 6000–6083.

Developmental Disabilities Assistance and Bill of Rights Act of 1975, PL 94-103, 42 U.S.C. §§ 6000–6083.

Dinerstein, R., Herr, S.S., & O'Sullivan, J. (1999). *A guide to consent.* Washington, DC: American Association on Mental Retardation.

Disability Discrimination Act, 1995, ch. 50 (Eng.).

Disabled People's International, Inclusion International, World Blind Union, World Federation of the Deaf, & World Psychiatric Users Federation. (1998). "All human beings are born free and equal in dignity and rights" Are disabled people included? London: Disability Awareness in Action.

Dybwad, G. (1985). Aging and mental retardation: An international perspective. In C.M. Gaitz & T. Samorajski (Eds.), *Aging 2000: Our health care destiny: Vol. 1. Biomedical issues* (pp. 465–475). New York: Springer-Verlag New York.

Education for All Handicapped Children Act of 1975, PL 94-142, 20 U.S.C. §§ 1400–1491.

Employers' Forum on Disability. (1998). The employers' agenda on disability: Ten points for action. London: Author. (Available from Employers' Forum on Disability, 60 Gainsford Street, London SE1 2NY, United Kingdom)

Erikson, E.H. (1968). *Identity, youth and crisis.* New York: W.W. Norton.

Erös, T. (1991). Lebenssituation erwachsener Menschen mit geistiger Behinderung in ihren Herkunftsfamilien [Situation of the life of adult persons with mental retardation in their natural families]. Unpublished thesis, Institute of Psychology, University of Vienna.

Factor, A.R. (1993). Translating policy into practice. In E. Sutton, A.R. Factor, B.A. Hawkins, T. Heller, & G.B. Seltzer (Eds.), *Older adults with developmental disabilities: Optimizing choice and change* (pp. 257–275). Baltimore: Paul H. Brookes Publishing Co.

Fair Housing Amendments Act of 1988, PL 100-430, 42 U.S.C. §§ 3601–3631 (1994 & Supp. I 1997).

Finally, new housing for the disabled [Editorial]. (1998, August 29). *New York Times*, A26.

Freedman, R.I., Krauss, W.M., & Seltzer, M.M. (1997). Aging parents' residential plans for adult children with mental retardation. *Mental Retardation, 35*, 114–123.

Glendenning, F. (1993). What is elder abuse and neglect? In P. Decalmer & F. Glendenning (Eds.), *The mistreatment of elderly people* (pp. 1–34). London: Sage Publications.

Griffiths, A., Roberts, G., & Williams, J. (1993). Elder abuse and the law. In P. Decalmer & F. Glendenning (Eds.), *The mistreatment of elderly people* (pp. 63–75). London: Sage Publications.

Hagner, D., Helm, D.T., & Butterworth, J. (1996). This is your meeting : A qualitative study of person-centered planning. *Developmental Disabilities, 34*, 159–171.

Henry, D., Keys, C., Balcazar, F., & Jopp, D. (1996). Attitudes of community-living staff members toward persons with developmental disabilities, mental illness, and dual diagnosis. *Developmental Disabilities, 34*, 367–379.

Herr, S.S. (1977). Rights into action: Protecting human rights of the mentally handicapped. *Catholic University Law Review, 26*, 203–318.

Herr, S.S. (1995). Maximizing autonomy: Reforming personal support laws in Sweden and the United States. *Journal of The Association for Persons with Severe Handicaps, 20*, 213–223.

Herr, S.S., & Hopkins, B.L. (1994). Health care decision making for persons with disabilities: An alternative to guardianship. *JAMA: Journal of the American Medical Association, 271*(13), 1017–1022.

Higgins, M. (1998, September). Assessing special needs: In fair-housing suits, tenants claim disabilities entitle them to anything from parking to pets. *American Bar Association Journal, 84*, 32–33.

Hogg, J., & Lambe, L. (1997). An ecological perspective on the quality of life of people with intellectual disabilities as they age. In R.I. Brown (Ed.), *Quality of life for people with disabilities: Models, research and practice* (2nd ed., pp. 201–227). Cheltenham, England: Stanley Thornes Publishers.

Holub, T.M. (1998, April). *Self-determination as a life-span issue*. Paper presented at the 19th Annual International Conference on Mental Retardation and Developmental Disabilities, New York City.

Immenschuh v. Paragon Group, Inc., No. SA-95-CA-0047 (W.D. Tex., May 1, 1998), reported in *Mental and Physical Disability Law Reporter, 22*, 493 (1998).

Inclusion International. (1998). *The beliefs, values and principles of self-advocacy*. Ferney-Voltaire, France: Author.

Individuals with Disabilities Education Act (IDEA) of 1990, PL 101-476, 20 U.S.C. §§ 1400 *et seq.*

James, B., Hobson, E., & Bradley, V. (1998, April). *Developing quality outcome measures: The New Hampshire approach*. Paper presented at the 19th Annual International Conference on Mental Retardation and Developmental Disabilities, New York City.

Janicki, M.P. (Ed.). (1996). *Help for caring for older people caring for an adult with a developmental disability: A manual for agencies aiding households with persons with a developmental disability*. Albany: New York State Developmental Disabilities Planning Council.

Jones, J., Dagnan, D., Trower, P., & Ruddick, L. (1996). People with learning disabilities living in community based homes: The relationship of quality of life with age and disability. *International Journal on Rehabilitation Research, 19*, 219–227.

Josephson, G. (1997). *Bus girl: Poems*. Cambridge, MA: Brookline Books.

Kryspin-Exner, I. (1997). Information, Schulung und emotionale Unterstützung für Angehörige und Pflegepersonal: Mögliche Anwendungen im Umfeld mit verwirrten und alten Personen mit geistiger Behinderung [Information, training, and emotional support: Potential applications in the area of confused and older persons with mental retardation]. In G. Weber (Ed.), *Psychische Störungen bei älteren Menschen mit geistiger Behinderung* [*Mental disorders in older persons with mental retardation*]. Bern, Switzerland: Verlag Hans Huber.

Kummer, S. (1998, August 10). Von der freiwilligen Sterbehilfe zum unfreiwilligen Gnadentod [From voluntary assisted death to involuntary mercy]. *Die Presse* [Vienna daily newspaper], p. 3.

La Rochefoucauld, F., duc de. (1885). *Reflections, or, Sentences and moral maxims* (J.W. Willis-Bund & J.H. Friswell, eds. & trans.). New York: Sampson Low, Marston, Searle & Rivington. (Original work published 1678)

Lachwitz, K. (1998). *1948–1998, fifty years of human rights: A guide through international human rights instruments for persons with an intellectual disability.* Ferney-Voltaire, France: Inclusion International.

Lebenshilfe Österreich [Austrian parents' association for people with mental retardation]. (1994). Ich möchte selbständig leben [I want to live by myself: A middle-age adult man giving his comments on a life after work]. Im *1. Oesterreichischer Kongress geistig behinderter Menschen, Kongressbericht* [In *Proceedings of the 1st Austrian Congress of People with Mental Retardation*]. Vienna: Author.

Lewin, T. (1990, October 28). As the retarded live longer, anxiety grips aging parents. *New York Times,* pp. 1, 32.

Longhurst, N.A. (1994). *The self-advocacy movement by people with developmental disabilities: A demographic study and directory of self-advocacy groups in the United States.* Washington, DC: American Association on Mental Retardation/People First of Illinois/Illinois University Affiliated Program in Developmental Disabilities.

Magrill, D., Handley, P., Gleeson, S., & Charles, D. (1997). *Crisis approaching! The situation facing Sheffield's elderly carers of people with learning disabilities.* Sheffield, England: Sharing Caring Project.

Massey, P.S., Johnson, J.E., & Kirk, J.E. (1992). *Making decisions: A practical guide for executives who manage programs for people with developmental disabilities.* Columbia: South Carolina Department of Mental Retardation.

Older Americans Act (OAA) of 1965, PL 89-73, 42 U.S.C. §§ 3001–3058ee (1994).

Organization of American States, *American Convention on Human Rights,* Off. Rec. OEA/Ser.L/V/II.23, Doc. 21, rev. 6 (1969), 9 I.L.M. 673 (1970), entered into force July 18, 1978.

Pennhurst State School & Hospital v. Halderman, 451 U.S. 1 (1981).

Perlin, M.L. (1994). *Law and mental disability.* Charlottesville, VA: Michie Co.

Polister, B.H., Blake, E.M., Prouty, R.W., & Lakin, K.C. (1998). *Reinventing quality. The 1998 sourcebook of innovative programs for the quality assurance and quality improvement of community services.* Minneapolis: University of Minnesota, Research and Training Center on Community Living, Institute on Community Integration, University Affiliated Program.

Potomac Group Home Corp. v. Montgomery County, 823 F. Supp. 1285 (D. Md. 1993).

Sands, D.J., Kozleski, E.B., & Goodwin, L.D. (1991). Whose needs are we meeting? Results of a consumer satisfaction survey of persons with developmental disabilities in Colorado. *Research in Developmental Disabilities, 12,* 297–314.

Seltzer, M.M., & Janicki, M.P. (1991). Commentary and recommendations. In M.P. Janicki & M.M. Seltzer (Eds.), *Proceedings of the Boston roundtable on research issues and applications in aging and developmental disabilities* (pp. 101–104). Washington, DC: American Association on Mental Retardation, Special Interest Group on Aging.

Sundram, C.J. (1994). Quality assurance in an era of consumer empowerment and choice. *Developmental Disabilities, 32,* 371–374.

Sundram, C.J. (1999). Pitfalls in the pursuit of life, liberty and happiness. *Mental Retardation, 37*(1), 62–67.

Sutton, E., Heller, T., Sterns, H., Factor, A.R., & Miklos, S. (1997). *Person centered planning for later life: A curriculum for adults with mental retardation.* Akron, OH: University of Akron, The Clearinghouse on Aging and Developmental Disabilities.

Turnbull, R.H., III. (1981). *The least restrictive alternative: Principles and practices.* Washington, DC: American Association on Mental Deficiency.

United Nations (UN). (1966). *International covenant on civil and political rights,* G.A. Res. 2200 A (XXI), 21 GAOR, Supp. 16, U.N. Doc. A/6316, at 52 (1966), 999 U.N.T.S. 171, entered into force March 23, 1976.

United Nations (UN). (1966). *International covenant on economic, social, and cultural rights,* G.A. res. 2200A (XXI), 21 U.N. GAOR Supp. (No. 16) at 49, U.N. Doc A/6316 (1966), 993 U.N.T.S. 3, entered into force January 3, 1976.

United Nations (UN). (1971). *Declaration on the rights of mentally retarded persons: Resolution adopted by General Assembly.* G.A. Res. 2856, 26 U.N. GAOR, Supp. (No. 29) 93–94, U.N. Doc. A18429.

United Nations (UN). (1975). *Declaration on the rights of disabled persons: Resolution adopted by General Assembly,* G.A. Res. 3447, 30 U.N. GAOR Supp. (No. 34) 88–89, U.N. Doc. 10034.

United Nations (UN). (1989). *Convention on the rights of the child.* G.A. res., 44/25, Annex, 44 U.N. GAOR Supp. (No. 49) at 167, U.N. Doc.A/44/49 (1989), entered into force September 2, 1990.

United Nations (UN). (1993). *Standard rules on the equalization of opportunities for persons with disabilities: Resolution adopted by General Assembly.* U.N. GAOR, 48th Sess., Agenda Item 109, at 28, U.N. Doc. A/Res/48/96.

United Nations, Department of Public Information. (1992). *The United Nations Principles for Older Persons* (DPI/1261-August 1992-6M). New York: Author.

Weber, G., & Rett, A. (1991). *Down Syndrom im Erwachsenenalter (Down syndrome in adulthood).* Bern, Switzerland: Verlag Hans Huber.

White House Conference on Aging. (1996). *The road to an aging policy for the 21st century (Final report).* Washington, DC: U.S. Department of Health and Human Services.

Wolfe, A. (1998). Is civil society obsolete? Revisiting predictions of the decline of civil society in *Whose Keeper.* In E.J. Dionne, Jr. (Ed.), *Community works: The revival of civil society in America* (pp. 17–23). Washington: Brookings Institution Press.

Wyatt v. Rodgers, 985 F. Supp. 1356 (M.D. Ala. 1997).

Wyatt v. Stickney, 344 F. Supp. 387 (M.D. Ala. 1972), aff'd sub nom. Wyatt v. Aderholt, 503 F.2d 1305 (5th Cir. 1974).

Index